PLANNING EUROPE'S CAPITAL CITIES

Planning, History and the Environment series

Editor:
Emeritus Professor Dennis Hardy, High Peak, UK

Editorial Board:
Professor Arturo Almandoz, Universidad Simón Bolivar, Caracas, Venezuela and Pontificia Universidad Católica de Chile, Santiago, Chile
Professor Gregory Andrusz, London, UK
Professor Nezar AlSayyad, University of California, Berkeley, USA
Professor Robert Bruegmann, University of Illinois at Chicago, USA
Professor Meredith Clausen, University of Washington, Seattle, USA
Professor Robert Freestone, University of New South Wales, Sydney, Australia
Professor John Gold, Oxford Brookes University, Oxford, UK
Professor Sir Peter Hall, University College London, UK
Professor Peter Larkham, University of Central England, Birmingham, UK
Emeritus Professor Anthony Sutcliffe, Nottingham, UK

Technical Editor
Ann Rudkin, Alexandrine Press, Marcham, Oxon, UK

PLANNING EUROPE'S CAPITAL CITIES

Aspects of Nineteenth Century Urban Development

THOMAS HALL

Routledge
Taylor & Francis Group

LONDON AND NEW YORK

First published 1997 by E&FN Spon

This paperback edition first published 2010
by Routledge
2 Park Square, Milton Park, Abingdon, Oxon, OX14 4RN

Simultaneously published in the USA and Canada
by Routledge
270 Madison Avenue, New York, NY 10016

Routledge is an imprint of the Taylor & Francis Group, an informa business

© 1997, 2010 Thomas Hall

Typeset in Great Britain by Cambrian Typesetters, Frimley, Surrey
Printed and bound in Great Britain by TJ International Ltd, Padstow, Cornwall

This book was commissioned and edited by Alexandrine Press, Marcham, Oxfordshire

British Library Cataloguing in Publication Data
A catalogue record for this book is available from the British Library

Library of Congress Cataloging-in-Publication Data
Library of Congress catalog card number 97-66869

ISBN10: 0-415-55249-4 (pbk)
ISBN10: 0-203-44956-8 (ebk)

ISBN13: 978-0-415-55249-3 (pbk)
ISBN13: 978-0-203-44956-1 (ebk)

Contents

CONCLUDING REMARKS

FOREWORD

Thomas Hall's *Planning Europe's Capital Cities* is a labour of love and a major contribution to the burgeoning international literature on planning history. The product of many years of research, first published in German in 1986 and in English in 1997, is now again revised in a form that will bring it to a wider English-speaking academic world. And this is important, since English-speaking academics are perhaps less likely than German-speaking ones to access the vast range of sources on which Hall has based his work.

It is important, as the author stresses at the outset in his own Introduction (Chapter 1), to stress what he has sought to do and what not to do. This is an account of European city planning between 1800 and 1900 but in particular between 1850 and 1880: a first golden age of planning, but one that strictly acted as precursor to the twentieth-century history that most students of planning know. It was as different from modern planning as it is possible to imagine; it was concerned centrally with form and appearance, very little with social objective or social content. It was, therefore, a late manifestation of a long movement in urban affairs, that – as Hall shows in Chapter 3 – had started with the ancient Greeks and Romans and had flowered again in the Renaissance; it was an end rather than a beginning.

Yet, as he demonstrates in the first of the general analytic chapters that conclude the book (Chapter 18), it was very much impelled by the same pressures and the same incentives to action; above all, the unprecedented growth that overtook one European city after another, as high birth rates allied with agrarian and industrial revolutions to take people off the land and into the towns. Deliberately, Hall does not treat these pressures in detail; he takes them as given. Nor does he treat the results in terms of peripheral expansion and suburban deconcentration, enabled and propelled by the new nineteenth-century transport technologies; those seeking an account of these processes must find it elsewhere. Again quite deliberately, he treats of only the innermost city that had come into being by about 1850 or at latest 1880: the area today characterized as the central business district, together with selected inner suburbs.

Within this area, as he shows, there were acute pressures, above all of public health and traffic: as more and more people poured in, poor as well as rich, housing densities increased and housing conditions deteriorated; traffic congealed, crammed on to medieval streets, above all on the approaches to the new railway stations. The response, in city after city, was the cutting of new streets and the rebuilding of the blocks between them, often without regard for the fates of those displaced; and plans for urban extensions in the form of geometrically regular apartment blocks separated by wide streets. Overall, perhaps, an improvement – though, as often as not, overwhelmed by a new flood of in-migrants.

In virtually every city, this general story is the same. And usually, Hall shows, the agent was a regal or imperial power, concerned in the process to assert itself and commemorate itself by means of a grand design. The partnership of Napoleon III and Haussmann, in Paris, is known to every student; one of the greatest contributions of Hall's book is to throw light on other great nineteenth-century planners, whose reputations have too long lain buried in their own lands and languages. Outstanding among them was the achievement of Ildefonso Cerdá, whose reconstruction of Barcelona invites comparison with Haussmann; but Hall reveals other extraordinary achievements, by Lechner and Feszl in Budapest, by Ehrenström in Helsinki, by von Förster and van der Nüll and von Sicardsburg in Vienna, and by the hugely but unfairly vilified Holbrecht in Berlin.

The Emperor Franz-Joseph, who presided over two of the greatest of these reconstructions – the Vienna Ring and the lesser-known but equally-magnificent ring and radial avenues in Budapest – succinctly stated the objectives: *Erweiterung, Regulierung, Verschönerung*, extension, regulation, beautification. To these, and to the others described in Thomas Hall's book, we owe much of the quality of the great European capitals that we so much enjoy – whether as residents or, more often, as informed tourists – in the first decades of the twenty-first century and beyond. To have brought together all these stories, in their depth and historic complexity, required a rare combination of historical and linguistic ability, and prodigious application. Scholars of urbanism throughout the English-speaking world owe Thomas Hall a debt of gratitude that will take a long time to replay.

Peter Hall
University College London
2009

PREFACE

Why write a book on planning in European capital cities during the nineteenth century, and why write it in Stockholm? At the end of the 1970s a cross-disciplinary research project was launched at the University of Stockholm under the title 'The Swedish Urban Environment: Building and Housing over the Past Hundred Years'. The project was led by Professor Ingrid Hammarström; the present author acted as research co-ordinator. One of the main purposes of the project was to chart the development of Stockholm's inner city area, a topic which was discussed in a number of studies and from a variety of angles. Excursions were also arranged to other cities of a similar character both in Sweden and elsewhere. In the course of working on this project I became increasingly interested in the role of planning in the development of these cities. In Stockholm a grand renewal and extension project – known as the Lindhagen Plan – was presented in 1866, and similar schemes were launched in several other capital cities. But I found there was no comparative study of these projects, and gradually I began to collect material as a basis for lectures and excursions. That a book finally emerged from these activities was due to a great extent to inspiring discussions which I was able to have with three scholars who visited Stockholm around the beginning of the 1980s, namely Anthony Sutcliffe, Peter Hall and David R. Goldfield, all of whom had demonstrated in their own research how rewarding internationally oriented comparative studies can be. David Goldfield's participation in 'The Swedish Urban Environment', which continued for more than a year, was particularly important.

A first version of the present book was published in German in 1986 as *Planung europäischer Hauptstädte, Zur Entwicklung des Städtebaues im 19. Jh* (Stockholm: Almqvist & Wiksell), under the auspices of Kungl. Vitterhets Historie och Antikvitets Akademien in Stockholm. Soon afterwards the late Gordon E. Cherry suggested that it should also be published in an English version in the series *Studies in History, Planning and the Environment*. For a variety of reasons this enterprise was delayed for some years, by which time a great many publications of importance to the project had appeared, and on several counts my own perspectives had shifted or become more sharply focused. The English edition should thus be regarded as a new book partially based on the German edition. My text was finished just before the end of 1995.

At different stages in this lengthy project many colleagues have read sections of the manuscript and I would like to thank them all for their helpful criticisms, ideas and comments. Apart from the editors of the series, Gordon Cherry and Anthony Sutcliffe, these include Gerd Albers, Peter Hall, Björn Linn, Torgil Magnuson, John Reps, Ingrid Sjöström and John Sjöström. I am particularly grateful to Erik Lorange, who not only allowed me to choose freely among his reconstruction plans, but has also adapted them for me for the purposes of this book.

It would have been impossible to write this book without the generous and patient co-operation of colleagues in many of the cities discussed here, who have shared with me their knowledge and their research findings. Several of them have also read the relevant sections in manuscript form. In particular I would like to mention the following: on Amsterdam Elisabeth de Bièvre, Michiel Wagenaar and Auke van der Woud; on Athens Manos Biris, Hermann J. Kienast, Angeliki Kokkou, Johannes M. Michael and Joannis Travlos; on Barcelona Fco Javier Monclús, Manuel de Solá-Morales and Salvator Tarragó Cid; on Brussels Piet M.J.L. Lombaerde, Yvon Leblicq, Marcel Smets, Jos Vandenbreeden and Herwig Delraux; on Budapest György Kelényi, Bertalan Kery, Károly Polóni and Alajos Sódor; on Copenhagen Ole Hyldtoft, Tim Knudsen and Poul Strømstad; on Helsinki Mikael Sundman; on London Stefan Muthesius; on Madrid Paloma Barreiro Pereira, Alberto Campo Bazea, Javier Frechilla Camoiras and Estanislao Pérez-Pita; on Oslo Erik Lorange and Jan Eivind Myhre; on Rome Tomas Larsson and Torgil Magnuson; on Stockholm Gösta Selling and on Vienna Rudolph Wurzer. To all these I proffer my heartfelt thanks. Any remaining errors or misunderstandings are of course entirely my own responsibility.

The work on the earlier German version of this book was financed by The Swedish Research Council for Humanities and Social Sciences. The Research Council has also made possible the present revision. The following funds have helped to finance the translation: Helge Ax:son Johnsons stiftelse, Elna Bengtssons fond, Magn. Bergvalls stiftelse, Berit Wallenbergs stiftelse and Marianne och Marcus Wallenbergs stiftelse. I would like in particular to thank the former president of the Stockholm University, Inge Jonsson, whose assistance in seeking funds for this purpose was crucial. I would also like to thank Bo Grandien for his willing support.

It is of great value to any author to be able to discuss all the problems that can arise in working on a manuscript, with someone familiar with the various topics and who is also committed to the enterprise. In the present case I have had the good fortune to find such a collaborator in my translator, Nancy Adler, herself an architectural historian. It has been a great pleasure to work with her on this English version. We have discussed what probably amounts to hundreds of questions, by no means all of them limited to the purely linguistic.

Two other people have been deeply involved in this book at various stages in its history. In particular this applies to my collaborator of many years, the architect Dieter Künkel who translated my first rough Swedish version into German. In a variety of ways he has also contributed to the present book, among other things adjusting many points in that first version before the present translation began, doing much work on the bibliography, creating the index and checking innumerable facts. The late architect George Lázár compiled and translated the source material for the sections on Budapest and Madrid. He also made the redrawn maps, unless otherwise stated.

Finally I would like to thank Lempi BorgWik, another colleague of many years for continually acting as my partner in discussions and my sounding-board for problems, and who has often produced constructive solutions to the most varied of problems. This has meant very much to the result and to my own pleasure in the work.

Thomas Hall
Stockholm

1

INTRODUCTION

During the nineteenth century many capital cities and other large towns in Europe were subject to vast improvement and expansion programmes, which still affect their physical appearance today. It was during this period that many features were created – such as the avenues and boulevards in Paris or the Ringstraße in Vienna – which now seem quintessential characteristics of the cities in question.

The aim of this study is to describe and compare planning in a number of capital cities, and in particular to address the following questions.

- When and why did planning begin, and what problems was it meant to solve?

- Who developed the projects, and how, and who made the decisions?

- What urban ideas are expressed in the projects?

- What were the legal consequences of the plans, and how did they actually affect subsequent urban development in the individual cities?

- What similarities or differences can be identified between the various schemes?

- How do these projects compare with earlier planning, and how did they affect the subsequent development of urban planning in general?

Separate chapters have been devoted to most of the European towns which were, or became, national capitals during the later nineteenth century, namely Amsterdam (a capital in name only), Athens, Berlin, Brussels, Budapest, Christiania (Oslo), Copenhagen, Helsinki (Helsingfors), London, Madrid, Paris, Rome, Stockholm and Vienna. Barcelona has also been given a chapter of its own. Bern, Istanbul, Lisbon and St Petersburg have not been included, nor have any of the towns – Bucharest and Sofia for instance – which acquired capital city status with the liberation of the Balkan states towards the end of the nineteenth century. Towns which were regarded as national centres without being the capital of a sovereign state during the relevant period such as Dublin, Prague and Warsaw, and the capitals of countries which later came to be part of the Italian or German states have been excluded. Towns like Florence which became capitals for a brief period have also been disregarded.

There would obviously have been some advantages in working with a wider range of examples. The amount of time this would have required was against it, but this was not the only reason for limiting myself to the present selection. Nineteenth-century planning in the central and eastern European capital cities, with the exception of Budapest, does not seem to have been the subject of extensive research, possibly due to lack of major planning projects of the kind discussed here.

St Petersburg, which was included in the earlier German version of the present book, has been excluded for the same reason. During

the eighteenth century the national government in Russia was probably more engaged in
the creation of an urban environment than any
of its counterparts in the other capital cities at
that time, though its aim was not to furnish
acceptable conditions for the populace, but to
provide a splendid framework for the exercise
of imperial power. Public control over urban
development began to weaken as early as the
1840s, however, and it was soon to cease
altogether. During the second half of the
nineteenth century no attempt appears to have
been made at any kind of overall planning, and
building controls were weak or non-existent.
This applied even to the grander areas which
had previously been protected by special
decrees. '. . . by 1913 all types of noxious
industries were found in those parts of the city
which earlier had been something of a sanctuary
from the sight and smell of factory production',
as Bater puts it.[1] Nor was much done about the
water supply or the sewage system. Street
standards were extremely low; some streets
had no paving at all.

Dublin enjoyed a genuine golden age in
urban development during the second half of
the eighteenth century, and through the good
offices of the Wide Streets Commissioners
appointed in 1752, probably benefited from
planning of a more advanced kind than any
other capital city at that period. But in 1800
the Irish parliament was dissolved, which
meant that Dublin lost its most important
capital city function and entered upon a long
period of decline in terms of planning and
building, even though the Wide Streets
Commissioners continued to function in a
more modest way until 1851. It was not until
1922 when Dublin became the capital city of
the sovereign state of Ireland, that any major
new projects appeared on the agenda. For this
reason Dublin has not been included among
my examples. Lisbon is in a different category:
the Avenida da Liberdade and the Avenida
Almirante Reis certainly qualify as striking
examples of large-scale planning, but in this

case it has not been possible to acquire
adequate material.

The inclusion of Barcelona is obviously
inconsistent with the title of the book. The
main reason for making this exception was not
the town's special historical role as the provincial capital of Catalonia, but the status of
Ildefonso Cerdá's remarkable extension plan
for the town. It would have felt strange to write
about mid-nineteenth-century planning without discussing this project.

It might be argued that the capital city
function is not necessarily the best selection
criterion for inclusion in a study of this kind.
The situation of capital cities varies so much,
and – perhaps most importantly – they also
differ so greatly in size, that comparisons might
seem rather meaningless. Moreover, some
capitals – in the Nordic countries, for instance
– can hardly qualify as large cities in European
terms. But if one city from every country is to
be chosen for a comparative study, the capital
city nonetheless seems to be an apt choice. It is
also reasonable to suppose that the capitals do
have some conditions and features in common
in the way they have developed, which justify
their being treated as a single group.[2] Nor is
the comparison concerned primarily with the
towns as such; the emphasis is on the planning
activities in the most important cities politically
speaking in their respective countries, cities
which in most cases were also the largest in the
country as well as the leading centre for trade
and industry.

It would have been interesting to have
established a control group by choosing one
other city for comparison with the capital in
each country. However, this was not possible
to realize within the frames of the present
study; nor was it possible to include non-
European capital cities as comparative
material.

The study thus focuses on a series of major
projects which appeared in the third quarter of
the nineteenth century, roughly speaking
between 1850 and 1880. But it would not have

been reasonable to disregard the planning of Athens and Helsinki, which acquired capital city status in the first half of the century, or various activities that occurred in the other cities before 1850. Thus 1800 can be regarded as an approximate starting date for the study.

Around 1910 modern town planning can be said to have established itself. That is to say, the shaping of the urban environment was to be subject to plans binding on those owning land, produced by professional experts and based on scientifically grounded urban development ideas.[3] At the same time planners were beginning to think along broader lines in order to coordinate communications, industry, the location of residential areas etc, in other words everything that today would be included in the concept of regional planning, which meant that planning was divided between the more detailed planning of the physical design of the built environment on the one hand, and structure planning paying particular attention to land use on the other. A crucial question to be addressed in this study concerns the importance of the role played by the capital city projects in this whole development. The 1880s can therefore be taken as, roughly, the closing date of the period studied as regards what was actually happening in the capital cities, while we follow the evolution of planning ideas to a slightly later date.

Nineteenth-century planning must be viewed in light of earlier events. The presentation of each city thus starts with a brief review of the town's urban development history, while the book itself opens with a chapter entitled 'From Hippodamus to Haussmann. Town planning in a historical perspective', in which the primary aim is to position nineteenth-century planning in a historical context.

It should be emphasized once again that the focus here is on the major planning projects; the aim is not to address planning developments as a whole in the studied cities. The reason for the relatively summary treatment of London is just the absence of any such comprehensive

projects, even though the various planning inputs taken together may well have amounted to the same volume of planning as elsewhere. In this context it may seem illogical that by far the most detailed city chapter is devoted to Paris, which also lacked an approved overall plan. But the redevelopment of Paris under the Second Empire can nonetheless be regarded as a single project, in comparison with the street improvements in London. Furthermore, this study refers primarily to public planning, conducted by municipal or national bodies. In several cases private land-owners have been responsible for the planning of extensive areas, but such undertakings have been mentioned here only in passing, when special reasons have warranted it. In London a large proportion of the planning came about under private auspices, which also explains why the biggest city has been treated in one of the shortest chapters in the book.

I would also like to add a few words about what this book does *not* set out to do. It would certainly have been interesting to compare the design of the buildings – both residential housing and public buildings – in the different capital cities, and public buildings are of course an important part of the capital city image.[4] But this would have meant entering another vast subject area, and would have made the study totally unwieldy.

Some readers may also miss an account of the urbanization process as such during the nineteenth century, or a section on the capital city as a phenomenon.[5] Both these themes have some relevance to the main issues addressed in the book, but they are too complex to handle briefly in any meaningful way. Local transport – first horse-drawn omnibuses, then horse-trams followed by steam and at the turn of the century electric trams – made life in the big cities more comfortable, at any rate for those who could afford to use the new facilities. But of these, the electric trams were the first to alter the conditions for planning in any more radical way. For this reason I have not included local transport developments in this book. I have also largely disregarded the suburban growth which appeared towards the end of the period studied, which also meant ignoring the impact of the railways on urban development patterns beyond the inner cities.

It has thus been my ambition to concentrate on the planning of what in the nineteenth century were the capital cities proper – areas which today largely represent the central or inner city districts – and to refer to related subjects and problems only when the context so motivates. One further point: it was first towards the end of the period considered here that active intervention in working-class housing came to be regarded as one of planning's central tasks; for much of the century planning and housing questions were divorced from one another. In the present survey the latter thus occupy a minor role.

The prime sources for this study have consisted of various scholarly works and printed original sources, supplemented as far as possible by on-site observations and by discussions with colleagues in the respective cities. The state of research varies very much from one town to another, and for each one a first footnote provides a survey of the literature.[6] In several cities the investigation of nineteenth-century planning seems to have passed through much the same stages. Following a few very preliminary works a basic study is published, charting the main lines of the development. Several more publications then appear, repeating the substance of the basic study more or less closely, including mistakes, and without very much further source research. Finally, a more extensive and comprehensive study is published, using the entire source material. The full story is reconsidered on a great many points. This stage has been reached in the case of, for instance Athens (Papageorgiou-Venetas, 1994), Paris (Pinkney, 1958 and other later works), Vienna (Mollik, Reining and Wurzer, 1980) and, perhaps, Stockholm (Selling, 1970). On Madrid such a work has

been produced (by Javier Frechilla Camoiras) but has not so far been published. But in most cities such a basic work still remains to be written.

'Source-steered' research has long been regarded as a particularly dubious variety of scholarly study, and those who employ this approach have frequently been placed lowest in the special purgatory for scholars. Nonetheless I willingly confess that the following descriptions have to no small extent been steered by the sources. Ideally, perhaps, the descriptions of every capital city should have been organized according to a uniform model, and should have included the same kind of information. That this was not feasible depended not only on variations in the quality and state of the source material, and on the different opportunities for obtaining information, but also on the simple fact that no town is like any other. In Helsinki the formative period occurred during the 1810s, in Paris during the 1850s and 1860s, and in Rome during the 1870s and 1880s. In some of the capital cities the population ran into tens of thousands, in others into millions. In some cases planning activities were primarily concerned with street improvements, in others largely with extending the existing town. Sometimes the national government involved itself by making substantial resources available, in other cases more 'liberal' non-interventionist ideas left it to individual actors to do what they considered best in their own interests. I thus hope I will be excused for allowing the diversity of the source material, and of the capital cities themselves, to determine the shape of my exposition.

That I have been working on the book for several years has also inevitably meant that horizons have shifted in the course of the voyage. Thus the descriptive chapters in the book could be suitably regarded as a series of essays on a common theme, each one with its own individual design. Nevertheless, as I hope the second part of the book will show, certain general patterns – or what could be called middle-range theories – in planning and urban development do emerge from the material, and this seems to me to be a satisfactory outcome for a study of this kind. My descriptions are a series of case studies in which the conditions are so diverse that it would hardly have been meaningful to suggest or to test more general laws or models.

During recent decades a great many works have been published on planning in various cities during the nineteenth century. These have generally been in the form of monographs. Very little, on the other hand, has been written on nineteenth-century urban planning in a comparative perspective. A work which aroused considerable attention at the time of its publication, and which has been translated into several languages, is Leonardo Benevolo's *Le origini dell'urbanistica moderna* (1963).[7] However, this work focuses on utopian projects and on attempts to found 'model cities'; big-city planning is only addressed at a fairly superficial level. Françoise Choay's *The Modern City: Planning in the Nineteenth Century* (1969) is an interesting but on several counts questionable attempt to systematize perspectives on nineteenth-century town planning. A major breakthrough for planning historical research, on the other hand, came with Anthony Sutcliffe's *Towards the Planned City: Germany, Britain, the United States and France, 1780–1914* (1981b). The focus of interest in Sutcliffe's book is town planning as an administrative phenomenon, i.e. the evolution of legislation, an administrative apparatus and a professional group responsible for planning. Less attention is paid to the plans and their design. I should like to emphasize here that Sutcliffe's book – and indeed his other writings as well – have been a vital source of inspiration for the present study.

When the German version of the present book was published I had not yet come across the slightly earlier *Stadterweiterungen 1800–1875: Von den Anfängen des modernen Städtebaues in Deutschland* (1983) edited by Gerhard Fehl and Juan Rodriguez-Lores. If I have understood the main thesis of their book correctly, it is that an earlier planning tradition stemming from the royal courts and imbued with a sense of social responsibility and high aesthetic standards, was losing ground at the beginning of the nineteenth century. It was to be followed by a period of speculation and chaos, in which weak authorities were content to try to impose a superficial veil of order over a chaotic real world. Only towards the end of the century did a type of planning evolve which was once again capable of producing order of a more solid kind. All through this process, the conditions of land ownership had played a decisive part. By and large this is also my own picture of developments in the same period. This first book was followed by another, in two volumes, in 1985, namely *Städtebaureform 1865–1900: Von Licht, Luft und Ordnung in der Stadt der Gründerzeit* which also up to a point addresses the same issues as are taken up here, albeit mainly during the period after the major capital city projects.[8]

Not until the English version of my own book was virtually finished did I become aware of Walter Kieß's *Urbanismus im Industriezeitalter: Von der klassizistischen Stadt zur Garden City* (1991). This book – which provides the most exhaustive documentation and analysis hitherto of nineteenth-century urban development, including capital city planning – would have supplied me with valuable reference material. Recently Gerhard Fehl and Juan Rodriguez-Lores have published *Stadt-Umbau: Die planmäßige Erneuerung europäischer Großstädte zwischen Wiener Kongreß und Weimarer Republik* (1995) in their impressive *Stadt Planung Geschichte* series, covering in part the same material as I do here. Whereas their earlier volumes primarily address urban extensions, the focus this time is on improvement and redevelopment projects.

Two alternatives seemed possible to me when it came to the organization of the book.

One was to present each town on its own, and to gather the comparative aspects together in a concluding section. The second was to compare the towns thematically, without any previous monographic description. Both alternatives have their disadvantages. But the first variant proved the most manageable; it also means that anyone seeking information about a particular city will find their way about more easily. On the other hand it has been impossible to avoid some repetition. It should also be noted that the sources acknowledged in the city chapters are not generally repeated in the comparative sections, except in the case of a direct quotation. All quotations in languages other than English have been translated in the text.

Anyone trying to conduct international comparative studies of twentieth-century planning will be confronted by a mass of plans of various kinds, whose designations are difficult to translate, since terms that sound similar can imply something quite different in different countries. In the case of nineteenth-century planning this problem is not quite so acute, since so many different types of plan had not yet emerged. In the following pages the terms 'plan', 'town plan', 'overall plan' and 'master plan' have been used largely synonymously to designate projects for the design of urban areas of varying sizes, or of whole cities, plans concerned primarily with dividing the land into streets and blocks.

The names of the various official bodies or titles of those persons involved in the planning also cause terminological problems. Such terms are usually given below in English translation (in some cases with the original name in brackets). The risk of this procedure is that authorities or positions which in fact have little in common may be designated in translation by the same term, whereby the reader might get the impression that the different countries are more alike than is actually the case.

One of the many things which can turn a planning historian's hair white overnight, is the habit of changing the names of squares and streets: in Central and Eastern Europe it was a case of depriving the leaders of the 'People's Democracies' of their fame and restoring streets to their previous names, and in Barcelona it meant giving streets Catalan names as their official designation. Throughout the book my aim has been to use the current names.

The projects studied are reproduced whenever possible, and in most cases there are also maps showing the situation before the nineteenth-century planning interventions. On the other hand there are no maps showing the situation after implementation of the plans. It should not be too difficult for readers to find such maps for themselves.

NOTES

1. Bater (1976), p. 400 *et passim*.
2. The same argument is put forward by Anthony Sutcliffe in a comparison between London, Paris and Berlin (1979*b*). It is important in this context to mention the book which originally inspired me to embark on the present study, and which has provided a tantalizing but unmatchable model, namely Peter Hall's *The World Cities*. This book devotes a great deal of attention to capital cities even though it is not aimed specifically at this category.
3. This is one of the main points in Sutcliffe (1981*b*).
4. This theme is pursued in Vale (1992), which aims to 'explore the ways that a variety of national regimes have used architecture and urban design to express political power' (p. VIII). The perspective is global and the emphasis is on towns which have become capitals since World War II, but the political iconography of several European capitals is also discussed in a fruitful way.
5. An analysis of the importance to urban development of the capital city function is provided in Mykland (1984), where it is exemplified by the case of Christiania.
6. Anthony Sutcliffe's *The History of Urban and Regional Planning: An Annotated Bibliography* (1981*a*) has been an indispensable aid. One

problem for authors writing books of this kind while living at the edge of Europe, is that it is often difficult to get hold of documents and other material published in other countries. On the whole this problem has been solved, but there remain some books which I have not been able to see, although I consider them to be relevant to the study.

7. English edition 1967 (cited version 1968).

8. Some of the works mentioned here will be discussed further below, pp. 361 ff. Mention should also be made of Donald J. Olsen's inspiring book *The City as a Work of Art: London, Paris, Vienna (1986)*, which appeared in the same year as the original version of the present study. Sections on nineteenth-century planning – some more detailed than others – can be found in various surveys of planning history (cf. pp. 48 f). Several surveys of architectural history also devote considerable attention to town planning during the nineteenth century, such as Leonardo Benevolo's *Geschichte der Architektur des 19. und 20. Jahrhunderts* and Sigfried Giedion's *Space, Time and Architecture*. Choay (1965), Dybdahl (1973) and Albers (1975a) are compilations of texts on urban development collected from various countries and cities.

2

FROM HIPPODAMUS TO HAUSSMANN: TOWN PLANNING IN A HISTORICAL PERSPECTIVE

On 29 June 1853 Georges-Eugène Haussmann assumed the post of *Préfet de la Seine*, i.e. he became the chief officer of the public administration in Paris. One important reason for this promotion was that Napoleon III saw in Haussmann the administrative capacity and energy required to execute his own comprehensive renewal and building plans for Paris. And, as we know, Haussmann proved worthy of the Emperor's expectations. Over the coming decades great expansion and redevelopment projects were also launched in many other European cities as well as in Paris.

Did the planning of the large nineteenth-century cities represent something essentially new? Or did it imply the fulfilment of earlier planning methods and ideas, was it one stage in a continuum? As these are among the key questions that will be addressed below, it seems appropriate to start with a brief but obviously selective retrospective survey of the history of urban planning.[1] The selection largely coincides with the traditional examples which reappear in practically every such survey, and which seem to have been generally adopted as signposts on the journey through urban planning history. A fundamental question here, of course, is whether this established set of examples actually provides a picture of *development* as such, or whether it represents a

collection of odd but inspiring special cases. However, it is not my intention to address this problem here. And, since the focus in the present survey is on ideas and innovations in themselves rather than on their *de facto* effects or their dissemination, there is at least some justification for adopting the conventional set of accepted episodes in the story of urban planning.

When Haussmann was embarking on his activities in Paris, the concept of 'town planning' or 'urban planning' had not yet become established. Other expressions such as 'extension', 'improvement' and 'embellishment' were generally used at the time.[2] Not until the last decades of the nineteenth century did people begin to speak of 'town planning' (*Städtebau*, *Urbanisme* etc) and this was also when planning entered its 'modern' phase (see pp. 360 ff). But the planning of whole towns, districts and building ensembles had, as we shall see, a much longer history than this might suggest. A number of more or less sophisticated typological systems have been suggested for systematizing and analysing this earlier planning.[3] It is not my intention to add yet another attempt here, when for purely instrumental purposes I speak of three categories, namely grid planning, ideal city planning, and local design planning.

Grid planning[4] refers to the creation of plans

consisting mainly of rectilinear blocks and straight streets, generally with a square created by leaving a block or part of a block unbuilt; most of the planned cities from Antiquity to the nineteenth century could be included in this category. Characteristic of such planning is its practical nature: the aim is to divide the urban area in an appropriate manner into blocks and streets, while aesthetic ambitions are of little or no importance.

Ideal city planning refers either to the creation of model projects illustrating theoretical concepts of the ideal form and function of the town, or to towns created under the inspiration of such notions.[5]

Local design planning implies the inclusion of monumental accents such as squares or streets, generally within an existing urban structure, or it involves attempts to create an architectural setting round a building or a group of buildings. This type of planning is often aimed primarily at providing for ceremonial functions, creating a splendid setting for a prince or for ecclesiastical or temporal institutions, or for the city itself; aesthetic considerations are thus crucial.[6]

It should be emphasized yet again that these categories cannot be regarded as pigeon-holes into which all projects and planners can be fitted. On the contrary, many projects include features characteristic of two or all three types of plan. A grid street plan may also contain architectural accents, and a project of the 'ideal' type may become so simplified at the implementation stage that it begins to resemble a simple grid. Alternatively, the pure grid and the pure architectural project can be regarded as the end points on a scale along which most plans could be placed somewhere in between.

Unplanned or spontaneous urban development is determined by factors such as topography, existing paths or tracks and buildings, traffic flows, ownership boundaries etc. This often results in winding streets and irregular plots. Early towns and districts in the different periods of urbanisation are generally characterized by such spontaneously evolving arrangements, which are not always very functional. Consequently, in planned expansions or new foundations at a later stage, efforts were often made to create straight streets intersecting at right angles, and regular blocks divided into uniform plots.[7] Tuscany, for instance, offers a variety of examples of both types: on the one hand the spontaneous growth of the hill towns where the streets are determined by the topography, and on the other the planned rectilinear medieval towns built on flat ground.

The ambition was probably to produce rectilinear plots according to predetermined units of measurement, which was the basic idea of grid planning. The Greek planner Hippodamus of Miletus, who was active around the middle of the fifth century BC is generally regarded as the pioneer of this type of planning.[8] To generalize slightly, we could say that the desire for uniformity and rectilinearity has informed most planned urban expansions from the time of Hippodamus until the end of the nineteenth century.[9] Naturally this does not mean that all plans are alike; the possibilities for variation are great, even under conditions of strict rectilinearity.

During Antiquity Hippodamus was regarded as the author of the grid plan for Piraeus, which was probably constructed towards the middle of the fifth century BC, and the principles ascribed to him were applied in Rhodes, Olynthus, Priene and elsewhere, and subsequently in a number of Hellenistic towns. Nothing written by him has come down to us, but the appropriate design for cities was discussed by several Greek authors, such as Hippocrates and Aristotle.[10] With the advent of the Roman Empire the rectangular town planning model was disseminated throughout much of the then known world, not least in the Transalpine provinces. One feature of the Roman town plan, which may have been inspired by the organization of Roman military

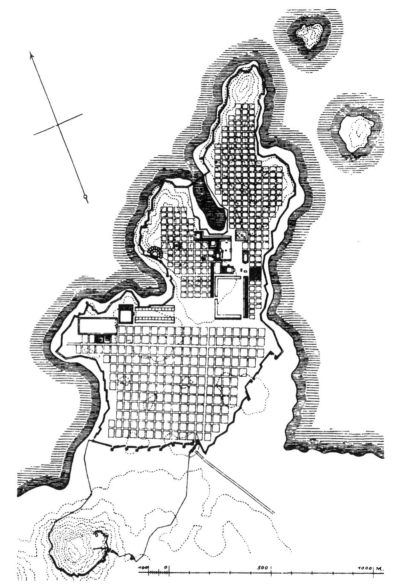

Figure 2.1 *Miletus, one of the classical examples of grid planning in Antiquity. The northern section came into being in the early fifth century BC and the southern part possibly at a later stage. Hippodamus, designated by both classical and modern writers as the originator of the grid plan idea, may have taken part in the planning as a young man, but he is hardly likely to have occupied a leading position. [From Gerkan (1924)]*

camps,[11] was the north-south and east-west street axes, which have been dubbed by posterity the *cardo maximus* and the *decumanus maximus*.[12] Close to or in connection with the intersection of these two streets, but as an enclosed enclave, lay the town's forum. The town was divided into uniform *insulae* by way of a rectilinear street network. The Roman plans can still be discerned in several cities north of the Alps, for example in Bordeaux and Strasbourg, and are well preserved in several north Italian towns such as Florence, Verona, Turin, Como and Bologna. Those responsible for the planning were a corps of qualified *mensores*, or land surveyors. The first book in Vitruvius' *De architectura* gives us

Figure 2.2 *Manhattan, New York, up to 59th Street. The uniform street network continues for more than another 100 streets to the north, interrupted only by Central Park. The map, which shows the south at the top, describes the present situation, but the block structure agrees by and large with a plan proposal submitted in 1811 for the expansion of the area north of Washington Square (the area with the narrow, east-west oriented blocks). From Miletus to Manhattan, from the fifth century BC to the nineteenth century AD, the rectangular street system with uniform blocks is a constantly recurring theme in planned urban development. It should be noted that the committee which produced the plan for Manhattan justified its rectilinear form primarily on the grounds that this made it possible to have the most convenient and cheapest housing. Aristotle said essentially the same thing, when he commented on Hippodamus's ideas during the fourth century BC. [Redrawn from a tourist map]*

some idea of the outlines of a Roman urban development theory. However, it should be noted that Vitruvius' compendium reflects conditions under the Republic, not during the great transalpine wave of expansions.

When Roman rule was replaced by the German kingdoms during the fifth century AD, the situation of the towns changed.[13] The compact built area shrank, tending to dissolve into an 'urban landscape' with many small settlements clustered round various nuclei, primarily cathedrals and monasteries. The rectangular street network was not maintained; many streets were shifted sideways and others disappeared altogether. This applies particularly north of the Alps; in southern Europe depopulation did not go as far, and so the structures of the plans survived better.

The High Middle Ages represented a new period of expansion in the history of the town in central and western Europe. The population was growing, agricultural methods were being improved and the area of cultivated land extended. At the same time trade was developing, thus re-creating the conditions necessary for urban growth. The period between the second half of the tenth century and the first half of the twelfth was characterized by the emergence of the medieval town. Part of this process took place on the legal plane: the inhabitants of the urban communities – growing richer as trade expanded – succeeded in strengthening their position *vis-à-vis* their lords and achieving a kind of collective vassal status with autonomy in internal affairs. The end point in this development lay in the characteristic late medieval city commune. Parallel with this process, the multi-cored urban landscapes solidified into coherent urban structures, and existing links between the various small settlements became permanent streets. By the end of the twelfth century the large medieval cities of western Europe had, without any apparent overall systematic planning, acquired the physical structure which was to last until the Industrial Revolution, and in many cases even longer.

Thus, by the twelfth century the town had become a fact in a physical as well as a legal sense. Whereas older towns had evolved gradually, new towns could now be systematically founded and planned by various patrons or lords. Lübeck is an important twelfth-century example. Like other towns from the twelfth or early thirteenth centuries, Lübeck has obviously sought to create a clear arrangement of blocks and streets, while at the same time many irregularities reveal that planning was still in its infancy. Moreover the basic structure in the different districts varies noticeably, which suggests that expansion proceeded piecemeal, rather than in accordance with a predetermined plan covering the whole town.

North of the Alps the number of chartered 'towns' multiplied during the thirteenth century. While the older towns had grown into centres for trade with distant places, a network of small or medium-sized towns was now being created which could provide territorial security as well as functioning as centres for local and regional trade. At the same time rationalistic grid planning was emerging and becoming more common, particularly in northern Italy, central Europe, south-west France and Wales. In these regions a large number of towns were established according to predetermined plans, and like the Roman towns they were characterized by their rectangular street networks and a desire for uniform blocks, although the results were not generally as consistent as their predecessors in the ancient world.[14] German examples which can be mentioned include Neubrandenburg and Frankfurt an der Oder, as well as Thorn, Elbing and Memel, these last all founded by the Teutonic Knights. In south-western France a great many *bastides* were founded by English or French kings and by feudal lords, primarily for reasons of territorial policy. The best known examples include Carcassonne (figure 2.3), Aigues-Mortes, Montpazier and Sainte-Foy-la-Grande. In Wales Edward I (1272–1307) established a series of small fortified towns obviously striving to follow rectilinear plans, the most important of which was Caernarvon. In England Salisbury under the patronage of its bishop represents the thirteenth century's most remarkable planning enterprise, while Gattinara can be mentioned as an example of the *terrae muratae* in northern Italy. Tuscany was a centre of medieval Italian town planning – with a number of carefully designed rectilinear cities.[15] There were also some systematically planned urban expansions, for example the rectilinear thirteenth-century Città Nuova in Massa Marittima.

New foundations appear to have followed a

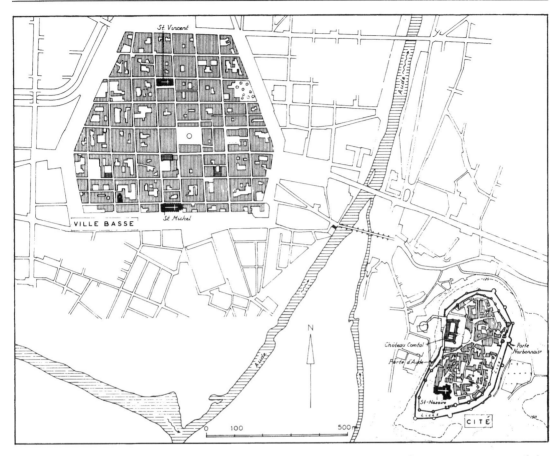

Figure 2.3 *Carcassonne, founded in the middle of the thirteen century by St. Louis, is one of the many examples of medieval grid planning. It is towns of this type, not those with winding streets and irregular blocks, that express the medieval town planning ideal. The old city, the* Cité, *southeast of the new one, can exemplify the type of medieval town that had grown 'spontaneously'. [Drawing by Erik Lorange]*

fairly regular routine. A suitable site was chosen, the requisite privileges issued, the plan and the plots marked out (in some cases we still have information about the original dimensions of the plots), and inhabitants were either attracted to the new foundation by favourable conditions or were compelled under threat to move in from another town. In some cases the work of foundation was led by the founders themselves, in others the task was transferred to agents, some of whom were probably more or less professional experts in urban foundations. In either case the local lord, as owner of the land, could decide the kind of town plan to be adopted. We can see from the case of Edward I just how seriously this activity was taken: on several occasions in 1296 and 1297 the king tried to assemble experts for a colloquium to discuss the best way to plan and order a city for the greatest convenience of the merchants and others who were to live there[16] – a town planning conference a good 600 years ahead of RIBA's 1910 meeting generally considered to be the first of its kind.

Towards the end of the thirteenth century the rate of town foundations slackened, and after the Black Death in the middle of the fourteenth century the Late Middle Ages can be regarded as a period of stagnation in European urban development. Little change was made in existing urban structures and major foundations or expansions were rare.

The medieval approach to urban building appears to have been pragmatic and technical; it is hardly possible to speak of medieval urban development theory. During the Renaissance interest grew in theoretical considerations about how towns ought to be designed, and a number of suggestions for 'ideal' cities were presented.[17] Two factors, to some extent interrelated, contributed to this interest in planning towns. The first was the rapid development of more powerful artillery and the consequent changes in fortification technology with bastions and broad earthworks instead of high walls. This meant that towns intended as strategic strongholds either had to be surrounded by new fortifications or they had to be founded *ex novo* and complete with the new type of defence system. Secondly, the independence of the towns was declining and the power of the territorial lords growing, which meant that many ideal projects were envisaged as the residence of a prince. Even the earliest of the great architectural treatises, Alberti's *De re aedificatoria* (published 1485 but written a few decades before), devoted a considerable amount of attention to the design of the town, albeit without producing any concrete or complete proposals.[18] Moreover, there were no illustrations in the original edition of Alberti's work. The first great ideal project was Filarete's Sforzinda (figure 2.4) presented with both text and drawings in *Trattato d'architettura*, which was probably written about 1460. A few decades later came Francesco di Giorgio Martini's architectural treatise, overflowing with sketchy outlines, among them a large

number of town plans.[19] Over the following century Italian architects and fortification engineers, such as Pietro Cataneo and Francesco de Marchi, presented numerous ideal projects.

One of the main issues addressed by the architects and urban development theorists of the Renaissance concerned the design of town plans in Antiquity. However, they sought the answer to this question not by studying surviving plan structures but by turning to Vitruvius. Several of their projects – but only in a few isolated instances were any cities actually built – have radial plans, i.e. the street network consists of streets radiating from a central focus, combined with streets arranged concentrically according to a concept first devised by Filarete (figure 2.4). At the street intersections there are often piazzas, sometimes with closed corners. By rhythmically varying the space between the streets and the size and design of the piazzas, it was possible to create sophisticated compositions whose purpose was aesthetic rather than practical.

The radial street system, though clearly a Renaissance invention, probably claimed its legitimacy from a misinterpreted passage in Vitruvius,[20] and was obviously regarded by many as aesthetically superior to the grid scheme, an urban design equivalent to the much admired centralized type of plan for churches. It also brought practical advantages, above all more effective control of the town and rapid communications between the centre and all points on the periphery, which was important in case of sieges. From the point of view of fortification technology a polygonal form was also desirable (most ideal city projects were surrounded by bastions), which may also be one reason why radial street networks were preferred, anyhow in theory, to chequerboard plans which did not lend themselves as naturally to enclosure within a polygon. Geometrical considerations and astrological notions, at any rate at first, may also have favoured radial solutions. But there were also rectangular street networks inspired by ideal city thinking

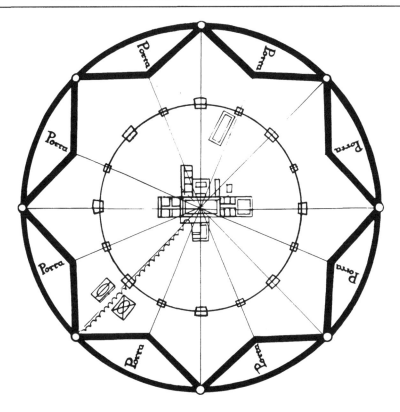

Figure 2.4 *Sforzinda. The so-called 'ideal projects' of the Renaissance often deviate from uniform rectilinearity. For the authors of these plans it was a question of translating the emerging absolutist ideas – whereby the town as a whole was regarded as a princely residence and was supposed in addition to function as a fortress – into a new urban form. For this purpose, centralizing solutions seemed eminently appropriate. With its radiating streets Filarete's plan for the imaginary town of Sforzinda, significantly named for the architect's patron Francesco Sforza, provides an important model. Further, whereas the castle in medieval towns was generally located at the periphery and lacked direct contact with the buildings in the town as such, thus expressing the political dualism between the lord on the one hand and the burghers as a municipal corporation on the other, the residence in Sforzinda has been placed in the centre – albeit not in a dominating position. The central square is rectangular – in later projects by other architects it would be given a design to match the outline of the town. Filarete's sketches should be regarded as preliminary drafts, but they demonstrate an ingenuity that is often lacking in the sometimes stereotyped projects of his successors. [From Rosenau (1974)]*

for example a well-known project by Scamozzi in the early seventeenth century (figure 2.5). The later 'model cities' were almost without exception envisaged as fortresses, and should perhaps be regarded as exercises in fortification engineering rather than manifestations of local design planning. In Italy a few towns were built according to the intentions of the theorists. Well-known examples include Palmanova in the 1590s and Grammichele about a hundred years later, both of which have radial plans, as well as Sabbioneta in the second half of the sixteenth century and Livorno in the late sixteenth century, both with rectilinear plans.

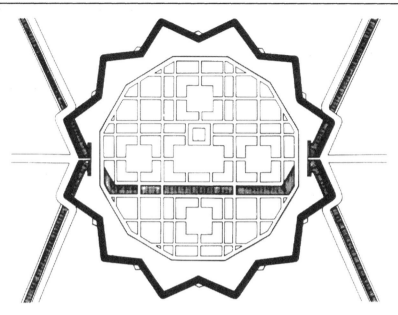

Figure 2.5 *Most model projects were intended for fortress towns, where streets and squares are distributed according to an often rather dry geometrical aesthetic. This category can be exemplified here by a proposal of Vincenzo Scamozzi dated 1615. With few exceptions the towns which were actually laid out according to a model project also had strategic objectives. The burghers were expected to participate in the maintenance and defence of the garrison and the fortifications. [From Rosenau (1974)]*

With its sophisticated block divisions and its square closed at the corners, this last town certainly smacks of an ideal project.[21] An impressive fortress town with a regular grid plan is Valletta on Malta, founded in 1566 by The Order of the Knights of St John.

In France and Germany a few 'ideal' projects assumed a different form and had a different motive, namely to offer a haven to the victims of religious persecution, in some cases providing a setting for alternative Christian ways of life. However, such examples as were realized were still clearly princely residence towns, where the lord expected his protection to be repaid by loyalty and revenue-generating enterprise. One source of inspiration for developments in Germany was Albrecht Dürer's project for a fortified town (figure 2.7) in *Etliche vnderricht, zu befestigung der Stett, Schloß vnd flecken* (1527). Here a number of

rectangular rows of houses were assembled in larger blocks intended for different purposes and different social groups; the blocks were then organized in turn round a square castle complex which dominated the town. The town's outline is also square. Dürer's ideas were taken up among others by Johan Valentin Andreae in *Reipublicae Christianopolitanae descriptio* (1619). Andreae produces a Christianopolis with narrow blocks which are laid out next to each other and linked at the corners, so that only one street on every side leads to the sacred building at the centre of the town, which has replaced the castle in Dürer's project. More conventional plans, many of which are similar in type to those in the Italian treatises, are to be found in Daniel Speckle's *Architectvra Von Vestungen* from 1584, or in Wilhelm Dilich-Schäffer's *Peribologia oder Bericht Wilhelmi Dilichii Hist. von Vestungs-Geweben*

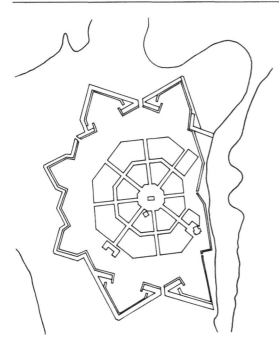

Figure 2.6 *The few towns with radial plans which have actually been realised can be represented here by Fredrikshamn in Finland, begun during the 1720s as a border fort against Russia, instead of the more familiar and often reproduced Palmanova, laid out a good hundred years earlier in Italy. [Redrawn excerpt from a 1741 map in Nordenstreng (1908)]*

(figure 2.30*a*) published roughly 50 years later, to mention only a few of many examples.[22] The towns envisaged in the schemes suggested in these publications are primarily fortresses; in other words, as in Italy, there is a shift away from architectural and social considerations and towards aspects concerned with fortification engineering. The best known German example of a project of the ideal type, which was actually built, is Freudenstadt, founded in 1599 by Duke Friedrich I of Württemberg as a mining town that was also to provide a haven for Protestant exiles from their own countries. The plan, which was produced by Heinrich Schickardt (figure 2.8), was never fully realized.

The first proposal seems to have been inspired by Dürer, and the final version has blocks arranged in the same way as in Andreae's not-then-published Christianopolis.

Two French authors of model city plans should also be mentioned, namely Jacques Perret and Sébastien Vauban, the second of whom was the leading fortification engineer in France under Louis XIV and the originator of a number of fortified towns, of which Neuf-Brisach is the most notable example. Perhaps the best known French town in the 'ideal' tradition is Richelieu, built in the 1630s by the famous cardinal with the quite clear intention of trying to create a model town. It was preceded by the fortified towns of Vitry-le-François (1544) and Charleville (1606). In Holland discussions of the ideal city took a practical turn and were geared to engineering considerations. Here the foremost theorist was Symon Stevin.

'Ideal city' projects which were fully realized according to the plan were rare, although it is sometimes difficult – and perhaps not always meaningful – to distinguish between 'ideal cities' and others. In many cases it is a question of a difference in degree rather than of two essentially different types. 'Ideal' projects may well have influenced more 'ordinary' urban development proposals which cannot in themselves be described as ideal cities. Moreover, many ideal models were certainly envisaged as theoretical examples rather than projects to be realized exactly. But even if the immediate practical importance of these ideas was not very great, the ideal projects represent a step on the way to modern town planning, being based on a theoretical concept of how the town should be designed and how it should function.

The type of planning which is referred to here as local design planning has not yet been touched upon, although there is considerable evidence of its occurrence in classical times, for example in the agora and forum ensembles. Nor was monumental local planning entirely absent during the Middle Ages. In Tuscany,

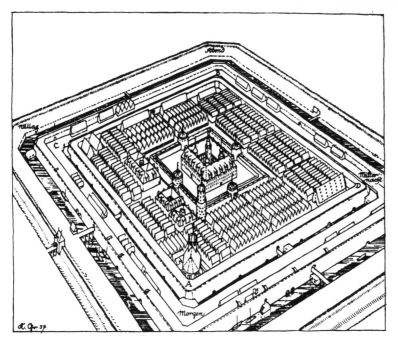

Figure 2.7 *Dürer's project for a model town published in 1527, redrawn by Gruber. Here, and in related projects, the geometrical town plan emerges as a consistent expression of a hierarchical social order, in which towns come into being by decree of a prince and form part of the power system. This proposal should be regarded as a theoretical exercise without any great implications for subsequent developments. [From Gruber (1952)]*

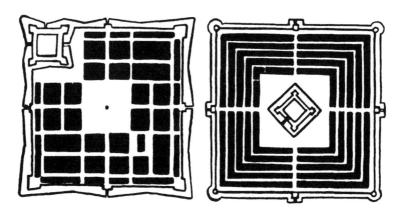

Figure 2.8 *Freudenstadt can represent the towns founded for refugees from religious persecution. The original plan, which has survived, was drawn in 1599 by the architect and master builder Heinrich Schickhardt. The first version (to the left), which is closely related to Dürer's model project, apart from the fact that the castle is not in the middle but is located in one corner of the square town, was rejected by Schickhardt's patron, the Duke of Württemberg. The approved version (to the right), with its narrow blocks and the large open area in the centre, represents a unique planning solution which was not reproduced in subsequent developments. The castle, probably for reasons of defence, has been turned 90 degrees so that its corners are oriented towards the entry roads. It was never realized. The project is reproduced here in a redrawing by Eimer. [From Eimer (1961)]*

for instance, several cities reveal an ambition to surround the most distinguished square with imposing buildings, as is superbly illustrated by the Piazza del Campo in Siena.[23]

In the early Renaissance a building was regarded largely as an isolated object, and not as one element in a broader setting. However, during the second half of the fifteenth century attempts were made to create architecturally coherent building ensembles. For example Bernardo Rossellino, probably in close co-operation with Alberti, transformed the small town of Corsignano into a splendid setting for Pius II (1458–64), who renamed it Pienza (figure 2.9).[24] Here it was clearly a case of inserting a monumentally designed milieu – a piazza surrounded by buildings – into what was otherwise a traditional Tuscan urban fabric. Mention should also be made of the project

initiated by Pope Nicholas V (1447–55) for redesigning Borgo Leonino, with straight streets surrounded by colonnades and a monumental piazza in front of St Peter's. During the sixteenth century more attention gradually came to be paid to the conception of an architectural environment as an integral whole. Michelangelo's Campidoglio project with its political connotations was an important step in this direction (figure 2.10). One of the characteristics that distinguishes the Baroque from the early Renaissance is just this growing ambition to incorporate the individual buildings into a coherent architectural context. Vistas, eye-catching foci and architectural ensembles became important ingredients in this approach, which thus heralded the monumentalizing of urban design, particularly of squares and streets, which were often designed as accents in

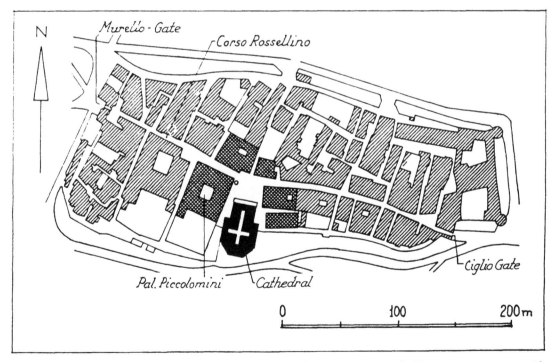

Figure 2.9 *Pienza. A Tuscan hill town transformed for Pius II, probably in cooperation with Alberti, to produce a milieu informed by current Renaissance design ideals. [Redrawing by Erik Lorange]*

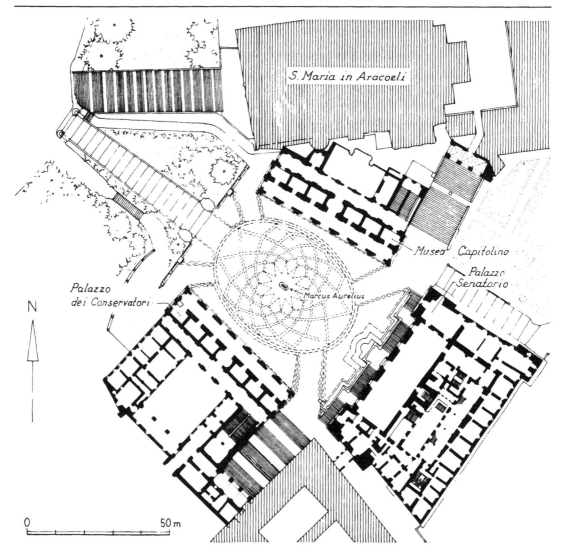

Figure 2.10 *Rome. While the buildings in medieval squares could be changed over the years, the typical monumental square is an outdoor room, conceived as an essentially unalterable unit (which does not mean that the final version might not be the result of a long evolution). Nothing can exemplify this better than Michelangelo's Campidoglio, which was followed by a whole series of individually designed Roman monumental places, often the result of the work of several generations of architects. [Drawing by Erik Lorange]*

existing urban structures. It should be added, however, that even if aesthetic ideas were important, they were seldom the only motive behind great urban embellishment projects. From the beginning a desire to enhance the

functional and sanitary standard was always part of the picture.

Let us first look at the role of the square or piazza as components in the plan. In the medieval planned town the square or marketplace generally consisted of a vacant block or part of a block, and was not surrounded by any coherently designed group of buildings. When a more distinguished square ensemble was desired, one obvious idea was to enhance the space thus created by the introduction of uniform architecture, preferably conceived as a whole. Inspiration may have come from medieval cloisters and Italian palace courtyards, as well as from earlier north Italian ensembles such as the Piazza San Marco in Venice and the Piazza del Campo in Siena. Important steps towards the uniformly designed square were taken by the Piazza della Santissima Annunziata in Florence and the Piazza Ducale in Vigevano, attributed to Bramante.[25] A further stage in the evolution of the Italian piazza was reached with the central piazza in Livorno around 1600. This has a uniform rectangular design and closed corners, but the

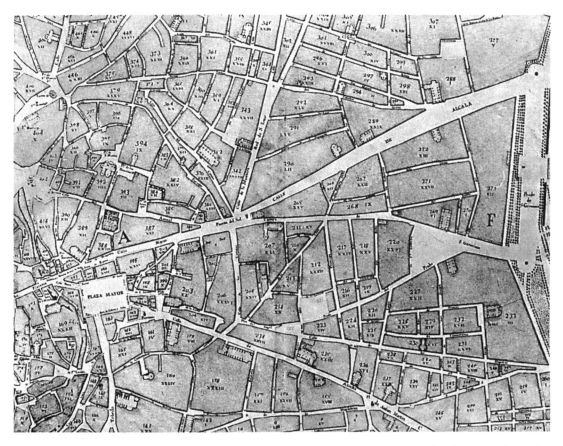

Figure 2.11 *Madrid. The term 'local design planning' refers in the present book primarily to the design of places or squares. An early example outside Italy is the Plaza Mayor in Madrid, a kind of city improvement project begun in the 1580s which aimed to create a place embracing both ceremonial and practical functions. Together with the Place des Vosges it established the 'royal' place in the European urban development tradition. Excerpt from* Plano Topographico de la Villa y Corte de Madrid, *1769, drawn by Antonio Espinosa de los Monteros. [From* Cartografía básica de la Ciudad de Madrid*]*

effect is somewhat diminished by the streets that run into it.

Something of a starting-point for the genesis of the square outside Italy came with the vast Plaza Mayor[26] in Madrid (figure 2.11), originally planned as early as the beginning of the 1580s by Juan de Herrera but realized in stages. In the 1610s a new plan was made by Juan Gómez de Mora but even this was not the end of the story. The Plaza Mayor as we see it today is the outcome of a whole series of fires and redevelopments, the latest of them towards the end of the eighteenth century.[27] The surrounding streets, which run into the square aslant and asymmetrically, still show that the square was partly cut out of an existing structure. The Plaza Mayor in Madrid provided the inspiration for a number of similar ensembles in other Spanish towns.

Even more important were the two places constructed in Paris during the first decade of the seventeenth century, namely the Place des Vosges (figure 2.12) and the Place Dauphine (see p. 56), both on the initiative of Henri IV (1598–1610). The first of these in particular reveals a kinship with the Plaza Mayor. Like the Plaza Mayor the Place des Vosges is incorporated into an existing urban structure, and both squares are surrounded by uniform architecture with arcades and embellished with royal equestrian statues. The Parisian squares are thus a little later than the earliest proposals for the Plaza Mayor. On the other hand they acquired their final form immediately, and the Place des Vosges is still largely intact. No study appears to have been made of the relation between the Plaza Mayor and the Place des Vosges. Perhaps Henri IV, through his links with Navarra and Spain may have known about the plans under way in Madrid and have been inspired by them. And possibly in its later stages the Plaza Mayor in Madrid may have been influenced by Place des Vosges, even though both squares share an important common predecessor in the Italian piazzas. With these two squares a model was established

for the ceremonial square worthy of a capital city, a *place* which was not just a crossroads for traffic but an enclosed urban room. During the 1630s London acquired a slightly simplified variant in the Piazza in Covent Garden, planned by Inigo Jones (figure 2.13). This ensemble heralded the type of square which later functioned more or less as a module in the subsequent expansion of London (cf. pp. 84 f).

There is thus no immediate prototype in Rome for the standard type of closed monumental square surrounded by arcaded buildings of uniform architectural design. Naturally at a more general level the Roman squares have functioned as a source of inspiration, but each one separately represents a unique solution contingent on unique opportunities and constraints and is thus too special to allow for imitation.[28] When it comes to monumental streets Rome has perhaps been more important as a model. It is in Rome that we find street improvements which were not only among the first but were also some of the most extensive before Haussmann.[29] These improvements were partly inspired by the need to cope with the great crowds of pilgrims who came to Rome every twenty-fifth year from 1450 onwards to celebrate Holy Year. It is thought that in 1600 more than half a million pilgrims came to the Holy City. They visited the churches and other holy places, often in long processions for which the existing network of narrow twisting streets were quite unsuited. Added to this, the numerous ecclesiastical institutions and foreign legates also generated a lot of traffic. In the sixteenth century there are supposed to have been more carriages here than in any other city in Europe. Charles Borromeo once commented that a necessary condition for succeeding in Rome, apart from the love of God, was the possession of a carriage.[30]

These chaotic conditions encouraged a whole succession of popes to undertake major street improvements, presumably modelled on Via del Corso, the Via Lata of Antiquity. Experience of earlier street improvements in

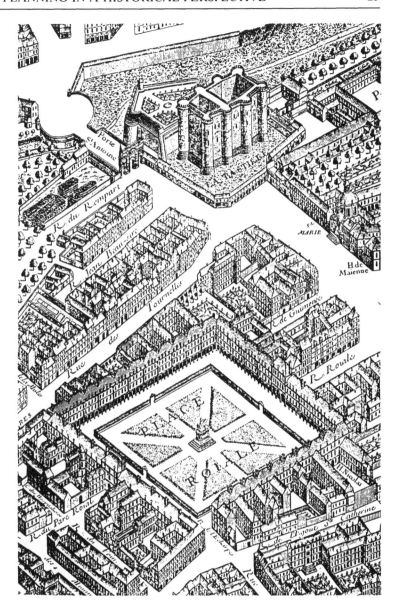

Figure 2.12 *Place des Vosges, Paris. This place, well preserved to the present day, was incorporated into an existing urban structure and became a model for the design of monumental urban squares. Detail of a map from the 1730s. [From Josephson (1943)]*

Florence may also have been a source of inspiration.[31] The first of the more substantial street developments was carried out under Sixtus IV (1471–84) in time for the Holy Year in 1475. The first completely straight street was Via Alessandrina, later called Borgo Nuovo, which was constructed under Alexander VI (1492–1503) in 1499 for the Holy Year 1500.

This ran from Castel Sant'Angelo direct to the main entrance of the Vatican Palace, corresponding more or less to the north side of the present-day Via della Conciliazione. Under Julius II (1503–13) the Via Giulia was created; it runs straight as an arrow and was perhaps meant to complement Via della Lungara on the other side of the Tiber. Under Leo X

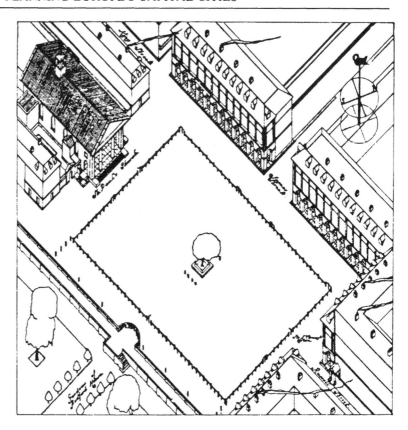

Figure 2.13 *In London there was no interest in grand monumental places of the continental type. Instead the first planned place – Inigo Jones's 'piazza' in Covent Garden, shown here in a perspective reconstruction – represents the first step towards a specifically English type, generally described as a square, namely an open space with more or less uniform buildings round a park-like green area reserved for the residents. [From Summerson (1978)]*

(1513–21) the Via di Ripetta was laid out from Piazza del Popolo to the church of S. Luigi dei Francesi.[32] Via del Babuino was not yet planned; not until it was built about ten years later under Clement VII (1523–34), was the series of streets radiating out from the Piazza del Popolo complete. The pattern, which would become a favourite motive in artistic urban design, was repeated on a smaller scale by the streets leading to Ponte Sant'Angelo.

A climax in grand-scale planning was reached during Sixtus V's pontificate (1585–90), with the vision of a street network stretching from S. Maria Maggiore across the whole of the ancient urban area (see p. 255). Only parts of the grandiose system of streets radiating out from S. Maria Maggiore, the Lateran Basilica and Colloseum were ever realized (figure 2.14).[33] The straight street was certainly re-

garded as aesthetically pleasing, but it is also a simple truth that the shortest route between two points is a straight line, and this was probably the deciding factor.[34] Knowledge of the newly built straight streets of Rome would then have spread across Europe; no other European town was international in quite the same way as the Holy City. The pontificate of Alexander VII (1655–67) represented a further peak in Roman building, including the planting of trees along a number of streets, perhaps the first time this had occurred on a large scale in any city.[35]

Many sixteenth-century streets in Rome terminated in front of a monumental building, which thus provided a dramatic visible marker from afar; this was another feature which would prove to be influential in the future. During Paul III's pontificate (1534–49), for

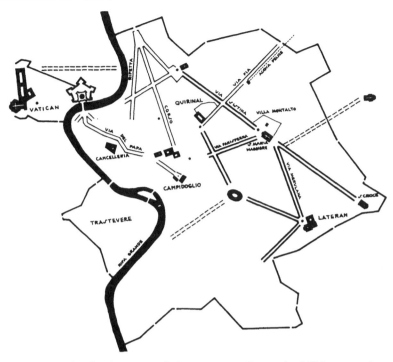

Figure 2.14 *Following the final return of the popes to Rome in 1420, extensive regulation and expansion plans soon began to be considered. Street planning was set seriously in motion during the second half of the century, and was aimed in a first phase at facilitating communications in the densely built-up area in the Campus Martius and between this and the Vatican. In the 1580s under Sixtus V, planning embarked on a second and more wide-ranging phase, and a system of completely straight streets was planned by the pope and his architect Domenico Fontana, as communicating links between the great titular churches. The figure shows the streets planned by Sixtus (dashed lines = streets not realized). The pope's project differs from earlier planning in its grand scale and in the fact that the new streets were to serve primarily as traffic routes. A similar focus also characterises many nineteenth-century projects, above all Haussmann's transformation of Paris. Common to both is the desire to enliven long street prospects with focal accents. [From Magnuson (1982)]*

example, the church of Trinità dei Monti, the Palazzo Farnese and the Palazzo Senatorio were all focused in this way, and under Pius IV (1559–65) the Porta Pia became the focal point of the new Via Pia, now Via XX Settembre. An innovation that appeared during Sixtus V's pontificate (1585–90) was the placing of obelisks instead of columns as an eye-catching marker at the end of a street. The obelisk raised in the Piazza S. Pietro in 1586 was probably not intended to function in this way, but it obviously gave birth to the idea which was then tried out the very next year, when an obelisk was placed in front of the apse of S. Maria Maggiore as a marker for the Via delle Quattro Fontane. Then in 1588 another obelisk was raised in front of the transept of the Lateran Basilica, at the intersection of Via Merulana and Via di S. Giovanni in Laterano, while a year later again yet another was positioned in the Piazza del Popolo, just where the potential of this visual device in the urban landscape could be exploited to the full: the obelisk draws the three streets together into a coherent ensemble, transforming what might have been a trivial junction into one of the most frequently imitated planning solutions in Europe.

In several cases attempts have also clearly been made to achieve uniformity in the design of the buildings along a street, although it was not generally possible to carry this through consistently. The street vista created by Vasari between the two wings of the Uffizi in Florence gives us some notion of the contemporary ideal.[36] During the later sixteenth century the criteria for enhancing a city street and giving it an air of distinction were thus established in Rome and would persist until the end of the nineteenth century: such streets should be straight and should end in an eye-catching accent such as a building, a monument or a column; they should also ideally be lined by buildings of uniform design. And this applied both to the redevelopment of existing structures and to the creation of entirely new ensembles.

It was only in exceptional cases that a complete urban setting could be created on architectural terms alone; to find the grand planning enterprises unhampered by reality, we have to turn primarily to landscape gardening. An example of combined landscape and townscape planning at the most exalted level is Versailles, which consists of a palace ensemble flanked by a park on one side and a town on the other (figure 2.15). Thus it is no longer a question of a residence in a town, but a town within a residence complex. The three principal thoroughfares of the town radiate out

from the palace square or Place d'Armes, repeating the pattern of the Piazza del Popolo in Rome. Thus the architectural heart of the town is the square before the palace, and not – as was almost always the case in the ideal plans – the geographical centre. However, streets and squares in Versailles have been designed in such a way as to recall the Italian ideal plans. Among other things there are several places with closed corners.[37]

Louis XIV's Versailles gave the other princes of Europe no peace. Many are the imitations and variants, both great and small. After Versailles, the most systematic attempt to integrate a town, a palace and a park into one great ensemble is Karlsruhe, which was planned at the beginning of the eighteenth century (figure 2.16).[38] At the centre of the original structure – for which no architect can be named with certainty, although a detailed programme appears to have been made by Karl Wilhelm Markgraf von Baden–Durlach – was a palace tower surrounded by thirty-two radiating avenues. Over the next few decades the project seems to have been extended and the finished palace complex consists of a short central block from which two long wings stretch away at an angle of 45 degrees. Between these wings a forecourt was planned, and beyond this – but within the sector created by avenues bordered on their outer sides by public buildings and continuing in the same direction as the palace wings – were envisaged first a formal garden with parterres and shrubberies, and then a town cut through by a broad street at right angles to the central axis from the palace facade. The larger sector outside the palace

Figure 2.15 *Versailles is not only a palace and a park, but also a town planned as a second capital city for France. The three sections are arranged round a common axis passing through the king's bedchamber, where the ritual robing and disrobing ceremonies took place. The plan, which shows a relatively early stage in the extension and rebuilding activities, is one of the many important drawings connected with the history of Versailles, which are to be found in the Nationalmuseum, Stockholm.*

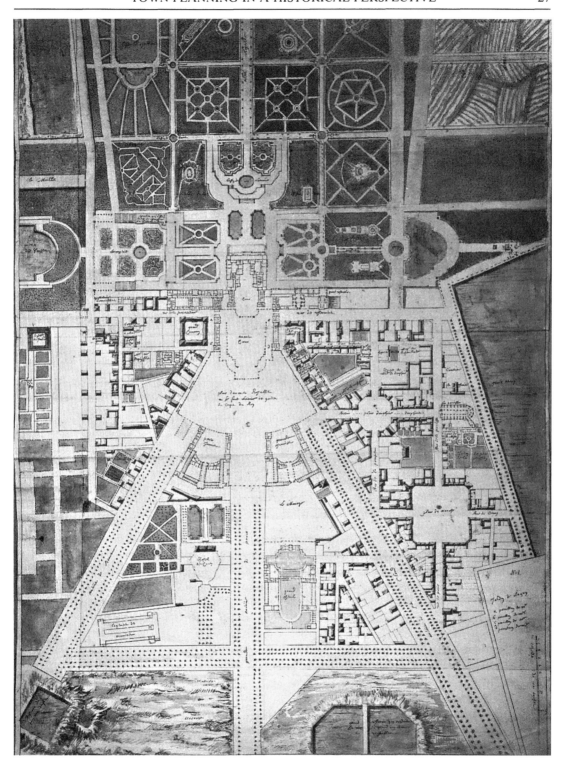

Figure 2.16 *Karlsruhe, especially in the form originally envisaged, is the most extreme example of a plan totally determined by the royal residence function: a tower belonging to the palace constitutes the central point in a radial scheme to which everything should be subject except the main street of the town, which intersects one of the streets starting from the palace at a right angle. The figure shows the planning status around 1740 in an engraving by J.M. Steidlin.*

wings, which thus comprised three-quarters of the circle, was occupied by a hunting park. The strong impression of a closed ensemble clustered round its central point, the palace tower, was reinforced by a circular road cutting through the town and the hunting park. Most of this project was realized. At the beginning of the nineteenth century some major expansion proposals were put forward, among others by Friedrich Weinbrenner. According to these plans, which largely remained on the drawing board, the town was to be extended by a system of avenues in a manner that would clearly have conflicted with the idea of the original ensemble, since it would have violated the centrality of the palace.[39]

Like Versailles, Karlsruhe was a unique manifestation of sovereignty, the supreme example of what in German is called *landesfürstliche Planung* and had no particular implications for later urban developments. It should be observed, however, that in both cases the palace lies outside the densely built-up area, and not in its centre as several authors of ideal projects suggested. By distancing it from the noisy activities of the town, the desired architectural and symbolical dominance would be easier to achieve, as would also the coordination of the palace and the parkland. This notion was to be followed during the nineteenth century, for instance in the proposals for Helsinki, Athens and Christiania.

The towns of Versailles and Karlsruhe were products of advanced planning, even though the aim was primarily to create not an ideal urban environment but an architectural and functional complement to the palaces. Ambitious planning enterprises had occurred earlier, albeit without any corresponding aesthetic aims and mainly with a view to dividing up future building land in a functional way, in some cases inspired by 'ideal' projects. The first post-medieval example of a comprehensive planned urban expansion was probably the *addizione erculea* in Ferrara, designed with considerable foresight by the architect Biagio Rossetti for Ercole I d'Este during the 1490s (figure 2.17). This enterprise, which more than

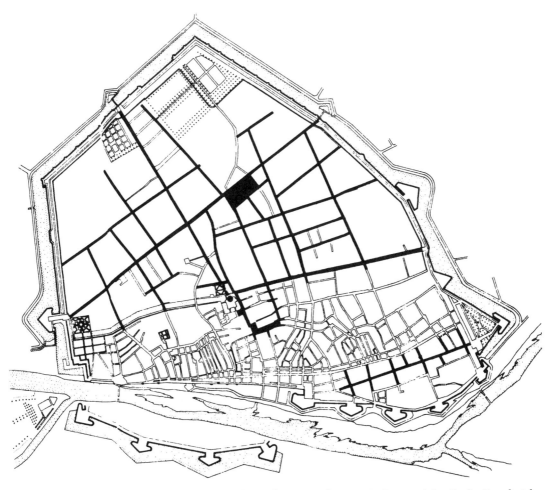

Figure 2.17 *Ferrara.* Addizione erculea, *planned in 1492 by Biagio Rossetti for Duke Ercole (the black lines in the northern part of the town). The proposal is unusual in that greater priority was given to the smooth adjustment of the new district to the old town, rather than concentrating on complete rectilinearity. [From Benevolo (1980)]*

doubled the area of Ferrara, was informed to a greater degree than many later expansions in other places with an ambition to adapt the new district and its street network – both organically and in its design – to the old city.[40] More stereotyped in its rectangularity and more of a new town than an urban expansion, was the Ville-Neuve in Nancy planned in 1588 by Girolamo Citoni; its realization required an extensive redevelopment of earlier buildings and streets. Later the two halves of the town were joined by a splendid square ensemble.[41] Rectangularity is also evident in Neustadt in Hanau from the beginning of the seventeenth century,[42] as well as in the almost contemporary Mannheim; both of these are typical fortified towns. Mannheim was destroyed by the French in 1689, and was rebuilt later on an even bigger scale, but according to a more formalistic 'chequerboard' plan.[43]

During the seventeenth century there were urban expansions or new foundations of various kinds and with varying levels of aesthetic ambition in several parts of Europe. Many more examples could be cited. However, let us turn instead to the Nordic countries, which provide us with rather a special case. By the middle of the seventeenth century, as a result of reforms and military successes, Sweden had achieved a leading position in northern Europe. At that time the country still had relatively few towns, and even fewer which exhibited much sign of progress. Under the influence of mercantilistic ideas Sweden's political leaders saw the redevelopment of the urban system as an important way of fulfilling the country's new role. Moreover, during the campaigns on the continent they had seen many splendid and flourishing European towns, and now they wanted to create something similar at home.

Swedish seventeenth-century urban policy comprised a number of different measures.[44] First, a large number of new towns were founded. Secondly, towns were to be activated by way of administrative reforms, trading privileges and large donations of land. Thirdly,

there was also a desire to modernise the physical form of the towns by way of town planning improvements. As one step in these efforts a large number of towns were mapped and new town plans drawn up.[45] These plans generally lacked any aesthetic ambition; they consisted of plain, rectilinear street networks and rectangular blocks, only scantily adapted to topographical realities. Thus, with a few exceptions, the Swedish plans were examples of grid planning, often of a rather simple kind; any kinship with the advanced compositions of the theorists was remote. The Swedish towns also differed from the ideal models in that, with the exception of the border provinces, they were not fortified, even if plan drawings were often decorated with bastions. The plans were generally made by fortification officers and land surveyors; only exceptionally were architects involved and then mainly for local design planning. In some although by no means all cases the improvement plans were realized wholly or partly by being imposed on the citizens, by initiating ruthless and often summary expropriations, demolitions and so on.[46] Attempts were also made to exploit the situation after a fire had destroyed a town or part of a town, by embarking on radical redevelopments.

Swedish seventeenth-century planning can best be studied in the new foundations. Gothenburg represents the paramount example; much of the plan inspired by Dutch town planning has survived, except that a few of the canals have been filled in. In the case of Kalmar the town was moved from its medieval site immediately in front of the castle to Kvarnholmen: here, too, a well preserved seventeenth-century structure can still be discerned (figure 2.19). But the greatest efforts were made in Stockholm, where all the suburbs were completely redeveloped (see p. 301). In Uppsala, too, wholesale street renewal was undertaken.[47] The fortified towns represent a special group, planned during the last decades of the seventeenth century, in particular

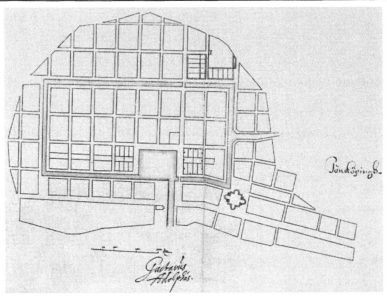

Figure 2.18 *Jönköping. Town plan approved by Gustavus II Adolphus, made around 1620 and attributed to the Dutchman Arvid Hand. The project, which came up in connection with the removal of the town to a new site after the Swedish-Danish war in 1611–13, is the most obvious example together with Gothenburg of Dutch influence on Nordic town planning as the canal systems in particular indicate. Unlike Gothenburg, this town was built in a much simpler way than had been originally envisaged. [Krigsarkivet, Stockholm]*

Karlskrona and Landskrona. In the many plan variants for these towns the inspiration of continental fortification and urban planning theoreticians is evident. Mention should also be made of Fredrikshamn (Hamina) in the Finnish part of the kingdom; from 1721 it was a border town facing Russia. As a result of its important site, the town was rebuilt according to a radial plan, the only systematically realized plan of this type in the North (figure 2.6).[48]

In the Danish-Norwegian kingdom improvements and planned expansions also occurred, albeit a little earlier and particularly under Christian IV (1588–1648). Among the most important of these was the new foundation of Christiania (Oslo) in Norway (figure 7.1), according to the kind of rectilinear plan typical of the times, and Kristianstad in Skåne (Swedish since 1658). In Copenhagen, too, several expansions were undertaken.[49] In

Germany the extension of Berlin represents a close parallel to that of Stockholm. It is probable that Sweden may have been a model for Frederick William (1640–88), the Great Elector, in his efforts to improve the status of Brandenburg. An important part of this policy was the improvement of Berlin (see p. 187). The new districts have plans of much the same type as those for Stockholm's *malmar* (cf. figures 12.1 and 13.1), which may have provided inspiration. It is not perhaps altogether impossible the Swedish urban development enterprises may have been one source of inspiration for the extensive town planning activities in Russia which were launched under Catherine II (cf. pp. 39 f).

The discussions in London after the Great Fire in 1666 represent one of the most noted episodes in the history of town planning.[50] Nine days after the outbreak of the fire and

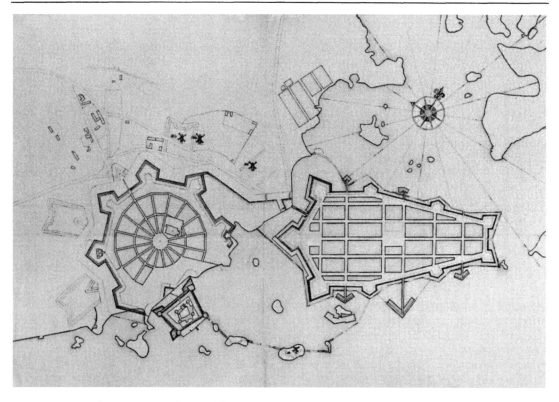

Figure 2.19 *Kalmar. During the Middle Ages Kalmar was one of Sweden's most important towns, as well as being a major border fort facing Denmark. During the Danish-Swedish war of 1611–13 the town was badly damaged, and was to be rebuilt according to a radial plan, made by the Dutchman Andries Sersanders. In 1647 Kalmar was ravaged by a devastating fire, after which the idea – already mooted earlier – of moving the town eastwards to Kvarnholmen and out of shooting-range of the fort, was put into effect. The new plan, whose author was probably the fortification officer Johan Wärnschiöld, had a rectangular street network of the more conventional type. On this map made in the 1640s the two alternatives have been brought together. Thus it shows side by side one unique and one more typical example of Nordic urban development during the seventeenth century. [Krigsarkivet, Stockholm]*

before it had even been fully extinguished, Sir Christopher Wren submitted a radical redevelopment proposal, complete with a written commentary. This was soon followed by proposals from John Evelyn, Valentine Knight, Robert Hooke and others. Wren's plan is one of the first attempts to combine a rectangular street network with diagonal avenues (figure 2.20). With its rectilinear blocks, its broad embankments and thoroughfares, and its star-shaped 'squares', this was a precursor of nineteenth-century planning, and was still regarded during the nineteenth century as exemplary.[51] The three alternatives submitted by Evelyn were structurally more complicated, favouring diagonal streets and squares of different shapes. Evelyn's ambition seems to have been to make a display of fashionable ideas rather than to allow for the prevailing conditions. Hooke's proposal (figure 2.30*b*) consists

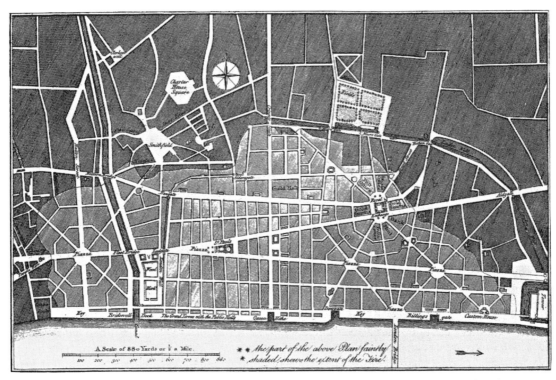

Figure 2.20 *London. Christopher Wren's proposal for the rebuilding of London after the Great Fire of 1666 is of central importance in town planning history. The western part of the urban area has been divided into a rectilinear grid, while the eastern part constitutes a system of polygonal squares from which streets radiate out. In the largest square lies the Royal Exchange, to which ten streets lead. The two parts are linked by broad thoroughfares which part at St Paul's. [From Yarwood (1976)]*

of a pure grid plan with occasional accents, in particular four large squares with closed corners. The streets are all of equal width. This project exhibits resemblance to the Nordic seventeenth-century town plans. All these projects were unrealistic, however, in so far as they paid too little attention to topography, existing street networks or ownership boundaries. This applied not least to Wren's proposal.[52] King Charles II (1660–85) seems to have been sympathetic to the idea of radical measures, but just how serious the plans were remains unclear. Be that as it may, the reconstruction basically retained the old planning structure. There were no legal instruments for controlling developments, and the necessary opportunities for financing such proposals and the administrative apparatus for implementing them were both lacking. However, a new building law produced by a committee, appointed jointly by the king and the City, and adopted by parliament in 1667, gave some guarantee of improved building standards and the widening of certain streets.[53] It is interesting to compare the relatively meagre results of the planning discussions in London with the great redevelopment of Stockholm's *malmar* which was just being completed at the same time. The difference probably depended on the fact that in Stockholm the centre of the city itself was not involved; moreover, the Swedish national government probably had a stronger position *vis-à-vis* Stockholm than the English government had with regard to London, and could therefore act more decisively.

The most important urban development projects of the eighteenth century include St Petersburg, Bath, Edinburgh and Lisbon, all of which possess certain unique features and have no direct parallels. St Petersburg is the only one of the towns discussed here which was founded intentionally as a capital city, and which had no connection with any earlier urban settlement; moreover it can probably be described as the most successful post-medieval urban foundation in Europe, at least in terms of population growth.[54] The building operations began in 1703 on directives from Peter the Great, as one step in his campaign to bring Russia politically, economically and culturally closer to Western Europe. The city was founded in a delta-like area at the mouth of the river Neva. Amsterdam, where Peter had stayed during his European journey, is said to have provided the model. The difficulties were enormous, not least due to the clayey and marshy terrain. Tens of thousands of enforced labourers, most of them peasants, carried out extensive channelling and pile-driving operations – an even greater manifestation of absolutism than had been seen during the building of Versailles a few decades earlier. Experts were called in from outside to answer for the planning and architectural design. Jean-Baptiste Le Blond was appointed chief architect in 1716, when he also drew up an imaginative master plan for the new town (figure 2.21). However, this plan appears to be more in the nature of a theoretical construct than a practicable building plan, and it probably had little impact on subsequent developments.[55]

The first moves towards creating a more impressive environment were made in 1737, when a new town plan was drawn up and a commission appointed to be responsible for planning developments. Particular attention was paid to the district on the south bank of the river, Admiraltéjskaja, where the idea was to create an area of imposing residential buildings, by forbidding either factories or wooden buildings to be erected there. It was also at this time that the system of three boulevards radiating from the place in front of the Admiralty emerged, with the Admiralty tower as focal point: the Nevskiy Prospekt and the present-day Gorokhovaya Ulitsa and the Voznesenskiy Prospekt.[56] The reign of Catherine II (1762–96) was a specially important period, during which the architectural character of the town was taking shape. Particularly significant was the establishment in 1762 of a commission concerned with brick building in St Petersburg and Moscow. The commission arranged an urban planning competition which produced several valuable ideas for the future; for a long time it was also to act as un urban development authority.[57] At the beginning of the nineteenth century, under Alexander I, the central parts of St Petersburg presented a homogeneous townscape punctuated by a number of magnificent architectural markers (figure 2.22). The more peripheral districts, on the other hand, were of a very low standard.

Of the other three, we can start with Bath, which on account of its thermal springs had long been England's leading spa. Here, in the course of roughly half a century from the mid-1720s, the two John Woods – father and son – skilfully exploited the topographical conditions to create a richly designed architectural environment in the spirit of English Palladianism, with Queen Square, the Circus and Royal Crescent as the chief jewels in a sequence of movement and variation (figure 2.23).[58] The Square and the Circus are formal and 'closed', while the Crescent is open to extensive views, a difference which reflects a shift towards the more romantic concept of nature that is also manifest in landscape gardening. Town planning and the design of buildings complemented one another in a manner unusual for the times,

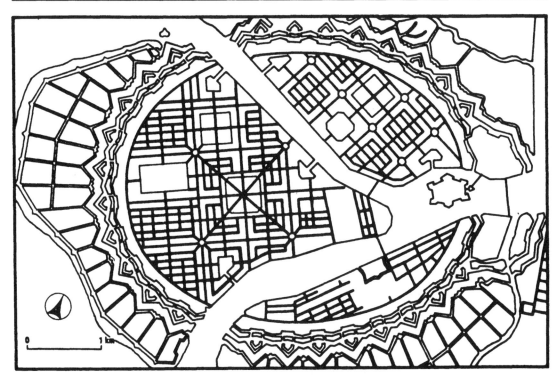

Figure 2.21 *Le Blond's visionary plan of St Petersburg. The streets radiating from the Admiralty are not yet envisaged; this solution evolved gradually in the course of the successive expansions. [From Bater (1976)]*

while at the same time landscape was integrated into the townscape in a way that had rarely if ever been seen before. Bath differs from London's West End with its contemporary rectangular squares by displaying a dynamic variation between different spatial forms (here the Woods were especially innovative) and by its creators' ambition to integrate the parts into an overall urbanistic context. Perhaps, to use the planning categories suggested above, we could say that local design planning has been extended here to embrace a whole urban environment.

Edinburgh provides another famous example. The old town lay within its walls on a mountain ridge, and by the eighteenth century there was already a pressing need to expand. By draining a marsh it became possible to build a 'new town' on another ridge to the north of the old one. The two parts were to be linked by a bridge over the area of the former marshland. In 1766, nearly two decades after the competition for the present Place de la Concorde in Paris (see pp. 61 f) and three years after a competition had been held for St Petersburg (see p. 34), Edinburgh organized a planning competition which inspired six proposals. The winner was the architect James Craig. His project, which was adopted by the city after some revisions, was not particularly remarkable: a principal street, the future George Street, was surrounded on both sides by four blocks and terminated at both ends in an open place, (today Charlotte Square and St Andrew Square), each with a church to close the prospect (figure 2.24). The new town was

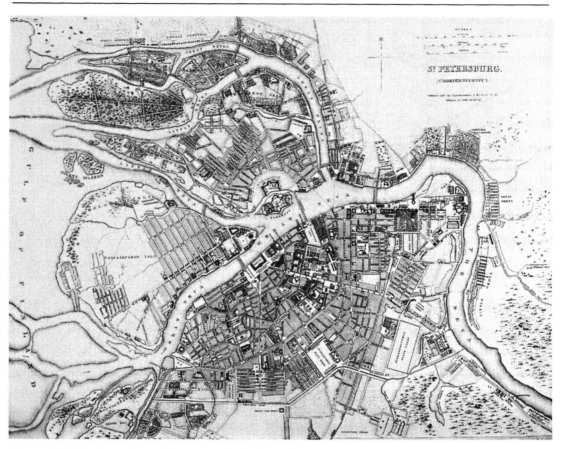

Figure 2.22 *St Petersburg. The map, which dates from 1834, shows the result of a good hundred years of conscientious planning. Along the bank of the Neva is the ceremonial centre with the Admiralty, the Winter Palace, the General Staff Building etc. and a sequence of squares. From the open place in front of the Admiralty the three main streets radiate out, connecting the centre with the peripheral areas. These streets are crossed by a number of concentric streets creating a rational structure. The tower of the Admiralty plays an important role by visually drawing together the different parts of the town rather as the obelisk in the Piazza del Popolo does in Rome. [Photo from Krigsarkivet, Stockholm]*

bordered on both sides by streets (the Princes Street and Queen Street of today), which were to be left unbuilt on their outer sides, to open up the view over the countryside below – something that was ascribed great importance in a way that is reminiscent of Bath. Narrower service streets then divided the eight main blocks into sixteen lesser blocks in a clear attempt at differentiation between streets. This

proposal was largely realized, and subsequently proved to be no more than a first step. During the nineteenth century it was followed by several magnificent extensions, including a system of squares, crescents and circuses, obviously inspired by Bath. A good deal of the space was used for parks and planted areas, by far the largest of these being Queen Street Gardens, which forms a block-wide belt separ-

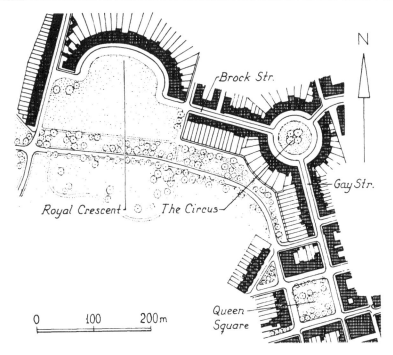

Figure 2.23 *Bath. In architectural schemes rather reminiscent of stage scenery, with façades concealing individually designed houses, it has been possible to create spatial effects in which architecture, terrain and landscaped prospects interact to create a townscape full of varied interest. [Redrawing by Erik Lorange]*

ating the original New Town from the later expansion area. The buildings were ultimately given an unusually uniform appearance in classicist guise.[59] What primarily distinguishes Edinburgh's New Town from most contemporary urban development projects, and even from earlier ones, was the active role played by the town and the consistency with which the great enterprise was realized, although it was a long time in the making. The impression here is of a homogeneous whole and not, as in London's West End, of a number of separate parts. One significant consequence of the building of the New Town was that a great many people belonging to the upper and middle social strata left the old urban core, which thus became increasingly slum-like.

Finally, mention should also be made of the rebuilding of Lisbon after the earthquake of 1755, which according to some estimates cost 30,000 people their lives and destroyed 9,000 houses. The worst of the destruction was in the central part of the town, Baixa, a district lying in a dip between two higher areas where the buildings were hit less hard. By royal command the work of reconstruction was led with supreme energy by the Marquês de Pombal. Several people were involved in the planning procedure, but the most important contribution was that of the architect-engineers Manuel da Maia and Eugénio dos Santos. The new plan was based on a rectangular system of narrow blocks and broad streets (figure 2.25). Architectural distinction was provided by squares on the two short sides, the Praça do Comércio facing the River Tagus to the south,

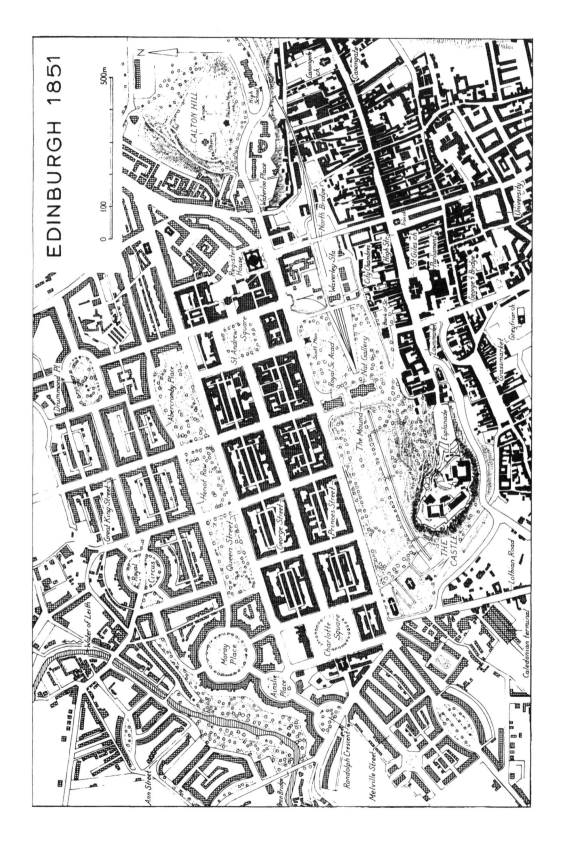

EDINBURGH 1851

and the Praça de Dom Pedro IV and the Praça de Figueria to the north.[60] Thanks both to its site and its architecture, the Praça do Comércio is one of the most impressive squares in any European capital city.

Hitherto little attention has been paid to the unique enterprise undertaken by the Wide Street Commissioners in Dublin during the second half of the eighteenth century. This body came to function as a kind of *de facto* planning authority 'empowered to approve or disapprove of all new streets made by private authorities'. It also carried out a number of street improvements of its own, which are today a characteristic feature of the centre of Dublin including Parliament Street, Dame Street, Westmoreland Street and D'Olier Street. Their intervention is of a kind that herald's the regularizations of the nineteenth century.[61]

Too little attention has also been paid in Western Europe to the intensive urban development and improvement projects which were launched in Russia after the fire in Tver in 1764, in areas where there had previously been few towns of any great size or importance. A commission in St Petersburg produced plans for a large number of towns. In 1793 the planning function was decentralized to the local governments, but the town planning operations continued, and in 1839 a volume of town plans was published as an appendix to the Russian statute book. Model drawings for town plans and the disposition of blocks were also made. This Russian town planning reveals a great wealth of variety; it made much use of

diagonal streets, and radial plans were sometimes used. Squares in different shapes and streets of varying width were also important elements. From the beginning of the nineteenth century onwards tree-planted thoroughfares also were a standard requirement in any large town. As we shall see below, Russian planning exerted a powerful influence in Finland, which ceased to be part of the Swedish kingdom in 1809 and became a Russian grand duchy under the Tsar.[62]

Antiquity and the Middle Ages both saw extensive rectangular planning in what could be called 'colonial towns', i.e. communities founded in some other area by a town, a state or an organization for strategic and/or economic purposes. Towns of this kind had to be made immediately habitable and defensible, which in turn required a number of measures including the construction of walls and the marking out of streets and plots within the future urban area. Later colonization outside Europe similarly led to a number of urban foundations, particularly in south and north America as well as in Asia.[63] For the same reasons these town plans were generally rectilinear; indeed, this solution was recommended in contemporary publications such as *Milicia y descripción de las Indias escrito por el capitán D. Bernardo de Vargas Machuca* (1599).

The laws promulgated by Philip II (1556–98) in 1573 for the 'Indias' were of great importance, providing detailed prescriptions for town plans and urban foundations. For instance: 'The plan of the place, with its squares, streets and building lots is to be outlined by means of

Figure 2.24 *Edinburgh. The central section consists of the New Town, created on the initiative of the mayor, George Drummond, planned by James Craig and built in the decades around 1800. Princes Street, 1.2 km in length and 30 m wide, became the main street owing to its position closest to the Old Town, of which it affords a magnificent view. On Calton Hill a 36-metre high tower was erected in 1819 in honour of Admiral Nelson, rising up against the sky like a vertical prolongation of Princes Street. Just after 1800 work began on a new district north of the New Town, along the axis of Great King Street and, slightly later, on a series of squares in the spirit of Bath in the north-west. [Redrawing by Erik Lorange]*

Figure 2.25 *Lisbon. The central part of the city, Baixa, was completely destroyed in the earthquake of 1755, after which the older street plan was replaced by the present grid. In the nineteenth century the two grand streets, Avenida Almirante Reis and Avenida da Liberdade, were created. The latter, 90 m wide and 1.5 km long, together with the star-shaped place of Praça Marquês de Pombal and the axially arranged park, Parque de Eduardo VII, extending a further 600 metres, forms one of the most prodigious ensembles of the nineteenth century. [Redrawing by Erik Lorange]*

measuring, by cord and ruler beginning with the main square from which streets are to run to the gates and principal roads and leaving sufficient open space so that even if the town grows it can always spread in a symmetrical manner.' Furthermore the ideal proportions for the width and length of a square were given as 2:3.[64] Naturally these and other prescriptions

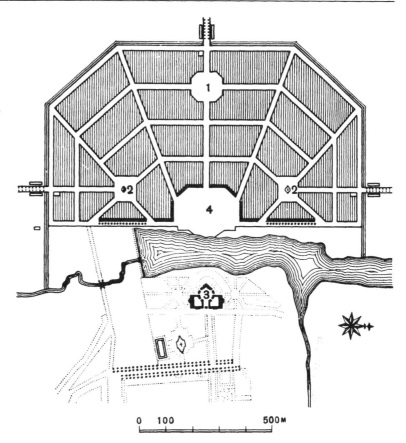

Figure 2.26 *Bogoroditsk. Town planning on a scale without parallel in Western Europe was undertaken in Russia during the decades around 1800. In 1839, 416 ratified plans were published as part of the official Russian statute book. The example shown here is the project ratified in 1778 for Bogoroditsk by E. Starov. Russian planning was influential not only in Finland but indirectly also in Sweden: Key:*
1. *The market place.*
2. *The church squares.*
3. *The palace.*
4. *The main square.*
[From Bunin (1961)]

for town planning in the colonies were based on experience gathered in Europe, but perceptions probably also flowed in the opposite direction, so that experience gained from establishing colonial towns was exploited in European urban development.[65]

Over the following centuries a number of towns were to be founded with rectilinear plans in north America.[66] Philadelphia, built according to a plan made by William Penn in 1682, represented an important prototype (figure 2.27). In his dual role as landowner and English governor, Penn organized the birth of this town with a firm hand, and the enterprise was a success from the start.[67] The population consisted mainly of Quakers, who found a

haven in the town. According to the original plan the rectilinear urban area was divided into four sections by main streets starting from the sides of the central square with its closed corners. Each of these four urban districts had its own small park. The residential roads ran parallel to the main streets, and divided the town into a great many blocks of varying length. The main features of this plan were realized. It shows an obvious kinship with Nordic seventeenth-century projects, for instance, thus showing that these ideas were part of a widely accepted approach.

Several of the many later towns built to rectilinear plans deserve mention: New Orleans in the 1720s and St Louis in 1764, both started

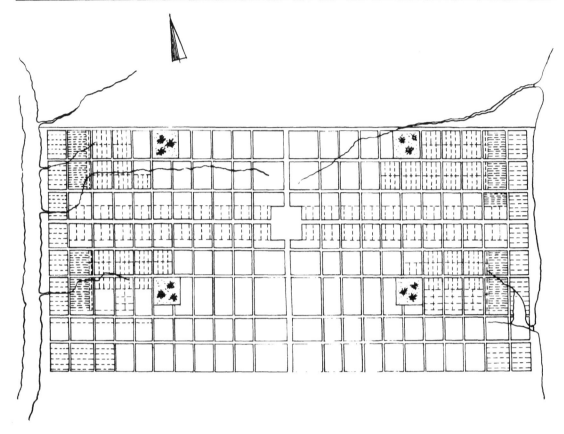

Figure 2.27 *Philadelphia. With its consistent rectilinearity, William Penn's 1682 project can represent the many towns founded in European colonies. At the same time the town became an influential model for hundreds of American foundations over the following centuries. [A slightly simplified redrawing after the reproduction in Reps (1965)]*

by companies in what was then French territory, Pittsburgh founded by William Penn's descendants in the 1780s and Cincinnati by land speculators around 1790. But by far the most consistent example of rectilinear block planning concerned the great expansion plan for New York whereby the whole of Manhattan north of Washington Square was to be covered by a uniform street and block system (figure 2.2). This plan, which was presented in 1811 and was subsequently largely realized, represents the greatest triumph of the rectangular school in any country. European visitors were impressed by the 'perfect regularity of the American

towns'; one traveller wrote at the end of the eighteenth century that in his view the rectangular plan was 'by far the best way of laying out a city . . . All the modern built towns in America are on this principle'.[68] That it was possible to realize the rectilinear plans so consistently was partly due to the absence of any earlier building which had to be considered; but more important was the fact that – with the important exception of New York – the land was generally owned by a single company or person who was responsible for marking out and distributing the plots.

But there were also some projects which

exhibited more obvious architectural ambitions, in particular the 1791 plan for Washington by the French major and architect Pierre Charles L'Enfant (figure 2.28), and Judge Augustus Brevoort Woodward's proposal for the reconstruction of Detroit after the fire in 1805 (figure 2.29). In the first of these, diagonal avenues cut through a rectangular street network; and in the second, streets radiating out from great circular places were combined with concentric streets creating polygonal encirclements rather than simple rings. This meticulously worked-out solution meant that most plots were rectangular or at least four-sided, and pointed plots could be largely avoided. Furthermore, it was possible to link

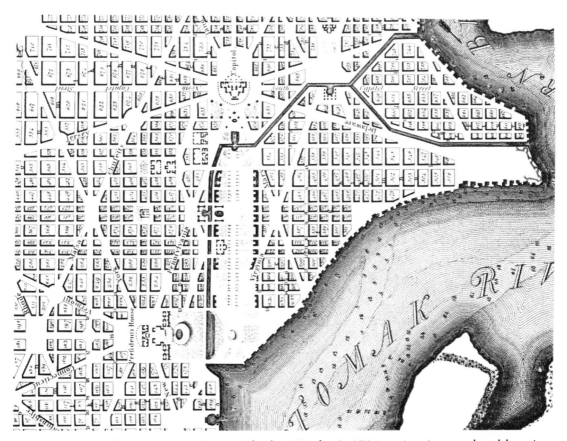

Figure 2.28 *Washington. Major Pierre Charles L'Enfant's 1791 project is reproduced here in a somewhat revised printed version from 1792. It was a question of designing a capital city for the newly created federation, and it was obviously felt that the inclusion of diagonal streets, which may recall Wren's plan for London, was a way of endowing an otherwise conventional rectilinear plan with some of the character of a capital. L'Enfant had more success than his countryman Le Blond had enjoyed at the beginning of the century with a similar commission: while Le Blond's plan for St Petersburg remained mainly on paper, L'Enfant's project for Washington was largely realized. However, it made very little impact on American urbanism during the nineteenth century until it was 'rediscovered' towards 1900 and became the source of inspiration for the City Beautiful Movement. [From Bacon (1974)]*

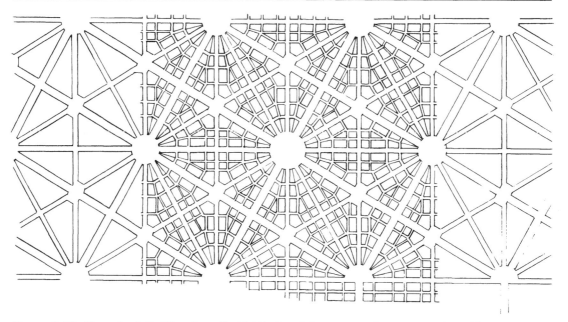

Figure 2.29 *Detroit. A.B. Woodward's 1807 plan. The project shows an undeniably innovative, albeit rather complicated variation on the radial theme. Hardly surprisingly, it had no immediate successors. [Redrawing after Reps (1965)]*

several radial systems together.[69] This was one of the more innovative variants on the radial theme to appear since this concept was first launched at the end of the fifteenth century.

Let us now return to Europe. Industrialization began in England during the last decades of the eighteenth century, but did not reach continental Europe until a good deal later. Heavy industrialization did not appear in Belgium until the 1820s, in Germany until the second half of the nineteenth century, and in the Nordic countries until nearly its end. But some changes had started much earlier: trade and commerce were expanding, the constraints on business establishment were being eased, production units were growing bigger and communications had improved. In many European towns in the eighteenth century populations were already increasing rapidly. Generally, owing to the obstruction of now obsolete fortifications or the legal obstacles surrounding the exploitation of land, this

growth led to the more intensive exploitation of existing built areas. In other words houses were being erected on or adjoining what had previously been courtyards.

The increasing population density served to emphasize the already obvious deficiencies of the urban environments. This, combined with the emergence of the more critical and analytical ideas of the Enlightenment, led to a debate about town plan redevelopment and urban improvements, although a traditional desire to create a distinguished setting was combined with these sanitary and functional considerations. Several early manifestations of this – in the ideas of Voltaire, Pierre Patte and Abbé Laugier, for example – were concerned primarily with Paris (see pp. 59 ff).[70] We shall see below that under Napoleon I a number of important urban development enterprises – among others the Rue de Rivoli – were in fact started. And in London at about the same time the first plans for Regent Street were being launched (see pp. 85 ff). Helsinki and Athens, both essentially new foundations, are other examples of the urban development ideas of the early nineteenth century. And in many towns surrounded by fortifications the demolition of the defence system came up for discussion. Where urban planning theory had previously been much concerned to allow for the necessities of defence, a main topic now was how to clear away the old fortifications and get rid of their negative effects.

Redevelopment and planned new foundations provided one way of improving the conditions of urban life. Another was to create towns of a new type, whose physical design would break with the traditional model, and where life would be organized along different lines. Ideas of this kind began to be discussed as early as the eighteenth century. A pioneer of what we could perhaps call the second wave of 'ideal cities' – model communities would perhaps be a more fitting designation – was the architect Claude-Nicolas Ledoux with his project for Chaux, an industrial village for salt production. The final project was adopted in 1774. The factory buildings form a straight baseline, in relation to which the dwellings are arranged in a semi-circle. In a treatise published twenty years later, *L'architecture considérée sous le rapport de l'art, des mœurs, et de la législation* Ledoux revised and extended his original project into something resembling a visionary ideal city. It is at this point that the semi-circle became an ellipse.[71] While Chaux represents a shift in approach as regards the exhaustive nature of the theoretical motivation behind urban development projects, it is also part of a tradition of industrial community planning in a paternalistic spirit, which has not yet been sufficiently investigated. The tradition seems to have appeared in various parts of Europe, including for instance the Nordic countries,[72] and it constitutes one of the fundamental factors behind nineteenth-century thinking on 'model' towns.

Where Ledoux argued primarily from the architect's angle, Charles Fourier was a philosopher and social critic seeking an alternative way of living. His ideal community, the *phalanstère*, which he described in several publications from 1822 onwards, could perhaps be defined as a large-scale collective and basically self-supporting organization in the shape of an enormous building complex, which could have been looking something like a blend of a hospital and a palace. Jean-Baptiste André Godin's *familistère* in Guise was an attempt at realizing Fourier's programme. During the first decades of the nineteenth century Robert Owen in New Lanark in Scotland tried to realize his own ideas for an ideal community, aiming not to maximize profits but to create conditions of greater equality and to provide the workers with a meaningful existence. Significant steps were taken to improve the housing conditions of the workers. But the basic physical structure was fixed by existing buildings, and in 1824 Owen launched a new model town in the United States – New Harmony in Indiana. But not even here was his ideal concept fully realized – a village with terraces in a large rectangle round an open area containing some public buildings, and with factories and workshops located outside the rectangle. A further British example on Utopian lines is J.S. Buckingham's model town Victoria, which was presented in *National Evils and Practical Remedies* (1849). The project consists of narrow blocks inside one another, creating a 'Chinese box' effect, in much the same way as in Christianopolis and Freudenstadt (cf. pp. 17 f).

Different ideas lay behind the first successful model town, Saltaire, founded in the middle of the century by the industrialist Titus Salt. A good environment and organized social conditions would, Salt assumed, promote effective production. In Saltaire the houses – of good quality for the times – were separated from the factory buildings, and the community was equipped with various communal facilities such as schools, hospital, laundries, homes for the

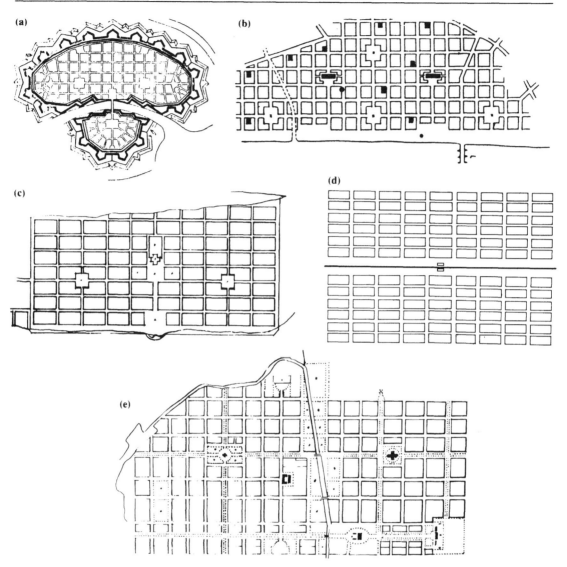

Figure 2.30 *Three centuries of rectilinear block planning. (a) Johan Wilhelm Dilich-Schäffer: Proposal for a fortress city, from the 1630s. [From Münter (1957)] (b) Robert Hooke: Regulation proposal for London 1666. [From Morini (1963)] (c) Carl Johan Cronstedt: Project for Kaskö in Finland, 1767. [Redrawing after Lilius (1967)] (d) Standard plan for railway towns used by the Illinois Central Railroad during the 1850s. [Redrawing after Reps (1965)] (e) Ernst Bernhard Lohrmann: Unrealized proposal for the reconstruction of Vasa in Finland after the fire in 1852. [Redrawing after Lilius (1967)]. The most fundamental difference between the grid planning of the Middle Ages and that of the sixteenth and seventeenth centuries is probably due to the different types of defensive systems, and to the fact that during the later period there was a stronger ambition to organise the urban structure symmetrically and to give it a geometrical shape (but it should be remembered that we have little in the way of medieval project drawings and do not therefore know how it was intended that the towns should look). During the eighteenth century*

elderly and a public meeting-house known as the Institute. The historical importance of Saltaire lay in the demonstration that planned alternatives to haphazard growth in industrial environments could be realized within the prevailing social and economic system.[73] It meant far more to subsequent developments than the various Utopian experiments mentioned above, despite the awed reverence with which these are always treated.

Thus, if we look at the state of urban planning at the beginning of the nineteenth century, we find that a great many of the towns then existing had come about 'spontaneously', i.e. without any preceding planning. But whenever a new town or district was the result of a deliberate decision, then the aim was also to achieve rational plot and block divisions, which generally resulted in rectilinear streets networks. The examples are so many and so scattered in time and place, that we are justified in speaking of a kind of pan-European planning tradition stretching from the thirteenth to the nineteenth century. Rectilinear planning was still regarded in the middle of the last century as the natural and rational model for new towns and districts,[74] even though ideas about broad tree-lined thoroughfares, embankment roads and parks had been in the air for some time.

Alongside the rational and sometimes mechanically rectilinear grid plans we have also seen a number of towns inspired by 'ideal' projects. Each of these last, scattered in both time and place, was virtually unique. We have also seen examples of a local design planning, intended to endow squares and groups of buildings or, in a few special cases, whole towns with a more splendid architectural dress.

Although taste changed with the years when it came to the design of buildings, the basic aesthetic ideals of urban planning had persisted more or less unaltered since the sixteenth century. Uniform and straight streets, vistas and enclosed squares were regular ingredients in any planning intended to create an imposing townscape from the Renaissance to the nineteenth century, albeit supplemented during the Baroque period by more dynamic features, such as dramatic prospects and diagonal avenues, frequently extending as straight roads out into the countryside.

Thus it is difficult to claim that at the beginning of the nineteenth century there was any systematic urban planning theory; on the other hand there were various long-established concepts and ideas about appropriate ways of making town plans. Since the middle of the eighteenth century, however, there had been a growing interest in urban improvement, i.e. the sanitary and functional conditions of the cities. The evils of the big-city environment were becoming increasingly obvious and ways of tackling them, with redevelopment or new communities as the principal alternatives, were being discussed in some circles. During the nineteenth century populations continued to grow; quite often the number of inhabitants in a town would double in the course of 30 or 40 years. This meant that town planning was facing problems and demands that were both quantitatively and qualitatively new. In the following pages a number of capital city projects will be described in an attempt to clarify the organization and forms of planning activity in the nineteenth century, and to discuss the interplay between practice and theory.

---

the fortifications began to disappear from the plans, while at the same time embankment roads were given greater importance and streets were made wider. During the nineteenth century tree-planted streets and parks became common elements even in the simple rectilinear plans. But despite fundamental difference between projects from different periods, continuity and similarity are the most noticeable feature.

EXCURSUS: GENERAL WORKS ON PLANNING HISTORY

Among the pioneers in the field of planning history Pierre Lavedan is in a class of his own. The first attempt to grasp the evolution of planning as a whole was his *Histoire de l'urbanisme* published in three parts in 1926, 1941 and 1952. These have been replaced successively by fully revised versions produced in collaboration with Jeanne Hugueney and published in 1966, 1974 and 1982. In retrospect several objections can be made regarding the first version of the *Histoire de l'urbanisme*, for example the predominance of the French material and the many omissions when it came to other countries, the often rough typological classifications of the plans studied, the lack of historical background and the paucity of reference sources. On all these counts the later volumes represent a clear improvement.

The second multi-volume town planning history, Ernst Egli's *Geschichte des Städtebaues* (1959, 1962 and 1967), is divided into periods as well as national 'areas', which in turn are divided into different countries. The author presents a series of often rather scanty descriptions of individual towns, in a manner somewhat reminiscent of an encyclopedia. The main strength of this work lies in its wide coverage, even though there are some surprising gaps; there is also little in the way of a general chronological overview. E.A. Gutkind's *International History of City Development* (1964 onwards) also runs to several volumes. For every country the author provides a general survey of urban development and descriptions of a number of towns. The emphasis is generally on the pre-nineteenth-century periods. His descriptions are generally informative but the material sometimes seem to have been selected rather haphazardly and the reference sources are often rather sparse. It is an impressive achievement, but as a basis for further research it has obvious weaknesses.

The history of town planning has also been addressed in various works of more limited scope. In terms of the number of pages, Leonardo Benevolo's *Storia della Città* (1975, English version 1980) leaves nothing to be desired; in this respect it can compete with the above-mentioned works. But its great length is due to an unassorted mass of pictures which sometimes reveal only a slight connection with the text which, despite all this illustrative support, still fails to convince – even in the case of the Italian material. A.E.J. Morris' *History of Urban Form* (1987, originally published in 1979) provides a reliable and largely chronological account of the evolution of town planning prior to industrialization, including general surveys and analyses of individual towns. Mark Girouard's *Cities & People* (1987, first published in 1985) is a popular but comprehensive overview of urban development; it offers many fresh insights which throw light particularly on the economic conditions and social consequences of urban development, while planning as such receives less attention. While these books are organized chronologically, at least in principle, Spiro Kostof's *The City Shaped* (1991) is divided into five main chapters, each with its own more or less chronological structure: ' "Organic" patterns', 'The grid', 'The city as diagram', 'The grand manner' and 'The urban skyline'. Each chapter thus spans essentially the whole course of urban development, with examples taken mainly from Europe and North America. The book contains many interesting juxtapositions and reflections, and the illustrations are of high quality. But the categorization of the material sometimes feels rather arbitrary and one wonders where the investigation is really leading – which is regrettable in view of the great learning it represents. This work has been complemented by a further book, *The City Assembled* (1992), in which the approach is morphological, focusing on such things as the city edge; princely, spiritual and commercial environments within cities; various types of public places; streets etc. The perspective in time and space is as comprehensive as in the first book.

Other works have taken up selected aspects of the subject, without any pretensions to providing a complete historical survey. In *Abendländische Stadtbaukunst, Herrschaftsform und Stadtbaugestalt* (1977; English edition *Urban Design in Western Europe*, 1988), Braunfels describes a number of towns with considerable insight, but presents little in the way of general conclusions on his stated theme, namely the relation between form of government and form of townscape. Bacon's *Design of Cities* (1974, first published in 1967) analyses a wide range of examples of what is referred to in the present book as 'local design planning'. Bacon includes extremely clear and instructive plans and perspective architectural drawings, eminently well suited to his purpose. The illustrations make this an indispensable handbook. Rasmussen's *Byer og Bygninger* (1949; English edition *Towns and Buildings*, 1951) in some respects resembles Bacon's book. Here too architecturally interesting solutions are analysed, in this case with the help of the author's own sketches. Erik Lorange's two-volume town planning history, hitherto only available in Norwegian, successfully combines facts and sensibility in an analysis of the visual qualities of the plans discussed (Lorange 1990 and 1995). Mention should also be made of Reinisch (1984), a book with many interesting observations, though the material is forced into a Marxist uniform in a way customary in the former GDR.

In some works the historical perspective is used mainly as a point of departure for the analysis of more topical planning issues. This applies for example to Geoffrey Broadbent's *Emerging Concepts in Urban Space* (1990), which offers a short survey of 'Urban space design in history' without, however, adding much to what had already been said in earlier works. The same applies to Jonathan Barnett's *The Elusive City* (1986).

Among older works mention can be made of Joseph Gantner's now apparently forgotten *Grundformen der europäischen Stadt* (1928), which represents a not uninteresting attempt to apply to the *Grundbegriffe* proposed by his teacher Heinrich Wölflin.

A general survey of works concerned with the early history of town planning can be found in Hall (1978, pp. 8 ff). What is said there about the medieval sections in the books reviewed also applies by and large to the chapters of sections concerned with later periods.

NOTES

1. Concerning the research development, see Excursus, pp. 48 f.
2. See e.g. Franz Joseph's *Handschreiben* concerning the planning of the glacis area in Vienna (pp. 72 f), where all three terms are used (in German *Erweiterung*, *Regulierung* and *Verschönerung*). Haussmann himself used the verb *régulariser* to describe his activities, and during the eighteenth century the expression *embellissement* was also used in France to designate urban improvements. However, it must be remembered that all these expressions were used with reference to implementation, not to the planning phase. There were obviously no terms indicating clearly that it was a question of planning rather than execution. Nor was any terminological distinction made between survey and project plans.

One of the many terminological problems connected with this book has concerned the word *reglering*, which with slight variations in the spelling appears in many European languages to designate rectifying operations, particularly the cutting of streets through existing blocks. In the following chapters 'improvement' has generally been used as equivalent of *reglering*, alternating in a few instances 'regularization', 'renewal' or 'redevelopment'.
3. Both Lavedan and Egli developed sophisticated typologies for the analysis of medieval towns in particular (cf. Hall (1978), pp. 8 ff). Recently

Kostof has introduced a kind of topological system (cf. p. 48).

4. The first work to examine the grid plan as a special type was probably Stanislawski (1946). Most recently Kostof in *The City Shaped* (1991) has devoted a chapter to the grid plan.

5. Several works treat this type of plan (see note 17).

6. Bacon (1974) is devoted to this type of planning.

7. Rather than speaking of cities as 'planned' or 'evolving spontaneously' Lorange suggests the concept of towns planned 'from above' or 'from below': 'The first group have been shaped by rulers and powerful authorities. The second are often the product of a kind of self-determination on the part of the inhabitants.' (Lorange, 1990, p. 13.)

8. Hippodamus is an elusive figure, and it is difficult to be precise about either his person or his activities. Our most important source is Aristotle (*Politica* II:V and VII:X). From the pages of Aristotle Hippodamus emerges as a benevolent but somewhat eccentric social philosopher. His activities as a planner of physical environments are not described in any great detail, but it is said that he invented the idea of dividing towns into blocks, and that he cut up Piraeus in this way. Aristotle also claims that it is most convenient, and best serves the public interest, to locate private houses on straight streets in the way that 'has been invented by Hippodamus'. According to Aristotle Hippodamus came from Miletus. Thus he might have taken part in the planning and rebuilding of this town after its destruction by the Persians in 479, but, if so, he would have been far too young to have had any leading position. Since Miletus was almost certainly regarded in its time as an unusually systematic example of rectangular planning, Hippodamus may have derived his ideas from it and may even have become identified with the lessons to be learnt there. Some other classical sources, above all Strabo and Aristophanes, indicate that Hippodamus had a firm reputation as the inventor of the rectangular town plan, even though this was quite clearly an overestimation of his achievements (cf. following note). On Hippodamus and Greek town planning, see in particular Castagnoli (1971), Wycherley

(1973), pp. 17 ff *et passim* and Ward-Perkins (1974), pp. 14 ff. Owens (1992) provides a more recent survey.

9. In fact this applied not only after but even before Hippodamus. On earlier grid planning, see Lampl (1968) and Kostof (1991), pp. 103 f.

10. Aristophanes' jokes at the expense of a planner in *The Birds*, show that town planning was treated with no more awe in Ancient Greece than it has been in recent times (cf. Castagnoli (1971), pp. 67 f).

11. This is a debatable point. So too is the relation between Roman planning on the one hand and Etruscan or Hellenistic planning on the other.

12. A good overview of Roman town planning is provided in Ward-Perkins (1974), pp. 27 ff, where among other things the concepts of the *cardo* and *decumanus* are discussed. These are really land surveying terms designating the north-south and east-west demarcation lines, whereby the land as a whole was divided into large squares. The street network in the towns was organized according to this overriding division, and perhaps efforts were also made to locate towns at the crossing of a *cardo* and a *decumanus* so that these could coincide with the main streets.

13. As regards developments north of the Alps during the Middle Ages, cf. Hall (1978) and the bibliography provided there. This work also includes a great many plans.

14. These developments were not influenced by ancient plans, however (although some remaining Roman streets may have served as models). In a study of the relation between medieval and classical grid plans, Lilius has rejected on good grounds the idea that existing classical town plans were still being imitated during the Middle Ages. Rather, referring to Lang (1955) and others, he claims that the medieval rectangular plan was largely a result of scholastic studies of Antiquity. 'The ancient world exerted its influence by way of the texts of, above all, Aristotle, Hyginus and Vitruvius' (Lilius (1968), especially pp. 31 f). This is a dubious stance. Certainly the rectangular town corresponded to Thomas Aquinas's idea of 'ordo', and naturally what Aristotle and others said about towns was known. But this does not necessarily mean that the idea of the rectangular plan came from the ancient writings; nor is there

any clear and unequivocal description of a town plan in the texts that had survived. The grid type of plan was indubitably inspired by practical considerations; experience had shown that it was the most appropriate solution. Nor did it appear out of the blue: rather, it was the result of a long medieval evolution towards an increasingly systematic way of dividing up urban areas. If the writings of Antiquity did play a part, it was not as the originator of ideas or as a starting-point, but as another way of justifying the use of a plan type which would have been used in any case. On the other hand it is possible, as Lilius points out, that better knowledge of the Roman art of surveying may have facilitated the marking out of plans.

15. See Friedman (1988).

16. Hall (1978), p. 126.

17. An early work on ideal cities is Münter (1929), reissued in 1957 in Berlin (DDR), where the material is 'pressed into a scheme of rather homespun Marxism' (Eimer (1961), p. 148). More recent publications on this topic include Eimer (1961), pp. 43–146 and Rosenau (1974). De la Croix (1972) focuses on the defence aspects of urban planning. The following passage on ideal cities is based mainly on these works. The most recent book on the theme is Kruft (1989), which concentrates on a selection of 'ideal' cities. It should be noted that the term 'ideal city' or *città ideale* as a general designation for a series of very different projects is a modern invention. Perhaps 'model town' would have been a better term. In the present book the term 'ideal city' is used in a wider sense than in Rosenau (1974, pp. 13 f) or – even more markedly – than in Kruft (1989, pp. 9 ff). Kruft has chosen to reserve the concept for towns which have actually been built. Here, instead, the term refers to city projects or actual cities which have been influenced by theoretical concepts regarding the creation of something superior to conventional town-building.

In the following discussion mention is made of several treatises and projects, in which physical shape and design were crucial factors. But even in works of a more social-theoretical focus, the design of the city was a key issue. Examples include Thomas More's *Utopia* (1516), Francis Bacon's *The New Atlantis* (1622), and Tommaso Campanella's *Città del sole* (1623). The last of these seems to have played a part as a source of inspiration for some of the nineteenth-century urban development theorists (Girouard (1987), pp. 350 ff).

18. In his Fourth Book Alberti recommends for a small town a street that winds along with the gentle curves of a river, and he justifies this in a way that recalls his much later successor, Sitte. In the Eighth Book, on the other hand, he obviously presupposes that streets are straight; here the basic features are developed in what could be called an urban design programme of the Renaissance, whereby the city was established as a work art and, consequently, artistic quality became one of the main goals of planning (cf. Kruft (1989), p. 13).

19. From the end of the fifteenth century onwards a great many fortification projects for existing towns were also produced, among others by Leonardo da Vinci and Michelangelo.

20. The idea that Vitruvius recommended radial street networks has also been adopted by several modern writers (for instance in Broadbent (1990), p. 37, reference is made to 'a Vitruvian circular plan'). This notion is apparently based on a misinterpretation of the classical author's admittedly rather complicated argument regarding the orientation of the town plan in relation to the winds (I:6). It seems very unlikely that Vitruvius would have suggested a plan form which had no roots in the Roman town planning tradition. Hamberg has shown in an unprinted paper how this misapprehension probably arose. The first edition of Vitruvius to be illustrated with a town plan showing radial streets was Caesare Caesariano's translation, published in Como in 1521. This pattern, which aimed to elucidate Vitruvius' exposition on the direction of the winds, was subsequently repeated in a number of later editions (Hamberg (1955), pp. 21 ff). But when Caesariano's edition was published, the radial plan was probably already quite a well-known concept in the relevant circles. Thus it appears that the radial plan was invented independently of Vitruvius, and only later became associated with his name after a misunderstanding of his intentions. In another passage (I:V,2) Vitruvius says that the town 'should not be square . . . but rounded, so that the enemy can be discovered from several positions'. Perhaps even this statement, which can hardly have had

any foundation in urban building practice in Vitruvius' times, may have been interpreted as support for radial plans.

21. Argan (1969), pp. 104 f.

22. Pollak (1991) lists seventy-three European treatises on fortification, and then only those in The Newberry Library in Chicago are included.

23. In Braunfels (1953) and Friedman (1988) the importance and distinctive nature of the medieval planning activities in Tuscany are emphasized. Even north of the Alps an early instance of aesthetic ambitions can be discerned in the design of the central parts of some cities (cf. Hall (1978), pp. 99 ff).

24. Argan (1969), p. 30 and Benevolo (1980), pp. 536 ff. The well-known townscape paintings in the Palazzo Ducale in Urbino, previously attributed to Francesco di Giorgio Martini, can give us some idea of how people in Alberti's times might have envisaged the ideal design for the ceremonial centre of a town (cf. Saalman (1968), pp. 376 ff, where these paintings are attributed to Cosimo Rosselli). In both cases we see buildings arranged along an open space penetrating deep into the picture, and in both cases the prospect is broken by large rather vaguely located monumental buildings. The buildings along the sides of this space are designed individually, but in some cases their cornices are of equal height. There is a sense of tranquil and harmonious spaciousness; there are absolutely no dynamic effects. Later representations of townscapes, for example Serlio's drawings for theatrical decors, also provide a complement to contemporary ideal city plans.

25. On the piazza in Vigevano, see Bruschi (1969), pp. 647 ff.

26. A forerunner of the Plaza Mayor in Madrid was the uniformly designed Plaza Mayor in Valladolid built in the 1560s.

27. *Guía de arquitectura y urbanismo de Madrid* (1982), pp. 36 ff; cf. Kubler and Soria (1959), p. 21.

28. On squares, see also pp. 309 ff.

29. As regards the street improvements in Rome, see Schück, Sjöqvist and Magnuson (1956), pp. 140 ff, 270 ff, 287 ff *et passim*, Magnuson (1958), pp. 21 ff, Frommel (1973), pp. 11 ff and Magnuson (1982), pp. 16 ff and (1986), pp. 230 ff.

30. Lotz (1973), pp. 247 ff.

31. In Florence extensive street improvements were already being undertaken during the final decades of the thirteenth century. The new streets included Borgo Ognissanti (1278), Via Palazzoulo (1279), Via Maggio (1295) and the present Via Cavour (Friedman (1988), pp. 207 ff).

32. Frommel has pointed out that the Via di Ripetta was probably intended originally as a principal street of greater importance than the Corso, since the roads which cross it do so at right angles (1973, p. 20).

33. On Sixtus V's urban development programme, see Magnuson (1982, pp. 16 ff) and Gamrath (1987). It is not only the straight streets and visual accents in this pope's projects which recall Haussmann. Like Haussmann's programme this also included major improvements in the water supply; it was Sixtus V's water acqueducts and water pipes which first made it possible for people to live on Rome's hills again. He also hoped to subdue unrest among the unemployed by providing public works – another parallel with France under the Second Empire.

34. Another impressive Italian example of street improvement from roughly the same time is Strada Nuova, built in the 1560s (today Via Garibaldi) in Genoa (Argan (1969), Fig. 90).

35. Magnuson (1986), pp. 230 ff. Krautheimer also stresses the political significance of Alexander's enterprises, which included St Peter's Square as well as a redevelopment of the Piazza del Popolo and the construction of its twin churches: 'Alexander's vision of a Rome renewed and reborn and outshining all the royal capitals of Europe wants to be understood on a wider plan still, as a political statment' (Krautheimer (1985), p. 138). 'A new grand "image" of Rome was needed to impress . . . on both Romans and the world abroad and primarily on visitors to Rome' (*ibidem*, p. 142). The same could be said of the rebuilding of Paris under Napoleon III, and of several other grand nineteenth-century capital development projects.

36. Girouard draws an illuminating parallel with Vincenzo Scamozzi's decor sketches for the Teatro Olimpico, which show very similar street perspectives (Girouard (1987), pp. 119 ff).

37. See for example Lavedan (1960), p. 103 ff.

38. See Valdenaire (1926), pp. 77 ff and Fehl (1983), pp. 137 ff.

39. See Tschira (1959).

40. Argan (1969), pp. 31 f and Benevolo (1980), pp. 556 ff. In this connection it can also be mentioned that in the 1560s Pius IV laid out an entirely new area, Borgo Pio, outside Borgo Leonino, where the rectangularity was carried out more consistently than in Ferrara's new district (see Gamrath (1976)).

41. *Histoire de Nancy*, p. 133; Lavedan (1960), pp. 100 f.

42. Egli (1967), p. 99.

43. Münter (1957), pp. 73 and 81 ff. Münter also discusses Mühlheim, more or less Mannheim's contemporary, which had a similar plan. On Mannheim, see also Egli (1967), pp. 101 ff.

44. The basic survey of seventeenth-century urban policy in Sweden and the research on this topic, is Ericsson (1977).

45. The seminal work on Swedish urban development policy during the seventeenth century is Eimer (1961), which also provides abundant illustrations. See also Hall (1991), pp. 170 ff. Swedish seventeenth-century planning was concerned with the location of the streets and, sometimes, the division of the blocks into plots. On the other hand, the plans say nothing about the design of the buildings. Directives on this point came instead from a long series of decrees from the national government, mainly concerned to replace wooden buildings by brick houses. However, this ambition was largely unfulfilled, perhaps mainly for the simple reason that brick houses were too expensive for the burghers.

46. That urban redevelopment of this kind was possible at all was at least partly due to the timbering technique in general use in Sweden, which meant that houses could be dismantled relatively easily and put up again elsewhere.

47. On Uppsala, see *Scandinavian Atlas of Historic Towns*, No. 4.

48. See Nordenstreng (1908), pp. 191 ff (which pays little attention to the plan, however), and *Suomen kaupunkilaitoksen historia*, I, pp. 323 ff. At one stage during the seventeenth century a radial plan was considered for Kalmar (see Hall (1991), p. 172, Fig 5.4).

49. See Lorenzen II (1951), pp. 144 ff *et passim* and Hartmann and Villadsen (1979), pp. 21 ff,

Larsson and Thomassen (1991), pp. 8 ff and Lorange and Myhre (1991), pp. 118 ff.

50. See for instance Rasmussen (1973), pp. 84 f, Hibbert (1969), pp. 67 ff, Morris (1987), pp. 217 ff and Milne (1990).

51. For example Wren's proposal was discussed in connection with the creation of a plan after the fire in Hamburg in 1842 (Schumacher (1920), pp. 5 f). The London plan has also been mentioned as a possible source of inspiration for Louis Napoleon's decision to rebuild Paris.

52. Morris claims that 'Wren's plan was totally irrelevant to the needs of the City'. 'It is surely not possible to see Wren's plan as more than an overnight exercise based on the use of undigested continental Renaissance planmotifs.' (Morris (1987), pp. 220 f.) The first comment may be correct, but the second is definitely misleading. The project is an attempt to create a rational urban structure, and it points forward rather than back.

53. The Rebuilding Act of 1667 is reproduced in Milne (1990), pp. 117 ff.

54. The main work on St Petersburg is Bater (1976), which provides a detailed description of the Russian capital city up to 1914. The emphasis is on the industrialization process and its economic and social effects, but the author also considers the physical environment. Planning and the architectural development of the town are also discussed in Hamilton (1954) and Egorov (1969).

55. Bater considers that Peter's urban development programme can be subsumed under five basic principles: 'the streets were to be straight and the buildings of brick or stone; in the overall plan the waterways were to be used to advantage; once determined the plan must be adhered to rigidly; within the city particular groups were to be assigned to specific areas; the management of city affairs would be concentrated in the hands of the resident commercial and industrial élite' (Bater (1976), p. 21).

56. Bater (1976), pp. 28 ff and Map 7.

57. *Ibidem*, p. 31.

58. Egli (1967), pp. 133 ff and Lavedan, Hugueney and Henrat (1982), pp. 189 ff; cf. also Neale (1990).

59. *Edinburgh, New Town Guide* and Meade (1971). The standard work on Edinburgh is Youngson (1966).

60. Egli (1967), pp. 81 f and Williams (1984), pp. 74 ff.

61. Craig (1992), pp. 172 ff; cf. also McParland (1972) and McCullough (1989), pp. 74 ff.

62. This passage is based on the exhibition catalogue *Mönsterstäder* (1974), with a text by Göran Lindahl; cf. also Bunin (1961), pp. 107 ff. The volume of plates mentioned here is called: *Polone sobranie zakonov rossijskoj imperiy 1839 kniga tserteshei i risunkov* (*Plany gorodov*).

63. For a survey of urban foundations during the period of colonisation outside Europe, see Egli (1967), pp. 224 ff. Cf. for India also Nilsson (1968), in particular pp. 40 ff.

64. Quoted from Reps (1965), p. 29, who strongly emphasizes the importance of this regulation, 'virtually unchanged throughout the entire period of Spanish rule', for the towns founded by Spain in America. See also Stanislawski (1947) and Crouch, Garr and Mundigo (1982).

65. Josephson has indicated the plan of Batavia (Djakarta) as a possible parallell to Gothenburg (Josephson (1918), p. 95).

66. For developments in the USA, see Reps (1965) and Scully (1969). The following passage is based mainly on Reps (1965).

67. Reps (1965), pp. 157 ff.

68. Quoted from Reps (1965, p. 294). The traveller concerned, Francis Baily, however, later found that the rectilinearity had been pushed too far, and that sometimes there was 'a sacrifice of beauty to prejudice', but above all he criticized the fact that it was applied 'without any regard to the situation of the ground'. To apply a rigid grid plan on inappropriate terrain could sometimes lead to very odd results (something which every visitor to San Francisco has reason to note). In 1772 a visitor to the place where New Orleans was to be founded noted that the engineer who was responsible for the work 'has just shown me a plan of his own invention; but it will not be so easy to put into execution as it has been to draw it out upon paper' (*ibidem*, p. 81). It can be added

that during the discussions in the 1830s about the plan for Athens, reference was made to the 'regular Quarrés à la Washington, New York and Philadelphia' as bad examples (Russack (1942), p. 21).

69. Reps (1965), pp. 240 ff and 266 ff.

70. Equivalents in the case of London are John Gwynn's *London and Westminster Improved* published in 1766 and George Dance the Younger's scheme for an extensive redeployment on both sides of London Bridge (Rosenau (1974), pp. 115 ff). A similar debate also occurred in Vienna (see p. 171).

71. On Chaux, see Kruft (1989), pp. 112 ff.

72. On the Swedish *bruk*, see Hall (1991), pp. 174 ff. and Fig. 5.9.

73. On model communities during the late eighteenth century and the early nineteenth century, see e.g. Egli (1967), Benevolo (1968), Bell (1969), Choay (1969) and Rosenau (1974).

74. The commission which submitted the great master plan proposal for New York in 1811 wrote, for example, perhaps with the above-mentioned projects for Washington and Detroit in mind: 'That one of the first objects that claimed their attention, was the form and manner in which the business should be conducted; that is to say, whether they should confine themselves to rectilinear and rectangular streets, or whether they should adapt some of those supposed improvements, by circles, ovals, and stars, which certainly embellish a plan, what ever may be their effects as to convenience and utility. In considering that subject, they could not but bear in mind that a city is to be composed principally of the habitations of men, and that strait sided, and right angled houses are the most cheap to build, and the most convenient to live in. The effect of these plain simple reflections was decisive.' (Quoted from Reps (1965), p. 297.) This and similar examples show that the consistent rectangular plan without any aesthetic ambitions was still the alternative preferred by many.

3

PARIS

An American study, of perfectly serious intent, has used a sophisticated points system to compare some of the world's greatest cities, and to discover which one is regarded as the most attractive. It is no great surprise to find that Paris[1] received the greatest number of points.[2] Generations of Europeans and Americans have assumed without question that Paris is the most beautiful and exciting city in the world. This idea of Paris as a town in a class by itself is not in fact very old; it goes back to the second Empire, and perhaps more exactly to 1867. This was when Napoleon III's collapsing régime gathered itself together for one last glorious fling, namely the second French *Exposition universelle*. The year of the exhibition established Paris's reputation as the city of luxury and sin, but also as the city of magnificent scenic effects. Only a few decades earlier, in the first half of the nineteenth century, Paris had been regarded as one of the dirtiest places in Europe. The explanation of this astonishing change lay in the radical transformation effected under Georges-Eugène Haussmann. If other nineteenth-century planning efforts have attracted little attention – at any rate until quite recently – 'Haussmann's Paris' has become a recognized concept. No other planner in any other country or from any other period has achieved such fame, not only in professional circles but in the world at large. Paris is therefore the obvious point of departure for a survey of nineteenth-century capital city planning.

The problems confronting Haussmann were

a legacy from the Middle Ages, so it seems sensible to begin our story with a brief retrospective survey. The embryo of Paris was a Roman settlement sprawling on both banks of the Seine, but concentrated during Late Antiquity to the Île de la Cité.[3] During the second half of the third century AD the town was fortified, like almost all Roman towns in Gaul. As was customary the medieval marketplace grew up outside the Roman walls, in this case on the right bank of the Seine. Round the fortified core several ecclesiastical buildings appeared, while the cathedral was built inside the walls. Here, too, Paris was following the usual pattern in Gallic towns. Paris had one advantage in being close to Flanders and the famous markets of Champagne, but most important to its future development was its role as residence of the royal dynasty of the Capetians, which was gradually strengthening its position and extending its ambitions towards the creation of a French national state. During the eleventh and twelfth centuries the population of Paris increased and the built area was extended, above all on the right bank. The old roads out of town, particularly Rue St-Honoré, Rue St-Denis and Rue St-Martin assumed the character of principal thoroughfares. Around 1200 a wall was made to enclose the built area (figure 3.1), as in many other towns at about the same time.

The stagnation suffered by many large towns during the fourteenth century does not seem to have inhibited the development of Paris, obviously depending on its growing importance as a

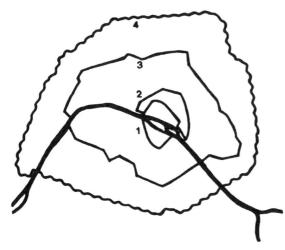

Figure 3.1 *Paris. 1. The first medieval town wall, built around 1200. 2. The second medieval wall from the end of the fourteenth century, which under Louis XIV made way for the promenades which would become the* grands boulevards *of today. 3. The tariff wall of 1780, demolished in the 1860s and replaced by the* boulevards extérieurs. *4. The ring of fortifications of the 1840s, later in 1860 to become the municipal and tariff border. Today roughly the site of the* boulevards périphériques *just outside the present municipal border.*

'capital city'. And whereas many towns, such as the two largest medieval cities in northern Europe, Cologne and Bruges, were a bit too generous when they built their walls and never quite managed to fill the space created Paris was becoming unbearably cramped. Around 1370 a new city wall was built on the northern side, which substantially increased the fortified area (figure 3.1). A further expansion of the fortified area occurred on the north-western side as late as about 1600. By the end of the Middle Ages Paris had become a complex urban structure consisting of several core settlements now joined to one another. Apart from some of the churches there were practically no monumental accents. The old, spontaneously evolving network of narrow and twisty streets, most of which ran parallel or away

from the bank of the river, was already inadequate. Over-population and the absence of open public spaces added to the unhealthy character of the town and must have made it a pretty unpleasant place in which to live.[4]

A new era in the building history of the town[5] began under Henri IV with the construction of two squares, the Place des Vosges (1605, originally the Place Royale) on the eastern edge of the northern side of the town, and the three-cornered Place Dauphine (1607) at the western point of the Île de la Cité (see figure 3.10). This last was part of an ensemble including a new bridge of a post-medieval type, the Pont Neuf, an equestrian statue of the king and a new street through the south bank, Rue Dauphine. Both squares were surrounded by buildings in a uniform style and were intended to create a worthy capital for the French monarchy, as well as functioning as outdoor rooms in the life of the city. This applies particularly to the centrally situated Place Dauphine with its many shops and busy commercial activities, while the Place des Vosges acquired a more aristocratic stamp, though originally intended as a centre for the production of silk.[6] Place des Vosges and Place Dauphine were typical examples of the local design planning which was to characterize urban development in Paris up to the Second Empire. A third *place* project, Place de France, never left the drawing-board. It was to have been a semi-star-shaped *place* with eight radiating streets; as regards size it could have rivalled Haussmann's plans. If this project had been realized, the layout of north-eastern Paris would have been quite different. One remnant of it has survived in the Rue de Turenne which was intended to link the new *place* with the Place des Vosges.[7]

Towards the end of the seventeenth century Paris, together with Vienna, was probably the most heavily developed town in Europe. Houses were being built higher and higher, the courtyards becoming more cramped and the traffic more chaotic in the narrow streets.

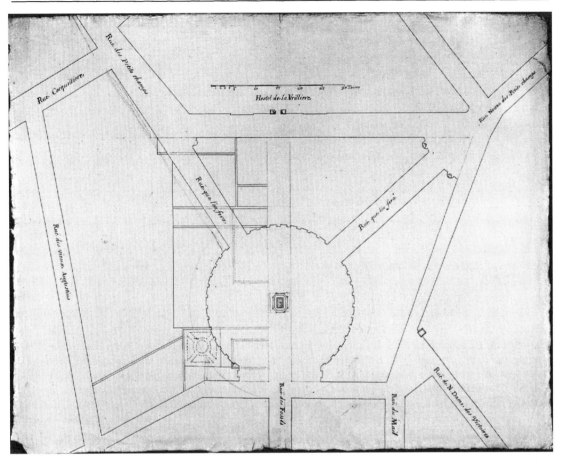

Figure 3.2 *Paris. Place des Victoires, designed and built in the 1680s under the direction of J.H. Mansart by order of the Maréchal de la Feuillade. The architecture was of uniform design, and the centre of the square was occupied by a statue of Louis XIV being crowned with a laurel wreath by a flying figure of Victory. The plan shown here, which is part of a large corpus of French drawings from the seventeenth and eighteenth centuries in the Nationalmuseum in Stockholm, shows how the square – the first one to be executed in circular form – was incorporated into an existing architectural structure. This involved some demolition, but was also effected by practical adaptations to existing conditions. In view of the modest forma – the diameter is 39 m – and the few streets leading into the square, it would perhaps be more appropriate to describe this as a 'circus' than as an* étoile. *[Nationalmuseum, Stockholm]*

During the 1680s two more squares were started, the Place des Victoires (figure 3.2) and the Place Vendôme (figure 3.3), both envisaged as a homage to Louis XIV and as monumental outdoor rooms in an urban structure that was otherwise not one of great splendour. Both were also commercial operations – the image of royalty probably provided a way of promoting the projects as much as a means for honouring the king. The property-owners could build their houses as they wanted, but had to follow the uniform facade design. In

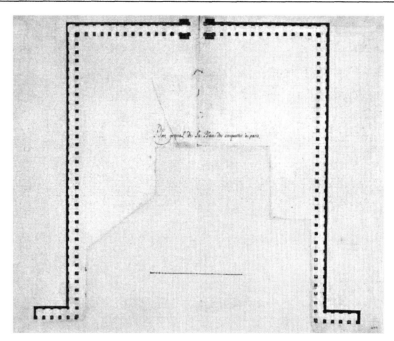

Figure 3.3 Plan général de La Place des Conquêtes à Paris. *Place des Conquêtes, later Place Vendôme, was begun in 1683 on the initiative of the Marquis Louvois, who succeeded Colbert in that year as royal superintendent. The Place des Conquêtes was envisaged as a rival to the Place des Victoires and conceived to celebrate Louis XIV's conquests. The picture shows the original project consisting of a rectangular square with buildings on three sides. The façades were built first, after which interested speculators could buy and build on the desired number of plot modules. The enterprise was not a success, and the façades that were built were demolished and replaced by a square with bevelled corners, that is to say, the Place Vendôme of today. [Nationalmuseum, Stockholm]*

the case of the Place Vendôme the facades were even erected separately before the buildings went up, thus showing that 'facadism' was by no means a discovery of the 1980s.[8]

But such occasional interventions had a cosmetic effect only. Far more radical efforts were needed to get to grips with the substandard urban environment and the heavy exploitation. And, as we have seen, large-scale urban development schemes were in fact not unheard-of in the seventeenth century. The regularization of Stockholm provides an excellent example. In Copenhagen and Berlin, too, far-reaching expansion projects were realized, while in London Christopher Wren among others was planning a vast improvement programme after the Great Fire of 1666, albeit little of this ever got beyond the drawing-board stage.

If any prince in Europe had the resources to transform his capital city, it was Louis XIV. And perhaps in the early days of his reign there were plans for something of the sort, but instead Louis gradually turned his attention to making Versailles the new political and administrative centre of France. Some French scholars have tried to explain this by reference to the humiliating experiences suffered by Louis as a young man in Paris, particularly under the Fronde, and to happy early visits to

Versailles when the house was little more than a hunting lodge.[9] Perhaps some of this may have played a part. But it seems likely that the wretched conditions in Paris and the difficulty of creating anything grand enough there, was the main reason why the Sun King focused his ambitions on Versailles. Here, unhindered by the cramped conditions in the old capital, he could plan the kind of setting he wanted for the ceremonial cult which surrounded his person and the exercise of his power. The problems of Paris were left for posterity to tackle.[10]

Of great importance to later developments, however, was the decision in 1670 to demolish the fortifications, which were replaced by tree-lined roads on the northern side of the town. Thus the roads which are known today as the *grands boulevards* appeared (see figures 3.1 and 3.6), and the type of street came into being which was to be known as boulevard. This ring road was originally intended primarily as a place for elegant outings on foot or by carriage, but it gradually became an important part of Paris's otherwise inadequate communications system, thus introducing the ring road as a recognized element in urban planning. Although it would be some time before the ring of boulevards in Paris acquired the character of city streets with buildings on both sides, the broad tree-planted road nonetheless became an established ingredient in the urban scene there, and subsequently in other capital cities as well.

The seeds of the future ceremonial parade – the Louvre, the Champs Élysées, the hill of Chaillot (Place de l'Étoile), La Défense – can also be dated to Louis XIV's time, in the shape of a project for the Jardin des Tuileries designed by André Le Nôtre. The garden was built round a clearly marked central axis pointing towards the hill on which the Arc de Triomphe was later to be built. Several French leaders have subsequently demonstrated their own glory in the building and enhancement of this axis: Louis XV, Napoleon I, Napoleon III,

Charles de Gaulle and most recently François Mitterrand.

In the eighteenth century conditions in Paris continued to deteriorate as a result of the constantly growing pressure of population. By the turn of the century the town had about half a million inhabitants. Although there were no longer any fortifications to prevent the spread of building, Paris retained its old structure with the population concentrated in the central parts. In this respect Paris differed from London, which had about twice as many inhabitants but enjoyed a more scattered structure with several core areas and lower densities overall.

Characteristically it was during the Enlightenment that the question of the embellishment of Paris – *Des Embellissements de Paris*, to quote the title of a pamphlet published by Voltaire in 1749 – seriously began to be discussed, and here the concept of *embellissements* included measures to make Paris a more healthy, convenient and efficiently functioning town. The shortcomings and disorder of the urban environment were identified and described, and remedies suggested. In particular the writings of the architectural theorists Abbé Laugier and, more especially, Pierre Patte reflect a growing understanding of the need to adapt the town to new conditions, by improving its street network and creating efficient marketplaces and buildings for public activities.[11] According to Patte tree-planted avenues and star-shaped *places* should be important elements in the making of a town. Like Laugier he even called for a *plan général* for the regularization of Paris. This is perhaps the first time the concept of the general or master plan was used in its modern sense.[12] He also prescribed water mains and sewage systems.

Even Voltaire, who seems to have launched the public debate on Paris, is surprisingly concrete. He declares that Parisians should be ashamed of living in the richest town in the world, where there are only two properly functioning fountains and where food has to be

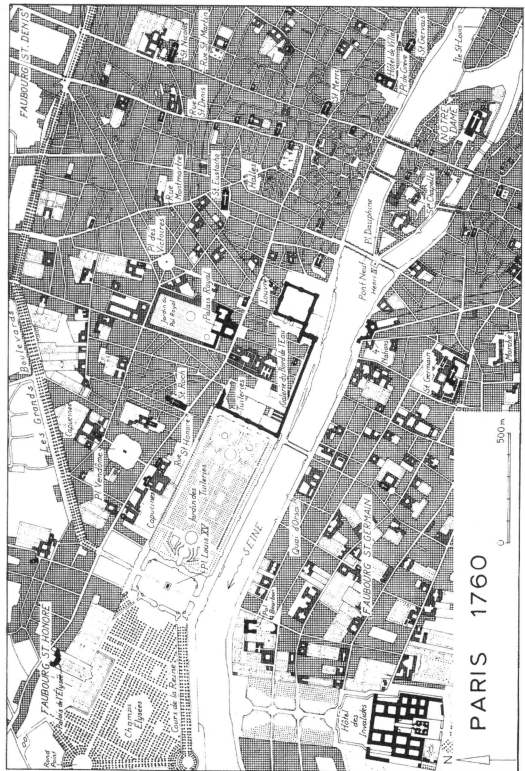

Figure 3.4 *Paris in the 1760s.* [*Redrawing by Erik Lorange*]

bought in narrow, polluted streets. And he calls for 'public marketplaces, fountains that really provide water and regular blocks . . . The narrow infected streets must be widened . . . We have enough to buy a whole kingdom, and we can see every day what is lacking in our town, and yet we do nothing but mumble about it.' Voltaire was aware that such a programme required economic resources; he went on to demand a proportional tax to finance the embellishment of Paris.[13] He was writing around 1750, a hundred years before Louis Napoleon came to power. But Voltaire's pamphlet could have provided a programme for the transformation of the city which was finally realized under the Second Empire.

The ideas thus launched by Voltaire, Laugier, Patte and others, did not at first lead to any concrete results. Little was done in the reign of Louis XV, although people had now become more aware that action was essential. The biggest project, the Place de la Concorde (1755–75, originally Place Louis XV), designed by Ange-Jacques Gabriel, was even more of an architectural show-piece than the earlier squares had been. In the competition which preceded the creation of the Place de la Concorde, however, several projects which could have involved major improvements were produced. These have survived in one of Pierre Patte's publications (figure 3.5).[14]

Recent years have witnessed much lively debate on the changes wrought by the French Revolution, and critical voices have warned against overestimating its importance as a pioneer of new ideas. In the case of the street improvements in Paris, there does seem to have been something of a breakthrough during the last decade of the ancien régime. 1783 saw the ratification of what might be called a building code, with stipulations regarding the width of streets, the height of buildings and building permits. That same year Louis XVI authorized the preparations for a town map. A few years later a street improvement proposal was submitted by the royal architect, Charles de Wailly, providing for several new principal streets on the south side of the town and a new street running from the Louvre to Rue St-Antoine.[15] Sutcliffe regards these measures as a turning-point in the planning history of Paris. 'The shaping of nineteenth-century Paris begins in the 1780s.'[16]

After the Revolution work on a master plan continued under the auspices of a *Commission des Artistes* appointed by the Convention in 1793. Extensive areas had been taken over by the state, primarily from the Church, and it was now a question of exploiting this land as far as possible for new streets. The Commission based its proposal – referred to in the literature as the *plan des artistes* – on ideas derived from both Patte and de Wailly. As in de Wailly's proposal the emphasis is on the less heavily exploited southern part of the town, and again like de Wailly, this plan envisages a new main east-west thoroughfare running parallel with the Seine on the north side. Avenues and star-shaped *places* are important ingredients prescribed by Patte. A large star-shaped *place* was planned in the south in the region of the Observatory, and another slightly smaller one to the east, at the Place de la Bastille.[17] However, the situation was altogether too chaotic for any really significant achievement. The opportunity for using the nationalized land for public spaces was also missed; instead it was sold for development.

The most influential urban design theorist in Paris around 1800 was J.N.L. Durand, who advocated that solutions to current problems be sought in the Greek and Roman art of urban planning. He emphasized particularly the important role of loggias along streets and round open *places*.[18] References to Rome naturally appealed to Napoleon, who saw himself not only as a builder of empires but also as a builder of towns.[19] One of Napoleon's most important contributions to the planning history of Paris was to start the building of the Rue de Rivoli, i.e. the east-west axis which had been suggested by the Comte de Wailly and

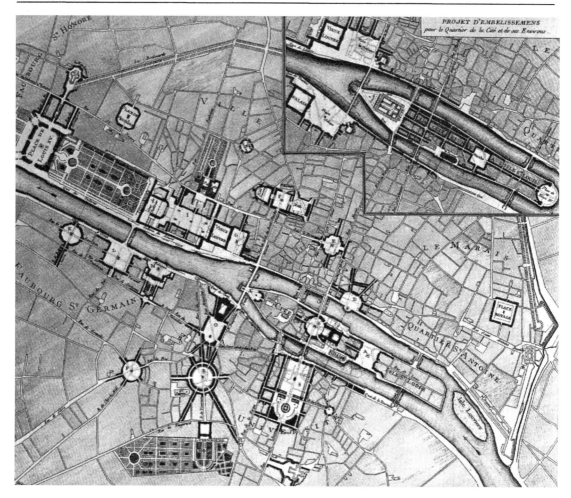

Figure 3.5 *Paris. Various proposals for the Place Louis XV. [From Patte (1765)]*

included in the *plan des artistes*. Under Napoleon the least complicated part was built, namely the section from Place de la Concorde along the Jardin des Tuileries to the Louvre, bordered on the north side by Charles Percier's and P.F.L. Fontaine's austere, strictly uniform façades with open arcades. The difficult problem of extending the street from the Louvre, through the confused conglomeration of houses, and on to the Place de la Bastille was left to the future, but as Sutcliffe has pointed

out, what was done was enough 'to establish the Rue de Rivoli as a paradigm for later improvements'.[20] Another undertaking which added a decisive marker to the townscape was the construction of the Arc de Triomphe (begun in 1806 and finished in 1836) on the hill of Chaillot, the future Place de l'Étoile. This involved the realization of some earlier ideas, while at the same time meeting the ideological requirement that Paris should be designed as a successor to Rome. The completion of the

Madeleine church, with its strict neoclassical temple façade providing a backcloth to the Rue Royale and closing the ensemble of Place de la Concorde to the north, should also be mentioned. As a companion-piece to the south a Corinthian temple front was added like a screen before the existing Palais Bourbon on the other side of the Seine, creating a magnificent transverse axis. But not everything revolved round monumental effects. Like the Roman Emperors in their time, Napoleon also planned streets, water conduits and other things necessary to make his capital a more comfortable city to live in. But by 1812 few of these projects had even been started, and those which had been begun, like the planned east-west axis, generally remained half-finished.

During the first half of the nineteenth century the population of Paris increased from 548,000 to 1,053,000, i.e. on an average by about 10,000 inhabitants per year, a figure which at that time corresponded to the population of a medium-sized city. But the street network in the centre was still medieval, and of a very poor standard. Important approach roads such as the Rue St-Denis and the Rue St-Honoré grew narrower towards the centre, and other streets were simply blind alleys. Several central streets were so narrow that two carriages could hardly pass, and yet they were supposed to cope with both local and through traffic. Even for pedestrians progress was difficult. Often there were no pavements, and in many places drains spilt out into the streets, where 37,000 horses (in 1850) also left traces of their passage.[21] These badly paved and muddy streets were also the location for busy food markets. Much of the building in the centre was undeniably slummy; the high narrow houses were badly maintained and dreadfully overcrowded. Almost all areas were densely built; light and fresh air could barely reach the interior of the blocks. Water was not only of poor quality, it was also in very short supply. The most important source was the Seine, into

which sewage also ran. And all these conditions were aggravated by the constantly rising pressure of a growing population.

The person responsible for the administration of the town, and consequently for seeing that the required action was taken, was a state official, the *Préfet de la Seine*, appointed by, and responsible to, the national government. There was also a kind of municipal council, the *Commission municipale* (later renamed the *Conseil municipal*), but this too was appointed by the government, which was thus in a powerful position for influencing what happened in Paris. It could even be claimed that, given this administrative construction, the initiative for reform had to come from the central government.

During the Restoration no major urban building enterprises were undertaken, although there was a good deal of housing construction under private auspices, particularly on the northern side of the city. In a map of Paris from 1834 (figure 3.6), for example, we can see that the Rue de Rivoli still ends on the west side of the Louvre.[22] Epidemics, social unrest and chaotic traffic conditions made it difficult to avoid taking action, however, and under Louis Philippe attempts were begun to improve conditions in the inner city, albeit on a small scale. The water and sewage systems were enlarged, and some street improvements were implemented, of which the most important was the construction of the Rue de Rambuteau which runs east from the central marketplace. This street was named after the Count de Rambuteau who was *Préfet de la Seine* for most of the period of the July Monarchy. No new overall master plan was made; the *plan des artistes* still seems to have been regarded as an unofficial version of such a plan. The dominating urban development issue of the 1840s concerned the central wholesale market, Les Halles, which generated a great deal of traffic in the centre of the city. The hygienic conditions there were also extremely unsatisfactory. Two alternative solutions were discussed, namely to

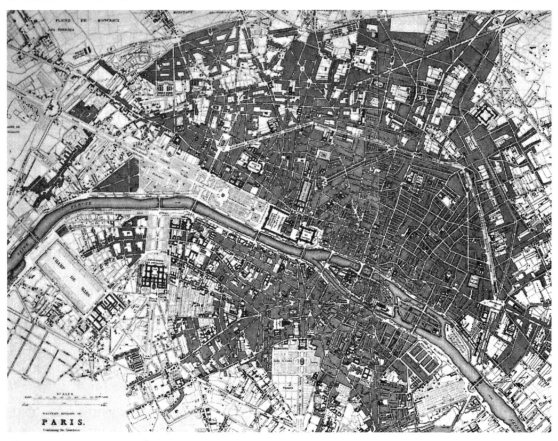

Figure 3.6 *Paris. Part of a 1834 map.*

let the market remain where it was and to build
new market halls, or to move it away from the
centre. Rambuteau supported the first option.
The disagreement about Les Halles also held
up any other action in the centre. The definitive
decision to keep the wholesale market where it
was and to build new covered markets on the
traditional site was not finalized until 1847, just
about a year before the July Monarchy fell.[23]
As a result it became absolutely vital that the
capacity of the streets into and around the
market should be increased, and some moves
towards achieving this were made in 1847.

Louis Napoleon seems to have been interested in urban development issues even during
his exile, and as soon as he assumed power he

was determined to initiate radical action in
Paris. It was a question of encouraging
progressive investments in development and
infrastructure, of creating jobs and improving
conditions for the masses. But it was certainly
just as important to Louis to demonstrate his
own forcefulness and to complete his famous
uncle's great urban development project which
had been lying fallow during the allegedly
feeble régimes of the interim period.[24] In 1839
he published a paper entitled *Des idées
napoléoniennes* (simultaneously published in
English as *The Napoleonic Idea*), in which he
wrote: 'The Napoleonic idea attaches importance only to deeds; it hates useless words. The
action which others discuss for ten years, it

executes in a single year.'[25] And an excellent example of a question which had been endlessly discussed without anything happening was just this, namely the improvement and redevelopment of Paris.

Thus when Louis Napoleon assumed power in 1848, important planning decisions were made and some projects launched. During his presidency he had to content himself with exerting impatient pressure on the new prefect, Jean-Jacques Berger, to resume work on the Rue de Rivoli and to speed up the street improvement around Les Halles. But Louis was not satisfied with completing plans already started; he also wanted to launch his own projects. After the *coup d'état* in December 1851 a start was also made on the Boulevard de Strasbourg and the Rue de Rennes, with a view to opening up communications between the Gare de l'Est and the *grands boulevards* on the one hand and the Gare Montparnasse and the centre of the city on the other. But this was not nearly enough to content the new Emperor, who demanded further measures to be financed by loans. Berger, however, opposed on principle the idea of taking up loans to extend the improvement programme – an attitude which made him popular in the municipal council. After a long-drawn-out struggle on this issue the situation became untenable, and Berger was compelled to leave his post.

It was now a question of choosing a less timid and more dynamic successor to the difficult but prestigious post of prefect of Paris. Great care seems to have been taken over finding a man of authority and energy to realize the Emperor's intentions. In Bordeaux there was a prefect by name Georges-Eugène Haussmann, a man admittedly lacking any extensive experience of urban development questions, but one who was known to be a ruthless and skilful administrator, as well as a loyal Bonapartist.[26] He was now summoned to Paris. The Minister of the Interior, Persigny, who was responsible for the 'job interview', has described his first impression of Haussmann

in his memoirs, as 'big, strong, vigorous, energetic and at the same time shrewd and wily, with a fertile and resourceful spirit . . . As for myself, while this absorbing personality displayed itself to me with a sort of brutal cynicism, I was unable to contain my lively satisfaction . . . I was enjoying in advance the idea of throwing this great feline animal to the troop of foxes and wolves assembled against all the noble aspirations of the Empire.'[27]

In July 1853 Haussmann was appointed *Préfet de la Seine*. As we have noted, the prefect was directly accountable to the national government, i.e. at this particular time, the Emperor. His powers were considerable. The municipal council could delay or possibly even stop new projects by refusing to allocate the necessary funds. But its members were not elected; they were, as mentioned above, appointed by the Emperor on the recommendation of the prefect. There was thus plenty of opportunity to create a compliant council.

Haussmann began his career as an urban developer by improving the efficiency of the municipal administration, and by mapping and levelling the whole of Paris.[28] The lack of any survey or topographical levelling had been causing serious problems during the current work on the Rue de Rivoli. Presumably at this stage certain overall aspects of the planning programme were also discussed. On the very day that Haussmann was sworn in as prefect, Napoleon III is said to have handed him a map of Paris on which he had shown, in four colours, the streets which were to be constructed. The colours indicated the priorities. This map has unfortunately been lost; on the other hand a reconstruction made in 1867 for William I of Prussia has survived, but it probably differs in various essential ways from the original.[29] It may seem surprising that no overall master plan was drawn up and published, as was to be done later in other capital cities.[30] This may have been partly because it was feared that the extent of the planned

Figure 3.7 *'Le baron
Haussmann'. [From*
L'Œuvre du baron
Haussmann*]*

inverventions would arouse protests, and because the street improvement proposals were
regarded as a package of measures rather than
as parts of an overall plan. Perhaps, too, it was
hoped in this way to prevent speculation. But
there does not even seem to have been a
master plan for internal use, apart from the
Emperor's outline.

In Haussmann's first year in office work
continued on the Rue de Rivoli, which was
extended to the Rue St-Antoine in order to
link up with the ring of boulevards. At the
same time planning began for a main north-
south axis, which together with the Rue de
Rivoli was to create a street system which
Haussmann called the *grande croisée de Paris*.
One possibility had been to widen either the
Rue St-Denis or the Rue St-Martin. But
instead Haussmann decided to extend the
Boulevard de Strasbourg through the blocks

between these two streets (figure 3.8). A
decisive reason for this was of course that it
allowed a straight continuation of the
Boulevard de Strasbourg, which had been
begun in 1851. But if the new street was taken
through the interior of the blocks, where the
buildings were the worst and the land values
least, the clearance effect would also be greater
and the cost of acquiring the land lower.
Further, in this way a street could be created
with new buildings on both sides. If an existing
street was being widened, the old buildings on
one side could be retained, which would bring
down the values of the new properties on the
other side. This idea of constructing new
streets as far as possible through the interior of
the old blocks, became a characteristic feature
of subsequent street improvement schemes.[31]

The new north-south thoroughfare –
Boulevard de Sébastopol – was extended across

Figure 3.8 *Paris. Aerial photograph showing Rue St-Denis, Boulevard de Sébastopol and Rue St-Martin. One possibility would have been to widen one of the existing streets, Rue St-Denis or Rue St-Martin, but instead a completely new street – Boulevard de Sébastopol – was cut through the middle of the blocks. [From Cars and Pinon (1991)]*

the Île de la Cité under the name Boulevard du Palais and, on the south bank of the Seine, as the Boulevard St-Michel.[32] However, the *grande croisée* with its linked streets was only the beginning. During the barely seventeen years of Haussmann's prefecture, a building and street regularization programme was implemented which in its sheer size has few if any rivals. A map of Haussmann's streets (figure 3.9) conveys an impressive albeit somewhat confusing impression. However, a closer examination does reveal, if not any superordinate plan, at least a guiding idea, namely to facilitate communications within the central

parts of Paris and between these areas and the peripheral districts of the city.

Under Haussmann the centre proper consisted, roughly speaking, of the Île de la Cité and the area around Les Halles and the Hôtel de Ville. Round this core there was an inner zone, bordered on the north side by the *grand boulevards*. Then came an intermediate zone extending to the tariff wall and the outer ring of boulevards; most of this area had been built up during the first half of the nineteenth century. The adjoining outer zone was defined by the fortifications erected in the 1840s. In 1860 the city and the tariff boundary were

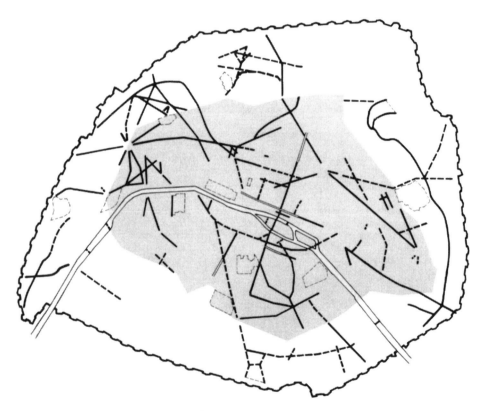

Figure 3.9 *Paris. Streets included in Haussmann's improvement and regularization programme. White sections of street were built before 1854, solid black sections before 1870 and dotted sections after the fall of the Second Empire, but still largely in accordance with Haussmann's intentions. The hatched area indicates the municipality of Paris up to 1860, when the municipal boundary was extended to the outer fortification ring. [Map drawn by Katarina Strömdahl-Lillfeir on a basis of maps in Cars and Pinon (1991)]*

moved out to this defence ring (figure 3.1). The central zone was heavily developed, while vacant land for housing construction, industrial establishments etc. was to be found above all in the outer zone. As a result of the wretched conditions in the urban core and its lack of good communications with the surrounding districts, the functional city centre was beginning to shift westwards. This had already been recognized in the 1840s, when the *déplacement de Paris* was discussed, together with possible ways of counteracting it.[33]

Patte and others had previously recommended that communications between the different parts of the town should be improved and some street projects had been carried out, albeit mainly in peripheral areas such as the Quartier de l'Europe. What was new in the programme outlined by Napoleon and realized by Haussmann, apart from its sheer size, was the systematic investment in good communications between the centre and the periphery. 'In order to render accessible and habitable the vast empty spaces which have remained unproductive on the furthermost edges of the town, it will be necessary first to pierce it right through, thus ripping open the centre,' wrote Haussmann, describing his thoughts on the first day of his appointment.[34] Thus conditions in the centre were to be improved by exploiting the outer zones more efficiently. Here we can discern a 'hierarchic' conception of the urban structure, rather similar to the view underlying the transformation of Stockholm City in the 1960s, for example.[35]

Mention should also be made of the railways at this point. The French railway network, on which serious construction had begun in the 1840s, consisted like its English and Prussian counterparts of a number of lines radiating out from the capital city; each regional system had its own terminus. In Paris, as in most other places, these stations were located on the outskirts of the most densely built area. Thus the town acquired a number of peripherally located dead-end stations, which had poor

communications with the centre (figure 18.2*a*). One of Haussmann's responsibilities was seemingly to do something about this problem – an aim which coincided with his ambition to improve communications between the centre and the periphery.

If we limit ourselves to the central zone, the measures planned and/or executed under Haussmann can be summarized under four main headings:

1. Extensive redevelopment on the Île de la Cité (figure 3.10) and around *Les Halles* to make the centre both accessible and functional.
2. The *grande croisée de Paris* with the Rue de Rivoli as the east-west axis and the four boulevards – Strasbourg, Sébastopol, du Palais and St-Michel – as the main north-south axis. These thoroughfares were to improve the traffic situation in the central zone, as well as communications between the centre and the outer zones. The principal north-south axis also gave the Gare de l'Est, and albeit to a lesser extent the Gare du Nord, excellent communications with the centre. Haussmann often refers to the *grande croisée* in his memoirs, and it is clear that he regarded it as providing the fundamental bones of his communication system.
3. An extension of the *grands boulevards* over the Seine in the southern part of the city, to create a ring of boulevards around the central zone (this was not realized until the Third Republic).
4. Diagonal streets through the central zone, such as the Rue de Turbigo and the Avenue de l'Opéra (this last was not completed until the Third Republic).

As well as the street improvement inside the central zone a series of traffic arteries from this zone and through the outer zones were also created, for example the Rue de Rennes to Gare Montparnasse (started before Haussmann's time); Avenue Daumesnil and Boulevard Voltaire through the eastern outskirts;

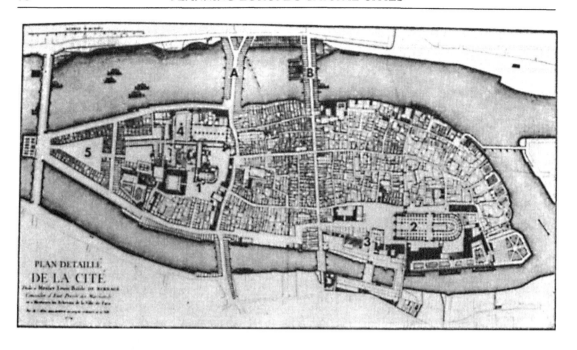

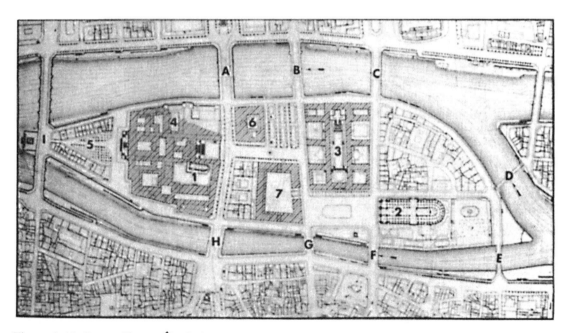

Figure 3.10 *Paris.* Above: *Île de la Cité, 1754.* Below: *after Haussmann's regulations. 1. Sainte Chapelle. 2. Notre-Dame. 3. Hôtel-Dieu. 4. Palais de Justice. 5. Place Dauphine. 6. Tribunal de Commerce. 7. Caserne de la Cité (now Préfecture de Police). The letters designate bridges. [From Lameyre (1958)]*

Rue la Fayette, Rue de Rome, Boulevard Malesherbes, Boulevard de Magenta and its extension in the Boulevard Barbès and the Boulevard Ornano through the northern area; and Avenue Foch, Avenue de Friedland and Boulevard Haussmann through the western parts. The incorporations of 1860 seem to have resulted, rather naturally, in a shift of emphasis from the redevelopment in the centre to creating roads out to the periphery.

In some places Haussmann's streets are so intimately interconnected that they could be said to be street systems. One such focus is to be found in the south-east, in what is now the thirteenth *arrondissement*. Here several streets meet at the crossing of Avenue des Gobelins and Boulevard Arago/Boulevard Saint Marcel, but there is no particular ambition to create a monumental *place* or any other grand effect, presumably because of the topography and the social character of the area.

Elsewhere, on the other hand, the impression of monumentality is all the greater. In this respect Place Charles de Gaulle (Place de l'Étoile) is in a class all its own. By linking eight streets into a symmetrical pattern with the four which already terminated at this point, Haussmann created a monumental setting on a scale that would be difficult to surpass, although strictly speaking it can only be fully perceived from the air (figure 3.11). In this way he orchestrated a splendid finale to a long-continuing project in Parisian planning, namely the building of an east-west axis, a *via triumphalis*, from the Louvre to l'Étoile. As we have seen, this idea was first launched by Le Nôtre for Louis XIV; it then continued in Gabriel's planning of the Place de la Concorde and in the construction of the Arc de Triomphe which started under Napoleon I. It must have been extremely satisfying for Napoleon III and his prefect to be able to complete this project with its imperial overtones and its associations with France's great rulers. A similar star-shaped *place* was created in the eastern part of the city, the Place de la Nation (originally Place du Trône), again by enhancing an existing structure. Ideally, of course, the two star-shaped *places* should have been equidistant from the crossing of Rue de Rivoli and Boulevard de Sébastopol, and a direct link-up with this central point in the new street network would have been desirable; but it was a question of adjusting to realities.

Haussmann's main contribution to the planning history of Paris thus consisted of creating new streets through existing urban structures. On the outskirts the level of development was lower. Here, more local planning should have been possible but no such ambition appears to have existed, even after the legal city boundary was moved out to the defence ring in 1860 and

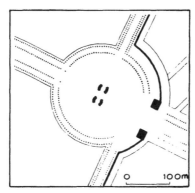
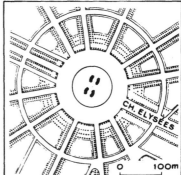

Figure 3.11 *Paris. Place Charles de Gaulle (Place de l'Étoile) before and after Haussmann's rebuilding. The thick line on the left plan shows the tariff wall. [From Lavedan (1975)]*

substantial unbuilt areas thus came under the city's jurisdiction. Local planning was left to landowners and the market forces, which is presumably why the plans in many places are so unstructured. The absence of tradition and legal instruments may have played a part, but would have been unlikely to restrain Haussmann if he had considered such planning to be urgent. An exception has to be made, however, in the case of the north-western area beyond Parc Monceau where an impressive district was created with several star-shaped *places* and broad avenues as part of an upper-class zone extending from the Avenue des Champs Élysées. The lack of interest was even more marked outside the 1860 city limits. Over the coming decades suburban building, much of it low standard housing, spread over this area – the *banlieue* – virtually unhindered.[36]

A typical feature of urban development activities during the Second Empire was the rapid progress from the preparatory to the implementation stage. Planning proper seems to have been kept to an absolute minimum; what was required was an immediate concrete result, not theoretical deliberations or committee discussions of various options. Many streets seem to have acquired their definitive location and extent almost by chance. Haussmann was a born improviser, always ready to grab opportunities as they arose. It is also obvious from his memoirs that he considered the different street projects one by one, not as part of an organic whole.

The first step in the process of implementation was to acquire the ownership rights to the land which was going to be affected by the planned streets. Following evacuation and the demolition of existing buildings, the new street and the necessary pipes were laid down. The property-owners and developers were then responsible for new building. This was the way the street improvements were to proceed, through cooperation between public and private interests.

To begin with this system seems to have

worked as intended, benefiting from the economic boom that immediately followed Napoleon's *coup d'état*. But difficulties soon arose. One problem was that the sums of money needed for acquiring the land, which were determined by a kind of jury, tended to be very high, particularly in the 1860s when the value of land was rising. Moreover, there was ample scope for manipulations with a view to forcing up the expropriation compensation. This, together with the high cost of demolition and the construction of streets, meant that the urban renewal scheme was becoming extremely expensive. By 1869, according to Haussmann's calculations, Paris had invested 2½ billion francs in urban improvements since 1851. The fact that this sum was forty-five times greater than the city's total costs in 1851, gives us some idea of the enormous size of the amounts involved.[37]

Naturally it was extremely difficult to finance an enterprise of this magnitude. We have seen that Berger, Haussmann's predecessor, felt dubious about relying on loans. His view was that the street improvements should cost no more than could be covered by the city's current revenues from custom dues and property taxation. Napoleon and Haussmann, on the other hand, found it perfectly justifiable to borrow for making improvements in the city: it was a question of a productive investment which would increase revenues in the long run. A first loan of 60 million francs had been taken up as far back as 1852, i.e. under Berger and despite his opposition, and another of the same size followed in 1855.

Another source of funding was provided by state grants, which could also be used for stimulating the city's own willingness to invest. The streets that formed part of the *grande croisée*, which Haussmann referred to as the *premier réseau*, was partly financed by government allocations. The same applied, according to an agreement between the town and the state in 1858, to a further twenty-one streets, mainly principal thoroughfares between the centre and the peripheral districts. Here the state paid 50 million of an estimated cost of 180 million francs; but the actual cost turned out to be 410 million. Haussmann called these streets the *second réseau*. For other streets the city had to provide the funding itself. This last category represented Haussmann's *troisième réseau*.[38] Napoleon III would certainly have liked the state subsidies to have been more generous, but the legislative body which had to approve such things was dominated by provincial representatives, who were not prepared to grant favours to Paris. Moreover, the opposition was constantly looking for ways of scuttling Napoleon's projects.

It had probably been reckoned that the street redevelopment would be largely self-financing, at least in the long term, as a result of growth and higher tax revenues, but also owing to the increase in the value of the plots lying along the new roads. However, this was assuming that the town owned the plots, and the right to expropriate more land than was needed for the actual streets with a view to future sales, was a controversial and complicated issue. A law enacted in 1807, to quote Sutcliffe, 'empowered all towns to draw up plans showing the desired *alignements* of all their streets . . . Lands ceded to the highway in execution of the *alignement* were to be compensated at their assessed value only, with no indemnity paid for disturbance.'[39] The system of *alignements*, whereby in principle property-owners were expected to effect the necessary improvements, never worked as intended. In 1841 a law had been introduced which enabled the expropriation of land for the *travaux d'utilité public*, referring in the first instance to railways. An expropriation act passed in 1850 (the *loi Armand de Melun*) made it possible to expropriate substandard housing for clearance. However, this law was difficult to apply, and had little effect. An important extension of the compulsory purchase prerogative was introduced by a decree-law in 1852, 'which allowed the complete expropriation of properties, part

of which was needed for the works, when the remainder was too small for the erection of "healthy houses".'[40] In the same year it was decided that expropriation permits according to the 1841 law were to be granted by the executive authorities and not, as before, by the legislature.

The town had thus acquired the right to expropriate land along a planned street, when this was necessary for the building of healthy dwellings. Whatever was not needed for the street the town could then resell, and could retain the added value. This right, which was of fundamental importance to the funding of the street improvements, was undermined in 1858 by a decision in the *Conseil d'État*. As a result of this decision the town was henceforth frequently compelled to return land not definitely used for streets to the previous owner, who could thus benefit from the whole of the increase in the land value. A decision in the *Cour de cassation* in 1860, regarding the compensation due to the tenants of expropriated housing, also went against the town, which led to further expense.[41] Thus trading in plots never became as important a source of financing for the street improvements as had been hoped. The city bore the whole cost but received little of the revenue. At the same time a wave of uninhibited speculation was pushing up the price of the land.[42]

Thus it became necessary to take up further loans. But even loans had to be approved both by the municipal council and by the legislative body; moreover, the market for municipal bonds was not unlimited. Nonetheless Haussmann managed to arrange a loan for 130 million francs in 1860 and another for 250 million in 1865. However, this money was chiefly intended for work within the area incorporated in 1860 between the old tariff wall and the new fortifications.[43]

But Haussmann was not prepared to limit himself to what could be done with the help of conventional funding. On the contrary, the urban renewal scheme was assuming increasingly gigantic proportions. In 1858, 129 properties were condemned to make way for public works; in 1860 the corresponding figure was 398 and in 1865 it was 691. The process peaked in 1866 when 848 properties were demolished in a single year.[44] This can be compared with the radical rebuilding of Stockholm's CBD during the 1950s and 1960s, which affected about 400 properties.[45] Naturally a project on such an enormous scale caused financial as well as administrative problems. From the end of the 1850s the regularization operations were being increasingly handed over to entrepreneurs, who became responsible for the entire process of implementation, including expropriations, and who supplied the town with finished streets.[46] The work was ordered on credit, i.e. the town would not begin to pay until the streets in question were complete, and then only in annual instalments. The developers, who were thus effectively granting loans to the city, themselves had difficulty in finding sufficient funds, and a system was established whereby payment orders (*bons de délégation*) were issued and made payable to the occupant, with the city as drawee. Haussmann signed these documents, not as acceptances but as proof that the delegation bonds corresponded to a demand on the city. The agreements were then discounted by the state mortgage bank, the *Crédit Foncier*. In some cases this happened before the work had even started, which was naturally rather a dubious procedure. These transactions and others of an equally dubious kind were facilitated by the municipal *Caisse des Travaux de Paris*, which had some borrowing rights and could thus make advance payments.

To begin with nobody outside the inner circle of the initiates had any insight into these financial methods. However, from 1865 it became clear to the public that Haussmann had, *de facto*, taken up large loans without the authorization of the legislative body. At the same time Napoleon III's position was being

seriously undermined; his régime had suffered a number of setbacks, and attempts to counteract criticism by introducing liberal measures only led to new demands for change. Haussmann seems to have been one of the critics' favourite targets. With his autocratic behaviour and evasion of political control, he personified much of what people disliked about the current constitution, and since they could not criticize Napoleon openly they had to shoot at his collaborators instead.[47]

In the end the enormous burden of debt in the shape of delegation bonds was too much for Haussmann, particularly when repayments began to fall due in 1868. In April that year a government bill proposed that the legislative body should approve an agreement between Paris and the *Crédit Foncier*, according to which the bank's claim on Paris for 398 million francs in the form of *bons de délégation* should be converted into a long-term bond loan. The reaction to what was regarded as official confirmation of Haussmann's abuses was a powerful one, and it heralded one of the greatest scandals of the Second Empire. Thiers, a conservative politician and the foremost representative of the opposition, described Haussmann's borrowing activities in the legislative body as 'a flagrant violation of the law, . . . the most amazing . . . ever committed.'[48] When after much delay the question was finally taken up in the legislative body, the government was compelled to make a number of concessions, which meant essentially that they were disavowing Haussmann. However, the prefect remained in his post until January 1870. By resigning then, he avoided being drawn into the events following the fall of the Empire, and was able to pass his last twenty years as a widely respected pensioner.

Haussmann's importance as an administrator and his skills in implementing plans cannot be questioned, but how should we evaluate his contribution as a planner, i.e. as an urban development ideologist and a shaper of urban space? And how important was Napoleon III in this context?

There is no simple answer to these questions. Naturally some of the most spectacular street constructions of the Second Empire can be traced back to earlier bouts of planning. This applies particularly to the Rue de Rivoli, although the street was located differently in the earlier proposals. The north-south principal axis did not appear in the *plan des artistes*, but it was included in the map which the Emperor gave to Haussmann in 1853. But the communication link as such had already been discussed at the time of the July Monarchy. Nonetheless, we should not make too much of the connection with earlier deliberations and plans. The *plan des artistes* not only lacked most of the streets which Haussmann realized, but its main focus lay in the southern part of the city. And the debate during the July Monarchy was primarily concerned with individual streets and minor projects only. What Napoleon and Haussmann did take over from earlier planning efforts was perhaps the idea of creating a network of broad, straight streets by means of street improvements, but they did not inherit concrete solutions. And in its scope and its radical nature the planning undertaken during the Second Empire surpassed all earlier serious proposals.[49]

It would be difficult, and is perhaps not really necessary, to separate Napoleon III's contribution from Haussmann's. As we have noted, Napoleon's sketch has been lost, and the street projects were discussed in frequent meetings between the Emperor and the prefect, but their deliberations do not seem to have been recorded apart from occasional notes in Haussmann's *Mémoires*. Nonetheless it is clear that the Emperor did play a decisive part. The idea of street improvement was in the air; Napoleon's contribution was to take it up and carry it through on a scale hitherto unknown, by giving Haussmann the requisite authority and by continuing to support him even when the critical voices grew louder. It also seems

reasonable to accept the Emperor as the main designator of the approximate locations of the principal streets in the central area.[50] And it should be remembered here that similar street improvements – without Haussmann – were also being realized in several other French towns during the Second Empire (see pp. 352 f).

But ideas are one thing; realizing them is another. The prefect probably had plenty of scope for his own judgement as regards both the exact location of the streets and their width and design – an opportunity which he certainly did not fail to exploit. And Napoleon's interest was presumably limited mainly to the principal streets in the centre; it was assuredly Haussmann himself who took the initiative when it came to the other streets.[51] The case of Pont de Sully shows that Haussmann did not hesitate to back his own opinion when it diverged from that of the Emperor. Haussmann, whose classicism was more dogmatic than the Emperor's, wanted the bridge to act as a straight extension of the Boulevard Henri IV, connecting it with the Place de la Bastille without interrupting the prospect towards the column in the square and the dome of the Pantheon.[52] Accessibility, too, would have benefited from this solution. But Napoleon wanted the bridge to cross the river at right angles, like the other bridges in the city. This conflict between the two men seems to have been one of the reasons why the bridge was not built at all under the Second Empire; when it was finally realized, it was Haussmann's alternative that won the day creating one of most impressive vistas in Paris.[53]

Naturally the work carried out under Haussmann would not have been possible without a team of efficient helpers. This applies particularly to the two engineers Adolphe Alphand, who was responsible for the parks and gardens, and Eugène Belgrand who was an expert on water and sewage questions, both of whom made sure in their own publications that their contribution would not be forgotten.[54] Mention should also be made of the architects Jacques-Ignace Hittorff, who was responsible for the local planning of the Place de l'Étoile, and Victor Baltard, who designed Les Halles. Haussmann seems to have preferred Baltard; moreover he apparently felt that he should patronize him as a former schoolmate. In fact, however, he was critical of them both, as well as of other contemporary architects. He complained that no architects of any real substance were available to him.

But Haussmann would certainly have reserved the right to make all the important decisions himself. He emerges unrivalled as the chief actor in the improvement programme. His office as prefect alone placed him in a position of power, and this was reinforced by the support of the Emperor. But the amazing results could not have been achieved without that combination of sensitivity to realities and a nose for unconventional solutions,[55] of pedantry and an ability to think big, of arrogant ruthlessness and diplomatic tact – all of which seem to have imbued his actions.

When Haussmann retired from the prefecture in 1870, several of the planned streets were little more than embryos. Work had ceased almost entirely in 1869 on account of the financing problems. Despite all the criticism levelled at Haussmann during the Second Empire, the following régime proceeded with the programme of urban renewal according to his intentions. This can be partly explained by the fact that projects once started had to be finished, that Haussmann left behind him a loyal team of colleagues in the municipal administration, and certainly also because his plans had obvious merits. Several of the streets which we regard as being particularly typical of Haussmann were in fact realized or at least completed after his time. Examples are Avenue de l'Opéra (figure 3.12), Boulevard Raspail, Boulevard St-Germain and Boulevard Haussmann.[56]

Finally it should be reaffirmed that Haussmann was by no means only, or even mainly, engaged in road construction. He undertook various other measures to improve living conditions in Paris, and to adapt the town to cope with the huge increase in its population from 1,277,000 in 1851 to 1,970,000 in 1870, that is with 700,000 inhabitants.[57]

One remarkable component in the urban environment thus being created was its parks – Bois de Boulogne, Bois de Vincennes, Buttes Chaumont and many other smaller areas of greenery (figures 3.13, 22.7f and 22.8b). In 1850 Paris had very little in the way of green spaces; by 1870 it had a park system unparalleled in continental Europe. Here Napoleon III does appear to have been particularly engaged, at least in the case of the Bois de Boulogne.

Another crucial question concerned the water supply. Even in the 1850s most drinking water was still taken from the Seine, which was also the town's main sewer. Nor, of course, was there any efficient purification system. Water mains can hardly make the same spectacular impression as great streets and parks, but despite Napoleon's lack of positive interest, Haussmann succeeded in building two aqueducts, 200 kilometres long, and relying like their Roman prototypes on the the force of gravity to carry 150 million litres of spring water into Paris every day. And he did this against the solid opposition of the municipal council, for example, which claimed that water from the Seine had always sufficed and would continue to do so in the future too. Nor did Haussmann get any support for this project from the medical community.[58] Another enormous investment undertaken on Haussmann's initiative and closely connected with the street improvements, was a radical improvement in the sewage system, which transformed sanitary conditions in the town.[59] Further, a great many public buildings were erected, such as Les Halles, the Bibliothèque Nationale, the Opera (completed after Haussmann's time), parts of the Louvre and so on. To these should be

Figure 3.12 *Paris. View from the roof of the Opera around 1870. At the time of the fall of the Empire only a minor breach had been forced through the sea of houses towards the Louvre, but even in a city with more modest pretensions than Paris, it would hardly have been possible to stop at that. And the project was in fact continued according to Haussmann's intentions, creating the street which we regard today as perhaps the most Haussmannian of all – Avenue de l'Opéra. [From Cars and Pinon (1991)]*

added a couple of major hospitals, seventy schools in the area incorporated in 1860 alone, markets, churches and town halls.[60]

Paris at the beginning of the 1850s was, according to Pinkney, a city of 'alley-like streets without issue, slums without light and air, houses without water, boulevards without trees, crowding unrelieved by parks, and sewers spreading noxious odours.'[61] Admittedly not all the problems had been solved by the time Haussmann left his post in January 1870, but great results had been achieved in the shape of new streets and parks, a new sewage system and a greatly improved water supply. Medieval Paris had been transformed into a modern city,

no longer a warning example but a model for others.

*   *   *

We have now described the general lines of the great urban development scheme of the Second Empire. But where did the ideas come from? What did the protagonists hope to achieve? And how has the result been judged?

As for the ideas, we have already noted that they were by no means new; on the contrary, ever since Voltaire the kind of action that the Second Empire realized had been the subject of discussion. And certain measures had been

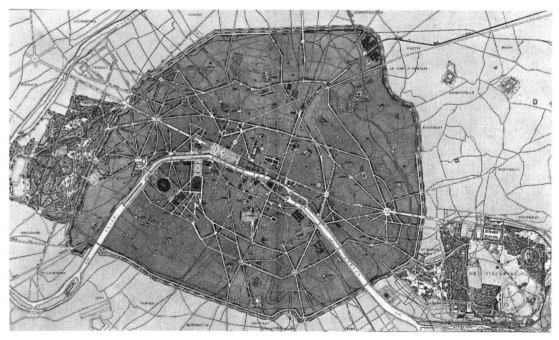

Figure 3.13 *Paris after Haussmann. [From Alphand (1867–73)]*

attempted earlier, particularly under Napoleon I. For his nephew this was a significant factor; Louis Napoleon was obviously deeply anxious to gain legitimacy and eager to appear a worthy heir, not only to his famous uncle but also to the great French thinkers and politicians of the *grand siècle* and the Enlightenment.

How was this great enterprise ever possible? The answer must be sought in Napoleon III's situation and his political programme. When it came to action he was a romantic: energy and drive were crucial components in the image he wanted to project. In this respect he anticipated such later rulers as Mussolini; if it was not possible to demonstrate his strength in spectacular successes on the battlefield or in foreign policy, achievements at home would have to do instead. During an important visit to Bordeaux in 1852 a few months before the new empire was proclaimed, Louis Napoleon declared that the 'conquests' he intended to make would be

harbours made deeper, canals dug out and railways completed.[62]

An additional factor was unemployment, which was sometimes very high in Paris. This was one of the must important reasons for the discontent that exploded periodically and which had often been exploited to generate political upheaval. One way of combating unemployment and stabilizing the political situation was to engage in great public investments. Street improvements were an ideal instrument for tackling unemployment; they generated an enormous number of jobs, not only in demolition and street construction work, but also and more importantly in the subsequent building operations. The fact that almost 20 per cent of the people in work in Paris in the middle of the 1860s, were engaged in the building trade is proof enough of the importance of the building boom in this context.[63]

But it would be misleading to interpret the

huge public investments simply as an attempt to keep the masses quiet. Napoleon did have a genuine interest in social issues, and he was influenced by several of the writers usually described as Utopian socialists, above all Saint-Simon. The idea that public works were the most effective means against endemic poverty was not unusual at this time, and Napoleon saw the Empire as particularly well fitted to make extensive public investments and thus to improve the conditions of the people. Apart from his book on 'the Napoleonic ideas' mentioned above, the Emperor's writings included a slightly socialistic pamphlet – *L'Extinction du paupérisme* (The Elimination of Poverty) – and a voluminous life of Julius Caesar. These three works can tell us something about the lines along which he thought. A kind of vague socialism, a desire to show energy and drive, and a romantic vision of empire combined with a liberal faith in the free market were the cornerstones of Napoleon's rather muddled political ideology – but it was also a brew which proved explosive. As far back as the middle of the eighteenth century many people had realized what Paris needed. But it was not until the flowering of Napoleon's social Caesarism that things really began to move.

Napoleon's own position and his political programme thus provided the conditions for urban renewal in Paris, but the great enterprise would hardly have been so successful if he had not had the luck, or possibly the good judgement, to choose the right person as his prefect. Haussmann combined persistence and a strong will with considerable flexibility and tactical skill, as well as an ability to enthuse others and win over opponents to his own way of thinking. And Haussmann obviously felt a strong attachment to Paris, where he had grown up and been educated. But he would certainly have committed himself just as eagerly to any other great task. Haussmann appears as the typical workaholic: an extremely able man who gives meaning to his life by organizing and leading great projects. To quote Jules Ferry, one of Haussmann's harshest critics: 'He is a powerful man, more than a great personality; rather, he is one of the basic institutions of our times.'[64]

The picture conjured up here may seem remarkably lacking in shadows. Were no mistakes made? Of course they were, and one rather surprising error which is often cited is that several of the great railway stations were not given adequate communications with the city centre. This is particularly noticeable in the case of Gare St-Lazare with its enormous volume of traffic.

Another criticism which can be levelled at Haussmann's urban development policy is that so little was done to improve the housing of the workers. There was great interest in demolishing the slums, but no attempt was ever made to provide alternative arrangements. Haussmann's clearances simply meant that the slums were shifted from one area to another. But the same thing happened in every slum clearance scheme in Europe in the nineteenth century – in some instances as late as the 1930s or even after. In this context we can only say that Haussmann was a child of his times.

Haussmann's Paris became a source of inspiration, influencing developments in many other cities. For most of our own century, right up to the end of the 1960s, the big-city environments of the nineteenth century have usually been judged harshly. They have been condemned by generations of writers representing different schools of urban development. But looking at Paris herself, several of the city's otherwise most rabid critics have found it difficult to quell a certain, albeit perhaps unwilling, admiration. For instance, writing in *Town Planning Review* in 1913, Patrick Abercrombie said 'Haussmann's modernisation of Paris is the most brilliant piece of Town Planning in the world.'[65]

One last point: Haussmann and Napoleon III were nationalists and patriots. It was abundantly clear to them both that France should lead developments in Europe; and it was equally self-evident that Paris was the centre of the world, the heir to Rome. To create a modern version of the metropolis of the ancient world – that, neither more nor less, was their ambition. And in *that* respect we can only say they succeeded.

NOTES

1. The municipal archive material on Haussmann's operations in Paris was lost in 1871, when the Hôtel de Ville was destroyed by a fire during the disturbances of the Paris Commune. However, a substantial amount of published source material is reported in Pinkney's bibliography (Pinkney (1958), pp. 224 ff; cf. also Sutcliffe (1970), pp. 335 ff). Among the printed sources there are several publications written by the actors themselves, in the first instance the *Mémoires du Baron Haussmann* (I–III, 1890, 1890 and 1893), which runs to 1,500 pages; further examples include Alphand (1867–73) and Belgrand (1873–77). Naturally the aim of this work – written long after the events described – is to explain and defend the author's own contributions and the urban development policy which he adopted in Paris during the Second Empire, but it is marked at the same time by the demand of the impartial official for completeness and exactitude. It also contains many striking accounts of illuminating episodes, which help to bring these great projects and their actors to life for posterity.

The seminal account of the transformation of Paris during the Second Empire is Pinkney (1958), which has been the main source of the present chapter. Pinkney (1955 and 1957) are essays more or less agreeing with the corresponding sections in Pinkney (1958). Chapman (1957) also provides a good review of Haussmann's career and activities. Among early French works mention should be made in the first instance of the collection of essays *L' Œuvre du baron Haussmann* (1954) and Lameyre (1958). Saalman (1971) provides a brief review accompanied by a considerable amount of pictorial material. In Lavedan's great book on urban development in Paris, a great deal of space is devoted to the interventions during the Second Empire (Lavedan, 1975). In a number of works Anthony

Sutcliffe discusses various questions concerning the great urban improvement programme in Paris and has located it in a longer development perspective (Sutcliffe (1970), particularly pp. 6–42 and the two 1979 publications, as well as the author's 1993 book). In the autumn of 1991 an exhibition on Haussmann was mounted in Paris, *Paris Haussmann, 'Le Pari d'Haussmann'* at the Pavillon de l'Arsenal, for which a splendidly illustrated book was produced (Cars and Pinon, 1991). Other recent works include François Loyer's *Paris Nineteenth Century, Architecture and Urbanism* (1988), Anthony Sutcliffe's abovementioned Paris, *An Architectural History* (1993) and David van Zanten's *Building Paris, Architectural Institutions and the Transformation of the French Capital, 1830–1870* (1994). The first focuses on the architectural development during the nineteenth century, while the second is a survey of building and planning in Paris from medieval times to the present, stressing the strong tradition of classical design. Van Zanten's book explores the interplay between state authorities, municipal agencies and private enterprise in the shaping of Paris. Planning developments, although not the main theme, are still treated extensively. The projects are discussed as parts of a three-dimensional scenography for the social life of the imperial capital, a point of view clear also in Sutcliffe's work. Plessis (1989) provides a survey of political and economic developments during the Second Empire.

2. Cf. Fried (1973), p. 6.
3. On the early developments, see Lavedan (1975), pp. 71–173 and Couperie (1968).
4. In Sjoberg (1960) Paris is cited as an example of the miserable street conditions in pre-industrial towns: 'The usual street, as opposed to the few main thoroughfares, is narrow, winding, unpaved, poorly drained, and apt to turn to mud during periods of snow and rain, making transportation slow and uncomfortable. Medieval Paris was notorious in this respect' (pp. 92 f).
5. On the development of Paris from the Renaissance to Neo-Classicism, see e.g. Lavedan (1975), pp. 177–393, Couperie (1968) and Sutcliffe (1993). An excellent work on this period which should be mentioned is Josephson (1943), which has unfortunately only been published in Swedish.
6. An extensive survey of the planning and

building in Paris during Henri IV's reign has recently been published by Ballon (1991). Comparing Henri's projects with Sixtus V's slightly earlier plans for Rome, she points out that Henri failed 'to pierce avenues across the capital'. Henri's programme, according to Ballon, was 'devoted to the daily activities of Parisian residents' rather than to 'movement through the city' (Ballon (1991), pp. 252 f).

7. Ballon (1991), pp. 199 ff; Sutcliffe (1993), pp. 20 ff.

8. The two *places* are discussed in Sutcliffe (1993), pp. 41 ff and, most recently, in Berger (1994), pp. 154 ff. Place Vendôme in particular appears to have been the subject of what can only be called negotiating planning in the sense of the term adopted in recent decades, for instance as regards a royal library.

9. Cf. for instance Hautecœur (1948), p. 264.

10. It should be mentioned that although Louis XIV's interest in Paris soon diminished, and little was done to improve conditions, nonetheless several important public buildings were created during his reign, e.g. the Hôtel des Invalides complex, and a great many magnificent private palaces. Bernard, who has devoted a study to Louis XIV's Paris, claims that Paris 'emerged' during this period, pointing out for instance that the majority of the most characteristic buildings in the centre of the city were begun then (Bernard (1970), pp. 289 f). There is of course something in this, but the meagre outcome of Bernard's obvious efforts to seek out every last attempt at radical change in the urban environment, reveals little more than isolated fancies on the part of Colbert and his architects Pierre Bullet and François Blondell.

11. Important critical works include Abbé Laugier's *Essai sur l'architecture* (1753), and *Observations sur l'architecture* (1765) as well as Pierre Patte's *Monumens érigés en France à la gloire de Louis XV* (1765) and *Mémoire sur les objets les plus importants de l'architecture* (1769); cf. Herrmann (1985), particularly pp. 131 ff and Sutcliffe (1993), p. 52.

In a recently published comprehensive study of French eighteenth-century urbanism Harouel has extended the perspective, focusing on provincial towns as well as Paris. The investigation, which deals primarily with legal and administrative aspects, demonstrates the existence of impressive town building activity in France even outside the capital (Harouel, 1993).

12. Patte's views on Paris are summarized in the chapter 'Des embellissemens de Paris' (pp. 212–229) in *Monumens érigés en France à la gloire de Louis XV* (1765). He describes here among other things how Paris was 'a mass of houses piled up pell mell, where it seems that chance alone has presided . . . There are whole blocks which have practically no communication with the others: all that can be seen are tortuous and narrow streets, which everywhere breathe of dirt and filth, where the meeting of vehicles continually puts the lives of the citizens in danger and constantly cause inconvenience.' After this Patte points out that a great deal of Paris has been built during the last 50 years, but without a *plan général*. He then proceeds to criticize the rotten air, the poor water supply, and the fact that the graveyards have been allowed to remain within the urban area. He advocates a radical renewal of parts of Paris, and claims that, although expensive, this would be possible to realize. 'If, for example a skilful architect had suggested to Louis XIII in 1620 to make of his house at Versailles a place whose magnificence would surpass anything that had ever been made of this kind, it is certain that such a project would have been rejected; the genius of the artist would have been admired, but his design would have remained unrealized'. And yet the work was carried out within a period of thirty years. In the same way, claims Patte, a plan for Paris could be successively executed. On Patte's urban development theories, see Picon (1992), pp. 186 ff and Sutcliffe (1993), p. 52.

13. Voltaire (1879).

14. The competition entries are reproduced in *Monumens érigés en France à la gloire de Louis XV*, (1765, pp. 187 ff).

15. Sutcliffe (1970), p. 12.

16. Sutcliffe (1993), p. 66.

17. The *plan des artistes* has not survived, but it was reconstructed towards the end of the nineteenth century on a basis of descriptions. The reconstruction is reproduced in Lavedan (1975), p. 300.

18. Cf. Josephson (1943), pp. 183 ff.

19. On Napoleon's plans for recreating parts of ancient Rome, see Jonsson (1986), pp. 41 ff.

20. Sutcliffe (1979a), p. 90. Several other streets were also constructed or started during Napoleon's reign, for example Rue de la Paix and Rue de Castiglione. In addition to this, extensive work was undertaken on quays and four new bridges were built. The slaughterhouse was also moved out of town from its site near Les Halles, and the water supply was improved. Even the graveyards were moved out of the central area (cf. Pinkney (1958), p. 33 and Sutcliffe (1970), pp. 13 f; a detailed description in Poisson (1964)).

21. Sanitary conditions in Paris around 1850 are described in Pinkney (1958), pp. 3–24.

22. From the end of the eighteenth century attempts had been made to produce the desired widening of the streets by voluntary clearance and renewal by the land-owners, after stipulating minimum widths; however this was largely a failure (Sutcliffe (1970), p. 13).

23. On developments immediately before Haussmann's time, see Sutcliffe (1970), pp. 14 ff; cf. also Pinkney (1958), pp. 75 ff.

24. Cf. Pinkney's views on the background to Napoleon's commitment to urban renewal in Paris (Pinkney (1958), pp. 29 ff).

25. Quoted from Lameyre (1958), p. 97.

26. When Napoleon visited Bordeaux as prince-president in October 1852, Haussmann saw to it that he was received like an Emperor. This visit to Bordeaux was an important step on the way towards the establishment of the Empire a few months later (cf. Agulhon (1983), p. 38).

27. Persigny (1896), pp. 253 ff.

28. The man responsible for the mapping was the architect and cartographer Deschamps, one of Haussmann's most respected collaborators. The great survey plan which was created under his guidance was engraved in the form of a series of maps on a scale 1:5,000. According to Haussmann's own words, he had these sheets 'framed and mounted on a little wagon in the middle of my office, for all to see' (Haussmann (1893), III, p. 15).

29. Pinkney (1958), pp. 25 ff.

30. Haussmann himself seems to have regarded the Emperor's outline as what we might now call a master plan: he speaks of 'the imperial plan' and 'the initial project' (Haussmann (1893), III, pp. 48 and 55). In the third part of his memoirs there are chapters entitled 'Plan de Paris'. The

word 'plan' has here been used to refer to the physical structure of the city and to the survey map of this structure rather than to a carto-graphical compilation of the planned inter-ventions.

31. Cf. Sutcliffe (1970), pp. 29 ff.

32. A review of the street works carried out during Haussmann's time is provided in Pinkney (1958), pp. 49–74; cf. also Lavedan (1975), pp. 427 ff.

33. Lavedan (1969) and (1975), pp. 398 ff.

34. Haussmann (1890), II, p. 33. Cf. also Sutcliffe (1970), p. 33.

35. Cf. for example Allpass and Agergaard (1979) and Hall (1985).

36. See for example Hall (1977), pp. 59 ff and Bastié (1964).

37. Pinkney (1957), p. 45. Pinkney does not indicate how far comparability is affected by changes in the value of money.

38. Haussmann (1890), II, pp. 303 f and (1893), III, pp. 55 f and 59 ff; cf. Pinkney (1958), pp. 58 ff.

39. Sutcliffe (1981b), p. 128.

40. Sutcliffe (1970), p. 26.

41. Lavedan (1975), pp. 422 ff.

42. In several of his novels Zola has provided dramatic descriptions of what could happen (see note 46).

43. On Haussmann's loan transactions, see Pinkney (1957) and (1958), pp. 174–221.

44. Pinkney (1958), p. 188.

45. See Hall (1985). Plot sizes and property values cannot of course be compared accurately, but in Stockholm too it was largely a question of small plots.

46. The procedure is described in Zola's *Au bonheur des dames*, pp. 77 ff; it refers there to Rue 4 Septembre. The transformation of the city is described in several other parts of *Les Rougon-Macquart*, above all in *La Curée* (pp. 82 ff *et passim*).

47. Mention should be made of the republican deputy Jules Ferry's work, which aroused much attention in its time, *Comptes fantastiques d'Haussmann*, composed of a series of newspaper articles published during 1867–68. The series of articles, whose title alludes to Offenbach's opera *Les Contes d'Hoffmann* was important in arous-ing opinion against Haussmann.

48. Quoted from Pinkney (1958), p. 204.

49. One of the main lines in Lavedan's exposition is that 'the work of the Second Empire emerged largely from investigations and the discussions that arose between 1840 and 1850' (Lavedan (1975), pp. 404 ff). However, Lavedan clearly overemphasizes the importance of the earlier projects to urban development under the Second Empire.

50. Haussmann himself touches upon his relationship with the Emperor in several places in his memoirs. With not unjustified self-awareness he comments as follows, for example: 'I would never have been able, on my own, to pursue nor, in particular, to complete the mission which He imposed upon me, and for the accomplishment of which He gave me increasing confidence, and gradually the liberty to make even major decisions. I would never have been able to battle successfully against the inherent difficulties, if I had not had the expression, the means, the instrument of a grand idea conceived by Him, for which above all I must give Him the credit, and whose realisation He supported with a firmness that never failed.' (Haussmann (1890), II, pp. 58 f)

51. According to Haussmann's memoirs the Boulevard St-Germain was not included in the Emperor's original plan (Haussmann (1893), III, pp. 48 f). If this is correct, then it was Haussmann who took the initiative to create this boulevard.

52. Regarding the aesthetics of urban development, their attitudes – Lavedan claims – were different. 'If Napoleon III can pass for a romantic, then Haussmann is a classicist.' (Lavedan (1975), p. 420.)

53. Haussmann (1890), II, pp. 522 f and Pinkney (1958), p. 29.

54. Alphand (1867–73) and Belgrand (1873–77).

55. As, for example, to build the Boulevard Richard Lenoir over the Canal St-Martin.

56. See for example Sutcliffe (1970), pp. 43 ff and Evenson (1979), p. 21.

57. Pinkney (1958), p. 152. The number of inhabitants for 1851 includes the area incorporated in 1860.

58. Pinkney (1958), pp. 105 ff.

59. *Ibidem*, pp. 127 ff.

60. *Ibidem*, pp. 75 ff.

61. *Ibidem*, pp. 24.

62. Agulhon (1983), p. 185.

63. *Ibidem*, p. 6.

64. Quoted from Lameyre (1958), p. 198.

65. Quoted from Sutcliffe (1981b) p. 193.

4

LONDON

London,[1] perhaps together with Rome, surely has the most complicated building history of all Europe's capital cities. And the starting-point was a Roman town, Londinium, embracing what is known today as the City. Up to our own day the City of London has remained an autonomous municipal unit, concerned primarily with its own interests rather than those of the emerging metropolitan area. Westminster, which grew up round Edward the Confessor's palace and his abbey church, came to represent a second nucleus. At the beginning of the sixteenth century 'London' consisted of two towns, London itself and Westminster, linked together in the first instance by the Thames but also by a street – more or less a highway and to some extent built up – along the stretch now comprising Whitehall, the Strand and Fleet Street. There were also a few castle complexes and villages.[2]

In the early modern period the land in what was to become the West End was largely owned by monasteries and Church foundations. By way of purchase and expropriation Henry VIII acquired most of this area, which he needed among other things to ensure the supply of water to his new palace in Whitehall. A little later parts of the area, which was the obvious space into which London could expand, were sold or granted to some of the highest-born noble families in the country. At the time most of the land here was still devoted to agriculture. However, as London's population grew, the demand for housing also increased. Suburban building of a simple kind began to appear despite the royal prohibition.[3]

The first person to recognize the opportunities of exploiting the agricultural land for building purposes seems to have been the fourth Earl of Bedford, who was responsible for the planning of Covent Garden and its neighbouring streets during the 1630s (cf. pp. 22 ff, figure 2.13). Similar exploitation projects were undertaken over the following centuries by various families – the Bedfords, Grosvenors, Portlands, Portmans, Russells and Southamptons among others – or by institutions such as the Church of England and the Foundling Hospital. According to the usual 'leasehold' system, which had no parallel in the other capital cities discussed in this book, the landowner did not surrender ownership of the land but simply leased it for a given period, usually ninety-nine years, after which the right not only to the land itself but also to any buildings which had been erected upon it, returned to him in full. When the stipulated period ran out, the landowner could either renew the lease on the existing buildings or he could demolish the buildings and allow the next leaseholder to erect new ones.

In this way, and as a result of detailed regulations in the contracts as regards the design and use of the buildings, it was possible to guard against deterioration or the possible development of slums in the area. Typically, too, as Olsen (1964) has pointed out, the estates covered large areas with a great many plots, and the landowners were wealthy people more interested in a long-term increase in value than in any immediate return on capital. One of the main points which Olsen makes, and one which had not hitherto been sufficiently observed, is that within these estates planning activities were both continual and comprehensive, their aim being to create and maintain an environment capable of attracting wealthy and socially 'desirable' people to the area. The classical example was Bedford Square, started in 1776 and surrounded by uniform façades with discreet classicizing decoration, and a garden square in the middle. Numerous squares were later designed according to this model.

But, however detailed it may have been, the planning in these estates affected only one part of that conglomeration of mostly small and heterogeneous units which constituted metropolitan London. A first attempt at public planning was made after the Great Fire of 1666. As we have seen, the results of this were rather meagre (see pp. 31 ff). During the 1790s the idea was mooted of making a street to Marylebone Park (the future Regent's Park), to promote the building of high-quality houses there. The park, together with the neighbouring areas, was the Crown's largest landholding in the capital city. The idea was supported by the Prince Regent, later George IV, who wanted to enjoy a monumental approach to his residence, Carlton House. The new street was

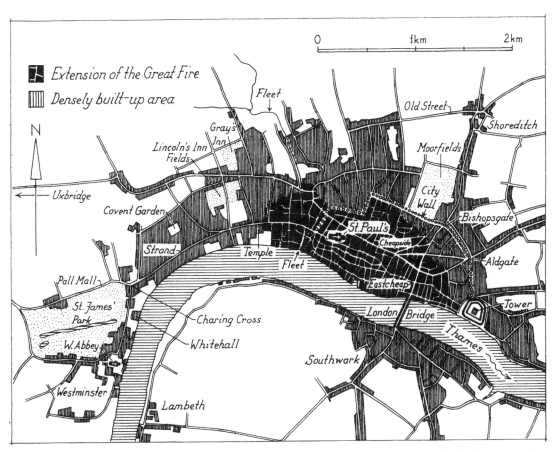

Figure 4.1 *London before the Great Fire of 1666. The oblong urban shape is wholly determined by the Thames. [Map redrawn by Erik Lorange]*

planned by John Nash. In his 1812 proposal (figure 4.2) the full width of Portland Place has been extended to Oxford Street, where it ends in a round place roughly where Oxford Circus is today. The street then continues, still as wide but now in a somewhat more easterly direction. This part was to be furnished with colonnades and shops. The street ends at the corner of a square, almost entirely occupied by a public building, and then continues from the diagonally opposite corner via a round place at the crossing with Piccadilly (roughly the present Piccadilly Circus) and on to Carlton House.[4]

Work on the future Regent Street started in 1814, following an alternative plan also made by Nash (figure 4.3). In this the square had been abandoned and the new street north of Piccadilly led in a wide curve round some plots whose acquisition had proved too expensive. Great difficulties faced the implementation of the project, but an important factor was that the Crown owned more than half the plots involved. However a great many plots still had to be expropriated and many leases purchased. That the street could be completed at all, was largely due to Nash's own skill. Not only did he plan the street and many of the buildings, but he was also personally involved in several major transactions to do with buying and selling the land. As work

proceeded, however, substantial changes were made in the original plans. For instance, as George IV the former Prince Regent lost interest in Carlton House and became more concerned about Buckingham Palace. Carlton House, a fundamental component of the original scheme, was thus demolished to make room for Carlton House Terrace, which can hardly be said to provide a fitting termination to the new street.

What made Regent Street one of the major achievements of nineteenth-century urban design was its central section, the Quadrant, where Nash developed the crescent model by introducing houses on both sides and lining his street with colonnades. Nash built the Quadrant at his own expense, when no-one else was willing to take the project on, which meant that it could be given the architectural unity the rest of the street lacks. The Quadrant has a dynamic force which can still be felt despite major alterations, and it provides an excellent validation of the thesis that brilliant architectural solutions are often the result of difficult conditions.

In its original form Regent Street presented a varied but nonetheless coherent picture, lacking the monumentality of its contemporary relative, the Rue de Rivoli, but also without the formal character of the Parisian street.

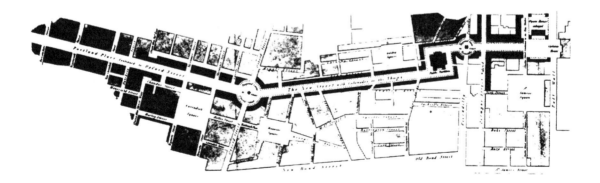

Figure 4.2 *London. John Nash's project, 1812, for a street between Portland Place and Carlton House. [From Mace (1976)]*

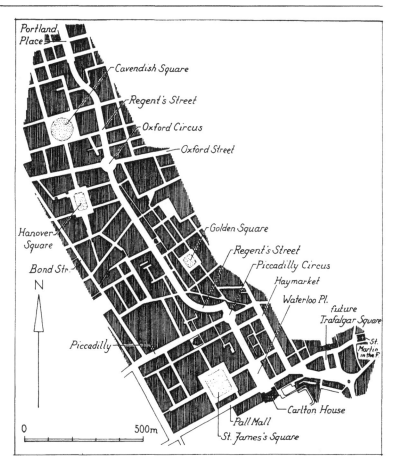

Figure 4.3 *London. Regent's Street as realized. [Map redrawn by Erik Lorange]*

However, while the Rue de Rivoli retained its original architectural design when it was extended under the Second Empire, many of Regent Street's façades were altered and their height increased before the end of the century, while early in the new century several of its buildings were replaced by larger ones. Thus the present-day visitor can hardly envisage the enchanting and festive nature of Nash's street scene, as he created it in a series of masterly improvisations under complicated conditions.

As early as 1812, in a first report, Nash had pointed out that an open place was desirable at Charing Cross, perhaps the most important junction in London. Here Whitehall from Westminster and the Strand from the City joined up with a street leading to the Haymarket and, via Pall Mall, to the planned Regent Street. Furthermore St Martin's Lane, an important link with the north-eastern parts of the town, ended at the Strand by Charing Cross. At the time the area intended for a square was occupied by the Royal Stables. Some time around 1820 this idea was taken up again, and in 1826 Nash presented a proposal for a square which would include a 'National Gallery of Painting and Sculpture', more or less on the site where the present National Gallery was later built. Work on the square began towards the end of the 1820s, and in 1830 it was given its name, Trafalgar Square.

The question of a monument in honour of Nelson was raised later in the decade.[5]

By 1800 the London area, with something over a million inhabitants, was already a colossal agglomeration. Fifty years later the population had risen to 2,700,000, which meant that London had surpassed all other contemporary or earlier towns in size. Over the next twenty years the population was to grow by a further million. At any rate until the middle of the century this growth was occurring without any accompanying overall physical planning or any other type of coordination. It was estimated at the time that London was governed by no less than 300 different bodies – 'an infinity of divisions, districts and areas . . . deriving power from about 250 different local Acts' – many of them with vaguely defined areas of competence, small resources, and very little authority.[6] The only local administration worthy of the name was in the City of London, and it was opposed to the establishment of any new efficient units.[7] As Olsen has put it, the town consisted of 'a collection of autonomous villages, many of which [had] been carefully planned within themselves but with little reference to the adjoining villages'.[8] People were aware of this at the time; in 1856, for example, London was described by one observer as 'the result of a gigantic accident'.[9]

As elsewhere demands for change were triggered by wretched sanitary conditions, cholera epidemics, chaotic traffic conditions etc. Significantly, the first major improvements after Regent Street were carried out by the only authority within metropolitan London with the power and the means, namely the City Corporation. Between 1825 and 1831 an extensive street building programme was under way in the City; impressive even in European terms, it included King William Street, Moorgate, Gresham Street and Farringdon Street.[10] Elsewhere in London developments were slower and more hesitant. John Nash had suggested a number of a new streets which were never seriously considered for imple-

mentation. Nash's successor as London's leading planning expert was Sir James Pennethorne, who presented some visionary proposals, particularly for a 'Great Central Thoroughfare' north of the Strand and Fleet Street, connecting the West End and the City. But outside the City any street improvement required national backing and *ad hoc* committees. Several times before the middle of the century select committees were appointed by Parliament – and once a Royal Commission by the Government – to discuss a variety of street improvements, some of which were subsequently implemented: New Oxford Street, Cranbourn Street, Endell Street, Commercial Street and Victoria Street, for instance. Pennethorne was involved in all these undertakings and in several other projects in his capacity as 'Architect and Surveyor for Metropolitan Improvements', although his schemes were constantly being reduced and distorted due to lack of funds. Mention could be made, for instance, of plans for an oblong polygonal square – a little reminiscent of Puerta del Sol in Madrid – in the crossing of New Oxford Street and Dyatt Street; if realized this square would doubtless have been of importance for the area.[11]

The aim of these alterations was not only, or even mainly, to improve communications; 'far more important', as a committee report pointed out in 1835, were the effects of cutting a new street on 'the health of that part of the capital through which it would be made, by the removal of a description of buildings that have long been a hotbed of disease, misery and crime.'[12] The location and direction of the new streets also seems to have been determined to a great extent by a desire to get rid of slum areas; apparently those involved had great confidence in street improvements as a drastic remedy for a wretched urban environment.

Although substantial results were achieved before the middle of the century, they still fell far short of what was needed. It was obvious that in order to plan more efficiently and, even

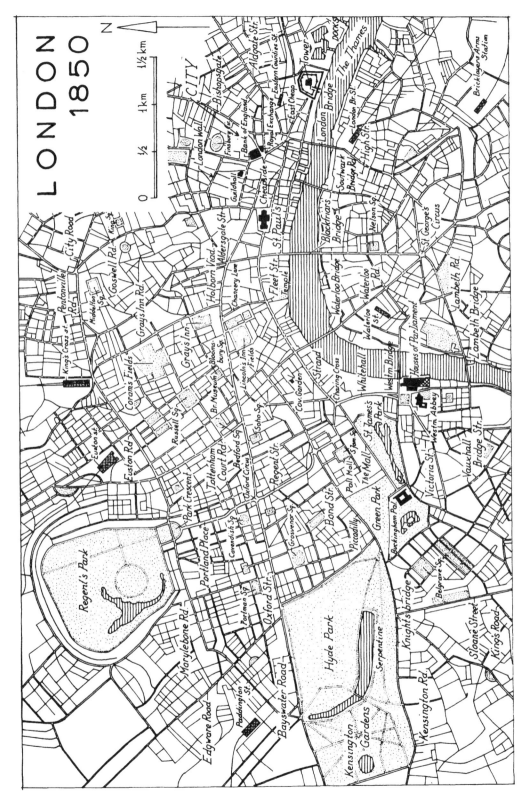

Figure 4.4 *London in the middle of the nineteenth century.* [*Drawing by Erik Lorange*]

Figure 4.5 *London. Outline of streets created during the nineteenth century. Solid black streets were built in the nineteenth century; dotted streets were improved during the nineteenth century; white streets are either earlier or later.*

more important, to see that plans were implemented, it was essential that a permanent joint body for the whole sprawling capital city should be created. For a long time certain planning functions had been assigned to Her Majesty's Office of Woods, Forests and Land Revenues, but the first real planning authority was the Metropolitan Board of Works which was established after a decision in Parliament in 1855.[13] This authority, whose members were elected by the local bodies according to a complicated system of rules, was to be responsible for the major streets, building regulations, sewers etc. Its main sources of income were the proceeds from a tax on coal and wine and a kind of property tax.[14]

The Metropolitan Board of Works pursued the same type of street improvement policy that had been adopted in the decades immediately before its own establishment, and following much the same principles as before, i.e. with a view to demolishing as much slum property as possible while also creating the necessary communications. Among the most important streets dating from this period, none of which can rival Regent Street, we find Charing Cross Road, Shaftesbury Avenue, Queen Victoria Street, Northumberland

Avenue, Southwark Street, and the Victoria, Albert and Chelsea Embankments. In addition to all this the new body made substantial improvements in the sewage system, perhaps its most successful venture.[15] But their efforts were still inadequate. Limited resources and insufficient authority rendered any really effective action impossible.

The Metropolitan Board of Works had a relatively short life. When local government was reorganized and a new system of county councils was introduced, the Metropolitan Board was replaced in 1889 by the London County Council. This new body, whose members were directly elected, produced some substantial results. Among other things it saw to the building of workers' housing as well as adopting building regulations which helped to raise the housing standard. But when it came to physical planning, it does not seem to have achieved anything very much, over and above what had been initiated under the Metropolitan Board. Nor does a municipal reform in 1899, whereby London's many vestries and districts were replaced by twenty-eight boroughs, seem to have changed anything in this respect. The numerous suburbs which were springing up outside the London County Council area were also a growing problem.[16]

A survey (figure 4.5)[17] can give us some idea of the changes in the street network in central London during the nineteenth century, which were certainly no less extensive than in other major capital cities. That the transformation of Paris appears so much more dramatic depends on its concentration to a relatively short time, whereas the operations in London were spread over a longer period. Nor can we claim that the measures adopted in London during this period were any more unplanned than elsewhere; the extension of individual streets was often preceded by comprehensive investigation and discussion in various committees and bodies, and the great estates were certainly engaged in well-considered 'planning' activities. But what does distinguish London from most other capital cities is the lack of any overall plan, although this does not necessarily mean – any more than in Paris where there was no overall plan either – that some sort of general conception of the planning and shaping of the city did not exist.[18] The absence of an overall plan can be explained in part by the fragmentation of the city's administration and the non-interventionist tradition which was characteristic of English public life at the time. The passive attitude of the English government to conditions in the capital city contrasts sharply with the situation in many other countries, in particular of course with France, where the national government took it upon itself to see that comprehensive changes were accomplished.

Towards the end of the nineteenth century the division between a West End and an East End was a fact, and a formless suburban landscape had grown up beyond central London with little if any public control, making the capital the largest and most sprawling metropolitan area the world had hitherto seen. This process, which was made possible to a great extent by various railway systems, will not be discussed here.[19] Suffice it to say that these areas were about to provoke London's most important contribution to the town planning creed, namely Ebenezer Howard's *Garden Cities of Tomorrow*.

NOTES

1. The seminal work on urban development in London is Rasmussen (1973, first published in 1934), which has also appeared in several English editions and printings (for instance 1988; the first 1937). It is doubtful whether any other urban monograph on building history has achieved as much fame as this book. The book is informed by the author's ambition to identify the unique features in London's development, and to find explanations outside the traditional architectural discourse on design and stylistic influences. The importance of social conditions and land owner-

ship patterns is stressed as influential factors. Naturally it is now out of date on several points as a result of more recent research but will long remain an inspiring introduction to London's complex building history. As regards the formation of the West End from the seventeenth century onwards, the reader should turn to Olsen's two works (1976 and, in particular, 1964); see also Summerson (1978). There does not seem to be any detailed survey of planning and street construction in the nineteenth century, but the subject has been touched upon in a couple of essays, e.g. Dyos (1957) and Sutcliffe (1979b). The more recent Young and Garside (1982) does not say very much about London's physical planning. And finally mention should be made of Ashworth (1954), which provides a basic survey of the genesis and development of English urban planning, and thus refers frequently to London, and Hibbert (1969), which provides a brief survey of London's history, with some attention to the physical development of the town.

2. For early developments in London, see primarily Rasmussen (1973) and Hibbert (1969).

3. This process is described for example, in Olsen (1964). The following presentation is based mainly on this work.

4. The Regent Street project has been discussed in a number of works. The basic facts of the genesis of this street are to be found in Rasmussen's London book, first published in 1934; here we find analyses of the architecture and urban character of the street, as well as a description of later changes (Rasmussen (1973), pp. 255 ff). Rasmussen's presentation has been complemented by various editions of Summerson's Nash biography (see for instance 1980, pp. 75 ff and 130 ff) and the same author's *Georgian London* (1978, first published in 1945), pp. 177 ff. Hobhouse (1975) provides a wealth of pictures from the history of Regent Street. Mention should also be made of Mansbridge (1991), pp. 130 ff, Mace (1976), pp. 31 ff and Saunders (1969).

5. Mace (1976) describes the discussions on Trafalgar Square and the lengthy history of the Nelson monument, and – the main topic of the book – the function of this square in London's political life. Nash's above-mentioned proposal for the design of the square is reproduced on p. 38 of Mace's book.

6. Olsen (1964), p. viii; quotation from *The Times* 20th March 1855, taken here from Young and Garside (1982), p. 21.

7. Sutcliffe (1979b) p. 76.

8. Olsen (1964), p. 5.

9. *Ibidem*, p. 6.

10. Tyack (1992), p. 44.

11. Tyack (1992), pp. 43 ff (Pennethorne's projects for a 'Great Central Thoroughfare' are reproduced on p. 48 f); cf. also Dyos (1957).

12. Quoted from Dyos (1957), p. 262.

13. As early as 1848 a Commission of Sewers had been established, the first joint body for the whole of London.

14. See Sutcliffe (1979b), p. 77.

15. Hibbert (1969), pp. 188 f.

16. Sutcliffe (1979b) pp. 77 f.

17. The data for this map were collected by Peter Rees, Director of Planning, City of London Corporation, to whom I would like to express my thanks.

18. Cf. the following comment in Sutcliffe (1979b) p. 77, as regards the Metropolitan Board of Works: 'It began to undertake a series of major street improvements which, though less obviously elements of a coherent plan than those of Paris, nevertheless corresponded to the general scheme which had emerged from earlier studies.' See also Barker and Robbins, I, (1975), pp. 10 ff *et passim*.

19. Cf. Garside (1984), pp. 229 ff.

5

HELSINKI

Helsinki (Helsingfors), like St Petersburg a century earlier, was planned as a capital city, albeit not from scratch.[1] Finland had been part of the Kingdom of Sweden since the Middle Ages, but after the war between Sweden and Russia in 1808–9, Finland became an autonomous grand duchy under the Russian tsar. Åbo (Turku) had long been a kind of *de facto* capital city in the Finnish region of the Swedish kingdom, but shortly after the end of the war the idea was launched of moving the government to Helsinki, a town of hitherto minor importance. In Helsinki's favour, however, was its location closer to St Petersburg and further away from the old mother country; moreover, a fire in 1808 had destroyed much of the town, which meant that the opportunities for creating an imposing townscape were better here than in Åbo. Even before the transfer of the government had begun to be seriously considered, a building committee for the reconstruction of Helsinki had been appointed, consisting of representatives of the burghers and chaired by the county governor. In 1810 the committee produced a plan proposal drawn by Lieutenant Anders Kocke.[2] This implied some extension of the existing urban area but no radical changes in the old plan (figure 5.1), the main lines of which had been created during the seventeenth century by Anders Torstensson (see pp. 201 f).[3]

The new plan was approved by Tsar Alexander I in 1811, but it was obviously not regarded as altogether satisfactory, particularly as the idea of transforming Helsinki into a capital city was now gaining ground. The proposal was therefore revised, and at the beginning of 1812 Johan Albrecht Ehrenström was asked to write a report on the revised version, which does not appear to have survived.

Ehrenström was a fortifications officer, diplomat and courtier. Born in Helsinki, he moved early to Sweden, and during the last three years of Gustav III's reign was the Swedish king's trusted aide. A few years after the death of the king he was accused on flimsy grounds of conspiring with Russia; he was condemned to death but later pardoned. In the autumn of 1811 he returned to Finland, where his acknowledged skills were welcomed. He evidently had no experience of town planning, although fortification officers had often been involved in the layout of towns, and the making of plans was an issue in fortification theory. But when through the good offices of a friend he was asked to report on the Helsinki plan, it was clearly not because of any planning expertise, but simply because he was a person of broad experience and accustomed to writing reports.

However, Ehrenström produced a detailed and to some extent critical analysis of the proposed plan.[4] He saw Helsinki as the obvious capital city for the new grand duchy, a fact which should be taken into account in the planning so as to preclude the necessity of embarking on costly alterations later. One of the main ideas in his report was that only brick houses should be permitted in the 'town

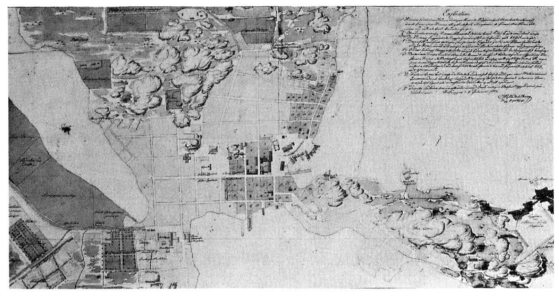

Figure 5.1 *Helsinki at the beginning of the nineteenth century. Detail of a map made after the fire of 1808. [Helsingfors stadsmuseum]*

proper'; anyone wishing to build in wood should be relegated to the suburban area, which would be separated from the main town by a canal. This was by no means an original idea. In Christiania (Oslo), as we shall see, wooden houses had never been permitted since the foundation of the town in 1624, and ever since the sixteenth century the authorities had been issuing ordinances against wooden buildings in Stockholm and other Swedish towns. Even the Helsinki building committee had intended the central parts of the town to be built in brick; however, dispensations for wooden houses were already being given. Ehrenström was much more definite on this point: the town proper was to consist exclusively of brick buildings and should be clearly separated from the wooden buildings of the suburbs. No exceptions were to be made. To a modern reader of this report it may seem surprising that Ehrenström gives no specific motivation for this very firm requirement as regards brick building. But for his contemporaries no such motivation would have been necessary; fire precautions, and the desire to create worthy townscapes, were well-known factors. Furthermore Ehrenström emphasized the importance of building the streets – even the side streets – straight and crossing one another at right angles. Topographical conditions, which in some places were awkward, should not be allowed to interfere with this design. He also advocated canals and broad embankments, and stressed the importance of basing the plan on a careful survey.

Ehrenström's views on the building committee's plan proposal met with a positive response, and he was asked to incorporate his ideas in an alternative proposal. This was soon completed and was approved in April 1812 by Alexander I, when Helsinki was also officially proclaimed as the capital city.[5] At the same time Ehrenström was appointed chairman of the building committee, in which position he was to remain chiefly responsible for the physical development of Helsinki until the mid-1820s.

After his appointment Ehrenström went on

with his planning activities and produced a proposal for the southern suburb;[6] the two projects were combined in a master plan (figure 5.2) which was approved by the Tsar in 1817.[7] The most notable feature of this plan is a broad unbuilt zone edged by double rows of trees and separating the town proper from the suburb, or in other words the high-density central core from the wooden town beyond. Right from the start this belt was designated as Esplanaden. A canal was to run along its northern border. The central square, Senatstorget, had now acquired a more monumental character. Its site and plan were apparently taken over from the building committee's second lost proposal, but Ehrenström adds to its splendour with his suggestion for a centralized church on the hill to the north of the square instead of the imperial residence which the building committee had planned there.[8] The short sides of the square were to be lined by public buildings of uniform design. The

Tsar's residence has been located instead, together with gardens and parkland, in the north-western section of the town. The street network is strictly rectilinear and as far as possible the streets run right across the town without a break.

In the suburbs the nature of the terrain has made it necessary to design two different street networks: the main axis in the western section is a tree-lined road, the present Bulevarden, which together with the Esplanaden creates an unbroken stretch across the whole peninsula, with harbourside squares at each end. The central square, the present Kaserntorget, which is located in the eastern section, was not designed in any special way but simply consists of an unbuilt block.[9] It acquired its architectonic character with the raising of Carl Ludwig Engel's barracks.

Ehrenström's project from the second decade of the nineteenth century could still in all essentials provide a useful guide to the central

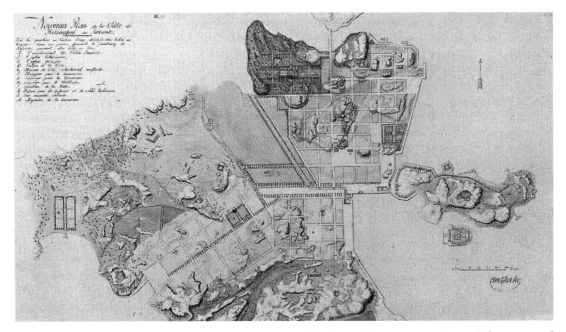

Figure 5.2 *J.A. Ehrenström's master plan for Helsinki. Preliminary version of the proposal approved by the Tsar in 1817. [Helsingfors stadsmuseum]*

parts of Helsinki today; few if any of the proposals discussed here have been realized as fully as this one. This is not only because of qualities in the actual plan, but also because for more than a decade Ehrenström himself was in charge of the building operations, and the authoritarian regime gave him far-reaching powers. In achieving this result, which is unique also in architectural terms, Ehrenström was fortunate in being able to collaborate with an architect of the quality of Carl Ludwig Engel, who set a uniform stamp on the townscape in the particular variant of neo-classicism which in the Nordic countries is referred to as 'empire' (*empir*).[10]

Ehrenström's rebuilding of Helsinki had far-reaching implications for the social structure of the town, as Sven-Erik Åström has shown in a major study.[11] Craftsmen and 'humble folk' without the resources for building in accordance with the ordinances, were largely compelled to leave the 'town proper' – and the poorer they were, the further out they generally had to move. The town centre thus came to be populated mainly by an upper class consisting of the nobility, various high-ranking officials, wholesalers, a few manufacturers and others who to a large extent lived in houses built with the financial support of the government. Ehrenström and his principals were obviously well aware of this effect and regarded it in a positive light. As early as 1571 the Swedish king, Johan III, had decreed 'that all those who are, if not exactly rich at least of reasonable wealth, should build in brick, if they desire to be inhabitants of the town; those others who have not the intention, the possibility or the means for such houses, should live apart.'[12] In other words it had long been recognized that such segregation was an inevitable consequence of raising the standard of building, but while this was clearly regarded as an added advantage it was not the prime purpose of the improvements. It is therefore questionable whether, as Åström suggests, we can really speak of social planning here.

Perhaps it is more a question of physical planning which – as in almost all such – had social consequences.

At least until the beginning of the twentieth century Helsinki's subsequent planning history lacks the sweeping visions of Ehrenström's time. The first real extension of the planned area occurred during the 1830s; this was in Gloet, the area to the west of Senatstorget and north of the Esplanaden.[13] Gloet was originally a bay which as late as the second decade of the nineteenth century almost reached what would later be the northern side of the Esplanaden. As we have seen, Ehrenström's original idea was to link Gloet with the southern harbour by a canal which for part of its length ran alongside the Esplanaden. But this idea was abandoned and Gloet was gradually drained and built, which meant that the street and the block network in Kronohagen, the district around Senatstorget, could be extended to the west. By the middle of the century the planned area was essentially complete, although some plots still remained unbuilt.[14]

During the third quarter of the century the new era was beginning to make its mark on Helsinki, with accelerating population increases, incipient industrialization, the first railway communications and so on. Apart from the location of the railway station and its links with the street network, planning discussions now focused mainly on the southern half of the peninsula and the area Skatudden, for which a series of projects had been appearing since the 1830s.[15] A new master plan which embraced the whole town (figure 5.3), and which this time was the responsibility of the municipal administration, was ratified in 1875.[16] Basically this plan, which was a combination of various subprojects, meant extending the existing block and street system, whereby one broad tree-lined street provided the main artery through the southern districts, while the hilly area south of Rödbergen was left as a park.

However, the 1875 plan affected subsequent developments to a limited extent only. On the

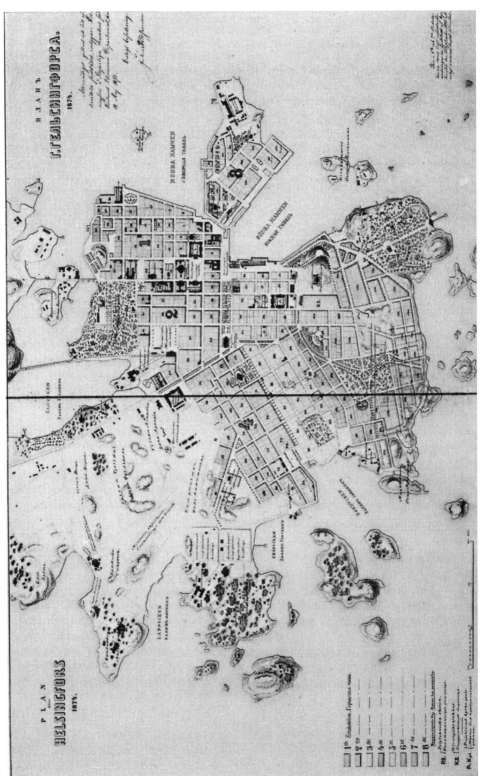

Figure 5.3 *Town Plan for Helsinki, ratified 1875. [Helsingfors stadsarkiv]*

urban peninsula, the area to the south-east –
i.e. north-west of Brunnsparken and south-
west of the Observatory Hill – development
was realized largely according to the plan. The
buildings consist primarily of large blocks of
flats built by private developers. In the south-
west, on the other hand, a more exclusive area
– Eira – was created according to a plan
produced in 1907 along quite different lines. In
the spirit of Camillo Sitte great attention was
paid by its authors – Bertel Jung, Armas
Lindgren and Lars Sonck – to exploiting the
topographical opportunities for creating a
varied urban landscape.[17] The final plan for
the district of Skatudden was not ratified until
1895, and most of the building began during
the first decade of the twentieth century.

Why did the 1875 plan remain largely unrealized? Åström seems to imply that it was
due to a combination of factors: under the
liberal values prevailing in the late nineteenth
century the position of the planners was weaker
than it had been under the more authoritarian
systems of the previous century; nor was the
plan adapted to the new political, economic or
technical realities.[18]

Around the turn of the century planning
discussions turned among other things on
further expansion towards the north-west over
Främre Tölö and Bortre Tölö, and an interesting Sitte-inspired plan was made for this area in
1902 by Gustaf Nyström and Lars Sonck.[19]
Several residential suburbs were also planned
in the same manner, for example Brändö by
Lars Sonck.[20] The area to the north of the
urban peninsula, Berghäll-Sörnäs, was somewhat problematic. As well as a residential area,
Djurgården, there were also large working-
class areas here which had developed quite
spontaneously. Thus it was a question of
raising the overall standard with the help of
redevelopment and complementary build-
ings.[21] '. . . the "better" districts were planned
in advance and the working-class suburbs in
retrospect,' as Åström puts it. 'Before 1910
workers' housing never had a chance of domin-

ating an area for which a plan already existed,
where building land was expensive and freedom
to build strictly circumscribed . . .'[22] Åström's
words could probably be applied to many
Nordic towns.

No serious attention was paid to the regional
aspect until around 1910.[23] A little later (1915)
Eliel Saarinen presented his inventive and
internationally famous proposal for Munksnäs-
Haga[24] to be followed (1918) by a master plan
for greater Helsinki, which was a *tour de force*
of Nordic planning.[25]

NOTES

1. The major work on the physical development
of Helsinki during the nineteenth century is
Åström (1957b). The prime goal of his study,
however, is not to describe the development of
the town plan but to analyse the interaction
between the spontaneous and planned genesis of
regions in a social-ecological perspective. Åström
(1979) provides a summary in English of the main
argument of the earlier book. Lindberg and Rein
(1950) give a detailed account of the planning and
building operations. Johan Albrecht Ehrenström's
life and his work in various fields are described in
Blomstedt (1966). The planning of Helsinki is
also discussed in *Suomen kaupunkilaitoksen
historia* (1981, 1983 and 1984), which is the basic
standard work on the history of physical development of Finnish towns. An extensive collection of
old plans can be found in *Helsingfors stadsplanehistoriska atlas* (1969), a very useful publication.
Mention should also be made of Sundman (1982),
which shows the extent of the built area at
different dates, namely in 1700, 1800, 1850, 1900,
1940, 1960 and 1980. Sundman (1991) provides a
wide-ranging survey of the Finnish town planning
with many references to Helsinki, but with the
main focus on the twentieth century.
2. *Helsingfors stadsplanehistoriska atlas*, No. 71.
3. *Ibidem*, No. 3; cf. also Eimer (1961), pp. 272 f
et passim.
4. Reproduced in Åström (1957a).
5. *Helsingfors stadsplanehistoriska atlas*, No. 72.
The plan was drawn by Anders Kocke. The

accompanying report is published in Åström (1957*b*), pp. 343 ff.

6. *Helsingfors stadsplanehistoriska atlas*, No. 73.

7. *Ibidem*, No. 74; the ratified version is reproduced as No. 77.

8. Ehrenström had already proposed this when he submitted his report on the building committee's plan.

9. Although they were still speaking of 'the town' and 'the suburb', there was already an indication in the 1817 plan of the division into five districts, each with its own square, which for a long time was to represent the administrative divisions in the town: Kronohagen with Elisabetsskvären, Gloet with Senatstorget, Gardesstaden with Kaserntorget, Kampen with Sandvikstorget and Rödbergen with the triangular Trekantens skvär. Not until 1875 did a further district, namely Eira, began to be considered. Skatudden, with its more modest buildings, was referred to for a long time simply as 'the eastern district' and was not counted as a district proper.

10. Engel also worked as a planner; among other things he made a new plan for Åbo after the fire of 1827.

11. Cf. Åström (1957*b*), pp. 58 ff *et passim*, and *idem* (1979).

12. Quoted from Josephson (1918), p. 260.

13. Cf. *Helsingfors stadsplanehistoriska atlas*, Nos. 100–104.

14. Cf. Sundman (1982), p. 33.

15. Cf. *Helsingfors stadsplanehistoriska atlas*, Nos. 90, 92, 93, 110, 111, 113, 120, 121, 128, 140, 151, 158, 174 and 190.

16. *Ibidem*, No. 143. See also Åström (1957*b*), pp. 129 ff. A revised version was ratified in 1887 (*Helsingfors stadsplanehistoriska atlas*, No. 156).

17. *Helsingfors stadsplanehistoriska atlas*, Nos. 200 and 201 and Sundman (1991), pp. 73 f. In this connection it should be mentioned that the architect Gustaf Strengell published *Staden som konstverk* (1922), which sums up the current urban design debate and advocates an artistic town planning with a classical signature.

18. Åström (1957*b*), pp. 220 ff, and *idem* (1979), pp. 63 ff.

19. *Helsingfors stadsplanehistoriska atlas*, No. 192; cf. also No. 193 and Sundman (1991), pp. 71 ff.

20. *Helsingfors stadsplanehistoriska atlas*, No. 206 and Sundman (1991), pp. 74 ff.

21. Cf. *Helsingfors stadsplanehistoriska atlas*, No. 188.

22. Åström (1957*b*), p. 262.

23. Cf. *Helsingfors stadsplanehistoriska atlas*, Nos. 210 and 213.

24. *Ibidem*, No. 218 and Sundman (1991), pp. 76 ff.

25. *Helsingfors stadsplanehistoriska atlas*, No. 222; cf. No. 219 and Sundman (1991), pp. 78 f.

6

ATHENS

Athens[1] became a capital city in the modern sense of the term relatively late. Following its struggle for freedom in the 1820s Greece was declared a sovereign state in the Second London Protocol issued by the Great Powers in 1830. In 1832 the crown was offered to Prince Otto of Bavaria, at that date still a minor. In 1833, following discussions during which other towns were also considered, it was decided that Athens should be the capital city of the new kingdom. No other solution would really have been possible, since the Europeans who had backed Greece during its wars had always regarded Athens as the cradle of European civilization, and their feelings had to be respected.

At the time Athens was a fairly insignificant place. Its population, which at the beginning of the nineteenth century was about 9,000–10,000, may have fallen to as little as 4,000 during the struggles of the 1820s. Much of the built area was destroyed, and only about 100 houses are said to have been habitable. The ancient ruins had been damaged in the frequent wars over the centuries; many had been incorporated into other structures during the Turkish period or were completely covered by later buildings. Towards the end of the war of liberation the Acropolis had even served as a fortress, which had naturally hastened its decline. Thus it was a town illustrious in name but hardly in fact, which was now to become the centre of a modern Greek state. A radical programme of clearance and expansion was therefore needed.

The task of drawing up a master plan for the new Athens was entrusted to two architects, Gustav Eduard Schaubert and Stamatios Kleanthes, the former from Silesia and the latter from Thessaly.[2] Both were pupils of Schinkel, and during the second half of the 1820s they had both pursued successful studies at the Berliner Bauakademie. They had both been employed for a short time as state architects in Greece before they undertook to make a detailed survey of Athens and its classical remains in 1831–32, together with a small group of archeologists (figure 6.1). The two architects probably began to prepare a master plan for the new town at this stage. They received the official commission from the provisional government to produce such a plan – apparently following a proposition by Kleanthes[3] – in May 1832.

There were evidently no directives, apart from a wish that the plan should 'reflect the ancient fame and glory of the town and be worthy of the century in which we now live.'[4] In a memorandum attached to their plan the architects explain: '. . . we did not know whether we were to envisage Athens as a future capital city or simply as a provincial town, nor – whichever it was to be – did we know the extent of the resources which the government would make available for the building of the new city.' However, they had assumed that the town was to be the capital, 'in view of the general opinion in Greece and the universal expectations of the Hellenes.'[5] At the beginning of the following year, 1833, the two

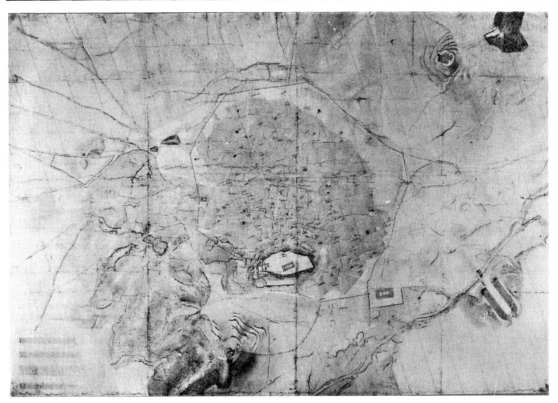

Figure 6.1 *Map of Athens made in 1831 and 1832 by the architects Schaubert and Kleanthes.*
[Photo provided by A. Papageorgiou-Venetas, Athens]

architects submitted a first version of their proposal. A revised version of the plan was ratified in July the same year, with some reservations and alterations, and at the same time the formal decision that Athens should be the capital was approved.[6] During the autumn of 1833, the plan was ratified a second time after some revisions.[7] The approved originals seem to have disappeared, but the architects' proposals are known from several other versions, which despite some deviations reproduce basically the same plan.[8]

In classical times the centre of Athens lay to the north of the Acropolis, an area which was now largely covered by buildings from the Middle Ages and later and divided by narrow irregular streets. In 1778 a city wall had been constructed, and at the beginning of the nineteenth century the built area was bounded by the Acropolis on the northern and eastern sides. The fundamental question which Schaubert and Kleanthes had to address was whether to regulate and extend the existing street and block structure, or whether to build a new urban core – and if so where. One possibility had been to build the town on low ground south of the Acropolis, where the level character of the terrain would have been immediately favourable and no hills would have hampered future expansion. Another possibility had been to build the town on the Acropolis itself and on the hills to the southwest of it. As we shall see, this solution had its advocates.

The architects decided, however, to build the new town on the north side of the Acropolis but outside the central parts of the ancient urban area, which was to be left free as an archeological zone. A decisive factor in this choice of site was certainly a desire to link the new town topographically with the ancient city. The argument in favour of retaining an archeological zone is one of the main items in the memorandum accompanying the plan: 'If the present situation in Greece [is unable to accommodate the immediate excavation of the area], then future generations will certainly reproach us for our lack of foresight in not allowing for this at some time in the future.' And should the archeological finds prove less abundant than expected, the memorandum continues in typical nineteenth-century spirit, then such ancient glories as the Monument of Lysicrates, the Tower of the Winds and the Gymnasium of Hadrian would at least be freed from 'the proximity of wretched sheds and modern houses . . . whose presence only serves to cloud and disturb the impact on the spectator.'[9] The area was then to be planted and developed as a kind of archeological park.

The point of departure for the new plan (figure 6.2) was the Acropolis – symbol of the leading role with which history had endowed the city of Athens in Greece. In counterpoint to this the royal palace was to be located to the north of the Acropolis hill, linked to it by a series of squares and a broad tree-planted road; the Propylaea and the Cave of Pan would then provide focal points for this street, which would lead from the centre of the new town and up to the entrance to the Acropolis through the ancient city. In this way the palace and the Acropolis, the two dominating features of the town, were linked in an axial system. This main axis was to be flanked by parallel streets, which, according to the architects' memorandum, would have as their focal points 'the Tower of the Winds and the centre of the Acropolis hill, above whose pinnacles the ruins of the Parthenon could be glimpsed on the one

hand, the ruins of the Gymnasium of the Ptolemeys and the ancient and illustrious "crown" of the Areopagus hill on the other.'[10]

It was intended that on each side of this central axis the town should be laid out in two essentially symmetrical parts. Each half of the town had its own broad main street, which radiated out from the square in front of the palace and continued to its own star-shaped open place. Here, too, the highways beyond should end. The two star-shaped places were then linked by a narrower street, which passed the edge of the archeological zone and formed the base of an equilateral triangle of streets.[11] Between the archeological zone and the new urban blocks the street network was to be redeveloped, but in such a way as to allow some of the old buildings to be preserved. The solutions varied somewhat in the different versions of the plan. As a result of the introduction of these diagonal streets – the future Stadiou and Pireos – the city as envisaged here seems to open itself to the ancient town and at the same time to embrace it.

The blocks in the central part were oriented in relation to the central axis, and those in the flanking areas in relation to the diagonal streets. Two diagonally located squares with public buildings provided the transition between the two block orientations, which meant that it was largely possible to avoid the blocks narrowing down to a point. A tree-lined street, 38 metres broad and called the 'Boulevard', linked these two squares, continuing as the major peripheral communication link round the palace area and describing a large roughly square configuration. In most versions of the plan there was a further square on the future Pireos, south-west of the square mentioned above. Furthermore, a park was suggested north of the palace as well as a large number of public buildings, although these were not located so as to provide focal points along the streets. The idea was obviously not to divert attention from the palace and the classical monuments, although these last, as

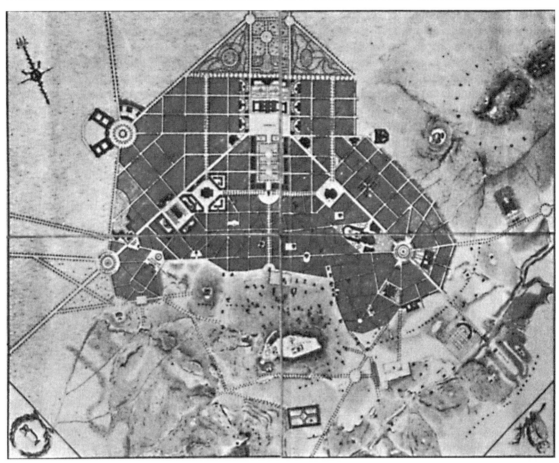

Figure 6.2 *Athens. Proposal by the architects Schaubert and Kleanthes for the regularization and extension of the new town. [Reproduction of the lithograph made in Athens and Munich]*

Kühn has accurately claimed, 'were not demoted to the status of a showcase . . . At an appropriate distance they remain encompassed in their own sphere' (cf. figure 6.5).[12] Buildings associated with commercial operations such as customs and post, as well as courts, were to be located along Pireos or in the two squares in this street; cultural institutions such as the university and the library would be on Stadiou, while government, parliament and the central administrative authorities such as the various ministries, were to be located in the neighbourhood of the palace. Theatres, the

stock exchange, the casino and the bazaar were to be in the large square on the street leading from the palace to the Acropolis.[13] Dwelling-houses should be low, intended for about ten people, and surrounded by gardens.[14]

Schaubert and Kleanthes's project appears to be well conceived, satisfying both aesthetic and functional requirements and leaving open the possibility of further expansion.[15] It also seems to be well-adapted to the topographical conditions. It is reminiscent of palace towns such as Karlsruhe and, in particular, Versailles.[16] Thus the main streets running diagonally from the open space in front of the palace have their counterparts in Versailles,[17] and so does the location of the palace in relation to the town and the park. But the topographical conditions have certainly played just as large a part here as any desire to follow the French example. In some respects the Athens project also recalls the plan that Rovira i Trias was to make for Barcelona a few decades later (see pp. 132 f). In both cases it is a question of aesthetically designed extensions more or less in the shape of new towns.

The enlargement of Athens was one of the most widely noted and comprehensive planning enterprises in Europe during the first half of the nineteenth century. It may seem surprising that the project was entrusted to two relatively untried architects, and that they succeeded in carrying it out so successfully even though they lacked experience of urban planning. Building on an idea touched upon by Russak,[18] Kühn suggests that they did not resolve the problem entirely alone, but had help behind the scenes. She believes that their teacher, Schinkel, whose interest in Athens was manifest in the remarkable palace project for the Acropolis, for instance,[19] may have put the finishing touches to their plan and introduced some significant improvements. However, there is no definite support for this hypothesis.[20].

As we have seen, Schaubert and Kleanthes's plan was ratified in 1833, and in April 1834 King Otto laid the foundation stone of the palace at the site suggested in their project. However, problems arose soon after the plan was decided upon. The land within the area of the plan had been purchased by speculators when the previous Turkish owners had moved out, and a violent rise in values made it difficult to lay down streets and squares.[21] The political and social situation was also turbulent, with a German king and a largely German group of administrators on the one hand, and on the other a rapidly growing Greek population. There was little of the stability and clear leadership which had been the prerequisite for

the successful refoundation of Helsinki in the decades immediately before.

In the summer of 1834 the architect Leo von Klenze was in Athens, sent by Otto's father Louis I of Bavaria as a diplomatic envoy, and also to supervise planning issues and organize the protection of the classical monuments.[22] Almost any architect who is given the chance to have a say in revising a major prestigious project, will take it. Klenze was no exception. In a comment on the approved plan, obviously written much later after his return to Munich, he developed an approach to urban building which deviates significantly from the principles current at the time. 'It seems,' he writes, 'that modern city-builders try to achieve the kind of regular structures and variously complicated geometrical figures that provide so much pleasure to the eye, without recognizing that this effect cannot be perceived on the ground, once the city is built.' The rest of his comment, including ideas that almost seem to foreshadow the Sitte school, is worth quoting *in extenso*:

If we consider the ordering of the streets, the squares and the buildings in Pompeii and even the few fragments remaining on the Capitol of the plan of Rome, the ancient capital of the world, then we must admit that the old cities, even when like Pompeii they lay on a plain or like Rome on slightly hilly ground, deviate greatly from the straight regularity of our so-called beautiful urban structures such as Turin, Nancy, St Petersburg, Mannheim, Karlsruhe etc.

But, to a fresh eye receptive to picturesque (*malerisch*) charm, what do these towns have to offer with their monotonously fatiguing effects, their straight phalanxes of dreary grey façades, their insignificant *points de vue*, their grandiloquent architectural set-pieces, when set against the rich painterly grouping of ancient buildings, without any geometrical rules but arranged – even jumbled – together alongside and above one another.

According to these observations on the particularities of the area, which were a given factor in the rebuilding of Athens, and given my own ideas about architectural beauty, it would have been my most sincere wish to designate for the building of the new city the heights on the western and southern side of the Acropolis, and the open area lying higher and open to the winds from the sea, stretching from the Mouseion to Kalirrhoe, and from there to Lykabettos.

Unfortunately, though, I was no longer free to choose!

The authors of the approved plan for the new Athens reveal – I admit it – a taste diametrically opposed to my own regarding the beauty of urban structures, when they use only part of the high area at the foot of the Lykabettos, and consign the new town to the very lowest and flattest area by the former Acharnaian gate, the outer Kerameikos and towards the Dipylon gate. Almost without any consideration for the nature of the terrain with its heights and depths, indeed often directly contrary to it, long and excessively broad roads with great squares and buildings have been planned, all of which seem to have no connection with the needs of the new city.

Klenze's conclusion is that 'the conception of the plan according to the historical and poetic idea, should be considered suitable for the earlier and the present historical development of the venerable town of Athens.'[23]

How, then, was this romantic programme applied in practice? Implementation of Schaubert and Kleanthes's plan had already started. Klenze's wish to locate the new town on the western and southern sides of the Acropolis, where it would lie higher and 'open to the winds from the sea, stretching from the Mouseion to Kalirrhoe, and from there to Lykabettos', was not realistic. Instead he had to be satisfied, as he put it, with 'improving the geometrical inadequacies of the plan with . . . painterly ideas.'[24] One of the most important alterations in the project submitted by Klenze (figure 6.3) was that the palace was moved to the southern end of the western diagonal street, close to the Theseion. Among other

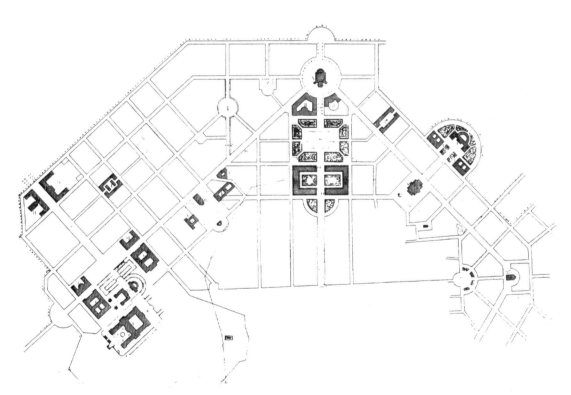

Figure 6.3 *Athens. Leo von Klenze's alternative project for the new town. [From Biris (1966)]*

things this would give a better view of the ancient monuments. The site suggested by Schaubert and Kleanthes was, in Klenze's view, unsuitable on topographical grounds, nor would it have allowed for the outlook envisaged. The rectangular square to which Pireos and Stadiou should lead, was replaced by a round one in which a church was to provide a focal point; the urban blocks were oriented in relation to the diagonal streets, which meant that even fewer of them narrowed down to a point. The central area was given a different design compared to the previous proposal, and most of the old buildings were preserved. Nor did the Stadiou have the straight extension envisaged by Schaubert and Kleanthes. On the contrary, in an intentional reaction against the earlier suggestion, the prospect was actually cut off, in that the street runs diagonally into a semi-circular place where yet another church was to be located.[25] Klenze wanted to reduce the width of the streets, and he also recommended buildings in several storeys and arranged more compactly than Schaubert and Kleanthes had envisaged. Schaubert and Kleanthes's plan had obviously aroused considerable opposition, and the high level of development may perhaps have provided a way of making the new plan more attractive to the owners of the land. Altogether this and other changes involved a radical transformation of the main principles of the approved proposal.

By September 1834 Klenze's plan had already been approved.[26] But conditions in Athens seem to have been pretty chaotic, and it is hard to get any clear idea of how the rebuilding was organized, which makes it difficult to assess the real importance of Klenze's plan. Perhaps it lay above all in the fact that the developers were no longer bound by Schaubert and Kleanthes's project.

It makes an interesting study to compare the two projects with the structure that was actually realized.[27] The triangle of streets, which was a fundamental element in Schaubert and

Kleanthes's project and which was also adopted by Klenze, was built largely according to the two architects' intentions in the shape of the present-day Stadiou, Pireos and Ermou. The two diagonally located squares were also realized, albeit with certain modifications and in an arrangement that is not wholly symmetrical (Platia Eleftherias and Klafthmonos). The blocks were divided in a different, less regular way than Schaubert and Kleanthes had intended, but the reality is closer to their project than to Klenze's. The tree-planted four-sided street configuration around the centre in Schaubert and Kleanthes's proposal was not realized. A great part of the old city area was left as it was, in compliance with the Klenze plan. The archeological zone of Schaubert and Kleanthes's plan, which Klenze had reduced a little, remained at the project stage; not until the excavations in the Agora during the 1930s, 1940s and 1950s were some of these intentions realized. The squares on the central axis, which were included in both proposals, also remained on paper, except for the Platia Kotzia and the present-day Agora. Of the splendid axial construction towards the Propylaea only the present-day Athinas came into being. Of the two streets parallel with this one, which were an important element particularly in Klenze's project,[28] the present-day Eolou was built to the east. Its northern section commands a magnificent view towards the Erechtheion and the Parthenon, just as the architects had intended. The western parallel street was never built out to its full extent, possibly because it would not have offered a corresponding vista. Thus Athinas, Eolou and Ermou exemplify the kind of streets that cut through whole areas with the precision of arrows and which were later to appear in many of the capital cities of Europe, although the buildings along these streets in Athens were simpler and the streets themselves narrower.[29]

The palace, when it was finally built, was located at the southern end of the Stadiou. In other words none of the projects were fulfilled here, although Klenzes's suggestion has presumably affected the choice of the ultimate site. His round open space to the north was long included in the plans for the town,[30] but when the Omonia square was finally constructed during the 1860s, it was given a rectangular, almost square shape. Whether or not this can be interpreted as a return to Schaubert and Kleanthes's plan remains an open question; but the present-day Omonia certainly has little in common with the palace square as originally proposed, and in the absence of any major monumental building it cannot function in the urban scene in the way the architects intended. The streets do not run into the square as had been envisaged, nor is there any central point from which the ensemble can be comprehended. Moreover, more streets run into the square than its size and form can really support. This unsatisfactory balance is further aggravated by the fact that Athinas does not lead into the centre of the square. Nor is the connection with Panepistimiou very successful. At the present time Omonia leaves a confused impression, further reinforced by the architecture which is very mixed in both scale and style.

Before we leave the question of the two plans approved during the 1830s and their impact on subsequent developments, something should also be said about the width of the streets. One of Klenze's main ideas was to make the streets narrower, and thus more picturesque; moreover they would not occupy so much expensive ground. In so far as these intentions were in fact realized, they did the town a real disservice, as we see things today. 'In the years to come this attenuation of the streets and the reduction in the size of the squares proved to have a distinctly inhibiting effect on subsequent urban development in Athens,' Kühn claims.[31]

However, according to the available material, Klenze's proposal apparently referred mainly to the secondary streets, which were to be reduced from 12.5 to 10 metres,

thus cutting the expropriation costs by one-fifth.[32] The width of the main axes was only slightly constricted.[33] Furthermore, the width of some streets had been reduced as far back as the autumn of 1833, at the time of the second approval of Schaubert and Kleanthes's project. On the other hand, Klenze's intervention did presumably affect the decision not to implement the proposed improvement of the street network in the old urban core.

By the late 1830s urban development in Athens was already deviating in crucial ways from both the approved master plans.[34] A major reason for this was the building of the palace, which began in 1836 according to Friedrich von Gärtner's plans on a site not previously included in any plan. In front of the palace, and oriented in relation to it, was a large open place, the present Syntagma, which meant that the Stadiou and the Panepistimiou had to bend in a rather unsatisfactory way in order to approach the square at a right angle. The inclusion of this previously unplanned square involved a shift in the centre of gravity in the urban structure: the centre of the town was to be here rather than, as had been envisaged, at Omonia square. Moreover Panepistimiou, the street running parallel to Stadiou, acquired greater dignity than had previously been intended, since a series of classically inspired buildings for various cultural institutions – the University, the Academy and the National Library – were located along its length.[35] The first to be built was H.C. Hansen's university building in 1837. And the street was constructed during the second half of the 1830s on broader lines than had been laid down in the approved plans; on a map dated 1837 it is called the 'Boulevard'.[36]

During the 1840s, according to Michael, a great many alterations and enlargements were made in the current town plan, mainly in the shape of 'planning provisions', that is to say 'street plans for small sections, which the engineers at the Office of Public Works were generally compelled to employ in order to handle and legalize various drawbacks and defects that had appeared.' 'These announcements thus complemented Klenze's plan, and together formed the basis of Athens' present central area.'[37]

A first attempt to produce a new overall plan was made in 1843, but it does not seem to have had much impact.[38] In 1846 a commission was appointed on the initiative of the government to devise a new plan. When the constitution had been revised in 1843, all foreigners in the Greek public service had been dismissed, and there was a shortage of Greeks with the appropriate education to fill the public posts. This meant that many such posts in the administration were filled by officers from the armed forces. The chairman of the 1846 commission was Colonel L. Smolenski; the other members were two more officers and two architects, Lysandros Kaftanzoglou[39] and

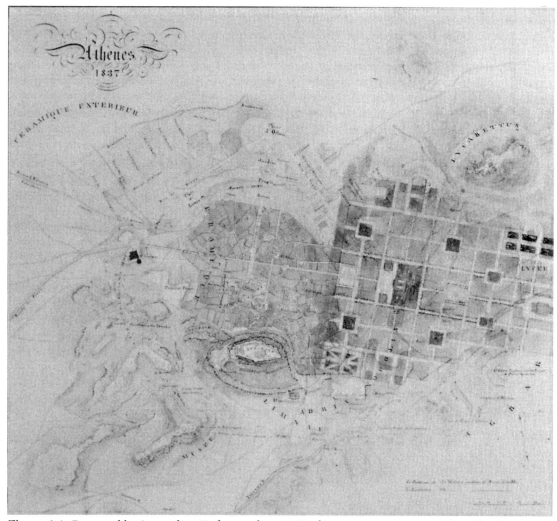

Figure 6.4 *Proposal by Lysandros Kaftanzoglou, 1839, for an extension east of the old urban area in the form of a uniform grid plan. [Photo provided by A. Papageorgiou-Venetas, Athens]*

Theophil von Hansen, who had remained in Athens as a private architect. The commission's recommendation, which was ready in 1847, involved no structural changes but various adjustments to details and some supplementary suggestions. On the east side of the city the street Akadimias was indicated, and the royal park south of the palace. On the western side, where Klenze's palace project had been abandoned, the plan was revised accordingly and more adequate allowance was made for the topography. Blocks were also laid out in the Kerameikos area. In the centre Klenze's project was simplified: a new open place flanked by two U-shaped bazaar buildings was envisaged between the future Euripidou and Sophocleous and, to the north of this complex but without any architectural relationship with it, there was to be a park. The future Omonia can still be seen, in the form planned by Klenze. Leoforos Amalias started from Syntagma as part of a tree-planted ring boulevard around the Acropolis. The 1847 plan was never officially adopted, but did nonetheless exert some influence on subsequent developments.[40]

As in the preceding decade some details in the plan were altered during the 1850s, often with the support of Queen Amalia (1836–62) who was interested in urban planning issues and who acted as regent for several long periods. Between 1856 and 1858 about thirty such alterations were made, for example minor changes to widen some streets, or the slight enlargement of some church squares in the old city area. One decision in particular should be mentioned, namely to widen the western sections of Ermou from 10 to 15 metres, to provide a better link between the town centre and the terminus of the Piraeus railway station. Implementation was difficult, however, as the idea was violently opposed by the landowners.

As the 1847 plan failed to achieve the effects intended, it was obvious that a new overall plan was required. In 1858 the municipality of Athens called for a new plan to be made. In 1860 a commission was appointed under one Colonel D. Stavridis. The members consisted of one more military officer, the mayor of the city, the head of the health department in the Ministry of the Interior, a bridge-construction engineer and a few architects; they were later joined by an archeologist. The commission submitted its report at the end of 1860. The area of the plan had been divided into four sections by the two streets, Ermou and Eolou. The plan recommended some improvements in the street network, affecting the Mitropoleos among others, and several new squares: the future Kolonaki, Kanigos, Monastiraki and others. Omonia was given a new shape, very close to the final solution. Locations for markets, schools and various public buildings were suggested in all districts. The Greek Agora and its Roman follower were to form a coherent archeological zone together. Some enlargement of the built-up area was also included.

The 1860 plan met with harsh criticism, mainly because insufficient consideration had been paid to questions of compensation. The plan was rejected as impracticable, as it would have involved the municipality in far too much expense. However, the municipal administration did approve the recommendation regarding the archeological zone, but the ministry turned it down on the grounds that it was as unrealistic as the rest of the recommendations. The plan was thus not ratified. Instead it was handed over to the Military Urban Planning Office for revision.[42]

In 1862 Otto I abdicated after a period of political unrest and the 'interregnum' before George I assumed the crown the following year was marked by instability. During this period a number of decisions were rushed through, favouring the interests of the landowners; among other things the width of some streets was reduced. Omonia, too, was diminished in order to increase the building area available on the neighbouring plots.[43] By 1864 the revised

Figure 6.5 *Prospect from Eolou towards the Erechtheion. Old photograph showing the townscape which emerged from Schaubert and Kleanthes's and Klenze's plans. [Photo provided by the Swedish Institute, Athens]*

plan drawn up by the military administration was finished, apparently involving fairly insignificant changes to the 1860 proposals. The plan was ratified in 1864–65, except for its south-western section which was postponed in view of problems connected with expropriations in the archeological area. The three approved sections remained valid for more than seventy years in the areas concerned, i.e. largely the central part of the town.[44]

The last decades of the nineteenth century saw a comparatively rapid increase in the population: the number of inhabitants rose from 44,500 in 1870 to 123,000 in 1896.[45] During the same period some industrialization also began. Better water supplies, street lighting, horse-drawn trams etc. were introduced.[46]

The railway line to Piraeus was opened in 1869 and to Laurion in 1885. On the political stage, the period was one of far-reaching parliamentarianism and liberal beliefs.

As a result of the expansion to the north of the city from the 1860s onwards, the road starting as Eolou and continuing as Patission acquired crucial importance as a communicating link between the old town, the new town which emerged around the middle of the century, and the suburban area which was developing to the north of it. The importance of Patission was increased by the establishment there of the Technical University and the National Archeological Museum, both of which were begun during the 1860s. In 1869 the planned area was extended northwards along

Patission as far as Pipinou, and beyond this line two suburbs were planned in 1871 and 1879, with largely rectilinear street networks. These were Ano and Kato Patisia.[47] As a consequence of this development Omonia became even more important as a traffic junction, and began to take on something of the 'centre' character that Schaubert and Kleanthes had intended, although it was mainly commercial operations which established themselves in the area rather than the public authorities which the architects had envisaged.

Apart from the planning measures discussed above, no serious attempts were made to control developments.[48] The built area spread in all directions, sometimes in accordance with the plans of private developers ratified by the authorities without any overall consideration of the need for public facilities or communications, and sometimes without any approved plan or building permission but simply with a view to satisfying the interests of the landowners themselves.[49]

In 1878 planning issues were transferred to the civilian arena, and a new state administrative authority for public works was established. This meant a further restriction on the opportunities for controlling developments in the service of the public good. Unlike the military, it was easy to dismiss the civilian officials; thus it was more difficult for them to withstand pressure from politicians and various other interested parties, particularly as it was regarded as the natural thing to satisfy the wishes of the landowners. Nor did the politicians assume responsibility for the physical development of the town. There was thus considerable scope for narrow short-sighted landowner interests to have free play. During the 22 years between 1878 and 1900, 173 amplifications and alterations were made in the 1864 plan, without being subjected to any overall view. Together, but uncoordinatedly, these registered rather than controlled developments during this period.[50]

The influence of one man, G. Genisarlis, city engineer and professor at the Technical University, was to prove of particular importance to the future of the city. He recognized a serious weakness in the earlier plans, i.e. that the street network was not adequately linked to the surrounding highway system, and he argued that the town would be suffocated by its lack of traffic arteries.[51] In 1876–78 Genisarlis succeeded in having two broad boulevards built, Leoforos Alexandras and Syngrou. The first provided communications between the north-eastern and north-western areas, between the Kifissos and Illissos basins, while the other provided an exit road of considerable capacity towards the south, towards Phaleron and Piraeus. Genisarlis also seems to have been the prime mover when it came to extending Leoforos Vasilissis Sophias to Leoforos Alexandras, to create a suitable traffic route for the built area around Lykabettos. These street projects were largely outside the planned area, and were implemented not by the municipality but by the military Engineering Office of Public Works. The boulevards had considerable influence on subsequent developments, since the detailed plans were adapted to them.[52]

During the first decades of the twentieth century several ambitious plans were published. Two international authorities were approached, first Ludwig Hoffmann, municipal building director (*Stadtbaurat*) in Berlin, and later the English urban planner Thomas Mawson, both of whom presented comprehensive projects.[53] But no overall plan was ever approved, and developments continued essentially along the same lines as during the late nineteenth century.[54] And we may well ask ourselves whether things are any different today. If we disregard those parts of Greater Athens where topographical or archeological factors have made building impossible, the town seems to stretch for miles and miles in a monotonous street network and with very little in the way of former villages or modern planned suburbs and green areas to relieve the dull impression.

Developments in Athens during the twentieth century seem to be characterized, perhaps more than in any of the other examples discussed in the present book, by a persisting libertarian attitude left over from the previous century; apart from a rectilinear street network, there seems to have been hardly any systematic control at all. The extraordinary view from the crest of the Philopappos Hill gives some idea of the vastness of this sea of houses stretching away in all directions; towards Piraeus in particular the streets look like a series of endless straight ditches cutting between the solid mass of the buildings.

EXCURSUS: ON SCHINKEL'S POSSIBLE CONTRIBUTION TO URBAN PLANNING IN ATHENS

Margarete Kühn claims with some force that Schaubert and Kleanthes's plan was revised by Schinkel. This thesis triggers a number of questions. First we can look briefly at Kühn's own argument, which starts from the fact that in the former royal collection in Berlin there is a variant of Schaubert and Kleanthes's project for Athens (reproduced in Kühn (1979), p. 510). According to Kühn this represents a preliminary stage, not the final plan, since 'in its urbanistic and architectural form it has to yield to the second version in several essential ways' (p. 511). Among other things the central axis between the Acropolis and the palace is more strongly articulated, and the transition to the diagonally arranged blocks in the flanking areas has been improved in the second version by the addition of the two symmetrically placed squares. Furthermore, in several important respects the Berlin variant agrees better than the alleged later version with the architects' description. As early as January 1832 Schaubert had mentioned in a letter to a colleague in Berlin that he would like to have Schinkel's opinion on a plan for the new Athens. In July the following year Schaubert was in Berlin, and according to Kühn the main purpose of this trip was to consult Schinkel. In this case Schaubert would have brought the variant of the plan preserved in Berlin. However, it cannot be proved that a meeting did in fact take place between Schaubert and Schinkel; by 4th July at the latest Schinkel had left Berlin on a fairly lengthy trip connected with his work. But

Kühn posits that some form of contact occurred, perhaps just a discussion, during which Schinkel could have recommended certain improvements. 'That the architects themselves would have evolved such a differentiated and articulated reformulation, more of an organism, thus eliciting a resonant urbanistic and architectural character from the possibilities available in their own earlier plan, seems to us unlikely' she writes (p. 516). She also claims to recognize signs of Schinkel's 'handwriting' in some parts in the final variant, particularly in the structures north of the palace and in the design of some of the squares (p. 516).

Thus far Kühn's argument. It certainly seems clear that the plan in Berlin represents an early stage in the planning of Athens, and it is very probable that the architects' memorandum belongs to this variant. It seems most unlikely, on the other hand, that it would have been this variant that was submitted to the government in 1833 for ratification. The plan appears too makeshift for the architects to have intended it as their final version. It is also significant that for this version they used not their own survey but a printed map. They would not presumably have adopted such a procedure for a version to be submitted to the government for final evaluation. Fountoulaki (1979) suggests a solution to this problem. Apparently quite independently of Kühn, Fountoulaki discovered that the memorandum belongs to the Berlin variant of the plan. But while Kühn appears to regard the Berlin plan as the variant approved in the summer of 1833, Fountoulaki sees it as a preliminary version which was submitted for comment at the beginning of the same year – a hypothesis which seems plausible.

It is more difficult to say anything definite about Schinkel's possible contribution. We do know that the architects considered consulting their teacher, as was natural in view of the importance of their task. It also seems probable that Schaubert brought the variant preserved in Berlin with him on his visit in 1833, and that he did so primarily in order to seek Schinkel's opinion. What raises doubt is above all the chronology of these events. According to Kühn, Schaubert arrived in Berlin in July 1833 – the journal *Museum* is quoted as the source of this – while Schinkel left Berlin at the beginning of the month. The briefness of the time available is alone enough to cause doubt. But the main objection is that if it was the revised version which was ratified in Athens in the summer of the same year – and everything suggests that it was – then this excludes the possibility of Schinkel's collaboration if we accept Kühn's dates; the plan was approved at the very time when Schaubert was arriving in Berlin allegedly to ask his teacher's advice. According to Fountoulaki's 'timetable', on the other hand, Schaubert came to Berlin 'at the beginning of 1833' and 'was there for six months' (Fountoulaki (1979), p. 38). However, this information does not entirely agree with note 172 in the same book, referring to a letter according to which Schaubert was 'on leave in Germany' from 29th March/11th April 1833 until September the same year. If the second dating is correct, then Schaubert could have managed within a three-month period to travel to Berlin, to consult Schinkel and to pass on his suggestions and corrections to Greece sufficiently quickly for the revised plan to be ratified there on 29th June/11th July. This does not seem entirely impossible, although it would have been a close thing. However, it is beyond the scope of the present book to try to dispel the obscurities surrounding Schaubert's trip to Germany.

Kühn is undoubtedly right in that certain details in the revised plan bring Schinkel readily to mind. But Schinkel-inspired features are hardly definite proof of the older architect's direct participation; both the younger men had trained under him and were naturally influenced by his ideas on urban design. Nor does the fact that the final version of the plan was superior to the preliminary one provide any binding proof that Schinkel had contributed to it. For the time being the question must be left open: the idea of an intervention on Schinkel's part cannot be excluded, but there is no proof that the two architects were not exclusively responsible for the revised version. Papageorgiou-Venetas, who has recently addressed the question of Schinkel's collaboration (1994, pp. 36 ff), adopts a cautiously sceptical position. He also adds some new arguments against this possibility, in the first instance that Schaubert and Kleanthes would hardly have failed to refer to Schinkel when their project was being criticized, if this well-known architect had indeed been involved. He also points out the obvious discrepancy between the respect which Schaubert and Kleanthes's plan demonstrates for the classical remains on the one hand, and Schinkel's more or less contemporary project for the unrestricted transformation of the Acropolis. Moreover, Klenze would certainly have heard of any contribution on Schinkel's part, and there is nothing in his report to indicate that he had.

NOTES

1. In the first period of urban planning in modern Athens, German architects played an important role, and several German scholars have shown an interest in this era of the city's history. A seminal work is Russack (1942), which also reproduces the memorandum attached to Schaubert and Kleanthes's plan. Kühn (1979) is largely devoted to an attempt to show that the plan submitted by

Schaubert and Kleanthes had been revised by Schinkel (cf. Excursus, pp. 112 f). Klenze's contribution is discussed in the monograph on this architect – Hederer (1964). Naturally Greek writers have also taken up the relevant issues.

In German Sinos (1974) deals with the various discussions in the 1830s but adds little to Russack (1942), apart from mention of a previously neglected plan proposal (cf. note 26). Two dissertations submitted at German universities should also be mentioned here, namely Michael (1969) and Fountoulaki (1979). The first of these, however, does not treat the issue in depth, but addresses the nineteenth century as a whole. The second is a monograph on Kleanthes which provides a good survey of the architect's involvement in the planning of Athens together with Schaubert, relying to some extent on previously uninvestigated sources and on several points complementing earlier works. *Athen-München* (1980), a modest publication from the Bavarian National Museum, also deserves mention. It briefly summarizes Athens' urban development in a section written by Angeliki Kokkou.

There is also a good deal of literature in Greek, covering in particular developments since 1840, which are dealt with either summarily or not at all in the literature in German. Among Kostas Biris's many publications, special reference should be made of his great work published in 1966, which must be regarded as the seminal study of the physical development of Athens in modern times. Another scholar of central importance is Joannis Travlos, whose book published in 1960 explores the topographical development of Athens right up to the nineteenth and twentieth centuries. Bodil Nordström has given me valuable help in making translations from modern Greek.

More recently, a magnificent work on Athens by Alexander Papageorgiou-Venetas appeared, *Hauptstadt Athen, Ein Stadtgedanke des Klassizismus* (1994). This meticulous study provides a far more detailed and well-supported picture of the first planning phase in Athens than has hitherto been available, but it does not alter the main lines opened up by earlier research.

2. The section on Schaubert and Kleanthes is based mainly on Russack (1942) and Kühn (1979), and on the two architects' memorandum which Russack reproduces.

3. Biris (1966), pp. 22 f.

4. Quoted from *Athen-München*, p. 17.

5. Quoted from Russack (1942), p. 177. Starting from the idea that Athens was to be the capital city, the architects further assumed that they must scale their plan to a population of 'at least 35–40 thousand inhabitants' (*ibidem*, p. 178).

6. The decision was made on 29th June/11th July 1833. The first date refers to the Julian calendar. According to Biris (1966) the plan was submitted for ratification as early as the end of 1832 (p. 236). On the relation between the two versions of the plan, see Excursus, pp. 112 f.

7. Cf. note 21.

8. Several variants of the plan have been published, but often without any analysis or even a proper account of where the originals are to be found. Thus Russack (1942) reproduces three variants and Biris (1966) four. A tentative attempt to sort out this sometimes confusing material suggests that the plan in Berlin (published in Kühn (1979), p. 510), which deviates significantly from other plans, is obviously a preliminary version (the reasons for this conclusion are given in the Excursus, pp. 112 f). One of the plans published in Russack (1942, p. 29), might represent the next stage in the processing of the proposal. The crucial question then is, which of the other surviving plans comes closest to – or possibly constitutes – the plan approved on 29th June/11th July 1833. Biris claims that it is a plan in the Municipal Library in Athens; this map is large-scale (1:2,000) and is very carefully executed (reproduced in Biris (1966), p. 27). Fountoulaki, on the other hand, considers that the plan which most closely resembles the approved version is a drawing in Munich, made to be the model for the lithographs mentioned below. The German Archeological Institute in Athens owns a version which is very close to the plans just mentioned (reproduced in Russack (1942), p. 180, Biris (1966), p. 33, Kühn (1979), p. 511, and Fountoulaki (1979), p. 224). Fountoulaki regards this plan as the immediate predecessor of the plan approved in 1833, while Biris regards it as the version revised and approved in the autumn of the same year (cf. note 21). Minor deviations from these three closely related maps appear in the two almost identical plans reproduced in Russack (1942), p.

27 and Biris (1966), p. 28. A lithograph version was published in both Munich and Athens (reproduced here as figure 6.2). None of the surviving plans can be identified with certainty as the revised version approved in the autumn of 1833.

The planning material has been studied most recently by Papageorgiou-Venetas (1994). However, this author does not provide a systematic catalogue surveying all the surviving plan maps and providing a complete account of where they are published and discussed. In view of the design and ambitions of the book, such a survey should have been a natural ingredient.

9. Quoted from Russack (1942), pp. 178 f.

10. *Ibidem*, p. 181. The Gymnasium of the Ptolemeys was the name given to some ruins in the area where the Agora was later excavated. However, they are not in fact from that Ptolemey's time, but date from around 400 AD. The most striking element consisted of the four giants taken from Agrippa's Odeon (see *The Athenian Agora*, p. 33, plan, and pp. 110 ff and Travlos (1971), pp. 233 ff). Many of these monuments would have required extensive excavations if they were to be seen from a distance, and even so, in view of their modest size and the nature of the terrain, they could hardly have served as visual foci.

11. In an earlier version of the plan (cf. note 8 and Excursus, pp. 112 f), this street would have had the same width as the diagonal street; by making it narrower, the border with the historical core became less marked (cf. Kühn (1979), p. 515).

12. Kühn (1979), p. 519.

13. This presentation is based on the architects' memorandum. However, this does not agree – particularly as regards the central axis – with the version reproduced here; it refers instead to the first suggestion (cf. note 8 and Excursus, pp. 112 f).

14. Both Russack and Sinos obviously want to interpret Schaubert and Kleanthes's proposal as the first garden city project in the late nineteenth century sense. Sinos writes: '. . . in the development of the garden cities in Europe this should have its deserved place' (Sinos (1974), p. 47; cf. Russack (1942), p. 28). This is surely to go one step too far. Free-standing houses with gardens

are by no means unusual in pre-industrial towns. In Athens, as both authors do point out, this was presumably the natural solution in view of the local building tradition.

15. The importance of opportunities for expansion was emphasized by the two architects themselves in their memorandum (cf. Russack (1942), p. 178).

16. Great importance was assigned in the proposal to the incorporation of the palace in a system of sight-lines, and in the memorandum it is pointed out that 'the balcony of the royal palace looks at the same time out over the beautiful shape of Lykabettos, the Panathenian Stadion of Herodes Atticus, the Acropolis with its abundance of proud memories, the warships and merchant vessels at Piraeus and the Eleusinian road' (Russack (1942), pp. 179 f). But this description was unrealistic; the absence of sight-lines was to be one of the main points in Klenze's criticism of the location of the palace.

17. Kühn's comparison with the roundabout at Hallesches Tor in Berlin seems less pertinent (1979, p. 513).

18. Russack (1942). p. 26.

19. See Forssman (1981), pp. 216 ff.

20. Cf. Excursus, pp. 112 f.

21. As a result of the opposition to the plan the building area was increased by reducing the size of some of the streets and squares, after which the plan was approved again in October 1833 (Biris (1966), p. 32; Fountoulaki (1979), p. 40). Biris's description of the changes seems to be based not on documents but on the map, which is in the German Archeological Institute, and which in his opinion reproduces the plan approved in October. On this assumption he claims that, among other things, Stadiou and Pireos were reduced from 22 to 20 metres, other streets from 15 to 12 and the northern stretch of Athinas from 40 to 20, while the southern part was broadened so that the street was 20 metres wide for its full length. He also says that a market square was abandoned in the Psyrris area, and that the southern limit for building was moved at the future Klafthmonos and Eleftherias squares, at Platia Klafthmonos by 20 metres.

22. On Klenze's Greek journey and his contribution to Athens' planning history, see Hederer (1964), pp. 53 ff and 140 ff.

23. Quoted from Hederer (1964), pp. 142 ff.
24. Quoted from Kühn (1979), p. 520. In 1833 the architect Ferdinand von Quast developed an argument in the German journal *Museum, Blätter für bildende Kunst* which is related to Klenze's ideas. Among other things he points out that the plain to the north of the Acropolis would be suitable for a new town, but adds the following question: 'Would such a town, however, be justified in bearing the name of Athens? This name is irrevocably linked with the Acropolis. Only at Acropolis does the name of Athens have the resonance we all desire.' He then argues that the town should be located in the hilly area around the Acropolis: 'How beautifully the districts are grouped on the different hills, how all life is concentrated to the valleys! The king could return to the old citadel of Kekrops and build his house close to that of Erechtheus . . . The houses then climb the hillside in painterly groups, merging with the greenery, in terraces up and over the hills, with long rows of villas, painterly situated in gardens, continuing as far as the neighbouring port.' (Quoted from Russack (1942), pp. 21 ff.) The text was published a second time together with Schinkel's proposal for a royal palace on the Acropolis in a brochure called *Mittheilungen über Alt und Neu Athen* (Notes on Ancient and New Athens). Perhaps Papageorgiou-Venetas takes von Quast's vision – which never assumed concrete form in a drawing – too seriously; it appears to consist of rather vague reflections (1994, pp. 103 ff). A more interesting question, addressed in the same chapter, is whether Schinkel regarded his palace proposal as an isolated project or whether it was part of an urbanistic concept and, if so, what shape such a concept assumed. It seems that this will have to remain an open question, due to the absence of information on the subject in the surviving documentary evidence.
25. Sinos points out pertinently that Klenze's plan 'is designed more as an urban expansion and less as a new foundation.' It is more difficult, on the other hand, to understand his idea that Klenze's plan 'must ideologically speaking be regarded as much closer to the idea of absolute monarchy than the solution presented in Schaubert and Kleanthes's plan' (Sinos (1974), p. 48). After all, the palace dominates the town

much more in their plan than it does in his.
26. *Athen-München*, p. 18. In protest Schaubert and Kleanthes both submitted their resignation from their posts as chief architects and directors of the civil building administration in Athens, but Schaubert was soon back in the service of the state (cf. Russack (1942), pp. 35 f). Sinos has noted that there was yet another plan for the new Athens. This was executed by August Traxel and engraved in Paris in 1836 (Sinos (1974), pp. 48 ff, and Fig. 4; see also Fountoulaki (1979), pp. 63 ff). The project is influenced both by Schaubert and Kleanthes's and by Klenze's proposals, but still appears to tackle the task in its own way. However, this proposal does not seem to have made any impact on the development of Athens, and will not therefore be discussed here. It could be added that Papageorgiou-Venetas is extremely critical of Traxel's proposal, which he regards as 'rubbish, a fantasy, the product of a confused and publicity-hungry brain' (Papageorgiou-Venetas (1994), pp. 193 ff).
27. See in this context the figure on p. 29 in Biris (1966), where Schaubert and Kleanthes's project has been incorporated into the existing town plan.
28. This idea played a bigger part in Schaubert and Kleanthes's first version than in their second.
29. The closest parallel in time and type to the Athens examples is probably the Carrer de Ferran in Barcelona.
30. Cf. the 1847 and 1854 plans, reproduced in Biris (1966), pp. 87 and 100.
31. Kühn (1979), p. 521; cf. Biris (1966), pp. 35 f.
32. According to information from Alexander Papageorgiou-Venetas. See also the memorandum on the street widths in Athens from August 1834, probably by Klenze (reproduced in Papageorgiou-Venetas (1994), pp. 330 f).
33. Schaubert and Kleanthes themselves say that the widest streets in the plan 'are 60–70 English feet wide', which is equivalent to 18–21 metres (Russack (1942), p. 181). In fact, according to their plan, the Pireos and Stadiou streets were envisaged as being 22.5 metres wide; but their final width was – and still is – 20 metres, in compliance with the revised version of their plan (cf. note 21). Euripidou, Eolou and Ermou,

however, were reduced from 12.5 to 10 metres, as were some of the other streets crossing Athinas. The latter was intended to be 32 metres wide in both the Schaubert-Klanthes and the Klenze projects; when implemented, it was 24 metres wide. Following Klenze's ideas the dimensions of the public squares were also reduced (I am grateful to Alexander Papageorgiou-Venetas for helping me to sort out the problems connected with the street widths).

34. Since there were no resources available for the expropriation of the land for the planned archeological zone, the present-day Plaka, the government felt compelled to allow the rebuilding. In 1836 Schaubert and H.C. Hansen drew up a plan for the area with much the same street network as before (*Athen-München*, p. 18).

35. The area thus acquired something of the character of a cultural centre, which had been Schaubert and Kleanthes's intention.

36. Reproduced in Biris (1966), p. 71. In the City of Athens Museum there is an interesting 1:1,000 scale model, made in 1977–79 under the guidance of Joannis Travlos. It shows the town in 1842. As can be seen, the building of the new town had barely started.

37. Michael (1969), pp. 40 f.

38. *Athen-München*, p. 19. Biris (1966) does not mention this plan. However, the plan cannot be found (according to verbal information from Angeliki Kokkou). Can the plan reproduced in Biris (1966), p. 86, possibly reflect the ideas in this proposal? The plan seems to some extent to foreshadow the 1847 proposal.

39. On this architect, who took part in the discussions on the planning of Athens during the 1830s, and who advocated locating the new town with a systematic grid plan west of the Acropolis, see Michael (1969), pp. 33 ff, and more importantly Papageorgiou–Venetas (1994), who has succeeded in rediscovering the plan, which was previously known only from Kaftanzoglou's description. However, the plan (figure 6.4) does not appear to have attracted much notice when it was presented as a contribution to the debate, and thus made no impact on subsequent developments.

40. Biris (1966), pp. 82 ff. The following presentation is based mainly on this work.

41. Biris (1966), pp. 88 f. An attempt made in 1872 to prevent this widening was warded off by I. Genisarlis among others (Biris (1966), pp. 163 f; on Genisarlis, cf. *ibidem*, pp. 188 ff).

42. Biris (1966), pp. 108 ff. Cf. also Michael (1969), pp. 41 ff.

43. Biris (1966), p. 159. There were even far advanced plans to demolish Kapnikarea, the Byzantine church on Ermou, but these were averted at the last minute.

44. Biris (1966), pp. 161 ff. It was, regrettably, not possible to obtain reproducible pictures of this and the other later plans for Athens discussed here.

45. Michael (1969), pp. 49 ff provides a survey of developments during the second half of the nineteenth century (population figures from *ibidem*, p. 68).

46. Biris (1966), pp. 193 ff.

47. Biris (1966), p. 163.

48. It was typical of the lack of foresight that in 1881 a plan was approved for the suburb of Kato Patisia which involved breaking the straight stretch of Tritis Septemvriou and the eastern parallel streets at Agiou Meletiou, although the municipal planning boundary at that time was at Kodrictonos (Biris (1966), p. 163).

49. Biris (1966), p. 163.

50. *Ibidem*, pp. 190 f. Cf. also Biris's three examples of short-sighted planning.

51. *Ibidem*, pp. 188 ff. An example of this was the bad connection between Omonia and the streets Liossion and Acharnon which Genisarlis tried to improve.

52. Biris (1966), pp. 188 ff. The planning situation in 1900 can be seen from the map in Biris (1966), p. 240, where the building demarcation lines approved at that point are shown.

53. Michael (1969), pp. 54 ff. On Hoffmann's plan, see also Schmidt (1979).

54. The successive widening of the rectilinear street network over an increasingly large area is strikingly illustrated on a map in Biris (1966), p. 319.

7

CHRISTIANIA

Oslo[1] was a town of some importance during the Middle Ages, with a bishop, several monasteries and extensive trade. And as far back as the fourteenth century it functioned as a 'capital city'. The union with Denmark, which was established definitively in 1450, combined with the Reformation, led to a decline in the standing of the Norwegian towns; in addition to which a good deal of trade had been lost to German merchants. In the early modern period Oslo was frequently damaged by siege and fire, and it was after a fire in 1624 that Christian IV decided to transfer the town from its original site east of the Akerselva river – the area now called Gamlebyen – to a new foundation west of the river and close to Akershus Castle (figure 7.1). It was in connection with this move that the name of the town was changed to Christiania (the name Oslo was revived in 1925).[2]

Christiania was planned according to the ideas prevailing at the time, with straight streets and rectangular blocks. Towards the Akershus Castle a square was laid out, with closed corners on three sides, and next to this the new city church was built in 1639. An important factor in the subsequent development of the town was that only brick buildings were allowed within the urban area, with the result that extensive districts of wooden houses grew up on the outskirts. To begin with Christiania was a fortified town, but as early as 1686 the ramparts were demolished after a fire. At the same time the church, which had been badly damaged in the fire, was also pulled down for reasons of defence; it was considered too close to Akershus Castle. Instead a new church – the present cathedral – was built north of the former ramparts and consecrated in 1697. Around 1730 a new market square was laid out, the present Stortorvet, with the church to the east and the former city gate on Kongens gate on its south side. Thus Christiania

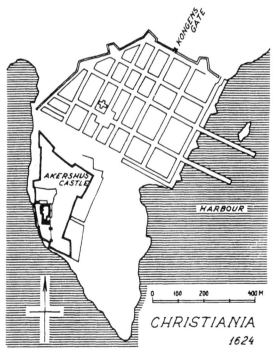

Figure 7.1 *Christiania at the time of the new foundation in 1624. [Map drawn by Erik Lorange]*

had acquired a new centre between the planned town of brick and the spontaneously evolving suburbs, whose population sometimes exceeded that of the city proper (figure 7.2).

In 1814 Norway was separated from Denmark, but was compelled at the same time to accept the Swedish king as its monarch. Christiania thus became one of two capital cities in a dual monarchy, i.e. it acquired a status not unlike that of Budapest half a century later. However, Norway had full command over internal affairs, and building legislation for example developed along different lines from those applying in Sweden. As early as 1821 a building act was proposed but was

never debated in the *Stortinget*, the Norwegian parliament. In 1827, however, the *Stortinget* approved a proposal for a special building act for Christiania. This Act prescribed among other things that a committee should be appointed 'to establish which places, squares and public exit roads should be extended or straightened in Christiania, or in suburbs on town ground, at the expense of the city purse.'[3] This became the starting-point for a permanent municipal planning body – the *regulerings-kommisjon* – comprising both politicians and officials. The survey prescribed in the Act was undertaken after much delay in the autumn of 1829. It took the form of a collection of

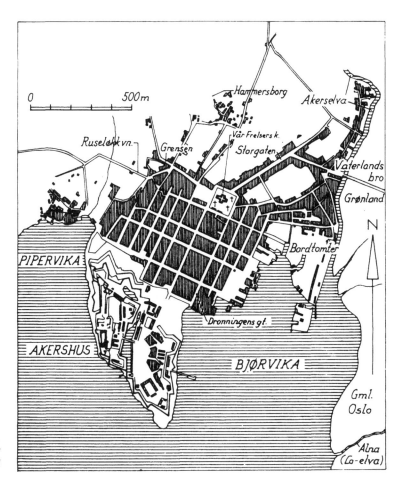

Figure 7.2 *Christiania, 1800. [Map drawn by Erik Lorange]*

proceedings, an inventory of requirements, in which all the desired changes were presented. However, the various suggestions referred mainly to details and were virtually limited to the existing urban structure. And no plan was made.

Ever since the sixteenth century the export of wood products had been an important factor in the economy of the Norwegian capital; numerous sawmills lay along the Akerselva with its many little waterfalls. The trade in wood products became increasingly important during the eighteenth century; it was not based primarily on the local sawmills but on the supply of board from the interior of the country. During the 1840s more modern types of industry began to appear, in particular textiles and engineering workshops. Christiania became by far the most important industrial town in Norway. The first railway line, from Christiania to Eidsvoll, was opened in 1854. In 1800 the population was a little over 10,000. By the middle of the century the town and its suburbs had 40,000 inhabitants. The new status as capital city had been of decisive importance in this context, since it meant that public funds were available for building, and that there was now a greater concentration of new administrative positions and operations in the town.[4]

As a result the built area naturally grew, in density as well as in extent. During the 1830s it became increasingly obvious that large sections of the surviving open spaces around Christiania would soon be exploited. These spaces consisted mainly of the so-called *løkkene*, or unbuilt private areas which had originally been part of the town's common land. However no overall plan was made, although the need for such a plan appears to have been recognized. For example, in 1836 someone proposed in the city council that a competition should be arranged to produce a plan. But this initiative came to nothing. Instead the *regulerings-kommisjon* had to judge every expansion project separately as it came up. Nor did the

committee have the resources or the control instruments to be able to exert much influence on individual projects.[5] Thus the urban structure evolved as the result of a series of development projects which had very little connection with one another.

It is possible to mention only a few of these here. Youngsløkken was developed according to a plan (figure 7.3) made by the town architect Chr.H. Grosch in 1839. A large square, the present Youngstorget, and several rectangular blocks were to be inserted between Storgata and Møllergata, two existing roads which together form a slightly irregular V. A year earlier, in 1838, the architect of the royal palace H.D. Linstow had submitted a proposal for systematizing the area between the palace and the town (figure 7.4). The palace was in process of construction at the time, and the area between the town and the palace had remained undeveloped. Linstow's main idea was that a road running along an axis from the palace should be linked on a slight bend with one of the existing seventeenth-century streets, creating a main thoroughfare right across the town. Round a grand square in the middle of the new district the university and other important institutional buildings were to be located. This street, the future Karl Johans gate, and the others parallel to it, were realized according to Linstow's intentions, as was the diagonal street, St Olavs Gate. The university was built more or less where Linstow intended, but the square was never completed in accordance with his ideas. The landowners on the north side of the Karl Johans Gate bought up the plots on the southern side and donated them to the town, on condition that nothing should be built on them. In this way the central park, Studenterlunden, was created. The parliament building, the *Stortinget*, rose at the eastern end of the park. At a later stage and after much discussion the *Nationalteatret* was built inside the park itself. The replacement of the buildings originally intended by a park has altered the prospect from the street towards

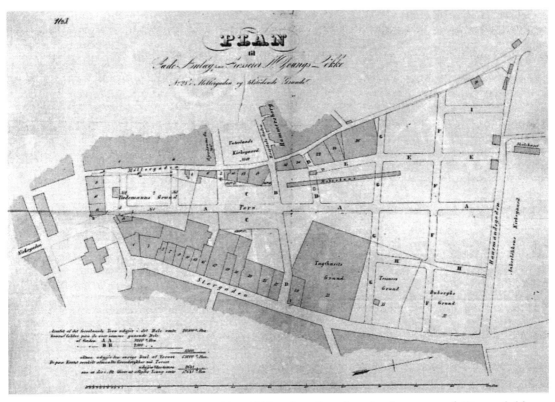

Figure 7.3 *Christiania. C.H. Grosch's 1839 plan for the development of Youngsløkken.* *[Riksarkivet, Oslo]*

the palace, as compared with Linstow's conception, although the trees of the Studenterlunden do give the street a kind of semitransparent 'wall'. The slight slope of Karl Johans Gate and the elevated site of the palace combine to produce an unusually impressive vista.[6]

However, it was becoming increasingly clear that an overall plan was needed, and when the Building Act for Christiania was being revised in 1841 it was suggested that the *regulerings-kommisjon* should be instructed to make such a plan 'to prevent the irregularity that at present occurs when buildings are erected, because, to the great detriment of the town, buildings are built quite arbitrarily, without any consideration of the street setting.' In the *Stortinget* an

even more stringent proposal was composed, and the clause as ratified ran as follows: 'The *reguleringskommisjon* is to make a plan immediately for straightening, extending and laying out streets and public squares for various districts in the town and its immediate neighbourhood, and the plan is to be submitted to the representatives of the municipality, after which the king's approval is to be sought.'[7]

Thus, at least on paper, the conditions were created for progressive planning in a way that was unusual for the time; none of the other capital cities discussed in this book had any permanent planning body at such an early stage, nor any equivalent building legislation. But the results were nil. The town architect, Grosch, did subsequently present a proposal

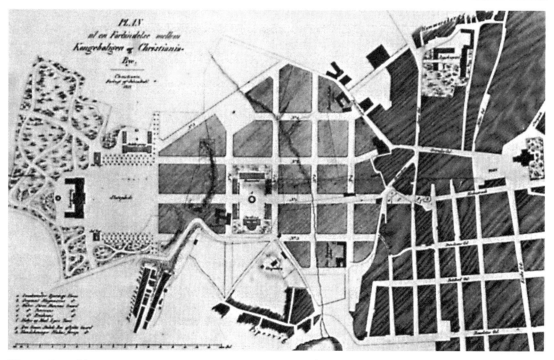

Figure 7.4 *Christiania. H.D. Linstow's 1838 project for the surroundings of the palace. [From Kavli and Hjelde (1973)]*

for a master plan in 1843, but it was referred by the *reguleringskommisjon* to a subcommittee which does not seem to have done anything about it. The issue of the plan was not raised again, despite the perfectly clear wording of the Act. In 1855 one of the members of the commission demanded that the plan prescribed in the Act be made as soon as possible; this, too, failed to achieve the intended result. But in the course of these various moves, a permanent working subcommittee was appointed, which gave the activities of the commission a firmer basis. Two years later the *reguleringskommisjon* decided, probably on the initiative of this subcommittee, to engage a part-time official whose brief would include the execution of a master plan. However, the new appointee, the architect G.A. Bull, was kept fully occupied by routine business.

In 1861 the town lost an important expropriation case. The court ruled that expropriation could only be effected in accordance with an approved and ratified town plan, and no such plan existed. Instead of being spurred at last to launch a planning campaign, the municipality asked to be freed from the mandatory requirement to produce a master plan. The *reguleringskommisjon* declared that the financial and technical problems of such a plan were anyway insuperable and that step-by-step planning was to be preferred. The *Stortinget* complied with the wishes of the municipality: the law was revised and the town granted the right to decide whether, and for which areas, plans should be made. If there were no plans, the requirements of the *reguleringskommisjon* should apply. Thus, as Juhasz points out, the earlier and often criticised 'fragmentary improvement' mode had now been legally endorsed.[8]

During the 1860s and 1870s planning continued, bit by bit, albeit sometimes for fairly large areas at a time. Two of the areas planned by Bull, who had now succeeded Grosch as town architect, were the working-class district of Grünerløkken with blocks of flats of the continental type, and the residential area north-west of the palace, Homansbyen. Factors such as topography, ownership boundaries, municipal boundaries and earlier building often played a more important part than any ideas about the overall structure of the town.[9] Towards the end of the century the debate on planning issues grew more lively. Various issues were discussed, such as the Akershus area, the harbour and the quays, and the location of the railway stations, including a suggestion for the transfer of the eastern

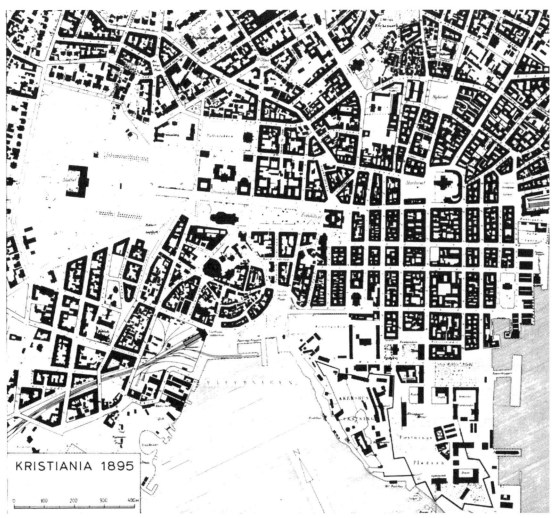

Figure 7.5 *Christiania towards the end of the nineteenth century. [Official map, revised by Erik Lorange]*

station Østbanestasjon (the present Sentral-stasjon).

An examination of a late nineteenth-century map of Christiania (figure 7.5) reveals remarkably little of the typical urban planning features of those times; there is hardly a single tree-planted street worthy of the name of boulevard or avenue, few central park areas apart from the Studenterlunden, little in the way of rectilinear areas and only one or two attempts to create monumental squares. St Olavs Blass, for instance, could be described as a kind of star-shaped place, although this effect has been spoilt by later development. Christian IV's rectangular plan is well preserved, forming a homogeneous area in the centre. Otherwise, as Juhasz puts it, 'the street network in the middle of Oslo today looks as though it were broken up into pieces of varying sizes,'[10] a natural result of the absence of any overall planning. This may seem surprising in view of the fact that on several occasions the government and the *Stortinget* took the initiative to launch planning activities, and that Christiania was the only one of the capital cities studied here which had a permanent body for planning and street improvement for most of the nineteenth century. Several factors in combination may explain this situation. Topographical features and earlier buildings certainly imposed their own constraints. The lack of any competent administrator and uncertainty about how to define the area to be planned, must also have played their part. But when it came down to it, the most important thing was that neither the *reguleringskommisjon* nor the municipality wanted to accept the costs to the public purse or the intervention in the rights of landowners regarding their own property, which any overall plan worthy of the name would have involved. In a country like Norway which in certain respects was progressive and democratic for the times, liberalistic values obviously represented a more powerful obstacle than they did in countries under more authoritarian rule.

NOTES

1. Little has been written about urban development in Christiania during the nineteenth century. The following presentation is primarily based on Juhasz (1965), which describes the activities of the *reguleringskommisjon* up to about 1860, and Pedersen (1965), which provides an overview of the evolution of planning in Christiania. Jensen (1980) adds little of importance about Christiania during the period that is relevant to us here. The seminal work on Oslo's general development during the nineteenth century is Myhre (1990); *idem* (1984) is a short survey of the same period.
2. In 1877 the spelling was changed to Kristiania.
3. Quoted by Juhasz (1965), p. 14.
4. Cf. Mykland (1984).
5. The problems were described by the *reguleringskommisjon* itself as follows: 'With regard to the regular construction of streets, the commission cannot generally be active other than by advising or recommending what seems appropriate. The Building Act does not give the commission any formal power to compel the owner to follow a particular plan or to lay down streets in such places as it requires; only if some owner or owners call for the construction of a street, can the commission see that such a street has the qualities required by the law and an appropriate orientation, or otherwise refuse to permit its construction. Only when the owner of a fairly large piece of land demands a street before dividing into plots, is the commission relatively free to determine the orientation of the street; however, this seldom occurs since most owners of large pieces of land first sell as many plots as possible along existing streets, and only after these are built do they finally demand the construction of a new street; but by that time the options are already very restricted. The only possibility of achieving any kind of regular planning is therefore to buy the land for the construction of the streets; but the funds available for this are extremely limited.' (Quoted by Juhasz (1965), p. 22.)
6. Linstow's long involvement in the creation of the area around the palace – a first study probably appeared as early as 1825 – have been explored in Pedersen (1961) and Kavli and Hjelde (1973), pp. 45 ff; cf. also Lorange's

analysis of the area (1984), pp. 128 ff. Obviously Linstow hoped from the start to create a new imposing district to link the palace and the town, but a more central piece of land for building in front of the Akershus Castle was at the disposal of the state, and it was therefore difficult to get much support for developing what at that time was a rather peripheral district. However, in 1836 it was decided that Akershus should be taken into use again for defence purposes, and further building in the neighbourhood was therefore forbidden. Thus Linstow had a good opportunity to relaunch his old idea. That same year he went to Germany, where among other places he visited Berlin and Munich. He invoked Ludwigstrasse in Munich as a model, and naturally also took an interest in Schinkel's architecture and planning (when the university building – actually designed by Grosch – was being planned, Schinkel was consulted and the building acquired certain obvious Schinkel-inspired features). It is more doubtful whether, as Kühn suggests, Linstow's project for Christiania could be linked with Schaubert and Kleanthes's plan for Athens (Kühn (1979), p. 519, note 20). Even if Linstow saw the Athens plan when he visited Schinkel – which does not appear to have been confirmed – he had already been working for a long time on the idea of a street on the same axis as the palace. And of course, the topographical conditions in Athens and Christiania were quite different.

7. Quoted by Juhasz (1965), pp. 24 f.

8. *Ibidem*, p. 34.

9. Of particular importance here was the *murgrensen*, the boundary within which it was mandatory to build in brick. This boundary, and the not quite identical juridical town boundary, was twice moved further out, in 1858–59 and in 1878. On the first occasion areas of poor-quality wooden building grew up just outside the boundary; on the second occasion this was avoided by forbidding any building outside the town in the vicinity of the boundary.

10. Quoted by Juhasz (1965), p. 23.

8

BARCELONA

Barcelona[1] occupies a position of special interest in the history of urban planning on two counts in particular: first because of the extension of the city – the *ensanche*[2] – which was planned around 1860 and then carried out with a consistency unusual in such contexts, and secondly on account of its urban core where much of the structure and many of the buildings from earlier development phases have been preserved.

The Barcelona of Roman times could probably have been described as a minor provincial town.[3] The ancient structure can still be glimpsed in the present street network. The direction of the two main streets has survived in the Carrer de la Llibrería (the *decumanus*) and the Carrer del Bisbe (the *cardo*). And, in addition to this, portions of the Roman Wall still exist. Barcelona's development into a major medieval town began in 801, when the town was reconquered by the Christians and became the most important outpost south of the Pyrenees. In the following period the counts of Barcelona successively extended their territory in frequent battles with the Moors. In 985 the county of Barcelona became an independent state, embracing a large part of present-day Catalonia. In the twelfth century it became united by marriage with the kingdom of Aragon, in which Barcelona was the seat of the ruler. By this time Barcelona had also become one of the leading merchant cities in the Mediterranean area. Around the Roman town a number of *vilanovas* had grown up, of which the most important was Vilanova de la Mar along the present Carrer Argentería. During the second half of the thirteenth century a city wall was built, enclosing the suburbs and running on the western[4] side along the river bed which would later become La Rambla.

In the course of the fifteenth century competition with other trading cities in the western Mediterranean grew increasingly keen, and in the later decades of the century certain events occurred which in the long run were to have negative consequences for the town. Ferdinand II's marriage with Isabella of Castile in 1469 created a united Spain, a country whose political centres would come to lie in Castile. Then, after the discovery of America in 1492, Mediterranean trade was superseded by the Atlantic route, and Barcelona was replaced by Cádiz as the leading port. For Barcelona the sixteenth and seventeenth centuries were a period of stagnation and decline. Little building was undertaken. During the fifteenth century, however, the town wall was modernised and extended, which meant that the area west of the Rambla was now fortified. For a long time this district remained sparsely built, and the buildings that did exist were mainly ecclesiastical.

During the War of the Spanish Succession (1701–1713) Barcelona supported the imperial side, which meant that the town was treated with extreme severity by Philip V. Catalonia lost its former autonomy, and much of the eastern urban area of Barcelona was demolished and replaced by a citadel. To house those who were made homeless by this development,

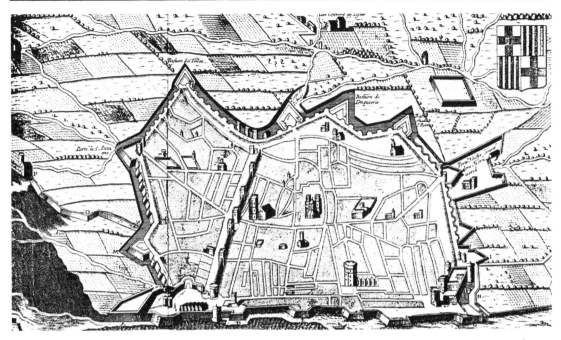

Figure 8.1 *Barcelona. This map (detail),* Herauß Gegeben von Matth. Seutter Kay. Geogr., *shows the earlier development phases in the town's history: in the centre there is the Roman town, whose walls to some extent have survived. This centre is surrounded by the medieval suburbs, which in the thirteenth century were enclosed by a new defence wall; this still existed when the map was made, following La Rambla, a water conduit running through the town. The area west of La Rambla was fortified by an extension of the town wall in the fifteenth century. [Uppsala universitetsbibliotek]*

the suburb of Barceloneta was built outside the walls, planned by the French architect Prospère de Verboom and begun around the middle of the eighteenth century. Today this district presents a strange picture with its narrow rectangular blocks and streets, and houses that seem high in relation to the streets between them. But at the time it was envisaged as a progressive alternative to the deep blocks of the old town. Every house was to look out over two streets and the buildings were to be low, to provide a good environment. However, during the 1850s the restrictions on building were dropped, and the original idea was spoilt as a result of excessive exploitation.

During the later years of the eighteenth century Barcelona became increasingly important as a commercial and manufacturing town, with accompanying population growth and a good deal of building activity within its remaining fortified walls. It was now that La Rambla acquired the character of a promenade, as the watercourses were covered and trees were planted. During the 1820s a major alteration was introduced in the street network: the roughly 10-metre broad Carrer de Ferran was built straight across the old street structure and continued as the Carrer de la Pricesa. The planner was the architect Josep Mas i Vila.[5]

Industrialization began comparatively late in Spain. The antiquated social structure, in which the Church and the landowning aristocracy held sway, impeded any rapid change.

However, in Barcelona large factories founded on steam technology were being established as early as the 1830s. At the same time Barcelona's importance as a port and trading city was growing, and by the middle of the century the town had become a major industrial and trading centre. It was also an important fort, still enclosed within its old fortifications, with the result that exploitation within the walls was intense and hygiene was poor. Towards the middle of the nineteenth century conditions in Barcelona in this respect were probably among the worst in Europe. Outside the town a broad glacis band remained unbuilt for reasons of defence. Beyond this zone lay several villages, of which the most important was Gràcia to the north. As early as the 1830s expansion plans involving the transfer of a small section of the fortifications were being discussed. A number of proposals were put forward, for instance an extension project by Josep Mª. Planas (figure 8.2), but the discussions broke down as agreement could not be reached on the design of the plan and objections were raised about land ownership rights.[6] It was also becoming increasingly clear that a minor expansion would be inadequate, and that more radical measures would be necessary. In 1853 a commission was appointed to draw up a petition to the government regarding the demolition of the fortifications – an idea that met with powerful opposition from the military just as it did in the other fortified capital cities. However, following a severe cholera epidemic, a decision regarding the demolition of the fortified area was taken in 1854.[7]

It was at this point that Ildefonso Cerdá appeared on the scene.[8] Cerdá was born on a country estate in Catalonia and had studied mathematics and architecture in Barcelona, after which he attended the College of Road, Canal and Harbour Building in Madrid. During the 1840s as a member of the state engineering corps – *Corporación de ingenieros de caminos, canales y puertos* – he received a number of commissions connected with the building of roads and railways in Catalonia and elsewhere. After coming into an inheritance he withdrew from active service in 1848 to study issues of urban development.

Spain's history during the nineteenth century is marked by violent political conflict and a series of shifts between progressive and reactionary régimes. At the national level the 1850s was a period of constitutionalism and liberalization. For the progressive party, the *Partido Progresista*, it was first and foremost a question of modernizing Spanish society and making it more efficient. But there was also a more radical group, the *Partido Democrático*, which wanted social reforms. Cerdá sympathized with the demand for greater democracy and for improving the situation of the workers. At the beginning of the 1850s he was given several political commissions, as a member of the parliament or *Cortes* and in the local administration of Barcelona. At the local level, however, conservative groups assumed the leadership and the town was shaken by violent unrest in 1854 and 1855.

Cerdá's first official planning task in Barcelona was to make a survey of the town's surroundings. The survey, which he made at his own expense, was completed by 1855 and was regarded in professional circles as a masterpiece of its kind (figure 8.3). On his own initiative Cerdá made a tracing from this map, with a proposal for a town plan for the area of flat land outside the town walls. Unfortunately this has been lost, although the accompanying commentary has been found.[9] Over the next few years Cerdá continued to work on his proposal, at the same time involving himself in various activities to improve the conditions of the workers in Barcelona. This resulted in a scientific study – *Monografía estadística de la clase obrera de Barcelona en 1856* – which presented comprehensive statistical data of a complete and methodical kind probably without parallel elsewhere at the time. As well as being published separately, this was also included as a supplement to the second volume

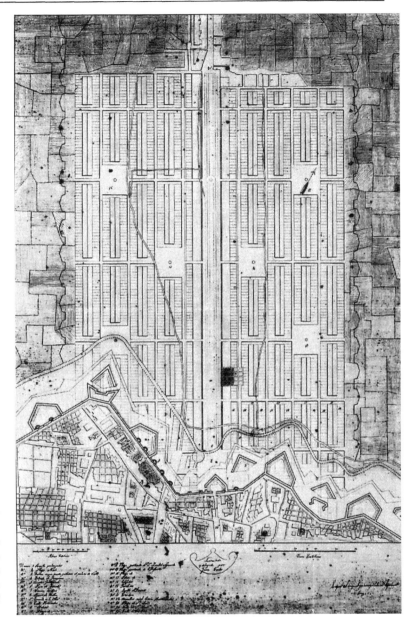

Figure 8.2 *Barcelona. Project from the 1850s by Josep Mª. Planas for an extension between the city and the suburb Gràcia along the promenade Passeig de Gràcia. [Photo from Colegio Oficial de Arquitectos de Cataluña y Baleares, Barcelona]*

of *Teoría general de la urbanización* (see pp. 134 ff and 363).

At last in 1858 came the final decision that the military should cede the fortification area, less than a year after a similar decision had been proclaimed in Vienna. It would have seemed natural at this point to consult Cerdá – the municipal leadership was probably well aware that he had gone on developing his own proposal of 1855. But the conservative-minded

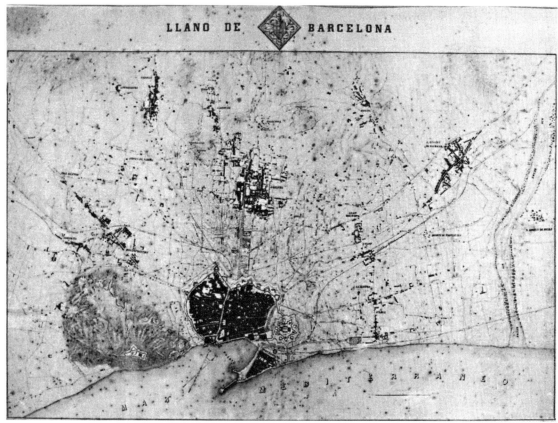

Figure 8.3 *Ildefonso Cerdá's survey of the plain around Barcelona, 1855. [Photo from Colegio Oficial de Arquitectos de Cataluña y Baleares, Barcelona]*

municipal authorities had apparently lost confidence in him, and preferred to implement the expansion of the town along the lines suggested by the city architect Miquel Garriga i Roca in a plan commissioned by the municipal council and approved in April 1858 (figure 8.4).[10]

Cerdá, however, regarded the planning of Barcelona as his mission in life, and was by no means inclined to surrender. Instead, he applied to the government in Madrid and in February 1859 secured permission to draw up a plan without receiving any financial remuneration. As we have seen, Cerdá was well prepared and his proposal (figure 8.7) was approved by the government on 7th June the same year. But

Barcelona municipal council was not willing simply to accept this intervention in what they regarded as the municipality's internal affairs. In the spring of 1859 they had announced a town planning competition, in which Cerdá did not take part. Thus when the competition closed in August 1859, a plan approved by central government already existed. Fourteen proposals had been submitted to a jury chaired by the chancellor of the university and consisting, apart from its chairman, of four architects, one physician, one engineer, one lawyer and a professor of physics. The first prize went by unanimous decision to a proposal submitted by the city architect Antoni Rovira i Trias (figure

8.5),[11] the second to the engineer Francesc Soler i Glòria (figure 8.6). After a chaotic local debate, in which Cerdá involved himself energetically the government in Madrid rejected Rovira i Trias's plan and Cerdá's proposal was approved once again in 1860.

The various twists and turns in this comedy are difficult to follow,[12] but there were evidently at least four sources of conflict: first, a conflict between the central and local governments regarding competence and power; secondly a political conflict between progressive and conservative groups; thirdly, and closely related to the political conflicts, there was a difference of opinion in urban development ideology between those who wanted an imposing town of the traditional type and those who preferred something new and rational; and fourthly, a professional conflict between two vocational groups, the engineers and the architects (who, as we have seen, were strongly represented on the prize jury). To this must be added certain economic ingredients: Cerdá's project may well have appeared to be several sizes too large as well as unreasonably costly in the eyes the city, and unfavourable in the eyes of some of the landowners. The fact that Cerdá's plan could be pushed through despite the local opposition was due to his ability, his excellent reputation as an engineer, his pugnacity and persistence, his extensive preparations for the task, his overwhelming expertise and, not least, his private means which enabled him to work full-time and without pay to produce his project with the help of anything up to seven assistants, and to lobby for it.

Let us now examine the main proposals. The

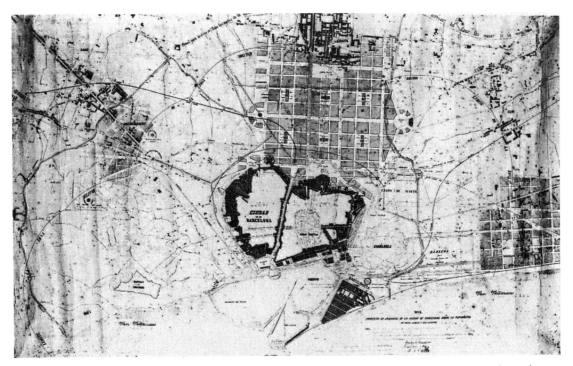

Figure 8.4 *Miquel Garriga i Roca's proposal for the expansion of Barcelona, 1857. [Photo from Colegio Oficial de Arquitectos de Cataluña y Baleares, Barcelona]*

first, by Garriga i Roca, is not very remarkable (figure 8.4). For the area between the old city and the village of Gràcia a plan consisting of square or almost square blocks is proposed. These blocks are grouped in turn in six larger blocks marked out by broader main streets, to be compared with the other streets which are only half as wide. In every such large block the middle section has been reserved as a square and embellished with a public building. A big rectangular square was planned on the central axis of the new district, immediately outside the old city, further to the east than the present Plaça de Catalunya. A similar open place was envisaged to the north, by Gràcia. In the west and east *plazas* were also indicated, the first forming a half-star and the second star-shaped. There are no parks at all. Several streets have

been marked more faintly, extending beyond the planning area proper and indicating further expansion. The street running past the old town is reminiscent of the later Gran Via de les Corts Catalanes; it continues to the west through a faintly sketched-in star-shaped *plaza*. An interesting question, which does not seem to have been discussed in the literature, is whether Garriga i Roca's plan draws on Cerdá's lost project of 1855. Perhaps the shape of the blocks and the long, faintly indicated street axes may derive from Cerdá.

Rovira i Trias's proposal is more sophisticated and indicates an attempt to combine a traditional design language with the demands of a modern town (figure 8.5). The new urban area is divided by a series of main streets, radiating out from the old town in trapezoid

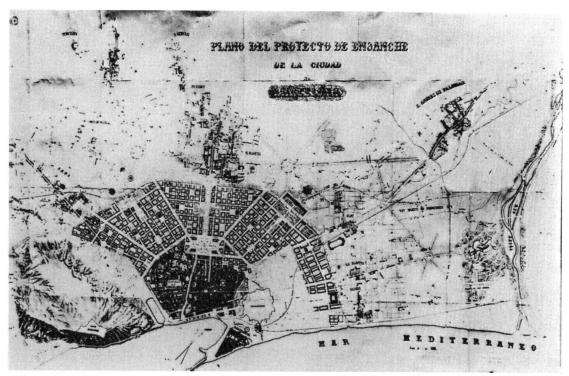

Figure 8.5 *Antonio Rovira i Trias's prize-winning proposal for the expansion of Barcelona, 1859.* [*Photo from Colegio Oficial de Arquitectos de Cataluña y Baleares, Barcelona*]

sectors, in a way that is reminiscent of the radial plans of the planning theorists. A magnificent monumental square, Foro de Isabel, is envisaged as a common centre for the old and new towns, located immediately adjacent to the old town. From this square a park-like street – a cousin of the Esplanade in Helsinki – leads north to Gràcia. This road, Passeig de Gràcia, had been laid out as early as the beginning of the nineteenth century, and it appears in several of the proposals. By this avenue, whose middle section has been expanded to form a large planted space, the central part of the town is divided into two symmetrical halves. The flanking sectors combine with this central sector to create a symmetrical whole. The two outer sectors are also divided, albeit not symmetrically, by one axis each of squares and small parks. In the case of the middle sections, various public buildings such as schools, museums, hospitals and market halls are proposed around many parks and squares. The arrangement of museums and other institutional buildings grouped around the outer squares in the central axes of the flanking sectors, recalls the future Maria Theresien-Platz in the entry submitted by von Sicardsburg and van der Nüll to the Ringstraße competition the year before. The old town centre has been surrounded by a street designated *Bulevar*. To the east a street network of a simpler kind has been created, and further opportunities for expansion in different directions have been indicated, for instance in some star-shaped *plazas* outside the city area proper. A prison has also been planned on the western side. Many streets are narrow, but almost all the blocks face an open space on one side, either a square, the boulevard or one of the broad radial streets.[13] Rovira i Trias's proposal follows the competition brief very closely. Among other things this had called for a large open place outside the old town, as already suggested in Garriga i Roca's project, as well as for straight exit roads and architectural monumentality.[14]

Rovira i Trias's project seems more like an ideal plan than a feasible alternative for a large growing city. Nonetheless it certainly satisfied several of the demands which a new plan could be expected to fulfil, for example allowing for good communications with the surrounding villages, some of which were already more or less urbanized. This plan also provided for a number of grand settings. It is not difficult to see why leading groups in Barcelona were attracted by the plan, which they obviously found more impressive, more appropriate to their needs and more realistic than Cerdá's gigantic project. The fact that there were four architects on the jury probably also favoured a proposal like Rovira's, with its wealth of architectural variety.

Francesc Soler i Glòria's proposal has two grids with different orientations, several large parks and a number of broad thoroughfares (figure 8.6). One of the main ideas in this proposal was that a large inner dock should be constructed to the west of the old town, something which was regarded as unsatisfactory from the point of view of hygiene. The project is an obvious 'engineer's plan' without any architectural pretensions, but also lacking the consistency that characterizes Rovira i Trias's and Cerdá's proposals (although in almost every other respect these two are each other's opposite). The third prize-winning project, submitted by Josep Fontserè, freely combines star-shaped plazas, diagonal streets and rectangular blocks.[15]

So now let us turn to Cerdá's proposal – certainly one of the most remarkable urban development projects of the nineteenth century (figure 8.7). If Rovira i Trias's project could be described as an obvious 'architect's plan', then Cerdá's proposal is an equally evident 'engineer's plan'. All the free space between the town and the surrounding mountains and villages has been filled with square blocks, all the same size (113 x 113 metres) and with the same cut-off corners, separated by streets of uniform width (20 metres). For once the term

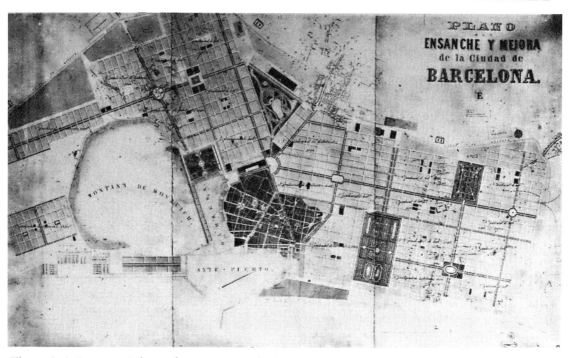

Figure 8.6 *Francesc Soler i Glòria's proposal which was awarded second prize in the competition for the extension of Barcelona. [Photo from Colegio Oficial de Arquitectos de Cataluña y Baleares, Barcelona]*

'chessboard plan' is fully justified. The grid is crossed by a few much broader thoroughfares (50 metres), which run either parallel or diagonal to the other streets. At the crossing of the two large diagonal streets, there is an enormous square. The plan indicates not only the boundaries of the blocks but also the site of the buildings within them. Most of the blocks were to be built only on two sides, with single rows of houses. The remaining areas of the blocks would consist mainly of planted open spaces. Several parks were also proposed, and other public structures such as market halls, churches, hospitals and so on. A large park borders the built-up area in the east, and in the west the Montjuich mountain was intended to serve as a corresponding park.

In the sheer size of its planned area Cerdá's project for Barcelona is overwhelming, while its open blocks are a radical innovation. The uniform shape of the blocks was not new, however, nor were the diagonal streets. Despite some variety in the grouping of the buildings, the general impression of the plan is monotonous; there are no scenic variations or architectural effects, nor is there any attempt to achieve such features. The large central square appears obviously weak both in its design and its function in the traffic network.

What places Cerdá's project in a class of its own is less its architectural merits than its theoretical underpinning and its author's scientific working method. In this respect the Barcelona plan marks something of a historical breakthrough. Never before had an urban planning venture been preceded by the assembling of so much data or been given such a comprehensive theoretical basis. Every detail in the plan has its reason; nothing was added at random. Cerdá saw planning as a technique to be used for finding functionally optimal solutions, based on the scientific analysis of the collected data. Solutions of this kind should in his view have universal applicability. The empirical basis was derived from the case of Barcelona, but the goal was wider, namely to formulate general principles for the rational design of cities. He presented his ideas in a number of publications, of which the most important is his 'General theory on urban development and the application of its principles and doctrines to the redevelopment and extension of Barcelona' (*Teoría general de la urbanización y aplicación de sus principios y doctrinas a la reforma y ensanche de Barcelona*, 1867). But this work, which was published long after the planning stage was over, had been preceded by memoranda more directly associated with the proposals.[16] There was thus a continual interaction between the evolution of the Barcelona plan on the one hand, and the building of a body of theory on the other. The theory was used to justify the plan, and the plan to elucidate the theory. We may well wonder how far the evolution of his theories preceded the plan, and how far it was a retrospective rationalization. But it is probably no more possible to answer this question than to solve the classic poser about the chicken and the egg.[17]

Cerdá's writings, like many similar manifestos, are full of a sometimes confusing mixture of theoretical abstractions and concrete details, of visionary generalizations and technical particularities. It does not fall within the scope of the present study to examine the content of his theories in any great detail.[18] Suffice it to say that Cerdá regarded the town as a combination of two fundamental elements, namely *urbe o continente* and *contenido o población*, that is to say a physical structure as a container, and the population and activities that give this its contents. The essential elements in every urban situation, according to Cerdá, were the street and the block, or to use his own terminology the *via* and the *intervia*. One of his basic ideas was that the streets, which were perceived as parts of an infinite system of communications, should be straight and of equal width, crossing one another at right angles, and that the blocks should have a uniformly equal-sided design. Just this uniformity was of cardinal importance to Cerdá. All the different parts of the town should be designed according to the same principles and should have the same value, and it should be possible to extend the urban area *ad infinitum* by adding new blocks – an idea that foreshadows Otto Wagner's 'infinite' city. Cerdá also endeavoured to see that the main streets represented a direct continuation of the chief entry roads into the city.

The streets were to be 20 metres wide: the carriageway should be 10 metres broad to allow four carriages alongside one another, and the space assigned to pedestrians should be no less, i.e. there should be two pavements, each one 5 metres broad. The buildings should not be higher than the width of the street, although Cerdá appears to have preferred one- or two-storey houses.[19] He also pays great attention to the orientation of the streets in relation to wind and sun conditions.

The street width and the permitted height of the houses does not differ significantly from the dimensions to be found in other inner city areas; the difference lies mainly in the fact that Cerdá provided fuller and more profound motivations. On other points, however, Cerdá's ideas went beyond currently recognized concepts. The requirement regarding cut-off block corners occurred in several large cities during the later nineteenth century, but in the Barcelona plan the corners of the blocks have been drawn back to such an extent that every crossroads assumes the appearance of an octagonal place, in which every side measures 20 metres. Cerdá set great store by this point, partly on grounds of traffic efficiency but also for social reasons: the street corners were to

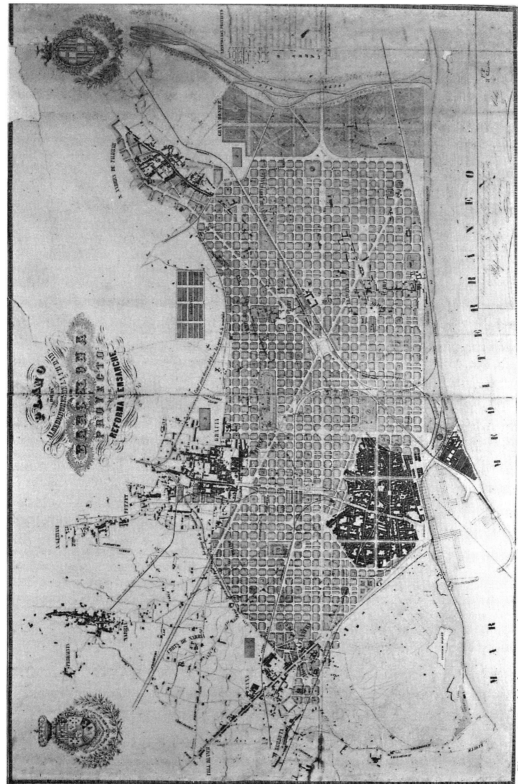

Figure 8.7 *Ildefonso Cerdá's proposal for the expansion of Barcelona, 1859. [Photo from Colegio Oficial de Arquitectos de Cataluña y Baleares, Barcelona]*

function as meeting points, provide shop sites etc. Another of Cerdá's basic requirements was that every street should be planted with trees at 8-metre intervals along the edge of the pavement, with 65 trees round every block. Elsewhere trees planted along the main streets had to suffice. According to Cerdá, even facilities such as clocks, wells and so on should be regarded as part of the urban setting.

The most radical but also the most controversial point in Cerdá's programme, however, was that the blocks should be built only along two sides and should consist of low buildings no deeper than 20–24 metres. The rest should

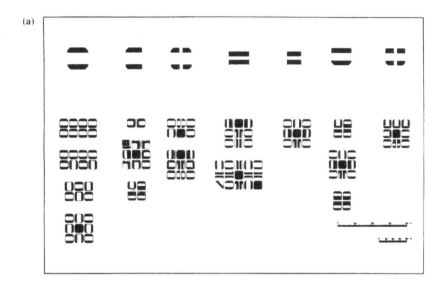

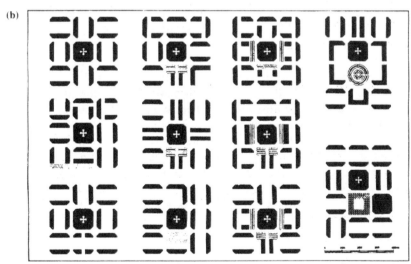

Figure 8.8 *Barcelona. Example from Cerdá's plan for* (a) *parallel rows of buildings, and* (b) *different forms of neighbourhood units.* [From Lotus international, No. 23, 1979]

be left open for gardens etc. As regards the placing of the buildings in the blocks the main model involved parallel rows, but rows at right angles to one another also appear. Both models allow for some variation, but the rows were generally placed parallel along the outside of the blocks (cf. figure 8.8*a*). The two types of block are combined in different ways, to contribute to the overall pattern in the urban fabric. Thus the blocks are grouped in what could be described as neighbourhood units around a centre with public buildings such as a church, a school, a market hall etc. (figure 8.8*b*); and these neighbourhood units are in turn combined into eight large district blocks.[20] In some cases several block modules were assembled in larger units for industries, parks and other space-demanding structures.

A comparison between Cerdá's plan and a modern map of Barcelona immediately reveals that the layout of both streets and blocks is remarkably similar. The most obvious difference is that the present grid does not stretch nearly as far towards the east as the grid in Cerdá's plan; the main part of the eastern half of the project was never implemented. But the western section of the existing grid reveals few deviations from the plan. The 50-metre broad west-east axis, the present Gran Via de les Corts Catalanes, has been realized, and so have the other planned main streets, in particular the long, 50-metre broad north-west/south-east diagonal street, the Avinguda de la Diagonal. The corresponding south-west/north-east diagonal, the Avinguda de la Meridiana, has only been realized in part.[21] Passeig de Gràcia already existed and, with its oblique orientation and greater width, it slightly disturbs the rectilinear grid.

A closer examination reveals, however, that it is only the division into blocks and the orientation of the streets that has followed Cerdá's plan. The content of the blocks is different; essentially, exploitation has been as intensive as in other big cities. Only a few isolated and stunted passages through the

blocks remain as faint reminders of Cerdá's intentions. Special mention should be made of the Passatge Permanyer, with its terraces and gardens. Further, almost all the parks have disappeared between planning and implementation. Nor was the huge square which would have been the centre of the town, Plaça de les Glòries Catalanes, ever realized. For decades, it has been little more than an unpleasant crossing of traffic routes. Instead the new centre, without ever having been planned as such, has evolved at the meeting between the old and the new towns, i.e. around the present Plaça de Catalunya and along the Avinguda del Portal de l'Àngel and its extension through the *ensanche*, the Passeig de Gràcia. Along and around this stretch of road there are department stores, shops, banks, offices and some of the architecturally most important buildings from the turn of the century, for example Gaudí's *Casa Milá*. We should here remember that Rovira i Trias envisaged a large square next to the old town centre, and that such a *plaza* was one of the requirements of the competition brief. However, the Plaça de Catalunya should be seen as the result of the free play of developments rather than as a planned adjustment to the Cerdá plan. Cerdá's intention was that the *ensanche* should be a completely new town, of which the old town centre would be one part; but he underestimated the importance of the traditional centre in the life of the city.

The extensive literature on the Barcelona plan has focused mainly on Cerdá's intentions, while less attention seems to have been devoted to the implementation process, which was slow and arduous.[22] The land within the planned area was owned mainly by Church foundations and private individuals, and its exploitation was conducted by several different companies. The municipality's concern was apparently, as elsewhere, directed mainly towards the construction of streets. Public control over private building seems to have been exercised by way of building ordinances and to have been

limited to checking that the indicated boundaries for blocks and buildings were observed,
and that the permitted maximum heights were
not exceeded. On the other hand there seems
to have been no legal possibility of preventing
more aggressive exploitation than Cerdá had
intended, nor was there apparently any political
will to do so. As early as 1859, when Cerdá's
plan was approved, the *Ministerio de Fomento*
decreed that blocks built on three sides should
be allowed,[23] and the government subsequently
approved such exploitation as had already
occurred in conflict with the plan. Cerdá seems
to have accepted this development. There is a
variant of the Barcelona plan dated 1863,
which is evidently regarded as the work of
Cerdá himself, and in which most blocks are
built on three sides or even all round.[24] It
would be interesting to have more information
about its origins, and Cerdá's own role in the
expansion process. For example, in 1863–64 he
made a local plan for two blocks for the
developers *La Sociedad Fomento del Ensanche
de Barcelona*, which included buildings on
three sides facing one another in a U
shape.[25]

A survey plan dated 1890 (figure 8.9) shows
that considerable progress had been made in
the development of the central area around
Gran Via and Passeig de Gràcia, and that

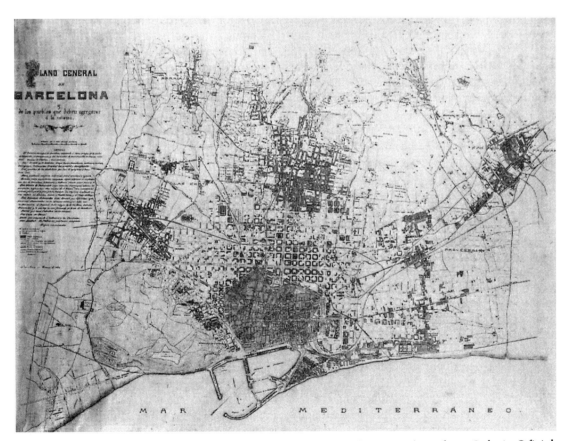

Figure 8.9 *Barcelona. Map of the city and its suburbs around 1890. [Photo from Colegio Oficial
de Arquitectos de Cataluña y Baleares, Barcelona]*

many blocks were now built on all four sides.[26] This section, known as the *Quadrat d'Or* ('the Golden District'), soon developed from a simple start to the most fashionable region of Barcelona.[27] On ground outside the Avinguda de la Diagonal which Cerdá had allocated as a hippodrome, building had begun on the *Sagrada Família*. In more peripheral areas of the Cerdá grid, on the other hand, exploitation had not yet started. Expansion eastwards was hampered by railways; moreover quite a lot of the building development took place in the suburbs outside the plan.[28] After the revolution of 1868, the municipality acquired the *Ciutadella* land, an area Cerdá had envisaged as being divided into blocks but which was now designed as a park and used for the 1888 World Fair. In connection with this exhibition investments were made in the embellishment of the city with splendid prospects and visual markers. Most important of these was the Columbus monument which was the focal point of the Rambla and the Passeig de Colom, the second of which was not conceived in Cerdá's plan.[29]

Towards the end of the nineteenth century regional problems began to make themselves felt. The surrounding villages were more or less fully urbanized and were successively incorporated. In 1903 a town plan competition was organized, with a view among other things to improving communications between the *ensanche* and the surrounding building agglomerations.[30] The reference map for the competition shows that large parts of the area planned by Cerdá were still unbuilt,[31] but the plan was still being followed, at least as regards streets and blocks, right up to the 1930s, and remained formally in force until 1953. It is also possible to describe the recently completed development of the eastern shore area – the Olympic village and, in particular, some of the new blocks next to it – as basically in accordance with Cerdá's conception. And finally the large central square, the Plaça de les Glòries Catalanes, seems to be acquiring, albeit in an altogether different shape, some of the importance envisaged by Cerdá with the erection of an auditorium and a new national theatre.

As regards the old town, Cerdá proposed three streets to cut through it, opening up communications between the town centre and the *ensanche*, namely the present Via Laietana, a corresponding street on the western side as an extension of the present Carrer de Muntaner and, at right angles to these streets, another one on the same site and with the same orientation as the present Avinguda de la Catedral. In 1889 a plan was approved for the town centre. It was drawn up by Àngel Josep Baixeras and was largely based on Cerdá's project.[32] However, there was powerful opposition from the landowners, and the Via Laietana was not started until 1908.[33] The parallel street on the western side was never realized, and the cross-connection remained a fragment, consisting only of the Avinguda de la Catedral and Avinguda de Francesc Cambó. A contributory factor here seems to have been a growing recognition of the cultural and historical values which would be lost if this street systematization went through.

The differences between Cerdá's vision of the *ensanche* and the urban structure as it has actually evolved, have often been pointed out. But in fact what is more remarkable is the extent to which the plan has been followed when it comes to the street network and the division into blocks. In none of the other towns studied in this book have the intentions of the original projects been so fully realised in this respect, creating a grid without parallel in Europe. To find parallels or prototypes it is necessary to turn to the Americas. 'Perhaps the engineer's greatest invention and success was to have made evident that a colonial model might serve for the new industrial metropolis, the new business city,' Frechilla points out.[34] It is also evident from Cerdá's commentary reports that Spanish-American towns from different periods have provided models and prototypes, and among them Buenos Aires in particular.[35]

Various publications on Cerdá over the last few decades have sought to see in him the predecessor of later planning ideologies. In his scientific approach to planning and in his partiality for uniformity and green areas Cerdá obviously foreshadowed functionalism,[36] but his housing ideals are closer to the garden city concept than to the high-rise visions of Le Corbusier and Gropius, and his concept of an egalitarian city is the opposite of the separation of functions prescribed by the CIAM-architects. And Cerdá was to a great extent a child of his times: in his optimism, in his analytical approach to problems, and in his confidence in technology he was a typical nineteenth-century man. To this can be added his inexhaustible energy, his capacity for work, and his conviction that he was in the right.[37] Outside Spain Cerdá does not seem to have been the subject of study until quite recently, and he has exerted hardly any influence on developments in the rest of Europe. Nonetheless it certainly seems justified to see in him one of the outstanding figures of modern town planning.

NOTES

1. Over the last twenty years or so a good deal has been written about Barcelona's nineteenth-century plan and its originator, Ildefonso Cerdá. Of the projects dealt with in this book, it has thus become one of the two – the other is Paris – to attract the most attention. However, it has mainly been a question of articles or relatively short pieces; a fundamental and authoritative survey of the conditions of the Barcelona plan and its genesis and implementation is, surprisingly, still lacking. The liveliness of Cerdá research over the last decade was triggered by the facsimile publication of his main work, *Teoría general de la urbanización y aplicación de sus principios y doctrinas á la reforma y ensanche de Barcelona*, which was published in 1968, thus

missing the centenary of its original publication in 1867 by one year. Of considerable importance, too, was the great Cerdá exhibition in 1976, and its catalogue *Ildefonso Cerdá (1815–1876), Catalogo de la exposición conmemorativa del centenario de su muerte.*

Perhaps we could speak of two waves of publications on Cerdá, a first one around 1980 with pioneering studies in the form of journal articles and simply printed books, and a second one during the early 1990s with lavish publications mirroring Cerdás transformation from an oddity of planning history to a Catalan cult personality. Let us begin with a look at the first period. Among journal issues devoted mainly to Cerdá can be mentioned *Cuadernos de arquitectura y urbanismo*, 100 and 101 (1974), and *2C – Construcción de la Ciudad*, 6–7 (1977). The 2C group of architects published an analysis of the Cerdá plan in *Lotus international*, No. 23 (1979), which devotes considerable attention to the design of the blocks and the way the buildings are grouped within the blocks, and to the theoretical background of the plan. The early works on Cerdá also include the collection of essays, Solá-Morales *et al.* (1978), which adopts an urban development and historical perspective, referring to other plans for city expansions, mostly in Spain but also elsewhere. The development of Cerdá's urban theories is discussed in Soria y Puig (1979), one of the main contributions to the Cerdá bibliography. *Ildefonso Cerdá, La théorie générale de l'urbanisation* (1979) is a selection from the *Teoría general de la urbanización* translated into French, with an introduction by Antonio Lopez de Aberasturi. Rodriguez-Lores (1980) seeks among other things to place Cerdá in a political and historical context.

To the second phase belong two collections of essays: *La formació de l'Eixample de Barcelona* (1990) and *Treballs sobre Cerdà i el seu Eixample a Barcelona* (with English translation), which deal with Cerdá and Barcelona from different aspects. An abundance of excellent nineteenth century photographs is presented in Garcia Espuche (1990). Furthermore, two large volumes of Cerdás own writings have been published: *Teoría de la construcción de las ciudades, Cerdà y Barcelona* (1991) and *Teoría de la viabilidad urbana, Cerdá y Madrid* (1991). The most recent publication is the exhibition catalogue, *Cerdà, Urbs i territori: una visió de futur*.

There are two publications of historical plans of Barcelona. The most comprehensive is *Atlas de Barcelona* (1972). Another collection of plans appears in Torres, Puig and Llobet (1985), covering the period 1750–1930.

Mention should also be made of Martorell Portas, Florensa Ferrer and Martorell Otzet (1970), a survey of planning development in Barcelona during the nineteenth and twentieth centuries which describes the background to Cerdás plan and its role in subsequent urban developments. The Cerdá plan is discussed in comparative Spanish context by Wynn (1984).

2. In the following pages the Castilian form *ensanche* will be used rather than the Catalan *eixample*, since Cerdá wrote in Castilian and the term *ensanche* is established internationally. Cerdá is written with an acute accent in Castilian and a grave accent in Catalan. Here I have adopted the Castilian form, which is the one used internationally; it was also the spelling used by Cerdá himself. Exceptions arc made for direct quotations and the titles of books or articles, which are given in the original version. Street names are given in Catalan in accordance with my stated principle of using as far as possible the forms in use locally in the early 1990s.

3. The historical survey is based in the first instance on Strauss (1974). See also *Vivienda y Urbanismo en España* (1982).

4. Almost all maps of Barcelona are shown with the north-east uppermost. The streets in the *ensanche*, which on the map appear to be orientated north-south and east-west, really run northwest-southeast and northeast-southwest. To avoid confusion the orientation of the map has been followed here, i.e. 'north' is used when 'north-west' would really be more accurate.

5. In the map by Mas i Vila reproduced on page 17 in Hernández-Cros, Mora and Pouplana (1973), we can see that the Carrer de Ferran has not yet been extended all the way to the Plaça Sant Jaume, but it is shown in its whole length in the maps made in connection with the discussions of urban development at the end of the 1850s.

6. See Martorell Portas, Florensa Ferrer and Martorell Otzet (1970), pp. 17 ff.

7. *Ibidem*, pp. 19 f.

8. A comparatively detailed account of Cerdá's career and situation in Barcelona around the middle of the nineteenth century can be found in Rodriguez-Lores (1980).

9. Cerdá's first proposal seems to have been widely known when it first appeared and was available for Carlos Maria de Castro in the *Ministerio de Fomento* (see pp. 151 f).

10. *Atlas de Barcelona*, p. 421. The approved plan was one of four versions produced by Garriga.

11. *Atlas de Barcelona*, Nos. 169 and 170. Both Rovira i Trias and Garriga i Roca are called *arquitecto municipal*. As several architects were apparently 'municipal architects' it is probable that this title should be regarded as a municipal 'authorization' rather than the designation of a post.

12. A survey of the developments in Soria y Puig (1992).

13. As a curious detail it can be mentioned that a canal was envisaged encircling both the new and old urban area. Similar ideas were still around in Budapest, as we shall see below, at an even later stage.

14. The competition brief is reproduced in Solá-Morales *et al.* (1978), pp. 48 ff.

15. *Atlas de Barcelona*, No. 171.

16. The commentary report *Ensanche de la ciudad de Barcelona, Memoria descriptiva de los trabajos facultativos y estudios estadísticos hechos de orden del gobierno y consideraciones que se han tenido presentes en la formación del anteproyecto para el emplazamiento y distribución del nuevo caserío* (1855) accompanied the first version of the Barcelona plan, while the *Teoría de la construcción de las ciudades aplicada al proyecto de reforma y ensanche de Barcelona* (1859) accompanied the second. Cerdá's other major reports include the *Teoría del enlace del movimiento de las vías marítimas y terrestres, con aplicación al puerto de Barcelona* (1863) and *Teoría de la viabilidad urbana y reforma de la de Madrid* (1861). This material was never printed during Cerdá's lifetime, but has been rediscovered in the course of research in the last few decades. It has now been published in the two volumes, *Teoriá de la construcción de las ciudades, Cerdà y Barcelona* (1991) and *Teoriá de la viabilidad urbana, Cerdá y Madrid* (1991), which represent

a virtually complete publication of Cerdá's written works. As has been noted above (note 9), the main content of Cerdá's memoranda were presumably familiar in professional circles. But Cerdá also published several papers in the engineering journal *Revista de Obras Publicas*.

17. The evolution of Cerdás theories is discussed in Puig (1990).

18. The following presentation is based mainly on *Lotus international*, No. 23.

19. As an analysis in *Lotus international*, No. 23 (pp. 85 f) shows, it is possible to read into the Barcelona plan a complicated geometrical pattern. However, there seems to be no support for this construction in Cerdá's writings.

20. Cf. *Lotus international*, No. 23, p. 83, Fig. 7.

The analysis of Cerdá's intentions is complicated by the fact that there are several variants showing the same block and street networks, but with considerable differences when it comes to the buildings in the block (three variants are reproduced in Solá-Morales *et al.* (1978), pp. 39–41). The plan reproduced above, which is the one that was approved by the government in 1859 and subsequently published, can be regarded as the main proposal.

21. The other main streets, too, such as Avinguda del Parallel, Avinguda de Roma, Passeig de Sant Joan and Carrer d'Aragó, were laid down mainly in accordance with Cerdá's intentions. This also goes for *las rondas*, the ring road round the old town, although there was a proposal for a very much broader boulevard (see Martorell Portas, Florensa Ferrer and Martorell Otzet (1970), pp. 38 ff).

22. This is emphasized by Espuche, Guardia, Monclús and Oyón (1991): 'the lack of effective legal, technical and operational mechanisms, tensions between the municipal and central governments, and the angry resistance of the private interests affected, hindered the development process' (p. 142). The building trade, as elsewhere, was subject to severe fluctuations with slumps and peaks (pp. 142 f).

23. *Atlas de Barcelona*, p. 473.

24. *Ibidem*, No. 185.

25. *Ibidem*, No. 186.

26. *Ibidem*, No. 227.

27. See Espuche (1990). The development of the

ensanche up to 1890 is possible to follow in a series of maps published in this work.

28. Fco Javier Monclús and Luis Oyón (1990) stress that the suburbanization of the neighbouring villages for residential and industrial use was a process parallel to the development of the *ensanche*, thus establishing a radial and concentric development along the railways contrary to Cerdás intentions.

29. Espuche, Guardia, Monclús and Oyón (1991).

30. The competition was won by Léon Jaussely (cf. *Atlas de Barcelona*, No. 245).

31. *Atlas de Barcelona*, No. 242.

32. *Ibidem*, No. 225.

33. Cf. *ibidem*, Nos. 255 and 257.

34. Frechilla (1992), p. 357.

35. In *Teoría de la construcción de las ciudades aplicada al proyecto de reforma y ensanche de Barcelona* (1859) Cerdá writes: 'The city of Buenos Aires is built on the quadrangular system. The direction of its streets is perpendicular or parallel to the Plate River forming a system of equal, perfectly square blocks with sides of 116 metres. The buildings generally stand between gardens; their depth is some 20 m, the width of the streets being the same. Each administrative quarter has 16 blocks; each law court, each police section, each parish has three quarters.' And further: '. . . the Spanish captains who conquered a New World for this monarchy, founded their beautiful cities under a plan so rational and philosophical, that they may serve and in fact have served as models' (quoted from Frechilla (1992), p. 360).

36. In the master plan for Barcelona, known as the *Plan Maciá* which was made at the beginning of the 1930s by the G.A.T.C.P.A.C. (*Grup d'Arquitectes i Técnics Catalans per al Progrés de l'Arquitectura Contemporània*) group of architects together with Le Corbusier, reference was once again made – significantly – to Cerdá (cf. Martorell Portas, Florensa Ferrer and Martorell Otzet (1970), pp. 103 ff and *Ildefonso Cerdá, Catalogo de la Exposición conmemorativa*, p. 119).

37. A list of Cerdá's many publications, compiled by Arturo Soria y Puig, is to be found in [Cerdá] (1991), *Teoría de la construcción de las cuidades*.

9

MADRID

In the Middle Ages Madrid[1] was a town of secondary importance, which had grown up round an originally Moorish Alcázar on the site of the present palace.[2] Its transformation from a provincial town to a capital city began in 1561, when Philip II moved his court from Toledo to Madrid. This seems to have been regarded as a temporary arrangement at the time, but apart from a short period around 1600 Madrid was to remain the royal residence from then on. The development of the capital city functions led to rapid growth; during Philip II's reign (1556–98) alone the population of the town trebled. The early decades of the seventeenth century saw a major urban development project in the construction of the Plaza Mayor (cf. pp. 21 f), which gave the town a location for trade and for the staging of important events (figure 2.11). The medieval town wall surrounded a fairly small area around Plaza de la Villa. During the 1620s a new wall was built, but the main motivation behind this was fiscal.

There can have been very little splendour about Madrid during the seventeenth and early eighteenth centuries apart from a few fairly grand buildings; most houses were low and simple, and the streets were poor. The court had access to more pleasant surroundings at the out-of-town palace, Buen Retiro, east of Madrid and at other residences elsewhere, such as the Escorial. It was not until the eighteenth century, after Spain's period as a Great Power had come to an end, that the idea of transforming Madrid into a worthy capital city was seriously launched. In 1734 the old

palace burnt down, which provided an opportunity to begin planning a new palace complex similar to those in Paris, Berlin and Stockholm. During the reign of Charles III (1759–1788) a great many new buildings, among them the Prado, were erected. At the same time some effort was being made to improve the standard of the street network, the water supply and so on. Another important development was the construction of a promenade, the Paseo del Prado, which lies between the town and the Retiro Park and provides the start of Madrid's present north-south axis, Paseo de la Castellana.

During the first half of the nineteenth century little seems to have been done to improve the physical environment of Madrid, despite a continually growing population.[3] The unstable political conditions may have been one reason for this, and the insignificant level of industrial development another. Furthermore, large areas were released for building within the old urban structure as a result of the secularization of church property in 1835, so that the need to extend the town did not seem so immediately acute. In 1846, however, a company called *La Urbana* had been established for such a purpose and it had also presented a proposal for the expansion of the city. This was rejected by the town authorities, however, as being unnecessary and unrealistic. The authorities were more interested in a plan for the existing town.[4] However, no such plan was produced, and the opportunity to use the land released by the secularization process for making improvements in the planning of the town was wasted, just as it was in Paris after the Revolution.

Ten years later the question of the extension of the city came up again, perhaps because it was recognized that any scheme for improving the existing town would be too difficult to realize. The uninterrupted growth in the population and the need for space for public buildings were other important factors. There was also a desire to prevent unplanned urban sprawl. Following a recommendation by Claudio Moyano, the minister of development *(Ministro de Fomento)*, a committee under Carlos de Castro was appointed in 1857. Castro was an engineer in the public service and had previously been involved in the construction of the first railway line out of Madrid (to Aranjuez). He had also been given various assignments connected with the capital city during the 1850s.[5] The committee seems to have been a working group rather than a steering body.[6] Certain rather general guidelines for its work were laid down by royal decree, stressing issues of hygiene and the importance of creating a capital worthy of the Spanish monarchy.[7] Castro started by measuring and levelling the area of the plan, and as early as August the following year a decision was reached on one section of the northern area of the *ensanche* (figure 9.1). In 1859 the proposal as a whole was complete, together with a detailed report, the *Memoria descriptiva del ante-proyecto de Ensanche de Madrid* or descriptive memorandum for the preparatory planning of the area for the extension of Madrid (figure 9.2). In May 1860 Castro was requested by the Public Works Office *(Dirección General de Obras Públicas)* to revise the northern section of his proposal.[8] The final plan and memorandum[9] were published later the same year, having been ratified by the government in July, apparently without much discussion or the introduction of any further major changes (figure 9.3).[10] But the proposal had already been approved by

Madrid's municipal executive board and county council (the *Ayuntamiento y Diputación provincial de Madrid*), by the responsible ministries, and by the advisory committee for roads, canals and harbours (the *Junta consultativa de Caminos, Canales y Puertos*).[11]

In the published lithograph the ratified plan – modestly referred to as the *ante-proyecto*, thus emphasizing that it was to be regarded as a draft version which was to be further developed – appears somewhat unstructured, at least at a first glance. The old town has been surrounded on three sides by large areas comprising new blocks and embraced by a ring boulevard, whose perimeter forms a polygon with Puerta del Sol approximately at its centre. As far as possible the blocks have been given a uniform design, either rectangular or square. Two types of street dominate, one narrower variant with no trees and another broader version planted with trees. The narrower type, referred to in the report as 'streets of the third order', were to be 15 metres wide, while the tree-lined version, designated 'streets of the second order', were to be 20 metres. Every second, third or, in a few cases, fourth street is of the broader kind. A third type of street, 'streets of the first order', are also mentioned in the memorandum: these were to be 30 metres wide with double rows of trees along the pavements. In fact only the ring boulevard belongs to this type.[12] There are no broad monumental streets which could have provided communicating links between the different parts of the town, except for the existing extension of Paseo del Prado which has been retained with three rows of trees on one side and four on the other. This artery, Paseo de la Castellana, was to terminate rather disappointingly in the north in a large area of parkland instead of being extended to the ring road.[13] Another big park, which was also to boast a lake, a hippodrome and a bullring, was planned east of the Retiro Park as a kind of enlargement of the palace grounds; in this way the extension, or the *ensanche*, was to be

Figure 9.1 *Madrid. Project by Carlos Maria de Castro for the northern area of the planned extension, 1858. [From Frechilla (1992)]*

divided into two parts. Several smaller parks were dotted about the town. There were no great monumental squares, but proposals were made for several smaller *plazas*, often created by cutting off the corners of the blocks, either in a straight line or on a curve. Public buildings have been marked in several places, often occupying one or more blocks.

In the original version of Castro's plan a number of existing roads were retained, cutting diagonally across the new grid, particularly to the north of the old urban area where the proposal obviously tallied with the partial project approved in 1858 (figure 9.1).[14] But according to the revised plan agreed upon in July 1860 these diagonal streets were not to be kept. One of the main theses in Javier Frechilla's argument is that – inspired by the French architectural theorist Léonce Reynaud's *Traité d'architecture* – Castro had wanted from the start to create a system of radiating roads, mainly to enhance the imposing character of

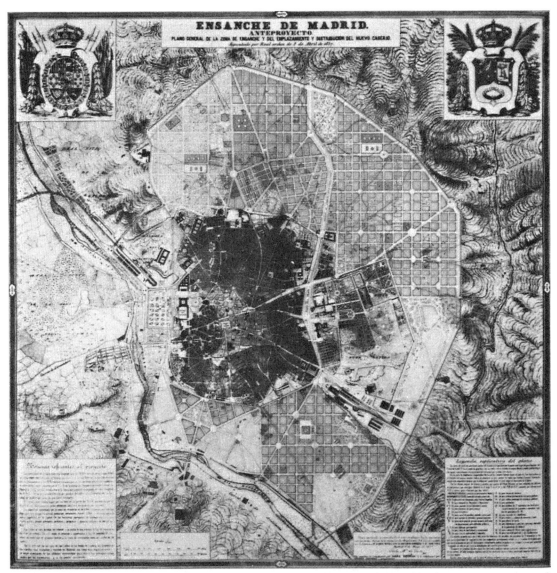

Figure 9.2 *Madrid. The preliminary version of Castro's master plan for the new extension of Madrid as reconstructed by Javier Frechilla. [From Frechilla (1992)]*

the city. This is certainly an attractive idea: in the nineteenth century broad, radial streets seem to have been regarded as particularly appropriate to capital cities – or at any rate to large cities in general. But there is one obvious objection to Javier Frechilla's interpretation, namely that Castro's diagonal roads consisted of streets that were already there, and they can thus be explained equally well as an adaptation to existing conditions as the expression of an intentional element in the plan.

No changes are proposed in the existing

Figure 9.3 *Madrid. Final proposal for a master plan, executed under the guidance of Carlos Maria de Castro, 1859. [From* Cartografía básica de la Ciudad de Madrid]

urban structure in either version. However, the square Puerta del Sol has the same shape on the plan that it would acquire as the result of a renewal scheme decided upon at the same time.[15] As part of this scheme the Calle de Preciados was continued northwards to the Plaza del Callao, forming a symmetrical complement to the much older Calle de la Montera. As early as 1862 it was decided that the Calle de Preciados should be extended to what is today the Plaze de España. This extension was not realized immediately, but later became

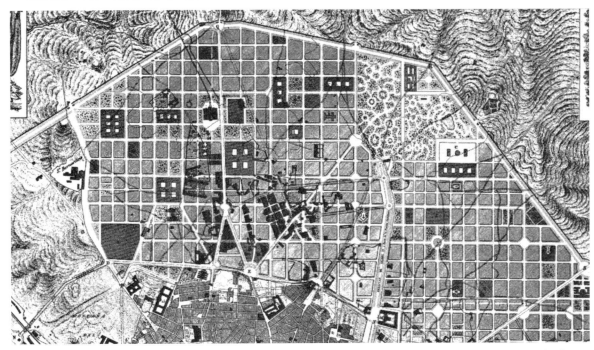

Figure 9.4 *Detail of figure 9.3, showing the northern section of Castro's master plan for Madrid.*

part of a larger project, namely the Gran Via. Due to problems with the financing and the necessary expropriations, it was some time before this more radical construction could be undertaken. It was begun in a westward direction from Calle de Alcalá in 1910 and was not completely finished until the 1940s. The street was envisaged as a communicating link between the new districts to the east and west of the old urban core.[16] But this thoroughfare, which in both character and architecture recalls the roughly contemporary Kungsgatan in Stockholm, had nothing to do with Castro's plan.

A weakness of Castro's plan as well as of several of the other projects discussed in this book, is that the communications between the existing parts of the town and those being planned, were not satisfactorily organized, even though we can see from the memorandum that Castro was aware of the problem.[17] But it would have involved extensive alterations of the existing urban structure, which would have meant in turn that Castro was overstepping the terms of reference he had been given. Even communications between the different parts within the new urban area do not seem to have been solved particularly well.

But perhaps Castro did not after all consider rapid communications between the different parts of the town to be an urgent matter. Here, more consciously than in other places, social and functional segmentation was sought: functional zoning was to be combined with residential segregation. In fact this was one of the main goals of Castro's plan. The planned area was to be divided into a number of districts, all intended for particular social groups or functions. Chamberi, the district north of the old town, was intended as a factory and industrial zone. It was an area which had already been partly developed, evidently with fairly simple buildings, and it was now to provide the location for extensive complexes such as military barracks and depots, a slaughterhouse, market-halls, prisons etc. But there were also to be a fair number of parks.

Immediately to the west of Paseo de la Castellana another zone was envisaged for the aristocracy, complete with villas and gardens, and suitably close to this great fashionable promenade. The social status of this district is enhanced by a series of squares along the street running parallel to Paseo de la Castellana. Salamanca, the area between this street and the present Calle de Alcalá, was planned as a residential district for the bourgeoisie. Here we find several squares and parks, a theatre and concert hall complex and a grammar school. The area south of Calle de Alcalá and east of the Retiro Park was to be a working-class district. Reading between the lines of Castro's memorandum, it is obvious that the peripheral location of this district was seen as an advantage. There are several parks in the centre of the district and three semi-circular open places on each side of it. There are no large public buildings apart from a church and, in one corner of the area, a hospital and a gaol 'for prisoners in custody or in transit' – evidently as an admonitory reminder to the local inhabitants. South of the working class district is the park area mentioned above, and beyond that a railway station that was already in existence (the present Estación de Atocha). South of the Retiro Park and the old town there is a district intended for commercial functions such as warehouses, offices, factories, hotels etc. This district has been designed along simpler lines, with few open squares. The area to the southwest, according to Castro, was not suitable for building on account of the awkward terrain. Here he suggested orchards and vegetable patches.[18]

When it comes to the streets and blocks, the different areas have been designed in much the same way. Squares and parks are also distrib-uted fairly evenly throughout the town, except that there are few squares in the district south of the Retiro Park and none at all in Chamberi, both areas intended mainly for non-residential use. On the other hand the distribution of the public buildings has been guided by the intended zoning, although a reading of the map alone would hardly tell us this. It should also be noted that barracks and other military buildings have been scattered throughout the new urban area; it looks as though the idea was to be able to muster the troops quickly to suppress possible riots. All districts, except those intended as residential areas for the refined classes, also have their own jail.

The systematic zoning of the urban area seems to have been Castro's own idea; nothing is said about it in the planning directives.[19] Nor does Castro offer any detailed explanation in his memorandum; evidently he regarded such zoning as too natural to call for any special motivation. Several factors may have contrib-uted to this situation: Spain was still a highly class-based society, the social structure of Madrid was antiquated and rigidly conven-tional, and Castro personally was of a conserv-ative cast of mind. This would mean that he saw the working class as a potential threat to the established order, a threat which could be reduced by concentrating the relevant groups to a single district in the town. But his systematic zoning could also be seen as an expression of the nineteenth century's search for rational and ordered solutions.

Castro's ideas about the design of the blocks are given in the memorandum and two illustra-tions attached to it. Different patterns are indicated for the arrangement of the buildings. According to one variant, the block would be 'closed' towards the streets in the traditional way, with continuous house façades; the houses themselves would be grouped round a large inner courtyard, a model anticipating the *Großhof* model common in many European cities in the 1920s. Another version was based on a freer design, with buildings and forecourts facing onto the street alternately (see figure 9.5).[20]

It is interesting to compare Castro's plan for Madrid with Cerdá's for Barcelona, which was commissioned slightly later than Castro's. Both were finally approved the same year, however, namely in 1860. But it is worth noting that Cerdá had presented, and even published preparatory studies for his Barcelona plan and that Castro expressly refers to these as a model.[21] Castro had much the same background as Cerdá: both were architects and engineers, and their professional experience was similar. Castro did not share Cerdá's politically progressive stance, however; on the contrary, he exhibited, as we have seen, a more conservative attitude.

The relation between Castro's project for Madrid and Cerdá's for Barcelona is a complicated one, studied most recently by Frechilla. Thus, when Castro refers to the Barcelona plan, he is thinking not of the final version but of the preliminary 1855 project (see p. 128) which was available in Madrid. To enhance the

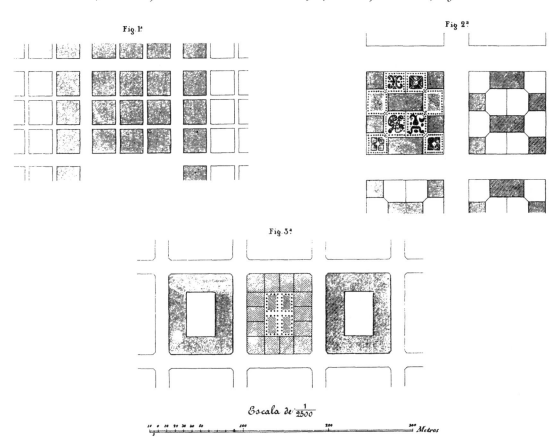

Figure 9.5 *Madrid. Proposal for the design of the blocks in Castro's project. [From* Plan Castro*]*

status of his own project, according to Frechilla, he borrowed not specific local solutions or the overall planning conception but a good deal of the technical explanations and other general background comments presented in Cerdá's memorandum.[22] But even the final version of Cerdá's Barcelona plan seems to have had some influence on the fate of Castro's proposal. It may have been the reason why Castro was asked in 1860 to revise his project in the northern section and to replace the diagonal avenues by an orthogonal grid (see pp. 145 ff). Or, in the words of the directives, to see that 'the direction of the streets and the surface area of the blocks be in harmony with those of the rest of the extension'. At the time when these directives were being issued, Cerdá's plan was also just being dealt with; it was ratified nine days later. So it is perfectly possible, even probable, that the two projects were compared and it was felt that Cerdá's consistent grid was more appropriate.[23]

The two final plans – Cerdá's for Barcelona and Castro's for Madrid – have one common feature apart from their grid networks: both lack the aesthetic architectural ambition that characterized, for example, Rovira i Trias's plan for Barcelona. Otherwise the differences are more striking than the similarities, and it is difficult to identify any concrete features which Castro could be said to have derived from Cerdá.[24] Cerdá's project reveals a magnificent conception; it is consistent and based on a particular planning theory. Castro's plan does not have the same coherent character – even though he obviously understood it was a central part of his job to give a certain dignity to the townscape[25] – and apart from its social zoning seems to be a rather *ad hoc* affair. One of Cerdá's main goals seems to have been to avoid just this kind of segmentation; his aim was that all parts of the town should be assigned equal value and given a similar design – in other words his approach was the opposite of Castro's. Moreover, Barcelona is an 'open' town; the idea was that it should be possible to

add new districts to those currently planned. The Madrid plan, due to its enclosing boulevard, creates the impression of a town turned in on itself. But this was not Castro's idea. On the contrary, in his memorandum he criticized this aspect of his own plan, and claimed that the government's directives had compelled him to adopt this solution. For fiscal reasons the authorities wanted clear and distinct town boundaries and a limited number of approach roads where entry tolls could be taken up.[26]

The differences between the Barcelona and Madrid projects stem from the different attitudes of the authors of the plans, and on the different conditions surrounding them. Cerdá was something of a Utopian visionary, while Castro – to quote Correa – was 'a pragmatic technician, a conformist bureaucrat.'[27] Barcelona was a growing commercial and industrial town, and its topography was favourable to building. Madrid, on the other hand, was a centre of administration with an old-fashioned social structure and more difficult topographical conditions. Furthermore, the Retiro Park and other existing structures obstructed certain developments.[28]

One may well wonder why Cerdá was not asked to produce a plan for Madrid. His interest in urban building was well known, and his reputation in the professional community was high. Moreover he appears to have enjoyed the confidence of the government. But it may have been felt that he was already fully occupied with Barcelona. And maybe Castro was thought to have closer links with Madrid. Perhaps, too, some may have felt that radical ideas could more suitably be tried out elsewhere, rather than in the capital city. But Cerdá expressed great interest in the planning of Madrid, and in February 1860 he obtained royal permission to study the planning problems in the old urban area of the capital. His main ambition seems to have been to improve communications, both within the central area and between this and the *ensanche*. Extensive documentation, consisting of memoranda and drawings, has recently been discovered. One of Cerdá's suggestions was to cover the whole existing urban area with a grid of square blocks, deviating 45° from the north-south axis (figure 9.6). In this radical and ruthless approach Cerdá anticipates Le Corbusier. Another more realistic suggestion embraced a number of street improvement schemes, including a street that closely followed the later extent of the Gran Via (see pp. 148 f).[29] Whether there is any direct connection here must remain an open question.[30]

Castro's plan was thus ratified in 1860, but little more than a start seems to have been made on its implementation during the 1860s. The idea seems to have spread around that it was unrealistic. In the municipal archives (Archivo Histórico de la Villa) there is a simplified variant of the plan, which was probably made at the beginning of the 1860s. This version deviates from the published proposal, among other things in that the public buildings have not been indicated, there are fewer parks, and the ring boulevard follows a slightly different course.[31] After the revolution of 1868 Castro was dismissed from his position as *director del ensanche*,[32] and a new plan was made by Angel Fernandez de los Rios. This,

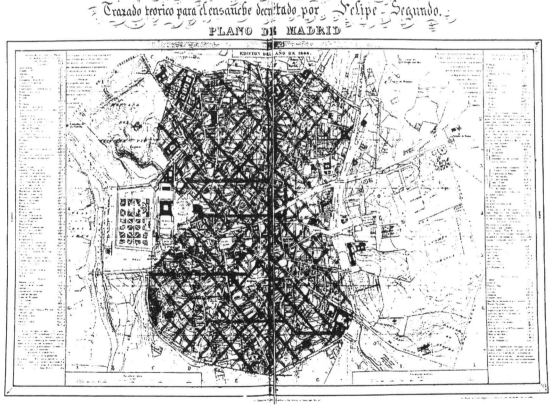

Figure 9.6 *Madrid. Ildefonso Cerdá's proposal for a radical redevelopment of the old city area.* *[From Frechilla (1992)]*

according to Correa, meant 'a conception and
a scheme that were quite different from Castro's
project, if not its exact opposite.'[33] During the
revolution the toll wall from the seventeenth
century began to be demolished. After the
restoration of 1869, Castro's plan was taken up
again. But in the course of its implementation,
about which little has been written so far, many
far-reaching concessions were made to various
interests, particularly those of the property
owners and developers.[34] A particular important role during the 1850s and 1860s was played
by the Marques de Salamanca, a banker and
landowner. As Correa puts it, the plan was
distorted and ultimately destroyed by the
constantly growing speculation in real estate.[35]

To what extent has Castro's project affected
the actual shape of the town plan? Exploitation
was much more ruthless than Castro had
envisaged, with the result that there are far
fewer parks and squares. Nor, with a few
exceptions, are the public buildings located
according to Castro's proposals. The ring
boulevard, on the other hand, was partly built
according to the intentions of the plan. Paseo
de la Castellana and the residential areas north
and east of the Retiro Park have also been
influenced by Castro's plan, at least as regards
the basic structure of the street network and
the block divisions. However, the open areas
in the blocks were smaller than intended,
although in two of the earliest blocks we can
still see large interior courtyards designed in
accordance with Castro's ideas.[36] North of the
old town there are only very general similarities
between the plan proposal and its implementation, and to the south the deviations from the
plan are even more evident. On the north side,
and to some extent on the south, existing roads
and tree-lined alleys were retained as streets,
contrary to the ratified version of Castro's plan
but apparently in agreement with the first
version. The orientation of the district north of
Calle de Sagasta deviates from the plan for this
reason, and to the south two eighteenth-
century alleys were retained as main roads and

diagonal streets. Also retained were some
existing round *plazas* such as the present
Glorieta Santa Maria de la Cabeza. To the
south-west – south of the present Ronda de
Toledo – a park-like area with round open
places and tree-lined alleys was planned. This
was largely realized, except that the area was
more intensively developed than Castro had
intended. Thus, all in all, we can say that the
version of Castro's plan that was published,
and which had been ratified by the authorities,
made only a limited impact.

However, things look slightly different if we
turn instead to the plan in the Archivo Histórico,
which is seemingly a revised version of the
published edition.[37] Here several adjustments
have been made to the existing street networks, while at the same time the majority of
the parks and public buildings have been
removed. This variant of the plan agrees much
better with the actual outcome, but even here
there are a number of deviations. In comparison
with the situation in Barcelona, where the
street pattern suggested in Cerdá's plan was
followed with great consistency, these are in
fact considerable. Powerful libertarian values
combined with the absence of effective instruments of control and an ambition to hasten the
initially slow development of the *ensanche*,
may have been the principal reasons why the
developers found it easy to get their demands
accepted. At the same time no attempt seems
to have been made to acquire an overall view
of the urban structure with the help of a new
plan.[38]

The social zoning outlined by Castro seems,
at least in part, to agree with the structure
which was to evolve in the *ensanche*, and which
still characterizes the area today.[39] Does this
mean that the plan did steer developments, or
that Castro foresaw what direction developments would take? The answer is probably a
bit of both. The location of the working class
and middle class districts can probably be seen
at least partly as an effect of the planning
activities. But in other instances Castro was

simply promoting a development that was already under way, for instance in the case of the Chamberi district and the upper-class area east of Paseo de la Castellana.

At the beginning of the twentieth century the outermost parts of the *ensanche* were still undeveloped, but beyond the town boundary a number of working-class areas had grown up. One of the main points in Castro's brief had been to create a closed city with few exit roads. This goal was partly fulfilled, with the result that communications between the town and the growing suburbs were inadequate. In 1910 P. Nuñez Granés presented a new plan, which aimed among other things to rectify this.[40] In the early decades of the twentieth century a major street improvement project was carried out in the central area, namely the construction of the Gran Via. As we have seen, this had been under discussion ever since the 1860s and it remained in essence a typical nineteenth-century project.

NOTES

1. For a long time little attention was paid even by Spanish scholars to nineteenth-century urban planning in Madrid. Only recently have works on this subject been published. The first scholarly study was the *Plan Castro*, which reproduces Castro's plan and the accompanying memorandum, together with a 'preliminary' introduction by Antonio Bonet Correa. Mention can also be made of two journal articles, namely Ferrán and Frechilla Camoiras (1980) and Pérez-Pita (1980). Madrid's urban development can be followed in the lavishly produced atlas *Cartografía básica de la Ciudad de Madrid*. In 1990 a voluminous doctoral thesis was presented at ETSAM in Madrid by Javier Frechilla Camoiras, on the evolution of the *ensanche*, *La construcción del Ensanche de Madrid*. It is based on extremely comprehensive archival researches, and on many important counts should change the earlier ideas about Castro's contribution to nineteenth-century planning in Madrid. Unfortunately it has not yet been published and only a few copies exist. A sort

of summary of the thesis has appeared in *Treballs sobre Cerdà i el seu Exiample a Barcelona* (Frechilla, 1992), but the argument is so compressed that it is difficult to follow it in detail. Publication of Frechilla's work, preferably in English, is much to be desired. I have had to content myself here with intimating his new interpretations of a few points only.

2. Madrid's early development can be traced in the maps in *Cartografía básica de la Ciudad de Madrid*.

3. During the reign of Joseph Bonaparte, however, some schemes were executed, in particular the creation of the Plaza de Oriente (see *Guía de arquitectura y urbanismo de Madrid*, 1982, pp. 37 ff).

4. *Plan Castro*, p. XXII.

5. Cf. the biographical chronology in *Plan Castro*, pp. LVI f. In 1854 Castro became responsible for paving operations in Madrid. On this subject he also published a work in 1857: *Apuntes acerca de los empedrados de Madrid* (Notes on paving operations in Madrid). Furthermore since 1854 Castro was head of the planning archives at the Ministry of Development (the *depósito de planos del Ministerio de Fomento*). Thus the choice of Castro to be responsible for the planning operations was probably a fairly natural one.

6. Most of the names listed on p. 16 in *Plan Castro* seem to be assistants of various kinds.

7. *Plan Castro*, pp. 5 ff and Frechilla (1992), pp. 354 and 357, note 3.

8. See Frechilla (1992).

9. Twenty-four large-scale district plans also form part of this project, but they appear to have been lost (Ferrán and Frechilla Camoiras, 1980).

10. The complicated story of the plan's genesis has been examined in Frechilla (1992), and much more fully in the same author's unpublished doctoral thesis (1992, p. 169). According to Frechilla certain passages in the printed memorandum refer to the first version of the plan. Thus we have here a situation recalling that in Athens, where Schaubert and Kleanthes's memorandum has proved to refer to a preliminary study for the final plan.

11. *Plan Castro*, p. 178.

12. Cf. the sections on Lám.ª 3ª (Plate 3) in *Plan Castro*.

13. In the original proposal, according to

Frechilla's reconstruction (see Frechilla (1992), p. 169), it led on to the ring road.

14. Frechilla (1992), particularly the reconstruction on p. 169.

15. According to Correa, Castro planned the new buildings on the north side of this square, thus contributing to the creation of what is still regarded as the true centre of Madrid (*Plan Castro*, pp. VIII and XII ff and the figures on the unnumbered pages following LXV). This statement does not appear in any other source, however, and in the *Guía de arquitectura y urbanismo de Madrid* (1982) the buildings in question are assigned to other authors. The same applies to Sambricio (1988), who does not connect Castro's name with the planning of Puerta del Sol or its surrounding buildings either.

16. *Guía de arquitectura y urbanismo de Madrid* (1982), pp. 59 ff.

17. *Ibidem*, pp. 115 f; cf. also pp. 136 f.

18. Castro's own description can be found in *Plan Castro*, pp. 104 ff; cf. also Correas' comments, *Plan Castro*, pp. XXVI ff. and Pérez-Pita (1980), p. 26.

19. To some extent the zoning proposed by Castro coincided with existing and established conditions. Thus, for example, there were already some factories in Chamberi. Frechilla suggests that the idea of social zoning may have been inspired by Léonce Reynaud's *Traité d'architecture* (Frechilla (1992), p. 161).

20. For the design of the block, see *Plan Castro*, pp. 161 ff; cf. pp. XXXIII f.

21. 'To our good fortune the work has been going on for some time in the Ministry for Development, similar to the task we have been commissioned to do. It refers to the building of a new area in Barcelona, and it is so completely and meticulously executed, it is in such a well arranged state and so full of valuable details, that we have not hesitated for a moment to choose it and to follow it step by step in those respects that are possible to realize in the locations where they are to be.' (Quoted from *Plan Castro*, p. 93).

22. According to Frechilla, Castro 'confined himself to using the index of the analytical part of the Cerdá document in order to establish, *a posteriori*, the justification for his project, adapting each section to the case of Madrid, even copying most of the statistical data – errors

included – furnished by Cerdà' (Frechilla (1992), p. 355).

23. Frechilla (1992), p. 356.

24. One might feel that Correa overemphasizes Cerdá's importance with regard to the Madrid plan, for example in the following statement: 'Without Cerdá, Castro's preparatory plan would have been different, and would at any rate have lacked the inner coherence, the consistent and regular shape of the blocks and the extensive open green areas . . .' (*Plan Castro*, p. XXX). Green zones and open spaces were among the standard elements in contemporary planning as were rectangular grids; however, Castro may have been influenced by Cerdá as regards the design of the blocks.

25. This is one of the main theses in Frechilla (1992). See for instance pp. 356 and 357, note 3.

26. *Plan Castro*, pp. 13 and 96 'We would be prepared to abstain from this and to let the town be entirely open . . . Nevertheless we are compelled to follow the express content of the royal decree.' Cf. also Ferrán and Frechilla Camoiras (1980), p. 6.

27. *Plan Castro*, p. VII. Cf. also *ibidem*, p. XV: 'His intervention was made by virtue of his position as Chief Engineer, and his task was to design a plan for the new built area, with a view to glorifying, honouring and modernizing an old and shabby town, the residence and capital of a monarchy also recently revived.'

28. See further Correa's presentation, in which one section is devoted to a comparison of planning in Madrid and Barcelona (*Plan Castro*, pp. XXXIV ff).

29. See Frechilla (1992). The project is reproduced by Frechilla on page 171.

30. Cerdá's attempt to intervene in the planning of Madrid is discussed in *Plan Castro*, pp. XXX ff by Correa, who does not consider that Cerdá's intervention had any very great practical importance. In 1862, however, the municipal administration appears to have had far-advanced plans to make Cerdá leader of the expansion project, an idea which according to Correa was presumably prevented by the provincial government (p. XXXII).

31. The plan is reproduced in Ferrán and Frechilla Camoiras (1980), Fig. 2. Correa considers that this plan, which like the published version is

dated 1859, should be regarded as a preliminary version (*Plan Castro*, p. XXIV), while Ferrán and Frechilla Camoiras believe that it was not made until 1863, although they give no reason for their supposition. With respect to several of the points on which the two plans diverge, the variant in the *Archivo Histórico* comes closest to the plan as realized, for example as regards the course of the ring boulevard, the area north of Calle de Sagasta and the street network in the south. It should therefore be regarded as a reworking of the published plan, which means that the latter date is probably more credible.

32. *Plan Castro*, p. XXXVII. Castro appears to have had this commission as early as 1865 (cf. *ibidem*, p. LVIII).

33. *Plan Castro*, p. XXV.

34. *Ibidem*, p. XXXIV.

35. *Ibidem*, pp. XXXVI ff.

36. Cf. aerial photograph in the same number of *Arquitectura* (1980, No. 222) as Pérez-Pita (1980). The blocks are defined by Calle de Serrano and Calle de Claudio Coello, and by Calle de Villanueva and Calle de Goya.

37. See note 25.

38. The main features in the development can be seen in the maps in *Cartografía básica de la Ciudad de Madrid*.

39. Cf. Pérez-Pita (1980), p. 26: 'It is incredible how faithfully the guiding principles specified by *ingeniero* Castro have been maintained.'

40. Reproduced in *Cartografía básica de la Ciudad de Madrid*.

10

COPENHAGEN

In earlier times Copenhagen[1] developed along much the same lines as Berlin and Stockholm, with a medieval core to which new planned districts were added during the seventeenth and eighteenth centuries, with rectilinear street networks (figure 10.1).[2] But unlike Berlin and Stockholm, Copenhagen retained its defensive function into the nineteenth century. This meant not only that the town was enclosed by a system of defences, but also that the only buildings permitted in a broad area outside the ramparts were simple half-timbered houses. Nor were any suburbs of any size built beyond the demarcation line which defined the prohibited area, as in Vienna. As Rasmussen puts it: 'With a steadily growing population the only way the town could expand was by building higher and more densely, so that it became more and more overcrowded and cramped.'[3] During the first half of the nineteenth century, however, population growth was moderate; the number of inhabitants rose from a little over 100,000 in 1800 to about 120,000 in 1840. From then on, growth was more rapid; in 1870 the figure was 181,000 and at the beginning of the next century just under 360,000.[4]

In the 1840s land was granted beyond the ramparts for a pleasure-ground, the nucleus of Copenhagen's famous Tivoli. Apart from this the prohibition against building was maintained until 1852, when the demarcation line was moved in to the Søerne (the Lakes). The area that was thus released was already largely in private ownership, and following the repeal of the prohibition landowners were able to make

big profits. Over the next few decades speculative building led to a ring of suburbs (*Broerne*, literally the Bridges) beyond the Lakes.[5] An attempt at public control came too late; when a plan was finally approved in 1857, most of the streets were already in existence.[6] The web of streets between the old exit roads still has an unorganized look about it. There were no attempts at all at any monumental building. This unplanned exploitation came to consist mainly of industrial premises and worker's housing.

Towards the middle of the 1850s it became clear that even the area between the *Søerne* and the city proper should be released for building. The cholera epidemic of 1853, which reaped almost 5,000 victims within a period of four months,[7] demonstrated just how inappropriate to the times was the demand on the part of the military that the town should remain enclosed within its defensive earthworks. The relevant area consisted of two zones, one girdle of fortifications proper, with ramparts and moats, and outside this belt a *glacis*-zone where building was restricted to simple structures that would easily be demolished later. The state laid claim to possession of the first of these zones, while the second was largely in private ownership.

This time the aim was to avoid the kind of unplanned building that had occurred in the *Broerne* district. As early as 1854 a first proposal for the expansion of the town was produced, involving a rather unimaginative division of the area into uniform rectangular

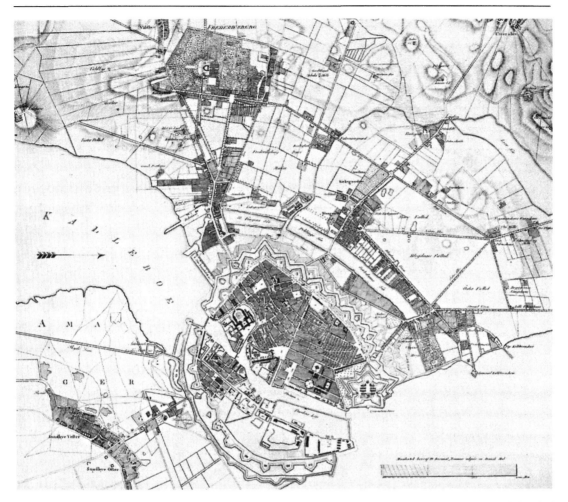

Figure 10.1 *Copenhagen. On this map dated 1817 we can see the medieval town (the left half of the built-up area within the bastion system), with later planned extensions (on the right and below on the left). Outside the bastions* (Voldene), *we can see the moats and an unbuilt strip of land. Then comes the* Søerne *and a broad area in which only simple building was allowed.* [Københavns stadsarkiv]

blocks.[8] Conrad Seidelin's 1857 proposal (figure 10.3) was more carefully thought out, with all the usual attributes such as tree-planted principal thoroughfares, monumental buildings and a great many squares, some of which would be planted. There were also several round or semi-circular open places with sculptures or fountains in the centre, and a suggestion of radiating streets. Further, a ring

boulevard was proposed along the *Søerne*; in an interesting commentary it was explained why a ring-road should be located here rather than more centrally, an option that had obviously also been discussed.[9] The centre of the new district was a large square surrounded by monumental buildings. The proposal shows that Seidelin was familiar with the urban design ideas of the times; his plan brings to mind

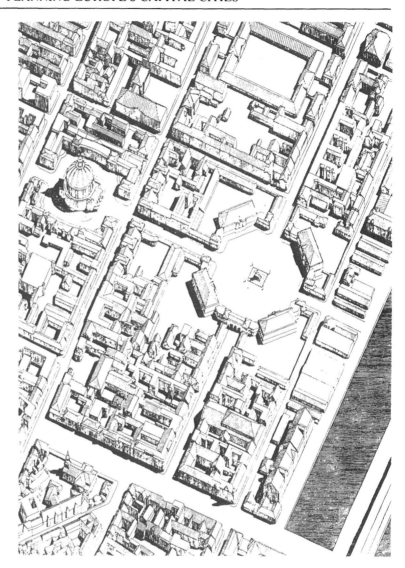

Figure 10.2 *Copenhagen. Amalienborg Plads, designed by Nicolai Eigtved around 1750, is – possibly together with the Senatstorget in Helsinki – the most outstanding square architecturally speaking in the Nordic capitals. [Redrawing by Erik Lorange]*

several of the entries for the competition in Vienna the following year[10], and his aesthetic approach recalls Hausmann's. But the absence of parks in the proposal is surprising.

Before exploitation of the demarcation area could begin, it had to be decided whether those enjoying the usufruct should profit from the whole of the increase in value, as they had done in the case of the *Broerne* area. The opinion of the military was that the state should expropriate the land, and then finance a new outer ring of fortifications by selling it. But many people found such a suggestion unconstitutional, and it was rejected by the *folketinget*, the Danish parliament.

The military's ideas about how the area should be exploited were demonstrated in a project proposed by the 'rampart demolition committee' (*sløjfningskommissionen*) in 1865 (figure 10.4). One of the premises of this plan

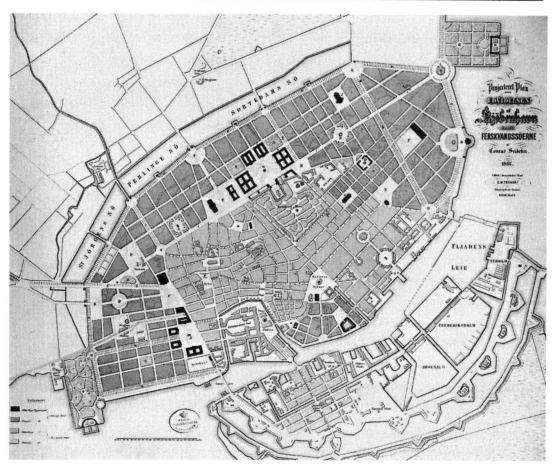

Figure 10.3 *The architect Conrad Seidelin's 1857 plan for the expansion of Copenhagen.*
[Københavns stadsarkiv]

was that by exploiting the area to the maximum, it would be possible to restrain further expansion beyond the *Søerne*, and at the same time to make a satisfactory profit from a future sale of building plots. The planned district is criss-crossed by tree-planted streets of varying widths. In the middle is a park, the Botanisk Have, with part of the old moat as a lake. This feature had already been decided, and was to form a continuation of Kongens Have. On the inner side of Sortedams Sø the Copenhagen municipal hospital, finished in 1863, has been included in the plan. The streets generally

intersect at right angles. There is no inner ring road here, nor any outer ring boulevard, unless the narrow street along the Lakes can be regarded as such. There are a few attempts to create some special accents, but on the whole architectural effects are used more sparingly than in Seidelin's plan. If his design could perhaps be described as a typical architect's proposal, we could call the commission's proposal more of an engineer's scheme. Nonetheless, the commission has included a good deal more greenery than Seidelin. Common to both proposals is the fact that the old urban

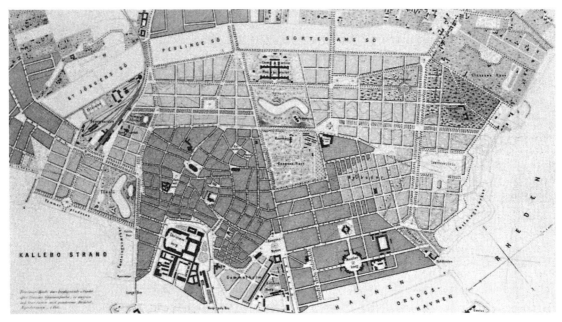

Figure 10.4 *Copenhagen. The demolition committee's 1865 proposal. [Københavns stadsarkiv]*

structure is left intact, which naturally caused problems when it came to linking it with the new areas. In both cases, however, some effort does seem to have been made to find a solution to this problem, particularly in the demolition committee's proposal.

The demolition committee's proposal was publicly displayed in 1865, and was criticized for its high level of exploitation. Among those submitting comments, the Academy of Art declared that the area of the ramparts proper should be laid out as a girdle of parkland round the centre of the city. This proposal, which was probably launched first by the city engineer L.A. Colding,[11] was presented in a schematic plan made by Ferdinand Meldahl, who was a professor at the Academy and at the time one of Denmark's leading architects.[12] The moat was to be retained, an idea which also appeared in a plan submitted the following year by a municipal expert committee, but possibly executed prior to Meldahl's (figure 10.5). In this plan the area of the moat has been kept

more or less intact, while the rest is organized in a rather unimaginative grid without open places or broad streets.

When Meldahl was elected to the town council he was able to put his ideas forward from within the municipal system. There were thus two clearly formulated alternatives to discuss: one involved heavier exploitation, but claimed to avoid too great a spread of suburban building, while the other would provide a girdle of parkland round the old city but more suburban spread. The advocates of the first solution wanted to avoid dividing the town into two, and to minimize distances, which was considered important in military circles, while those who supported the second alternative did so mainly on hygienic grounds.[13] It should also be mentioned that the demolition committee was further criticized for concentrating exclusively on residential blocks and paying insufficient attention to the needs of business and industry.

When the demolition committee presented

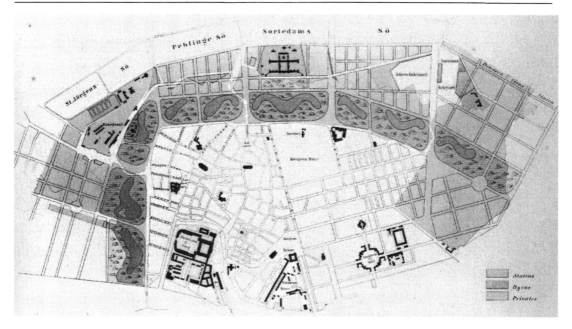

Figure 10.5 *Copenhagen. Exploitation of the area of the fortifications according to the expert committee's 1866 proposal. [Københavns stadsarkiv]*

their proposal, it was already obvious that on economic as well as legal grounds a single overall project of this type had little chance of being realized. A precondition had been the expropriation of all the land which was not in public ownership, and a proposal along these lines had already been rejected. In 1867 a law was passed whereby the owners of the land between the ramparts and the *Søerne* were given the right to retain their property, in return for paying half the increase in value that would arise from the abolition of the building prohibition. The result of this was that state and landowners had a common interest in seeing land values rise as much as possible, and consequently favoured heavy exploitation. Furthermore, the law gave the government the right to sell the area of the fortifications proper to the municipality, and this was done at a price which made it impossible to lay out the whole area as parkland. But it was included in their agreement that a certain area, albeit rather a small one, should be kept as a park.

As soon as this decision had been made, the planning could enter a more definitive phase. 1868 saw ratification of a street plan produced by a committee of state and municipal representatives, while in 1871 a municipal committee presented a proposal (figure 10.6) which was ratified the following year. The question of a ring-road was solved by creating a broad boulevard between the old urban area and the new district, consisting of the present Øster Voldgade, Nørre Voldgade and H.C. Andersens Boulevard. Another narrower street described an arc through the new district somewhat further to the west. Substantial parts of the fortification area itself remained unbuilt, forming a series of parks. But there is practically nothing of Seidelin's grand star-shaped places or his street prospects; in fact there is very little of the visionary about this plan: grand gestures seem to have been inhibited by plot boundaries,

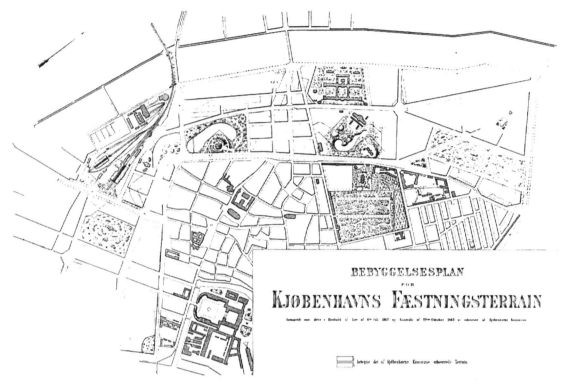

Figure 10.6 *Copenhagen. The city administration's ratified plan for the area of the fortifications, 1872. In a revised version dated 1885 the western boulevard (the present H.C. Andersens Boulevard) was straightened somewhat, which meant that the Tivoli area could be kept intact. [Københavns stadsarkiv]*

topographical conditions and existing buildings and other structures. The only square simply consists of an empty block, the present Israels Plads. Block divisions are indicated round this square only. In 1885 a slightly revised version of the plan was ratified; the changes referred mainly to the parks and H.C. Andersens Boulevard, which now acquired its present extension.[14]

The demolition of the ramparts and the subsequent exploitation began during the 1870s, but the whole area was not built until the beginning of the present century.[15] Most of the building in the southern section consists of blocks of flats built by private developers. Large and medium-sized flats are built along the street, while smaller flats look out over the courtyards. In the northern section between Øster Søgade and Øster Farimagsgade, terraced houses were built between 1873 and 1879 for workers under the auspices of the *Arbejdernes byggeforening*. This area, with its long narrow blocks, is unique in capital city planning and seems to herald later urban development ideas.[16] The three large parks, Ørstedsparken, Botanisk Have and Østre Anlæg, follow in the main the 1885 plan. Østre Anlæg was even enlarged quite considerably. In all three parks substantial sections of the moat were retained as ponds and lakes. Several public buildings were also built in the former glacis area, e.g. Ny Carlsberg Glyptotek,

Statens Museum for Kunst and the town hall, built in 1892–1905 and recognized as the masterpiece of the architect Martin Nyrop. All in all the area on the town side of the *Søerne* was built to a much higher standard than the *Broerne* area, although even there the difference between, for instance, the buildings in the splendid Søtorvet and on Nørre Farimagsgade on the one hand and those along the more humble Nansens gade on the other, is very striking.

Mention should also be made of the plans for Gammelholm, a central area within the fortified town which had previously been used by the navy. Several suggestions were made for this district, including one by Seidelin which included broad streets and architecturally designed squares. However, when exploitation began in 1861 it followed a plan by Meldahl, which had no particular architectural ambitions. The area was exploited as heavily as current building ordinances permitted.[17]

During the nineteenth century little seems to have been done about cutting streets through the older urban structure. However, around 1900 a combined clearance and street improvement project was launched (Kristen Bernikows Gade, Bremerholm, Knippelsbro, Torvegade), although it was not finished until very much later.[18] But this thoroughfare lacks the touch of a ruthless Haussmann: it winds its way through the old urban structure much as the Corso Vittorio Emmanuele does in Rome. As in other cities the question of the railway played an important part in the planning. For most of the time when the area on the town side of Søerne was being discussed, the railway station was located in the western corner of this district, representing an awkward obstacle to any overall solution. The central station was finally moved to its present site southeast of Vesterbrogade after 20 years of discussion, following a decision reached in 1901.[19] At the same time it was decided to construct a north-south railway connection in a tunnel under Voldgaderne. Residential areas for prosperous families were built close to the centre, albeit outside the municipal border, in Frederiksberg and Gentofte. Around the turn of the century a more progressive approach to urban development questions began to emerge in Copenhagen. Here as in many other towns regional aspects were now beginning to be considered. In 1908 an international town plan competition was held.

Copenhagen's situation in the middle of the nineteenth century was not unique. Several cities in Europe at this time were in the position – so favourable from the planning point of view – of possessing extensive unbuilt areas where their defences had once been located. Of the capital cities Vienna provides the most obvious parallel, but developments nonetheless moved in very different directions in the two towns. Vienna was still the capital of an empire, whose leaders intended from the start to create a new district of great splendour. And their plans were favoured by the fact that the state laid claim to ownership of the land. Moreover, industry was largely located in the suburbs. In Denmark royal absolutism had disappeared in 1849, and the position of the recently established municipal administration in Copenhagen was comparatively weak. Its ambitions as well as its resources were more modest than those in Vienna, and there was plenty of scope for the free play of market forces. The attempts at overall planning, perfectly reasonable in themselves, failed because the landowning situation was often unclear, ownership was fragmented, and 'liberal' ideas about ownership rights obtained.[20] Where Vienna created an imperial and ceremonial theatre, Copenhagen acquired a more ordinary nineteenth-century townscape, full of blocks of flats of varying standard. Even though a good deal of the area was laid out as parks, and some public buildings were included, there is little to recall Vienna. But perhaps the example of the Habsburg's capital city may have had one effect, that despite everything a ring-road was finally achieved.

NOTES

1. A basic work on Copenhagen's building
history is Rasmussen (1969), although this publication cannot be compared with the same
author's well-known book on London. Its organization in thematic chapters, the absence of
references, and the often personal and polemical
opinions, make it difficult to get a clear idea of
the town's development during the nineteenth
century from this book. An overview of building
development and planning from 1840 to 1940 is
provided in Rasmussen and Bredsdorff (1941),
which has been one of the main sources for this
chapter; cf. also Johansen's two essays in the
same volume (1941*a,b*) which provide a good
deal of information on housing construction.
Rasmussen (1949, pp. 129 ff) provides a description of the planning of the fortification and
demarcation area, which is shorter but otherwise
agrees with the description in Rasmussen and
Bredsdorff (1941). Langberg (1952) looks at the
expansion of the town in a longer time perspective. *Københavns historie*, IV (Jensen and Smidt
(1982), pp. 150 ff) and *Danmarks arkitektur,
Byens huse – Byens plan* (Hartmann and
Willadsen, 1979) add little new in the way of
facts, but they link the discussions on urban
development in Copenhagen with the history of
the town and with the history of Danish urban
development as a whole. The latter also applies
to Larsson and Thomassen (1991). Copenhagen's
physical development during the period of
industrialization is addressed in a theoretical
perspective by Hyldtoft (1979). The most recent
study is Knudsen (1988*b*), a wide-ranging survey
of how the physical structure of Copenhagen was
transformed and modernized during the period
1840–1917, focusing in particular on the activities
of the municipal administration. Some of his
results are presented and further developed in
English in Knudsen (1988*a*) and Knudsen (1992).
2. In the middle of the eighteenth century an
outstanding architectural ensemble was created –
the eight-pointed Amalienborg Plads surrounded
by four uniformly designed palaces, with Frederik
V's equestrian statue as its central point and the
Marmorkirken in the background (figure 10.2) –
a royal square to rival the French models.

3. Rasmussen (1969), p. 246.
4. Population figures from Johansen (1941*a*),
p. 39 ff.
5. This sequence of events has been described in
Hansen (1977).
6. Rasmussen and Bredsdorff (1941), p. 14.
7. Johansen (1941*b*), p. 67.
8. Picture in Rasmussen and Bredsdorff (1941),
p. 17.
9. In a comment on his plan Seidelin writes:
'Many people would like to have seen the
ramparts transformed into boulevards (carriageways separated by trees down the middle), in
order to improve the air circulation. We believe
that such boulevards, which would have to follow
the old twisting line of the ramparts, would
favour the free movement of air less than the
many broad uniform streets crossing one another
at right angles, and the great places which are
intended for the very site of the old ramparts and
bastions. Nor could a boulevard across a town
offer strollers the same benefits that the boulevard
suggested for the lakeside would do, because the
traffic continually crossing from the other streets
would cause both crowding and noise, and
because the trees would not thrive in a large city,
particularly if it is lit by gas light. And for half the
year it would still be unpleasant to have to walk
across these dark streets in the evenings, as such
boulevards are always dark at night . . . All these
disadvantages disappear in a boulevard along the
waterside. Furthermore the streets in the plan are
so ample . . . that it will be possible to have a
sufficient flow of air into the town from these
boulevards which are open to the water along
their whole length.' (Quoted from Dybdahl
(1973), pp. 53 f.)
10. This has been noted by Rasmussen and
Bredsdorff (1941), p. 18.
11. According to information from Tim
Knudsen.
12. Cf. Dybdahl (1973), pp. 54 ff.
13. Cf. Rasmussen and Bredsdorff (1941), p. 19.
14. Picture *ibidem*, p. 23.
15. On the development process, see Johansen
(1941*b*), pp. 24 f.
16. Cf. Rasmussen (1969), p. 108.
17. Reproduction of these plans in Rasmussen
and Bredsdorff (1941), pp. 24 f. Knudsen (1988*b*,

pp. 57 ff) also provides an account of these events that is critical of Meldahl.

18. Rasmussen (1969), p. 152.

19. Cf. Rasmussen and Bredsdorff (1941), pp. 28 f. On the planning of this area, which dragged on for several more decades, see *ibidem*, pp. 30 ff.

20. However, industrial establishment on the town side of the Søerne was largely prevented, mainly on account of easement stipulations (information provided by Ole Hyldtoft).

11

VIENNA

Large cities often comprise areas whose complex structures are difficult to capture or describe in simple models. Vienna[1] is to some extent an exception to this. The city consists of a core, the medieval town, surrounded by three concentric rings: the Ringstraße district, the inner suburban zone and the outer suburbs (see figure 11.1b). These four urban regions are clearly defined in relation to one another, as well as having distinct street networks and a different character of building.

The historical core – the medieval town – goes back to Roman times. Vindobona, the future Vienna, was one of the Roman Empire's many border towns along the Rhine and the Danube. The rectilinear Roman settlement, which can still be divined in the orientation of some of the streets, occupied only part of the area of the medieval town. Roman Vienna could probably be described as a minor garrison town.[2]

It can be assumed that like most Roman towns Vienna lost its urban functions during the early Middle Ages, and thus also a large part of its population, after the collapse of the Roman Empire. At this time Vienna was not even an episcopal see, a function which in many other towns helped to preserve at least a little of the urban character. During the tenth and eleventh centuries the former Roman towns began to expand anew, a process generally completed by the building of a new wall round the extended urban area. Most of these walls were built during the thirteenth century. Vienna appears by and large to have followed

the usual pattern. By the time the town had acquired its surrounding wall, around 1200, the urban area was about four times as large as it had been under the Romans. As usual the medieval town plan was determined by the topography and by existing tracks or paths and buildings. As far back as the twelfth century Vienna was what we could call the seat of the Babenberg dynasty. Towards the end of the thirteenth century the ruling power switched to the Habsburgs, and the town soon became the leading centre of the Habsburg lands. From the fifteenth century onwards Vienna was almost uninterruptedly the seat of the German Emperors. The Turkish siege of 1529, which the Viennese managed to withstand, was an event of great significance. Vienna had now acquired a special status as the bulwark of Western civilization against the threat of the Crescent, and was surrounded by new modern fortifications. A feature that would be important to the physical development of the town in the future was the prohibition, on grounds of defence, of any building in the area just outside the town. After various extensions this unbuilt zone – the *glacis* – formed a girdle almost 500 metres wide (figure 11.1a).

The strength of Vienna's position as the 'capital city' of the Holy Roman Empire and of the Habsburg hereditary domains increased steadily. There was thus a pressing need for the town to expand, a need which could not be satisfied by extensions because of the building prohibition around the ramparts. Instead this resulted in more intensive land development

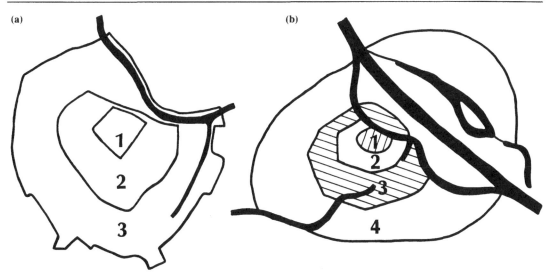

Figure 11.1 *Schematic subdivision of Vienna. (a) The inner city: 1. The area of the Roman town. 2. The area of the medieval extensions. 3. The Ringstraße district (the former rampart area or glacis). (b) Greater Vienna: 1. The inner city core. 2. The Ringstraße area. 3. The inner suburban area, bounded by the Gürtel on the site of the outer rampart (the* Linienwall*) from 1704. 4. The outer suburbs.*

inside the walls and to a relatively rapid process of redevelopment. Suburbs also began to grow along the exit roads beyond the prohibited building zone. The availability of land, the lower land values, and perhaps above all freedom from the town toll, all added to the considerable attractions of the suburbs.

A second Turkish siege occurred in 1683; this time too the danger was averted, although practically all the buildings outside the walls were razed to the ground by one side or the other. Vienna now began its definitive expansion beyond the medieval core, even though the building prohibition around the fortifications was still strictly upheld. The suburbs were built up again along the exit roads, but now on a more permanent basis. Craftsmen and traders also established themselves there in increasing numbers. The fortified town became more exclusively the centre of administration and the upper reaches of commerce, and the residential district of the nobility and established burgher classes. In 1704 Vienna was surrounded by another defensive rampart (the *Linienwall*)

around 2000 metres beyond the old fortifications. This meant that the suburbs now lost their freedom from the toll, but at the same time they acquired at least *de facto* status as part of a kind of 'Greater Vienna' (see figure 11.1*b*).

The early eighteenth century was a period of lively building activity on both sides of the *glacis*, the unbuilt girdle surrounding the town. Due to shortage of space the greatest building enterprises, namely Karlskirche by Johann Bernhard Fischer von Erlach and Prince Eugene's Belvedere by Lukas von Hildebrandt, were located beyond the inner fortification systems. During the later years of Maria Theresa's reign, the administration, the judicial system, education and so on all now assumed more organized forms; it is perhaps at this time that Vienna can be said to have emerged as a capital city in the modern sense of the term. The Empress's greatest building enterprise, begun before the start of her reign, was the palace of Schönbrunn, which despite its enormous size served merely as an out-of-town residence. In this respect it differed from its model, Versailles, which was Louis XIV's permanent residence. The palace of Schönbrunn was built beyond the outer ring of fortifications. The nobility also built themselves great summer palaces in the immediate vicinity of Vienna, of which the Belvedere was the most magnificent example. Towards the end of the century the fortified core found itself surrounded by a townscape of a very distinctive character consisting of suburbs, palaces and parklands, agricultural villages and areas of cultivation, and to the north, south and west by vineyards and their villages.

The period of the Napoleonic Wars did nothing to enhance Vienna's position, despite the great congress held there in 1814–15. Around the middle of the nineteenth century the Emperor's regime suffered various setbacks, but the 1860s brought the beginning of the most splendid period in the history of Vienna, from 1867 the principal capital of the Austro-Hungarian Dual Monarchy. The population had been growing apace even before the middle of the century, however, and from 247,000 in 1800 had risen to 444,000 by 1850.[3] The population pressure on the fortified heart of the city was thus increasing. In 1827 there

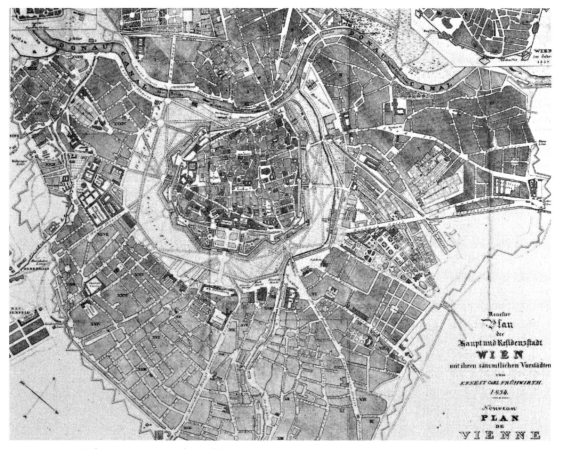

Figure 11.2 *'The most recent plan of Vienna, capital city and imperial seat, with all its suburbs, by E.C. Frühwirth 1834.' Extract. [Photo from Kungliga biblioteket, Stockholm]*

had been an average of 37 people in every house; by 1857 the figure had risen to 54.[4] The problems were particularly great in Vienna, since the urban area had already been heavily exploited during the previous centuries.[5]

The most obvious solution was to develop the unbuilt girdle surrounding the fortifications, which would also allow for the building of a more splendid setting for the imperial power. Hofburg, the imperial residence, consisted of a haphazard series of buildings from different periods, altogether lacking in the uniformity or grandeur of the great royal palaces in such cities as Paris, Berlin, Madrid or Stockholm. During the second half of the eighteenth century there had been some general discussion about the 'embellishment' of Vienna, and this had immediately triggered the idea of building on the land beyond the ramparts. This, to quote a pamphlet dated 1776, would make Vienna within a few years into 'a second Paris'.[6] The French capital was thus the great example to follow, and it was probably the series of boulevards on the north side of Paris (see p. 59) which now inspired the idea of a tree-lined ring road around Vienna's central core. This, it was claimed in 1787, could be 'the most splendid street in Europe'.[7] As in the contemporary French debate about the embellishment of Paris, these visions of splendour were mixed with surprisingly far-sighted comments on the improvements in sanitation and hygiene that could also be won. At this early stage, too, the possibility of covering costs by selling plots within the rampart area was mooted.[8] At the time, however, these various proposals did not lead to any concrete results, despite the recognition that several other capitals were unfortified towns. In Berlin, for instance, demolition of the fortifications had begun as far back as the 1730s, and in Paris no post-medieval fortifications had ever been built. Nonetheless, the abolition of the fortification system was apparently never seriously considered in Vienna; perhaps the Turkish siege of 1683 was still too fresh in memory.[9]

The Napoleonic Wars finally demonstrated the obsolete nature of the Viennese defences. French troops took the city on two occasions, and after the briefest of sieges. As a result of these events and of the growing population pressure during the first half of the nineteenth century, calls for building on the land beneath the ramparts were frequently heard, and several projects were suggested; most of these, however, referred to small sections of the area only.[10] Among others, proposals were submitted as early as 1843 by Ludwig Förster, who was later to play an important part in the final planning work. Despite all this activity, still nothing happened – perhaps mainly because of resistance on the part of the military inflamed by the revolutionary events of 1848, but possibly also because of the generally conservative spirit in Metternich's Vienna.

Nonetheless around 1840 the new times began to make their mark, with the building of railways and the beginnings of industrialization. The upheavals of 1848 and the reforms – albeit only temporary ones – that followed, and Franz Joseph's accession to the throne the same year, did bring some political renewal, at least compared with the previous reactionary period. And this in turn had implications for Vienna's urban development. In 1850 the municipality of Vienna decided to incorporate the suburbs that lay within the outer ramparts (the *Linienwall*), although imperial sanction was not given until 1861. As early as 1852, however, Franz Joseph had appointed a committee to make a proposal for the expansion of the town. From that point on, it was a question of *how* rather than *whether* the land outside the ramparts should be built.

There were several reasons for this. The Emperor himself must have felt an urgent need to compensate for the setbacks in foreign policy by creating a magnificent setting for the imperial seat of power – a setting which could rival or even surpass the splendour displayed by other monarchs. The housing shortage was also becoming increasingly difficult to ignore.

And even though building on the empty land surrounding the town would mainly satisfy the 'housing needs of the prosperous classes', as one memorandum put it, it could not be denied that 'such a vast increase in dwellings must have a favourable effect on the housing needs of the less prosperous groups in the population as well.'[11] The great urban development programme in Napoleon III's Paris was also something of a challenge.[12] However, the deciding factor must have been that the retention of the fortifications could no longer be justified on military grounds; their only importance now was to provide protection against riots among the population of the suburbs.[13]

The military did not abandon their opposition, however: they were only prepared to approve the demolition of the old fortifications if a new system was built between the inner city and the suburbs. But the idea of building in the fortification area had the support of several ministers, in particular the Minister of the Interior, Alexander von Bach, a forceful politician who clearly played a very important role as an instigator of the project. The Emperor, too, seems to have been convinced that the town must be allowed to expand, and in 1857 the whole question entered a decisive phase. After lengthy preparations, a paper – referred to as *Handschreiben* – was produced in the finance and interior ministries, which Franz Joseph dispatched in the form of an official letter to the Minister of the Interior on 20 December. This paper, which was published in *Wiener Zeitung* on 25 December, was of crucial importance to subsequent developments and will therefore be reproduced in full:[14]

Dear Freiherr v. Bach,

It is Our desire that the extension of the inner city of Vienna should be undertaken as soon as possible, that at the same time it should be linked to the suburbs, and that in so doing the improvement and embellishment of Our residence city and capital should be a matter of concern. For this purpose We grant the use of the area of the ramparts and fortifications round the inner town and the moats around these.

The land thus acquired – and which according to the master plan that should be made is not to be reserved for any other purpose – is to be used for building lots, and the sales revenues thus generated should serve to establish a building fund, which will cover the state's expenses for the project, and in particular the cost of the public buildings and the transfer of such military facilities and buildings as are still necessary.

In executing this master plan and in realizing the extension of the city after Our approval of this same plan, the following should be considered:

The removal of the ramparts and the filling in of the moats, should allow for the creation of a broad embankment along the Donaukanal in the area from the Biberbastei to the Volksgarten wall, while the area acquired from the Schottentor to the Volksgarten can be used partly to enlarge the parade-ground.

Between these given points the extension of the inner city should be effected mainly towards Rossau and Alservorstadt, on the one hand following the Donaukanal and on the other the boundaries of the parade-ground, but allowing a suitable setting for the Votivkirche now under construction.

In planning this new district attention should be paid in the first instance to the building of a fortified barracks, which should also house the large military bakery and the military prison, and this barracks should be located at a distance of eighty (80) *Wiener Klafter*[15] from the Augarten-Brücke, on the extension of the future main ring road.

The open place in front of Our castle and the existing gardens on each side of this, are to be left unaltered in their present condition until further instructions are given.

The area outside the Burgtor and up to the imperial stables should be left free. Similarly, that part of the main rampart (Biberbastei) on which are located the barracks bearing Our name, should remain intact.

The further extension of the inner city should be effected at the Kärntnertor, and this on both sides of it, towards the Elisabeth- and the Mondschein-Brücke and as far as the Karolinentor.

The erection of public buildings should also be taken into account, namely a new building for the general staff, an office for the town commandant, an opera house, a national archive, a library, a town hall, as well as the necessary buildings for museums and galleries, and the chosen sites for these shall be given with exact details concerning the area to be covered.

The area from the Karolinentor up to the Donaukanal should also be left free, as well as the great parade ground of the garrison from the square in front of the Burgtor and almost as far as the Schottentor, and the parade ground should be adjacent to this square.

From the fortified barracks by the Donaukanal and to the large parade ground an area running in a straight line and with a width of one hundred (100) *Wiener Klafter* should remain free and unbuilt. Furthermore, a traffic belt, connected with the embankment along the Donaukanal, should be constructed around the inner city, on the rampart area with a width of at least forty (40) *Klafter*, consisting of a carriageway flanked on either side by tracks and paths for walking and riding, and this girdle is to be given the appropriate embellishment with alternating buildings and open parks.

The other main streets should be planned to have an appropriate width, and even side-streets should be no less than eight *Klafter* wide.

The construction of covered markets, and their distribution throughout the town, should be given no less consideration.

At the same time appropriate attention should be paid to the regularization of the inner city when the master plan for the extension of the town is executed, and particularly the opening of suitable exit roads from the inner city linking up with the main traffic arteries to the suburbs, as well the construction of new bridges for these thoroughfares.

In order to produce a master plan a competition should be arranged and a programme published according to the principles prescribed here, but it should be added that competitors are otherwise free to elaborate their own plans, and that suitable recommendations over and above those given here should not be excluded.

A commission should be appointed to evaluate the plans submitted, with representatives from the Ministry of the Interior and the Ministry for Trade, as well as from Our central military chancellery and the supreme police authority; one member of the governmental board of Lower Austria should also be included as well as the mayor of Vienna; in addition suitable experts appointed by the Ministry of the Interior in agreement with the other central authorities mentioned here, and the commission should be under the chairmanship of a section head

at the Ministry of the Interior. The three best proposals chosen by this commission should be awarded prizes, namely the sum of 2,000, 1,000 and 500 gold ducats in the Imperial and Royal mint.

The proposals which are thus regarded as the three best should be referred to Us for a decision, as well as the subsequent measures concerning the realization should in due form be submitted to Our approval.

For the execution of this Our instructions, you are immediately to take the necessary action.

Vienna, the 20th day of December 1857.
Franz Joseph m.p.

The main points thus agreed with what had already been discussed in the eighteenth century: a ring road of the boulevard type, a number of public buildings and financing by the sale of plots. But there was a greater awareness now of the importance that the new district would have in the system of communications between the old city and the suburbs. One novelty was the idea of a competition. The document reads like a coherent summary of the discussions about the area of the ramparts, and it appears well suited to provide a basis for subsequent developments. We may well wonder whether any other large city in nineteenth-century Europe could boast of an improvement scheme with such a systematic programme as its starting-point.

Preparations for the competition seem to have been well under way when the missive was dispatched; by January 1858 it had already been officially announced as the first major town planning competition of the nineteenth century.[16] Referring to the Emperor's letter, the aim was defined as follows: '. . . to give the experts the opportunity . . . to present their proposals for the aims and measures, according to which the extension and town plan re-developments were to be carried out, in light of the practical needs of the population in technical and aesthetic respects.'[17] Apart from this a number of detailed directives were given, for instance regarding the desired floor area of

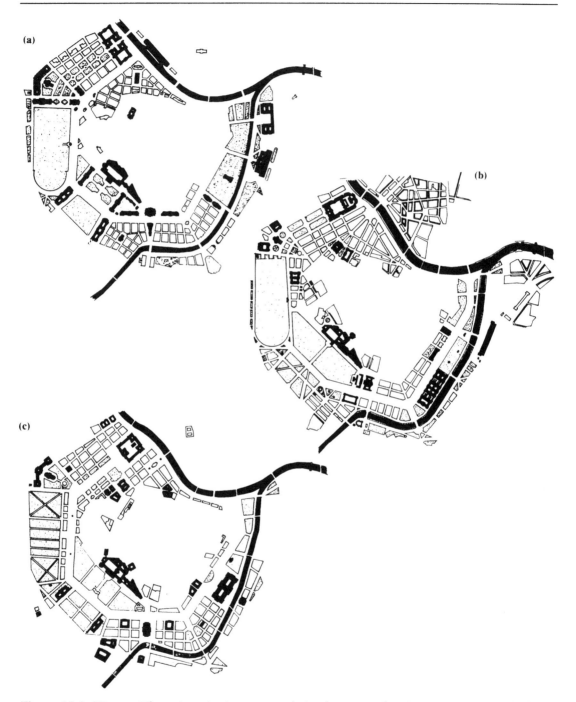

Figure 11.3 *Vienna. The prize-winning proposals in the town planning competition, 1858. (a) Sicardsburg and van der Nüll. (b) Förster. (c) Stache. Public buildings solid black, green areas dotted. [Simplified drawings after the reproductions in Mollik, Reining and Wurzer (1980)]*

Figure 11.4 *The*
Grundplan *for the*
extension of Vienna,
approved by the Emperor
in 1859. Public buildings
solid black, green areas
dotted. [Simplified
drawing after the
reproduction in Mollik,
Reining and Wurzer
(1980)]

the various public buildings and the organization of the entries. Extensive cartographical
material was available to the competitors.

The competition aroused great interest;
altogether the brief was distributed to 509
interested parties. By the closing date, 31 July
1858, eighty-five entries had been received.
Representatives of various ministries and
authorities predominated among the judges,
but a few master-builders and architects, as
well as two representatives of the municipality
of Vienna, were also included. Practical and
functional aspects seem to have been of central
interest, in what was obviously a very thorough
scrutiny of the entries. In December 1858 it
was announced that three proposals were to be
awarded prizes without any ranking being
made between them. The authors of these
proposals were Friedrich von Stache, Ludwig
von Förster and Eduard van der Null together
with August von Sicardsburg (figure 11.3).
They were all architects, and apart from Stache
were all professors at the Akademie der

bildenden Künste in Vienna. Six other proposals were also mentioned for consideration,
one of which was the work of the landscape
gardener, Peter Josef Lenné, who had
previously been involved in planning in Berlin
(see pp. 192 f and 317 f).

The authors of the three prize-winning
projects had all, in different ways, previously
been engaged in the discussions on the urban
development of Vienna. This applied particularly to Förster, who had presented various
proposals for the expansion of the city. The
prize-winning entries all display good
knowledge of the town, realism and skill in
architectural design. Many of the other
proposals seem amateurish, carelessly put
together, or generally unrealistic. The committee of judges felt able to dismiss them with
comments such as 'totally impossible' or 'not to
be considered'. Stache, and above all Förster,
showed considerable foresight in their proposals concerning the comprehensive planning
of Vienna; both suggested a railway ring

around the town and a system of radial streets through the suburbs. Förster's explanatory commentary on his project is worth particular mention, as it reveals a well-thought-out view of Vienna's future development.[18] The competition aroused a good deal of interest in the press. This, the first major 'modern' town planning competition, appears to have been arranged along lines that are surprisingly similar to the way such things are organized today.

By December 1858 a committee had already been appointed to process the proposals and to produce a final master plan. This committee was composed according to much the same principles as the committee of judges, but Förster, Sicardsburg and Stache were now also included. By April 1859 the committee had prepared a proposal for a master plan (*Grundplan*)[19] which the Emperor ratified, after a few minor alterations, in the autumn of the same year (figure 11.4). Thus the entire planning process had taken less than two years.

The same year 1859, preparations began for realizing the project.[20] A 'Commission for the Expansion of the Town' (*Stadterweiterungs-Commission*) was appointed to see to the administrative coordination, including representatives from the Ministry of the Interior and the authorities affected. The municipal administration was represented by members of the executive board (the *Magistrat*) and the town building office (the *Stadtbauamt*). This committee was essentially restricted to preparing the decision base; the decisions themselves were made by the Minister of the Interior and, ultimately, the Emperor. But the committee still played an important role as a coordinating body, examining all proposals in relation to the *Grundplan*. Further, a 'fund for the expansion of the town' (*Stadterweiterungsfond*) was established, in which the revenues from the sale of plots, buildings and demolition material were to be placed, in order to finance the necessary expropriations, the demolition of the fortifications, some of the construction of quays and bridges and the erection of the new public

buildings. The 'Committee for National Buildings' (*Baucomité für öffentliche Bauten*) was responsible, as the name implies, for public buildings. The 'Vienna Building Committee' (*Wiener Baucommission*), on the other hand, which was also dominated by representatives of the state administration, was a kind of building authority whose task was to implement the building ordinances of 1859.

The town was in a weak bargaining position. The municipal authorities claimed that the state had no right to direct the planning, and that the rampart area had originally been handed over for reasons of defence and should therefore now be returned to the municipality, when it was no longer required for this end. But these views met with no response at the national level. Furthermore the town was expected to pay for street works, the construction of drains and water-mains, the laying out of parkland and, naturally, the building of its own town hall. The Ringstraße project would also call for extensive investment on the part of private developers, but they were given the benefit of long-term exemption from taxes; this generally covered both municipal and national taxes for a period of thirty years.

Construction of the Ringstraße began in earnest in 1860; work on the Franz-Joseph embankment and its extension along the Donaukanal, as well as the demolition of the fortifications, had been started the year before.[21] In the course of a single decade, between 1860 and 1870, practically the whole Ringstraße was built and a major part of the fortifications demolished. In addition, about 190 blocks of flats were put up. During the next decade, up to 1880, more than 200 more were added, and public building was also forging ahead. Around 1890 housing construction, which had been characterized by the same powerful fluctuations as Ingrid Hammarström has described in the case of Stockholm,[22] was largely finished; so too were most of the public buildings. Almost the whole Ringstraße project was completed within about 30 years from its start; after 1890 it was mainly a question of additions only, albeit in some cases such as the new palace wing (*Neue Hofburg*), important ones. The revenues accruing to the fund for the expansion of the town between 1858 and 1914 amounted to 112,525,831 *Gulden*, and the costs were 102,329,686 *Gulden*. Municipal expenditure in connection with the project amounted during the same period to 27,609,619 *Gulden*.[23] This great development enterprise was thus an economic success, at least from the government's point of view.

By the time the area was fully developed, it could boast 590 blocks of flats, some of them also providing space for shops and offices. Large flats predominated; small flats accounted for a tiny proportion only of the total dwelling area. The high prices for land had erected an effective barrier to working-class and middle-class housing; social segregation was thus built into the environment. There were also a number of public buildings, including two theatres (Hofoper and Burgtheater), several museums (Kunsthistorisches and Natur-historisches Museum as well as Museum für angewandte Kunst) and an exhibition building (Sezession), the parliament, the university, a concert hall (Musikverein), the town hall, the Justizpalast and a church (Votivkirche). In addition there were a few other buildings of a public kind, and of course streets and several large green spaces.

The master plan or *Grundplan* ratified by the Emperor in 1859 played a central role in the subsequent developments, even though it seems to have been regarded as a set of guidelines rather than a binding document. During the actual process of expansion devi-ations occurred in almost all parts of the planned area, due to various rearrangements or the need to satisfy the wishes of different interested parties. Thus the planning of the Ringstraße area can be said to have fallen into four stages. The first was the formulation of the programme in the Emperor's letter and the supplementary directives to the competition

entrants. The second was the selection of the three winning proposals (figure 11.3). The third consisted of work on the *Grundplan* (figure 11.4), and the fourth of the final planning of local details, as manifest in the built environment.[24]

The task facing the planners was subject to several important constraints. The area to be planned consisted of a circular belt, 450 metres across at its widest but in other sections considerably narrower. The kind of urban space design that was customary at the time, with long straight streets and a right-angled grid, was thus rendered difficult if not imposs-ible by the general topographical conditions. This showed up all too clearly in some of the less successful competition entries. Nor was it possible to allow for large star-shaped places. The building programme was also exceptionally extensive. Apart from parks and a great many public buildings, a ring road and good com-munications between the old town and the suburbs had to be allowed for, as well as the housing which was to finance the project. And in addition to all this the parade ground in the north-west was to be extended. The topography and various existing buildings also had to be taken into account.

One fundamental problem concerned the location of the ring road. The programme gave no lead on this point. One solution could have been to locate it close to the old town, which would have meant leaving the greatest possible uninterrupted space between this road and the suburban district beyond the *glacis*. Two of the three winning proposals – the Sicardsburg/van der Null and the Stache projects – by and large followed this solution, while Förster gave his ring road a more central position in the planned area, but made it much narrower in its north-western section.[25] The planning com-mittee chose Förster's location, except that the road was to retain its full width – 57 metres – for the whole of its length round the inner city. It may perhaps have been felt that a centrally located road would be better for traffic purposes; it would also be easier to give it an appropriate front facing the old town. Further, it would not have been possible to build a street close to the old town until the fortification system as a whole had been demolished. Apart from a few marginal adjustments the Ringstraße was constructed as set out in the *Grundplan*, and was thus one of the few elements in the plan to be realized without any significant changes.

One novelty in the *Grundplan* was a 'heavy load road' (*Lastenstraße*) which was to run parallel with the Ringstraße along the periphery of the area. It was to take care of heavy traffic so as not to spoil the distinguished ambience of the Ringstraße. This road was built, but only in the north-west. Förster's proposal had included a road in an equivalent location in the south-eastern section of the planned area.

A paramount question concerned the design of the area outside the *Hofburg*. In the Emperor's missive it was decreed that the space in front of the castle should be left unaltered and that the neighbouring area further out beyond the freestanding *Burgtor* up to the imperial stables was to be left unbuilt. Sicardsburg and van der Nüll suggested that these areas should be used for a large imperial square, consisting of two large, planted sections, one on each side of the planned ring road. The short ends of both the sections should be closed by monumental buildings, which at the same time would form the long sides of the whole complex, diverging slightly towards the imperial stables which were outside the planned area proper. Stache produced a similar solution but, as suggested in the programme, without buildings on the short sides of the inner section immediately in front of the castle. Förster – and here he followed the programme closely – proposed a park area without any buildings; attention in his project focused on the existing *Burgtor*. In this instance the *Grundplan* mainly follows the Sicardsburg/van der Nüll proposal, apart from the fact that

the flanking buildings do not diverge towards the imperial stables. However, discussion about this part of the area certainly did not stop just because there was now a *Grundplan*; on the contrary, it continued well into the 1870s. In 1866 a competition was announced for the museum buildings, which had now been decided upon and which were to be built along the outer section of the square ensemble. When the entries were being judged, Gottfried Semper was called in as the expert assessor, and he presented revised proposals of his own. However, the final plan drawn up by Semper (figure 11.5), is basically a reworking of the Sicardsburg/van der Nüll proposal: the two museum buildings flank a park-like place (the future Maria Theresien-Platz), with the imperial stables in the background, and on the palace side of the Ringstraße two new palace wings create an inner square (the present Heldenplatz), of which only the one to the south-east was built.[26]

The design of the north-western section of the former *glacis* area was strictly governed by the programme. Military requirements and internal security were strikingly well catered for by a fortified 'defensive barracks' and the existing drill and parade ground; the two were to be linked – in accordance with the programme – by an intermediate rectangular open area. The rough position of the barracks had been indicated in the Emperor's missive, and the various proposals thus provide similar solutions for this part of the town. The Votivkirche was already being built, and a preliminary decision had been taken whereby the university was to provide a background for the church. This solution had been proposed as early as 1856 by Sicardsburg and van der Nüll. Several competition entries, including Sicardsburg/van der Nüll's and Stache's, as well as the *Grundplan*, thus suggested similar designs for this part of the town, based on the Sicardsburg/van der Nüll scheme. But the entire situation changed in 1868, when the Emperor gave permission for building on the

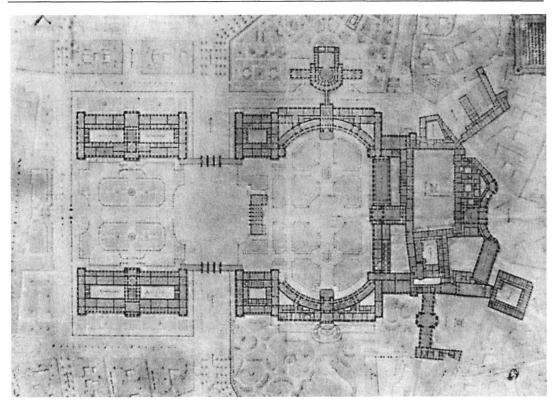

Figure 11.5 *Vienna. Gottfried Semper and Karl von Hasenauer: Project for the extension of the Hofburg, 1870–71. Two exedra-shaped wings, linked by triumphal arches over the Ringstraße with the museum buildings on the south-western side, create a magnificent imperial forum. [From Lhotsky (1941)]*

parade ground. The space thus freed was used for the town hall, the parliament building, the university, three buildings which together with the Burgtheater form a grand symmetrical ensemble, and a number of blocks with apartment houses.

The Sicardsburg/van der Null and the Förster projects both located the Imperial Opera House in roughly the position it later came to occupy, probably because an opera just here had already been discussed at the time of the competition. The former opera house, the Kärntnertortheater, was also close by. The definitive site was given in the *Grundplan*. The opera was in fact the first monumental building

to be started. Sicardsburg and van der Null had intended the opera as part of a group of grand buildings, an idea that the *Grundplan* did not adopt. Instead the arrangement of the blocks in the south-eastern section of the district in the *Grundplan* largely follows Förster's proposal, although his idea of collecting several institutions in one enormous building to the east was not accepted. On the eastern side of the rampart area all the proposals had included a green area along the River Wien, as suggested in the Emperor's brief; here the *Grundplan* followed Förster's outline with a park in roughly the same location as the future *Stadtpark*. All the projects also included, again

according to the programme directives, proposals for embankments along the Donaukanal.
Competition entrants were also invited to
recommend planning improvements for the
inner city, but the authors of the winning
projects were all very cautious here, and
limited themselves to a few interventions
around the Hofburg. In the *Grundplan* interest
focused exclusively on the rampart area.

All in all we can say that the ratified plan was
greatly influenced by both Sicardsburg/van der
Nüll's and Förster's proposals. However, it
cannot be described as a derivative compromise
wholly dependent on these two entries; it is an
autonomous product which also includes some
new ideas of its own. In the outcome, there is
little agreement between the plan and its
realization, when it comes to details; nonetheless the basic character has been largely
retained.[27]

In 1880 a book was published by the art
historian Albert Ilg in Vienna with the striking
title *Die Zukunft des Barockstils* (The Future
of Baroque Style), and it can hardly be
doubted that at that time the Baroque was
regarded as the most appropriate style for the
seat of imperial power. Several buildings, and
in particular the Neue Hofburg, are in the neo-
Baroque style, and the Baroque has also
influenced sculpture, painting and interior
decoration. Can we then speak of neo-Baroque
planning?[28] Hardly; at any rate not in the sense
that applies to Paris. As we have noted, it was
not possible in Vienna to create the same
straight streets and long integrated prospects.
Both the shape of the Ringstraße – an irregular
hexagon – and the trees that line it, preclude
the idea of uninterrupted vistas. 'In Vienna the
beauty lies at the corners, and mostly round
the corners,' as the Austrian writer Hans
Weigel aptly puts it when comparing the two
towns.[29] Here there is no uniform overall
solution, but a series of autonomous transverse
axes – of which the most magnificent,
Schwarzenbergplatz, was established before
the Ringstraße development – and building

ensembles. The grandest of these surrounded
the Maria Theresien-Platz/Heldenplatz, which
although never altogether finished, does work
as a coherent whole. Less coherent is the
arrangement round the Rathauspark with four
large building complexes, each in its own style,
with nothing in common except their location
round the same open space. The connecting
link for these many disparate elements is the
Ringstraße, which gives the area a kind of
unity. The great variety of the scenery along
the Ringstraße may reflect the way it came into
being, i.e. as a result of collaboration between
a number of experts and the representatives of
different interests.[30] But despite this the
Ringstraße as a whole – perhaps uniquely in
our material – is a *Gesamtkunstwerk*, an
example of 'total art' in which architecture,
landscape architecture, sculpture and even
interior decoration come together to create a
unified setting, a true expression of the
aesthetic, social and political values of the
times.

The *Grundplan* did not include new streets
in the city core, but a few street improvements
were subsequently carried out. A start was
made with the widening of the Graben Gasse
and the Stock im Eisen Platz in the 1860s,
which meant that an awkward obstacle to
traffic between Graben and Stephansplatz disappeared.[31] Later street improvements
involved the stretch including Kärntner Straße
and Rotenturmstraße, as well as Wipplinger
Straße. A major project was the creation of the
Michaelerplatz towards the end of the century
as a forecourt to the main entrance of the
Hofburg, an undertaking which ended in the
cause célèbre of the construction in 1910–11 of
the famous 'Looshaus'.[32]

In the later decades of the nineteenth century
the population of the Vienna region was
growing rapidly. The area between the
Ringstraße zone and the outer line of fortifications, subsequently indicated by the outer ring
road, the Gürtel, was becoming more densely
built, while beyond this boundary large areas

such as Hernals, Ottakring and Favoriten were being developed for industrial and residential purposes (figure 11.1*b*). However, in research and in the architectural debate it is the Ringstraße area that has attracted almost all the interest, although in fact the project represents only one part of the total building operations in nineteenth-century Greater Vienna. But although most efforts were concentrated on the Ringstraße, some attempts were also made to plan and control building in the outer reaches of the town and suburbs. As early as 1839 the architect Alois Pichl drew up a plan for part of the Favoriten district.[33] In 1862 the government made it mandatory on the municipalities in the Vienna region to produce master plans. Over the following years a series of such plans, generally

in a very simple form, were made for various parts of the urban area. They were 'just street network plans which, while maintaining the old traffic routes, introduced the successive widening and – in accordance with §7 of the 1859 building ordinances – straightening of certain existing streets, but which paid little attention to the creation of an efficient street network by letting streets cut through existing blocks and major planning improvements or reserving certain areas for gardens and squares'.[34] Förster and Sicardsburg were among the more ambitious plan-makers. In 1861, for example, Förster made a plan for Brigittenau which Sicardsburg revised a few years later, while Sicardsburg in turn contributed to the planning of Favoriten. The main features of Förster's project for Brigittenau (figure 11.6) are the

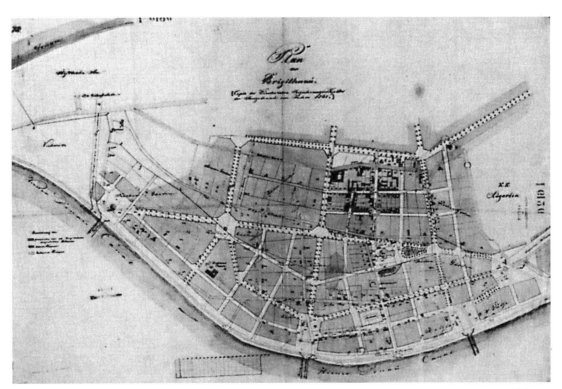

Figure 11.6 *Vienna. Förster's project for Brigittenau, 1861. [From* Die städtebauliche Entwicklung Wiens bis 1945*]*

monumental axial thoroughfares and the tree-planted streets; Sicardsburg's revision involved certain alterations to adjust to the topographical conditions and existing buildings.

In the outer suburban area several municipalities were responsible for planning, independently of one another and of the city of Vienna; this meant that comprehensive or general inter-municipal aspects of planning received very little attention at all. The plans were approved by the relevant municipal councils and were to be ratified by the Ministry of the Interior. But in fact the Ministry disregarded this opportunity to assume a coordinating role. These plans generally appear to have

consisted of rectilinear street networks and uniform blocks, laid out without much attention to topographical conditions (figure 11.7). In the Ringstraße area the state put all possible resources into the realization of the plan, but suburban development was generally left to make its own way and the schematic plans carried little legal clout. In one major suburban project, however, the state was the prime mover, namely in constructing the Gürtel, i.e. a boulevard following the line of the outer fortifications. This had been decided by the Emperor as early as 1861, but was only realized several decades later.

The rapid and largely unplanned growth of

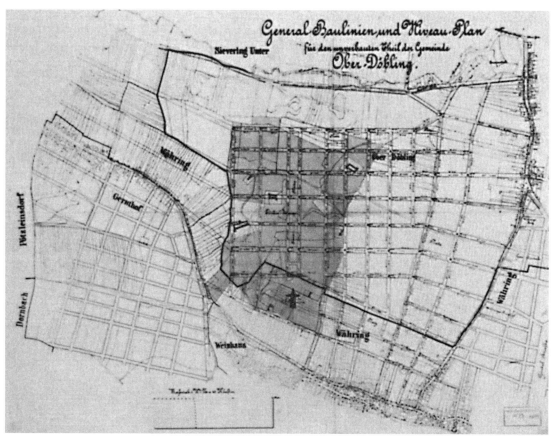

Figure 11.7 *Vienna. Block demarcation plan for Ober-Döbling, c. 1880. [From* Die städtebauliche Entwicklung Wiens bis 1945*]*

the suburbs created many problems, of which the Viennese municipal authorities were not unaware. In 1890 the suburbs were incorporated and two years later a competition for a comprehensive development plan (*Generalregulierungsplan*) for the entire Greater Vienna was announced in an ambitious attempt to create what today would be called a regional plan.[35] The competition – in which Joseph Stübben and Otto Wagner shared the first prize – aroused international interest as a kind of general inventory of the planning ideas of the times, but in Vienna it made little impact on future developments, with the possible exception of the building of the urban railway (the *Stadtbahn*) and the associated *Regulierung* of the River Wien. One of the new railway lines ran along the line of the former outer rampart, the *Linienwall*; together with the Gürtel this marks the boundary between the inner and outer suburbs (figure 11.1*b*).

After the First World War Vienna found herself no longer the capital city of an imperial empire of 52 million people, but simply the capital of a small republic of 6.4 million. Consequently rapid urban growth gave way to a steady population decline. This is one of the main reasons why there is no ring of inter-war residential areas round Vienna, or any encircling suburbs from the post-war period. Meadows and hilly vineyards still take over where the densely built-up city ends. The Ringstraße area has also remained surprisingly intact as regards both buildings and functions. It is doubtful whether any other capital can make us feel as close to the ambience of the late nineteenth century as Vienna does.

NOTES

1. A probably unrivalled cross-disciplinary series of publications has been devoted to that great urban development programme of nineteenth-century Vienna, namely the Ringstraße and all the buildings etc. pertaining to it: *Die Wiener Ringstraße, Bild einer Epoche*, edited by Renate Wagner-Rieger. The series consists of eleven parts and fifteen volumes. Different parts have been devoted to such things as planning, building technology, building materials, sculptural decoration, decorative painting, commerce, culture, social structure etc. The series also includes some architectural monographs. The first part was published in 1969 and the last appeared in 1981. The typographical design of the series is costly, and it is richly illustrated with top-quality photographs, old pictures, maps, diagrams, etc. All in all it represents an impressive achievement and several of its constituent parts maintain a very high standard. There has presumably been some difficulty in defining the scope of the different volumes, particularly as some adjustments in the overall design appear to have been made since the series was originally planned. There is thus a good deal of overlap, which is quite understandable and certainly represents no great drawback. On the other hand it would have been helpful if the authors had referred to one another more than they do, when addressing the same or related issues. For example the background, planning and execution of the Ringstraße project is a theme which is obviously addressed in varying detail in a number of the works in the series. This may have been partly because the volume devoted specifically to the planning aspect was not published until 1980, as one of the last in the series, namely Vol. III, *Planung und Verwirklichung der Wiener Ringstraßenzone* (Mollik, Reining and Wurzer, 1980). But planning and execution questions are also addressed in fairly elaborate detail in Vol. II, *Geschichte und Kulturleben der Wiener Ringstraße* (Springer, 1979), Vol. V, *Wirtschaft und Gesellschaft der Wiener Stadterweiterung* (Baltzarek, Hoffmann and Stekl, 1975) and Vol. VI, *Wirtschaftsfunktion und Sozialstruktur der Wiener Ringstraße* (Lichtenberger, 1970) as well as in the introductory part, Vol. I, *Das Kunstwerk im Bild* (Wagner-Rieger *et al.*, 1969). Mollik, Reining and Wurzer (1980) gives an extremely detailed account of the planning and execution process, and the work also contains a good deal of material on other towns for purposes of comparison, but its character is descriptive; there is not much analytical discussion. Nonetheless, owing to its thoroughness the book is in a class of its

own among monographs on urban planning during the nineteenth century and it has been the main source for the Vienna chapter here. There are two other basic works on Vienna which have no real equivalent in the literature concerning other towns, namely Bobek and Lichtenberger (1966) and Wagner-Rieger (1970). The first provides an excellent account in a historical-geographical perspective of Vienna's urban development from the middle of the nineteenth century, illustrated by a great many maps and diagrams. The second addresses Vienna's architectural development during the nineteenth century, focusing on stylistic matters. The Ringstraße has also been discussed in a number of other works, of which mention should be made of Eggert (1971), and the exhibition catalogue *Die städtebauliche Entwicklung Wiens bis 1945* (1978). Interesting aspects of the building pattern in different parts of the town are highlighted in Klaar (1971). A dissertation in German on Vienna was presented at the Royal College of Technology in Stockholm in 1976, but did not add anything new on the nineteenth-century planning. It was later published in Swedish (Wulz, 1979). Two excellent works address the cultural situation around the turn of the century, namely Janik and Toulmin (1973) and Schorske (1980). The main focus of these books is on the post-Ringstraße period, but the second one includes an account of the creation of the Ringstraße area, seeing it 'as a visual expression of a social class' (pp. 24 ff).

2. On Vienna's earlier history, see for example *Die städtebauliche Entwicklung Wiens bis 1945* and Mollik, Reining and Wurzer (1980).

3. See Table 18.1, p. 264.

4. Mollik, Reining and Wurzer (1980), p. 73.

5. Around the middle of the nineteenth century 85 per cent of the inner city area was built (Bobek and Lichtenberger (1966), p. 63), and 86 per cent of the houses were more than two storeys high, 58 per cent more than three (cf. Mollik, Reining and Wurzer (1980), p. 75)

6. From F.W. Taube: *Gedanken über Verschönerung der Städte mit einer historischen Nachricht, wie seit 1763 die vornehmsten Hauptstädte sich in Europa allmählich verbessert und verschönert haben* (1776) (Reflections on the embellishment of towns, with a historical account of the way in which the most distinguished capital cities in Europe have improved and beautified themselves since 1763), quoted here from Mollik, Reining and Wurzer (1980), p. 84. As early as 1716 Lady Mary Wortley Montague declared in a letter from Vienna that the town would be one of the most beautiful and best built in Europe, if the Emperor would allow the demolition of the ramparts and gates, in order to unite it with its suburbs (according to Lichtenberger (1970), p. 17).

7. Agostino Gerli: *Lettera al Signor Callani, Pittore e scultore in Roma Concernente vari progetti sopra la città di Vienna* (1787), quoted here from Mollik, Reining and Wurzer (1980), p. 85.

8. Suggestions about this were to be found in both Taube and Gerli (see previous notes).

9. In Hanover the fortifications were abandoned in 1763 and in Graz in 1784 (Lichtenberger (1970), p. 17). During the first half of the nineteenth century towns began to demolish their fortifications one after the other (see below, pp. 352 f).

10. Mollik, Reining and Wurzer (1980), pp. 87 ff.

11. Quoted from Mollik, Reining and Wurzer (1980), p. 110.

12. Cf. quotation from *Die Presse* (1857) in Springer (1979), p. 86.

13. Cf. Mollik, Reining and Wurzer (1980), p. 112.

14. Quoted from Springer (1979), pp. 94 ff. The missive is written in a bureaucratic and rather old-fashioned German, so a literal translation has not been attempted.

15. One *Wiener Klafter* is approximately equivalent to 1.9 metres.

16. The plans for organizing a competition seem to have emerged during the spring of 1857. In the main the account of the competition follows Springer (1979), pp. 99 ff and Mollik, Reining and Wurzer (1980), pp. 115 ff. For a discussion of a relation between the Ringstraße competition and other town planning competitions, see Breitling (1980).

17. Mollik, Reining and Wurzer (1980), p. 116.

18. The commentary is reproduced in Mollik, Reining and Wurzer (1980), pp. 472 ff. The views expressed in the competition proposals as regards

the area outside the Ringstraße district, and their implications for this area, are barely discussed in Mollik, Reining and Wurzer (1980), but are touched upon in Breitling (1980), p. 36.

19. The fact that it was possible to present a proposal so quickly, and one on which the committee was at any rate outwardly agreed, reveals a remarkable level of administrative efficiency. But that this was not achieved without bitter concessions can be seen from the following lines in a letter from Ludwig von Förster to the academy professor and art historian Rudolph Eitelberger von Edelberg. 'The ministerial plan is a distortion of my plan, mixed with some parts of other plans which by no means fit in with my revised concept; it is thus a hotchpotch and so incompetently put together, that in fact it contains not a single correct line. A lack of taste and understanding can be seen in every part of the plan. My heart bleeds to see that such a splendid opportunity, which at last even here could have done justice to art, has once again been frittered away by the bureaucracy. This botched plan will cause offence as every new building goes up, but to foresee this would have been beyond the capacities of such incompetent people as those who have pieced this plan together, and the whole dominating horde of officials . . .' Quoted from Springer (1979), p. 146.

20. The following account is based mainly on Mollik, Reining and Wurzer (1980), pp. 177 ff.

21. The following figures are quoted from Mollik, Reining and Wurzer (1980), pp. 189 ff, particularly Fig. 28, and Lichtenberger (1970), pp. 18 ff and pp. 220 f (Appendix 1).

22. Hammarström (1979). Cf. *ibidem*, Fig. 3 (p. 32) with Lichtenberger (1970), Fig. 1 (p. 19).

23. Mollik , Reining and Wurzer (1980), p. 187.

24. The analysis of the various phases of the planning process is facilitated by the cartographical material, particularly the comparative maps in Mollik, Reining and Wurzer (1980, Map Appendices Nos. 54, 55, 56 and 80). Cf. also the main text, p. 173 *et passim*.

25. The reason for this was obviously that just here the street ran close to the open area prescribed in the Emperor's missive between the 'defensive barracks' and the parade ground.

26. This course of events is described in Lhotsky (1941).

27. Wulz has claimed that the monumental buildings along the Ringstraße were supposed to have been located with a view to creating a symmetrical pattern in which the Hofburg would provide the middle axis. The symmetry was to apply to both grouping and functions (Wulz (1979), pp. 46 ff, especially figure on p. 47). This idea is interesting, but is probably an over-interpretation. In an assumed symmetrical scheme it might be possible – apart from the Art History and Natural History Museums – to include the Rossauer and Franz-Joseph barracks, the Votivkirche and the Karlskirche together with the Burgtheater and the Staatsoper. Other buildings could hardly be forced into this scheme. It also seems clear that several buildings which could be incorporated into such a scheme have in fact been located according to criteria other than an overall principle of symmetry. Moreover, if such a principle had existed, it would surely have been mentioned in the extensive material available on the planning and execution of the Ringstraße area. But Wulz has not referred to any such proof. It is also strange that he supports his theory entirely on the plan as executed, and does not take the previous planning activities into account, where any possible principle of symmetry would presumably have been more in evidence, particularly in the *Grundplan* ratified by the Emperor.

28. Choay regards Vienna as a typical example of neo-Baroque planning (1969) p. 12.

29. Weigel (1979), p. 21. Cf. the map of architectural vistas in Mollik, Reining and Wurzer (1980, Map Appendix No. 84), which, however, gives an exaggerated idea of what can actually be seen from the Ringstraße.

30. In this context it should be pointed out that the savage critic of the planning of Berlin, Werner Hegemann, emphasized that the Ringstraße project was the first step in a development towards what was later to be called *Städtebau* (Hegemann (1913), pp. 249 ff).

31. Banik-Schweitzer (1995), pp. 135. ff. This project turned out to be expensive for the municipality, and it did not again become seriously involved in inner-city street improvements until the second half of the 1890s, but even then

the lack of a functioning expropriation law turned out to be a serious obstacle (*Die städtebauliche Entwicklung Wiens bis 1945*, pp. 27 ff and 80 ff; Banik-Schweitzer 1995, pp. 141 ff).

32. Czech and Mistelbauer (1977).

33. Reproduced in *Die städtebauliche Entwicklung Wiens bis 1945*, p. 147. Despite a green space which has been reserved outside the built area, this plan appears behind the times. Squares and blocks have been arranged symmetrically in the spirit of the model projects of the Renaissance, but there is no modern street network.

34. *Die städtebauliche Entwicklung Wiens bis 1945*, p. 18. This seems to be the only work that also discusses the planning of the suburban areas; it has thus provided the basis for the following account.

35. On the competition, see Breitling (1980).

12

BERLIN

The embryo of Berlin[1] consisted of two small towns lying close to one another, Berlin and Kölln, both founded in the thirteenth century. Up to the Second World War most of the medieval plan structure had survived, particularly in Berlin. The transformation of Berlin-Kölln, two of many small towns east of the Elbe, into the leading city in central Europe, was closely bound up with the transformation of Brandenburg from a border province to become the dominating German state, and with the rise of the Hohenzollern dynasty from margraves to Emperors. An important period in this development was the reign of Frederick William the Great Elector (1640–88), which saw a number of reforms in the civil and military administration, as well as determined efforts to enhance the status of Berlin, now an important administrative and garrison city.[2] From 1658 onwards a system of bastions began to be built round the two towns and including the suburb of Friedrichswerder, which was granted its own town charter in 1662.

A little later trees began to be planted along the road between the fortified town and the royal hunting park, Tiergarten. When it was completed this ceremonial thoroughfare, Unter den Linden, was 1½ kilometres long and 60 metres wide. In the middle was a path for walking, flanked by three rows of trees and a carriageway on each side. Unter den Linden, which came into being about the same time as the ring of boulevards round the north of Paris, was to have great influence on subsequent developments. The west side of Berlin now

became indisputably the most elegant district. Unter den Linden was also the point of departure for much future planning: either during the eighteenth and early nineteenth centuries, when the centre was to be raised to monumental status, or under national socialism, when an east-west axis was to be created across the whole city.[3] In addition this thoroughfare was to serve as a link – still effective even today – between the east and west sides of town, and as a suitable setting for parades.

During the 1670s a fourth town, Dorotheenstadt, was added. It lay to the north of Unter den Linden, including even the blocks on the southern side of the thoroughfare. Dorotheenstadt became very much the district where the prosperous settled, and rows of grand town houses began to appear along Unter den Linden. Two decades later building began on another town, Friedrichstadt, to the south of Dorotheenstadt. It was intended mainly for the French Protestant immigrants who were offered a haven in Berlin after the revocation of the Edict of Nantes. Characteristic of this district is the regular pattern of the blocks, possibly inspired by the rather similar system that had been adopted recently in the town extensions in Sweden (cf. pp. 30 f). Two rows of short blocks are flanked by longer rows (see figure 12.1). When this district was being extended around 1730, it was embellished architecturally by the construction of three 'squares' just inside the town gates. To the south a round open place was created – Belle-Alliance-Platz, now Mehringplatz – where three streets meet

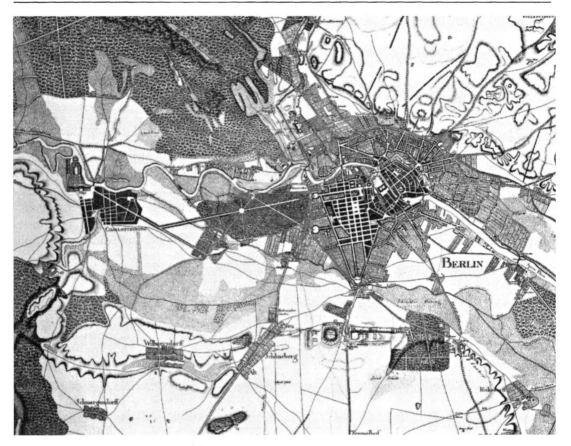

Figure 12.1 *'Plan of Berlin and the surrounding area 1798, published by J.F. Schneider.' Extract.*
[Kungliga biblioteket, Stockholm]

as in the Piazza del Popolo in Rome or in the Place d'Armes in front of the palace of Versailles. At the same time two further architecturally planned places were built, namely the octagonal Leipziger Platz at the end of Leipziger Straße and the square Pariser Platz at the end of Unter den Linden. Berlin had thus acquired its own version of the royal squares in Paris.[4]

In 1701 Frederick III had himself crowned as Frederick I of Prussia, with the result that although Berlin lay outside the actual borders of the new Kingdom, it became the seat of royal power. During the eighteenth century a number of proposals were made for altering the centre of Berlin, but most remained on paper. However, under Frederick the Great (1740–86) some projects were realized with a view to embellishing the city. In particular, mention should be made of two great places:

Figure 12.2 *Berlin. Master plan for the central area by Karl Friedrich Schinkel, dated 1817. Schinkel appears to have started from a total conception of the centre of Berlin, even when his particular commission was to plan individual buildings. [Staatliche Museen zu Berlin]*

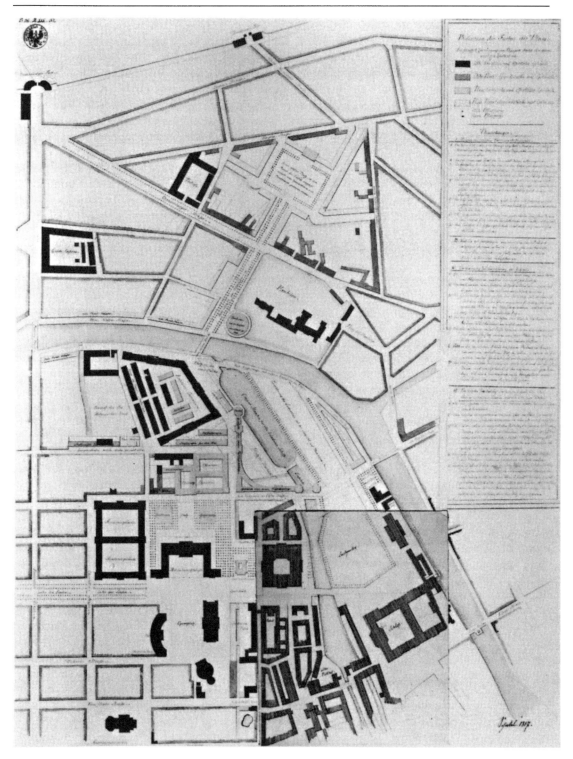

Gendarmenmarkt and Bebelplatz, this last being envisaged as a 'Forum Friedericianum'. However, this was largely a case of local design planning. There do not seem to have been any more plans for expansion after the establishment of Friedrichstadt, although Berlin's population during the eighteenth century increased from around 50,000 to almost 170,000. The formal merging of the five towns to create one unit occurred in 1709. Towards the middle of the century the fortification system had lost its defence function and was being successively demolished. In 1734 the town acquired a tariff wall. When the city's boundaries were moved out in 1737, its old area almost doubled.

Even at the beginning of the nineteenth century there were still no direct communications between the medieval urban core in the east and the new suburbs in the west. In a far-sighted 'master plan' dated 1817 (figure 12.2) Schinkel, with an analytical approach to both problems and needs, outlined a programme for improving communications between the two halves of the town, as one stage in the architectural and functional enhancement of Friedrichswerder and the *Schlossinsel*. Despite constant opposition he succeeded over the following decades in imposing certain changes on the urban structure in connection with various building projects. The construction of a museum building in the Lustgarten – the future Altes Museum – was combined with improvements in the northern part of the town and with the construction of a new warehouse (*Packhof*). In the southern area communications were improved, albeit far less systematically than Schinkel had wanted, between Friedrichstad and the principal street in the eastern district, Königstraße, when the Friedrich-Werdersche-Kirche was built in the second decade of the nineteenth century and the Bauakademie in the 1820s.[5]

The defeat of Prussia by Napoleon and the subsequent occupation of Berlin resulted in a period of national revival and extensive domestic reform, which transformed Prussia from a backward agrarian and military state into a modern society. The Congress of Vienna was a success for Prussia, and the country's political position was further reinforced by the dissolution of the Holy Roman Empire. A period of weakness around the middle of the century was followed by successful wars against Denmark, Austria and finally France. The German Empire was proclaimed in 1871 – the ultimate confirmation of Prussia's dominating position. Thus Berlin now became the centre of Central Europe, the capital of the Kingdom of Prussia and of the German Empire.

Around the middle of the nineteenth century the process of industrialization got seriously under way in Germany, and at quite an early stage Berlin acquired a substantial manufacturing industry. The geographical location of the town and its growing economic and political importance made it the centre of the German communications network, by rail, road and water. After 1871 there was also rapid industrial expansion, which made Berlin pre-eminent among German industrial towns. The population rose from a little over 170,000 in 1800 to about 420,000 in 1850 and to almost 1,900,000 in 1900. The number of inhabitants had thus multiplied more than tenfold during the nineteenth century.[6] In 1800 Berlin was one of several important towns in Germany and central Europe; by 1900 it was Europe's third city.

Naturally this population increase had radical implications for the physical structure of the town. To begin with the growing demand for space seems to have been met by increasing the exploitation of the old urban areas and by putting up simple buildings on the outskirts. The city's jurisdiction was extended on several occasions, and as we have seen the fortifications had already lost their original function in the eighteenth century. The main obstacles to expansion were legal. Not until the first half of the nineteenth century did it become possible to sell farming land for private exploitation.

Prussia's Common Code of Land Law (the *Allgemeines Landrecht*), 1784, obliged the police, as the state's local authority, to indicate the boundaries of new streets and blocks (*Fluchtlinien*) as towns expanded. When in 1808 Prussian towns acquired municipal autonomy as the result of a Town Administration Act (the *Städteordnung*), the police became answerable to the municipal bodies, which therefore took over indirect responsibility for street planning. An exception was made for Berlin, however, where police and town planning both remained directly under the state.[7]

In 1825 the *Baupolizei* in Berlin started to plan the unbuilt areas which were still to be found within the tariff walls. They turned their attention particularly to Köpenicker Feld, the

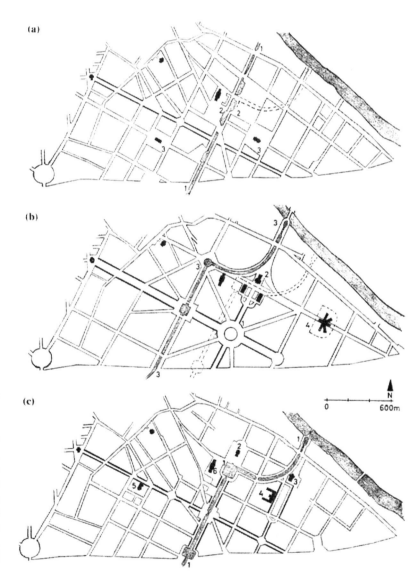

Figure 12.3 *Berlin. Various projects for the Köpenicker Feld, re-drawn by Schinz. (a) Geheimer Baurat Schmid's proposal, 1826, according to which exploitation began. (b) Alternative proposal, submitted by J.P. Lenné, in January 1840. (c) The final plan. [From Schinz (1964)]*

future Luisenstadt, an area of about 370 hectares and thus by far the largest available. Development appears to have started around 1830 according to a plan made by *Oberbaurat* J.C.L. Schmid (figure 12.3a).[8] This is a typical product of an 'engineering' approach, with no pretensions to aesthetic quality. The rectilinear block divisions largely follow the land ownership boundaries, and the area is divided by a canal between Spree and Landwehrgraben. The Crown Prince, the future Frederick William IV, presided over the meeting when the plan was presented to the ministry, and he personally produced an alternative plan which paid greater attention to architectural design. This plan was submitted to Schinkel who, in a report in January 1835, defended the original plan and criticized the prince's. The first plan, according to Schinkel, paid 'the greatest possible attention to the local conditions, which meant particularly that the existing boundaries of fields and garden plots were retained . . . since without this caution the compensation process would be endlessly complicated and costly.' He also noted that there were no sharp pointed blocks and that 'convenient communications and good connections' had been catered for.[9] However, the Crown Prince was not satisfied with Schinkel's statement, but commanded the surveyor of the royal gardens (*Gartendirektor*) J.P. Lenné to design a project which was presented in 1840 (figure 12.3b). This proposal was more in the grand manner dominated by a star-shaped place, suggested by the prince. In a revised version obviously in response to criticism from the *Baubehörde* (the building authority), the star-shaped place was omitted. Instead a square was created along the extension of the canal, in which the Michaelkirche provided a focal point. Another square, Mariannenplatz, was also added. The division into streets and blocks is pretty much the same as in the initial proposal (figure 12.3c).[10]

However, it seems to have been understood that extensive building activities could also be expected outside the tariff wall. As early as 1830 a plan for the surroundings of Berlin – part of which is now lost – was produced by Schmid for the Higher Building Board (the *Technische Oberbaudeputation*).[11] Ten years later, in 1840, Lenné produced his plan, *Projectirte Schmuckund Grenzzüge von Berlin mit nächster Umgegend*[12] (revised version 1843), which among other things proposed a ring of boulevards round the town. This project can be said to set the finishing point of the earlier planning of Berlin as a royal residence, but it also represented an attempt to allow for the requirements of an emerging industrial city.[13]

At the beginning of the 1850s the question of a new building plan was discussed in the police board (*Polizeipräsidium*), and in 1857 a report was presented on how to proceed. Among other things it was suggested that the planned area should be divided into fourteen 'departments' rather than the previous five. It was also claimed that several completed or ongoing building enterprises, including in particular the railway stations and their neighbouring areas of tracks, had rendered the earlier plans largely irrelevant. In 1859 the Minister of Trade put the issue before the King. He suggested that the state and the municipal authorities should share the costs between them, and emphasized the great urgency of the whole question. As a first step extensive surveying and levelling work was necessary. Working from this survey existing plans could then be revised and the street network extended into areas which had not been previously planned.[14]

When the responsible official in the police council fell ill, his task was transferred in 1858 to 32-year-old James Hobrecht, who had qualified as a hydraulic and civil engineer (*Baumeister für den Wasser-, Wege- und Eisenbahnbau*) the year before. Hobrecht had also previously studied to become a land-surveyor at the Bauakademie in Berlin. He seems to have obtained most of his practical professional experience in railway building. Later Hobrecht was to enjoy a successful career as a sewage

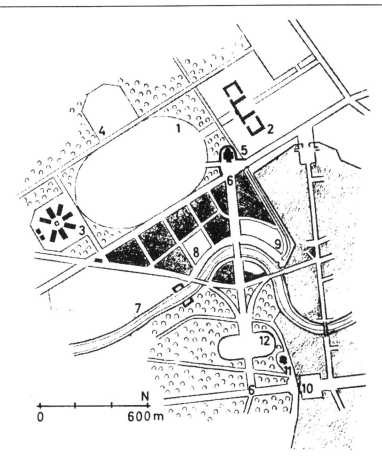

Figure 12.4 *Berlin. One of the most important planning issues towards the middle of the nineteenth century concerned the large area in Moabit which adjoins the existing urban structure and which had become available when a gunpowder factory was moved away. The picture shows an unrealized project by Schinkel from 1840, later reworked by Lenné. The plan is dominated by a large drill-ground (1). From north to south a street (6) runs, with a church (5) providing a focal accent. In the southern part this street passes a ceremonial place (12) in Tiergarten. Here, later, the ambitions of the German imperial era would take shape in the Königsplatz, with the* Siegessäule *as the central accent, and the parliament building, the* Reichstagsgebäude, *as the dominating building. Parallel with this proposed street runs the Neue Wilhelmstraße, with whose construction Schinkel was also involved. [From Schinz (1964)]*

expert in the building administration in Berlin. In 1858 he had no experience at all of urban development issues. That he was given the job in Berlin – in 1859 he was appointed formally as head of the commission for preparing plans for the surroundings of Berlin (*Kommissarium*

zur Ausarbeitung der Bebauungspläne für die Umgebung Berlins) – appears to have been partly a matter of chance. But perhaps it seemed a good idea to choose someone with competence in both land surveying and hydraulic engineering, since the present job would include making a proposal for the sewage system.[15] And anyway there were probably few suitable candidates. However, the choice of a person of such meagre experience suggests that the task was not regarded as particularly complicated or important. To quote a contemporary source, it really meant nothing more than producing 'a mass of local police provisions, that would determine the parts of the plots within the town's jurisdiction which should be built, and which should be left unbuilt and reserved for public streets and open places.'[16]

Hobrecht worked on the Berlin plan, with some interruptions, for about three and half years until December 1861, when he moved to Stettin to another job. He had several assistants at his disposal, and the work was obviously carried out in more or less constant communication with the police board and the local authorities. Hobrecht's instructions were brief, but included a number of points which he was to take into consideration in making the plan. Point 3 in the instructions is as follows:

The preparation of a building plan [should be carried out], utilizing all the hitherto collected material, and in the second place taking into consideration existing stipulations (*Feststellungen*), so long as these appear feasible and appropriate, and under the guidance of the following points:

(*a*) All street structures which can be expected to be required for future traffic should be planned, and in this planning the size of the blocks in Friedrichstadt in the street network between Behren- and Kochstraße should serve as a guideline;

(*b*) sharp-pointed blocks should be avoided as far as possible;

(*c*) according to their function as tree-lined thoroughfares (*Promenaden*), main streets, side streets or alleys, the streets should have a width of 13–15, 7–9, 5–6 or 3–4 *Ruthen* respectively, and a girdle ring road should be particularly considered. The new streets must be connected to the existing ones in an appropriate manner;

(*d*) it is advisable that the streets should have an orientation from south-west to north-east and north-

west to south-east respectively, and that they should lead to a church, a monument, some other important building, towards water or a wooded area or gardens;

(*e*) existing streets and roads, especially such as are legally ratified (confirmed by *Separations-Rezesse*), should only be changed for compelling reasons; furthermore the present boundaries or private plots should be pierced only with the greatest caution and leaving no unbuildable land fragments, which can generally be ensured by a slight adjustment of the new streets;

(*f*) open places shall be distributed according to needs as evenly as possible, and particularly if a church is being considered on this ground it should if possible be located at the highest point, or by a river, a canal or a harbour; suitable planting of these areas should also be considered;

(*g*) the construction of large reservoirs for the collection and purification of street water should be considered if possible in the proximity of the Spree, the Panke or the canals.[17]

Furthermore he should allow for the effects of earlier planning and sometimes also for the wishes of the plot-owners. Thus his freedom of action was circumscribed in various ways. The common view that he executed the plan more or less at his own discretion, is not correct.[18] The fourteen sub-plans were prepared successively and published after royal approval in 1862.[19]

Hobrecht's task differed in almost every way from Haussmann's. In Paris it was primarily a case of redeveloping and clearing existing buildings by constructing new streets; in Berlin, on the other hand, it was entirely a question of making plans for new building. In Paris one of the fundamental goals was to create an efficient street system through the centre; in Berlin the centre was not directly involved.[20] Here, due to earlier efforts the circumstances were more favourable than in Paris, at least in the western part of the central city, the Friedrichstadt. Haussmann wanted to create a city worthy of an empire. Hobrecht certainly had no such ambitions, despite the monumental squares he included. Moreover, the desire for magnificence was well catered for in the centre of the town. And while for Haussmann the emphasis was on the execution of the plan, Hobrecht's planning was intended primarily to indicate guidelines for future expansion in private hands.

At the centre of Hobrecht's plan (figures 12.5 and 12.6) lies the old urban structure, the Tiergarten and the now completed extension Köpenicker Feld. These areas are surrounded almost entirely by new buildings, although the greatest expansion is envisaged to the north and east. Exit roads cut through the new districts and the town is surrounded by a ring road, although on the west and southern sides this does not embrace the whole built area. To the north-east there are a number of concentric streets. The block divisions are not uniform; the blocks themselves vary in size and form, and particularly in peripheral sites are often very big. Several squares are also suggested in the plan. Some are simply unbuilt blocks or parts of blocks, but more ambitiously designed squares are also included, for example two star-shaped places on the north side, another square with closed, cut-off corners to the east, and a series of monumental squares along the

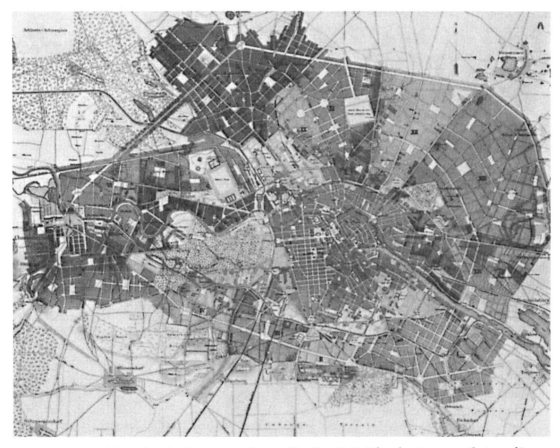

Figure 12.5 *Building plan for the surroundings of Berlin, 1862. The plan is a compilation of James Hobrecht's fourteen subplans. [From* Berlin, Stadtentwicklung im 19. Jahrhundert*]*

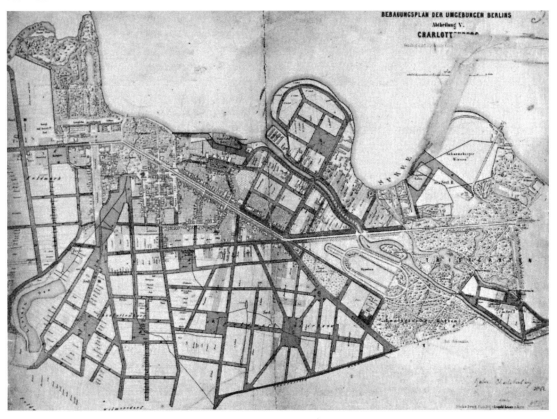

Figure 12.6 *Department V, Charlottenburg, in Hobrecht's building plan for the surroundings of Berlin. The present Savigny-Platz and the Steinplatz and their associated streets, were implemented largely according to the plan. [Photo from Landesbildstelle, Berlin]*

southern section of the ring road. Several of these architecturally conceived squares were to have monumental buildings as a focal point; this is something which shows up more clearly in the local plans than in the overall plan. What is very noticeable is the plain design of the large area to the north-east, the future district of Prenzlauer Berg. The eastern suburbs had little status and Hobrecht had obviously reckoned that the new blocks there would be occupied by workers' housing, while the more expensive housing was intended for the west and south where there were already many patrician homes.

The overall plan itself seems somewhat unstructured, as though there had been no overall guiding idea. The architectural ingredients such as squares and so on appear conventional and rather haphazard. The block divisions seem provisional and the ring road appears to lack any organizational connection with the urban structure which it encircles. But it should be remembered that Hobrecht did not start from any all-embracing concept, but from the conditions prevailing in the different areas to be planned. In fact Hobrecht did not even make the overall plan reproduced here for the whole of Berlin; it represents a compilation of his separate district plans put together by another hand. Naturally this does not mean that Hobrecht had no overall view at all, but simply that the prevailing local conditions provided an essential point of departure for his planning operation.

Thus an analysis and evaluation of Hobrecht's proposal should start not from the overall plan but from the local plans. What were the prevailing conditions, what were the problems, and how did Hobrecht proceed? A first attempt to answer these questions appears in Heinrich's study (1962), although this only looks at two of the sub-plans. Heinrich's conclusion is that Hobrecht adapted his proposal to a great extent to existing streets, buildings, property boundaries, topographical conditions etc.[21] And this, as we have seen, was his brief.

Further, according to Heinrich, Hobrecht's plan was intended primarily as a 'base on which the work could build'.[22] Nor was it ever realized in detail. Even a superficial comparison between the plan and a map of the town shows that the monumental conceptions were largely abandoned and that the block divisions and roads often deviate markedly from those planned.[23] Perhaps we could say that the plan as implemented was of the same kind as Hobrecht's, but was not his exactly. Its impact on developments was thus limited. An investigation of the implementation process might be able to explain the deviation, but so far no such study has been made.

As a result of a reform in Prussia in 1875, the introduction of the *Fluchtliniengesetz*, responsibility for street planning was transferred from the police to the town authorities. Towards the end of the nineteenth century several large German cities introduced *Staffelbauordnungen*, which could be described as building regulations allowing for different building heights in different districts, thus acting as a sort of zoning instrument. In Berlin, however, very little happened.[24] The Hobrecht plan remained formally in force until 1919, although various revisions were made at different times.[25]

Architects and planners who are the subject of criticism from their contemporaries, often

have to wait a long time for an objective evaluation. And the same applies to the built environments they create. The first negative judgements are repeated over and over again, sometimes for several generations. Attitudes to Hobrecht are an example of this phenomenon. From around 1870 and for roughly the next 40 years, the speculative building of *Mietskasernen* flourished, turning Berlin into 'the greatest city of tenements in the world'.[26] These tenements often provided wretched living conditions, with small simple flats grouped around cramped backyards. As far back as the 1870s it was being claimed that Hobrecht's plan fostered this type of building, and in Werner Hegemann's *Das steinerne Berlin*, which appeared in 1930, the planner was presented as though he were almost personally responsible for the spread of tenement building in Berlin. His plan is described as 'incredibly bad', representing the height of the Prussian government's 'Philistinism' and resulting in an environment 'so poor that neither the stupidest devil nor Berlin's most conscientious *Geheimrat* or speculative builder could have produced anything worse.' The criticism is not limited to Hobrecht's values and competence as a planner; the plan is also presented as a botched job, put together with 'infantile thoughtlessness' and making no allowance for existing conditions.[27] This picture of Hobrecht has persisted ever since. Schinz, for example, writes that 'his dreadful work has made his name immortal.'[28]

An unprejudiced evaluation of Hobrecht's activities should, to be fair, take account of his brief and the restricted freedom he was allowed, as well as his experience and the conditions in general. The first attempt at such an evaluation was Heinrich's article published on the centenary of the ratification of the Hobrecht plan, in which the author pointed out that Hobrecht did a competent job, and that the accusations of ignorance and nonchalance were unjustified. Furthermore, his principals did not expect him to produce any grand or radical solutions. On the contrary, the costs of implementation were

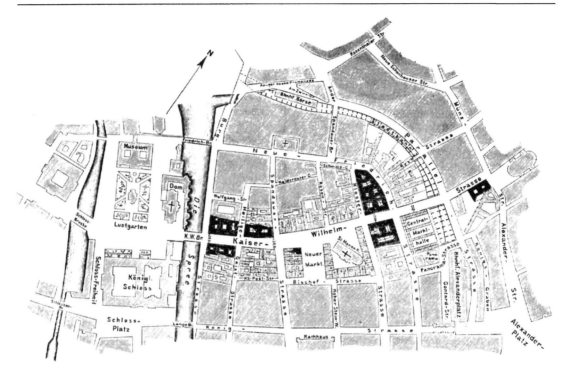

Figure 12.7 *Berlin, the central area around 1890. The Hobrecht plan has no real equivalent to Haussmann's great* percées. *However, some street cuttings – quite unconnected with Hobrecht's plan and its implementation – were realized in the old town in Berlin, mainly in the 1880s. The most important of these involved the Kaiser-Wilhelm-Straße, Neue Friedrichstraße and Parallel-straße. Otherwise any renewal under the* Gründerzeit *took place largely within the existing block structure. [From Engel (1976)]*

to be kept as low as possible by paying minute attention to property boundaries and topographical conditions. As we have just seen, this way of proceeding had been defended by Schinkel at an earlier stage. It would be unrealistic to expect a more radical approach on the part of an official on the threshold of his career – which does not mean that a planner of greater experience and ingenuity could not have produced a better plan.[29]

There is one obvious weakness in the plan, however, for which Hobrecht can perhaps be held responsible, and that is the size of the blocks – particularly as his brief stated that he was to follow the size already adopted in Friedrichstadt. But as Heinrich points out,

Hobrecht may have expected the blocks to be divided up further when they were built.[30] Moreover he may have assumed that the interiors would be left largely unbuilt to provide space for gardens and open areas.

But even if Hobrecht cannot be held personally responsible for doing a poor job, given the conditions under which he worked, his plan may of course have played a fatal role in subsequent developments, irrespective of the fact – largely ignored by his critics – that it was certainly not implemented in all its details. If this claim is to hold, however, it is reasonable to ask ourselves whether the density of the buildings in the inner city could have been avoided in any other plan – even a more imaginative one – given the conditions and, in particular the legal constraints that obtained during the relevant period. And the answer is that it would probably not have been possible. On slightly stronger grounds it might be claimed that the building ordinances which allowed for the heavy exploitation bore the responsibility for the way things later developed. But this supposition does not get at the fundamental causes either. In light of the building tradition and technical possibilities of the time, the densely built areas of blocks of flats were a natural answer to an economic and social situation.[31] Only when these changed did it become possible to create other types of residential milieus, such as the *Siedlungen* of the 1920s.

NOTES

1. The classical work on Berlin's urban development history is Hegemann (1930). But this book is extremely polemical, particularly as regards developments during the second half of the nineteenth century and the main actor, James Hobrecht. The book should be regarded today as a document of its own times, rather than a scholarly work. Schinz (1964) provides a good overview of the building history of the town, very well illustrated with reconstruction drawings and maps, but repeating the traditional denigration of Hobrecht's activities. The first attempt at a more objective analysis of Berlin's planning during the nineteenth century is Heinrich (1962; see also Heinrich 1960, which provides a survey of Berlin's urban development since the end of the eighteenth century). Extensive information on Berlin's nineteenth-century planning history is given in Geist and Kürvers (1980); this, despite a rather rhapsodic exposition, provides a good picture of Hobrecht's activities and the conditions under which he worked. A number of essays have also addressed the subject of nineteenth-century planning in Berlin in varying detail, of which Matzerath and Thienel (1977) and Sutcliffe (1979b) should be mentioned. But taken as a whole, surprisingly little research has been devoted to the Hobrecht plan, at least in comparison with what has been written about many of the other capital city plans. A major work on the physical development of Berlin during the period of industrialization is Thienel (1973), although this does not focus particularly on planning. A broader historical view of the same period is given in Masur (1970).

2. The following description of Berlin's early history largely follows Schinz (1964).

3. As regards the east-west axis, see Larsson (1978), pp. 55 ff.

4. Obviously pains were taken as far as possible to utilize church towers and palaces as foci for the streets (cf. the plan in Schinz (1964), p. 97).

5. On Schinkel's activities in Berlin, see Pundt (1972).

6. See p. 64; cf. also Thienel (1973), p. 369. The figures refer to the town of Berlin. Greater Berlin had over 2,700,000 inhabitants in 1900.

7. Sutcliffe (1981b), pp. 11 f.

8. According to Wenzel (1989), p. 71, Schmid made plans not only for the unbuilt areas inside the toll border but also for the entire surrounding area. But these plans do not seem to have been published.

9. Quoted from Schinz (1964), p. 224 f.

10. According to Schinz the final version is supposed to have been made by the *Baubehörde*. But on Lenné's 1840 master plan – *Projectirte Schmuck- und Grenzzüge von Berlin mit nächster Umgegend* – the design of Köpenicker Feld does not agree with the version given in Schinz as Lenné's draft, but is much closer to the final solution. Thus if Lenné himself is not responsible for the form of Köpenicker Feld on the 1840 master plan, another proposal with this design must have been completed the same year and incorporated in his proposal. However, Lenné is regarded as the author of the final plan, for example by Engel (1976), p. 50 and Wenzel (1989), pp. 75 ff. Lenné probably drew the plan, but adapted it to meet the requirements of the relevant authorities.

11. Geist and Kürvers (1980), p. 466.

12. The meaning is roughly: Roads planned along the borders as well as to beautify the city of Berlin and its neighbouring areas.

13. Geist and Kürvers (1980), pp. 476 ff. Lenné's contribution is also touched upon in Engel (1976), p. 50.

14. The description above is based primarily on Geist and Kürvers (1980), pp. 468 ff and Heinrich (1962).
15. Cf. Geist and Kürvers (1980), p. 485. The work did not start until April 1859.
16. Quoted from Heinrich (1962), p. 42.
17. Quoted from Geist and Kürvers (1980), pp. 485 f.
18. This is convincingly demonstrated in Geist and Kürvers (1980, pp. 485 ff) in an analysis of departments IX and XI in the plan (on the north side of the tariff wall, to the west of Schönhauser Allee).
19. See Heinrich (1962), p. 45.
20. Cf. Sutcliffe (1979b), p. 83. Independently of the execution of the Hobrecht plan, the municipality of Berlin initiated some street-cuttings through the old urban area, the most important being the Kaiser-Wilhelm-Straße constructed between 1877 and 1887. This enterprise wiped out the Gasse an der Königsmauer, notorious for its prostitutes and brothels (cf. figure 12.7 and Radicke, 1995).
21. Heinrich (1962), p. 55 *et passim*. Heinrich's interpretation is confirmed by Geist and Kürvers (1980), which comes to a similar conclusion.
22. Heinrich (1962), p. 55.
23. There does not seem to be any complete comparison of the plan and its result. Heinrich's conclusion is that Hobrecht's plan 'was admittedly implemented everywhere as regards the main lines it lays down, but only rarely when it comes to local solutions; in particular, the blocks in many places have been further divided or divided in quite a different way than was planned' (Heinrich (1962), p. 50).
24. Cf. Sutcliffe (1979b), pp. 83 f and (1981b), pp. 19 ff). Sutcliffe, as earlier Hegemann, suggests that as a result of his position in the Berlin building administration Hobrecht put the brakes on a more progressive type of planning. It should be pointed out here, however, that Hobrecht's later activities were devoted entirely to sewage facilities; there seems to be no concrete evidence suggesting that he sought to check progressive initiatives in the planning of Berlin.
25. On the continuous revisions in one of the 'departments', see Heinrich (1962), p. 45.
26. The quotation is the subtitle of Werner Hegemann's *Das steinerne Berlin*.
27. Hegemann (1930), p. 295 ff.
28. Schinz (1964), p. 121.
29. The revaluation of Hobrecht's contribution which was started by Heinrich, was supported by Geist and Kürver's study.
30. Heinrich (1962), p. 50.
31. Cf. *ibidem*, p. 52 *et passim*. Thienel (1973, p. 43) suggests a similar view.

13

STOCKHOLM

The history of Stockholm as a town goes back to the last decades of the thirteenth century.[1] The first town grew up on an island, later known as Stadsholmen, between Lake Mälaren and the Baltic. The oldest settlement was on the high triangular plateau of the island, and was surrounded by a simple wall. In the course of the fourteenth and fifteenth centuries the island grew, partly as a result of land elevation and partly as rubbish silted up the water, and it was at this time that the radial street network that is so typical of the old city (*Gamla stan*) emerged. At an early stage there was also some building on the mainland to the north and south of Stadsholmen, in what are known as the *malmar*, the suburban areas of Norrmalm and Södermalm outside the city wall. During the fifteenth century a new town wall was begun but never finished; in the course of the sixteenth century it lost any importance it had previously had.[2]

The middle of the seventeenth century saw intensive efforts to enhance the towns of Sweden (see pp. 30 f); an urban system of the continental type was regarded as essential to Sweden's new image – and indeed to its function – as a great European power. And Stockholm naturally attracted the most attention. The chancellor Axel Oxenstierna was convinced that 'if only Stockholm could grow and its population begin to swell', then 'the others would get on their legs as well.'[3] Stockholm was favoured, in that it received large donations of land, and the towns of northern Sweden were forbidden to engage in foreign trade; all goods had to be transported in or out via Stockholm or Åbo. But these benefits carried certain obligations. Among other things town planning improvement without parallel in Sweden – possibly with the exception of Uppsala – or elsewhere in Europe were instituted in Stockholm, according to directives issued by the government of Queen Christina's regency. The regularization of the town had started as early as the 1620s, when the western part of the medieval urban core acquired a new town plan after a fire. At the end of the 1630s the redevelopment of the suburbs began, and a few decades later the winding medieval street network had disappeared to make room for a systematically executed plan consisting of straight streets crossing each other at right angles and, so far as possible, regular blocks. Because of the topography, however, the street system had a different orientation in the different districts, each of which had its own market square (figure 13.1). The seventeenth-century street network remained comparatively intact until the redevelopments of recent decades, and even now much of it can be said to have survived as it was. The man mainly responsible for the seventeenth-century plans and their implementation was Anders Torstensson, who acted as town engineer from 1636, the first person to occupy such a position in Stockholm. Torstensson was also responsible for several other plans, for instance for Södertälje, Uppsala and Åbo. It seems reasonable to describe him as a professional planner, and this

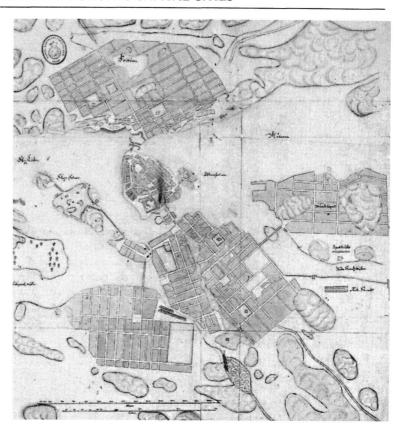

Figure 13.1 *Stockholm.*
Map showing
regularizations and
extensions implemented
and planned, c. 1660.
[Lantmäteriverkets arkiv,
Gävle]

is certainly also how his contemporaries saw him.

At the beginning of the nineteenth century Stockholm had about 90,000 inhabitants. The first 40 years of the century were characterized by the greatest population growth in Swedish history: the population of the country increased from 2.4 to 3.5 million. But the share of the urban population remained unchanged, representing about 10 per cent of the total. In Stockholm the population had risen to a little under 100,000 by 1850.

Industrialization in any real sense was late to start in Sweden, and there were few signs of it before the last decades of the nineteenth century. But as far back as the middle of the century a number of changes had occurred which affected conditions in the towns. The

guild system was abolished in 1846, and full freedom to trade was introduced in 1864. A Companies Act came into operation in 1848. In 1866 the old Estates had been replaced by a two-chamber parliament, albeit not one that was democratically elected. In 1862 a new system of municipal administration had been introduced. Another important factor was the building of the railways, which began in 1855. In 1862 the main western line between Stockholm and Gothenburg was finished, followed in 1864 by the southern line between Stockholm and Malmö via Falköping. Around 1860 the urban population began to increase relative to the size of the total for the whole country. From 10 per cent in 1850 it rose to 20 per cent around 1900 and 30 per cent around 1930. The population of Stockholm rose from about 100,000 in 1856 to 200,000 in 1884 and 300,000 by 1900. At the same time the town was undergoing rapid industrialization, which transformed it into the unrivalled leader among Sweden's industrial towns. Advanced mechanical production, food processing and the printing industry were all important there.[4]

As early as the seventeenth century a good deal of planning activity had taken place in Sweden, as we have already noted (see p. 201). The initiative came from the central government; the burghers' attitude to the proposals for improvements was generally negative. Most of the projects remained either wholly or partly on paper. Stockholm is one of the comparatively few examples of successfully implemented regularization schemes. Towards the end of the seventeenth century planning activities tailed off. Moreover, after the death of Charles XII in 1718, constitutional changes reduced the government's powers. Street improvements were also discussed during the eighteenth century, but almost without exception because destruction by fire forced the issue. The towns were now in a stronger position than during the previous century, and thus the changes were slight.[5] It was not until after the municipal reform of 1862 that the central authorities seriously re-addressed planning questions; as a result of the 1874 building ordinances, the towns were obliged to produce plans. Some plans had in fact already been made before that date, for example for Vänersborg, Karlstad and Umeå.[6] The first town planning competition in the country was held as early as 1861, with a view to producing a plan for Gothenburg.

Planning in Stockholm started relatively late, which by no means implies that the existing situation was satisfactory. On the contrary. In the middle of the nineteenth century the sanitary and building standards in Stockholm were wretched, although the situation varied from one district to another. Conditions were worst in the 'Town between the Bridges' (*Staden mellan broarna*), i.e. the medieval urban core. The streets were narrow, the traffic dense, green areas and public open spaces practically non-existent; houses were narrow, high and overcrowded. A visitor from the United States in 1857 complained that the streets were 'as dirty as in New York'.[7] In other words the problems were much the same as in many other large cities. In parts of the *malmar*, however, the environment was in some respects better. Development was less intensive, and the many gardens were a bright spot. Moreover, thanks to the seventeenth-century improvements, the streets were straight and relatively broad. But in some parts of the town the water was seriously polluted. The harbours were badly organized and the waterside blocked by tanneries and other activities. In addition to all this the water supply and the refuse disposal system were both poor, particularly of course in the central areas.

The city administration responsible for solving these problems was organized in an old-fashioned way, with the magistracy (*magistraten*) as the executive organ and The Fifty Elders as a kind of decision-making body. Furthermore the municipal revenues were small, and the administrative resources notably limited. The town governor (*överståthållaren*) appointed by the government was in a strong position, presiding over the meetings of the magistracy and the Elders; an energetic governor was essential if any concrete results were to be achieved.[8]

The 1850s appear to have been something of a turning-point in the history of urban development in Stockholm; a number of major projects were discussed, and began in part to be realized. At this time Stockholm was predominantly a shipping and trading town,[9] and the first major modernizing operations concerned the construction and equipping of quays and improving the harbours. Thus by the beginning of the 1850s Stadsholmen was surrounded on both sides by new quays. At about the same time the first gasworks were built, and water mains began to be planned. The question of

the railway also came up at this time. The state
railway company was responsible, in accordance with a decision in the *Riksdag*, for all
three long-distance main lines radiating out
from Stockholm (the so-called *stambanorna*).
The conditions were thus right for a single
centrally located mainline station, a possibility
which the chief railway building engineer Nils
Ericson was eager to exploit. The town preferred the idea of two reversing stations,
mainly because they feared that the planned
railway link over Lake Mälaren would have a
detrimental effect on conditions in the
harbours. However, Ericson's idea met with a
positive response from the central authorities,
and the mainline station was located on western
Norrmalm on what was previously the shore of
Klara sjö. The first stretch was opened in 1860,
and *sammanbindningsbanan*, the linking line
through the town, began to be built in 1863 and
came into operation in 1871. Thus Stockholm
acquired a station where all the main lines met,
and avoided the problems so often caused in
other capital cities which had reversing stations
on sites at the edge of town.

The question of the connecting line came to
be linked to plans for the extending of the
quays; most members of the magistracy and
The Fifty Elders wanted to obstruct the idea of
a connecting line by constructing quays on
Riddarholmen, but the government and the
governor compelled the town to invest instead
in a combined quay and esplanade project
along Nybroviken, the future Strandvägen.
The construction work began in 1861, and gave
Stockholm its first broad tree-lined road. For
traffic purposes Strandvägen was not perhaps
the most urgent project at the time, but for
many decades it was the most fashionable
street in town for strolling and taking the air.

The building of the railway lines and quays,
and the way in which railway and steamer
traffic should be linked together, were planning
issues that were crucial to the future development of the town, although no overall plan was
made. As early as 1846 a regularization plan

for parts of Stadsholmen had in fact been
prepared as the result of a private initiative.
This plan, the work of the architect G.Th.
Chiewitz, has not survived. But it was invoked
on several later occasions, for instance in 1857
in a debate on a public building proposal in the
Burghers' Estate in the *Riksdag*. One speaker,
referring to the then current works in Paris,
demanded that a plan should be made for the
regularization of Stadsholmen.[10] His demand
was satisfied, probably in a more radical way
than he had envisaged, in the proposal submitted by the master builder A.E. Rudberg in
1860,[11] and published in a revised version in
1862.[11] Here, apart from a few important
monuments, old buildings have been levelled
and replaced by straight streets and regular
blocks (figure 13.2). In a commentary on the
plan Rudberg summarized the reasons for his
approach, painting a gloomy picture of the
existing structure with all its many deficiencies.

Rudberg's activities did not win any immediate sympathy in the municipal administration.
However, as early as 1857 – the same year that
a regularization plan had been called for in the
Riksdag – a comb-maker named A.E.
Schuldheis had put forward a proposal at a
meeting of the magistracy and the Elders for 'a
plan for the . . . successive improvement and
embellishment of the town'; a planning competition should be arranged for this purpose.[12]
The idea was to embrace not only or even
primarily Stadsholmen, but the whole city.
However, Schuldheis's proposal was vague and
inadequately prepared; he was about to withdraw it, when another member declared that in
such a case he would adopt it as his own.
Schuldheis's suggestion was strongly criticized;
among other things it was said that a plan
would anyway be no more than a drawing-
board product committing nobody to anything.
Naturally people were also worried that a plan
would threaten property-owner interests;
added to which the idea conflicted with the
conservatism and caution that was typical of
municipal politics at the time. Despite all this it

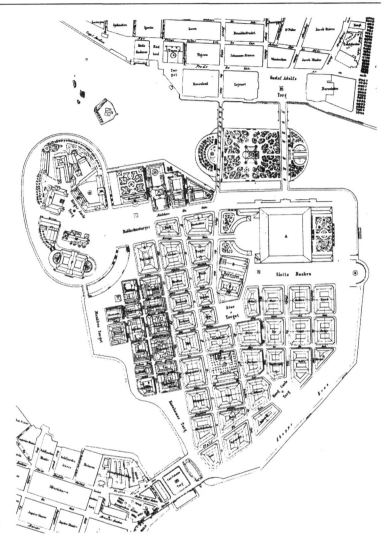

Figure 13.2 *Stockholm. A.E. Rudberg's proposal for the rebuilding of the 'Town between the Bridges', 1862. [Kungliga biblioteket, Stockholm]*

was decided by eighteen votes to thirteen that a committee should be appointed to examine the question. After more than eighteen months the committee produced a report, in which it supported and even elaborated Schuldheis's ideas: a plan was to be made for the comprehensive improvement of all quays, streets and squares; it should also include suggestions for new streets, the planting of trees and so on. But when the issue was discussed again by the

magistracy and The Fifty Elders a year later, in 1860, it was announced that the time was not yet ripe for making such a plan; mention was also made of the absence of any adequate survey on which to base it.

But radical changes were just round the corner. In 1862 the municipal reform mentioned above was finally passed, and the same year Gillis Bildt, a 41-year-old General and great grandfather of the former prime minister of Sweden, was appointed governor of Stockholm. Bildt was an energetic and progressive man, eager to press on with transforming Stockholm into a healthier and more efficiently functioning town. Perhaps he was inspired by Haussmann, who at that time was at the peak of his fame and had not yet been exposed to any serious criticism. At the beginning of 1863 Bildt sent an official letter to the town authorities, in which he referred to Schuldheis's proposal and emphasized the need to have a plan which would include areas hitherto unbuilt as well as improvements in the existing urban structure. It should also allow for adequate communications between the outskirts and the centre of the town and, as far as possible, for streets and quays on the periphery of the town. His missive also included concrete suggestions for improvement and new streets. An important point was that Bildt was prepared to exclude the 'Town between the Bridges' from the planning activities; he admitted that action was urgent there, but felt it would have to be so extensive and consequently very costly that it should be taken up as a separate project. In this Bildt diverged from Haussmann, to whom the clearance of the urban core was fundamental. On the other hand, the idea here – unlike Berlin and Copenhagen – was to 'puncture' parts of the existing urban structure with new streets in much the same way as Haussmann had done in Paris. The decision to exclude the 'Town between the Bridges' from the regularization programme was to have very important implications for the future of Stockholm. The medieval urban core was 'saved', according to the way we see things today, but was also doomed to lose its function as the city centre to Norrmalm, becoming simply 'the Old City'.[13]

As a result of the governor's letter the city engineer A.W. Wallström was asked to produce the requisite master plan, together with the builder mentioned above, Rudberg, 'who had made a meritorious plan for the building of the "Town between the Bridges" '.[14] The city

council (the *stadsfullmäktige*) allocated the necessary funds for the work. The proposal was successively presented in the shape of a series of seven area plans (cf. figure 13.3), the first of which was ready by the autumn of 1863. Thus, like the Hobrecht plan for Berlin a few years earlier, the sheet showing the plan for the whole town represents a secondary combination of a series of previous sub-plans.[15] This type of procedure, whereby each district is planned separately, can mean that overriding aspects are insufficiently observed; and Rudberg and Wallström do seem to have paid more attention to details than to the holistic view, something which can probably also be said of Hobrecht. Thus, the existing urban structure has been left largely intact, apart from some improvements near the planned central station.

No serious attempt has been made to establish adequate communications between the northern districts. Admittedly a tunnel under the Johannes district is suggested, but its capacity would have been meagre and it had no satisfactory link-up with the street network on the western side. New areas have been laid out by adding extensions – generally wider – to existing streets, but the width of the streets is everywhere quite modest. The creation of new crossing-streets has resulted in a somewhat unstructured network of large blocks; here, too, the system of through-roads does not appear to have received sufficient attention. Tree-lined streets and parks are mainly confined to the outer reaches of the city, and were to make hardly any real impact on conditions in the central districts. As in the Hobrecht plan for Berlin, a large section of the urban area is surrounded by a ring boulevard along the city border, as instructed by the governor himself. Market squares have been planned in several places. A number of star-shaped 'squares' are also included in the plan, mainly located on the ring boulevard. To summarize: Rudberg and Wallström's proposal was certainly made with the best intentions,

Figure 13.3 *Stockholm. A.E. Rudberg's and A.W. Wallström's project for improving the area around St Klara, one of the seven local plans for Stockholm, 1863. [Kungliga biblioteket, Stockholm]*

and its details are in many cases well thought-out, but it lacks the great radical vision required for any fundamental improvement in Stockholm's urban environment.

During 1864 Rudberg and Wallström's proposals were submitted successively by the governor to the newly established finance committee (*drätselnämnden*). This was a body under the city council, which had come into operation in 1863. Obviously the governor had

expected that the municipal authorities' handling of the issue would be mainly limited to allocating the necessary funds. But the finance committee was not prepared to approve the new plan just like that. Instead, in its turn, it appointed a special committee to examine the proposal. It must be left open whether the goal was primarily to have the plan assessed, or whether it was to demonstrate the new autonomy of the municipal government. However that may be, the work of this committee was dominated by Albert Lindhagen, permanent undersecretary of state (*expeditionschef*) and later member of the Supreme Court, who soon became its chairman. The outcome was that Rudberg and Wallström's project was declared unusable. The Lindhagen Committee's report took the form of a new proposal, presented in 1866 and published the following year.[16]

In its far-sightedness, its broad perspectives and its cogent presentation this proposal (figures 13.4 and 13.6) is a high-water mark in Stockholm's planning history. We should not uncritically accept the Lindhagen Committee's negative view of Rudberg and Wallström's project, however, since this certainly provided an important point of departure for the work of the Lindhagen Committee and gave it several concrete ideas to work on.

The most striking element in the Lindhagen Committee's proposal is a long 70-metre-wide avenue across the whole of Norrmalm from Brunnsviken to Gustav Adolfs Torg, 'a broad . . . artery for traffic, air and light.'[17] The northern section of this grand thoroughfare, one of the most grandiose street projects of the nineteenth century, ran mainly over ground that had hitherto been developed either little or not at all, but its southern length was to cut not only through the Brunkeberg, a ridge stretching from north to south across the northern parts of the town, but also across the built-up area of central Norrmalm. Among the buildings which would have to be demolished was Adolf Fredrik's church. To the east of this avenue a slightly narrower tree-lined street was planned, which would run straight as an arrow through the whole northern area of the city to the Berzelii Park. The east-west connection was catered for by a street which would run from a star-shaped place in the neighbourhood

of the present Fridhemsplan, cutting diagonally through the street network in Kungsholmen to join up at Norrmalm with the pattern of the existing network, and opening up communications through the Brunkeberg, after which it would cut diagonally across Östermalm to another new star-shaped place, roughly the present Karlaplan. On the southern side of Norrmalm a broad passage has been opened through the existing urban structure from Berzelii Park through Kungsträdgården and along the length of Jakobsgatan to the present Tegelbacken. The main routes in the north are Karlbergsvägen and a street roughly on the site of the present Odengatan. Other thoroughfares are also included, as well as quays and roads along the embankments and a boulevard encircling the built-up area on the north and east sides of the town.

On Södermalm the existing main streets, Hornsgatan and Götgatan, were to be widened and a ring road was to encompass the main part of the district. In this way, and with the help of a ramp road or viaduct leading up to Södermalmstorg it was possible to solve the awkward problem of linking the street network of inner Södermalm to the low-lying embankment, which was isolated from the interior of the district by several obstructive rocky outcrops. Rudberg and Wallström's proposal also included a ring road at the same site, but without any direct connection with the embankment. Instead tunnels were to cater for communications here.

On separate maps the Lindhagen Committee presented their proposals for linking the main street system to the road network in the surroundings of the city, and it was suggested that several roads should be straightened and new sections built.[18]

A remarkable feature of this proposal is the

Figure 13.4 *Stockholm. The Lindhagen Committee's proposal, 1866, for the improvement and expansion of the city. Above: the northern section. Below: the southern section. [From Selling (1970)]*

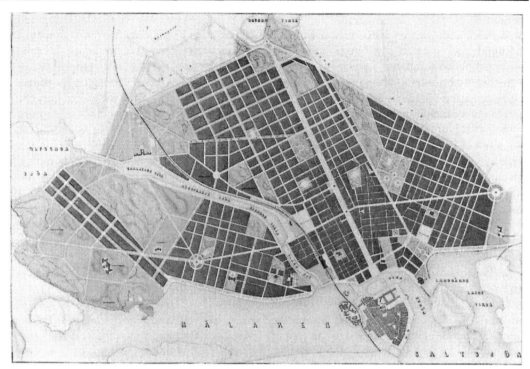

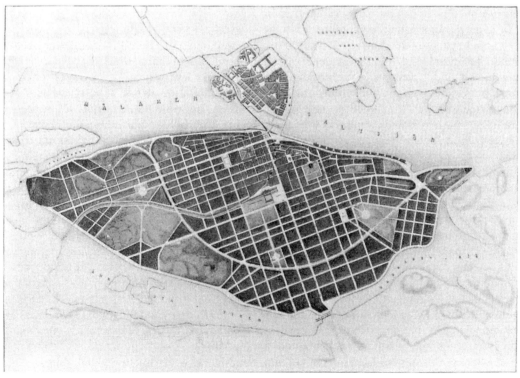

abundance of parks. In particular it can be noted that Humlegården is connected with the woodland and park areas beyond the ring boulevard by an unbroken stretch of green as far as the city boundary. From Humlegården a tree-lined avenue leads to Berzelii Park, which has also been substantially extended by filling in the whole of Nybroviken. This park is connected in turn with another one on Blasieholmen to the east of the National Museum and, via a further planted area in what is now Norrmalmstorg, also with Kungsträdgården. A number of other parks were also proposed, mainly located in places where the topography made it difficult to build.

On Norrmalm the Lindhagen Committee suggested two large market squares on much the same sites as Rudberg and Wallström had indicated: one in the neighbourhood of the present Norra Bantorget and one to the east of Nybroviken. As for the design of the blocks, the Lindhagen Committee proposal diverges hardly from that of Rudberg and Wallström; in both cases the blocks are rectangular throughout; some are also very large. It should be noted, however, that the Lindhagen version included planted forecourts in the blocks to the north of Karlbergsvägen and elsewhere. The Committee's proposal included no new public buildings, apart from indicating the sites for a few churches; in this respect it differs from most other capital city plans. Perhaps the Committee was influenced by all the financing problems and mounting costs that had arisen in connection with the recently completed building of the National Museum. But one or two public buildings could hardly have been more unrealistic than all those great broad thoroughfares.

That there was nothing random about the genesis of the Lindhagen Committee's plan is evident from the explanatory commentary accompanying it. Judging from experience in other countries the planners reckoned on a rapid increase in the population of Stockholm from 126,000 in 1865 to 200,000 in 1890 and 300,000 in 1915. This forecast proved to be astonishingly accurate: the figures were in fact 246,000 and 364,000 respectively. The Committee regarded this growth process as unfortunate, but impossible to prevent. Its negative consequences must therefore be guarded against, by way of far-sighted planning among other things. Efficient traffic routes and streets of appropriate width, if possible planted with trees, embankments and a large number of parks were regarded by the Committee as important remedies against 'all the wretched consequences in our towns, which undermine the health of the body and pollute and exhaust the mind.'[19]

Implementation of the plan is also discussed, and here the commentary is surprisingly defensive in tone, presumably as its authors were all too aware of what was politically possible. The plan was to be realized largely as a result of voluntary clearance and development by the land-owners; the town's activities were to be limited to acquiring ground for the streets and constructing them in stages as the new houses were built. Calculating from the amount of building which had taken place in the last few years, it was reckoned that implementation would take 63 years. During this period some houses would lie further back from the road than others in many of the streets, which the Committee did not consider to be a very serious disadvantage. Until the whole street had been widened, the unbuilt pockets thus formed could be used for planted forecourts. It is difficult not to feel that the Committee was making very light of the difficulties and costs connected with the proposed street works.

This great town plan proposal with its accompanying commentary was, formally, a committee product. Apart from Lindhagen the Committee included two architects (P.J. Ekman and Ludvig Hawerman), one engineering officer (F.W. Leijonancker) and one master builder and contractor (Axel Alm). All the members were local politicians. However, Selling regards Lindhagen as the main author of the plan, certainly with justification; this, too, is how his contemporaries appear to have regarded him. Moreover, the commentary has survived in an original hand-written version in Lindhagen's writing. As Selling suggests, the most important actor apart from Lindhagen, was probably Leijonancker, who was familiar from his extensive foreign travels with what was being done in towns abroad, and who also planned Stockholm's first water mains.[20]

Reactions to the Lindhagen Committee's proposal were mixed. *Stockholms Dagblad*, for instance, wrote: 'It is not unlikely that some people will regard this as mere "plan-mongering" on a colossal scale, and will consider that such radical and far-reaching redevelopment is utterly unnecessary, while others may well admit the appropriateness of the plan but will shrink from the thought of the costs involved.' But for its own part the newspaper felt that the proposal should be adopted as quickly as possible and not postponed to an uncertain future, as the difficulties of implementing it would simply grow.[21] Other judges were cautious or sceptical. Generally speaking, as *Stockholms Dagblad* feared, people seem to have found the plan 'too grand'.

Once the Lindhagen Committee had finished its work, the question of the town plan was left pending for eight years. There does not seem to be any obvious single explanation for this. One important factor may have been the slump in the housing market in the late 1860s;[22] thus the question of a master plan did not perhaps seem very urgent. Another explanation could be that the very size and complexity of the problems made people postpone tackling them as long as possible. Moreover, as Selling points out, there were also problems about how to handle the whole issue. The town had no expert officials in the relevant field apart from the town architect, who did not take part in the discussions on the plan since planning was not considered part of architecture, and the city

engineer whose own proposal had been turned down by the Lindhagen Committee. Added to which, both these men were accountable to the old trade and finance board (*handels- och ekonomikollegium*) under the magistracy, which supervised building activities in the town and which was not embraced by the new municipal organization.[23] Thus it was unclear who was to decide about what.

At the beginning of the 1870s building activity began to pick up again; in 1872, for example, two building and real estate development companies were founded, both with huge plans for their future operations.[24] Several local street improvement schemes were carried out under private auspices. It became clear that the town must act if it wanted to keep any control over developments. The finance committee was also urged by the town architect among others to take up its planning activities again. And the administrative problems were now being sorted out. In a building by-law ratified in 1870 it was decreed that questions 'regarding the construction of new blocks or the changing of old ones should be handled by the city council'. A commission was investigating the abolition of the old trade and finance board to put an end to the dual command of the old and new municipal bodies, and from 1874 onwards the new finance committee had a building director at its disposal as an expert. The 1874 building ordinances for all the towns in the country were also very important; they had been drawn up by Albert Lindhagen. It was stipulated that building issues should be dealt with by a special building committee, and not by a unit under the magistracy. Furthermore it became mandatory for the towns to make town plans.

In January 1874 the question of a master plan was finally taken up again. Thus began five years of proposals and counterproposals, referrals and comments, reservations, objections, compromises and votes, before the town plans could finally be accepted.[25] Planning issues were discussed first in a special working subcommittee of the finance committee, of which Lindhagen was a member, after which they moved on to the committee itself. Next the plan proposals were passed to the drafting committee (*beredningsutskottet*), which sent them out for comment to various bodies including the building committee, after which the proposals were submitted to the city council. And once the plan had been approved by the council, it had to be submitted by the governor to the government for ratification.

It is not possible here to describe in even the barest outlines the chequered career of the plan proposals, as they wound their way through the municipal apparatus. It was obvious at the very first meetings in the working subcommittee that opinions were many and various and conflict inevitable. In order to get things moving, and also to prevent unplanned development, a partial plan referring to a minor and largely unbuilt part of Östermalm was approved in 1875.[26] Essentially it followed the Lindhagen Committee's block divisions, but omitted the proposed diagonal street. This proved to be the first of several fatal blows to the Committee's proposal. Another was that the new city engineer, Rudolf Brodin, as well as the newly appointed building director, C.J. Knös, were commissioned at the beginning of 1876 to produce a new plan proposal. This project (figure 13.5), known as 'the delegates' proposal', aimed to simplify the Committee's proposed development schemes and to reduce their costs, and on some counts it accorded

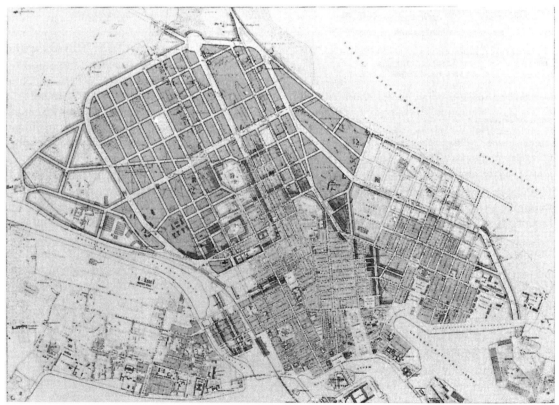

Figure 13.5 *Stockholm. The 'delegates' plan', 1876, for the expansion of Norrmalm. [From Selling (1970)]*

with Rudberg and Wallström's plan. All the main streets on the Lindhagen Committee proposal were either reduced in size, moved or eliminated. The street north-east of Humlegården was widened to become an esplanade, the present Karlavägen;[27] it was also intended to extend this street round the planned districts in the north of the town. The outer ring boulevard to the east was abandoned mainly because it would have touched on crown land, and the state bodies involved were rather ungenerously watching over their own interests. This attitude appears to have been shared by the government. There is a striking difference here compared with Vienna, for example, where the central government took it for granted that state-owned land should be exploited for the benefit and enhancement of the town.

The appointment of a new planning group was a severe setback for Lindhagen, but he was ready with an answer. Even before Brodin and Knös had completed their work, he had presented a new plan for Norrmalm based on the ideas in his committee's proposal.[28] Over the next few years the issue passed slowly through all the necessary levels; over and over again it was discussed at meetings, only to be shelved once more.[29] For instance, it took the town council eight meetings in November–December 1877 and three more the following year, before it had fully dealt with the Norrmalm plan. Discussion at all these meetings tended to revolve round details – the width or extension of streets and so on – rather than tackling the plan as a whole. Sometimes separate votes were even taken on different sections of one street. Votes were often won by small majorities, with supporters and opponents switching sides from one question to another, and decisions going one way at one level and another way at the next. Lindhagen seems to have been the only one of the politicians to have started from a well-thought-out overall view, and he fought persistently and indomitably for his proposal. Against him were ranged

the advocates of thrift, various real estate interests,[30] and pundits of all kinds. Gustaf Nerman, an engineer and writer who had won a prize in the 1862 competition for a town plan for Gothenburg, was a serious opponent. In many respects he held progressive views, but he seems to have disliked Lindhagen's long, broad streets. He also represented one of the above-mentioned real estate development companies. He criticized Lindhagen's proposal energetically, sometimes perhaps purely for reasons of prestige, and recommended instead the proposal put forward by the city engineer and the building director.

The fiercest struggles raged over the planned Birger Jarlsgatan, which according to Lindhagen should be extended to Nybroviken. One powerful constellation wanted to continue Sturegatan to Norrmalmstorg instead; this group included representatives of the two real estate companies, who were involved in the developments along this street and in the neighbouring area north-east of Humlegården. Lindhagen's line won the day, however, but by the smallest possible margin (46 to 45).[31] The upper part of Birger Jarlsgatan, on the other hand, was not to have the straight extension envisaged by Lindhagen. According to the delegates' proposal (figure 13.5) Odengatan was to be slightly displaced sideways at a square in the middle of its length (roughly the present Odenplan), but Lindhagen succeeded in achieving a straight street, albeit not as wide as he had wanted. This victory, too, was gained by a margin of one vote. In the Lindhagen Committee's proposal Karlaplan had been star-shaped. In the delegates' project this place was abandoned altogether, while the sub-committee recommended a rectangular 'square'. On this issue, too, Lindhagen achieved a majority in the town council and the star-shaped place was approved. Further, it was decided that Sveavägen should continue to Adolf Fredriks Kyrkogata, but its width was reduced from 70 to 48 metres; the westernmost section of Kungsgatan was also decided upon, but its width was reduced from 24 to 18 metres. On other important points, however, Lindhagen was totally defeated.

The plan for Kungsholmen also led to considerable debate, and the decision process followed a similar path. The main question was whether to accept the diagonal thoroughfare proposed by the Lindhagen Committee, cutting across the whole district by extending Drottningholmsvägen to Kungsgatan, or whether to follow the delegates' proposal which meant widening Fleminggatan and letting a short cross-street carry the traffic from there to Drottningholmsvägen. At first Lindhagen's alternative met with a favourable response, but one Kungsholm resident succeeded in demolishing this support by presenting a revised version of the delegates' proposal.[32]

The plan for Södermalm was less controversial and was dealt with at a single meeting of the city council. An important feature here was Ringvägen, which in variously modified forms had appeared in all the proposals. Hornsgatan was also to be widened.[33]

The Norrmalm plan was ratified in 1879, and the plans for Kungsholmen and Södermalm in 1880.[34] The three plans, with the possible exception of Södermalm, were typical products of compromise and were lacking in the consistency and broad perspective which characterized the proposal of the Lindhagen Committee. But the attempts which were nonetheless made to provide a traffic communication system were largely derived from Lindhagen's various proposals. It was to prove that on the whole the ratified plans were feasible and appropriate to the available resources. But many problems were allowed to rest for the time being, for example the redevelopment of existing built areas and the creation of good communications between the various districts.

These planning activities in Stockholm were completed just as the great building era was dawning. Over the following decades it was a rare year which saw fewer than 5,000 room units added to the stock; some years the figure was over 10,000.[35] With the street network that was ratified in 1879–80 the dense city core spread into old ramshackle areas and former gardens. The town's responsibility was generally restricted to constructing the streets, which necessarily involved it in an extensive trading in plots. As in Paris a few decades earlier it proved more profitable to buy up whole properties and to sell the plots after the streets were laid down, than to expropriate only the parts of the plots which were to be developed as streets. Thus by the end of 1895 the town had acquired plots amounting to a total area of almost 5,000,000 m² at a cost of something in excess of 32 million kronor. Only a small proportion of the ground had been resold by that date, but it had already become clear that the increase in land values would go a long way towards covering the cost of the street improvements.[36]

The plans ratified in 1879-80 had been largely implemented by the first decades of the twentieth century. But around the turn of the century other planning ideals were already emerging, and soon the chief representative of the Sitte School in Sweden, Per Olof Hallman, later director of town planning in Stockholm, was working on plans for some of the unbuilt rocky areas of the inner city.

Although the town succeeded in implementing the town plans, it turned out that both the 1874 building ordinances and the town plans based upon them lacked sufficient legal clout. In 1907 a Town Planning Act made it possible for town plans to include binding regulations regarding the design of the buildings.[37]

Several of the ideas in the Lindhagen Committee's proposal managed to survive the city council discussions of the 1870s. The extension of Kungsgatan to Stureplan was approved in 1887, and the extension of Sveavägen to Kungsgatan in 1896. In 1928 Albert Lilienberg, the newly appointed director of town planning, presented a master plan proposal, the most notable feature of which

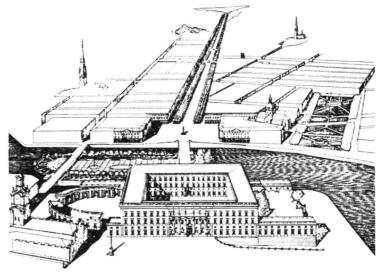

Figure 13.6 *Stockholm. Sveavägen according to the Lindhagen Committee's project. A perspective reconstruction by Tage William-Olsson. [From* Sankt Eriks årsbok *(1930)]*

was that Sveavägen should be extended to Gustav Adolfs Torg, albeit in a narrower version than that envisaged by Lindhagen. This remained the most controversial issue in Stockholm's planning debate right up to 1945, when the city council decided that Sveavägen should end at Klarabergsgatan. More recently Norrmalm has undergone a radical transformation according to city centre plans presented in 1947, 1962 and 1967.[38] In these plans many features from the Lindhagen Committees proposal reappeared, for example the traffic route over Strömmen and Blasieholmen, the broader version of Jakobsgatan, and the idea of creating an east-west communicating link from western Norrmalm to Östermalm.[39] This does not mean that modern plans have been derived from Lindhagen's. Rather, the problems have in many ways been the same and have consequently resulted in similar solutions.

NOTES

1. The seminal and essentially the only work on the planning of Stockholm during the second half of the nineteenth century is Selling (1970), which provides a thorough and detailed account of the decision processes. It has provided the main source for this section on Stockholm. Selling (1960) can be regarded as a preliminary study for the later work. Among works which touch on planning in Stockholm, albeit briefly, mention should be made of G. Paulsson (1950), Gejvall (1954), T. Paulsson (1959), Råberg (1979) and Hall (1991), p. 185. The seminal work on Stockholm's economic development as a commercial and industrial town during the relevant period is Hammarström (1970). William-Olsson (1937) provides an exemplary account of the economic-geographical developments. Developments in municipal policies are described in Lindberg (1980). Högberg (1981) comprises an overview of Stockholm's history, and devotes considerable space to urban development.
2. The basic work on medieval developments in Stockholm is Ahnlund (1953). Cf. Hall (1974), which provides a detailed bibliography.
3. On seventeenth-century improvements, see Hall (1970) and the literature referred to there; cf. also Råberg (1979 and 1987). Råberg presents a theory regarding a plan dating from the reign of Gustavus II Adolphus, against which objections can be raised. However, any discussion of this question lies outside the scope of our present subject.

4. On these developments, see in particular Hammarström (1970) and Ahlberg (1958).

5. On eighteenth-century planning in Sweden, see Nisser (1970).

6. Cf. Hall (1991), p. 174 and 189 ff. On Umeå, see Eriksson (1975).

7. Quoted from Selling (1970), p. 2. The following account is based largely on this work.

8. On the administrative organization of Stockholm at this time, see Höjer (1955 and 1967).

9. Cf. Hammarström (1970).

10. *Protocoll hållna hos vällofliga borgareståndet,* vid *lagtima riksdagen i Stockholm åren 1856 och 1857,* III, p. 257 (22nd April 1857).

11. Rudberg (1862). Cf. quotation from the commentary on this plan, see p. 297, note 20.

12. Quoted from Selling (1970), p. 4.

13. This process can be followed in the data reported in William-Olsson (1937). Selling has devoted a special study to the discussions on the 'Old City' issue (1973).

14. Quoted from Selling (1970), p. 6.

15. The combination of the partial plans (Plates 3 and 4) in Selling (1970) was produced on Selling's initiative. When the plans were being discussed during the 1860s, no such combination appears to have been made.

16. *Utlåtande med förslag till gatureglering i Stockholm.*

17. *Ibidem,* p. 42.

18. Published in Selling (1970), Plates 5 and 6.

19. *Utlåtande med förslag till gatureglering i Stockholm,* p. 4.

20. Selling (1970), pp. 13 and 47.

21. *Stockholms Dagblad* 15th June 1867, quoted here from Selling (1970), p. 13.

22. Cf. Hammarström (1979), pp. 33 ff and Fig. 4.

23. Selling (1970), pp. 13 ff.

24. Selling discusses these real estate development companies both in the work on Lindhagen (1970), pp. 16 ff and in a special paper (1975).

25. A number of the planning proposals appear in large-scale reproductions in Selling (1970).

26. Selling (1970), Plate 9.

27. This had been recommended by the Board of Public Works and Buildings (*överintendentsämbetet*) in its examination of the above-mentioned 1875 plan for part of Östermalm, with reference to the decree in the building ordinances regarding the esplanades (see p. 301).

28. Selling (1970), Plate 11.

29. *Ibidem,* Plates 12–16. See also pp. 279 ff.

30. Real estate interests had a strong position in the municipal bodies as a result of a weighted voting system, which meant that large property holdings gave a large number of votes in elections to the city council.

31. Selling has discovered that of the twelve city council members who were certainly shareholders in one of the companies, *Stockholms byggnadsförening,* there were ten who voted for the Sturegatan alternative and only one for Birger Jarlsgatan; the twelfth shareholder was not present (Selling (1975), p. 223).

32. Cf. Selling (1970), Plates 17–20.

33. *Ibidem,* Plates 21 and 22. On the recommendation of the delegates the city council reintroduced the tunnels planned by Rudberg and Wallström (although the eastern one in a different location); but when the plan was ratified by the government, they were excluded.

34. Cf. Selling (1970), Plates 23 and 24.

35. Hammarström (1979), Fig. 4. Cf. also *Stenstadens arkitekter* (1981), Diagram p. 3.

36. *Stockholm 1897,* II, pp. 242 ff. There does not appear to be any later evaluation of the outcome of the town's property transactions.

37. Cf. Hall (1991), p. 180.

38. Cf. Hall (1985).

39. In April 1887, at his last city council meeting, Albert Lindhagen presented a proposal for laying down a traffic route through the Brunkeberg ridge, from Norra Bantorget to Engelbrektsplan, as an alternative to the extension of Kungsgatan. The proposal was rejected, but as Selling has pointed out it anticipated Tunnelgatsleden in *City 67* (1970, pp. 44 f and 50).

14

BRUSSELS

In the Middle Ages Brussels[1] was already a town of some standing due to its situation on the trade route between Cologne and Bruges, and because of its role as the centre of the flourishing production of woollen cloth. At quite an early stage the town also became the seat of the dukes of Brabant. A first town wall was built around 1100, and another was constructed some time after the middle of the fourteenth century. Over 7 km in length, this second wall covered an area that in terms of medieval conditions was a large one, and one which was not in fact exploited in full until the nineteenth century. The urban area consisted of two parts, each with its own special topographical nature, on the one hand the *ville basse* and on the other the *ville haute* lying much higher on the hills to the east. The lower town, which grew up on both sides of the river Senne, was the medieval town of the burghers, while the upper town was dominated by the ducal stronghold on the Coudenberg. This division between a commercial city and an administrative royal seat has persisted to the present day.

Urban development in Brussels was given a major boost in the sixteenth century when the Willebroek Canal was built. Together with the rivers Rupel and Schelde it provided an excellent link with the sea. It was also during this century that Brussels acquired something of the status of a capital city in the Netherlands, which were incorporated into Philip II's Spanish Empire after the death of the Emperor Charles V. The Emperor's ambition to integrate the Netherlands into the Spanish kingdom triggered the events which led to a division between the southern Catholic provinces, which became a vassal state under Spain, and the Protestant north which ultimately became independent as Holland. In the eighteenth century the former Spanish Netherlands were first part of the Austrian Habsburg Empire, to be absorbed into France later after Napoleon's victories.[2]

In 1782 Joseph II decided to demolish the fortifications in all the towns of the southern Netherlands. But it was not until the Napoleonic period that Brussels began to replace its fortifications, which followed the line of the medieval wall, by a ring of boulevards.[3] This vast enterprise, which was to continue for much of the nineteenth century, resulted in what are known as the *boulevards de ceinture*.[4] Apart from a few sections these boulevards do not appear to have functioned as streets of central importance in the life of the town, in the same way as the *grandes boulevards* in Paris; they served above all to mark the boundaries between the town and its neighbouring municipalities, and as traffic routes; this last function was reinforced during the present century, when alterations transformed the *boulevards de ceinture* into a traffic artery pure and simple.

However, important urban development schemes had already started a little earlier. The creation of the Quartier du Parc and the Place Royale in the 1770s – the latter inspired by the *places royales* in Bordeaux, Nancy, Reims,

Rouen and other French towns – can be said to
have been the first step in the modern planning
history of Brussels. The general lines were thus
determined for subsequent developments not
only in the upper town but also in several of the
suburbs, as well as for certain streets in the
lower town (figure 14.2). During the 'Dutch
period' in the history of Brussels (1815–1830),
when the Congress of Vienna had established
the kingdom of the Netherlands under the

House of Orange-Nassau, the modernization
of the street network in the upper town was
launched with the extension of the Rue Royale
– bordering the Parc de Bruxelles – first to the
ring boulevards and later beyond the city
boundary, and the extension of the Rue de la
Régence as far as Notre-Dame-du-Sablon.
This last street represented a continuation of
one of the diagonal axes of the park, which at
the same time constituted the middle axis of

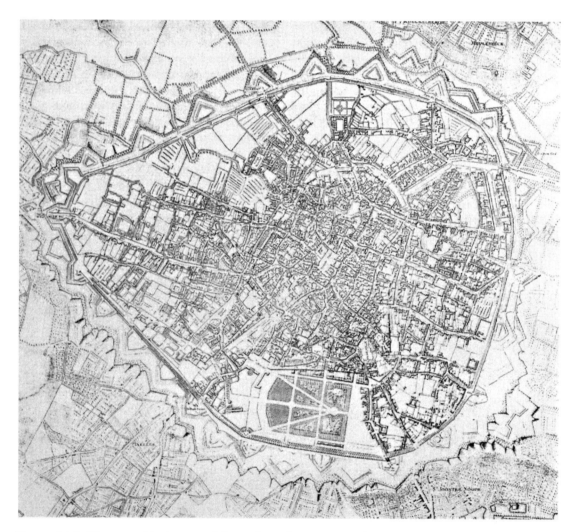

Figure 14.1 *Topographical map of Brussels and its surroundings. Engraving by L.A. Dupuis,
1777. [Photo from the Sint-Lukasarchief, Brussels]*

the Place Royale (figure 14.2). A few decades later both streets were to acquire dominating foci, the former in the Eglise Sainte-Marie (begun in 1845), and the latter in Poelaert's Palais de Justice (begun 1866).[5]

The Belgian revolution began in Brussels in 1830, and the following year Leopold I, the newly elected king, made his ceremonial entry into the town, now the capital city of an independent Belgium. The following decades were characterized by rapid industrialization, at an early date compared with other continental European countries, and by commercial expansion. This growth in trade was facilitated by the construction of many railways all converging on the town, which made Brussels

one of the most important junctions in northern Europe.

In the middle of the nineteenth century, however, Brussels proper still retained its medieval dimensions, and was bounded by the ring boulevards. This meant that a great deal of the urban expansion occurred outside the town boundaries. Brussels was surrounded by a number of villages which were all growing fast around the middle of the century. In 1838 a Belgian local government act granted the municipalities the right, among other things, to make local plans for the distribution of building blocks. One of the first examples of such plans, and probably one of the earliest developments in connection with a railway station, is

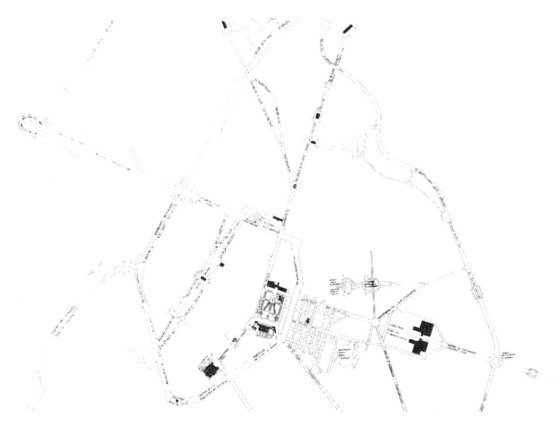

Figure 14.2 *Mapping of the axial streets, whose orientation are determined by the Parc de Bruxelles. [From* Bruxelles, construire et reconstruire]

the *plan générale* which was made for the area around the new Gare du Nord in the municipality of Schaerbeek. The first version of the plan is from 1838, the second and final one from 1840. The plan, which was drawn by François Coppens, seems to have been the result of cooperation between the municipality and the railway company. The urban blocks have been drawn across the old agrarian property boundaries, but not in a stereotyped grid pattern, and an attempt has been made instead to adapt to the prevailing conditions. Parallel with the railway there is a monumental thoroughfare, with two round places and one square with closed corners.[6]

Another early attempt at planned suburban expansion, this time on a grander scale, aiming to create a sumptuous environment for the urban elite, was made by a company created in 1837 and known as the *Société Civile pour l'agrandissement et l'embellissement de la capitale de la Belgique*. This company bought up an area lying between two villages and belonging to two different municipalities beyond the eastern section of the boulevard ring. It was also linked directly with the Quartier du Parc, which certainly contributed to the prestige of the project. For this new suburb, Quartier Léopold, the architect Tilman-François Suys made a plan which was

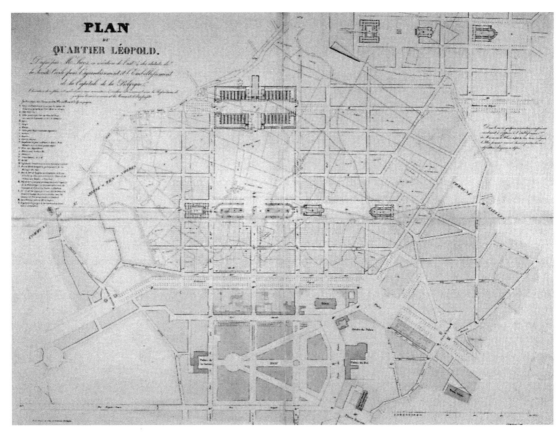

Figure 14.3 *Brussels. Project by T.-F. Suys, 1838, for the Quartier Léopold. [Photo from the Sint-Lukasarchief, Brussels.]*

adapted to the orientation of the pathways in the Parc de Bruxelles (figure 14.3). The plan represents an ambitious attempt to create, within the framework of a traditional grid, an impressive new urban area with a series of public buildings and parks arranged in a grand ensemble in the centre.

The Quartier Léopold was not an immediate success. Its development really only took off when the area was incorporated into Brussels in 1853 and the *Conseil communal* decided to extend the Rue de la Loi, the main link between the town and the suburb. But the original plan was much simplified, and the monumental centre was never realized. More attention was paid to architectural design when a new district – the Quartier Nord-Est – was added to the Quartier Léopold according to plans produced by the architect Gédéon Bordiau and approved by the *Conseil communal* in 1875, i.e. during the administration of Jules Anspach. Square Marie-Louise and Square Ambiorix, together with Avenue Palmerston linking them together, formed a grand complex of parks and squares – possibly slightly too large in relation to the urban structure surrounding it.[7] A development in design thinking can be clearly discerned here, from the slightly static grid planning in the Quartier Léopold to the Baroque dynamism of the Quartier Nord-Est, which can be said to herald the more grandiose planning under Leopold II.[8]

Another much discussed planning issue concerned the Avenue Louise. At the end of the 1840s two land developers acquired a concession to lay out a new avenue from the ring boulevard to the Bois de la Cambre. The project was felt to be important, as it would link the town to a wooded area suitable as a public park. The two developers were not able to realize their plans, but following persistent pressure from the government and the promise of financial support, the town took over the enterprise and it became possible to complete this avenue, 55 metres wide and almost 3 km

long. To compensate for its cost the town was also permitted – despite protests from the municipality of Ixelles – to incorporate the street and a zone extending about 40 to 100 metres on either side of it. Today Brussels still thrusts like a wedge into the neighbouring municipality. The Avenue Louise, lined on both sides by splendid mansions, soon became one of the most fashionable residential areas in Brussels.[9]

Ever since 1830 Brussels had been growing rapidly in both population and importance, and was well on the way to becoming one of the main commercial centres in Europe. But by the middle of the century its medieval street network was still intact, apart from the changes in the upper city mentioned above and a few minor adjustments in the low-lying districts. Thus, the first attempts at urban renewal comprising a number of properties was the construction of the shopping arcade Galeries St-Hubert (1836–45), one of the pioneers of its kind in Europe and still functioning today, and the long but rather narrow Rue Blaes cutting through the historic Marollen Quartier (1853–60).[10]

However, it was obvious to the governing bodies, who mainly represented the merchant élite of the town, that major interventions were required.[11] They could see that trade in luxury goods had been growing more slowly than in other towns, and that this commerce also tended to shift towards the suburbs to the east. Nor were there any suitable premises for stock-exchange dealings. During the 1850s the discussion about urban development in Brussels focused on two problems: the River Senne, and the creation of a north-south connecting link through the town. The Senne, along whose banks the town had originally grown up, wound its way with many offshoots all through the lower town. This caused a number of difficulties. The river was used more or less as the main sewer for the district; it thus constituted a serious sanitary problem, which was aggravated by the fact that at times it flowed

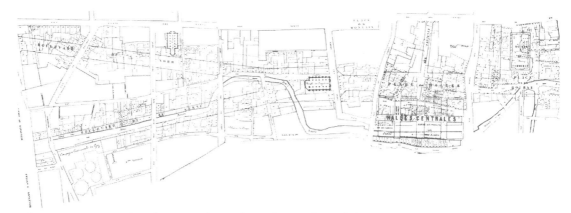

Figure 14.4 *Brussels. This map shows how the Boulevard du Centre cuts through the old urban 1867 was L. Suys.* [*From* Bruxelles, construire et reconstruire]

very sluggishly. An even more urgent question concerned the inundations which constantly threatened large areas of the town. Added to all this the winding course of the river made it difficult, if not impossible, to systematize the innumerable tiny plots and narrow alleys, thus effectively blocking any modernization of this picturesque but hardly distinguished heart of the growing capital city (figure 14.5). During the first half of the 1860s various ideas were suggested, ranging from the redirection of the river or covering it over, to the construction of an aqueduct.

The second major issue discussed concerned the construction of a north-south traffic link of adequate capacity through the town. During the Middle Ages the most important traffic artery – Steenweg – had run in a west-east direction along the route of the present Rue de Flandre, Rue Sainte-Catherine, Rue du Marché aux Poulets, Rue du Marché aux Herbes and continuing into the now vanished Montagne de la Cour (cf. p. 229). During the nineteenth century the north-south traffic flow became increasingly important, mainly due to the existence of two major railway stations located at each side of the town: the Gare du Nord immediately outside the northern section of the boulevard ring and thus also outside the town boundary in the present-day Place Rogier,

and the Gare du Midi inside the boulevard ring in what is today Place Rouppe. The Gare du Nord was the terminus for the lines from Holland, Germany, Antwerp and Liège, and the Gare du Midi for those from France, the south of Belgium and the Atlantic coast.

The two stations generated a good deal of traffic to and from the centre of the town and between their own two locations. But the north-south links which had to carry this traffic were totally inadequate. A first attempt at tackling the problem was the construction of the Rue du Midi, which was taken northwards from the south station in two stages. The Gare du Nord was reached by the seventeenth-century Rue Neuve, which had been slightly re-routed at its northernmost end. But the capacity of this chain of streets was poor, particularly in the very narrow central link, the Rue des Fripiers, where the church of St Nicolas still sticks out into the street. The situation was further complicated by preparations during the 1860s for relocating the Gare du Midi to a site outside the boulevard ring;[12] this would have made the communications between the two stations even worse. Various more or less realistic proposals were put forward for linking the Gare du Nord and the Gare du Midi, for example by running a double track along a broad street through the town.[13]

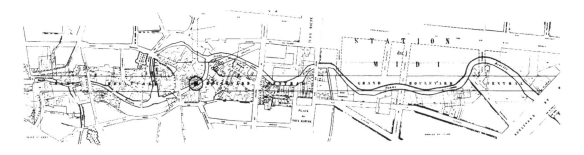

structure, and indicates the size of the expropriation zones. The author of the project submitted in

It was largely to the credit of one man that the many suggestions were finally transformed into a feasible project, and that the project itself could be realized. This man was Jules Anspach, a lawyer and politician who became mayor in 1863 at the age of only 34.

When Anspach took up his post many suggestions had thus already been aired, and there was much support for the idea of taking radical action. Anspach's own importance lies mainly in his recognition of the most practicable approach to solving two of the most urgent urban problems at one go, namely covering the Senne and building a north-south main road on the site. At the same time the sewage problem could be resolved by running drains parallel with the conduits intended for the river. The project was also to include a covered market and a stock exchange.[14] A decision in principle on this programme was reached by the *Conseil communal* in October 1865. The architect Léon Suys was responsible for planning the road. In his imposing 1867 plan a *Grand Boulevard Central* cuts through the town in a straight line to a simple rectangular square, where it branches out to form a Y; from here one arm of the boulevard follows the course of the Senne while the other leads to the Gare du Nord (figure 14.4). The long main boulevard was to be divided visually by a fountain; in its

northern section a great Bourse de Commerce was to be built on one side and the Halles Centrales market on the other, albeit not opposite one another.[15]

Anspach, who was a convinced liberal, obviously felt that the great enterprise could best be realized under private management. After negotiations with various interested parties, an agreement was reached with an English company created for the purpose, the Belgian Public Works Company, which for the price of 26 million Belgian francs was to take over all the projects involved, including the Stock Exchange, the Halles and the fountain. The town was to arrange the necessary expropriation permits, but the company would be responsible for compensating property-owners. In return the company would then have the right to profit from the rise in land values which the project would generate, by selling the new plots.[16] Anspach justified this procedure quite frankly to the *Conseil communal* by saying that 'the law puts numerous obstacles in the way of the public authorities . . . It would be difficult for a municipality to indulge in speculations of even the most honest kind, to seek out by way of special contracts the conditions from which private individuals can benefit; it would be difficult for a municipality to build houses with

Figure 14.5 *Brussels. Buildings along the Senne before it was covered over and the central boulevards were built. [Old photo from the Sint-Lukasarchief, Brussels]*

a view to making a profit, to make loans repayable in annuities, or, in a word, to utilize all those means which a property company can adopt to ensure the profitable exploitation of the land and, consequently, the ultimate success of the operation.'[17]

Work started in 1868, but the company soon came up against problems of liquidity and financing; after a time the town had to intervene and complete the project. When the boulevards were officially opened in November 1871, most of the plots were still unbuilt and subsequent development proceeded slowly. There were several reasons for this. Attempts to introduce apartment blocks on the Parisian model were not a success; there was no tradition behind this type of housing in Brussels, and many of those who could have afforded to live in the new apartments chose a villa in one of the fashionable suburbs instead. The town had to take over several apartment blocks after the company's bankruptcy. Furthermore, many of the plots were small or unsuitable in shape; during the expropriations too much attention

Figure 14.6 *Brussels. Place De Brouckère, where the central boulevard divides into two arms. At the end of the right arm the Gare du Nord can be glimpsed. The Anspach Fountain is under construction. [Old photo from the Sint-Lukasarchief, Brussels]*

had been paid to the winding course of the Senne and the earlier street network.

In various ways, including competitions for the most beautiful façade, the municipal authorities tried to hasten the building and to encourage architectural quality. In the southern part of the town they also involved themselves in the construction of a large covered market, the Palais du Midi, to bring some life into this area. And by and large the plan was realized – the most obvious exception being that the fountain was never built, which is one reason why the long axis, the Boulevard Anspach and the Boulevard Maurice Lemonnier, appears rather monotonous and uninteresting, particularly to anyone going south. The street is also relatively narrow, only 28 metres wide, and its two arms are even narrower so there is not enough room for rows of fully grown trees. It

should perhaps be added that very little was done, either by the town or the company, for the roughly 13,000 people who were made homeless as a result of the demolition of what had been largely a slum area.[18]

The construction of the boulevards through the centre of Brussels was of course inspired by the boulevard system in Paris. And Anspach certainly saw himself as a Belgian Haussmann: on at least one occasion he asked the advice of the Parisian prefect, and in contemporary reviews he was referred to as 'Ansmann'.[19] Like the master himself, Anspach tried to combine clearance, road construction and the building of a sewage system in a single package. The idea of handing over execution of the plans to private companies had also been tried in Paris. There, too, several boulevards were intended as traffic routes to the railway stations, and the Halles in Brussels were more or less a copy of those which Baltard planned for Haussmann.[20] But there were also differences: Anspach was a municipal official and not, like Haussmann, a special state appointee; moreover, the construction of the central boulevards in Brussels was a purely municipal project, which was not pushed through by the central authorities like the street improvements in Paris. Nor were the new boulevards in Brussels characterized by the architectural uniformity or the monumental accents that were a feature of the best of the Parisian models. In Anspach's position Haussman would certainly have been more deeply committed to ending the central boulevards with some architecturally organized focal points. In the event, only the present Boulevard Adolphe Max was treated in such a way, terminating at the Gare du Nord, but even then the boulevard approaches the station diagonally. Part of the explanation must have been that this was a municipal project; when the King in person intervened in the planning, the creation of an imposing city image was given greater prominence, as we shall see below.

In addition to some complementary alterations in connection with the central boulevards,[21] another major development enterprise was also undertaken during Anspach's term of office, namely the redevelopment of the Notre-Dame-aux-Neiges district in the north-eastern corner of the boulevard ring.[22] This project is interesting in that it was not contingent on the construction of roads, but was purely a question of clearance. The background to this undertaking was overpopulation in the district, a low standard of housing and a high morbidity rate. But there was obviously also a wish to open up the prospect from the boulevard ring towards the Colonne du Congrès which was erected during the 1850s, even though this would require extensive excavation operations. In the new plan two diagonal roads intersected in a centrally located square (figure 14.7). This development, which was carried out by a company created for the purpose, the Société Anonyme du quartier Notre-Dame-aux-Neiges, naturally provided no solution to the housing problems of those rendered homeless by the demolitions.[23]

A fundamental problem of urban development in Brussels concerned the highly limited area available within the city borders, which meant that much of the expansion occurred in neighbouring municipalities. In 1831 Brussels had about 100,000 inhabitants, while the surrounding eighteen municipalities together had 41,000, i.e. barely half as many, and none of these other municipalities had more than 5,000 inhabitants. When, around 1900, the population of the core town achieved its maximum size, roughly 185,000 inhabitants, it had not even doubled in size since 1831. During the same period the population in the surrounding municipalities had multiplied by more than ten times and now amounted to 442,000. Thus the population of the suburbs was more than twice as large as that of Brussels itself. The largest of these municipalities – Schaerbeek – had 63,000, corresponding to one-third of the population of the town proper.[24] Industry came to be located in the suburbs as well, mainly on the west side close to the harbour and the River Senne, and in the south.

Several capital cities and other large towns had similar problems, although Brussels is one of the most glaring examples. As a result of the very restricted area of the central municipality, developments in the neighbouring areas did not acquire a markedly suburban character as they generally did elsewhere, but instead became both functionally and visually an extension of the central city core. This may be one reason why Brussels appears to have recognized at an unusually early stage the disadvantages of urban growth unrestricted by any kind of overall control. One way of tackling this problem was by incorporation, and the municipal authorities in Brussels differed from many other towns in their positive attitude to such an idea – probably because the

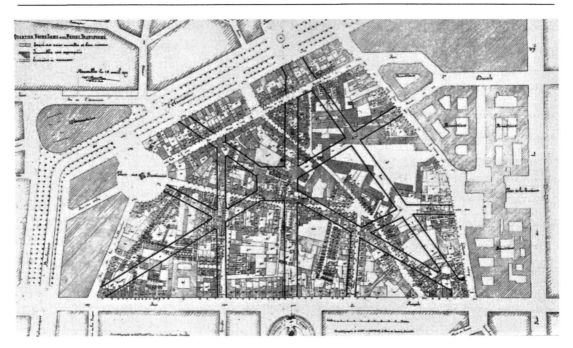

Figure 14.7 *Brussels. Project for the redevelopment of Notre-Dame-aux-Neiges, by G. Aigoin and A. Mennessier, 1874. [Photo from the Sint-Lukasarchief, Brussels]*

surrounding municipalities possessed desirable tracts of vacant land and little low-quality slum building. The suburban municipalities did not want to be incorporated, however, and in 1854 a government bill for extensive incorporation was rejected;[25] during the nineteenth century only three minor incorporations were effected, including the Quartier Léopold and the Avenue Louise which we have discussed above.

But other attempts were also made to control urban expansion. In 1859 a young land surveyor, Victor Besme, was appointed by the *Conseil Provincial du Brabant* as 'surveyor of the roads of the Faubourgs of Brussels' (*Inspecteur voyer dans les faubourgs de Bruxelles*), a post that he was to hold until 1903. Besme's real task was to coordinate road planning in the suburbs of Brussels, but what he actually tried to achieve can be described as something approaching inter-municipal regional planning, albeit the area of the capital

city itself was not included. He presented his ideas in a comprehensive report entitled 'The Suburbs of Brussels, Comprehensive plan for the extension and embellishment of the Brussels region' (*Faubourgs de Bruxelles, Plan d'ensemble pour l'extension et l'embellissement de l'agglomération bruxelloise*) published in a first version in 1863 and in a second in 1866 (figure 14.8). A basic principle in the Besme plan was that the entire metropolitan area was to be encompassed by a new high-capacity ring road, as a complement to the existing radial links, which were also to be added to. Furthermore, it indicates the location of industries and other structures and of parks and residential areas for different social groups. Besme's proposal could perhaps be described as an early attempt at zoning, although the legal instruments for its execution were lacking, and in many respects he was simply proceeding in accordance with existing trends.[26] Not even the

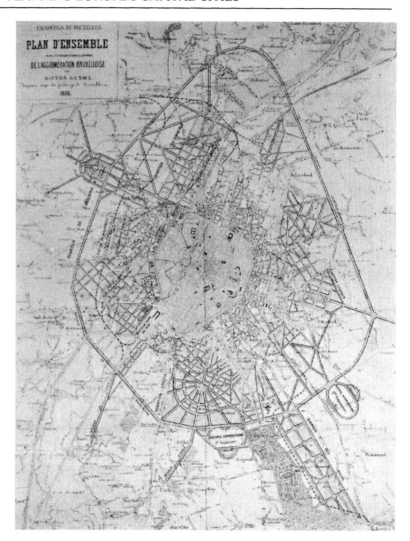

Figure 14.8 *Victor Besme's 'Regional Plan', 1866, for the suburban municipalities of Brussels. [Photo from the Sint-Lukasarchief, Brussels]*

main lines of his plan were ever really implemented, but it was nevertheless an important source of ideas, not least as a result of the author's long service at his post.

A third person apart from Ansbach and Besme also had a decisive influence on the physical evolution of Brussels, namely Leopold II. The King's ideas about what a city should look like probably agreed in full with Haussmann's. Ranieri summarizes his programme under three points: large green areas, broad thoroughfares, and a uniform design for private buildings.[27] To this we could also add a taste for grandiloquent public buildings and monuments.

Leopold does not seem to have taken an active part in the urban development enterprises of the Anspach period, although they certainly accorded well with his own ideas; but the King's support was obviously not needed and work began anyway, soon after he came to the throne in 1865. On the other hand, as Crown Prince and Duke of Brabant he had taken a personal interest in the execution of the plans for Avenue Louise. During the last two decades of the nineteenth century and the first decade of the twentieth, the King was engaged in various ways in a whole series of urban development projects. Ranieri lists twenty-four *interventions de Léopold II*.[28] The great majority of these were concerned with the suburban municipalities. The 'interventions' were often made in close collaboration with Besme. The fact that it was possible to construct at least part of an outer ring of boulevards was largely due to Leopold's support. Several of the major parks, such as the Parc de Saint-Gilles-Forest, the Parc public de Laeken, the Parc Josaphat, and the Parc de Woluwe, were created or enlarged at any rate partly thanks to the King, and the same could be said of some of the peripheral boulevards and avenues. The ostentatious ensemble consisting of the Parc, the Arcade and the Palais du Cinquantenaire was largely a royal project. Nor is it likely that the Basilique du Sacré-Cœur would have been built without the King's support; the church now provides an unusually impressive visual focus on the Boulevard Léopold II. Leopold II can probably be described as the last monarch to conduct urban policy on a grand scale.[29]

The structure planning was concerned mainly with routes for through traffic, and with parks and monumental accents. The respective municipalities, often in close collaboration with the land developers, were responsible for local planning such as the street networks between the major traffic arteries. The general pattern seems to have been that companies or individuals with plentiful resources first planned and parcelled out substantial areas, and that the houses were then built one by one by small builders. Houses of more than three storeys were not very common, and many of the buildings were single-family homes.[30] It is probably a justifiable claim that the districts built here in the second half of the nineteenth century and at the beginning of the twentieth, many of them with broad streets and extensive

green areas, generally present a more spacious and attractive face than their counterparts in most of the other capital cities discussed here.

Lastly, mention should be made of a project which was executed during our own century, but which was nonetheless dependent to a great extent on the nineteenth-century planning discourse. In the lower town communications had been improved with the construction of the central boulevards under Anspach, and in the upper town good north-south connections had been created in an earlier phase by extending the Rue Royale and the Rue de la Régence. But towards the end of the nineteenth century the links were still unsatisfactory between the two sides of the city, across the overpopulated districts occupying the rising grounds of the upper town. The most important of the existing streets, Montagne de la Cour which led up to the Place Royale, was steep and narrow and difficult to tackle with a horse and carriage. At the same time it was one of the city's main business streets, and the centre of the luxury retail trade. Alterations in this street had been discussed by the *Conseil communal* as far back as the early 1850s. In 1863 the municipal authorities examined twenty-six projects which had been produced since 1850, and ten years or so later a commission examined 162 similar recommendations. Reporting on these the commission declared that a straight connecting street could never be satisfactory on account of the different levels involved, and recommended instead a project by the architect Henri Maquet, involving a broad street describing a kind of wide semi-oval. This would mean relieving Montagne de la Cour of most of its traffic, thus limiting any necessary interventions along its length.[31]

But this project also came to nought, and in 1881 Leopold II's architect Alphonse Balat produced a radical project involving the monumentalization of the area by means of demolitions, the widening of streets, and the clearing of space round the existing institutional buildings – the museums, the library and the

Palais de l'Industrie. The idea was that the area around the Montagne de la Cour should be transformed: a noisy, disorganized and untidy city centre was to become a worthy approach to the royal *ville haute* on the heights above.

This suggestion was exactly to Leopold II's taste. However, in 1893 the municipal council under its mayor Charles Buls decided on a much reduced version of the suggested relief road combined with a slight widening of the narrowest part of the Montagne de la Cour. In practice this would have meant writing off Leopold's desired solution, and the monarch intervened resolutely to block the municipality's plans.[32] In face of a threat that expropriation permits would be withheld, Buls's recommendation was rejected by one vote in the *Conseil communal*. After this the municipal machine appears to have accepted the King's line, despite the mayor's opposition. The proposal outlined by Balat for what now began to be called the 'Mont des Arts' was developed by Maquet in a series of projects. In 1897 the demolition of the Saint-Roch quarter to the north of the Montagne de la Cour was begun, and after that the die was cast: a solution based on limited intervention was no longer feasible. Attempts to proceed with a series of gradual adjustments, in tune with the historical legacy of the area and on a compatible scale, had been forced to yield to a monumental urbanistic project promoted by the King and involving the total transformation of the nature and functions of the area; added to which it proved to be out of all proportion to what the town could bear. After further demolitions and the launching of various projects, the whole thing ground to a standstill, and in 1909 – with the following year's *Exposition universelle* in mind – a 'provisional' solution was adopted. This was to remain at the same 'provisional' stage for a long time; it was not until after the Second World War that the plans were realized, and then in a somewhat altered form.

A little more should be said about Charles Buls. His opposition to the King's far-reaching

plans was certainly dictated in part by concern for the town's already hard-pressed economy and by consideration for the voters whose operations were located in the area that would suffer. But his own ideas about urban development played at least as important a part, as did his keen interest in the preservation of historical buildings and milieus. His commitment to these issues emerges clearly from a brochure he published in 1893, *Esthétique des Villes*,[33] which is both a polemic against radical change in the area of the Montagne de la Cour and an attempt to conduct a principled discussion on urban development and renewal. He gives cogent expression to a number of ideas and values, which were beginning to spread in Europe around this time, in reaction to stereotyped planning and heavy-handed urban renewal projects. The nucleus of his message is that while a flourishing city must necessarily change 'in order to adapt to new traffic requirements, and to the exigencies of property, hygiene and comfort . . . this evolution should not be imposed by brute force; it should be conducted with filial respect for all those memorials of the past which can without inconvenience be preserved.'[34]

Buls's polemic, which according to his own words was written without knowledge of Sitte's *Der Städte-Bau nach seinen künstlerischen Grundsätzen* which had been published a few years before, aroused considerable interest, and a second edition had to be published a year later (the first edition had been a very small one). It was translated into English, and in Germany was the subject of an appreciative article by Joseph Stübben.[35] But despite the international interest, Buls was still unable to realize his ideas in Brussels, and in 1899 he resigned from office in protest.

The demolitions required for the King's 'Mont des Arts' project were not the only large undertaking to affect the centre of Brussels around the turn of the century. As far back as the middle of the nineteenth century the construction of a centrally located railway station, to which the line was to run via a tunnel from the Quartier Léopold, had been discussed, as had a linking track right across the town. Several of the projects which were suggested in the second half of the century for organizing communications between the upper and lower towns, included suggestions for stations at a variety of sites. In the last years of the century the government revived the idea of a track connecting the Gare du Nord and the Gare du Midi, to be combined with a central station. The town finally approved this plan, although with no great enthusiasm. An agreement was reached and extensive demolitions began in 1903. The project progressed slowly, however, and the new link did not come into operation until 1952.[36] Work on the 'Mont des Arts' has been going on for a very long time, and is not entirely finished yet. For much of the twentieth century central areas of Brussels have thus either been closed off or have been under construction – all as a result of nineteenth-century projects and ideas. There is no parallel to this situation in any of the other capital cities.[37] This long-drawn-out process of transformation has meant that much of the town's retail trade and other activities have shifted into other areas. And it seems all too likely that Buls would have felt justified in his warning of aesthetic impoverishment, if he could have seen the new Rue Cantersteen and the Marché au Bois today, or the great empty space below the Gare Central, an undefined vacuum which at least in visual terms fails to live up to its majestic name, the *Carrefour de l'Europe*.

NOTES

1. Three publications are of fundamental importance to the study of the modern planning history of Brussels. They have all been published in connection with exhibitions, namely *Bruxelles, construire et reconstruire, Architecture et aménagement urbain 1780–1914* (1979); *Poelaert et son temps* (1980) and *Pierres et rues, Bruxelles:*

croissance urbaine 1780–1980 (1982) (all three have also been published in Flemish). The first two were published by Crédit Communal de Belgique and deal with urban development as well as with architecture. *Bruxelles, construire et reconstruire* surveys a longer period, while *Poelaert et son temps* concentrates on architectural developments during the active years of Joseph Poelaert (the architect of the mammoth Palais de Justice), i.e. the later nineteenth century. Both these publications include excellent surveys of planning developments written by Yvon Leblicq; the former also has a long section by Jos Vandenbreeden and A. Hoppenbrouwers with an opening part on 'L'urbanisme à Bruxelles; les théories et la réalité'. *Pierres et rues* was published by Sint-Lukasarchief together with the Société Générale de Banque and is intended to describe 200 years (1780–1980) of urban and planning development; contributors include Jan Apers, Jos Vandenbreeden and Linda Van Santvoort. The book is based on extensive material about urban development in Brussels, which has been collected by Sint-Lukasarchief, and it is richly illustrated with old maps and photographs, as are the other two publications mentioned above. These works will be referred to below by their respective titles, and not by the authors' names. It should be mentioned that Yvon Leblicq has also published papers on planning developments in Brussels during the nineteenth century elsewhere, for example in *Bruxelles, Croissance d'une capitale* (1979). However, the most important of Leblicq's papers is probably the one published in 1982, 'L'urbanisation de Bruxelles aux XIXe et XXe siècles (1830–1952)'. Leblicq's various contributions have provided the basic material for this presentation of Brussels.

Monograph studies have been devoted to two of the main actors in the discussions on urban development in Brussels, namely Jules Anspach (Garsou, 1942) and Leopold II (Ranieri, 1973). The work on Anspach is organized on traditional biographical lines, and can hardly be described as an urbanistic study, even though a considerable amount of space is devoted to urban development policy, since Anspach made his most noted contribution in that area. Ranieri's study is steered to a great extent by the source material, the King's own archives, and adopts a very positive attitude towards Leopold's activities; it is the monarch rather than the town that is the central focus of the study. Consequently the book deals mainly with the surrounding municipalities, since the main part of the King's urbanistic activities were located there (Anspach, for example, is only mentioned once). Among earlier publications which address urban development in Brussels, mention can be made of Jacquemyns (1936) and Verniers (1958); this last, however, is somewhat rhapsodical in tone. Urban development in Brussels from the middle of the nineteenth century onwards is also addressed briefly in Krings (1984). The history of Brussels in a longer perspective is presented, for example, in Vanhamme (1968), *Histoire de Bruxelles* (1979) and *Bruxelles, Croissance d'une capitale* (1979). Finally mention can also be made of *100 ans de débat sur la ville* (1984), a collation of extracts from the minutes of the *Conseil communal* in Brussels concerned with a number of important urban development issues. The discussions on the construction of the central boulevards, for instance, are given considerable space.

2. On the earlier developments, see for example *Histoire de Bruxelles* as well as Henne and Wauters (1968–69).

3. Cf. Martiny (1980), p. 27.

4. *Pierres et rues*, p.21.

5. See *ibidem*, p. 24. During the 1820s several other major developments were undertaken, for example the Place des Barricades. This was planned by the engineer J.B. Vifquain as a round place surrounded by uniform and sparsely decorated architecture and with roads radiating from it in a star shape. But the uniform pattern is broken by a visually disturbing opening towards the ring boulevards. Mention should also be made of the Hospice de Pachéco, a work of the architect Henri Partoes built in the 1820s in the north-west of the city. The way in which the open space and the surrounding roads are incorporated into the urban structure bears witness to a sensitive design.

6. Muylle and van den Eynde (1989–90).

7. *Bruxelles, construire et reconstruire*, pp. 18 ff.

8. Developments in the area east of Quartier Léopold – Le Parc Léopold – where attempts were also made to create a zoological garden and where a natural history museum and other

scientific institutions were ultimately built, are discussed in Brauman and Demanet (1985).

9. *Bruxelles, construire et reconstruire*, pp. 32 ff.

10. Smets and D'Herde (1985), p. 451 and Smets (1983).

11. The following description of the genesis of the central boulevards is based mainly on *Bruxelles, construire et reconstruire*, pp. 41 ff, *Pierres et rues*, pp. 153 ff, and on the material published in *100 ans de débat sur la ville*, pp. 61 ff.

12. The area of the Avenue de Stalingrad was formerly occupied by the railway station, which explains its surprising width.

13. See, for example, Victor Besmes' project reproduced in *Bruxelles, construire et reconstruire*, p. 81.

14. This programme appears to have been largely complete by October 1864 (see *100 ans de débat sur la ville*, p. 91). It is not altogether clear from the available sources how far Anspach was personally responsible for the solution finally chosen.

15. A colour reproduction of the plan appears in *Pierres et rues*, following p. 42.

16. Unfortunately the contract has not been reproduced or reported in detail in the available literature (cf, however, Smets and D'Herde (1985) and *100 ans de débat sur la ville*, pp. 94 f). It should be mentioned that the project was sharply criticized in the *Conseil communal* on both technical and economic grounds.

17. Quoted from *100 ans de débat sur la ville*, p. 94.

18. This despite the fact that the company had undertaken in its contract to provide replacements for the expropriated housing (Smets and D'Herde (1985), pp. 456 ff). On the consequences of this project for the housing situation of the workers, see also Cassiers, de Beule, Forti and Miller (1989).

19. Cf. *Bruxelles, construire et reconstruire*, p. 42. The letter from Haussmann is reproduced in Garsou (1942), pp. 132 f.

20. As regards subsequent demolition, Brussels was ahead of Paris. *Les Halles du Centre* were demolished as early as 1956.

21. As well as streets made in connection with the building of Les Halles and the Bourse, there were also other minor street improvements, such as the Rue d'Anderlecht.

22. *Bruxelles, construire et reconstruire*, pp. 64 ff.
23. A contemporary critic of the project claimed in the *Conseil communal* that there was no proof of the necessity for such extensive interventions on grounds of clearance; in fact it was a question of satisfying 'concerns of luxury'. '. . . even if the prospect of the Colonne du Congrés from the Louvain gate may ravish the passerby, it still seems preferable to me to dispense with the view and to retain the interior of the *quartier* for the working population, leaving the present slopes, which are anyway not very steep.' (Quoted from Leblicq (1982), p. 347.)
24. This description is based on the table in *Bruxelles, Croissance d'une capitale*, pp. 174 f.
25. *Bruxelles, construire et reconstruire*, p. 31.
26. A good deal of attention is devoted to Besmes's activities in Ranieri (1973), pp. 61 ff *et passim*. See also *Bruxelles, Croissance d'une capitale*, pp. 268 f, and Smets and D'Herde (1985). On this subject I have also benefited from conversations with Professor Marcel Smets and with the architects, Herwig Delvaux and Jos Vandenbreeden.
27. Ranieri (1973), p. 14. In another context she writes: 'The love of beautiful parks and broad avenues summarizes under two headings the fundamental principles of the Leopoldine doctrine of urban design.'
28. See the map and the list in Ranieri (1973), pp. 344 f.
29. This remark has proved to be a little premature. At the time when this was written, the British Prince of Wales had already entered the lists as a royal participant in the urban development discourse. Like Leopold he represents a fundamentally classicizing aproach, but of an essentially more moderate kind and one that is combined with a strong sense of historical continuity. On projects such as the Sainsbury Wing in Trafalgar Square and the renewal of Pater Noster Square, the British heir to the throne has made an impact scarcely second to

that of Leopold, but without the powers that were available to the King.
30. Information provided by Professor Marcel Smets and the architects Herwig Delvaux and Jos Vandenbreeden. An impressive example of street planning in the suburban municipalities is the Avenue Rogier in Schaerbeek.
31. For a detailed account of the discussions concerning Montagne de la Cour, see Leblicq (1982), pp. 353 ff.
32. In a letter to the head of his cabinet the King wrote: 'I have by no means hidden from M. Buls the strength of my formal opposition to his idea, nor that I shall use all means available to me to defeat it.' The King also sent for Buls to attend upon him, in order to plead with him to withdraw the project (Leblicq (1982), pp. 360 f).
33. The second edition was published in facimile form in 1981 by Sint-Lukasarchief, together with the contemporary English and a modern Flemish translation.
34. Buls (1894), p. 19. Smets (1995) is a comprehensive study of Buls, which emphasizes the conflict in which he found himself, on the one hand accepting modernity in principle, and on the other distancing himself from certain of its cultural and social consequences.
35. Collins and Collins (1986), p. 50. It appears among other things that Buls translated Stübben's lecture at the World's Columbian Exposition in Chicago in 1893 into French.

The architect Jos Vandenbreeden suggested that some of Buls's articles published under a pseudonym suggest that he did know Sitte's work when he wrote *Esthétique des Villes*, although Buls himself later denied this.
36. For an account of the sequence of events, see Leblicq (1982), pp. 363 ff.
37. Large areas have also been closed to the public for long periods in Stockholm in pretty much the same way, but in this case due to more recent planning projects (cf. Hall, 1985).

15

AMSTERDAM

Amsterdam's history goes back to the thirteenth century.[1] The town developed where the River Amstel flowed out into the IJ, at that time still a bay in the Zuiderzee (previously part of the North sea, but during the present century cut off from it and renamed IJsselmeer). Around 1270 a barrier or *dam* was built in the Amstel, and this has given its name not only to the town itself but also to its central square, the Dam. The original settlement consisted of two streets parallel with the river, the Warmoesstraat and the Nieuwendijk of today. It was surrounded by simple defences, with the two moats, Nieuwezijds Voorburgwal (now a street) and Oudezijds Voorburgwal. Amsterdam flourished on fishing and the Baltic trade, and became an important port. Twice during the Middle Ages the town was extended, acquiring new streets and moats parallel with the Amstel, which gave medieval Amsterdam its long, thin appearance (figure 15.1).

Political and economic factors combined during the first half of the seventeenth century to transform Amsterdam into the leading European trading city, a development which had begun towards the end of the previous century. The self-confident patriciate of merchants, who enjoyed the greatest wealth of anyone in Europe outside the royal dynasties, considered their town to be cramped, inconvenient and lacking in the required dignity. Thus they decided in 1609 to embark on an unusually impressive urban extension scheme. On the western and southern sides of the old spool-shaped core a girdle was added consisting of three new canals – Herengracht, Keizersgracht and Prinsengracht – and the blocks between them. Outside this girdle to the west a new area – the Jordaan – was created. Its rectilinear street network was oriented diagonally in relation to the three new main canals. The whole project was realized within the space of two decades; by the beginning of the 1620s the canals appear to have been built and the blocks marked out. A rapid increase in the population, which rose from 50,000 in 1610 to 200,000 in 1650, favoured the realization of the project.[2]

It was intended that the physical and social structure of the Jordaan area and that of the blocks along the canals should be clearly differentiated. The town had acquired the land between the great canals, and was therefore able to distribute property there without having to consider any previous ownership boundaries. The new plots were sold on strict conditions regarding the design of the houses to be built there. In the Jordaan the town did not acquire the land in this way, and the street network was laid out according to existing ditches and ownership boundaries. Consequently the changes there were less dramatic, and by and large people could build as they liked. This is where crafts were to be concentrated, particularly those that caused unpleasant odours or polluted the water. The result was a kind of social zoning: the merchants occupied impressive sites along the new concentric canals, while craftsmen and their like were relegated to more peripheral locations.

Figure 15.1 *Amsterdam. This woodcut by Cornelis Anthoniszoon, 1544, shows the medieval town before the seventeenth-century extensions. [Photo from the Gemeentelijke Archiefdienst, Amsterdam]*

The most striking features of the plan are of course the canals. These had at least two practical purposes: to drain the marshy ground, and to provide transport routes for freight which was reloaded on to small boats in the harbour and shipped to the warehouses along the waterways. But they may also have been intended to enhance the image of the city. Communications between the centre and the new areas were conspicuously poor – something which does not seem to have been considered particularly important. Nor was there any interest in classical planning for grand effects, with focal accents and stately squares. An exception was the debate about the shaping of the Dam Square in the 1640s, in connection with the construction of the Stadhuis planned by Jacob van Campen.

In a first phase the plan was marked out as far as the Leidsegracht.[3] In a second phase, launched at the beginning of the 1660s,[4] the extension was continued eastwards, first to the Amstel and later two blocks further (figure 15.2). After this, however, nothing more happened, obviously because the boom in Amsterdam's economy had petered out. It seems fairly certain that as early as the second decade of the seventeenth century a general concept involving a girdle of canals embracing the whole of the old city did exist, even though no overall plan has survived from this period. But on a map dated 1613 the new system of

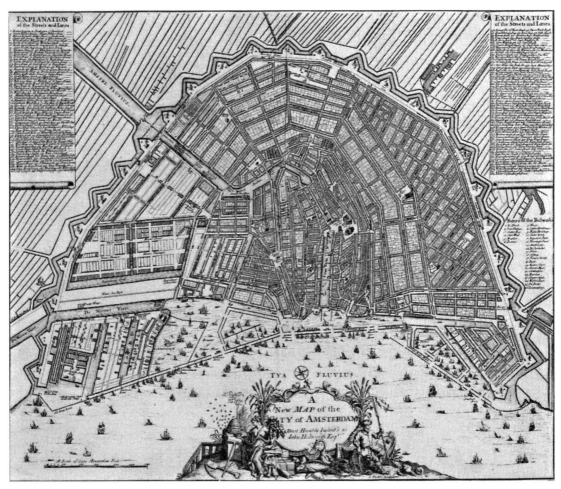

Figure 15.2 *Amsterdam. This map, which was printed in 1720, is one of many which show the city after the seventeenth-century extensions. [Photo from the Gemeentelijke Archiefdienst, Amsterdam]*

bastions is already marked in such a way as to suggest that the canals were to continue round the whole town.

This project is remarkable not only for its grand scale, but also because it represents an initiative launched by the town itself. Other seventeenth-century street improvements, for example in the Nordic countries, were pushed through by the central authorities, while in London it proved impossible to conduct any really radical regulations after the Great Fire of 1666, even though advanced plans had been made.

When it became evident that there was no need to extend the residential blocks along the whole of the east side, a promenade and recreation area – de Plantage – was laid out there during the 1680s. Here middle-class families could have a small plot of land for a garden or a little summer-house, but no permanent building was allowed.[5]

The powerful economic upsurge in Amsterdam in the seventeenth century was followed by a period of stagnation in the eighteenth, during which the town lost not only its leading position in world trade but, subsequently, its independence as well. There was something symbolical about Louis Napoleon's transformation of Jacob van Campen's town hall – originally, in the middle of the seventeenth century, an unsurpassed manifestation of municipal sovereignty – into a royal palace in 1808.

The first half of the seventeenth century was a period of relatively slow population growth in Amsterdam – with an increase from roughly 200,000 in 1800 to 224,000 in 1849[6] – and there was little building activity. In the middle of the century the structure of the town was still much as it had been at the end of the seventeenth century. The sanitary problems were appalling, not least because refuse was tipped into the canals; alarming reports were as frequent here as in other cities. In 1848 the town's defensive function was abolished – a decision made without any lengthy discussion; the demolition

of the fortifications had already begun and proceeded in stages. The last section was cleared in 1862. Some plans for a promenade and a park belt on the site of the walls were presented, but did not come to anything.[7] At much the same time the population began to grow more quickly, which also meant mounting pressure to extend the previous urban area.

The first attempts at planned exploitation outside the old urban area were made under private auspices. A remarkable initiative, without immediate parallel in other capital cities, was made by Samuel Sarphati, a doctor who hoped – with a mixture of commercialism and social commitment that was typical of the times – to create a kind of model district. In 1862 he produced a plan; its principal focus was to be a *Paleis voor Volksvlijt* surrounded by green areas (figure 15.3). Land was also reserved for commercial operations and residential facilities. The well-to-do were to live on their own in the series of short blocks while others would be housed in the row of long blocks. Sarphati was granted a concession from the municipal council to realize this plan; among other things he would be allowed to take over, at no cost, those parts of the relevant land at present in the possession of the municipality.[8]

The *Paleis voor Volksvlijt* was built between 1857 and 1864 as an exhibition hall in iron and glass, inspired by the Crystal Palace in London.[9] But apart from this Sarphati's project was dogged by difficulties, not the least of them financial. The privately owned land quickly rose in value and no resources were available to acquire it. An area dotted with windmills which lay along an old ditch through the intended residential area proved particularly problematic. In the end Sarphati had to relinquish his concession, and the development of the area was taken over by a building company, the *Nederlandsche Bouw-Maatschappij*; the basic structure and narrow blocks of the area between Gerard Doustraat and Ceintuurbaan – in everyday parlance known as 'de Pijp' – has

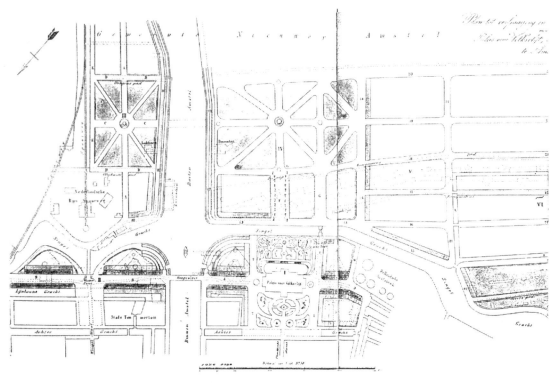

Figure 15.3 *Amsterdam. Plan for a development including an exhibition palace, the* Paleis voor Volksvlijt, *and adjoining commercial and residential areas, according to the intentions of Dr Samuel Sarphati. [From* Amsterdam in kaarten*]*

thus little to do with his plan. Sarphati had envisaged a large axially designed park area on both sides of the Amstel; this was reduced to a park occupying the equivalent of two blocks in a somewhat more westerly site, the present Sarphatipark.

A more successful enterprise, also under private auspices, was the Vondelpark,[10] a project planned and realized by a consortium of wealthy citizens on the same lines as Regent's Park in London, which may have been their inspiration. The purpose was two-pronged: to create an impressive park without any intervention by the municipality, and to generate income from the upgrading of the land. With this last in mind they bought up

more land than was needed for the park itself, so that neighbouring plots could be sold for expensive homes in a stately setting. The villas around Koningslaan, which merge into the park landscape, are particularly magnificent. The building of factories and blocks of flats for workers was naturally banned, and special provisions in the sales contracts guarded against any such possibility.

Towards the middle of the 1860s the municipal authorities began to see that they would have to take an active part in developments if they wanted to have any control over the expansion of the town, and J.G. van Niftrik, the city engineer, undertook to produce a plan. This was ready in 1866 and was printed the following year (figure 15.4).[11] In the plan the old polygonal town is surrounded by a belt of built-up areas. To the west of the Jordaan – the old workers' district – an area of workers' housing was envisaged, and next to it an extensive area reserved for factories. A broad belt of parkland was to separate the workers' district from the next residential area, intended for the middle classes. This last is divided first into a row of rectilinear blocks, followed by a series of blocks along streets radiating out from a round open place, and finishing with three more rows of rectilinear blocks. The Vondelpark separates this area from the upper class district with its radiating streets and its palatial buildings and free-standing villas in park-like surroundings. Here too a theatre and museum are planned. To the south-east another area has been reserved for industrial operations, with a neighbouring district for workers' housing. A striking ingredient in this plan is the amount of space allowed for parks and other green areas. All blocks with continuous facades would be grouped round large green courtyards, just as Carlos de Castro had suggested for Madrid a few years earlier.

Van Niftrik's project is indubitably an impressive attempt to create a town planned in detail, in which nothing was to be lacking. And yet it has the air of an obvious drawing-board product, added to which it was a little old-fashioned for its time. What van Niftrik produced was a number of residential areas without any organic coherence. He was more interested in architectural effects than in the urban function. Most striking is the lack of communications both within the newly planned area, and between this area and the centre. The railway station, to be located in the south-east close to the present Sarphatipark, does not seem to have been adequately integrated into the street network. A tree-planted ring road runs through the new districts but is too narrow to function efficiently as a traffic artery. The planned segregation and poor communications of van Niftrik's plan are to some extent reminiscent of Castro's proposal for Madrid, although the latter appears more carefully worked out.

Van Niftrik's plan met with powerful criticism – directed not so much at the poor communications, however, as at what were claimed to be the insuperable problems which the necessary acquisition of land would entail, and for which the town had neither the legal means nor the economic resources. State grants were out question. Another major objection concerned the location of the railway station, which it was felt would impoverish the old central area around and north of the Dam Square.[12] Eventually it was decided that the central station should be located on reclaimed land in the IJ, immediately north of the old urban core and thus also close to the Dam. Another advantage of this location was that the station (opened 1889) would be close to the harbour, where a boom in traffic was expected to follow the completion of the North Sea Channel (finally opened in 1876).

Thus after much discussion van Niftrik's plan was rejected, but the rapid expansion of the town during the 1870s – the population increased from approximately 224,000 to 511,000 during the second half of the nineteenth century – made some sort of plan necessary, and this time the task went to J. Kalff, recently appointed director of public works (*directeur van publieke werken*). His proposal, known as the General Expansion Plan for Amsterdam (*Het algemeen uitbreidingsplan voor Amsterdam*) and produced with the help of van Niftrik, was presented in 1876 and approved two years later (figure 15.5).[13] If van Niftrik's plan was inspired by a kind of vision, albeit a somewhat unrealistic one, Kalff's can be described as more of a pragmatic adjustment to prevailing conditions. In dividing the planned area into streets and blocks, the greatest possible attention has been paid to existing ownership boundaries and ditches. The green areas have practically disappeared, and no attempt has been made to locate different

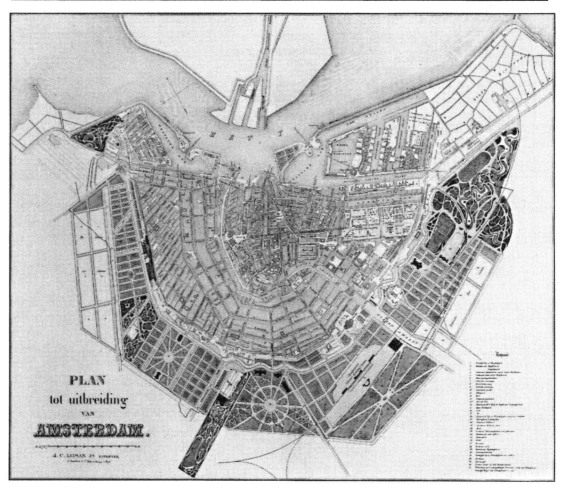

Figure 15.4 *Amsterdam. J.G. van Niftrik's 1866 plan for the extension of the city. [Photo from the Gemeentelijke Archiefdienst, Amsterdam]*

functions in separate parts of the urban area. However, a ring road – broader than the previous one – is suggested on the west side, extending to the Vondelpark, and corresponding more or less to the present Frederik Hendrikstraat, Bilderdijkstraat and Constantijn Huygensstraat. Surprisingly, the equivalent street on the eastern side – the Ceintuurbaan – was not envisaged in the plan. Kalff's plan seems more concerned to synthesize developments that were already under way, than to steer developments itself, and landowners de-mands for new streets to increase building densities were provided for. By the beginning of the present century the area of the plan had been built, largely following its suggestions, particularly on the west side.[14] Most of the buildings are blocks of flats of a fairly simple standard, built by speculators. Kalff's plan includes the Rijksmuseum, which had been started in 1877; it is designed as a large-scale propylaea, but its integration into the urban structure is disappointing. The proximity of the Vondelpark and the wealthy residential districts

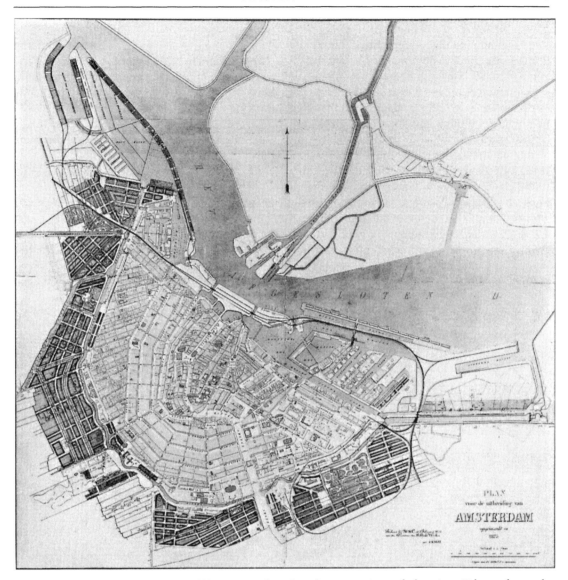

Figure 15.5 *Amsterdam. J. Kalff's 1875 plan for the extension of the city. [Photo from the Gemeentelijke Archiefdienst, Amsterdam]*

certainly affected the choice of site for the museum, and a little later for the Concertgebouw and the Stedelijk Museum as well. It is significant, however, that no attempt was made to exploit the opportunity for coordinating these buildings into an architectural ensemble.

During the last quarter of the nineteenth century a number of street improvements were carried out in the medieval centre of Amsterdam, with a view to preserving the attraction of the area for commercial activities. Amsterdam possessed a unique advantage in being able to create new and surprisingly broad streets without extensive demolition, simply by filling in the canals. Nieuwezijds Voorburgwal and Spuistraat are both examples of this; two others are Rokin and Damrak, the principal streets in the town centre, the second of which was constructed to link the Dam with the central station.[15] These streets opened up north-south links across the long narrow urban core, but communications through the surrounding seventeenth-century districts were poor. The Raadhuisstraat, built in the 1890s, was an attempt to correct this. Together with the Vijzelstraat constructed in 1916–22 it was Amsterdam's only major street cutting through existing structures in the manner of Paris (one section, however, is a filled in canal).[16] The

innermost section of the Raadhuisstraat closes with a visual focus, namely the back of the Royal Palace, the former town hall. Haussmann would have appreciated this, but he would not have approved of the wide curve imposed on the extension of the street in order to reduce the cost of acquiring land (as Nash made Regent's Street describe a curve for the same reason). However, this curve established a kind of contact between the Stadhuis and another masterpiece from the golden age of Dutch architecture, Hendrick de Keyser's Westerkerk, whose importance in the townscape was thus also enhanced.[17]

Compared with the seventeenth-century urban development project, this nineteenth-century planning appears half-hearted and

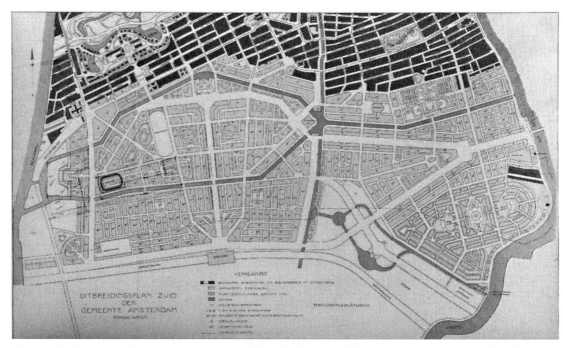

Figure 15.6 *Amsterdam. Berlage's second Plan-Zuid, 1915. The plan consists essentially of a grid with narrow streets and long narrow blocks crossed by broad streets. It is notably 'classical' and marks the rapid retreat from the winding, picturesque streets of the Sitte school which were characteristic of the previous proposal. At the same time there is a social dimension that was lacking before. [Photo from the Gemeentelijke Archiefdienst, Amsterdam]*

marginal, particularly the plans for expansion. Compared with most other capital cities, too, Amsterdam was obviously a backwater as regards urban development. However, this was soon to be changed.[18] As early as 1901 Holland acquired far-sighted legislation which made it possible for the municipalities to concern themselves with social housing. Amsterdam was already one step ahead: in 1900 the architect H.P. Berlage had been engaged as consultant.[19] A first version of Berlage's plan for the major expansion of Amsterdam to the south – *Plan Zuid* – was completed in 1904.[20] This plan is rather unstructured, however, and is encumbered with numerous winding streets of obvious Sittian inspiration, which seem particularly inappropriate in this flat terrain. Nor have communications with the older urban area been satisfactorily solved. With its sparse utilization of the available land, the plan lent itself to expensive housing but would have done little to solve the housing problems of the less well-to-do. This version was adopted by the town council in 1905, but with reservations. The issue was raised again a little less than ten years later, in 1913, and Berlage was asked to produce a new plan, a task he embarked on the following year. The revised and finally approved 1917 version (figure 15.6)[21] has quite another character. The basic structure of the plan is rectilinear with long narrow blocks, implying a big step towards functionalism. At the same time, however, with its subtle interplay of axes and visual accents it is also more Haussmannian than anything produced in Amsterdam during the preceding century.[22] The district was to become internationally recognized as a model for the 'good' environment, owing to its carefully designed buildings in the style known as the 'Amsterdam school'.

NOTES

1. The two main works on nineteenth-century planning are van der Valk (1989) and Wagenaar (1990). In van der Valk's work, which covers the period 1850–1900, the emphasis is on planning and decision processes, which are described in considerable detail. The author also seeks to test a theory that there are two kinds of planning, the 'sociocratic' and the 'technocratic' (see also note 22 below). Wagenaar whose study covers the period 1876–1914, addresses planning in some detail, but his chief purpose is to describe in a geographical perspective the change in land use, and to link this to changes in industrial activity and economic and social structures. A selection of the most important historical maps are reproduced in *Amsterdam in kaarten, Verandering van de stad in vier eeuwen cartografie* (1987). Professor Auke van der Woud has kindly allowed me to see in manuscript an unpublished essay on urban development in Amsterdam. This paper has been a main source for the chapter on Amsterdam.

2. Population figures from van der Woud's manuscript.

3. The first expansion stage is shown on a map, the original of which is dated 1612 (*Amsterdam in kaarten*, pp. 38 f).

4. The second main phase in the expansion project appears in a master plan dated 1662, reproduced in a somewhat later copy in *Amsterdam in kaarten*, pp. 86 f.

5. *Amsterdam in kaarten*, pp. 134 f.

6. Figures from the Amsterdam Office of Statistics, supplied by Auke van der Woud. There seems to be some uncertainty concerning population development during the first half the nineteenth century. According to Mitchell (1992) the population was 217,000 in 1800 and 224,000 in 1850, *i.e.* a very small increase. According to van der Valk (1989, table 1) the figure for 1849 was 247,000.

7. Information supplied by Michiel Wagenaar; cf. Prins (1993).

8. See van der Valk (1989), pp. 165 ff; Wagenaar (1990), pp. 258 ff and *Amsterdam in kaarten*, pp. 136 ff.

9. It was destroyed by fire in 1929, meeting the same fate as the Crystal Palace. Today the Nederlandsche Bank shoots up over the inner city skyline with its sterile 17-storey office tower.

10. See Wagenaar (1990), pp. 268 ff.

11. Van Niftrik's plan and its treatment by the municipal decision makers are described in detail in van der Valk (1989), pp. 223 ff. See also

Wagenaar (1990), pp. 247 ff. A brief but penetrating analysis of the plan appears in van der Woud's above-mentioned essay.

12. Information from Auke van der Woud.

13. The plan has been discussed by van der Valk (1989), pp. 293 ff.

14. This can be seen in the map dated 1905 in *Amsterdam in kaarten*, pp. 158 f.

15. Two project variants are reproduced in *Amsterdam in kaarten*, pp. 154 f.

16. The map of the project is reproduced in *Amsterdam in kaarten*, p. 155.

17. Information from Auke van der Woud.

18. Before this, however, a more conventional extension plan had been presented in 1897 by C.L.M. Lambrechtsen van Ritthem and van Niftrik (see van der Valk (1989), pp. 349 ff, picture on p. 355). This was heavily criticised and was rejected in 1900.

19. A vast amount has been published on Berlage. On his contribution to Amsterdam, see in particular *Berlage in Amsterdam*.

20. Reproduced in *Berlage in Amsterdam*, p. 43.

21. I am gratful to Dr. Michiel Wagenaar for sorting out the complicated story of the Berlage *Plan Zuid*.

22. Van der Valk presents an interesting argument based on what he calls the dichotomy between sociocratic and technocratic planning (pp. 417 ff and 565 f). 'Technocratic planning gives a key role to technicians and scientists, assumes a monolithic planning subject, centralized decision-making, comprehensiveness, blue-prints, a high degree of commitment to plans. It sees conformance to plan as the sole measure of effectiveness, rationality as a prescription for plan-making and the planning process as linear . . . Sociocratic planners perceive the planning subject to be a temporary coalition of actors. Planning should not only be the play ground for experts . . . Contextual limitations are taken into account. Planning is perceived as a cyclic process.' Van Niftrik and Berlage are counted as representatives of the first of these approaches to planning, and Kalff as a representative of the second. There is no doubt that van der Valk's sympathies are with Kalff and the type of planning he stands for, and his book is something of an apologia for Kalff's plan. Van der Valk's argument addresses a problem central to all planning. Most people today would probably disassociate themselves from purely technocratic planning. But the question is, how far is it possible to go in the opposite 'sociocratic' direction, without planning losing its identity and ending up as a feeble extrapolation of prevailing trends? Kalff's plan reveals the weaknesses rather than the strengths of 'sociocratic' planning. Nor is there any obvious link between the two approaches to planning methods and the quality of the results. The chosen examples demonstrate this with all possible clarity. Berlage's *Plan Zuid* produced an environment to which most people would probably react positively, while Kalff's plan did little to endow the relevant area much environmental quality.

16

BUDAPEST

Until 1873 Budapest consisted of two towns, Buda and Pest, situated on the western and eastern banks of the Danube.[1] The distinction was not only a legal one; it applied also to the structure of the urban landscape. No effort seems to have been made to coordinate building or planning before the first half of the nineteenth century, and any such coordination would have been difficult in view of the width of the river, which varies within the urban area between 290 and 500 metres. The topographical conditions are also essentially different: the Pest area is characterized by low-lying land with no evident variations in level, while on the Buda side the ground is hilly with the Castle Hill (Várhegy) and, just south of this, the Gellért Hill (Gellérthegy) as the most important peaks.

The history of Budapest began with the Roman town of Aquincum, which was situated north of the Castle Hill, in what was later to be Óbuda. Aquincum, which was a town of some importance in the first centuries of the Christian era, seems to have been completely abandoned during the barbarian incursions. The Hungarian kingdom was founded by Magyar tribes around 900; according to tradition the exact year is supposed to have been 896. Pest can trace its roots back to the early eleventh century, and Óbuda also gradually acquired the character of a town. Both were devastated by the Mongols in 1241, after which the fortified town of Buda was established on the Castle Hill. Pest, too, was restored, and it was at this time that there developed the division of functions between the two sister cities which was to persist and even to become more marked over the years: Buda was the fortified town, the centre of administration and the home of the aristocracy, while Pest was the home of the burghers and merchants. By the end of the Middle Ages Buda had become the most important town in the kingdom of Hungary, albeit not a capital city in a formal sense; Pest was a lively commercial centre, but could not compete with Buda in size or importance.

The Turkish occupation brought further devastation to the two towns, which from 1541 until 1686 were no more than marginal border towns in the Turkish Empire. In 1686 the Turks were superseded by the Habsburgs. From then until the middle of the nineteenth century Buda enjoyed the status of a provincial capital, with Pest complementing it as a commercial town. Growing trade thus favoured Pest. The following shows the resulting shift in the relative population figures of the two towns:

Year	Buda	Pest
1686	24,000–26,000	4,000
1696	2,205	1,708
1720	12,138	2,706
1777	22,019	13,040
1780	23,000	16,000
1799	24,306	29,870
1810	24,910	35,343
1831	38,565	64,137[2]

The rapid growth of Pest led to some attempts at planning as early as the 1780s.[3] But the plans were never realized. In 1804 the governor of the city, József Nádor, asked the architect János Hild to make a plan for improving and extending the city. Shortly afterwards, in 1808, a kind of board of works was established, whose name can be roughly translated as the 'embellishment committee' (*Szépitöbizottság*). Hild's project was concerned mainly with the northern suburb of Lipótváros, and provided for a simple plan based on straight lines, with rectangular blocks and three streets meeting in a round place (figure 16.1). Only part of the Hild plan was ever implemented. Over the following decades, however, substantial suburban building appeared on the outskirts of Pest. The embellishment committee appears to have been responsible for planning and supervising the building, and the principles applied were the same as those in the Hild plan: as far as possible streets were straight and blocks rectangular. Demolition of the city wall, which in parts had houses built on both sides, had started as far back as the eighteenth century. But outside the wall a broad zone had remained unbuilt, functioning mainly as a junction for the highways approaching from all directions. This ring road, which had thus come into being

quite spontaneously[4] (today the Kiskörút, or Little Ring, consisting of Károly körút, Múzeum körút and Vámház körút) provided a valuable point of departure for subsequent planning, and could be included in all later plans without any significant widening.

Until the middle of the nineteenth century a kind of pontoon bridge was the only connection between Buda and Pest not involving river transport. It was a primitive arrangement which could not cope with ice in winter or the rising waters of the spring. As the population increased rapidly with industrialization during the nineteenth century, and as both the towns grew in importance as administrative and cultural centres, this arrangement appeared increasingly irrational. At the same time Hungarian nationalism naturally required that the two towns together should form a capital city – Budapest. The first to suggest this was Count István Széchenyi in an article published in 1828. Széchenyi was also the driving-force behind the first bridge construction, the Széchenyi lánchíd or Chain Bridge, which was built between 1839 and 1849.

Little enthusiasm was shown in Vienna for this project which, significantly, was led by English engineers, as was the 350-metre long

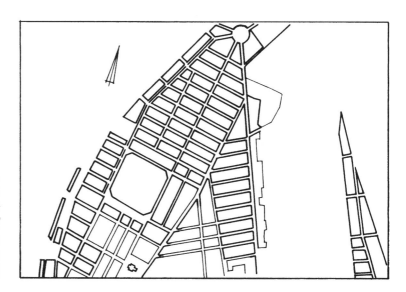

Figure 16.1 *Budapest. Northern part of an 1805 project for the street improvement and expansion of Pest, drawn by János Hild. [Redrawn from Preisich (1960)]*

tunnel (Alagút) under the Castle Hill, which links up with the bridge. This construction, which was finished in 1857, was probably the first traffic tunnel of such a size in Europe. The location of the Chain Bridge appears to have been decided in light of the availability of technically suitable land and the fact that an approach road to the Castle Hill already existed. Connections with Pest were not so good; the bridge lies on the edge of what in the nineteenth century was the centre of Pest instead of in the middle of the town where the river is narrowest, and where the Elizabeth Bridge (Erzsébet híd) was later built.

With the building of the Chain Bridge, which was financed by toll charges, it became easier for the two towns to avail themselves of one another, but the traditional functional division between a state administrative centre and a commercial centre became even more marked over the following decades. The impact of the bridge on the physical structure of the towns was perhaps more limited than might have been expected. On the Buda bank, however, the Krisztinaváros district expanded as a result of the splendid new communications with Pest, and on the Pest bank some large office blocks were subsequently built close to the bridge, evidently because of the proximity of the offices of the state administration. But there were no dramatic shifts in the activities of the city centre; the retailers remained at their old sites in the inner city.

During the year of revolutions, 1848, nationalists established a Hungarian régime under Lajos Kossuth. The revolt was crushed in the autumn of 1849, however, and Hungary was reincorporated into the Hapsburg Empire. The following period was one of reaction and stagnation, during which the country enjoyed little freedom. But suppressed energy was apparently building up until it exploded in 1867, when as a result of the *Ausgleich* or Constitutional Settlement Hungary won virtually equal status with Austria as part of the Dual Monarchy or Austro-Hungarian Empire.

Hungary now became part of the European economy, and industrialization was encouraged by the inflow of foreign capital. The development of railway construction can serve to illustrate this: between 1867 and 1873 over 4,000 kilometres of railway were laid down in the country. The industrialization of Hungary was largely concentrated to Budapest, where population growth in the decades around the turn of the century was exceptional even for those times: the number of inhabitants rose from 280,000 in 1869 to 733,000 in 1900. Rapid expansion was anticipated after the Constitutional Settlement, and the burning ambition of the Hungarian government was to give the city a distinctive physical appearance: if Hungary was to be the equal of Austria, the country should also have a capital to rival Vienna. A first step in this direction was to coordinate the towns in the juridical sense, and this was achieved in 1873. The Budapest which was thus created included, apart from Buda and Pest, also Óbuda and Margaret Island (Margit-sziget).

In order to control building developments in the capital city the prime minister, Gyula Andrássy, suggested that the former embellishment committee should be revived, and so it was recreated in a new guise modelled on the Metropolitan Board of Works in London.[5] The new body (the *Fövárosi közmunkatanács*), which came into operation in 1870, will be referred to below as the capital city's General Board of Works. Town and government were both represented on the Board, but the latter were in the majority. Buda had three representatives, Pest six, and the national administration nine, but the government also appointed a chairman and a vice-chairman. The Board was ranked above the municipal authorities, and had the right of decision on planning issues. Unlike the commissions which administered the Ringstraße project in Vienna, the General Board of Works in Budapest was a permanent body responsible for the whole town, and later also for developments in the neighbouring municipalities. In this way Budapest acquired a kind of regional planning system very early on. The Board survived the changes of the First World War and was not formally dissolved until 1947. Officials and large landowners from the aristocracy were predominant among its members, at least during the first decades of its life, and conflicts with the municipal authorities were frequent.[6]

At the time when the General Board of Works first began to operate, Pest had a relatively highly exploited urban core, the medieval town, with narrow irregular streets. This area was surrounded by a broad road, the future inner ring, from which a number of streets radiated, following the old highways (cf. figure 16.2). The buildings between these streets were predominantly one-storey houses. Some parts of the street network consisted of straight lines and right angles, but the streets were narrow, the blocks were small, and there was no coordination between the different areas. The highest standard of planning was to be found in the suburb Lipótváros, north of the inner city, which had been built according to Hild's plan. Naturally the water supply was inadequate, as were the drainage and communication systems. There were similar problems on the Buda bank, with the added complication of the topographical conditions there. Pest was attracting the most interest, however, and on the Buda side it was primarily a question of the Castle Hill, which was to be improved to such good effect that Budapest could match Vienna as imperial residence.

Quite soon after the Board of Works had been created, two important goals appear to have been established, which were to have an decisive impact on subsequent developments. These emerged from a remarkably far-sighted report, written by the engineer Ferenc Reitter in 1869 and commissioned by the prime minister, Andrássy, as part of his firm commitment to the improvement and planned expansion of Budapest. The first goal was that a ring road should be laid down, mainly following an old arm of the Danube and encircling most of the then built-up area of Pest.[7] The other was the construction of a new 'diagonal road', a grand avenue, which was to link the inner city with the City Park (Városliget) to the east of the town. At the time communications with the park were unsatisfactory, the only street being the Király utca.[8] In order to clarify the possibilities a competition was announced in 1871, based on the ring road and the radial road. Only ten proposals were submitted, and they were judged by a jury consisting of three representatives of the government, three from the Budapest Board of Works, one each from Pest, Buda, the Ministry of Trade and the Medical Association, and two foreign experts. The first prize went to Lajos Lechner, chief engineer of the Ministry of Works and Traffic. The second prize went to Frigyes Feszl for a proposal with the evocative title *Metropolis*, while the third was won by the London engineers S. Klein and Sándor Fraser.[9]

Unfortunately all the proposals submitted for this competition have been lost, except for a plan for Pest which was part of Klein and Fraser's project. There is thus little point in discussing them, since they can only be reconstructed with the help of the jury's descriptions. However, it is worth mentioning that Lechner's proposal paid particular attention to the physical and aesthetic enhancement of Buda, while his plan for Pest was more limited: he suggested virtually no major new streets over and above those prescribed in the competition brief, nor any radical street improvements. In his view parks were superfluous in the central areas of the town, since the Danube anyway supplied space and air. He was more progressive, though, in suggesting a belt of woodlands and parks around the city. Feszl's project concentrated on Pest, and the measures he suggested were far more radical, including new broader radial roads. Of these, a planned extension from Üllöi út through the old urban structure to the Chain Bridge is worth noting.

Figure 16.2 *Map of Buda and Pest, 1833. [Kungliga biblioteket, Stockholm]*

The greater restraint which Lechner showed may have brought him the first prize, but Feszl's proposal revealed an overall and well-reasoned view of the town which is reminiscent of Förster's entry for the Ringstraße competition. Soon after this competition Lechner was appointed Director of Works for the capital city.

Starting from the competition entries the General Board of Works now drew up a master plan. This was completed in 1872 and was published the following year (figure 16.3). The main points are once again the ring road and the new radial road. The ring road – today the Great Ring (Nagykörút) – was intended to sweep round most of the older built-up area in a wide semicircle (figure 16.4). In the north it was to be linked to the Buda bank by a new bridge, the Margaret Bridge (Margit híd), which would also be connected with Margaret Island. A formal approach was to be created at the abutment of the bridge. So far no bridge was being planned in the south. The road was to cut through the area of the Western Station (Nyugati pályudvar), but a new station building was to be erected a little further to the east, close to the new ring road and therefore offering excellent communications. The road was to be laid down largely on ground which had previously been built. Substantial demolition was therefore required, but it was mainly a question of simple, low buildings. The absence

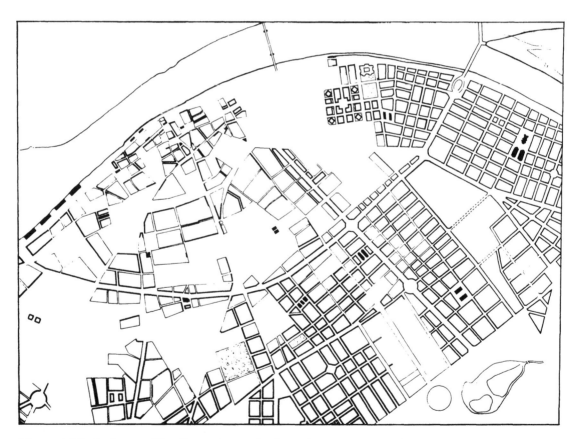

Figure 16.3 *Budapest. The General Board of Works' master plan for street regulation in Pest, 1872. [Redrawn from Siklóssy (1931)]*

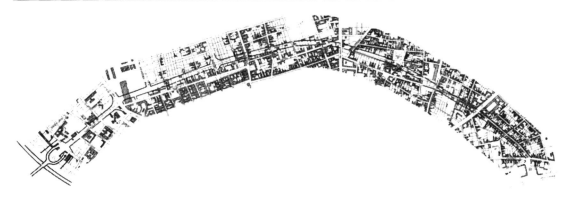

Figure 16.4 *Budapest. Project for the Great Ring. [From Preisich (1964)]*

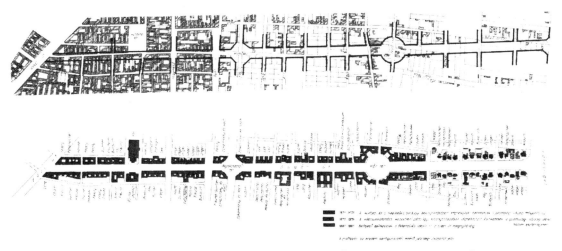

Figure 16.5 *Budapest. Project for the radial road, the Andrássy út. [From Preisich (1964)]*

of monumental accents is striking. No focal points or public buildings were planned, and the only suggestion of any kind of monumental square appears at the crossing with the new radial road, where cut-off corners are indicated. Thus the ring road is more of a traffic artery than a grand boulevard. It may seem surprising, in view of the level of ambition that presumably prevailed in the General Board of Works, that greater efforts were not made to give this street a more splendid appearance. A comparison with the Ringstraße in Vienna may spring to mind, but in fact the similarity in location and function between this ring road and the *grandes boulevards* in Paris is more striking.

A little more effort was made to achieve an imposing effect in the design for the radial road, which after the fall of the communist regime has recovered its original name, Andrássy út (figure 16.5).[10] This was to consist of three sections, created by the above-mentioned crossing with the ring road and a round place further to the east. Each section was to be broader than the previous one. The first was to be bordered by four-storey houses, the second by three-storey houses and the third by free-standing two-storey villas. The inner-most section would run through existing built-up areas, whereas the outer sections would not require much demolition. In 1873 it was decided that an opera house should be built on the inner section; this would represent the only grand public building there. The function of the street in the urban traffic system is unclear, something of which contemporary critics also complained. In the east it ends at the city park, without any proper continuation or termina-tion. In the west it ends diagonally and rather ignominiously in the present day Bajcsy-Zsilinszky út. Even today it lacks any really satisfactory continuation, despite the widening of József Attila utca. It seems particularly surprising that no attempt was made to exploit the Szent István bazilika, which was being built at the same time as the street was planned, as a point of focal interest.[11] A third grand avenue, the present-day Bajcsy-Zsilinszky út, which was to lead north from the inner ring, required no widening; here the existing exit road could be utilized. Remarkably little interest was shown in the crossing between this road and the Great Ring. A number of alterations were suggested inside the inner ring, while the area between this and the new ring was left largely intact. The old exit roads – mainly Üllöi út, Rákóczi út and Bajcsy-Zsilinszky út – were to serve as major traffic routes. The built area outside the new ring was planned in conven-tional rectangular blocks, which were to be surrounded by yet another 'outer' ring. The only new bridge was the Margaret Bridge, which has been mentioned above.

The plan, which necessitated extensive de-molition, was successively implemented in the course of the following decades under the management of the General Board of Works. Top priority was given to the radial road, the Andrássy út. Expropriation began in 1871, and building started two years later. By 1885 most of the plots along this street – almost two and a half kilometres long – were built. The project soon became associated with the celebrations

planned for the thousandth anniversary in 1896 of the founding of the kingdom of Hungary. An underground railway was built beneath the radial road in time for the world exhibition to be held during the anniversary year in the city park. This was the first electric underground railway in continental Europe. At the beginning of the present century the great Millennium Monument was erected at the termination of the street. The location of the opera house provided another sign of the fashionable char-acter of the street. The ring road – which was to be a little over four and a half kilometres long – was begun at about the same time as the radial road, but took longer to complete. It was not opened until 1896, and was not complete until 1906. The main sewer of the town was built beneath this road.

The radial road and the Great Ring were built largely according to the 1872 plan, but on other major points the plan was subject to alterations or additions. The street improve-ments inside the inner ring ran into big problems, as did communications across the Danube. A major project concerned the im-provement of the existing Rákóczi út, an old approach road which became more important when the Eastern Station (Keleti pályudvar) was built at its far end. An extension of this street through the inner city was to lead to a new planned bridge over the Danube, the Elizabeth Bridge. Around the turn of the century a star-shaped place in the very centre of the old urban core at the crossing of the new north-south and east-west main streets was being considered, but the square finally built, Felszabadulás tér, has a more modest and manageable design. On the other hand an arrangement with obviously grand connota-tions, whereby two sumptuous corner houses frame the approach road to the Elizabeth Bridge, was realized. The road itself cuts ruthlessly through the old city centre, passing close to the old city church, which could fortunately be preserved; the town hall, how-ever, had to be demolished. Not often is the collision of old and new so dramatically demonstrated as here.

A little earlier a bridge had also been built at the southern end of the inner ring, known as Freedom Bridge (Szabadság híd).[12] Another much debated planning issue at this time concerned the design of the large square, Szabadság tér, which was to replace the barracks then occupying the site.[13] The final result was a large planted area whose northern section forms a semi-star-shaped place.

As in most ports and river cities, major public investment during the nineteenth century included the construction of great quays and embankments, most of them later than 1871. Mention should also be made of Margaret Island which the city acquired in 1909. This two-and-a-half kilometre long island, with its oak trees, gardens, ruins and bathing facilities, is an oasis on a par with the great parks of Paris, and it is nearer the centre of town.

As in Vienna these various improvements were financed from a building fund, to which the Emperor Franz Joseph donated a large sum. The fund financed the expropriations, and received income from the sale of plots. But, as elsewhere, the rapid urban development of the city depended on private building speculation. The demand for apartments and premises of all kinds was so great, and the supply of capital so ample, that the expansion of the city spread to blocks and areas not included in the official plan.

Buildings erected before 1870 are today in a small minority; few capitals today present such a homogeneous picture, with most buildings dating from the decades around 1900. This applies particularly to Pest, but to some extent to Buda as well. There, however, transformations and public interventions were less comprehensive, apart from the buildings on Castle Hill and the extension of the Great Ring and the Margaret Bridge round part of the hill, but with less coherence and less grand-scale thinking than on the Pest side. Large industrial areas grew up along the Danube on the Pest bank

beyond the Great Ring, and more still on Csepel Island (Csepel-sziget) to the south of the city.

At the beginning of the present century planning focused on new peripheral industrial and residential areas in Pest; simultaneously on the hills of the Buda side vineyards were being replaced by exclusive residential areas with little public planning. One of the last major projects in the centre of the city was the magnificent neo-Gothic Parliament building, begun in 1884 and completed in 1904. Significantly a site was chosen on the Danube, rather than on one of the great avenues in the interior of Pest. It is no coincidence that the site and design of the building both evoke memories of the Houses of Parliament in London rather than of the pure classical Parliament in Vienna, though classicism otherwise was firmly rooted in Budapest. During the period when the Parliament was being built, the side of the castle facing the Danube was extended and – in a conscious effort to create a worthy capital city ambience – was given a more splendid appearance. What was really the back of the castle had now emphatically become its main facade. Hotels and office headquarters were also largely located along the embankment, including the imposing headquarters of Gresham, the English insurance company, opposite the Chain Bridge. The centre of the new capital city was not in the interior of Pest, but in the area where the two halves of the city face one another across the water. The Danube thus plays a unique role in the urban scene. It is this setting, enhanced by the dramatic topography of Buda, that creates the special character which distinguishes Budapest from the other large cities of the nineteenth century.

NOTES

1. The seminal work on late nineteenth-century planning in Budapest is Siklóssy (1931), published in connection with the sixtieth anniversary of the establishment of the General Board of Works.

Other important sources are Preisich (1960 and 1964), which describe urban development in Budapest between 1686 and 1919. A large number of plans and pictures illustrate these books. Excerpts from both of them have been provided by the architect George Lázár, without whose cooperation this section could not have been written. Mention should also be made of Broschek (1975), an unpublished dissertation from the University of Vienna on the radial road.

2. Figures from Preisich (1960), pp. 19 and 51 f. The nobility, the military and temporary students are not included in 1720, 1777 and 1780.

3. The project is reproduced in Preisich (1960), pp. 118 ff.

4. The genesis of the road as a traffic artery, and not as a *glacis* area, can be seen not least from the fact that it is widest between the northern and southern approach roads, and on the north side it does not lead down to the Danube.

5. Cf. Siklóssy (1931), pp. 80 ff.

6. On the General Board of Works in the capital city, see Siklóssy (1931).

7. It was perhaps less far-sighted that Reitter envisaged a canal as an alternative to this road. This idea may have been generated as a result of his responsibility for much of the construction of the embankments along the Danube.

8. Cf. Siklóssy (1931), pp. 140 ff.

9. The competition is discussed in Siklóssy (1931), pp. 117 ff.

10. During the communist period the street was known as Népköztársaság útja (the street of the People's Republic).

11. Various projects to provide the street with more interesting termination, for instance a national theatre in Erzsébet tér, have been discussed in recent years.

12. The Petöfi Bridge (Petöfi híd) on the extension of the Great Ring was not built until 1937.

13. Some proposals are reproduced in Preisich (1964), p. 178.

17

ROME

Last of all we turn to Rome – a town which is in certain respects unique but which nonetheless follows the general pattern of our capital cities in many ways.[1] The early building history of the town can be given only in the briefest outline here. The residential areas in ancient Rome were mainly on the hills, while almost all the large public buildings were located at the foot of the hills or between them. During the Middle Ages, when the city lived on as the centre of the Catholic Church and the most frequented place of pilgrimage in the West, the situation was pretty much the opposite: dwellings were mainly concentrated to the low-lying Campus Martius, while several important churches rose on the hills. It was the prominence of Rome as a place of pilgrimage, with the tombs of the apostles and martyrs and the other traditional holy sites, that lay behind the vast urban planning enterprises of the sixteenth century and, in particular of Sixtus V's pontificate (1585–90). It was now that the thoroughfares linking the major pilgrim churches and other important buildings were laid out: under Pius IV (1559–65) the Via Pia between Monte Cavallo and Porta Pia, under Gregory XIII (1572–85) the start of Via Merulana between the Lateran Palace and S. Maria Maggiore, and under Sixtus V the completion of this street and the construction of Via Panisperna and Via Sistina running from S. Maria Maggiore to Piazza Venezia and Trinità dei Monti respectively and from S. Maria Maggiore to S. Croce in Gerusalemme (cf. pp. 24 f). To begin with, however, these were little more

than connecting links, but they were envisaged as rectilinear streets, and those who chose to build houses along them were given special privileges. The grand innovative architectural schemes, which were subsequently studied throughout Europe, involved the insertion of monumental accents into the urban structure. These included the Campidoglio (figure 2.10), Piazza del Popolo with its three radiating streets, Piazza di S. Pietro and the Spanish Steps. During the Napoleonic era far-reaching plans were forged for the restoration and embellishment of the town, but most of them remained on the drawing board.[2]

By the middle of the nineteenth century Rome had still been barely affected by the kind of changes which were taking place in many other capital cities. As the centre of the Catholic Church, by far the most international organization in existence, and by virtue of its history and its monuments, the town enjoyed a kind of worldwide status. At the same time, as the chief city in the fairly highly centralized Papal States, it was also one of several Italian capital cities. In 1850 its population was about 175,000 – not perhaps a very impressive figure compared with London and Paris, but still a considerable number for the time. Building was still concentrated to the Campus Martius and Trastevere. Of the area within the Aurelian Wall, built in the third century AD, only about one-third was at all densely built.

In the course of the nineteenth century, as the era of the Papal States was drawing to a close, evidence of the new times gradually

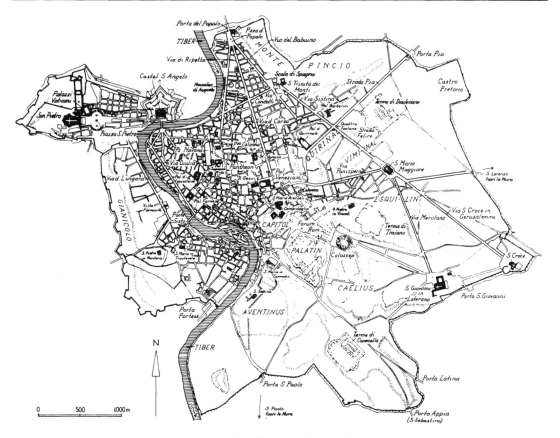

Figure 17.1 *Rome 1748. [Redrawing of Nolli's map by Erik Lorange]*

began to appear even in Rome. The arrival of the railway was an important factor; at the end of the 1850s the town was linked by rail to both Florence and Naples, and in 1867 work started on the Stazione Termini. Despite the absence of any major industry, the population of the town had been increasing since the second decade of the century; between 1850 and 1870 it rose by nearly 70,000.

But it was only after the end of the papal régime that serious change began. In the ranks of the *Risorgimento* it was taken for granted that Rome was to be the capital city of the new unified state. On 20 September 1870 Victor Emmanuel's troops broke through the wall at Porta Pia, and preparations for transferring the

functions of the capital from Florence to Rome were immediately launched. One of the first steps was to start work on a town plan. A *commissione di architetti-ingegneri* was appointed only ten days after the city fell; its task was 'to study the extension and embellishment of Rome and particularly the project for building new blocks in that part most readily adaptable to new construction.'[3] The main reason for acting so fast was probably the need to arrange offices for the public administration and homes for the civil servants, as well as organizing for the substantial increase in population that was also expected. Moreover, there was certainly a sense of urgency about transforming this venerable but rather dilapidated town into a city to rank alongside the other capitals of Europe. In the past Rome had often provided a model for Paris; now the situation was reversed. At one point there may even have been consultations with Haussmann.[4] Planning activities were facilitated by the town planning provisions included in the Expropriation Act adopted by the Italian state in 1865. In this act, mention was made of both regularization plans (*piano regolatore*) and extension plans (*piano di ampliamento*), and rules were laid down for the approval of plans and their legal implications.[5]

Work on the town plan continued for several years. A first proposal (figure 17.2) was submitted by the *commissione* under its chairman Pietro Camporesi as early as November 1870,

but this should be regarded as a kind of tentative initial outline only. 1871 was an eventful year: several plan proposals were submitted, including one by Camporesi himself. New committees were appointed, and by November the city council was able to approve a plan executed by the municipal building and planning office (*ufficio tecnico*), which represented a compromise between the earlier proposals. The chief author of the plan was the director of the *ufficio*, the engineer Alessandro Viviani. The approved plan was exhibited in January 1872, a procedure that was unusual at the time, and was submitted again in a revised version in 1873. Further discussions took place before the plan was approved for the second time in the autumn of the same year. But it was

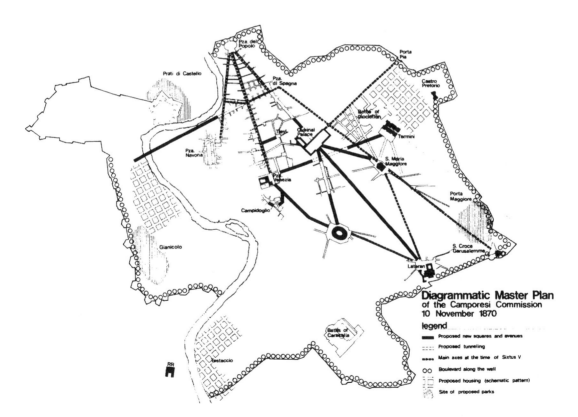

Figure 17.2 *Rome. Schematic reconstruction of the proposal of the Camporesi Committee in November 1870. [From Kostof (1976)]*

never ratified by the government. The main reason for this was probably some uncertainty as regards its financing. In 1880 the question was re-opened for discussion. Only after several more years of committees, reports, alterations and compromises was the plan for the improvement and extension of the city of Rome (*Piano regolatore e di ampliamento della città di Roma*) ratified by royal decree in March 1883 (figure 17.3). However, the main lines of this *piano* agreed with the earlier 1873 plan. Kostof has analysed the decision process and describes the plan as 'the product of endless debate and compromises, . . . an uneasy union between private gain and public good.'[6]

The main reason for the long delay was that a great many people and agencies were involved in the decision process, but no-one actually had sufficient power to get anything done. The municipal administration was weak and lacking in that authority which an established administrative tradition provides. The *giunta*, a kind of

municipal executive committee, was replaced several times during this period. And the city council's system of appointing temporary committees rather than permanent units to prepare the various plan proposals, further undermined the continuity. Several different municipal bodies were also involved in the planning work, and conflict arose not only between but also within them. Even in the office of the planning director, Viviani, an alternative to the official proposal was submitted. Regional and national authorities were also involved as developers and as controlling bodies. And last but not least, in that liberal age, landowners and speculators enjoyed considerable scope for their own manipulations. All these actors stood for different and sometimes incompatible interests.

The expectations associated with a plan which was meant to guide Rome's transformation from a picturesque relic of the past to a large modern city were naturally high. The

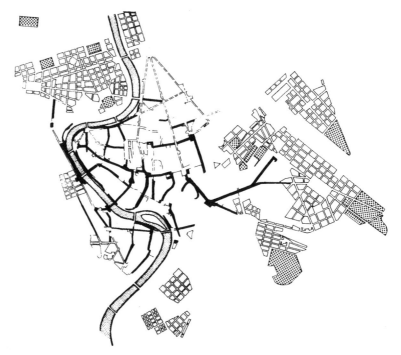

Figure 17.3 *Rome. The* piano regolatore *ratified in 1883. Dotted areas signify locations 'for government buildings and the exhibition palace'. As regards the existing urban structure, only the main streets are indicated. Unshaded streets already existed; shaded streets were to be created as a result of regulations. All blocks drawn in on the plan designate new building. [Redrawn simplified version, after the reproduction in* Roma, Città e piani*]*

plan was supposed to create imposing sites for the public buildings of the state, and to indicate suitable residential areas for the expected increase in the population. Further, it was to organize communications between the old centre in the Campus Martius and the eastern districts, where the new centre was being planned and the railway station had already been located. The distribution of functions between these two areas was also a crucial question. In connection with all this the planners had to decide how much of the earlier building in and around the Campus Martius should be demolished. There were also many restrictions: the topography was hardly suited to large-scale urban building; at the same time it was necessary to take a variety of historical buildings and monuments into consideration. Although the ancient ruins were not as yet being exploited as systematically as they were to be later during the Fascist régime, the ambition was certainly to cause as little damage as possible to the prestige which they gave to the town – or to lose the possibility of income from visitors. A first step was taken with the establishment of an archaeological zone, confirmed by law in 1887.

It is not possible to describe the various plans in detail here. The directives of the Camporesi Committee stated from the start that the emphasis should be on the building of new areas rather than on the improvement of the existing urban structure, obviously because such action would be too complicated and time-consuming. In the Committee's proposal of November 1870 (figure 17.2) the Palazzo del Quirinale, which had been reserved to become the royal residence, was given an important role. Three main thoroughfares radiated out from a broad place on its south-eastern side, leading to the Colosseum, the Lateran and the Basilica S. Maria Maggiore. The Piazza del Popolo with its three radiating streets was presumably the inspiration here. The middle avenue was to be continued through a tunnel under the Quirinal Palace linking it to Via Due

Macelli and Via del Babuino. Together these streets would provide a straight route for traffic across the town. Great emphasis was also placed on the central station, Stazione Termini, which was intended to be linked direct to Piazza Venezia by a thoroughfare proceeding through another tunnel under the Quirinal Hill and thus also under the three avenues mentioned above. Via del Corso has been extended as far as the Colosseum, while Via Condotti carries on to the Tiber and over to the other side via a new bridge. New residential areas were suggested north-east of Stazione Termini, in the Testaccio district and north-east of the Janiculum. Several parks were also included in the proposal.

The next important step is represented by the 1873 plan which, although it was never ratified as a legally binding document, functioned *de facto* as the master plan for Rome for the rest of the 1870s.[7] The system of streets running from the Palazzo del Quirinale has now been abandoned altogether, which can be seen as an expression of greater realism as well as showing that municipal interests were now asserting themselves more strongly. One of the main goals of this plan was to create a new centre in which the future Via Nazionale and the Via XX Settembre – both of which had appeared in earlier plans – would be the main thoroughfares. Via XX Settembre followed Pius IV's Via Pia, while under the papal régime a Belgian-born real estate speculator, Cardinal Xavier de Mérode, had already launched plans for the Via Nazionale. Its location was probably inspired by the idea of letting the exedra of Diocletian's baths provide the backdrop to a 'forecourt' to the street, the present Piazza della Repubblica. But this stretch was hardly compatible with the role of the street as a traffic artery leading to the Stazione Termini, even though the station was at first closer to the Piazza than it is now. A more decisive shortcoming, however, was probably that the topography and existing buildings made it difficult to link the street to Piazza Venezia – a problem which was not solved in the plan and which remains unsolved today. Thus the western side of the city had no good communications with the eastern side, which represented an obvious weakness here.[8]

A number of new streets were planned in the older parts of the town. Via Condotti, which was already sufficiently broad, was to be linked to Prati, the new district west of the Tiber, by a new street and a new bridge – the future Via Tomacelli and Ponte Cavour. But an envisaged extension of Via Condotti down to Largo dei Fiorentini was never realized, nor was a street from Piazza Borghese to Piazza della Rotonda in front of the Pantheon. Via Zanardelli, which runs from Ponte Umberto to Piazza di Tor Sanguigna, is included in the plan but was intended to end diagonally at the corner of Piazza Navona. Via del Tritone was also planned, as was its connection with Via Nazionale via a tunnel under the Quirinal. This part of the plan was largely realized. But a proposed street, in some parts quite a broad one, from Piazza di Trevi to Piazza della Rotonda, was never made.

The most remarkable of the suggested new streets cutting through the existing fabric, however, was the future Corso Vittorio Emanuele II (which starts as Via del Plebiscito), connecting the new centre in the east with the Vatican and Prati in the west. On its way through the Campus Martius it would pass some of the most important monuments of architectural history, including Palazzo Venezia, Il Gesù, S. Andrea della Valle, Palazzo Massimo, Palazzo della Cancelleria, Chiesa Nuova among others. Confronted by these monuments the planners were prepared to abandon their preference for straight streets, which was otherwise axiomatic in contemporary planning. Corso Vittorio Emanuele II wends its respectful way past churches and palaces in a series of bends and with frequent variations in width. The street was realized largely in accordance with the plan. Several redevelopment schemes were envisaged to the south of

it, but the communications between them and the new thoroughfare were poor. A street that is more typical of nineteenth-century planning is Via Cavour, whose most easterly section from the Stazione Termini to S. Maria Maggiore was to run through the new district on the Esquiline Hill, and then through existing built-up areas to the Forum Romanum. Here a new street was to lead to Piazza Venezia, but the idea was obviously also to let it continue as a viaduct over the Forum. In addition to the schemes mentioned here, several minor adjustments were also proposed.

The most important of the new areas for building in the 1873 plan is a district on the Esquiline, laid out round a large open place, the future Piazza Vittorio Emanuela.[9] Here the plans appear to have been worked out jointly by the town and the landowners. It is a street network of the conventional type, but the streets are fairly narrow in relation to the height of the houses, while the square is built on a surprisingly large scale (300 × 180 m). Despite its size it is possible to perceive it as a coherent whole, thanks to the architecture of the façades which have certain elements in common. The architect was Gaetano Koch, who was also responsible for the buildings round the exedra in the Piazza della Repubblica. In both cases loggias are an important ingredient in the overall scene – a feature with roots in ancient building traditions rather than in Roman Renaissance and Baroque. The type of square exemplified by Piazza Vittorio Emanuele also lacks Roman models, if indeed this rather over-blown square can be said to represent a 'type' at all.[10] A similar piazza was also proposed on the west bank of the Tiber, in the Prati area, which was intended to be the second important new residential district. Parks were also included in the plan, and an industrial area in Testaccio. Quays, embankments and several new bridges were other self-evident elements.

As we have seen, the 1873 plan was not ratified until ten years later, and then in a revised version (figure 17.3). However, the changes were not radical, but were chiefly in the nature of adjustments to what had actually happened in the interval.[11] Most of the street improvements suggested in the 1873 plan were also included here. But some proposed streets had now been abandoned, and important additions made; the street network system as a whole appears more carefully considered. This last applies particularly south of Corso Vittorio Emanuele II, where Via Arenula and its extension, Viale di Trastevere, can now be seen. Further links were proposed between Corso Vittorio Emanuele II and the streets along the Tiber, but these were not realized in accordance with the plan. Piazza Venezia was also to be reshaped and enlarged, and its connections with Via Cavour and Via del Colosseo to be designed on a grander scale than in the 1873 plan. It is not a very long step from this scheme to the pompous Via dei Fori Imperiali which was built under the Fascist régime.

If we try to assess the role played by the 1873 and 1883 plans in Rome's subsequent urban development, we find that not all the proposed schemes were realized. Nonetheless the end result – with thoroughfares such as Via del Tritone, Corso Vittorio Emanuele II, Via Arenula, Via Cavour and others – compared favourably with the achievements of several other capital cities. The new districts on the Esquiline and in Prati di Castello emerged in roughly the shape envisaged by the planners. On the other hand the buildings along the new main thoroughfare, Via Nazionale, were not given the monumental character intended. Moreover, a good deal was built which was not included in the plan, particularly outside the Aurelian Wall. The most striking addition to the urban scene during this period, the national monument for Victor Emmanuel II, for example, was not among the proposals.

The Roman planners were working under difficult conditions. The state was demanding street improvements and prime locations for its buildings, but it frequently ignored the plan, and was unwilling to release funds for its implementation. The municipal administration was weak, and had little local support. The landowners, on the other hand, had huge resources at their disposal and did more or less what they wanted. The ruthless exploitation of the parks and gardens round the old villas is perhaps the worst result of what Reed has justifiably called 'the third sack' of Rome.[12] The municipal authorities were faced with a *fait accompli*. The difference of opinion between those who wanted to concentrate on the improvement of the old town and those who wanted to give priority to the construction of new districts, obviously made it still more difficult to find constructive solutions. Under such conditions an offensive approach was impossible; planning had to be limited to making adjustments in what was actually being done. Active control was unachievable and perhaps not even desired.[13]

In 1909 a new plan was approved, but with its various star-shaped piazzas such as the future Piazza dei Re di Roma and Piazza Giuseppe Mazzini, for instance, it was still clearly a product of nineteenth-century thinking. This plan, too, was only partly realized. The same can be said of the 1930 plan which was ratified by Mussolini in 1931 when the Fascist régime celebrated its eighth anniversary.[14] Under the auspices of the state a number of spectacular projects were carried out, in particular the construction of the Via dei Fori Imperiali and Via della Conciliazione. Both these recall nineteenth-century planning principles, while also expressing a contemporary reaction against early nineteenth-century picturesque effects and a turning back towards the straight streets and monumental prospects of the century before. The aesthetic and functional importance of the Via della Conciliazione is highly debatable, while the Via dei Fori Imperiali attracts so much traffic into the Forum Romanum area that during the 1980s there was even talk of demolishing it.

NOTES

1. The most important source for the chapter on Rome has been Kostof (1976). Lindahl (1972) has also been very useful. Other major works are Meeks (1966), which brings historical aspects to bear on the planning and building of *Terza Roma*, and Insolera's two articles published in 1959, which include extensive pictorial material. Vanelli (1979) is a study of the economic aspects of the building developments. Rome's urban development in a longer perspective is described in Insolera (1971), which is the seminal work on the modern period. Traffic issues are discussed in Kostof (1973). Among works addressing the historical and economic development of the city during the relevant period, mention should be made of Caracciolo (1969 and 1974). Calabi (1980) provides a general overview of Italian planning and the conditions for planning during the nineteenth century and around 1900.

2. A survey of these developments is provided by Jonsson (1986), pp. 41 ff.

3. Quoted from Caracciolo (1974), p. 98.

4. See pp. 346 f.

5. On Italian planning legislation, see Calabi (1980).

6. Kostof (1976), p. 6.

7. Cf. *Roma, Città e piani*, the plate following p. 87. It was unfortunately not possible to find a reproduction of the 1873 plan of an acceptable standard. For this reason only the 1883 plan – which by and large agrees with the 1873 version – has been included here.

8. For the various proposals regarding Via Nazionale, see *Roma, Città e piani*, p. 98.

9. A detailed account of the genesis and structure of this district are given in Girardi, Gorio and Spagnesi (1974).

10. Meeks claims that this square and its architecture are related to Piazza dello Statuto in Turin (1966, p. 317).

11. This applies to the Viminal and the Quirinal, for example, where several national building projects conflicted with the 1873 plan (cf. the schematic plans in Kostof (1976), p.10).

12. Reed (1950). Cf. the map of 'The lost villas of Rome' in Fried (1973), p. 101.

13. While Kostof (1976) appears to believe that there was an express ambition to steer urban development with the help of planning, Fried (1973) seems to assume in a short overview of the late nineteenth century – as Caracciolo (1974) apparently does too – that the municipality did not really want any planning at all.

14. On later planning in Rome, see Fried (1973).

18

THE BACKGROUND AND MOTIVATION
FOR THE PLANS

We have seen how large-scale plans were made and to some extent implemented in a number of European capital cities in the decades after 1850. Important steps had of course already been taken in the first half of the century, for example Hild's 1804 plan for the suburb of Lipótváros in Budapest, the new planning of Helsinki in the second decade of the century, the planning of Köpenicker Feld in Berlin which was initiated during the 1820s, and the project plan for the expansion of Athens a few years later. Mention should also be made of the construction of the Rue de Rivoli in Paris, Regent Street in London, Carrer de Ferran in Barcelona and, albeit on a more modest scale, of Karl Johans gate in what was then Christiania. And of course in several places there were also discussions which did not lead to any concrete results. Paris is probably the prime example of this, since after the July Revolution the question of resuming Napoleon I's plans for street improvements was debated on several occasions; Napoleon's scheme in turn had been largely derived from the 1793 *Plan des artistes*. But the projects that were realized in the second half of the nineteenth century were on quite a different scale and of quite another type: it was no longer a question of creating splendid ceremonial towns for princes, but of building large, modern, efficient cities for a new age.

There thus seems good reason for us to look at the situation and the problems of the capital cities around 1850. A number of change-inducing factors were making themselves felt in all the towns studied here, albeit with greater force in some than in others. The most obvious of these was population growth, although this varied very much from one town to another (see table 18.1). In 1800 one city, London, already had over a million inhabitants, while another, Paris, had more than half a million. Nearly half the towns discussed here, however, had populations ranging from 100,000 to 250,000 (Amsterdam, Barcelona, Berlin, Copenhagen, Madrid, Rome and Vienna). Three had populations of between 54,000 and 76,000 (Brussels, Budapest and Stockholm), another three (Athens, Christiania and Helsinki) had around 10,000 inhabitants each. Six of the fifteen towns in this book, including the two largest and most important, experienced a population growth of between 75 and 150 per cent during the first half of the nineteenth century. In the case of Berlin, Helsinki and London this meant an increase of around 140 per cent, while for Madrid, Paris and Vienna it was around 80 per cent. Only four towns (Athens, Brussels, Budapest and Christiania), with populations under 100,000 in 1800, grew more rapidly than this, while three others (Barcelona, Copenhagen and Stockholm) grew more slowly, and two (Amsterdam and Rome) hardly experienced any growth at all (see table 18.1).

Thus in 1850 London had over 2.5 million inhabitants, while Paris had just passed the

Table 18.1. Population development in European capital cities between 1800 and 1900.

Town	Population (in thousands)			Percentage increase		
	1800	1850	1900	1800–1850	1850–1900	1800–1900
Amsterdam	217	224	511	3	128	135
Athens	12	31	111	158	258	825
Barcelona	115	175	533	52	205	363
Berlin	172	419	1,889	144	351	998
Brussels	66	251	599	280	139	808
Budapest	54	178	732	230	311	1,255
Christiania	10	28	228	180	714	2,180
Copenhagen	101	129	401	28	211	297
Helsinki	9	21	91	133	333	911
London	1,117	2,685	6,586	140	145	490
Madrid	160	281	540	76	92	238
Paris	581	1,053	2,714	81	158	367
Rome	163	175	463	7	165	184
Stockholm	76	93	301	22	224	296
Vienna	247	444	1,675	80	277	578

Source: Number of inhabitants from Mitchell (1992). It should be mentioned that the official boundaries of some towns were extended as a result of adjustments and annexations during this period, which affected the population figures. In the chapters on the individual towns above, different figures may be given due to the use of other sources.

million mark. Two towns had between 400,000 and 500,000 (Berlin and Vienna), and three had between 200,000 and 300,000 (Amsterdam, Brussels and Madrid). Four towns (Barcelona, Budapest, Copenhagen and Rome) found themselves in the 100,000–200,000 range. One town (Stockholm) had slightly less than 100,000 inhabitants, while three others (Athens, Christiania and Helsinki) were still relatively small, with populations of between 21,000 and 31,000.

During the second half of the century the population increase was to continue even more rapidly. In more than half the towns discussed here the number of inhabitants tripled or more than tripled during this period (Christiania's rate of growth was the greatest, at 714 per cent). Only one of them failed to double its population, namely Madrid. In absolute figures, however, there was considerable growth even there, with an increase of more than a quarter of a million. And percentage

rates can easily obscure the enormous differences in absolute terms. Helsinki, for instance, increased by 12,000 and London by a good 1.5 million during the first half of the nineteenth century, while the same two towns increased by 70,000 and nearly 4 million respectively during the second half.

There was obviously a general link between growth and a propensity for planning, but it is not possible to indicate any particular size or growth rate that can be said to have triggered planning directly. This is not perhaps surprising – an increase which would have a negligible effect in a large city, could have overwhelming implications for a small one. On the other hand there does seem to have been some correlation between the size of a town and the specific thrust of the planning. Some projects were primarily concerned with tackling the poor conditions resulting from earlier population growth by introducing a variety of improvements, while others aimed at extending the towns to adapt them to the population growth expected in the future. Although most projects were concerned with both improvements and extensions, improvements were rather naturally felt to be more important in towns which were already large and had recently experienced rapid growth, while extensions received more attention in smaller towns which could expect expansion in the future. Planning in London, and even more in Paris, concentrated in the first instance on new streets through the centre and others between the centre and the peripheral areas, but a related idea was to make it easier for outlying districts to cope with the rapid increase in population that was envisaged. In Athens, Berlin, Budapest, Amsterdam, Copenhagen, Rome and Stockholm, the last four of which at least had experienced a relatively low rate of growth during the first half of the century, the emphasis was rather on planning for growth. In Stockholm, for instance, the Lindhagen Committee was planning for an estimated increase in the population from 126,000 to 300,000 within 50 years, while Cerdá's plan for Barcelona was intended to cater for 800,000 inhabitants.

The population increase in the first half of the nineteenth century generally led to a more intensive use of the built areas and a higher population density per unit of space. In several of the cities expansion into new areas was hampered or prevented altogether by the existence of defensive works of various kinds (Amsterdam, Barcelona, Copenhagen, Vienna), or by legal obstacles to building in particular areas (as in Berlin). The absence of adequate communications technology was obviously another effective barrier to expansion. In Barcelona, for example, population density increased from 148 persons per hectare in 1718 to 800 in 1857, a trend which was probably much the same elsewhere. As a result, the wretched sanitary conditions of the pre-industrial city became increasingly evident: poor or non-existent sewage disposal or refuse-handling systems, inadequate access to fresh water often combined with poor water quality, as well as other health hazards such as polluting workshops, the ubiquitous presence of animals, centrally located cemeteries and so on. And added to all the deficiencies of the pre-industrial city there was now the increasing air and water pollution caused by the many factories. Problems of hygiene and sanitation were calling for urgent attention in all the towns discussed here,[1] albeit in some more than others.

Towards the middle of the nineteenth century many people began to realize that something had to be done, particularly as the consequences of the miserable sanitary standards affected everybody. Alarming reports appeared from one large city after another throughout Europe. Infectious diseases, and particularly cholera which was the greatest scourge of the nineteenth-century cities, were great catalysts of opinion. Cholera was endemic in India and in the course of the century appeared several times in Europe, for instance in 1834, 1853-59, 1866 and 1873. The cholera bacteria are transmitted by water and food, something which was not recognized at first, and for anyone exposed to infection the risk of becoming ill is very high. The symptoms are acute diarrhoea and vomiting, with consequent dehydration of the body. During the nineteenth century the mortality rate for cholera was over 50 per cent among those of working age and over 90 per cent for children and old people. But it was not only the terrifying death rate that made people afraid, but also the uncertainty about how the disease spread.[2] Although no one could feel safe, it was nonetheless obvious that the disease was more prevalent in districts with inadequate sanitary standards. The cholera epidemics indubitably helped to prepare public opinion for radical urban development measures, particularly the lengthy epidemics of the 1850s. In Barcelona, for example, a severe cholera epidemic appears to have been the direct cause of a first decision in 1854 to demolish the ramparts and to extend the town. In Copenhagen, too, there was a connection between the abolition of the inner line of fortifications, and a particularly severe cholera epidemic. Thus in most of the capital cities, and most noticeably in Paris, the planning projects can be regarded as part of a more comprehensive programme for raising the standard of hygiene.

Population growth and incipient industrialization were also putting more pressure on the street networks. In the centre of the towns many streets were still largely as they had been in medieval times, and even principal streets were often very narrow. The situation became chaotic when carriages, goods transport, pedestrians, stalls and booths etc. all had to fight for space on the wretched surfaces of these streets (figure 18.1). It was becoming increasingly obvious that straight, broad thoroughfares were required.[3]

The building of the railways aggravated the traffic problem. Each capital city became the centre of its country's railway network and the terminus of several lines. For various reasons, among other things the existence of several

Figure 18.1 *A pre-industrial main street under pressure from the big city's growing traffic. 'City', engraving by Gustave Doré. [From* London, a Pilgrimage *(1872)]*

different railway companies, separate stations were often built for each line or each regional system. These stations with their enormous hinterland of rails and platforms were generally located on the current edge of the densely built urban area. Thus Berlin, London, Paris and to some extent Vienna all came to be surrounded by a system of dead-end stations (see figure 18.2); in other cities one or two such stations were built. In Stockholm, where special topographical conditions made it possible to run a connecting link through the town, the location of the central station on Norrmalm hastened a shift of the city centre activities to this area. In Amsterdam too a single central station catering for through traffic was built on the edge of the city centre. Connecting links through the inner city were later to be built in Copenhagen, and more recently in several capitals – in the case of Brussels with particularly devastating implications for the physical structure of the town.

The effects of these stations on existing urban structures were largely indirect. The actual building of the stations generally required limited alterations only, but the new flow of traffic which they generated soon gave extra force to the argument for improving the capacity of the street network. In several cases the railway stations also became the starting-point for new streets. The most vigorous efforts to link the stations to the urban core were made – not surprisingly – in Paris, with the Boulevard de Strasbourg and its extension in the Boulevard de Sébastopol from the Gare de l'Est, and the Rue de Rennes from the Gare Montparnasse. But not even in Paris was the planning entirely consistent. Haussmann has often been criticized later for the poor access to the extremely busy Gare St Lazare, even though the construction of Rue Auber did link the station to the inner ring of boulevards.[4] The great station building complexes and their tracks also affected urban development in semi-central and peripheral areas, most markedly perhaps in Berlin, where the railway complex caused a number of changes in the Hobrecht plan. The tracks often came to function later as barriers dividing the areas of expansion into districts developing independently of each other, thus hampering overall planning.[5]

Thus around the middle of the nineteenth century a number of factors – population growth, increasing pressure on the street network for the transport of people and goods, together with a growing awareness of hygienic needs – made the pre-industrial urban structure with its narrow streets and many small properties appear increasingly obsolete. Around the same time other changes were also paving the way for radical urban measures. A new attitude towards land and land-owning was emerging and this was certainly an important factor: having formerly been regarded as a collective amenity, land was now – under the influence of liberalism – coming to be considered more and more as a 'commercial good'. Long-established legal barriers to development and building were being abandoned, and the way was opening for the investment in land and the speculative building on which all the large capital city projects were based. Moreover, development in artillery meant that the old fortifications of the capital cities had lost their importance long before the middle of the nineteenth century,[6] although in several cases – namely in Barcelona, Copenhagen and Vienna – demolition of the ramparts had been postponed by the opposition of the military. But by the middle of the century it was no longer possible to invoke the necessity of maintaining the old defence system, and during the 1850s it became clear that in these three towns the ramparts would be demolished. In Amsterdam the decision was taken in 1848 and in Brussels it had been decided as early as 1782 (see also pp. 352 ff).

Administrative reforms also played a part in these developments. The period 1850–1900 can be said to have seen a general improvement and enlargement of municipal operations and capacities, arising from the new and heavier

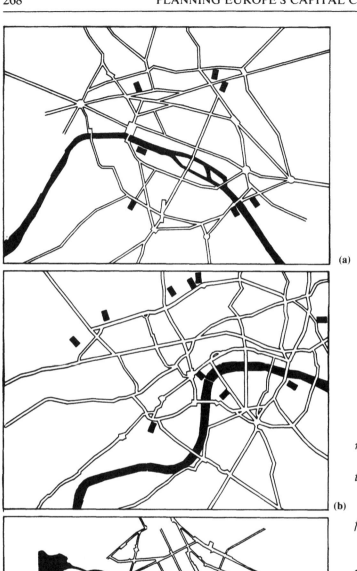

(a)

(b)

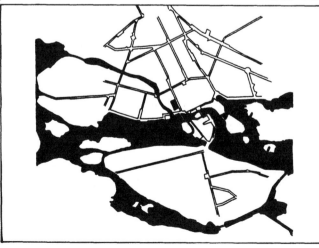

(c)

Figure 18.2 *Location of the railway stations. In smaller towns the railway with its station and tracks radically altered the urban structure; in many places in Europe a broad street can be found from the old urban core to a place in front of the station building. In the larger towns, where the urban core was already surrounded by a broad girdle of built-up areas, stations were generally located on the periphery, which resulted in huge traffic problems. Here we can see the location of the major railways stations in relation to a rough outline of the main street networks in Paris (a), London (b) and Stockholm (c). (The scale of the maps is not uniform.)*

demands to which the towns were now subject. There is clearly a close correlation between more efficient organizational forms of work on the one hand, and the major urban development undertakings on the other (see also p. 337).

Finally, it should be pointed out that in a number of cases political changes at the national level also acted as triggering factors. In Paris the renewal of the city was part of the programme whereby Napoleon III sought to maintain and strengthen his position. In Vienna and Madrid the planning projects were triggered by political changes and aimed at strengthening the position of the central government in an unstable situation. In Rome a town planning committee was appointed only ten days after Victor Emmanuel's troops had taken the city. In the case of Athens, Budapest, Christiania (Oslo) and Helsinki, the planning activities were also a direct consequence of the fact that the towns had acquired the status of capital cities. Another political change process, less dramatic but still important, was the transfer of power and influence to a growing and – in economic terms – increasingly strong 'bourgeois' group with a direct personal interest in shaping the environment in which they pursued their trades and spent their lives.[7]

The great urban development enterprises were a natural response to the problems plaguing many capital cities around the middle of the nineteenth century. But they are also typical manifestations of developments in society as a whole at the time, imbued as they were with a huge optimism, a spirit of enterprise and an eagerness to launch a variety of projects, combined with a positivist faith in man's capacity to cope with great problems by seeking rational solutions. At the same time it should be emphasized that these undertakings were by no means accepted without debate or criticism; on the contrary, they met constant opposition: on the one hand from those who believed in principle and on ideological grounds that public control should be kept to an absolute minimum, and on the other from those who opposed anything which might mean higher taxes or an infringement of the economic interests of the property-owning classes.

NOTES

1. Conditions in London around the middle of the nineteenth century have been vividly described by Hibbert as follows: 'In the hot dry summer of 1858 it was impossible to cross Westminster Bridge without a handkerchief pressed closely over nose and mouth, impossible to take a trip on a river steamer without feeling sick, impossible to breathe in the House of Commons until the windows had been covered with curtains soaked in chloride of lime. A few years before this, in 1849, the disgraceful state of London's drainage system – if so noisome a collection of leaking pipes, uncovered cess-pits, stinking gullies, rotting privies and gas-filled sewers could be called a system at all – combined with the disgusting state of its 218 acres of shallow and overcrowded burial grounds, and with the pall of smoke-filled, disease-spreading fog that hovered in the streets, produced a most fearful outbreak of cholera which at the height of its virulence killed four hundred people a day.' (Hibbert (1969), p. 187). Similar descriptions can be found of several of the towns discussed here, in both contemporary and modern works. There almost seems to have been a kind of unofficial competition between writers seeking to describe conditions in any one town as being particularly dire. Thus Barcelona, Paris, St Petersburg and Stockholm have each at some time or other been picked out as the most wretched town in Europe during the nineteenth century.
2. For a general survey of the cholera epidemic, see *Le Choléra, La première épidémie du XIXe siècle* and Longmate (1966). On cholera in Amsterdam, see *Amsterdam in kaarten*, pp. 128 ff, in Barcelona, *Atlas de Barcelona*, p. 571, in Brussels, Krings (1984, p. 90) and in Stockholm, Zacke (1971). Cf. also Knudsen's study of Copenhagen which seems to suggest that the importance of cholera in connection with urban improvements has been exaggerated. It was not – if I have understood his argument correctly – the

triggering factor, but was invoked in support of steps which were anyway desired (Knudsen (1988b), pp. 41 ff). But it was just this effect on public opinion which was important to several of the major urban development projects.

3. However, Berlin, Copenhagen and Stockholm already enjoyed quite extensive seventeenth-century areas where the streets were both straight and relatively broad, and in these three towns the authorities were content with minor alterations to the old urban structure.

4. In the mid-1850s a proposal for a broad street from the Gare du Nord and parallel with the Boulevard de Sébastopol was presented. This does not however appear to have gained Haussmann's support – hardly surprisingly, in view of the proximity of the Boulevard de Sébastopol.

5. During the present century a number of disused railway stations and tracks have provided opportunities for interesting urban development projects, in pretty much the same way as the fortification areas in the nineteenth century.

6. The inefficiency of the traditional defence works was demonstrated several times during the Napoleonic wars, for example during the British navy's shelling of Copenhagen in 1807, which left large parts of the city in ruins, and on the occasions when French troops captured Vienna.

7. Cf. Anspach's 1874 report to the Conseil Communal in Brussels, reproduced on p. 333, note 10.

19

THE AUTHORS OF THE PLANS

In the previous chapter an attempt was made to describe the background to nineteenth-century capital city planning, and to discuss some of the factors that appear to have triggered these activities. Let us now turn to the planning process itself. Theoretically a planning project can be divided into five phases: exploring the problems, drawing up a programme, making preparatory plans, deciding on a plan and executing it. However, this ideal scheme can hardly be applied to any of the examples discussed here, with the possible exception of the Ringstraße project. No real programmes appear to have been formulated, again with the possible exception of Vienna and Franz-Joseph's *Handschreiben*, his missive on the demolition of the fortifications of Vienna. Perhaps Ferenc Reitter's memorandum on the improvements in Budapest could also be called a kind of programme. Otherwise what usually happened was that some person or committee was asked to produce a plan. Some general guidelines might be given, but sometimes there were no directives at all.[1] After a certain amount of discussion and associated adjustment the plan was approved and ratified. It therefore seems justified to devote one chapter to the authors of these plans and another to the process of decision-making.

Planning in all the towns discussed here was influenced by a number of actors both at the preliminary planning stage and during implementation. There is not one example of a plan being executed in full agreement with the intentions of a single planner, with the possible exception of Ehrenström's plan for Helsinki. Sometimes changes were made before the plan was approved, sometimes during its realization. Some cases involved so many proposals and so many people that it is difficult to emphasize anyone in particular; in other cases it is possible to pick out certain people whose ideas and proposals did have a decisive influence on the final plan (table 19.1).

In some instances the projects accepted or ratified for execution can be regarded as the achievement of a single individual. This applies in particular to Castro's plan for Madrid, Cerdá's for Barcelona and Hobrecht's for Berlin, as well as the Klenze project for Athens (the preceding project had been the work of two people, Schaubert and Kleanthes). The same could be said of Ehrenström's plan for Helsinki, but this belongs to the beginning of our period and is in many ways the child of an earlier tradition. The Kalff plan for Amsterdam had a single author as well, but it was an account of current developments rather than a plan in the usual sense. But in other cases the genesis of the plans was more complex. In the case of Paris Napoleon III and Haussmann can be regarded as the fathers of the basic concept, although other people converted their intentions into concrete plans for execution. In Budapest the ratified plan was largely based on two projects, namely Lechner's and Feszl's competition entries. But important elements dating back to an earlier memorandum written by Ferenc Reitter at the request of the prime

Table 19.1. Originators of the plans discussed here.

AMSTERDAM	The first plan was produced by Jacobus Gerhardus van Niftrik (1833–1907), and the finally adopted one by J. Kalff.
ATHENS	Gustav Eduard Schaubert (1804–68) and Stamatios Kleanthes (1802–62); plan variant by Leo von Klenze (1784–1864).
BARCELONA	Ildefonso Cerdá (1816–76).
BERLIN	James Hobrecht (1825–1903).
BRUSSELS	Although he did not actually make the plan, Jules Anspach (1829–79) was the driving force as regards the central boulevards; the originator of the master plan for the suburbs was Victor Besme (1834–1904).
BUDAPEST	The plan made by the General Board of Works and adopted in 1873 was largely based on the competition entries of Lajos Lechner (1833–97) and Frigyes Feszl (1821–84), which in turn were based on a programme produced by Ferenc Reitter (1813–74).
CHRISTIANIA	A preliminary plan created by Christian Heinrich G. Grosch (1801–65) was never in fact discussed properly; no subsequent overall plan was ever made.
COPENHAGEN	Several different proposals; the decisive ones were submitted by committees. A proposal by Ferdinand Meldahl (1827–1908), however, was of considerable importance.
HELSINKI	Johan Albrecht Ehrenström (1762–1847).
LONDON	Regent Street was planned by John Nash (1752–1835) and several other streets by Sir James Pennethorne (1801–71). No master plan appears to have been made for the subsequent street improvements.
MADRID	Carlos Maria de Castro (1810–93).
PARIS	Napoleon III (1808–73); Georges-Eugène Haussmann (1804–91).
ROME	Alessandro Viviani (1825–1905); but many others were involved.
STOCKHOLM	Albert Lindhagen (1823–87), as chairman of a committee; the final plan was based only partly on Lindhagen's intentions
VIENNA	Architectural competition and committee; many involved, of whom Christian Friedrich Ludwig Ritter von Förster (1797–1863), Eduard van der Null (1812–68) and August Sic(c)ard von Sic(c)ardsburg (1813–68) merit special mention.

minister, were already determined before the competition. Lindhagen's name has been linked in accounts of planning in Stockholm with the great master plan presented in 1866, but this was based to some extent on a previous proposal; moreover Lindhagen was acting as chairman of a committee whose other members must have had some influence on the shape of the plan. And although this committee proposal greatly influenced the plan as finally ratified, many of its ingredients had in fact been changed or abandoned. In Rome the name of Viviani emerges as a key figure, but the existence of numerous committees and proposals make it difficult to define his contribution exactly. In Vienna and Copenhagen, too, several committees and many different people were involved in the planning, making it almost impossible to pick out any particular author.

By the middle of the nineteenth century urban planning had not yet become an established area of professional expertise. Previously town plans could be the work of fortification engineers for instance, or of land surveyors or architects.[2] The originators of the great capital city plans of the nineteenth century also had very different types of background. The training they had received, and the positions they held, fall into no regular pattern; the only feature common to them all, with the possible exception of Cerdá who had systematically studied planning on his own, was that they had no training in urban development matters. Haussmann and Lindhagen were trained in the law; Haussmann's ambition from an early stage was for a successful career in the administration, and by the time of his appointment as Prefect in Paris he had long been in the service of the state; Lindhagen was a judge who served for a period as a government official and who ended his career as a member of the supreme court. Some of our planners had a technical education; Castro, Cerdá and Hobrecht, for example, were civil engineers, and Lechner, Reitter, van Niftrik and Kalff appear to have had a similar background. It should be noted, however, that both Castro and Cerdá had studied architecture before turning to engineering.

Architects also took part in the planning process, particularly during the first half of the century, though not generally as the sole author of an adopted plan but by presenting proposals or submitting competition entries. Athens produced an exception to this, with the plan made by the architects Schaubert and Kleanthes ratified in 1833, and that of the architect Klenze ratified a year later. In Vienna the *Grundplan* for the Ringstraße area, ratified by the Emperor, was very largely based on the competition entries submitted by Förster and by van der Null and Sicardsburg. All three were architects and professors at the Academy.

In the competition for the Budapest plan the second prize was won by an architect, Frigyes Feszl, and many people considered his proposal to be the best. Mention should also be made of Antoni Rovira i Trias, who presented an interesting proposal for the expansion of Barcelona. In Copenhagen proposals were submitted by architects; in particular, a kind of layout plan for the area between the ramparts and the *Søerne* (the Lakes), and the final project for Gammelholm, were both the work of the prominent architect Ferdinand Meldahl. In many places in the middle years of the nineteenth century conflict between architects and engineers was common, with architects claiming that engineers lacked the artistic qualifications to design buildings and engineers declaring that architects lacked the necessary technical knowledge. Disputes of this kind seem to have affected developments, at least in the case of Barcelona. We will return later to the question of the possible differences between the plans of the architects and those of the engineers (p. 330).

What positions did the authors of these plans occupy? In Stockholm, Lindhagen participated in his role as an elected political representative, as well as on his own initiative. He was a member of the town council and of several municipal boards. Others became involved as administrators or experts, but in a variety of positions and at different levels. After a long career as an administrator, Haussmann had reached the very top of his particular hierarchy and his position gave him virtually ministerial status. He was probably chosen as prefect for his presumed capacity to administer major urban development projects. In contrast to this, when Hobrecht was commissioned to produce a plan for Berlin he had only recently completed his education, and his position was created solely for this task. Viviani was head of the authority in Rome which was responsible for urban planning, and his position was thus a more 'normal' one for the job. The same applies to van Niftrik and Kalff, who were city engineer and director of public works respectively. Castro was a member of the *Corporación de ingenieros de caminos, canales y puertos*, and had previously undertaken a variety of commissions in Madrid; he seems to have acted as a kind of city engineer and thus had the natural background for the task. Cerdá represents a special case. He had behind him almost twenty successful years as an engineer; he had also had political assignments at the national level as a member of the Spanish parliament, the *Cortes*, and at the local level in Barcelona. But by the time he undertook to make a plan for Barcelona he was no longer involved in active government service, nor was he working on any current municipal assignments. That he nonetheless became involved was probably due to his recognized expertise and his well-documented knowledge of Barcelona. His progressive political reputation may also have come into it, as well as the fact that he actively sought the job and was prepared to do it without any remuneration. Schaubert and Kleanthes were young and relatively inexperienced architects when, as a result of their own initiative, they were given the job of producing a plan for Athens. By the time the proposal was being processed, they had already quit their brief state employment. Klenze came to the task as a Bavarian legate and Bavarian court architect, but held no Greek position when he was working on his plan for Athens.

Many became involved in the planning projects as competition entrants, as members of committees or as people wont to take part in the public debate. Competitions were arranged in three of the cities discussed here, namely in Vienna (1858), Barcelona (1859) and Budapest (1871). In Vienna the Interior Ministry was responsible for the competition, and the ratified plan for the Ringstraße area – the *Grundplan* – was based to a great extent on the three winning entries. In Barcelona the competition was organized by the city in order to find an alternative to Cerdá's plan, which had been made with the concurrence of the government

in Madrid. The competition was won by Antoni Rovira i Trias, one of the city architects of Barcelona; the government nonetheless approved Cerdá's plan and Rovira's proposal had no influence on the outcome. In Budapest the competition was announced by the General Board of Works, and the final plan was a revision and compilation of the proposals which won the first three prizes.[3]

Several of the people we have just been discussing had a considerable theoretical interest in urban planning issues. This applies in particular to Cerdá, whose *Teoría general de la urbanización* (1867) is one of the most remarkable works of modern planning theory, albeit long disregarded outside Spain. Ludwig Förster, prize-winner in the Ringstraße competition, was also profoundly interested in the ideal spatial organization of the city, as was Lindhagen in Stockholm. Lindhagen did not go so far in his ideas as Cerdá, but he formulated a number of the principles that steered nineteenth-century planning in large cities, although again his work did not cross his own country's borders.

Finally it should be pointed out that the planning was also influenced by a number of politicians and decision-makers who, without being professional experts or actively participating in the creation of the plans, were deeply committed to urban development issues. Mention should be made of Napoleon III in Paris, Leopold II in Brussels, Alexander von Bach in Vienna, Gyula Andrássy in Budapest, Gillis Bildt in Stockholm and Claudio Moyano in Madrid. The General and politician Leopoldo O'Donnell, who pressed for the demolition of the fortifications in Barcelona, could perhaps be added to this list.

NOTES

1. Nevertheless, according to Frechilla, Castro's directives seem to have been fairly specific, and in his 1858 proposal Castro stresses the importance of detailed instructions for the production of

planning projects (Frechilla (1992), p. 173, note 8).

2. A survey of all the 171 ratified town plans in Sweden for towns outside Stockholm during the period 1850–1910, shows that 62 were made by people bearing the professional title of engineer or city engineer, 50 by others described as land surveyors, 8 by architects and 8 by officers. Five people had other titles, and 38 were given no titular designation. Particularly notable is the prominent position of the land surveyors, especially since many of those entitled 'engineer' were land surveyors (Hall (1991), p. 184).

3. Other master plan competitions included: Brno 1861, Mannheim 1872, Dresden 1878, Aachen 1878, Cologne 1880, Kassel 1883, Zürich 1883, Dessau 1888, Hanover 1891, Munich 1893, and the above-mentioned second competition in Vienna in 1893 (Breitling (1980), p. 33). In Gothenburg, Sweden's second largest city, a competition was arranged as early as 1861. At the beginning of the 20th century a new wave of competitions ensued, but now with a metropolitan focus. If the first Viennese competition can be described as a kind of starting-shot for inner city competitions, the second can be said to have triggered competitions for metropolitan regions.

20

THE DECISION PROCESS

This chapter is concerned primarily with decision-making during the planning phase itself, i.e. from the moment planning begins until a plan is finally decided and implementation can start. This process took quite different forms in the various cities. Comparisons are difficult without first making exhaustive studies of the legal frames and administrative arrangements in the relevant towns or countries.[1] The following exposition should be regarded as a preliminary attempt to identify some of the principal features involved. It seems clear that the towns studied here can be divided into two groups: one in which national bodies handled planning issues, and one in which responsibility fell to the municipal authorities. The most important examples in the first category are the capital cities in the countries whose monarchs enjoyed a strong personal standing, i.e. France, Prussia and Austria-Hungary. Amsterdam, Christiania, Copenhagen, Rome and Stockholm, on the other hand, belong to the second category. How did the decision making process differ between these two groups?

Paris is of course the prime example of effective, central decision making, whereby planning and implementation merge with one another; it is difficult to distinguish a separate planning phase. The exact decision path does not appear to have been studied yet, and naturally it varied according to the task of the moment. Furthermore, both rules and praxis changed over time: towards the end of the Empire, Napoleon III's personal position had become weaker and was not so different from

that of a constitutional monarch, while Haussmann's conduct became increasingly independent, not to say self-willed. As a rule the real decisions – about new streets for example – seem to have been made at frequent informal meetings between Haussmann and Napoleon, when it was generally a case of the Emperor approving the Prefect's suggestions. This, at least, is what the memoirs suggest. In many cases Haussmann was able to make decisions himself, and he seems to have avoided bringing up any question for discussion if he thought the Emperor might not follow his line. Not until the implementation stage were other decision-making bodies involved. Expropriations, national subsidies and municipal borrowing called for imperial decrees, but Napoleon rarely needed to fear objections on the part of his ministers. The municipal decision making assembly, *Conseil municipal*, only had to be consulted if the measures involved financial commitments on the part of the town. Moreover the *Conseil* was not elected but was appointed by the national government; oppositional members might thus risk losing their places. However, Haussmann controlled the *Conseil municipal* – at least if we believe his own account – not so much by employing the language of power as by using his tactical skill and ability to enthuse those around him. His recommendations were generally approved.[2] It was more difficult to manipulate the national assembly, which could reject or reduce any suggested state contributions or refuse to approve further municipal borrowing. And on several occasions this was exactly what they did. The legislative assembly was dominated by provincial representatives, unwilling to do the capital city any favours. Complicating operations in Paris was also a way of opposing Napoleon's régime. But national support was only required in certain special cases, and Haussmann eventually found ways of taking up loans without involving the national assembly. In view of all this it is not surprising that the decision process ran smoothly.

The mid-nineteenth century seems to have ushered in the age of the committees and commissions; as we have seen, committees of various kinds played an important part in the decision process in many towns. Even Napoleon had considered appointing a committee to discuss 'the plan for the general system of new public thoroughfares to be successively opened in Paris', and he informed Haussmann of his intention at their first meeting after the Prefect's appointment. This was an unforeseen blow to Haussmann, who according to his memoirs immediately decided to give the committee *le coup de la mort*. It would perhaps be justified to quote Haussmann's account of a discussion he had with the Emperor about this committee after its first meeting:

After the meeting the Emperor took me on one side and asked what I thought of it all: 'Sire,' I replied, 'the committee seems to me to be too big to be efficient. It is our habit, when there are too many of us, to let the slightest observations assume the form of a discourse, and instead of remaining brief, reports are transformed into learned dissertations. Work would proceed better and more quickly if the committee were composed of the Emperor as President, the *Préfet de la Seine* as Secretary responsible for analysing matters submitted to Your Majesty and for executing Your decisions and, finally, between the Sovereign and his very humble servant, the smallest possible number of other members.' – 'In other words, if there were no-one at all it would be best?' asked the Emperor, laughing. – 'That is indeed the essence of my idea', I answered. – 'I really believe,' replied His Majesty, 'that you are right'.

I heard no more about the *Commission des Grands Travaux de Paris*. It died of starvation, and its ephemeral existence left no trace or any regrets, apart from the disappointment that certain of its members must have felt at the end of its mandate.[3]

This account may smell of reconstruction after the event, but it is still significative of Haussmann's attitude to his job, and of the way in which the urban renewal programme did in fact function.[4]

In Vienna, unlike Paris, it is possible to distinguish clearly between a planning and an implementation phase. In both, the decision process functioned efficiently even though much of the work took place in committees, often quite big ones. There was great pressure to achieve the quick results the Emperor wanted, and most committee members were officials in an authoritarian, hierarchic administrative system. It was necessary to make far-reaching concessions, albeit not always without bitterness, as we have seen.[5] As in Paris, decisions were based on the will and power of the Emperor; conditions were also more favourable than in Paris, since the state already owned the land and it was a question of building on virgin ground. No-one in Vienna assumed a position of power of the kind Haussmann enjoyed in Paris. Franz Joseph did not involve himself personally in the same way as Napoleon III, and certainly lacked the French emperor's decided views on questions of urban development. Planning in Vienna thus provides an example of an efficient collective decision process. The standing of the municipal authorities in Vienna seems, as in Paris, to have been very weak. But in Paris the city was at least the formal principal as regards the street improvements, whereas the extension of the Ringstraße area was seen as a question of state responsibility.[6]

In Budapest, where the government appointed the General Board of Works of the Capital City, the decision-making process also worked efficiently. This Board, on which national representatives were in the majority, enjoyed a very strong position. Under the Minister for the Interior it was responsible not only for working out and adopting the 1872 overall plan as well as various subplans, but also for implementation. Thus all important decisions were made by the Board. Both Buda and Pest did in fact possess what we could call building councils, but their function seems to have been restricted to questions of minor importance and a kind of formal legal reviewing function as regards building permits; and some of their decisions still had to be submitted to the General Board of Works, to whom appeal could be made against any municipal decision on planning or building.[7] Thus the authority of the Board of Works differed greatly from that of its model, the Metropolitan Board of Works in London, which seems to have lacked any real 'authority' function and which acted more or less as an intermunicipal cooperative body. None of the other towns studied here had any equivalent body; the closest parallel to Budapest is the *Stadter-weiterungs-Commission* (Committee for the Expansion of the Town) in Vienna, although this was responsible for the expansion of the *glacis* area only. The function and standing of the Board of Works recalls Haussmann's position: in both cases it was a question of appointment by the government and of far-reaching authority. To begin with, under the force of Ferenc Reitter's personality, the activities of the Board followed a progressive line, but gradually it came to be an obstacle to development; it saw as its task the implementation of the 1872 plan with as few alterations as possible, and as late as the beginning of the present century it was still rejecting all proposals for the creation of a new plan.

In Berlin, in contrast to the three towns discussed above, the government did not regard the planning operations as an issue of great national interest. And the situation was anyway different: it was not a case here of planning the city centre or other districts of distinction, calling for stately architecture. The plan was executed by James Hobrecht, an official employed especially for the project who had recently qualified as a hydraulic and civil engineer; it was submitted to the King for ratification after receiving the approval of the police board. There was clearly never any mention of a planning committee, and no municipal body appears to have been involved in the planning process, although the plan was approved by the city. During implementation a great many changes were made in the plan, obviously without any particular fuss.

In the Spanish case, too, the final planning decisions were taken by the national government. In Barcelona the town actively opposed the proposal drawn up by Cerdá in consultation with the government, and a competition was arranged to find an alternative. In the end, however, they were forced to accept the Cerdá plan, which was subsequently respected to a degree that was quite unique, at any rate as regards the structure of the city blocks. But the very fact that the town did not immediately accept a proposal already approved by the government suggests that it had greater freedom – at least as regards this type of question – than was the case in Paris, Vienna or Berlin. Nor, of course, was Barcelona a capital city. In Madrid the government seems to have retained full control over planning. The *Ministerio de Fomento* took the initiative and appointed a committee , evidently without consulting the town. Despite the existence of this committee, Carlos Maria de Castro emerged as the man responsible for the proposal. This was approved by the government, after being submitted to the municipality and other bodies for comment; this last, however, seems to have been little more than a formality. But considerable importance was obviously ascribed to the consultative committee or *junta consultativa* of the official engineering body, the *Corporación de ingenieros de caminos, canales y puertos*. The junta fulfilled an expert function at the national level in a way that had no equivalent in the other countries discussed here.

Helsinki and Athens provide examples of decision making processes that were both quick and efficient. Ehrenström's 1812 town plan for the Finnish capital was submitted direct to the Tsar on completion, and was immediately approved. Schaubert and Kleanthes's project for Athens appears to have been approved by the government without any very extensive investigation or municipal involvement. Both these plans, and particularly the one for Helsinki, can be seen as late examples of purely royal decision-making.

While planning decisions were taken quickly and efficiently in all these towns, the opposite has to be said of Amsterdam, Copenhagen, Rome and Stockholm. In Stockholm it took seventeen years from the start of the planning activities until the final plans were ratified, and in Rome it took thirteen. Even in Copenhagen planning discussions lasted for considerably more than a decade. In Christiania, despite the question having been raised as early as 1836, it was never possible to produce a plan at all, even though the town was instructed by the national parliament or *Storting* to produce such a plan. Twenty-five years later, in 1861, Christiania asked to be freed from this demand, to which the *Storting* agreed. For the sake of comparison it is worth remembering that Haussmann's entire term of office lasted barely seventeen years.

Why did the planning process drag on for so long in these towns? We take Stockholm as our main example of this category, i.e. of towns where the municipality was responsible for planning. We find that the question of a plan to cover the whole town first appeared in the form of a private bill submitted in 1857. The proposal was criticized, and after three years of thinking it over, it was decided in 1860 that no action should be taken. However, the matter was brought up again three years later, this time by the city governor representing the central authorities; he referred to the earlier bill and instructed the town to see that a plan was made. This was the only time during

the nineteenth century that a state authority intervened in such a concrete way in the planning of Stockholm. The sequence of events that was thus launched can be divided into three phases: first an initial planning phase lasting almost four years, during which two proposals were prepared, followed by a period of seven years when work was at a standstill, and finally a discussion and decision phase lasting nearly seven years.

A first proposal was completed within about a year. That it was not immediately approved probably depended on the municipal reform which had just been introduced, granting the cities greater independence. The newly created finance committee (*drätselnämnden*), which functioned as a kind of municipal executive board, appointed a further committee which was supposed to comment on the proposed plan; instead, however, it produced a completely new plan of its own, which delayed things for another two years. A variety of factors then coincided in such a way that the whole issue lay dormant for seven years. The most important of these were probably the low level of building activity which made the idea of a plan seem less urgent, and uncertainty about the roles of the various officials involved.

In 1874 the final phase was launched, during which the plan was to wind its way through the complicated decision apparatus. First it had to be adopted by the city council, an assembly of a hundred elected members; after this it was ready for submission to the government for ratification, at which stage changes could also be introduced. The handling of this issue in the various municipal bodies was lengthy and fraught with conflict. The plan for Norrmalm alone, for instance, required eleven meetings of the city council. The decision process appears to have been chaotic; the broad outlines were swamped in an endless series of votes about the width or length of streets; the majorities were often small and the constellations of voters for and against were constantly shifting.

This situation can be explained in a number of ways. For example, there was as yet no established party system. Council members could not invoke a party line to support their own opinions, but this also relieved them of any 'party' loyalty and meant they could decide for themselves on every single point. Moreover, planning was not yet regarded as an activity reserved for professionals; anybody could – and did – have his own opinion about where streets should be built. Nor had the town yet acquired an administrative apparatus for dealing with planning issues.

We may well ask ourselves why these planning issues aroused such strong emotions. General conservativism and resistance to change were certainly part of the picture. It was always difficult to get expensive projects accepted, as they might mean an increase in taxes; the cheapest alternative could usually rely on the support of the eager savers, regardless of what it involved. And some people simply opposed on principle the idea that the town should involve itself in anything on the scale of the great street development projects. But not all reactions were negative; new suggestions were often floated during the discussions in the city council or the various boards; some were perhaps no more than a passing fancy, but others offered well-thought-out alternatives. Chance events and personal preferences played a large part in all this. For example, Kungsholmen – one of the central Stockholm districts – might well have looked quite different today if one particular individual, a new resident in the area, had not become interested and produced an alternative to the finance committee's proposal.

The decision process was also complicated by widespread speculation, with further delays as a result. During the period we are talking about it was not considered immoral to exploit knowledge of the city plans in one's own interests, or even to seek personal benefit from taking part in municipal decisions. We have seen how representatives of two development companies established in 1872, worked hard in the city council to see that certain important streets should be built just where it suited them. About another big developer who exploited his position as a council member to promote his own interests, the newspaper *Dagens Nyheter* wrote in March 1879: '. . . he is so desperately keen . . . that the whole of his powerful frame trembles with ill-concealed anxiety until the city council, with or without a vote, decides on the purchases.'[8] All this happened quite openly; what went on in secret, using front men and so on, has not yet been investigated and will probably now never be completely uncovered. It seems probable, however, that many members of the municipal boards and committees exploited their positions and their 'inside information' for personal speculations.

Land and building speculation – by which I mean transactions geared to a quick rise in value rather than a long-term profit – occurred in all the cities discussed here due to the rapid urban growth, albeit to a varying extent and in different ways. It could arise at any stage from the first tentative discussions and until the buildings were in place – and of course even later. In Paris there was large-scale speculation in future street locations, despite the uncommunicative and authoritarian nature of the decision process.[9] Nor could the authorities in Athens or Rome curb a powerful wave of speculation. In Vienna, where the state owned the land, there was far less scope for this kind of manipulation, as the rise in land values was realized at the time of the sale of the plots. In Stockholm the municipality traded extensively in building plots, partly in order to profit by a future rise in land values – something which critics within the city council regarded as unwholesome speculation. The dilemma was that towns were dependent on substantial private investment in building for the implementation of their plans, and it was therefore difficult to control the abuses effectively or to prevent most of the value increase ending up in the pockets of the speculators (see also p. 338).

It should be emphasized that none of the leading planners appears to have used his own position for his private advantage. Both Lindhagen and Haussmann were driven by their commitment to the matter at hand, convinced that their measures were in the public interest. The same could probably be said about most of the planners discussed in this study. Not even Hobrecht, who was otherwise criticized for almost everything, has been accused of acting for his own private profit.

It should also be pointed out in this context that decision making in most of the towns discussed here was a surprisingly open affair. In some cases both proposals and ratified plans were published (Copenhagen, Stockholm, Vienna), in others ratified plans alone (Athens, Barcelona, Berlin, Budapest, Madrid, Rome). Paris seems to have been the only one of our towns where systematic efforts were made to keep the public out of the planning process, albeit without much success.

Returning now to the final phase of the planning in Stockholm, we have seen how the hundred city councillors had to make up their minds under a barrage of differing opinions and opposing interests. Perhaps it is not surprising after all, that the whole process dragged on for so long.[10] And it was as one of this hundred that Albert Lindhagen tried to achieve a comprehensive solution and to save as much as possible of the principles embedded in the 1866 committee proposal. His political position does not seem to have been particularly strong; on some occasions he was close to losing his mandate.[11] Moreover, his work for the municipality was only one of his many commitments; apart from serving in the Supreme Court, he had various other obligations and for some years was a member of the *Riksdag*. Nonetheless he found time to produce several plan proposals of his own, and to write a series of detailed comments and reservations. As we have seen,

Lindhagen did not succeed in steering the decision process, but did manage to influence it in various important ways due to his expert knowledge, his integrity, his commitment, his skill in debate and, above all, because his suggestions were always based on a well-thought-out overall view.[12] It is much to Lindhagen's credit that the chaotic decision process did ultimately lead to an effective plan, in which posterity has found little to criticize.

In Rome the most important role was played by a competent official, Alessandro Viviani. In certain respects, however, the problems in Rome and Stockholm were akin: planning issues were being dealt with by newly established municipal assemblies; in both cities there was powerful pressure from speculators; conflict was rife both within and between the municipal actors involved; and, particularly in Rome, there were clashes between national and municipal interests. The Stockholm plans ratified in 1879 and 1880 could in fact be described in the words which Kostof uses to characterize the plan for Rome: it was, he said, 'the product of endless debate and compromises, . . . an uneasy union between private gain and public good.'[13]

In Copenhagen the town adopted a progressive approach, while the state and its agencies found various ways of obstructing the solutions which the municipality favoured. In Christiania, on the other hand, the municipal administration was obviously unwilling to make much effort to produce the plan requested by the state, and the *Storting* later withdrew its demand for a plan at the behest of the town. In Amsterdam too the decision process seems to have been both lengthy and chaotic.

London falls a little outside the general pattern: on the one hand, opposition to state intervention in local affairs seems to have been particularly strong there; on the other, London was divided into a large number of municipal units, which often lacked any administration worthy of the name. National initiatives were thus of particular importance, but the government's chief aim was to avoid costs. The position of the intermunicipal boards which were established – the Commission of Sewers in 1848 and the Metropolitan Board of Works in 1855 – was weak, and their resources insufficient. Under these circumstances it is hardly surprising that London lacked any real public overall planning, though some schemes were produced by John Nash, James Pennethorne and others.

In Athens, too, the conditions for planning were unfavourable. After a splendid prelude when the plans produced by Schaubert and Kleanthes in 1833 and by Klenze in 1834 received such quick approval, it became increasingly difficult to push plans through to the approval stage, due to the prevailing 'liberal' values and the sometimes chaotic conditions. A similar sequence of events can be observed elsewhere, with quick efficient decision making being replaced by processes that were both complicated and inefficient. Helsinki can provide an example: the 1812 town plan was produced and approved in the course of a few months, while it took numerous proposals and decades of investigations and discussions before a plan for the Skatudden district could be ratified in the second half of the century.

What, then, are the main conclusions to be drawn from these descriptions and comparisons? Generally, it was the national governments which initiated the planning process, although in Barcelona, Copenhagen and Vienna there was powerful local demand for the demolition of the fortifications and the exploitation of the surrounding unbuilt *glacis* areas. In Brussels, unusually, the city inaugurated several improvements, in particular the central boulevard; at a later stage, however, the national government launched various projects outside the borders of the municipality of Brussels. In most cases, too, problems and possible measures had been under discussion long before planning proper began. During the

initial planning and decision phases we have noted that two main models can be distinguished: in one, the process is directed by the national government and its representatives, while in the other the town occupies a stronger position and the government's role is limited to ratifying the municipality's plans. In the first group the decision process runs smoothly and quickly and is geared to an overall view; in the second, things proceed slowly and laboriously, while details are discussed at great length and numerous compromises have to be made. In the first category, planning in the capital city is regarded as a national issue; in the second, it is seen primarily as a municipal question, possibly with a certain national political dimension. In Copenhagen, for example, this meant that the state regarded the maximum profit accruing to itself as the most important criterion for its urban development policy in the capital city. Berlin is a special case: national bodies were responsible for planning, but they did not rank the project particularly high.

However, this suggested dichotomy should not conceal the disagreement which could arise between the different national bodies, in some cases between government and parliament, regarding the role of the state in the planning of the capital cities. Suspicion and envy of the capitals seems to have been a common feature in all the elected parliaments, where provincial representatives were in the majority; so too was opposition to the use of national funds for improving conditions in these cities.[14] It was sometimes difficult to overcome this opposition, even in authoritarian states such as France under the Second Empire, and even more difficult under a liberal constitution like the Italian. Moreover, landowner interests were strongly represented in the parliaments as a result of the voting eligibility rules and the voting restrictions; in the Danish *Folketing* a suggestion that private land in the *glacis* area should be expropriated was rejected as being incompatible with the constitution; the idea had been to reserve the increase in land values for the general public, when the earlier prohibition on building was lifted.

NOTES

1. It is largely for this reason that Stockholm has been allotted so much space in this chapter. However, the decision process in Stockholm – perhaps along with Amsterdam and Vienna – is probably also the one which has hitherto received the most exhaustive scholarly attention.

2. At the first meeting between Napoleon and Haussmann after the latter's appointment, the Emperor announced his intention of dissolving the *Conseil municipal* 'to remove those members who are a bad influence', and urged Haussmann to choose new members. However, according to the memoirs, the Prefect managed to persuade the Emperor that the best tactic would be to postpone any dissolution of the *Conseil* until he had taken a closer look at its composition. If it proved necessary to dissolve it, the best time to do so would be when it was opposing some popular proposal. But it was possible, Haussmann pointed out, that Berger – the former Prefect – had exaggerated the negative mood of the *Conseil* as an excuse for his own inactivity (Haussmann (1890), II, pp. 51 f).

3. Haussmann (1890), II, pp. 57 ff.

4. Camillo Sitte was just as critical of committees as Haussmann was, but in his case for artistic reasons. A fundamental requirement, according to Sitte, was that a single person should be responsible for the planning: 'It is simply impossible for several people working together in committees or offices to create works of art.' (1889, p. 132.)

5. See p. 185, note 19. It is also worth quoting von Sicardsburg's comment on the minutes of the final meeting of the committee which produced the *Grundplan* for the extension of the Ringstraße area: 'It is natural that there should be differences of opinion and diverging ideas. But it is a question of making progress in this matter, which means that it would not be meaningful to insist further on our own diverse opinions. I accept that this plan is now complete, and do not consider whether or not it agrees with my own ideas.' (Quoted from Mollik, Reining and Wurzer (1980), p. 337.)

6. When it came to the planning of the former parade ground, however, Cajetan von Felder, the mayor of Vienna, succeeded in influencing the final solution in such a way that it was possible, among other things, for the city to build its town hall in the area (cf. Mollik, Reining and Wurzer (1980), pp. 211 ff and 459 f).

7. Cf. A. Közmunkatanács alapokmánya, az. 1870, évi 10. t.- c. (Basic regulations for the capital city's General Board of Works, quoted in Siklóssy (1931), pp. 86 ff).

8. Quoted from Selling (1970), p. 53.

9. In his novel *La Curée*, Zola fiercely attacks land and building rackets.

10. Stockholm was not alone in this. On the contrary, in Swedish towns it seems to have been the rule rather than the exception that everything to do with overall planning took a long time to deal with, unless a fire disaster had occurred to compel speedier action. In the small town of Södertälje to the south-west of Stockholm, five years were to pass from the day the question of a plan was raised until a plan was finally ratified (Gelotte (1980), pp. 54 ff; cf. also Hall (1991), p. 185).

11. Cf. Selling (1970), p. 30.

12. Of some importance too was probably the authority that Lindhagen enjoyed as author of the 1874 building ordinances.

13. Kostof (1976), p. 6.

14. This point is made in Sutcliffe (1979b).

21

CONTENT AND PURPOSE OF THE PLANS

A number of problems were common to all nineteenth-century capital cities, for example the rapid growth in population, the low standard of hygiene and poor traffic conditions. At the same time, however, the differences between the towns were also striking. We need only mention size, topography, administrative procedures, the standard of the existing street network and so on. The demands facing the planners thus varied greatly from one town to another. Consequently the plans themselves also differ in many ways, as well as having several features in common.[1]

In the introduction to his missive on the subject of the Viennese fortification area, Emperor Franz Joseph spoke of the city's *Erweiterung* (expansion), *Regulierung* (improvement) and *Verschönerung* (embellishment).[2] Just these features could be described as the over-riding goals of urban planning at the time. Some projects such as Hobrecht's plan for Berlin, Castro's for Madrid and van Niftrik's for Amsterdam were concerned exclusively with expansion, while Haussmann's contributions to the planning of Paris were concerned mainly with improvement and embellishment, although one primary purpose for the urban redevelopments there was to make further expansion at the periphery possible. However, the nineteenth century saw no clear borderline between 'expansion' and 'improvement'; it was a question of two sides of the same coin, and the aim was to create

well-arranged and efficient urban environments. In many projects both the components were of course included, as in Viviani's plan for Rome and Lindhagen's for Stockholm, as well as Ildefonso Cerdá's plan for Barcelona. The plans for Rome and Barcelona thus embraced the whole town, both existing and planned areas, while the Stockholm plan covered everything except the urban core, the Town Between the Bridges.

But the terms 'expansion' and 'improvement' tell us little about the kind of urban environment that was desired or about the problems which had to be solved. Around the middle of the nineteenth century scientific planning theory was still in its infancy, and there was as yet little real debate on urban development questions. The creation of a town plan was regarded as a practical matter: the aim was to see that building plots were efficiently organized, that streets were of suitable width, and so on. Attitudes were essentially the same as they had been in previous centuries.

We can also learn a good deal about the prevailing planning ideas around the middle of the nineteenth century from the 1874 Swedish building ordinances, written by Albert Lindhagen who was also closely involved in the planning of Stockholm. According to these ordinances it was mandatory upon Swedish towns to make town plans, and the purpose of the plans was stipulated as follows:

The town plan should be made in such a way as to allow simultaneously for the space and convenience necessary for movement and the light and fresh air required for health; it should provide the greatest possible security against great fires, and the open spaces, variety and neatness so necessary to the sense of beauty.[3]

Smoothly running traffic, a good standard of hygiene, security against fire and a distinguished townscape were thus the goals to which, according to these ordinances, particular attention was to be paid, and they can be regarded as fundamental objectives for most nineteenth-century planning. Perhaps we should add the need for the clearance of substandard buildings, which was presumably implicit in the four stated goals, and the requirements of 'internal security'. This last, however, does not seem to have figured in Nordic town planning, and would in any case not have been a fitting ingredient in a statutory document.

Obviously the author of the Swedish building ordinances did not expect planning to be concerned with zoning, i.e. the location of different activities such as housing or industrial establishments. Such considerations played apparently an insignificant part in the projects discussed here and have not therefore been addressed in a separate section, although admittedly some plans such as Castro's proposal for Madrid and Schaubert and Kleanthes's project for Athens, revealed an obvious ambition to divide the town into zones for different activities. In a few cases, particularly in Helsinki and Madrid, we can speak of intended social zoning.

Nor is a special section devoted to fire safety, which was in fact an important consideration in the Swedish 1874 building ordinances. These were intended to apply not only to central Stockholm where most buildings were brick, but also to the other towns in Sweden where buildings were almost exclusively wooden and fires were a serious threat,[4] as indeed they were in Finnish and Norwegian towns too.[5] The broad tree-lined streets were meant to stop the spread of fire and thus to avoid major catastrophes. The risk of fire spreading was not so great among brick buildings, but even in the centre of large towns the broad streets were probably still regarded as a way of averting a possible risk. In the various planning discussions the fire safety factor was rarely specifically mentioned, but was certainly implicit.[6]

Let us now examine the main goals of the nineteenth-century capital planning.

TRAFFIC

'The warp of the plan for a town,' according to the Lindhagen Committee in Stockholm, should be 'the movement therein and the natural routes for this.'[7] Today this statement may seem something of a truism, but it is probably difficult for us now to imagine the chaos that often reigned on the narrow streets of Europe's larger towns in the nineteenth century, and how long it took to travel even short distances. The traffic aspect was also of central importance in many of the projects discussed here, but most of course in those chiefly concerned with street improvements. In Paris the primary goal of the redevelopment was to create high-capacity communications within the central parts of the city, and between these and the peripheral areas. In Brussels one of the main problems was to link the two railway stations which were located on opposite sides of the old city, to the north and south. In London too, traffic considerations played a decisive role in the improvement projects.

In the projects geared mainly to expansion traffic considerations were less crucial, although even here adequate communications

L'omnibus de la Bastille.

Figure 21.1 *Paris. 'L'Omnibus de la Bastille', Gustav Doré's xylograph in* Le Nouveau Paris *(1861). During the second half of the nineteenth century an increasingly complex network of buses and tramlines spread across the big cities, thus accentuating even more the need for broad, level, straight streets, but without having any radical effect on the urban structure. [From* L'Œuvre du baron Haussmann*]*

had to be arranged in the new districts and between these districts and the older parts of the town. The Lindhagen Committee's proposal for Stockholm solved these problems by extending the streets in the older areas through the new districts, and – more importantly – by planning for new main roads running through existing and planned areas alike. During the discussions which preceded acceptance of the final plans, however, several of these through roads were abandoned or reduced in size. Similar solutions were attempted in Rome;

there, however, planning was complicated by the awkward topography and the allowances that had to be made for buildings of cultural, historical and archeological interest. Cerdá's plan for Barcelona, on the other hand, included some streets in the *ensanche* which cut ruthlessly through the old city. Of these only Via Layetana was ever realized, however. In Budapest it was possible on the Pest side to start from existing streets and build a system of radial and concentric communications; there was less interest in the Buda side. In Vienna it was a question of exploiting the area beyond the ramparts – the *glacis* – to create good communications between the city core and the suburbs. This problem was solved by the Ringstraße, and by the fact that the old exit roads were extended into the new area; links through the old city core would have required radical redevelopment, and no attempt was made to apply a consistent solution to this problem in the *Grundplan*. Nor was any serious attempt made in Copenhagen to let streets run from the new districts through the older areas; in Madrid the situation was much the same.

It should be mentioned here that in several of the towns where the 'great projects' did not involve new streets cutting through old districts, this did in fact occur at a somewhat later stage to create links with and across the city centre. Examples are the Kärtnerstraße in Vienna, Kaiser-Wilhelm-Straße in Berlin, Gran Via in Madrid and Kristen Bernikows Gade and its extension in Copenhagen.

Ring roads were discussed in several of our capital cities; they were mainly intended for the periphery, where they would embrace all or at least the greater part of the built area (examples include Berlin, Brussels, Budapest, Copenhagen, Madrid and Stockholm). This reflected the still persistent perception of the town as a closed physical unit, with a definite boundary between itself and the surrounding countryside. Fiscal considerations also played a part, at least in Madrid; a 'border boulevard' would make it easier to collect tolls and to guard against smuggling. Such projects rarely went beyond the discussion stage, or were only partially realized; again, the example is Madrid. If the peripheral ring roads were thus sometimes motivated on grounds other than traffic, the inner rings which were built in Barcelona, Budapest, Copenhagen, Vienna and to some extent Amsterdam, as well as the one completed in Paris, were all the more important in

a traffic context. They could be combined with radial streets, often following the routes of the old exit roads. The combination of radial and concentric arteries appears to have been regarded as a particularly satisfactory solution; this ideal was perhaps realized best in Budapest with its three ring roads and many exit routes. Vienna, too, acquired a similar system in the outer ring on the site of the *Linienwall*. The attempt to combine radial and concentric arteries might seem a typical product of nineteenth-century rational thinking, but is actually something of a constantly recurring planner's gimmick. The early ideal city theorists played with such solutions, and they have reappeared in many twentieth-century projects.

What, then, were the current criteria for a good traffic road? The detailed design of streets will be discussed below (see pp. 99 ff), but some of the most fundamental requirements should be mentioned here. For instance, roads should be broad enough to allow rapid traffic to proceed unhampered by slow or parked vehicles. Pavements for pedestrians, which previously had been an exception, now became the rule, and this first step towards traffic segregation could be described as one of the greatest contributions of the nineteenth century to urban environment. Planted strips in the middle of a road or along its sides were considered highly desirable. Another important point was that roads should be straight, level and as long as possible, to speed up the flow of the traffic.[8] No solutions had yet been found for the problem of crossroads; squares were often created at major crossings, but not even in the star-shaped places was the circulation principle applied. Eugène Hénard launched this Columbus's egg a few decades later with his *carrefour à giration* (figure 21.2).[9] One of the big advantages of the planted ribbon down the middle of the roads was probably that it reduced the awkward problem of crossing traffic.

Figure 21.2 *Eugène Hénard's pioneering proposal for a* Carrefour à giration, *1906, used at the Place de l'Étoile since 1907. Until then there had been no rules for how to behave at cross-roads, which meant that conditions were chaotic at the major traffic junctions. It should be noted that Hénard also intended a lower level for pedestrians with various facilities; as we know, such arrangements became a recurring element in twentieth-century street planning, although pedestrians were seldom given the open space in the middle of the square, as Hénard envisaged. Among his many other ideas is a proposal for split-level crossings. [From Evenson (1979)]*

STANDARDS OF HYGIENE

During the second half of the nineteenth century it became increasingly urgent to improve the hygiene standards in the towns. The accelerating growth and increasing density of the urban population had aggravated the already low standards of hygiene in the pre-industrial towns. In Stockholm, for example, the average life expectancy for men during the 1850s was 20 years; for women it was 26. Every third child born living, died during the first year of its life. As late as the 1870s a 15-year-old male had only a 20 per cent chance of reaching 65.[10] In the rural areas mortality was lower and average life expectancy considerably higher. The figures for Stockholm were not unique; conditions were similar in the large towns in other countries.

In the middle years of the century people were becoming increasingly aware that the prevalence of disease and the short life expectancy in the cities were neither natural nor inevitable; they depended on the standards of hygiene and sanitation. This knowledge emerged partly as a result of the regular statistical compilations that were now being made, which revealed the hygienic conditions in the towns and the life expectancy of the people who lived there. Moreover, it was now easier for different countries or towns to communicate with each other, and the amount of information travelling between them was growing. It became evident that the problems were similar in all large cities. Any positive results achieved could now be passed on quickly to other countries in Europe, thus helping to break down the conservative opposition that modern novelties such as water mains, drainage systems and so on usually aroused. The English experience probably did a lot to alter attitudes, perhaps through the persuasive writings of Sir Edwin Chadwick and other representatives of the public health

Figure 21.3 *Berlin. As early as the 1790s a German doctor wrote: 'In general the poor housing, in which the ordinary people of Berlin have to live, greatly contributes to the diseases suffered by this industrious class of citizens . . .' The poor man 'has to manage in one room, where he not only carries on his trade but where he lives and sleeps together with the whole of his household.' This drawing from 1845 of a shoemaker's dwelling and workshop shows that conditions had not improved during the first half of the nineteenth century. [From Schinz (1964)]*

movement, but certainly through admiration of their effects. It was largely through Chadwick's efforts that England acquired a Public Health Act in 1848.[11] In many places, not least in Stockholm, medical associations fulfilled an important function in disseminating information; in Copenhagen the medical association became involved in a major project for the creation of healthier housing.[12] 'Indeed it may well be true' writes Fraser, 'that the medical profession did more to improve the nation's health by identifying the public health problem and generating interest in it than by any improved techniques in the treatment of patients.'[13] The effect of the cholera epidemics on public opinion has already been mentioned. There were two theories about the way disease spread: the supporters of contagion held that it was passed on by contact, the miasma supporters believed that changes in the quality of the air caused by miasma, i.e. particles from space or the interior of the earth, created a predisposition to infection. This second school particularly emphasized the importance of sanitary conditions and hygiene in combating the disease.

The public health programme – 'programme' referring here not to a manifesto but to various measures being recommended by progressive politicians and technologists – aimed at a radical transformation of the whole urban environment, to include better housing, parks and other open spaces, systems for the supply of gas and water, adequate drainage, organized refuse collection, better distribution of food by building market halls, and the removal out of the towns of establishments and activities unsuited to the urban environment. All these measures required planning, and all were interrelated. Haussmann's programme for Paris included practically everything, except direct measures for improving the standard of working-class housing (unless we count the extensive demolition of substandard housing). The sanitary objectives were of fundamental importance in most of the other planning schemes, particularly from the 1850s onwards.

What, then, was the specific contribution of town planning to the improvement of the urban environment, taking the term 'town plan' in a fairly limited sense? The answer is probably: to provide every district in the town with light and fresh air. 'The public gardens, the broad planted streets where the air can circulate freely, are absolutely necessary in the interior of the large cities, in the cause of sanitary conditions,' as Haussmann's collaborator Adolphe Alphand wrote in 1868.[14] Similar statements could certainly be quoted from reports and other documents on urban planning in different countries. The park and the broad tree-lined road can be considered the most important contribution to town planning in the period studied here. Certainly both parks and tree-lined streets had existed before, but only as occasional features, not as standard elements in the urban scene.

CLEARANCES

Good standards of hygiene, slum clearance and 'internal security', i.e. the creation of conditions for suppressing social unrest, were all closely interrelated in nineteenth-century planning. Linked to these are the attitude to social segregation. First let us examine the clearance problem. The main purpose of such urban redevelopments as had occurred since the seventeenth century, had generally been to replace what was regarded as inadequate buildings with others that were more worthy of the cities concerned. As a result of the rapid urbanization during the nineteenth century, the question of urban renewal acquired a new urgency; population density in the central districts was increasing, as was the pressure of traffic. At the same time the standard of building was declining as a result of more intensive exploitation; many buildings were being added to, while others were extended into open courtyards. In the course of the century the economically privileged classes increasingly abandoned the most densely populated and shabbiest areas, in order to settle in the new and more spacious districts. Thus slum areas were created: their inhabitants belonged to the least prosperous groups, living in areas plagued by over-crowding, poor building standards, and inadequate streets, water mains, sewage systems and so on.

These slum areas were often right in the centre of the cities; as late as the 1850s one of the worst areas in Paris lay between the Louvre and the Arc du Carrousel, and in London a particularly notorious one was near Trafalgar Square along St Martin's Lane, which was then a main road running from Charing Cross in a northerly direction. Such elements in the urban scene were naturally hard to combine with the desire for a clean, tidy and distinguished image. The slum areas were also regarded by the privileged classes as a threat to 'law and order', and as a danger to the established economic and social system. And they did in fact frequently become centres for criminals and prostitutes. The districts with the most miserable conditions also provided easy ingress for epidemic disease, which from there could spread to the more privileged areas. Moreover there was a growing conviction that society must assume responsibility for creating acceptable conditions for all its members, even those in the worst plight. And so the elimination of the slums became a major theme in the debate on urban development. But to undertake such actions under public auspices was no easy matter, above all for economic and legal reasons, and in any case was hardly compatible with the *laisser-faire* spirit that imbued many aspects of contemporary society. The persistent hope was that the free play of the economic forces would ultimately arrange everything for the best. The difficulties were particularly overwhelming and the opposition particularly strong when it came to redeveloping whole districts; street improvements were more obviously of general interest to the community as a whole and therefore struck a chord more easily. And as they created attractive plots, it was also easier to finance them. Street improvements were thus often regarded as a kind of universal solution to the problems of the cities.[15] The combination of clearance and the cutting of new streets is a basic feature in nineteenth-century planning.

The problems of wretched housing conditions were first noticed, quite naturally, in England, the birthplace of industrialism. It was there that the term 'slum' was first coined; and 'slums' and 'slum clearance' have probably been discussed more in England during the last 150 years than in any other European country. 'The attempt to contain the gap between an acceptable standard of housing and the status quo has been one of the main preoccupations of Britain's City Fathers since the problem began to be recognised in the first half of the nineteenth century,' writes Allan.[16]

Thus the clearance factor was an important element in the street improvement schemes in London during the nineteenth century. For example, in 1838 a select committee emphasized that streets did not only have 'the single purpose of obtaining increased facilities of communication,' but that their importance was 'in direct proportion to the degree in which they embrace all the great purposes of amendment in respect of health and morals . . . by the removal of congregations of vice and misery.' At about the same time it was also being claimed that the redevelopment programme should be judged according to the three following criteria: '1. The opening or enlarging of communications for the general convenience of public intercourse; 2. The improvement of certain districts, of which the present state is greatly injurious to the health of the inhabitants; 3. The melioration of the moral conditions of the labouring classes closely congregated in such districts.'[17] Such considerations thus determined not only which projects were to be supported, but also the location of the streets. Farringdon Road, New Oxford Street, Charing Cross Road and Victoria Street are among those roads which cut through areas considered to be in great need of improvement.[18]

If the urban renewal in London and Paris had anything in common, it was their attitude to clearances, which were assigned as much importance in Haussmann's Paris as in London. There, too, the route of a street was often determined by a desire to achieve maximum effect in terms of the demolition of substandard housing.[19] Why did just Paris and London, which were otherwise diametrically opposed in their administrative systems and planning policies, both experience extensive programmes of clearance and street-building in combination? The answer obviously lies in the size of the two towns, both in terms of population and area. There were simply so many slums there that it was more difficult to disregard them; added to which at least London wanted to project a splendid 'world metropolis' image. Moreover, on account of the great distances involved, good communications between the centre and the outlying areas were even more necessary here than in the other towns.

But in Paris – in contrast to London – vast areas in the centre were also totally cleared, namely Île de la Cité (figure 3.10) and the district of the market halls. Haussmann would certainly have extended this area of renewal even further if it had been possible. In Athens a radical redevelopment and extension scheme was planned in combination with total clearances; all older buildings which were not considered to be of archeological or historical value were to be demolished – a goal that was never reached; parts of the built area dating from the Turkish period were preserved, and the old street and plot pattern remained largely

the same. In Helsinki, too, radical renewal of the built areas was planned; the conditions were good, since large parts of the urban area had burnt down and the intentions of the scheme could be largely realized.

In the other projects discussed here the clearance factor seems to have played a secondary role, which does not mean that people were unaware of the problems. In Stockholm, for example, planning discussions started from the need to do something about the poor conditions in the urban core, the central part of the old city, and the first project was aimed at the complete renewal of the streets and buildings on Stadsholmen (see figure 13.2).[20] However, it soon became clear that such an operation would be far too complicated and expensive; efforts were subsequently redirected towards planning for urban expansion, combined with some street improvements in the existing structure. The same approach was also applied in Rome and Barcelona. In Berlin and Vienna, among others, combined clearance and street schemes were carried out, but not as part of the plans discussed here.

In all these towns, and in varying degrees in the other capital cities as well, there were central areas characterized by immense population density, extremely poor housing and wretched sanitary conditions. However, people preferred to postpone tackling these problems – except indirectly through any effects which could be achieved by street improvements[21] – even though they had all been the subject of numerous reports and discussions. Instead the tendency seemed to be to promote urban extension, which chiefly meant the exploitation of unbuilt land. One exception was the renewal of the Notre-Dame-aux-Neiges district of Brussels, which had no connection with any major street improvements. The central boulevards in this city, on the other hand, provide a typical example of slum clearance combined with a street project.

Finally it should be emphasized that 'clearance' in the nineteenth century existed only in the sense of demolishing undesirable housing; on the other hand, little was done to provide better alternatives for the people who were compelled to move. The result was generally that the victims of the demolitions were forced to move wherever rents were the lowest, i.e. to a similar sort of district, which in turn became even more overcrowded and wretched than it had been before.[22] In Brussels the company which was to carry out the construction of the central boulevards did in fact commit itself to finding houses for the evacuated population, but in the event nothing came of it. But the problem had at least been discussed several times in the *Conseil communal*.

INTERNAL SECURITY AS A PLANNING GOAL

As we have seen, an important idea behind the clearances which were undertaken, primarily in London and Paris, was the neutralization of districts which might be potential trouble spots. But how important was the security aspect in the planning, in the more limited sense of seeking to facilitate police and military action with a view to maintaining law and order? In several accounts, the street building programme in Paris is associated mainly with security considerations, i.e. the streets should be wide enough to make it difficult to set up barricades, and long and straight enough to be easily covered by artillery fire.[23]

Life for the labouring population of Paris was wretched: their wages were low, they lived in miserable conditions, and sometimes jobs were scarce. Between 1827 and 1849 barricades were raised on several occasions. Any regime, irrespective of its political principles, must have regarded the prevention of any further unrest which could be exploited to trigger a *coup d'état*, as a condition of survival. Napoleon III and Haussmann launched a comprehensive programme for improving the urban environment. Their public works, and the associated private building enterprises, also created a great many new jobs. In these and other ways attempts were being made to remove the causes of discontent. But obviously Haussmann and Napoleon would also have been anxious to discourage the construction of barricades and to make it easier to crush any riots. In several of the street improvement projects security aspects may have come into it, for example in the Rue de Rivoli and the Boulevard de Sébastopol, where it would be possible to move troops quickly to the centre of the city, and in the Boulevard Voltaire which cut a breach through the working-class district to the east of the inner city. Barracks were also located at strategic points; the most important was the Caserne Vérine with space for 2,000 soldiers at the Place de la République.

But it would hardly be accurate to claim that security aspects were a dominating, or even a particularly important, reason for the great urban transformation.[24] The references to national security which Haussmann himself made may have been largely tactical, to get the *Conseil municipal* and above all the *Corps legislatif* to approve the cost of the improvements.[25]

In some other towns, too, security aspects were taken up in the discussions, particularly in Vienna where the year of revolution, 1848, remained fresh in people's memory, and where the military invoked the risk of riots in the suburbs. They opposed the demolition of the Viennese fortifications as long as possible on the grounds that internal security required it, and finally set a number of conditions which were at least partly fulfilled, before they would agree to withdraw from the area of the ramparts. According to the Emperor's missive of December 1858, a large fortified barracks was to be built and linked with the existing drill-ground by an open area. Other military security requirements were also satisfied. Nonetheless they obviously came to be regarded as less and less important as the Ringstraße project proceeded: at the end of the 1860s the drill-ground was made available for building; later, at the turn of the century, the Franz Joseph barracks, built as recently as in the 1850s, was demolished to make room for Otto Wagner's *Postsparkasse*. Castro's plan for Madrid also paid great attention to internal security, not by way of broad streets but by distributing military installations all over the urban area. Few of them appear to have been built, however.[26]

To judge from the available accounts,

security aspects do not seem to have been assigned much importance in the other towns or, if they were, not for long. In Stockholm, for example, internal security does not appear to have been related in any way to planning issues, even though Strandvägen provided a first-class link between the barracks in Djurgården and the centre of the city. In Helsinki several barracks were scattered around the town, but hardly for reasons of internal security; nobody was likely to fear riots among the farm lads and maid-servants who had recently moved in from the countryside.

Segregated Housing and Social Zoning

Finally, was social zoning, in other words a deliberate segregation of housing, a goal of the planning activities? The complex question of segregation can only be touched upon briefly in our present context. First, however, it should be noted that even in the pre-industrial town it is possible to discern a certain segregation, often in that an economic and social élite was over-represented in the centre and the lower social groups on the periphery.[27] The urban redevelopments that occurred in earlier periods, particularly in the Nordic countries, and the building rules which were issued in many towns, probably tended to reinforce this pattern. This was something which the powers-that-be regarded as a positive development, in so far as such considerations arose at all.[28]

To a great extent, however, the big cities on the continent during the early years of the nineteenth century were characterized by a mixture of different activities and different social groupings. 'A single house', writes Sutcliffe, speaking of Paris, 'could contain ground-floor shops, a first-floor apartment for the landlord or a rich trader, several floors of lesser apartments, some of them occupied by working craftsmen, and servants' quarters in

the roof. And the courtyard or garden would often be filled with workshops. Within such an urban structure, segregation of classes was vertical rather than horizontal, although certain areas were more favoured by the rich than others.'[29] A similar pattern can be demonstrated at least in Berlin, St Petersburg and Stockholm.[30]

As the nineteenth century progressed, however, we have seen that families who were wealthy enough to leave the run-down, over-populated, unhealthy and industrialized areas, which were often centrally situated, generally did so; they would move to new districts or to residential suburbs along the railway, where there were no 'disturbing' activities. As a result of this process, which varied in its extent from town to town and assumed a variety of forms, different groups of the population were beginning to live further and further away from one another or, as we might put it today, housing was segregated.[31]

This was the result of considerations and measures which were regarded as natural and rational. In the grander locations in the town, along important streets and round the parks, the most attractive residential areas were to be

found; the plots here commanded the highest prices, and it made economic sense to use these locations for sumptuous buildings as powerful elements in society considered fitting. If any district possessed particularly attractive sites for houses, because of beautiful scenery or a good climate, or simply because there were no annoying activities in the area, then the price of the land rose. And it was natural for developers with plenty of capital to build houses there with spacious apartments for the privileged classes. A suburban residence was also far beyond the purses of the working-class, added to which the travel costs would have been too high. In this way the built environment was designed for segregated living, a feature which thus became incorporated into the urban structure.

This way of separating different sections of the town probably corresponded to the social ideas of the time, to the feeling for system and order. Naturally it also meant obvious benefits for the upper social strata; it was pleasant to be relieved of disturbing sights such as poor folk living too close, although some feared that the concentration of labourers in restricted areas could be a threat to the established social order.

Nonetheless, segregated housing, at least in the capital city projects we have been discussing here, was a consequence of other considerations rather than a primary planning goal in itself.[32] But there is one notable exception to this general statement, namely Castro's plan

Figure 21.4 This cross-section of a house in Stockholm around the middle of the 1870s — similar pictures could be found in other capital cities — illustrates the usual housing conditions of the time, namely that the finest dwelling was on the first floor, with simpler homes in the storeys above. This form of vertical segregation became increasingly rare towards the end of the century, when lifts made the higher floors more attractive. [From Kasper (1875)]

for Madrid. Castro envisaged the different population groups living each in its own area, which would then be designed with just this group in mind. Even Ehrenström's transformation of Helsinki can be said to involve a kind of social planning: the Esplanade was to separate the 'better' district with the brick houses of the wealthy from the wooden town of the poor.[33] At almost the same time John Nash was expressing similar ideas in connection with the planning of Regent Street: the street was to be 'a boundary and complete separation between the Street and Squares occupied by the Nobility and Gentry, and the narrow Streets and meaner Houses occupied by mechanics and the trading parts of the community.'[34] Among the projects described here we can find one example of a completely opposite view, namely in Cerdá's plan for Barcelona. Here the intention was to make all parts of the town uniform and equal, among other things to avoid the social separation of some regions from others.

NOTES

1. The presentation and technical organization of the plans obviously varies from one proposal to another; they were also drawn to different scales. Longitudinal sections and cross-sections of the streets were usual. In many cases the material was printed. Several plans were based on extensive studies, which were also published. The prime examples of this were Cerdá's project for Barcelona and Castro's for Madrid. A detailed motivation was also published with the Lindhagen Committee's proposal for Stockholm. In several cases the planning was preceded by detailed measurements and topographical levelling. Reliable maps do not generally appear to have existed previously. Here, too, Haussmann was in the vanguard, with an excellent mapping and topographical levelling of Paris. One of the reasons for this was that when the Rue de Rivoli was to be extended, it was discovered that the altitude had been misjudged, which led to a lot of costly extra work.

2. Similar formulations occurred in several other towns, for example in 1836 in a motion regarding a town planning competition in Christiania's town council (Juhasz (1965), p. 21).
3. *Kungl. byggnadsstadga* (1874), § 12. Almost fifty years before similar wording had been used in composing a building act for Christiania; there was talk of embellishment, convenience and traffic, health and fire safety (cf. Juhasz (1965), p. 13).
4. Right up to the end of the nineteenth century it was not unusual for towns to burn down, either wholly or in part, as Karlstad did in 1865, Gävle in 1869, and Umeå and Sundsvall on the same night in 1888 – to mention just a few of the best known examples (Hall (1991), pp. 181 ff).
5. Lorange and Myhre (1991), and Sundman (1991), pp. 65 ff.
6. On one occasion at any rate in the planning discussions in Stockholm reference was made to fire safety, in connection with the width of Odengatan (Selling (1970), p. 29).
7. *Utlåtande med förslag till gatureglering i Stockholm*, p. 8.
8. That the primacy of straight streets was not taken completely for granted, however, can be seen from the debates in the Stockholm City Council. Lindhagen's straight Birger Jarlsgatan was criticised on the grounds that north-westerly storms could sweep through it unhindered, and that snowdrifts could pile up there in the winter (Selling (1970), p. 28). Cf. also Klenze's objection quoted above (p. 104) against Schaubert and Kleanthes's plan for Athens, and below (pp. 324 f).
9. Evenson (1979), pp. 32 f.
10. Ahlberg (1958), pp. 62 ff.
11. An overview of developments in England in this field can be found in Fraser (1973), e.g. pp. 51 ff. Mention should also be made of Lewis (1952), in which Chadwick is discussed. On Shaftesbury, see Battiscombe (1974), pp. 219 ff and Finlayson (1981), pp. 276 ff and 352 ff.
12. Rasmussen (1969), pp. 104 f.
13. Fraser (1973), p. 56.
14. Alphand (1867–1873), [I], p. LIX.
15. Cf. Dyos (1957).
16. Allan (1965), p. 598. On the relation between the slum problem and physical planning, see also Tarn (1980), Smith (1980) and Sutcliffe (1981b).

17. Both examples from Dyos (1957), pp. 262 ff. Dyos also provides further examples.

18. Cf. Dyos (1957), pp. 212 ff.

19. Cf. Pinkney (1958), pp. 33 ff, 39 f *et passim*, as well as Sutcliffe (1970), pp. 29 f.

20. The situation in the Old City was described by A.E. Rudberg, the author of the first redevelopment plan as follows: 'From this labyrinth of narrow, twisting, dark streets and alleys, dripping on both sides with a constant stream of stinking fluids, . . . from these narrow courtyards surrounded by towering houses, wells of darkness . . . in whose depths all possible filth collects, whence poisonous fumes have risen for hundreds of years and still rise today, bearing the seed of innumerable diseases, penetrating with their stinking breath every corner of the surrounding dwellings, whose tightly packed inhabitants can open their windows and doors to let out the even fouler air from their rooms, but are denied any possibility of exchanging it for air that is fresh. Once these fumes have risen above the roofs or spread along the streets, they are carried by the wind, albeit in constantly thinner layers, to other parts of the town where, in the insanitary vapour to be found there, they find willing allies in executing their health-destroying mission among the other dwellers in the capital city . . . Moreover, after some sojourn here, the cheek pales, the eye dims, breath grows heavy, and pains and morbid symptoms appear, carrying their message of a premature death . . .

It is not only that its insalubriousness [i.e. in the district between the bridges] undermines the health of the body and thereby also destroys the power of the spirit, making of it an easy victim for temptation, but its overcrowding, its filth and darkness together make it a paradise for vice and crime; shy of the light, vice thrives here, finding fertile ground in homes, inns and even worse places, and dispatching its missionaries to the rest of the town . . . It is natural that for just these reasons a great many souls have been drawn into the vortex of crime, as they would not otherwise have been; and it is equally natural that many of those who move to other parishes take with them not only the physical diseases of this place, but also their moral decadence which then exerts its destructive influence on their new surroundings.' (Rudberg (1862), pp. 7 ff.)

21. In Rome several clearances of this kind were carried out during the Fascist era. Above all, the construction of the Via dei Fori Imperiali meant the destruction of many very simple housing blocks.

22. That the primary aim of the clearance was not to improve the conditions of the people living in the slum districts, is clearly stated in the introduction to A.E. Rudberg's redevelopment proposal for the Town between the Bridges: 'Here a possible misunderstanding must be cleared up immediately. It might occur to some that the inner district of the town, which is now mainly inhabited by the lower and poorer classes, should be rebuilt to provide healthier and more efficient dwellings for these people. But further consideration should demonstrate the unreasonableness of this idea. The core of a town, the centre of industry and trade, where all communications meet, cannot possibly provide suitable dwellings for the poor, for the plots are too expensive . . . Thus the meaning here is not directly to provide the poor with healthier and better dwellings, but rather to deprive them of the wretched and unhealthy homes, which are offered them in the centre of the town.' (Rudberg (1862), p. 2.)

23. This interpretation can even be found in scientific works, such as Ranieri (1973), p. 14 and Hojer (1974), p. 50). Ranieri, for example, writes: 'When Napoleon III, inspiring Haussmann, had the straight boulevards constructed, it was above all out of consideration for the public order, with the underlying idea that without too much difficulty these broad arteries could be covered by cannon fire in case of riots. But Leopold II had more peaceful concerns.'

24. In his memoirs Haussmann dismissed out of hand the idea that the Emperor had strategic intentions in connection with the street planning, i.e. to make local riots difficult. But, he continued, even if this was not the intention, as the opposition claimed, it was nevertheless 'the very happy consequence of all the great openings conceived by His Majesty for improving and cleansing the ancient city.' This result helped 'alongside a number of other good reasons', to motivate the states share of the high cost. But essentially we should accept Haussmann's word when he assures us: 'As for myself, the promoter

of the additions made to the initial project, I declare that, in combining them, I never had the slightest thought in the world as to their greater or lesser strategic importance.' (Haussmann (1893), III, pp. 184 ff.)

25. As regards this question, see for instance Pinkney (1958), pp. 35 ff, Chapman (1957), pp. 184 ff, Sutcliffe (1970), pp. 31 ff and Lavedan (1975), pp. 420 ff.

26. The security aspect seems to have played a pretty marginal role in the redevelopment of the city centre in Barcelona (cf., however, *Atlas de Barcelona*, p. 557). And Cerdá pointed out that an advantage of the grid type of plan was 'the possibilities of defence against un uprising' (quoted from Frechilla (1992), p. 177, note 33).

27. Cf. Sjoberg (1960), pp. 91 ff *et passim*. The Uppsala volume of the *Scandinavian Atlas of Historic Towns* provides a good example of this pattern as applied to Uppsala.

28. Cf. p. 96. In St Petersburg 'particular groups were to be assigned to specific areas' (Bater (1976), p. 21).

29. Sutcliffe (1970), p. 323. That people were aware of the social pattern can also be seen in Fig. 3 in Pinkney (1958), a cross-section of a block of flats in Paris dated 1850. Similar pictures can also be found elsewhere, for example in Stockholm (see figure 21.4).

30. Here we can refer to a famous passage in Strindberg's autobiographical novel, *Tjänstekvinnans son*, where he describes the 'vertical' segregation in the house where he spent part of his childhood (Strindberg (1962), p. 7). A more detailed description is provided by Herman Salomon Krook, under the pseudonym Herman Adam, in his novel *Nemesis* (1861), in which a five-storey house in the Old City is described as follows (pp. 1 ff): 'The lowest storey was occupied by shops for all kinds of drapery goods, mostly foreign things from England and France, . . . On the first floor dwelt affluence, rank, birth and riches; you could see this in the costly curtains, the chandeliers and the old portraits in oils on the walls . . . One floor above this dwelt general prosperity. Here too there was wealth, of the solid kind acquired by hard work and by taking thought. An easy comfort prevailed, but not without a certain stiffness . . . On the next floor

up dwelt the lower middle-class, industrious and conscientious ants, adding to their small stacks each day, happy and contented with little. . . . But on the fifth floor, there dwelt poverty, folk embroiled in a day-long struggle with care; labourers barely earning a day's wage despite sweating from morn to eve; widows and children sewing and embroidering for their meagre daily bread and young men fighting for their future, meeting the first hard knocks of reality . . . Perhaps we should stop here, but there was still an attic above . . . Here was sheer unadorned need . . . Here was the lowest end of society, here ran that narrow borderline beyond which one small step leads to the world of vice and crime.'

31. Due partly to the absence of a system of communications, St Petersburg seems to have maintained 'the traditional, essentially pre-industrial, admixture of classes and activities' until the beginning of the twentieth century (Bater (1976), pp. 401 ff).

32. Sutcliffe feels justified in claiming – admittedly for the period 1890–1914, i.e. the years immediately after the great capital city projects – that 'planning was . . . serving primarily the interests of the richer sections of the population. . . . In fact, in all four countries [Germany, Britain, the United States and France] we have been observing the efforts of technocratic or social elites to set up a painless method of social reform which would remove the grievances of the poor while educating them into the values of their social superiors' (1981*b*), p. 208).

33. When Åbo, Finland's second largest town, was to be rebuilt after the fire in 1827, three plot sizes were adopted, and the smallest plots were used only in the outermost parts of the town.

34. Quoted from Dyos (1957), p. 261; see also Mace (1976), pp. 33 f. Nash also declares that 'there would be no opening on the East side of the New Street . . . and the interior houses and the traffic from the Haymarket would be cut off from any communication with the New Street'; 'the Line of Separation between the inhabitants of the first classes of society, and those of the inferior classes is Swallow Street' (quoted from Mace).

22

ELEMENTS OF THE PLANS

In the previous chapter a passage was quoted from the 1874 building ordinances for Swedish towns, indicating the goals which the planning was expected to achieve (p. 285). The passage is followed in the original by a list of measures for fulfilling these goals, which can be summarized as follows: broad streets, of which some should be tree-lined; functional blocks, not too large; spacious squares; and public planted areas of varying size and type. Let us now look at the way streets, blocks, squares and parks have been designed.

STREETS

The Swedish building ordinances distinguish between two types of streets, on the one hand ordinary residential streets which were to be at least 18 metres wide, and the 'esplanades', which were to have two carriageways with trees between them. This distinction between residential or local roads and broad tree-planted thoroughfares for traffic and the enhancement of the townscape, is a fundamental feature of nineteenth-century planning.[1]

On the whole residential streets do not seem to have attracted much attention in the planning. If possible they were of course to be straight and level. The minimum width of 18 metres in the Swedish ordinances was probably fairly normal for residential districts in the second half of the nineteenth century; in the commentary on his project for Barcelona, for example, Cerdá recommended 20 metres as a suitable width, while in the Viennese Ringstraße area the width varied between 16 and 23 metres. Most residential streets intended for blocks of flats probably lay within this interval. The width of the carriageways for meeting traffic was generally 10 metres or a little more,

so that two horse-drawn carriages could pass one another between two stationary ones. The width of the pavement, previously a rarity, but now a self-evident part of the whole, was determined by that of the street; if this was 20 metres, the pavements were generally less than 5 metres wide; otherwise the preferred width was 5 metres or more. If a street was about 20 metres or more, rows of trees became possible; in Barcelona all pavements were tree-lined. In the other cities planted trees were exceptional in the purely residential streets, and were rare in any streets less than 25 metres wide. Pavements should have kerb stones raised about 10 cm above the level of the carriageway, to prevent traffic from disturbing pedestrians, and the carriageway itself should be convex so that water could run down into the gutters.[2]

The straight tree-lined principal street or thoroughfare, often lined with shops, restaurants and other public or commercial buildings, was the most cherished feature of nineteenth-century planning. Let us start by examining the terminology. Two designations are often used for these major streets, apart from the ordinary word for street in the various countries, namely 'avenue' and 'boulevard'. To these we can add the term 'esplanade', even though as the designation for a street this occurs almost exclusively in Finland and Sweden. In many places there is also the designation *allée* for principal tree-lined streets. 'Promenade', too, can also be used in this connotation. All these terms have French origins, and common to them all is the fact that they lack a clearly defined meaning.[3]

Boulevard (from the Dutch *bolwerc*, bulwark) originally meant, to quote *La Grande Encyclopédie*, 'defence works outside the wall and replacing the barbican of the Middle Ages'. The word gradually came to be used to designate tree-lined promenades on the site of former fortifications. The model was established when the boulevard ring round the northern part of Paris was opened in the reign of Louis XIV. The term 'boulevard' occurred in Vienna as early as the eighteenth century, referring to the street which was proposed for the area of the fortifications. Towards the middle of the nineteenth century 'boulevard' was used commonly in the sense of 'road running round a town', regardless of whether or not there had previously been any fortifications there. An early example appears in Schaubert and Kleanthes's project for Athens ratified in 1833, where the broad tree-lined street which was to surround the centre of the new city in the form of a rectangle, was called the 'boulevard', even though it did not follow the periphery of the town and was outside the existing built area. In Brussels the word was used both for the inner ring, which replaced earlier fortifications, and the outer ring which did not. In Barcelona the designation was used in its original sense, to apply to the monumental ring road which was proposed by Rovira i Trias. The much simpler street that was actually built, was called the *rondas*. In Berlin and Stockholm the term 'boulevard' emerged during the discussion and planning phase, referring to ring roads at the periphery,

although there had never been any fortifications where the streets were to be built. But the word 'boulevard' does not exist in Stockholm as part of the name of a street, nor so far as I know does it do so in Berlin. In Copenhagen, on the other hand, part of the road constructed over the former fortification area was christened H.C. Andersen's Boulevard; here the word was being used in its original sense.

In Paris the term 'boulevard' acquired a new meaning which it has kept ever since Haussmann's time, namely a tree-planted principal street. The north-south axis in the *grande croisée* was thus called Boulevard de Strasbourg, Boulevard de Sébastopol and Boulevard de St Michel, probably because it was regarded as an extension of the old boulevard network. Boulevard in this new extended meaning then became common in Paris and was used in the same way in Brussels as well, where the new streets through the centre of the town were called 'boulevards'. Outside France and Belgium, on the other hand, this connotation does not seem to have spread, apart from one or two isolated instances.[4]

An *avenue*, according to *La Grande Encyclopédie*, is 'an impressive and decorative approach to a palace, a chateau, a great public or religious building, to a triumphal memorial, to the ceremonial entrance to a town', preferably broad and 'lined with trees, with pavements and benches'. Early avenues included the streets leading towards the dome of the Invalides. In accordance with the above definition a number of streets leading up to the Arc de Triomphe were called avenues, as was the grand approach to the opera. But the term was not used consistently: one or two of the streets from the south-east leading into the town, for instance, were also called avenues, even though they lacked focal points. Some avenues were fairly modest, while others were broad and almost park-like, as indeed were some of the boulevards such as Boulevard Richard Lenoir. It was thus the direction and focus of the street rather than its appearance that decided whether it was called a boulevard or an avenue. 'Avenue' was used similarly in Brussels.

The term 'avenue' never became very common in the Nordic countries or in continental Europe.[5] The new grand approach to the ceremonial entrance to the old city area, created according to the 1886 plan for Gothenburg, was called Kungsportsavenyn, a correct usage of the term.[6] In Spain, at least in Madrid and Barcelona, some of the most important principal streets were called avenidas, even if they did not noticeably lead to a monument or a public building. In London the term appears sporadically, e.g. Shaftesbury Avenue, which admittedly leads to Piccadilly Circus and the statue of Eros, the memorial to Lord Shaftesbury, but it twists and turns and has not the width of a monumental street. In the United States the word 'avenue' is widely used, but in the sense of a main or broad street.

The word esplanade also comes originally from fortification terminology, and was used according to La Grande Encyclopédie to designate 'the part of a town extending from the defence works to the first houses on the edge of the built area or the areas between the houses in a town and its fortress'. According to the same source the modern use of the word is generally 'a vast square with alleys of trees widely spaced and arranged in front of a chateau or a palace'. In Paris the term is never applied to a street, but only to the open space between the Hôtel des Invalides and the Seine.

In Sweden and Finland, on the other hand, 'esplanade' has come to mean a broad street with two carriageways and trees planted between them. The word was first used to describe the 450-metre-long and 100-metre-wide parkway begun during the second decade of the nineteenth century in Helsinki, to separate the central area with the brick houses of the wealthy from the wooden town of the poor, and the term 'esplanade' appeared as far back as Ehrenström's first proposal in 1812. Broad, tree-planted fire-breaks then became a constant element of Finnish planning, and the

type is referred to in the 1856 building ordinances as esplanad.[7] The Swedish building ordinances of 1874, created by Albert Lindhagen, were strongly influenced by Finnish planning, and among other things they adopted the Finnish concept of the esplanad. It was decreed 'that broad esplanades with trees planted down the middle and carriageways on each side' should 'be constructed in the town, preferably in several places with different orientations.' The carriageways comprising the esplanade should be at least 12 metres wide, but no total width was indicated.[8] This decree resulted in the building of a number of esplanades in Swedish towns.[9] In Stockholm only Karlavägen and Narvavägen fulfilled the criteria of the esplanade, and at first this stretch of road was called Esplanaden; today the word is not included in any street names in Stockholm, but can still be found in some Swedish provincial towns.[10]

Finally, mention should be made of the term allée, which in French enjoys wide and varied usage, ranging from a garden promenade to a tree-lined ceremonial approach. In northern Europe and Germany the term can sometimes be used for tree-lined streets. In Anglo-American usage an 'alley' is a simple street, sometimes even a mere passage, or a walk in a garden or park lined with trees or flowers.

Thus the borderlines between the different terms are very fluid; there are no designations that apply throughout Europe. Esplanade, boulevard and avenue, depending on the terminological tradition in the different countries, can all be applied to streets which are relatively similar. Even within countries usage can vary, and there are no hard and fast definitions. Broad principal thoroughfares can also sometimes be described by the ordinary word for street. This is generally the case in Germany and Italy, where no difference is made between ordinary streets and principal streets; in both cases the term is Straße and via. In Spain the two terms via and gran via are used.

There is thus little point in trying to discuss

nineteenth-century principal streets on a basis of their contemporary designations. It is also difficult to pick out any general characteristics for this type of street. While residential streets run to more a standardized general pattern, the principal streets usually reveal a great variety of individualized designs.

A simple look at some street widths, which can vary from under 30 metres to almost three times as much, is enough to illustrate this diversity. At 100 metres wide the Esplanade in Helsinki is hardly to be regarded as a street any longer, and is not in fact considered as such. The Ringstraße in Vienna is 57 metres wide, and the Lastenstraße 23 metres. Vester, Nørre and Øster Voldgade in Copenhagen are all 50 metres wide. In the central parts of Paris street widths are fairly moderate, due to the price of land; the boulevard that bears Haussmann's name is only 30 metres wide and several others are no broader. Further out it was possible to build on a bigger scale: the Avenue de Wagram measures 40 metres, the Avenue de Clichy 46 metres and the Boulevard Auguste Blanqui 70 metres. This can be compared with the earlier Boulevard de la Madeleine which is 50 metres wide and the Avenue des Champs Élysées, 80 metres. In Brussels, too, the new streets cutting through the centre were relatively modest; the Boulevard Anspach is only 32 metres wide, while at the periphery the dimensions were much more generous, with the Boulevard du Midi for example measuring 60 metres and the Boulevard du Régent 80 metres. The Via Nazionale in Rome was only 22 metres wide, although it would have been perfectly possible to give it greater width. Shaftesbury Avenue in London is even narrower, namely 19.5 metres. In both cases cost-cutting fervour rather than efficiency was probably the guiding factor, which would have been typical of the indecisive planning in these two cities. In Budapest the ring road was 33 metres wide and the radial street (Andrássy út), for example, 45.5 metres.[11] In Barcelona the main streets were built according to Cerdá's prescriptions,

i.e. to a width of 50 metres. And, finally, peripheral streets in Stockholm such as Ringvägen and Valhallavägen were built on a substantial scale (48 and 65 metres respectively). The two 'esplanades' Karlavägen and Narvavägen were 48 and 44 metres wide respectively, while the principal streets in the centre, some of which were partly the result of street cuttings, could be about 30 metres wide like Odengatan and Birger Jarlsgatan, or in some cases even narrower like Hornsgatan. Sveavägen, the grand main street of the Lindhagen plan, varies in the version as built between a mere 32 and 36 metres. The fairly obvious pattern seems to have been that the streets were wider, the further they were from the city centre.

When it came to the cross-section of these streets, the variations were also considerable. The main alternative lay between having trees along the sides or down the middle, creating two carriageways (i.e. what the Finnish and Swedish building ordinances called an esplanade). A combination of the two systems was also possible, but only if the street was extremely wide. According to Stübben, trees flanking the carriageway represented the most common solution in France, while in Germany and Belgium the trees were generally in the middle. The advantage of the first alternative was that the whole thoroughfare formed a single prospect and the street appeared more splendid; the main disadvantages were that the tree-tops hid the façades, and the trees could obstruct passage between the road and the houses. The alternative of planting rows of trees down the middle provided a good view of the houses and was more convenient for pedestrians and residents, according to Stübben, but the street scene as a whole was less attractive.[12] In our examples, however, this alternative seems to have been rare.

On streets with a maximum width of 30 metres there were generally only two rows of trees, either along the edge of the pavement or in the middle of the street, where there might

Figure 22.1 *The paving of Birger Jarlsgatan in Stockholm. [Photo from Stockholms stadsbyggnadskontor]*

also be a bridlepath or a footpath. If a street was broader than this, it was possible to plant three or more rows of trees in the middle, and to allow for more paths for riding or walking. Flanking trees could also be planted in double rows to form an *allée* and sometimes, along the Ringstraße in Vienna for example, a special track could be made for local traffic between these trees and the pavement. If a street ran along the edge of a park, trees were sometimes only planted on one side. Sometimes, too, forecourts could be laid out in front of the houses, but this was less common. In other words there were a good many options, par-

ticularly when the streets were so wide that trees in the middle could be combined with trees at the sides (cf. figure 22.2, which illustrates a few only of the possible variants). Deciding factors were the available space, the traffic requirements, the financial constraints, the social character of the district and so on. Many streets shared the same fate, namely that en route from idea to realization their width was reduced and their appearance simplified. Sveavägen in Stockholm, for example, was originally envisaged as a 70-metre-wide thoroughfare, but was later reduced to 48 metres; when it was finally built it was even narrower.

Figure 22.2 *Principal
streets. Two basic types of
tree-lined street can be
distinguished, one with
double rows of trees in the
middle (a), and the second
with single rows of trees
along the kerb (b). These
two types can be varied
and combined in many
different ways. There may
be two rows of trees on
both sides of the road;
here an example from the
Avenue de Wagram in
Paris (c), and further
carriageways can be
constructed alongside, as
on the Ringstraße in
Vienna (d). In another
alternative the middle
section can be enhanced,
with tracks for riding and
walking and further rows
of trees, as for example on
the Avenue de Clichy (e),
or allées on the sides of the
road can be combined
with rows of trees in the
middle, as on the
Boulevard Auguste
Blanqui (the former
Boulevard d'Italie) (f),
both in Paris. [From
Stübben (1890)]*

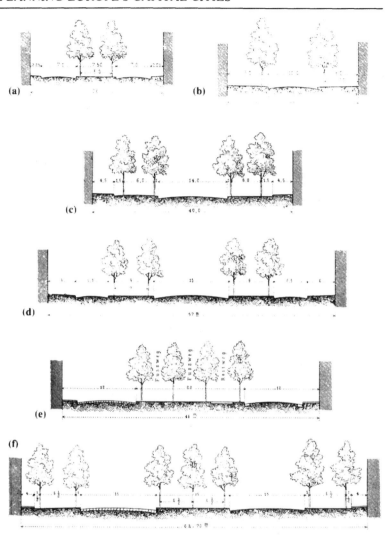

The ideal was that a principal thoroughfare should be absolutely straight. As Lameyre puts it, 'a Haussmannian street doesn't know how to bend'.[13] Most plan-makers of the nineteenth century probably shared this ambition, but as we have seen they often had to compromise. In Vienna a basic prerequisite was that the Ringstraße should form a polygon, and in Rome the Corso Vittorio Emanuele had to wend its way between churches and palaces. Elsewhere, for example in Stockholm, streets originally planned as straight became twisted or even moved at the decision or execution stages. Sometimes, too, the advantages of inflexible straightness were called in question.[14]

Another urgent question concerned the street gradient. In the regulations appended to the 1876 Prussian building act, the *Fluchtlinien-Gesetz*, it was decreed that the gradient of a principal thoroughfare should not exceed a ratio of 1:50, and even this gradient should occur only exceptionally in nineteenth-century main streets. Stübben recommended for the longitudinal profile a 'concave levelling' and mentions as examples the Champs Élysées and the Rue La Fayette in Paris, the Boulevard du Midi in Brussels and the Via Nazionale in Rome. 'Convex levelling' on the other hand, he describes is 'painful and ugly'.[15]

These broad tree-lined streets, often flanked by shops, cafés, and places of entertainment, where people were sometimes served on the pavement, introduced a new type of milieu into the cities, a place where it was possible to stroll without risk of getting dirty or being splashed, where you were unlikely to be disturbed by the society's poorer members or by vulgar activities of any kind; a milieu perceived as an attractive manifestation of modern life. For a few decades the new streets and their neighbouring parks furnished a stage on which an essential part of the life of the bourgeoisie could be played, providing space not only for traffic but also for walking, meeting and recreation (figures 22.3 and 22.4), until that plague of a later era, the motorcar, began to exhale its fumes into the air.[16]

Figure 22.3 In the parks and along the tree-lined main streets a rich street-life for strolling and meeting people developed, illustrated here and in figure 22.4 by two pictures of Stockholm during the 1860s. The picture to the right shows Karl XIIIs torg in Kungsträdgården in Stockholm. [From Ny illustrerad tidning (1869)]

Figure 22.4 *Stockholm. Berzelii park. [From* Ny illustrerad tidning *(1866)]*

City Blocks

Generally speaking planners during this period paid little attention to the design of the city blocks. On the one hand the number of possible variations was limited, and on the other the frame of reference for the planning generally only included the external shape of the blocks and the subdivision of public and private space. The internal design was the property owner's business.[17] The ideal was a network of similar rectilinear blocks, their width corresponding to two plots and their length often to roughly twice the width. Any divergence from the uniform rectangular pattern would generally be due to planning constraints such as topography, existing streets,

property boundaries and so on. During the second half of the century the level of exploitation and the size of the buildings both increased, which appears to have been a general trend in many of Europe's large towns. Building plots and city blocks thus also became bigger. The broad streets now being stipulated in many building ordinances also affected the picture: if the streets were not to take up a disproportionate amount of the space, the blocks had to be larger too. This probably explains the enormous blocks in Berlin, with innumerable small courtyards and many backyard buildings. The corners of the blocks were often cut off obliquely or, more rarely, rounded, to facilitate pedestrian and street traffic. In the Swedish building ordinances this was mandatory; in Barcelona the solution was so ubiquitous that every crossroads was designed as an octagonal 'square', with 20-metre-long sides (hardly an advantage for pedestrians who have to take a circuitous route at every crossroads).

When new thoroughfares broke through existing block structures, the strangest shapes could result, often with sharply pointed corners, which may make for an exciting cityscape but hardly create very practical building plots. Paris has numerous examples of this. It was difficult and expensive to exploit such plots. One of the main objections to the Lindhagen Committee's diagonal streets concerned this very point, i.e. that the streets broke up 'the intermediate blocks into shapes impossible to build in, with acute and obtuse angles'. In his reply Lindhagen was able to refer to the existence of such solutions in other capital cities, particularly in Paris.[18]

However, there was one exception to the planners' general lack of interest in the city block. For Cerdá the blocks were not simply the space between the streets, but the vital elements that should determine the urban fabric. The *Teoría general de la urbanización* devotes a good deal of attention to the design of the blocks. These, according to Cerdá, should be square. They would thus all be of equal value, and it would be possible to create a better relationship between streets, buildings and traffic. Furthermore, it would always be easy to extend the plan. Where necessary the block modules could be joined to form macro-blocks, to allow for parks, industrial zones, commercial facilities and so on. The most radical idea, however, was that the blocks should be built on two sides only and should otherwise be open to gardens or similar planted areas, to provide perfect ventilation for the air exhaled from the houses.[19] This idea was not practicable, but the square-shaped block did become a typical feature of Barcelona. Openings in the blocks were also prescribed in the 1874 Swedish building ordinances, which stated that 'where suitable, gardens should be laid out across the middle of the blocks, so that the parts intended for building are located on

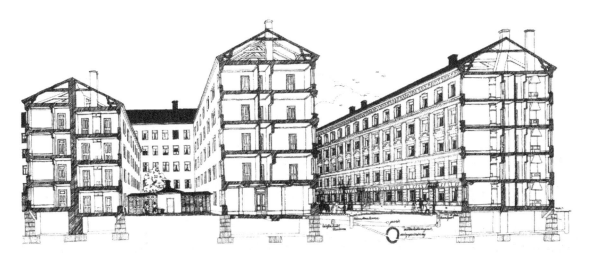

Figure 22.5 *Stockholm. Section of a block at the end of the nineteenth century (drawing by the Stockholm town-building office). The approved town plans indicated only the location of the streets and the shape of the blocks; the height and basic design of the houses, the size of the courtyards and so on were regulated by the 1874 building ordinances.*

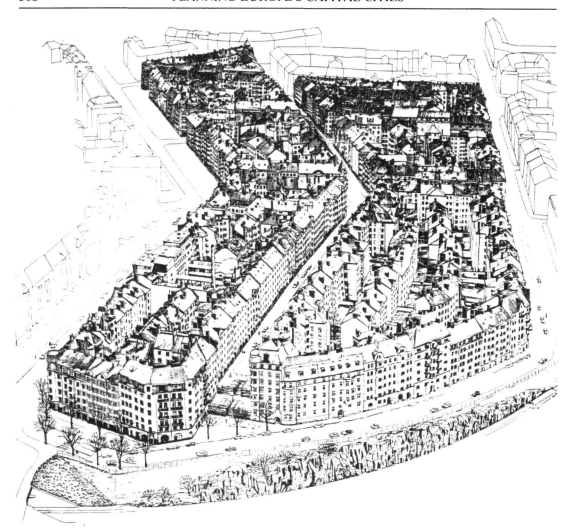

Figure 22.6 *Stockholm. Birkastaden from the west (in the middle Tomtebogatan, on the left Karlbergsvägen). The town plan for this district is largely based on the Lindhagen Committee's 1866 proposal, even though the expansion was not realized until the beginning of the twentieth century. This prospect, which was made by the Stockholm town-building office, can serve as an example of the way the interior of the block was filled with buildings. In this respect the Stockholm city blocks were not extreme, since according to the 1874 building ordinances one-third of the plot area was to be left unbuilt as a courtyard.*

either side of them'.[20] This recommendation met with little practical response of course, no more than the Lindhagen Committee's suggestion that 'small parks, corresponding to the English squares' should be laid out 'in great numbers' as part of the blocks and sometimes at their centre.[21] Open courtyards with greenery are also suggested in Castro's plan for Madrid and in van Niftrik's for Amsterdam; in Madrid two blocks of this type were built and have survived.

SQUARES

If the capital city projects were characterized by a certain lack of variety when it came to the design of local streets and blocks, the opposite seems to be true of the design of squares. In projects and in realized plans all kinds of squares are included, varying in both form and function. However, it should be emphasized that the overall projects discussed here generally only indicate the outlines of the squares, and that their design must therefore be regarded as a preliminary rather than a definitive proposal, in a way a kind of sample.

'The design of the public squares' was, as Stübben puts it, considered as 'the most important aesthetic task of the town-building process.'[22] Here too the inspiration of older models was most likely to make itself felt.[23] A brief look at earlier square design could therefore be appropriate (see also pp. 20 ff). First, it should be remembered that the architecturally created square was an exception in former times, occurring only in particularly important towns or districts. In early medieval towns, squares had usually developed organically as the product of historical continuity, often resulting in pleasing proportions and satisfying spatial effects, where irregular shapes were an advantage rather than a drawback, at least as we see things today. Most of the planned towns established in the later Middle Ages had a single large square, created by leaving one or more blocks – or parts of blocks – unbuilt. Here lay the town hall, and the surrounding private houses were generally among the most distinguished in the town. The church would be located close to – but generally not in – this square, which was also the given centre of the town, a place for trade and other activities. But there was still no conception of the square as an architecturally perceived whole.

The ideal city projects of the fifteenth and sixteenth centuries usually included several squares, some of them motivated on architectural rather than functional grounds; moreover,

these squares were usually designed as autonomous spaces, rather than representing an empty version of the built block. It was not unusual for the sides of such squares to meet at the corners, thus enhancing the impression of an enclosed space. While towns were growing in importance during the Renaissance as the residence of princes, with the local design planning that this entailed, the perception of the square changed. All parts and details were supposed to collaborate to produce an integral whole, complete and unchangeable: façades were designed to match or complement one another, and the relation between the size and form of the square and the 'walls' created by the surrounding buildings was subject to fixed regularities. The unrivalled example here is the Piazza del Campidoglio in Rome (figure 2.10), where the shape of the plan, the differences in altitude, the architecture of the enclosing buildings, the decoration of the 'floor' of the square and the location of the central equestrian statue, all combine to create a single unit, in which nothing can be altered without destroying the balance. Like many of the most famous Roman squares the Campidoglio represents a unique solution based on unique conditions. It could act as a source of inspiration, but could hardly be repeated.[24] The squares in Paris provided, as we have seen, answers to urban development problems that were more generally applicable and therefore made more impact as prototypes. The Place des Vosges is probably the most important model for the enclosed square in an urban structure, and the Place des Victoires the first realized – albeit rudimentary – example of the star-shaped variety.[25]

Turning to the seventeenth- and eighteenth-century overall town plans, for example the abundant seventeenth-century Nordic material, we frequently find square designs that differ little from the medieval praxis, i.e. the central square is created by leaving a block or part of a block unbuilt. In other cases the solutions and designs are more advanced, and there is sometimes an obvious desire to differentiate squares according to function.

The nineteenth-century plan-makers had to consider both the traditional functions of the square and other aspects that were either new or at any rate changed. The market function was still essential, supplying the towns with provisions, although covered market halls became an increasingly common alternative to open-air trading during the second half of the century. Many squares had always been traffic junctions, and as the volume of traffic increased their role as traffic filters became so significant as to merit description as a new function. Centrally located squares could also help to enhance the city's – and in some cases the government's – image; this was nothing new, but more squares and bigger ones were now required as part of the public display, often as the site of the many new public buildings – government departments and town-halls, museums, theatres and so on. As towns and their populations grew, and demands for a better urban environment grew with them, squares were also needed to provide space to breathe in, small oases in the surrounding neighbourhood. Such squares could be provided with flowerbeds or trees, and sometimes became almost indistinguishable from small parks. It was for this intermediate form that the English word 'square' first began to be used even outside England.[26]

In the following pages special attention will be paid to the square as a traffic junction and part of the overall traffic system, since this was also an aspect to which the town planners generally paid particular attention. The larger squares, together with the principal thoroughfares, were to provide the basic framework in the urban communication network, and thus an important element in overall planning. Smaller squares and the typically 'architectural' kind received their more definitive design first at the local planning stage, and the purely

utility squares were almost always kept very simple.

A quick look at the kinds of solution featuring in our capital city projects shows that the squares there deviated very little from the previous basic models. There are squares which are simply empty blocks, and squares which have been given a more independent architectural form. The first category includes most market squares and some of the small squares, planted or otherwise; most of them are rectangular. In the second category the most favoured kind seems to be the round or semi-circular version, often with streets radiating out from it. It was evidently felt that this type of square could most satisfactorily meet the traffic requirements as well as providing a distinguished setting. 'One of the attractive features of the star-shaped square,' wrote Stübben, 'is that from the centre of the square it is often possible to enjoy, one after the other, the views along its radiating streets, like a panorama of city prospects passing before the gaze of the spectator.'[27] Various other forms also appear in the projects belonging to the second category, of which the square with closed corners is but one example.

Hobrecht's plan for Berlin is a veritable sample card of squares, some circular and others regular polygons, but most of them consisting of an unbuilt block or sections of blocks without any particular architectural design. They were certainly not intended as definitive or detailed proposals. The Lindhagen Committee's project for Stockholm also includes the two main types, namely market squares consisting of unbuilt blocks and central squares in the new districts with a star-shaped form. Rovira i Trias's plan for Barcelona is an example of the systematic creation of architecturally planned squares, with some of the forms being repeated in symmetrical patterns. In Cerdá's alternative proposal every street-crossing qualifies as a square, one or two of them as large ones. But the enormous rectangular central square appears overgrown and does not seem to fit either aesthetically or functionally into the town plan. Castro's plan for Madrid includes several quite small squares, some of them unbuilt blocks and some semicircular. There are no real traffic squares. Van Niftrik's plan for Amsterdam likewise included a number of squares, aiming at creating a magnificent setting rather than good traffic conditions. But these fancies were to remain on the drawing-board.

Since there is many a slip between the first proposal for a square in an overall plan and its realization, it is hardly surprising that the most consistent solutions to the square problem are to be found in Paris, where planning and execution progressed hand in hand, and where it was not necessary to look for compromises in a series of different committees. Unsurpassed of its kind is the Place Charles de Gaulle (Place de l'Étoile), which dominates the whole northwestern part of Paris (figure 3.11), crowned by Napoleon's Arc de Triomphe at the centre of twelve great radiating avenues. The high ground and the enormous dimensions of the place itself with a diameter of more than 350 metres – all contribute to the effect. The surrounding buildings are on a smaller scale than Haussmann had wanted, but they are screened from the open space by trees, which fulfil the visual function of an enclosing wall, although only in a bird's eye view is it possible to perceive all the parts as an integral whole. Place Charles de Gaulle seems to have been regarded in its own time as an ideal solution to the problem of combining monumentality with efficiency in what we would now call traffic management.

Almost as large as Place Charles de Gaulle was its counterpart in the eastern half of the city, Place de la Nation, although here the topography and the surroundings did not allow for the same uniform monumental design, and some of the radiating streets were short blind alleys. One more large star-shaped place was also given its definitive form under Haussmann, namely Place d'Italie in the southern section

of the city. Of the smaller star-shaped places in Paris, Place de Wagram and in particular Place du Mal Juin (formerly Place Péreire) deserve mention; so too does the Place du Trocadéro with its semicircular design. On the other hand, the large rectangular traffic squares which acquired their final shape under the Second Empire, in particular the present Place de la République (figure 22.7b) and Place de la Bastille, have a fragmented air despite the monuments at their centre; the enormous open areas and the many broad streets leading into them do not really add up to any pattern that we can grasp. The same applies to Place de l'Alma, albeit to a lesser extent.

Several other capital cities confirm the difficulty of combining the traffic requirements of space and broad approaches, with a desire for monumentality and the sense of an enclosed 'room'. This applies to Breitscheidplatz, for example, and to a lesser extent to Wittenbergplatz and Nollendorfplatz in Berlin, which were realized largely according to the intentions of Hobrecht's plan. Their structure appears vague, they resemble incidental traffic junctions rather than proper squares. In London Nash's project for Regent Street precipitated three of the capital's most important traffic junctions: Oxford Circus, Piccadilly Circus and Trafalgar Square. The first two represent a special form, the round circus, more enclosed than the star-shaped 'square' with its many radiating streets. The London traffic circus can best be described as a circular arrangement carved out of the blocks at a street-crossing. Oxford Circus still offers the prospect of a planned space, while at Piccadilly the impression has been fractured by the building of Shaftesbury Avenue. Several projects have been suggested, but none have been realized. Trafalgar Square, at least at ground level, lacks any discernible structure, despite Nelson's Column and the colonnaded façades of some of the buildings (on aerial photographs it is easier to perceive some ambition to

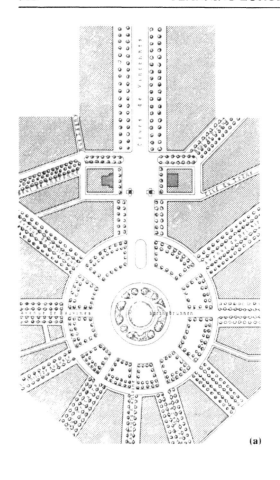

(a)

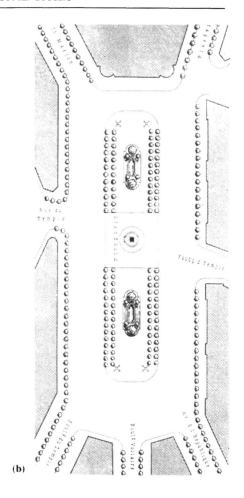

(b)

(c)

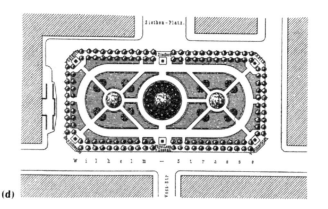

(d)

(e)

Figure 22.7 *Squares, parks and gardens. Place de la Nation (a) and Place de la République (b) in Paris are both examples of typical traffic junction squares, which due to their size and the many broad streets running into them, give very little impression of enclosed space. The greenery round St Johannis Church in Copenhagen (e) and Zionskirche in Berlin (c) can illustrate squares, whose purpose was to incorporate monumental buildings into the urban structure. A characteristic feature of the nineteenth century is that squares and public places are often supplied with a great deal of greenery; this broke with the traditional concept of the square since Renaissance times, not only because landscape gardening introduces a new dynamic means of expression, but more particularly because the masses of trees, shrubs and flowers changed the perception of the place as a room, and often contradicted it altogether. The greenery could be given either a fairly strict design, as in the Wilhelmplatz in Berlin with its surrounding public buildings (d), or a freer design as for example in the Square du Temple in Paris (f). [The scale of these examples is not altogether uniform, (a)–(e) from Stübben (1890), (f) from Alphand (1867–73)]*

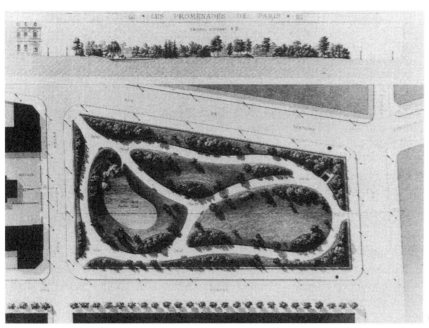

(f)

create a symmetrical arrangement of each side of the axis formed by Whitehall, the column and the portico of the National Gallery). The conditions were complicated: several streets run haphazardly into the square and the various monuments in it and surrounding it have no uniform scale. To create a uniform solution here would have required a building administration with much greater powers than then existed in London. Seidelin's plan for Copenhagen included several circuses of much the same type as in London, but they disappeared in the later proposals.

Apart from Paris, one of the relatively few examples of a star-shaped 'square' to be fairly consistently realized in a European capital, is Karlaplan in Stockholm, although its importance as a junction for traffic cannot rival that of the great star-shaped *places* in Paris. The star shape for Karlaplan was suggested at an early stage, namely in the Lindhagen Committee's project. During the lengthy travels of the project through the processing machinery of the municipality, alternative designs were discussed, but in the deciding vote the star-shaped place won. The conditions were favourable, since the site for the proposed square was largely unbuilt. But the counterpart to Karlaplan which Lindhagen had planned to the west on Kungsholmen was never realized.

In Vienna the problems were different. No need was apparently felt for any large squares as traffic junctions; traffic would be catered for by the Ringstraße. But a major task concerned the creation of the squares and gardens or parks which were to enhance the surroundings of the monumental buildings. They received their final shape at the local planning stage, generally after alternative proposals had been discussed.

Thus, if we try to summarize the nineteenth-century approach to the design of squares as it emerges from the projects discussed here, we find that to a great extent square design goes back to earlier forms, which have been rationalized and often applied on a larger scale; it is a

question of variations on certain archetypal themes rather than of the direct imitation of any specific prototypes. A type of square that must be described as typical of the nineteenth century is the pure traffic junction, a square that does not look in on itself but which opens outwards in many directions to facilitate optimal circulation. It may be strictly regular like the Place Charles de Gaulle or amorphous like Trafalgar Square. Another typically nineteenth-century type, which we have so far only noted in passing, is the small square, often with a garden or planted with trees and shrubs, and intended as an open space for a neighbourhood or as the forecourt to some public building.

In order to speak of a square being created in an architectural sense, it is not enough that the area concerned has a certain size or extent; there must also be a sense of defined space. Many of the nineteenth-century squares are so large that they can only be perceived as covering a vast surface but not as defining a space. Piazza Vittorio Emanuele in Rome is an example of this, as are the great *places* in Paris and the huge central square in Cerdá's plan for Barcelona. Where the approach roads are very broad, as they often were, this also reduces the sense of an enclosed room. Further, the surrounding buildings were generally designed with a view to satisfying the landowner interests rather than serving primarily as components in a uniform architectural entity. And it was just these attributes of nineteenth-century planning, the stereotype design of the squares and their lack of aesthetic quality, which aroused some of the severest criticism. The solution to the question of the layout of the square is one of the main themes of Camillo Sitte's *Der Städte-Bau nach seinen künstlerischen Grundsätzen* (1889), in which he attacks the lack of spatial effect or architectural design in contemporary squares, and compares them with the variety of the earlier squares and the sense they provided of being in an enclosed room. A number of factors had contributed to produce the development criticized by Sitte. The growth in the urban population and the increasingly heavy traffic called for larger squares and broader streets. The new administrative and institutional buildings often proved too big and pretentious to be components in an organized space. The main aim of the property owners was to achieve optimal return on capital, and there was little opportunity for controlling private building. A great many decision-makers were engaged in the genesis of a square in the role of developers, architects or public officials. The time had gone when a single patron and his architect could create a central town square according to their own ideas. But the great rectangular or circular squares with their many access roads doubtless reflected the technological approach to urban development that typified the age.

PARKS AND GARDENS

Parks and gardens,[28] according to progressive nineteenth-century town planners, were one of the most important components of the urban environment. Together with tree-lined streets they were a kind of universal means for 'banishing darkness, overcrowding, foul air and all that is unnatural' as well as 'the obnoxious influences that undermine the health of the body and sully and dull the spirit' as the Lindhagen Committee put it.[29] There should be parks, again according to the committee, 'along everyone's road and close to everyone's home'. 'The inestimable supply of life-giving fresh air and natural beauty which the outcrops of Stockholm provide in great abundance, would be ill-used were they to be monopolized by a few individuals . . . as a little more icing on their gingerbread, rather than being made available for the enjoyment of the whole population of the capital city.'[30] And similar ideas could be heard elsewhere. Parks were also thought to have a didactic, educational value, both ethically and aesthetically. They would counteract rebellious movements and bring tranquillity to people's souls.[31] It was indisputable, or so it was claimed in a city authority report in Berlin, that well-kept parks, 'are one of the most fitting means of relieving our minds from anxiety over material things and for assuaging, when it arises, a disposition for the coarse or brutal.'[32]

The idea that public parks should be a natural part of the urban environment was one of the most fundamental nineteenth-century additions to the urban development creed. A great many town parks were thus created, although the best and earliest examples are not always to be found in the capitals. Earlier there had either been no parks in towns at all, or they had been reserved for the few. Only exceptionally were parks open to all. A big step was taken when London's Hyde Park was opened to the public in the 1630s, and other royal parks gradually followed suit, Green Park among them. But when preliminary plans were made for Regent's Park in the 1810s, it was not intended that it should to be open to everyone, and there were still a great many private parks in London.

Nash's highly influential project for Regent's Park was the first great park project of the nineteenth century, and a milestone in the history of park planning, both as regards the way in which the park was integrated into the urban structure and in the overall design whereby terraces, crescents and splendid town houses have been combined with a rich, imposing park landscape. It took its place among the unique swathe of parks – Kensington Gardens, Hyde Park, Green Park and St James's Park – that cuts across London. The London parks made a great impression on Louis Napoleon during his exile.[33] As Emperor he was deeply committed to laying out or remodelling various parks, above all the Bois de Boulogne, followed by the Parc Monceau, the Bois de Vincennes, the Parc des Buttes Chaumont and Parc Montsouris (although this last was not completed until the Third Republic), as well as many smaller parks. The French example was taken up in Brussels, where large parks were laid out under Leopold II, albeit primarily in outlying areas. In the Ringstraße area in Vienna, too, parks were an important component; public parks occupied 5 per cent of the total area in the *Grundplan*. The English and French experience may have inspired the Lindhagen Committee to propose the many parks in the Stockholm plan. Both Lindhagen and Leijonancker, another member of the committee who was responsible for Stockholm's first water mains, were familiar with what was happening out in the world as a result of their travels and studies. Castro's proposal for Madrid is also well supplied with parks – two large ones and several smaller green areas.

There was not the same interest in parks in all the capital cities. In the Hobrecht plan for Berlin there seem to be no new parks of any importance. In Budapest planners abstained from parks on the grounds that the Danube provided adequate air circulation.[34] And, of course, parks tended to shrink or disappear altogether on their journey from proposal to realization. This was what happened in Stockholm, where only part of the area assigned to parks in the Lindhagen plan was actually used for that purpose. Improved blasting technology was probably a factor here. When it became possible to exploit the outcrops in Stockholm for building at low cost, the pressure to do so became too strong. In Copenhagen, too, the parks actually laid out were only part of the total park area which optimistic planners had envisaged. In Barcelona there are practically no parks at all in the *ensanche*, although Cerdá's plan included substantial park areas to complement the green belts cutting through and edging the blocks. In Rome there was a unique opportunity to provide the people with beautiful parks: it would only have been necessary to adapt parts of the existing gardens on the

Esquiline and Viminal Hills for public use. But parks were obviously not of primary interest at first, and when they became so most of the land had already been exploited. Only the Villa Borghese could be saved as a public park.[35] In Amsterdam van Niftrik's plan from 1866 suggested an abundance of park areas, most of which had disappeared in Kalff's plan ten years later, which was the one to be implemented. But in the Vondelpark Amsterdam enjoyed a fairly centrally situated park, which had been created under private auspices but which was open to the public. Like Regent's Park in London and several later English public parks, it was the result of a land development project, which combined the laying out of the park with the sale of building lots. Generally speaking, there were big variations between parks and between towns as regards the drivers of the projects. National and municipal bodies could be involved, as well as associations, companies and private individuals. Methods of financing also differed sharply from project to project.

One non-European example should also be mentioned, namely Central Park in New York, which came into being as the result of a campaign launched in 1844 in the *New York Evening Post* by the journalist William Cullen Bryant. He had recognized that the town would be an insufferable place to live in, if the buildings on Manhattan were allowed to spread beyond 42nd Street, which was then the boundary of the built area. When the city had gained possession of a vast area corresponding to about 150 blocks north of 59th Street and between 5th and 8th Avenues, a competition was arranged. It was won by Frederick Law Olmsted and Calvert Vaux. Work on this enormous park began in 1857.[36] Central Park was the starting-point of the American park movement, and it acquired imitators in several other American towns. 'It was in North America' writes Sutcliffe, 'that open space first emerged as a potential structural element for the entire city, while Europe continued to view the park as a reservoir or oasis in the middle of mass buildings.' 'American city parks,' according to Sutcliffe, 'began to out-strip those of Europe in both scale and quality of their design from the 1850s.' Alongside transport technology they represented America's greatest contribution to Europe when it came to urban development.[37] How-ever, the American influence first made a serious impact towards the turn of the century, i.e. after the period studied here.

Nineteenth-century town parks were not designed according to any standardized model. Even in size they could vary from huge suburban parks to small green areas covering less than a block, from large landscaped parks to tiny patches. In the suburban parks, like the Bois de Boulogne, it was possible to ride or drive in your carriage, while the larger parks inside the cities were intended for strollers, and the smallest ones as 'lungs' and meetings places for those living in the neighbourhood, or as frames round important buildings. The location and the social status of the expected visitors, as well as the economic resources, all affected the character of the park. Naturally the prestigious parks were designed differently from those in the working class districts. Some of the biggest parks consisted of a number of separately designed sections, creating some-thing we could call a park complex rather than a single park. The broad tree-lined principal thoroughfares were also regarded as parks of a kind, as links in a system of green areas.[38]

The planning and creation of a park was a complicated undertaking. It was one thing to include a park in an overall plan, and another to bring it into being. Specialists – many of whom were engineers, landscape architects, gardeners and administrators all in one – were responsible for their detailed layout and real-ization. Sir Joseph Paxton, England's foremost park planner around the middle of the century, was one such versatile character; Peter Josef Lenné in Berlin and Adolphe Alphand in Paris were others; Alphand had been carefully

selected by Haussmann himself, and he became one of the Prefect's closest collaborators. Naturally these men then had their own assist-ants and aides; in Paris Pierre Barillet-Deschamps was largely responsible for the detailed layout of the parks. Of the many other lesser-known names in this field in other towns, mention can be made of Knut Forsberg in Stockholm.[39]

The chief determining factor in designing a park was the topography: it was up to the planner to create an attractive and varied layout, exploiting the conditions imposed by the terrain. A lake was also an essential element in any large park, preferably a long rather than a round one, and best of all one that narrowed towards the ends or that twisted its way along in serpentine curves. Former moats lent themselves well to the creation of ponds, because of their zig-zag shape, which was happily exploited in Copenhagen for example. If the topography determined the basic character, the vegetation was obviously the other most important component: trees, bushes and flowers. Unusual species were favoured – often arranged as a kind of backdrop to provide the visitor with a pleasant milieu and to offer beautiful, varied and where possible surprising prospects. The dramatic and artistic aspect of the park could be further enhanced by architectural details such as build-ings, bridges, monuments etc., or by the careful arrangement of statues and fountains. Some-times part of a park could even be laid out as a scientific botanical garden. The paths should be arranged to provide people with the best possible experience of the park, and should be designed to cope with the estimated number of visitors. Fields for games were also part of the picture and, in larger parks, bridle-paths and perhaps even a race-course. Other important elements included eating places of various kinds and possibly a concert pavilion. In the summer people could row on the lakes and in winter skate on the ice. Parks were not only meant to provide green areas and fresh air;

they were also envisaged as a place for games and sports and informal social intercourse.

There were thus many ways of introducing variety, of which the parks in Paris in particular provide plenty of examples. The Parc Monceau, which was reopened in 1861, is an example of elegance and distinction in a park that would be difficult to surpass, with its exotic trees, its magnificent flower beds, its varied topography and wealth of architectural detail, not to mention the palatial appearance of the houses which surround it. The Parc des Buttes Chaumont (figure 22.8*b*), which began to be built in 1864 and was opened in time for the World Exhibition in 1867, is also unique. A park has been created at different levels in a disused quarry, a romantic vision of an Alpine landscape with dramatic rocky outcrops, sheer precipices, a waterfall, high suspension bridges and fantastic views.

London's parks were generally composed in a less extravagant mode, with fewer trees and bigger open areas. The French landscape gardener, Alphand, wrote: 'Their appearance is rather simple, compared to our Parisian promenades,'[40] but he was perhaps referring mainly to the older parks. Despite Alphand's words, English parks too could offer exciting prospects, but they generally also kept large areas for sports and games and, compared with their counterparts in France, were therefore better suited to the needs of the people. Among the town parks created during the Victorian era, mention should be made of Battersea Park in London (figure 22.8*a*). It was first planned by James Pennethorne and revised by John Gibson, and was laid out during the 1850s, a little after Victoria Park which was an offspring of the same architects.

The town parks and *Volksgärten* in German cities had similar goals; the model may have been the old ducal landscape gardens, but now in a version adapted to a mass public.[41] One prototype was the *Volksgarten* planned by Lenné in 1824 in Magdeburg, and an excellent example is provided by the *Volksgarten* laid

out by Adolf Kowallek in 1887–89 in Cologne.[42] Berlin's stock of parks was totally inadequate, and the example shown here, the Humboldthain (figure 22.8*c*), laid out by Gustav Meyer in 1869–75, does not appear very inspiring. The middle of the Humboldthain has gentle winding paths, while its outer reaches are more formally organized, and it is framed by straight roads lined with double rows of trees.

It was quite common for nineteenth-century parks to borrow in this way from a wide-ranging storehouse of forms. While the urban planner was bound by the demand for rectilinearity and rationality, the creator of a park could take another way, mixing and making, and freely combining or juxtaposing different modes in the same park. From the French tradition came the idea of a regular design. A formal layout could be used for instance surrounding buildings to insert them in the general concept of a park. Otherwise town parks seem to belong most happily to the English tradition, with its less formal organisation. But it is a long way from the subtle design of the gardens of England's stately homes, where the solitary stroller could dream away the hours, to the public town parks with their planned network of paths for crowds of visitors, their scenic effects of a topographical, horticultural or architectural kind, or their eating-places and other public facilities. Intermediate links, apart from Nash and his proposal for Regent's Park, were two landscape gardeners active at the beginning of the nineteenth century, namely Humphry Repton – on occasion Nash's partner – and John Claudius Loudon, both authors of noted written works. Repton was inspired by Lancelot Brown's type of landscape park where the idea was to refine nature's own beauty, but he gradually developed a moderated variant of the 'picturesque' style, whereby colours – much as the tints of the artist's palette – were used to create pleasing, sometimes gaudy 'pictures' of nature. Loudon is the principal name in the 'gardenesque' style, in which the individual

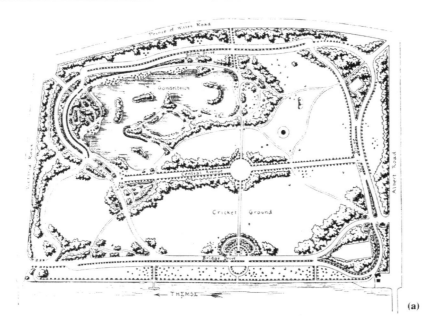

(a)

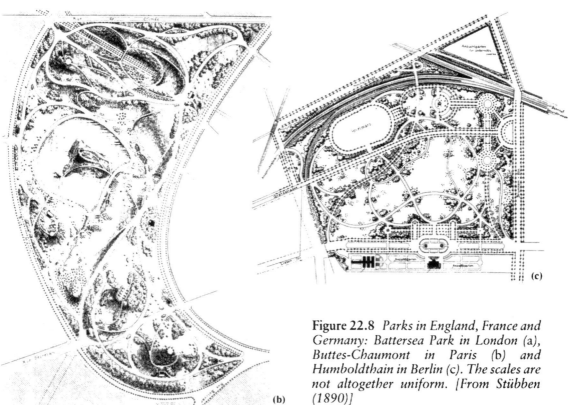

(b)

(c)

Figure 22.8 *Parks in England, France and Germany: Battersea Park in London (a), Buttes-Chaumont in Paris (b) and Humboldthain in Berlin (c). The scales are not altogether uniform.* [*From Stübben (1890)*]

Figure 22.9 *Stockholm. Café Blanch in Kungsträdgården, autumn 1874. [From* Ny illustrerad tidning *(1874)]*

plants rather than the whole ensemble are in the focus of attention. Every plant or tree was to be carefully placed and displayed so that its special quality and beauty could best be studied – a truly nineteenth-century approach.[43] Over the years park design evolved along many different lines, sometimes towards formal monumentality and sometimes towards highly dramatic effects as in Parc des Buttes Chaumont in Paris.

NOTES

1. It was also possible to distinguish between three types of street, as for example in the regulations appended 1875 to the Prussian *Fluchtlinien-Gesetz*, where streets were divided into 'side-streets with a width of 12–20 m, middle-ranking traffic roads with a width of 20–30 m and principal thoroughfares with a width of 30 m or more' (cf. Stübben (1890), pp. 67 f). Three classes were also used by Castro for his Madrid plan.

2. Cf. further Stübben (1890), pp. 80 ff., which is an important source for this chapter.

3. The following should not be regarded as an attempt to produce an exhaustive survey of the use of the relevant terms, even though a few other towns do serve as references.

4. In Helsinki the extension to the Esplanaden was rather surprisingly called Bulevarden from its start in the 1810s, although it was to be the main street of an entirely new district. This was thus in anticipation of the more unorthodox use of the word in Paris later. In discussions of the town plan in Budapest, the term 'boulevard' was used

not for the ring road but for the diagonal thoroughfare.

5. No streets in Stockholm, for instance, were called avenues.

6. On the other hand the name 'Nya allén' was given to the street constructed during the 1820s in the old fortification area in Gothenburg, according to a plan made by the city architect Carl Wilhelm Carlberg – although this is Sweden's only 'boulevard' in the traditional sense of the word.

7. Lilius (1968–69), pp. 90 ff. and *Mönsterstäder*, pp. 7 f.

8. *Kungl. byggnadsstadga*, 1874, §§ 12 and 13. In the Stockholm City Council, Lindhagen claimed the total width of an esplanade had to be 55 m (Selling (1970), p. 52).

9. Améen (1979); Hall (1991), pp. 187 ff and 248. However, esplanades had been planned and laid out before 1874 in Sweden. The street, wide as a block, which cuts through the west Swedish town of Vänersborg after a fire there in 1834, is akin to the esplanade in Helsinki and is certainly inspired by the Finnish example, although the function of the prototype, to act as a social barrier, is absent. Esplanades with the width of one block were also proposed for Gävle in 1869; one of them was subsequently realized. The Lindhagen Committee's proposal for Stockholm, on the other hand, included no esplanades, unless the future Sveavägen could be counted as such. The designation 'avenue' seems more relevant, and was also used by the committee itself. After approval of the 1874 building ordinances, the esplanades were generally given a simpler design, resembling broad thoroughfares rather than green belts.

10. Copenhagen and Hamburg each have a street known as 'Esplanade'; here esplanade is used as a name rather than the designation of a particular type of street. Both names seem to be unique in their respective cities, and so far as I know there is no other 'esplanade' in Denmark. In Germany the term seems to be very unusual. Copenhagen's esplanade was laid down between 1781 and 1785 along the length of an existing road, as a tree-lined 'promenade for the general public' between the citadel and the town; the name is contingent on the site and is used quite correctly here. This road was an important traffic artery, leading from the customs sheds at the harbour, past the citadel to the southernmost bastion, continuing at an obtuse angle to Østerport (according to John Erichsen, director of Københavns Bymuseum). Today only the southern leg of the angle bears the name Esplanaden. Its namesake in Hamburg is part of the ring road which was built in the former area of the fortifications. It can be mentioned as a curious detail, that New Orleans also has its esplanade, also laid out along the line of the former fortifications. This thoroughfare, with trees planted down the middle, does recall the Swedish and Finnish esplanades.

11. Data from Stübben (1890), pp. 80 ff.

12. *Ibidem*, especially p. 85.

13. Lameyre (1958), p. 101.

14. Cf. p. 296, note 8 and pp. 324 f.

15. Stübben (1890), pp. 77 f.

16. It seems justified to quote Alphand's description of the Champs Élysées here, although it is a park belt rather than a street, like Esplanaden in Helsinki: 'They provide, at one and the same time, a place for strolling and large leafy trees to give shade, regular hedges to edge the flowerbeds or to form broad avenues, flowers, clumps of elegant bushes, undulating lawns adorned with rare plants as solace to the eye, cafes and music hidden among the greenery, games and fountains playing – all these provide a harmonious scene. At night almost everything is lit up. The crowds jostling against one another among the trees, the music, the voices of the singers and the murmuring of the fountains together evoke a mood of magic along this entrancing promenade.' (Alphand (1867–73), [I], p. LIX.)

Bédarida and Sutcliffe have discussed the importance of the street in the life of Paris and London during the nineteenth century. Their conclusion is that, with its lower street network standard and its more scattered building structure, London never encouraged street life of the Parisian type 'In English, one may, "stroll" in a park, but hardly in a street.' (Bédarida and Sutcliffe (1981), p. 33.)

17. In the 1874 Swedish building ordinances it is stated that the town plan should be so designed that 'on the one hand the blocks should not take up so much room or contain so great a number of plots, that the necessary air circulation is obstructed or the extinguishing of fires prevented,

but on the other the building plots within the blocks should be sufficiently large to leave enough room not only for buildings but also for open and airy courtyards' (§ 12). The prescription is well-meaning, but gives little concrete guidance. On the subject of blocks, see also Stübben (1890), pp. 54 ff and Mollik, Reining and Wurzer (1980), pp. 169 ff. What is said above about the city blocks refers to the central areas of large cities of the type to which the plans discussed here refer. In residential suburbs and working-class areas on the outskirts of the town other types of block were certainly to be found.

18. Selling (1970), pp. 23, 30 and 32. In Stockholm the same criticism was raised a good 50 years later against Albert Lilienberg's proposal to extend Sveavägen to Gustav Adolfs torg (see Hall (1985), pp. 12 ff). It should also be remembered that Klenze's alternative proposal for Athens was intended among other things to reduce the number of blocks with sharp corners. The problem has thus been observed in quite different contexts and at different times. In Stübben's opinion sharp corners could sometimes provide 'the most desirable and best business location' (1890, p. 58).

19. *Lotus international* 23 (1979), p. 84.

20. *Kungl. byggnadsstadga* 1874, § 12.

21. *Utlåtande med förslag till gatureglering i Stockholm*, p. 35.

22. Stübben (1890), p. 189.

23. Most of Stübben's examples were taken from the period 1850–1890, but in the chapter entitled 'Public squares in an aesthetic perspective' he refers significantly enough to a whole series of earlier examples.

24. An exception must be made for the Piazza del Popolo, although it was only the pattern of the three streets radiating out from the square that was imitated, rather than the design of the piazza as a whole.

25. Henri IV had planned a semi-star *place*, which was never realized (see p. 56).

26. Stübben distinguishes between four categories of square: 'traffic junction squares, utility squares (including market places and *Volkplätze*), decorative squares (squares with greenery, English-type squares) and architectural (monumental) squares'. But, he continues, it is not impossible 'to realize two or more of these

goals in a single square construction' (Stübben (1890), p. 141).

27. Stübben (1890), p. 147. Stübben emphasizes, however, that 'big city life and very varied architecture' belong to this type of square. 'Without these the star-shaped *place* easily comes to resemble a roundabout, and is just as confusing.'

28. On the city park, see Chadwick (1966), Hennebo (1974), *L'Œuvre du Baron Haussmann*, pp. 91 ff. and Mollik, Reining and Wurzer (1980), pp. 284 ff; cf also Stübben (1890), pp. 492 ff. City parks are also discussed in some of the many essays in *The History of Garden Design: The Western Tradition from the Renaissance to the Present Day* (1991). Panzini (1993) is a recent work on the development of the public park in a European perspective. Mention should also be made of the series *Geschichte des Stadtgrüns*, edited by Dieter Hennebo. Vol. III, *Entwicklung des Stadtgrüns in England von den frühen Volkswiesen bis zu den öffentlichen Parks im 19. Jahrhundert* (Hennebo and Schmidt, 1977), and Vol. IV, *Stadtparkanlagen in der ersten Hälfte des 19. Jahrhunderts* (Nehring, 1979), are of particular interest in our present context.

29. *Utlåtande med förslag till gatureglering i Stockholm*, p. 4.

30. *Ibidem*, pp. 31 and 35.

31. Cf. Hennebo and Schmidt (1977), pp. 114 ff.

32. Quoted from Hennebo (1974), p. 81.

33. The more knowledgeable visitor, the landscape gardener Peter Josef Lenné from Berlin, on the other hand, was not impressed, but criticized London's parks which he found inferior to their continental counterparts. He also declared that the fences round the parks and the locked gates were typically English, as were the planted areas in squares (see Chadwick (1966), p. 32).

34. On Margaret Island there was a park that was laid out towards the end of the eighteenth century. The town did not buy the island until 1908. Also, Pest already had one of the oldest parks in Europe to be laid out under the auspices of the citizens themselves, namely Városliget from the early nineteenth century.

35. It should be pointed out, however, that as far back as the beginning of the nineteenth century Rome acquired a city park in the one which Napoleon had planned by Giuseppe Valadier on

Monte Pincio. Here, the exploitation of the slope recalls earlier Italian palace gardens, and it became the point of departure for the re-structuring of the Piazza del Popolo which was carried out over the following decades under the same architect.

36. Cf. among others Reps (1965), pp. 331 ff and Chadwick (1966), pp. 181 ff.

37. Sutcliffe (1981b), p. 197; cf. *ibidem*, p. 93.

38. Cf. map of the parks and tree-planted streets in Paris, in Alphand (1867–73), [IV].

39. According to Swedish accounts Forsberg is supposed to have won a competition for the design of the Bois de Boulogne at the beginning of Haussmann's period in office (the latest mention of this appears in Gyllenstierna (1982), p. 53, according to which Forsberg is said to have received a prize of 100,000 francs, a fabulous sum for the times, which he had wasted in feasting and drinking before he had left for home). However, no such competition is mentioned in French accounts nor in Haussmann's memoirs, and it seems all too likely that Forsberg made up the whole story.

40. Alphand (1867–73), [I], p. LVIII.

41. Hennebo (1974), pp. 77 f.

42. The plan is reproduced in Stübben (1890), p. 503 and Hennebo (1974), p. 78.

43. See Chadwick (1966), pp. 20 ff and 53 ff.

23

ATTITUDES TO THE CITYSCAPE

To what extent could the planners enhance the beauty of these cities, according to the ideas of their own times?

As we have seen, a variety of practical considerations often favoured the rectangular street network, cut through – sometimes diagonally – by broad tree-planted thoroughfares, as the best solution to functional problems. But plans of this kind were certainly also seen as a source of beauty.

What then did this 'beauty' consist of? The paragraph quoted in chapter 21 (page 285) above on 'goals' in the Swedish building ordinances of 1874, for example, speaks of 'the open spaces, variety and neatness so necessary to the sense of beauty'. Open spaces between the blocks in the shape of broad streets, squares and parks were thought to enhance the appearance of a town, while also making it a healthier and more efficient place to live in. In all the towns studied here we have found a strong desire to create 'open spaces'. In the Emperor's *Grundplan* for the Ringstraße project in Vienna, just over 20 per cent of the total planned section was occupied by the blocks and other built areas. A little less than 20 per cent was occupied by green areas, 10 per cent by water and 50 per cent by arrangements for traffic. The demand for open spaces was clearly well satisfied here.[1] Corresponding figures for other projects have not been easily available, but it is quite clear that nineteenth-century planning represented a noticeable new departure as regards the relative proportions of built and unbuilt areas, even though the unbuilt parts tended to shrink on the way from project to realization, and there were big variations between different projects and types of project. Haussmann's street improvements in Paris, for instance, involved opening up a compact urban structure and a noticeable increase in the unbuilt area, albeit much of this was in fact used to make room for traffic. Cerdá regarded the interplay between open and built areas as a fundamental element in shaping the urban environment,[2] although his plans for open passages along and through the blocks were not realized in the *ensanche* in Barcelona, and the unbuilt area was ultimately fairly small.

The second requirement in the Swedish building ordinances, variety, is not altogether easy to satisfy in a grid system, and the risk of monotony was obviously recognized. Klenze, for instance, had already spoken critically of the rectangular network, while Baumeister and Stübben both warned that a straight stretch of road that went on for too long could be tiring and ugly.[3] However, in some of the capital city projects the rectilinearity was broken by diagonal streets, as well as by ring roads which Baumeister and Stübben recommended but which Cerdá did not. In this context it can be noted that the Lindhagen Committee felt compelled in its report to pre-empt possible criticism of the priority given to the functional rather than the aesthetic aspect, in the following words: 'One or two elegantly arranged streets or open spaces could of course have made a pleasant impression, but in a town plan they are of little importance compared with the organization of streets into a coherent overall system of communications. A narrow twisting street can perhaps make for variety in the district through which it runs, providing it also with a certain quaintness and venerable air; but it is nonetheless to be condemned as conflicting with the demands for clean and unobstructed roads for traffic, and the imperative need for light and fresh air in human dwellings.'[4] It is interesting that the committee considered it necessary to make this statement at all; it shows that the rectangular pattern was not entirely safe from criticism.

One way of solving this could have been to let the surrounding buildings supply the variety. This was in fact what happened in Vienna, where the monumental buildings along the Ringstraße were distinguished by different architectural styles, although this was not of course primarily intended as a way of creating variety. As the nineteenth century saw it, the façades along a street were definitely not an appropriate means of introducing variation. Sometimes, as in Stockholm for instance, there was a tendency to design the dwelling-houses individually, albeit within the framework of a classical idiom. But, ideally, it was felt – at least until the third quarter of the century – that the façades of dwelling-houses should be characterized by uniformity and restraint. Uniformity went furthest in the new boulevards and avenues in Paris. Here the building ordinances provided exact instructions for the design of the façades. Sometimes regulations were even included in the sales contract for the plots, to guarantee that all cornices and windows along the side of a block or a street should be at the same level.[5]

Thus uniform façades along the streets were something which Haussmann, and no doubt most of his contemporaries, regarded as highly desirable. The same attitude lies behind the third criterion in the Swedish building ordinances, namely 'neatness'. Conspicuous façades, differing sharply from one another, were definitely not regarded as 'neat'. Variety should be produced by other means, perhaps by squares of various shapes, ideally boasting a monument of some kind, and by parks and planted areas, tree-planted streets and public buildings, preferably isolated from their surroundings to create a striking effect. Eye-catching accents were favoured, often consisting of a monument or an imposing building closing the prospect along an important street. If possible the monuments were placed in the centre of a square, where they were visible from several approaches.

The demand for 'neatness' also of course implied a desire to see that the environment is not disturbed by elements that are less 'neat', such as older buildings that clash with the surroundings, buildings with shabby façades and so on. In 1859 the Swedish engineer and urban development theorist Adolf Wilhelm Edelsvärd wrote in a commentary on a project for a model city: 'That which is useful and appropriate to its purpose is also the most beautiful.' Further: 'How much aesthetic pleasure, how much elevation of the spirit, is thrown away in the confusion, the congestion, the ugliness which still reign in many of our smaller towns.'[6]

Long vistas and striking markers were a crucial ingredient in Haussmann's urban design aesthetics, if not the most crucial. Prime examples include the Avenue de l'Opéra terminating in the opera house itself, the Boulevard Henri IV with the Panthéon and the Colonne de Juillet functioning as special accents and the Boulevard Malesherbes focusing on the façade of St Augustin. One cause of constant irritation to Haussmann was the fact that the Boulevard de Strasbourg, which had been started before he became Prefect, had not been built slightly further to the east, which would have given it, and in particular its extension as the Boulevard de Sébastopol, a splendid finale in the dome of the Sorbonne church. He tried to correct this oversight by locating the Tribunal du Commerce on the Île de la Cité, where its dome could provide the focal point he wanted.[7] One result of the street

Figure 23.1 *'Neighbours'.
A newly built house in
central Stockholm at the
beginning of the 1880s
and the interior of the
courtyard of the house
next door. Throughout
the later nineteenth
century the townscape in
many European capital
cities must have been
characterized by a mixture
of new 'modern' houses
and streets and earlier,
small-scale and often
slummy buildings. One of
the most important
aesthetic goals was to
demolish such disfiguring
sights. [Ny illustrerad
tidning (1882)]*

cuttings which Haussmann was unlikely to
have found aesthetically pleasing, was the
creation of blocks tapering to a narrow point –
sometimes resembling nothing more than a
slice of cake. For strollers in our own day,
however, they certainly help to produce a
varied and exciting urban scene.

In an oft-quoted passage Haussmann tells
how he was reproached by the Emperor for
paying too much attention to the appearance of
the townscape: 'The Emperor, who did sometimes show proof of taste about many things,
reproached me for being too artistic in matters
of building; for sacrificing too much to the
correction of alignments, for looking too hard
for prospects to justify the orientation of the
public thoroughfares. "In London," he told
me, "they are concerned only with satisfying
the demands of traffic in the best possible
way." My answer was invariably: "Sire, the

Parisians are not Englishmen; that is to their advantage".'[8] The story could certainly be true: not many of those engaged in urban development in the nineteenth century were as concerned about aesthetic aspects as Haussmann was.

Visual accents of this kind do not seem to have received as much attention in the other towns, with the possible exception of Brussels (figures 14.2 and 23.2). Hobrecht, however, in accordance with his instructions, had envisaged a number of churches as focal points for the ring road and its connecting streets in Berlin, and in some instances his intentions were realized. Kaiser-Wilhelm-Gedächtniskirche, for example, provided a focal point for several streets. In Vienna long prospects of the Parisian kind were impossible because of the topographical conditions, and the accents that were planned have often been obscured since by trees. The Lindhagen Committee does not

seem to have considered it important to introduce such eye-catching effects in Stockholm; at any rate, nothing is said about this in their report. In one or two instances, however, space was reserved for churches in particularly striking locations, e.g. at a point which more or less coincides with the site from which the later Gustaf Vasa Church was to provide a visual accent for Odengatan. Nor does there seem to have been much interest in such focal points in either Budapest, Copenhagen, Madrid or Barcelona. It seems surprising, for example, that St Stephen's Church, Budapest's great nineteenth-century temple, was not exploited as a backdrop for the so-called radial road, Andrássy út. In Cerdá's rational type of planning such effects were simply not considered, although a few focal points which had not been planned from the beginning did eventually appear in Barcelona.

One aim underlying the desire for beauty

Figure 23.2 *Brussels. The nineteenth-century predilection for dramatic focal accents can be illustrated here by Sainte-Marie in Brussels, which provides a background decor for the Rue Royale. Beyond the church the street continues to yet another visual accent, the town hall in Schaerbeek. [Photo from the Sint-Lukasarchief, Brussels]*

Figure 23.3 *Berlin. Tauentzienstraße with Kaiser-Wilhelm-Gedächtniskirche. This photograph, probably taken around 1900, illustrates the late nineteenth-century idea of an attractive townscape: the great width of the street conveys a sense of space, light and air. The church provides a striking accent and the trees help to create variety (here the trees were obviously fairly young, but in many streets in European capital cities they have now become so big that in the summer they obscure the architecture; it is debatable whether this corresponds to the intentions of the nineteenth century). Compared with the stricter aesthetic represented by Haussmann, for example, the houses here display a variety of designs, with no coordination in the height of their cornices and windows. [From* Album von Berlin und Potsdam*]*

was to make the town a pleasant and healthy place to live in, another was to provide a distinguished and impressive setting for the activities conducted there, a manifestation of the city's resources, power and taste.[9] The bourgeois class, growing steadily richer and more powerful, was naturally interested in the creation of an attractive urban townscape which could enhance the city's image.[10] What distinguishes some of the capital cities from other large towns is the presence there of a strong central power, with its special demands and ambitions. The grand finale of ceremonial monarchy was being staged in the second half of the nineteenth century. This was the age of Victoria, Franz Joseph, Napoleon III, William II, Victor Emmanuel, Leopold II and Oscar II. Several of these regents represented the unifying link in complex state structures consisting of several more or less autonomous units, each with their own interests. Franz Joseph, with an empire embracing many nationalities and constantly threatened by currents of nationalistic and liberal ideas, was the prime example – a situation which certainly encouraged his desire for an appropriately magnificent setting for the wielding of his power. The many official buildings created at this time in Vienna and

Figure 23.4 *Berlin. Lübbener Straße in Kreuzberg can provide an example of a more everyday urban scene. [Photo, 1926, from Landesbildstelle, Berlin]*

elsewhere often acquired prestige from the monarch, while also contributing by their design and ornamentation to the glorification of the monarchical system. In the most authoritarian societies, namely France and Austria, the construction of official monumental buildings was combined, as we have seen, with a desire for radical urban development measures. The following quotation from a report by Haussmann in 1868 expresses this ambition: 'If it is a work before which all political passions should be silent, towards which a sense of patriotism should direct all good will, it is assuredly the great enterprise which will make of Paris a Capital worthy of France, or even, one might say, of the civilized World.'[11] Significantly, in the less authoritarian

atmosphere of England, the most obvious manifestation of nationalism in the capital's urban structure, Trafalgar Square, was never given a uniform design; the square seems to have been created by chance.

Several of the most magnificent public buildings erected in the capitals during our period, such as the Opéra in Paris, Neue Hofburg in Vienna and so on, were drawing on Baroque prototypes. Is a similar influence apparent in planning? This question has already been touched upon in the chapter on Vienna above. The focal accents, the uniform street façades, the extended prospects and the monumental squares all represent elements which nineteenth-century planning has in common with the seventeenth century, and which were indeed sometimes inspired by projects in the earlier period. This applies particularly to Paris. It could even be said that in the Place de l'Étoile Haussmann has created one of the most magnificent projects of the 'Baroque' style. And it is in fact French Baroque Classicism rather than the Roman Baroque which influenced nineteenth-century planning. But the kinship between nineteenth-century planning and the Baroque should not be exaggerated. The features mentioned above should perhaps be regarded as more or less constant elements in the kind of planning that has aesthetic ambitions – in other words, planning in the grand manner. It should also be remembered that many of the planning projects which were actually executed during the seventeenth and eighteenth centuries lacked the monumental qualities which we term Baroque, as indeed did many of their nineteenth-century successors.

A difference can perhaps also be noted between the architects' plans in which questions of form were generally considered particularly important and the city as a whole was regarded as a work of art, and the engineers' proposals in which functional efficiency was the decisive factor. The main example of this second class is of course Cerdá's plan for Barcelona, in which it seems that aesthetic effects are systematically avoided. Examples of the first category, the architects' plans, can be found among the competition entries for the *glacis* area in Vienna; here too mention should be made of the Schaubert-Kleanthes and Klenze proposals for Athens, Rovira i Trias's project for Barcelona and Conrad Seidelin's plan for Copenhagen. In these projects considerable attention is paid to the design of squares as outdoor rooms and sequences of urban space, to the insertion of buildings in an attractive way in the townscape, to the creation of visual accents and a varied street pattern, in other words to providing the conditions for a pleasing urban setting.[12] These projects belong to the period before or around 1860; perhaps they

can be regarded as late examples of an earlier and more purely aesthetic overall planning tradition in a classicizing mode, which gave way after the middle of the century to a more technical and utility-oriented planning type. Rapid urban expansion called for vigorous action based on rational considerations: it was a case of creating, as far as was technically, legally and economically feasible, the good roads needed for traffic and the green areas and 'ventilation' needed for good hygiene. There was no longer the same scope for aesthetically ambitious overall solutions, nor were such solutions expected of current urban planning, which was largely concerned with whole cities or districts. There were of course some exceptions to this, particularly in the imperial capitals, Vienna and Paris, and sometimes also elsewhere, where an ambition to create splendid and beautiful urban settings was evident. And naturally the design and planning of the central districts were subject to higher expectations than were housing areas on the outskirts.

Thus, the shape and design of the town were not regarded by these planners or their principals as anything that necessarily called for an education in artistic matters or for designing ability; to plan a town was primarily a technical problem, in which the functional coincided with the beautiful. It was not until almost the end of the century that town planning was emancipated from its technical way of looking at things and opened up to the art of urban design, partly as a result of Camillo Sitte's *Der Städte-Bau nach seinen künstlerischen Grundsätzen* (1889) which was arousing considerable attention at the time.[13] Features in the planning of the previous decades which were particularly subject to criticism included the alleged predilection for 'squares' in the form of empty areas without any clear space-shaping limits, the lack of variety and the often stereotyped design of the plans with their uniform block modules, and the freestanding monumental buildings unrelated to the other buildings around them. Another objection, which was to be pointed out by Sitte's followers, was that the planners sought to adapt the terrain to the plan rather than the plan to the topographical conditions.

Urban planning has always swung between a technical-functional and an artistic pole, and in a planning-history perspective Sitte's work is important not only as a plea for a more aesthetic approach, but equally for the emphasis on what we have called 'local design planning'. Particularly important for him was the design of spaces, preferably in varying sequences, and the insertion of buildings organically in the spatial context. Did Sitte mean that the planner should assume responsibility for the city as a whole, or was it just a question of creating a number of local solutions? Sitte's attitude on this point is not entirely unequivocal. In the chapter 'The monotonous and unimaginative character of modern towns', he dramatically denounces the town planning of his own time with its alleged monotony, poverty and lack of artistic sense. Instead of designing spaces, planners have begun – according to Sitte – by laying out plots and blocks, and then letting what is left become streets and squares.[14] If Sitte is obviously referring here to towns as a whole, in the following chapter, 'Modern systems', he is careful to point out that when it comes to striving for artistic goals the task of the town planner does not apply to the whole town: 'The artist needs for his purposes only a few principal streets and squares, everything else can be abandoned to traffic and the material needs of everyday.' And 'The great mass of dwellings can be devoted to work, and here the town can show itself in its everyday dress, but the few principal places and streets should be able to display themselves in their Sunday best to the pride and joy of the population.'[15] The chapter entitled 'Improved modern systems', however, seems to apply essentially to the planning of whole districts. If the 'unfortunate parcelled-out blocks are once drawn in on the building plan,' Sitte says here, 'then nothing much can ever come of it.'[16]

Thus, Sitte gave hardly any clear instructions on overall planning. Nor was his book a planning manual, providing concrete solutions. It was left to his followers, Karl Henrici, Theodor Fischer, Per Olof Hallman and many others to convert the new ideas into practice, often in the form of *Jugend* inspired winding streets, for which there is little support in Sitte's text. And whereas the capital city projects, and almost all earlier town plans, had been envisaged in 'flat' terms regardless of the topographical conditions, the aim now was to try to exploit undulating terrain to create variations in the townscape.[17] But such picturesque street systems were little more than an interlude. A more traditional view also persisted and the usual rectilinearity soon came into favour again in both practical planning and doctrine, for example in Otto Wagner's book *Die Großstadt* (1911).

When *Der Städte-Bau* was published Sitte had no personal experience of overall planning. However, the reputation he rapidly acquired meant that he was soon being consulted by several towns and in 1893 was asked to produce an overall plan for Olmütz (Olomouc). This has been analysed by Rudolph Wurzer, who considers it to be well put together and in accord with the prescriptions in Sitte's book.[18] It is very striking, though, that it lacks the picturesque street system that we regard as typical of Sitte. Sitte's second overall plan, made in 1903 for Marienberg, does however include streets of this kind.[19] Here the planner seems to have been inspired by his interpreters, and to have become seriously 'Sittean' himself!

In retrospect we might perhaps ask ourselves whether the difference in kind between Sitte's aesthetic ideals and those of his predecessors' has not been exaggerated, both by his pupils and successors and by modern scholars. Focal accents and organised spatial design were fundamental elements in Sitte's urban theory, as they had been in all planning with any aesthetic ambitions for around 300 years. But whereas the capital city projects tended to excel at pompous grand-scale effects, Sitte represents what we could call the chamber music of urban design, an intimate art that had no use for long straight thoroughfares. Haussmann and his like sought to compose a princely setting to be enjoyed by carriage; Sitte wanted to create a rich and rewarding world for, literally, the man in the street.

During the nineteenth century there was widespread discussion about the principles of restoration, and some kind of institutionalized system for the preservation of the architectural heritage began to emerge. Interest focused chiefly on buildings which were in the nature of monuments, and in particular on medieval churches. The great urban transformations of the second half of the nineteenth century sometimes led to the demolition of buildings of considerable architectural quality, but above all it was many of the old urban milieus, generally of a low standard, which were razed to the ground. At first these drastic changes met with little opposition, but gradually the picturesque qualities of the areas doomed to disappear began to be recognized (cf. figure 23.1). The reaction was strongest where the transformation was most radical, namely in Paris.[20] In its early years the new photographic technology was best suited to unmoving subjects such as buildings and urban scenery, and soon comprehensive photographic documentation was helping to promote public interest in the earlier urban environment. Towards the end of the century a preservation movement began to take shape, not directly associated with Sitte, but nonetheless expressing ideas and themes related to his message. The most noted contribution was Charles Buls's *Esthétique des Villes*, published in 1893. The recognition that even simple urban milieus could have a cultural-historical value became more general during the first decades of the new century, only to be swept away by func-

tionalism's ahistorical passion for change and innovation.

It is interesting to note here that just as grand-scale rectangular planning with its Baroque-inspired visual accents was beginning to fall into disrepute in Europe, on grounds of its alleged lack of artistic qualities, the same type of planning was acquiring new life and new value in the United States in the City Beautiful movement, which found much of its inspiration in the classicizing exhibition buildings for the World's Columbian Exhibition in Chicago in 1893, known as the White City. In this movement aesthetic aspects occupied a central place, and traditional features such as tree-planted streets and great squares with focal monuments were regarded as important ingredients in the creation of beauty in the urban environment. 'Make no little plans, they have no magic to stir men's blood', ran the famous battle-cry of the foremost advocate of this planning school, Daniel H. Burnham, who applied his ideas to such gigantic plans as those for San Francisco (1905) and Chicago (1909).[21] Both plans reveal enormous areas of uniform rectangular blocks, cut through often diagonally by broad tree-planted arteries, and with vast squares embellished by monuments and surrounded by splendid buildings in the city centres. Extensive parks were also an important feature.

Burnham's plans seem to reflect ideas about the beautiful and well-organized big city that had been prevalent in Europe during the third quarter of the nineteenth century, although to some extent his urban planning programme had its roots in the American tradition, in particular L'Enfant's project for Washington. Moreover, unlike the slightly earlier European projects, his plans revealed a clear ambition to be regarded as artistic products. The main reason for the importance attached to aesthetic aspects in the United States around the turn of the century and later, lay in the extremely rapid urban expansion that had occurred after the Civil War, and which had resulted in many stereotyped and visually poor environments. The delicate and intimate effects of the Sitte school hardly offered a feasible alternative to those who, like Burnham and his compatriots, were planning for a further wave of rapid expansion; furthermore, the regular grid had still stronger roots in the United States than in Europe. Another important factor was that many leading American architects had been trained in Paris, and were thus familiar with the image of the city as created by Napoleon III and Haussmann. American planning at the beginning of the twentieth century, and the work of Burnham as its greatest example, can be seen as the final stage in a tradition going back at least to the seventeenth century, when Wren's plan for London was one of its first manifestations.

The hegemony of Sittean planning was thus short-lived. Before the First World War there was already a reaction against twisting streets, and the straight model came back into favour. The question is whether this can be seen as a sort of impulse to retreat from the City Beautiful movement. It is certainly possible that Burnham's project may have opened the eyes of European visitors to the qualities of their own towns. On the other hand, classicizing planning would surely have enjoyed a renaissance, even without the counter-example of the City Beautiful movement.

How then, with the eyes of posterity, can we evaluate the effects of the European capital city planning projects as creators of townscape. The question, ultimately, is whether a period should be judged by its worst or its best examples, by its shortcomings or its achievements. On the one hand the second half of the nineteenth century saw the emergence of vast areas, for example in Berlin, which can only be described as monotonous and dull in the extreme, lacking in any visual or inspiring qualities. On the other hand some parts of central Paris, for example, with their tree-lined streets, their buildings, traffic, cafés and shops, convey a powerful sense of a great city's pulse, rich in variety and displaying a synthesis of the qualities generally regarded as 'urban'. Today, too, another factor has come into play: the visual variety of the nineteenth-century city, and particularly of the more imposing districts, has emerged from its long concealment under the dull grey cloak of a century's soot and dirt, to be revealed in all its original festive apparel.

NOTES

1. Mollik, Reining and Wurzer (1980), p. 158.
2. Even Cerdá admits that 'cities built on the square system' are monotonous without 'open blocks, with their variety of combinations and gardens' (quoted from Frechilla (1992), p. 117, note 32).
3. Baumeister (1876), pp. 96 ff and Stübben (1890), pp. 74 ff. As regards critical views on rectangular street networks and straight streets, see above, p. 296, note 8.
4. *Utlåtande med förslag till gatureglering i Stockholm*, p. 8.
5. Cf. Sutcliffe (1979a).
6. Hall (1991), pp. 187 f.
7. Haussman (1890), II, p. 488 and (1893), III, pp. 60 f and 529 ff.
8. *Idem* (1890), II, p. 523.
9. That the two aims were regarded as two sides of the same coin is apparent from many statements, for instance this by Castro concerning the planning of Madrid: 'giving width to its so narrow streets, cutting into them spacious squares and laying out parks and gardens which, at the same as giving the capital of the Monarchy the appearance of beauty and importance it deserves, may contribute to its health and hygiene' (quoted from Frechilla (1992), p. 358).
10. In this context a statement made by Anspach in the Conseil Communal in Brussels can be quoted: 'It is our constant preoccupation to cleanse, to embellish our city, to make a joy of the agglomeration, the centre of industry, of commerce and wealth, without aggravating the drawbacks of city life, but on the contrary making them easier to support.' (Quoted from Leblicq (1982), p. 344.)
11. Haussmann (1890), II, p. XII.

12. Van Niftrik's plan for Amsterdam made in the mid-1860s is a special case. It reveals clear artistic ambitions, even though its author was an engineer. However, this was not manifest in any overall concept, but rather in a number of episodes without any obvious connection.

13. The seminal work on Sitte – and a paragon among studies of this kind – is Collins and Collins (1986), which takes up a number of aspects of Sitte's life and activities, looking at his writings and assessing his importance in a way that is both reliable and exhaustive. The book includes an English translation of *Der Städte-Bau*. The first edition of Collins and Collins appeared in 1965 and was a milestone in Sitte research, since it demonstrated convincingly that the traditional picture of Sitte as a sort of apologist for the medieval period was based on what can only be called a falsification of his book. It was Camille Martin's French translation (1902) of this work which toned down Sitte's references to the Baroque – which Sitte himself regarded as exemplary – and over-emphasized his references to medieval urban development as a model (but as Collins and Collins state on p. 65, there is no point in speaking of styles in connection with Sitte, since 'his reduction of the urban environment to essentials that underlie any or all period styles' is just what characterizes his approach). The space devoted to Vienna was reduced and Martin introduced a number of French examples. This translation became the internationally most widely distributed version of Sitte's work, which meant that it also greatly affected interpretations of his message (see Collins and Collins (1986), pp. 71 ff). The first translation of *Der Städte-Bau* into English was published in 1945, and was mainly based on the French translation. The first translation to follow Sitte's own text was Collins and Collins (1965), after which new translations appeared in many languages. What has inevitably been lost, at any rate in translating Sitte into English, is his inflated bureaucratic style which is such a contrast to the subtlety of his argument – which in turn gives the book its idiosyncratic air.

An important complement to Collins and Collins is provided by Wurzer (1989 and 1992), which is based on partly new material. During the decades round the turn of the century Vienna was the centre for major ventures in many spheres. In a cross-cultural study Carl Schorske has sought to identify patterns in this explosion of activity, and with great insight has linked the Ringstraße project, Sitte and Wagner together in their temporal and local relationships (1980, pp. 24 ff).

In 1990 a symposium was held in Venice on Sitte and his interpreters (*Camillo Sitte e i suoi interpreti*). This was later published in book form (1992), with contributors from a number of countries.

14. Sitte (1889), pp. 88 ff.

15. *Ibidem*, pp. 97 ff

16. *Ibidem*, p. 130. On p. 137 ff he outlines the main points which should be taken into account when making a plan. But then he emphasizes once again, that planning concerned with artistic goals need apply only to the more important squares and streets.

17. This depended partly on the new levelling techniques which made it possible to carry out a correct survey of the terrain. It was also at this time that town-plan models began to be used.

18. Wurzer (1989), pp. 16 ff.

19. Cf. Wurzer (1989), pp. 19 ff.

20. Cf. Sutcliffe (1970), pp. 179 ff.

21. On Burnham, see in particular Hines (1974, quotation from p. XVII). On the City Beautiful movement and its importance, see, apart from Hines (1974), Reps (1965), pp. 497 ff; Scott (1969), pp. 47 ff; Goldfield and Brownell (1979), pp. 214 ff; Wilson (1980) and Sutcliffe (1981b), p. 102 ff. Charles Mulford Robinson played an important part in introducing European planning to the United States in his 1903 book *Modern Civic Art, or the City Made Beautiful* (see Sutcliffe (1981b), pp. 103 ff). This book, like one or two more with a similar focus, was based on Robinson's experiences from study trips to Europe.

24

IMPLEMENTATION AND RESULTS

To make town plans is one thing, to realize them is another. This is probably an experience that urban planners in all periods have shared. A town planning project is by its very nature a complex, expensive and time-consuming enterprise, in which planning ideas and design aspects may not carry much weight. Many different decision-makers are usually involved, as authorities, politicians, landowners or developers. Moreover, because implementation is a lengthy process, the original plan may be considered passé before it is fully realized, with all the changes and further delays that this means. The planner of an individual building generally has far more opportunity to influence the final result since the project is smaller, its implementation takes less time, and the decision-making is often limited to a single developer.

This chapter has three sections. The first consists of a brief look at the implementation process in some of the capitals. The second is an attempt to indicate the main features of the administrative and legal conditions of planning in the nineteenth century. In the third I discuss the extent to which the capital city projects were realized.

The implementation process in some of our capital cities has already been touched upon in chapter 21, in connection with a discussion of decision mechanisms in the planning phase. The principal points raised there apply by and large to the implementation phase as well: where planning went smoothly, implementation generally did so too.[1]

In Vienna it was the state, as the owner of

the land, which assumed direct responsibility for the implementation of the Ringstraße project, and through a system of committees the decisions were entrenched in the various groups or authorities concerned. Of particular importance was the *Stadterweiterungs-Commission* (Committee for the Expansion of the Town) which could perhaps be described as a nineteenth-century precursor of the London Dockland Development Corporation as regards both function and powers. The development process, which was greatly facilitated by the fact that most of the land was in public ownership and unbuilt, seems to have proceeded without too much trouble, as the planning had done. Over 600 plots were sold to private individuals and companies, and within a few decades dwelling-houses had been built on them; the revenue from these sales was enough to cover extensive public building. The town acquired the land for streets at no expense, but had to be responsible for the costs of construction. Implementation of the plans for the suburbs and outlying areas does not appear to have proceeded in the same systematic way.

In Budapest a body established by the state, the General Board of Works, was responsible not only for planning but also for implementation. Thanks to its own extensive powers and a certain amount of state support combined with lottery profits, the Board kept a firm hold over the street operations; property transactions and construction works seem to have proceeded without problems.

In Paris the implementation process was

much more complicated and difficult to grasp as a whole. There was no ratified or public plan; the point of departure was an outline which the Emperor handed to Haussmann on his appointment as Prefect of Paris. The municipal administration was responsible for implementation under Haussmann. As the representative of the state he was the real driver, while as head of the municipal authority he led the transformation of the town. The problems in implementing the 'plan' were far greater than in Vienna, since the land on which the future streets were to be constructed was largely in private hands and already built. From the start Haussmann had evidently envisaged a 'rolling' and largely self-financing process: the town was to buy or expropriate more land than the streets themselves would require, so that after the streets had been laid down the new building plots could be sold. In this way the town would profit by the increase in land values, which in turn could help to finance both demolition and street construction.[2]

The system seems to have worked satisfactorily to begin with, but after a time serious problems arose. Haussmann could not control the wave of speculation which he himself had helped to encourage. Compensation for expropriations tended to be so high that the increase in land value had already been swallowed up, and the town even lost the right to expropriate more land than the streets themselves would require. Despite this setback the street improvements proceeded apace, and when the town's own financial and administrative resources were no longer adequate, the whole street package was put out to tender. This gigantic urban transformation enterprise was thus possible as a result of state support and extensive municipal involvement, and of big private investments in plots and building.

The Lindhagen Committee had intended its plan for Stockholm to be implemented by spontaneous renewal, albeit in organized forms. The pace of the urban redevelopment and its actual locations were to be determined by individual initiatives; the town would construct streets and parks as the urban expansion proceeded. As things turned out, however, the town chose to play a much more active part. New ideas and new vigorous actors in the municipal administration launched the acquisition of large tracts of land during the 1880s, to facilitate realization of the town plan. The town was able to construct the new streets and lay out the blocks on its own land, and to carry out the necessary technical work. Plots could then be resold ready for building. In this way the municipality could profit from part of the increase in land values, instead of being compelled to pay high compensation when streets had to be constructed, and making no profit at all. Streets and sewage systems could also be constructed in a more rational way as a single undertaking, rather than being dealt with piecemeal as the Lindhagen Committee had envisaged. The town's efforts were favoured by a high average level building activity, despite some powerful fluctuations, and the plans ratified in 1879 and 1880 had been largely realized by around 1910. Here the municipality can be said to have been in fairly firm command of implementation, even if as elsewhere it depended on individual investors' willingness to build.

As to the other towns: in some cases there are no implementation studies, in others the studies are difficult to access. However, the principle in most towns seems to have been the same, i.e. that the town was to be responsible for street construction as building proceeded as well as for new main streets through built-up areas. In Rome the town appears to have had very little control over developments; individual developers did more or less what they wanted, as indeed they also seem to have done in more recent times. The role of the municipality in Berlin remains an open question; implementation appears in any case to have proceeded without any active involvement on the part of the government and to a great extent on the investors' terms. The systematic way in which the grid plan was implemented in Barcelona shows that there must have been some effective control, although the market forces determined the design of the buildings. In Amsterdam, Athens, Christiania and Madrid, the authorities apparently allowed considerable scope for speculative operations to get the plans implemented. England differed from other countries in the strong position of its Parliament, which had a great deal of the responsibility and authority that in other countries belonged to the government. In London the various street projects were handled at first by committees appointed by Parliament; not until 1855 when the Metropolitan Board of Works, predecessor of the London County Council, was established, did the capital city acquire a permanent body for making and implementing town plans. The street improvements received no state financing, but had to be financed out of the municipal revenues and – to a lesser extent – by borrowing. Not even Regent Street was subsidised; it came into being as part of 'normal estate development, paid for out of the ordinary landed revenues'.[3] It should be added, however, that within the London estates there were extensive private planning activities which had no exact parallel in other capital cities.

To summarize: in a few towns active steps were taken to speed up the implementation of a plan, notably in Paris, Vienna, Budapest, Brussels and, to some extent, Stockholm. But generally speaking the authorities were restrained in Europe's capital cities during the second half of the nineteenth century, when it came to active public intervention in the implementation of plans. One of the main reasons for this was certainly the expropriation legislation which disadvantaged the towns; another was the weak legal force of the plans.

The problems confronting those who were responsible for implementing plans in nineteenth-century capital cities could be adminis-

trative, technical, economic or legal. Comparisons of such aspects between the capitals are complicated in that country differences are particularly marked when it comes to administrative frameworks and legal conditions. It is therefore more difficult to make national comparisons here than in the case of general background factors, planning ideas and aesthetic ideals.[4]

Let us look first at the administrative situation (cf. also pp. 267 ff). One fundamental condition for the realization of major planning projects was the presence of an efficient administrative body, appointed by the state or the municipality. In several of the countries discussed here municipal reforms were introduced during the nineteenth century, for example in Prussia in 1808 and 1850, in England in 1835, in France in 1837 (a first reform was carried out as early as 1789, but was soon fatally weakened). In Stockholm, the municipal reform first delayed planning but was at the same time creating an apparatus for its effective implementation. In Vienna, too, the municipal reform of 1860 was probably of some importance to the extension process.

But in the elected decision-making bodies opinions were often deeply divided on matters of fact, and in many instances there was a declared opposition to any extensive municipal intervention, particularly where this might threaten the interests of house- or plot-owners. Moreover, the municipal bodies had limited economic resources at their disposal and few officials to handle the complicated issues that inevitably arose in the implementation of major urban development projects. Consequently implementation was a lengthy process involving many compromises. Brussels, with its active municipal urban development policy, can be said to have deviated to some extent from this rule. The construction of the central boulevards and the redevelopment of the Notre-Dame-aux-Neiges district were implemented entirely on the city's initiative, even though the work itself was put out to private companies. The decisive factor here was probably that the mayor's position in the administration was constitutionally strong, and the office was held at the time by Jules Anspach, a man of unusual energy. In Stockholm, too, implementation proceeded satisfactorily under the auspices of the municipality, once it had started. Otherwise implementation was obviously most efficient when representatives of the state or the various national authorities were responsible for leading the operations, as in Paris, Vienna, Budapest and, at the beginning of the nineteenth century, Helsinki. Here planning and implementation went hand in hand.

Engineering aspects have not been discussed in the present study. It should be pointed out, however, that several of the relevant projects included technically complicated problems and solutions which would have been almost undreamt of a few decades before, such as the sewage system in Paris, the canal tunnel under the Boulevard Richard Lenoir, the covering of the river Senne in Brussels, the traffic tunnel under the Castle Hill in Budapest or the Holborn viaduct in London.

The financing problems were considerable and there were no easy solutions. Street improvements and urban expansion involved the towns in major financial commitments. In principle they were responsible for all the expenses connected with streets, squares and the related facilities, and often for parks as well, despite the consequent increase in land values which fell to the plot-owners along the new streets. In some cases the cost of expropriating land for future streets also had to be met. In order to finance their costs the towns had to rely on taxes and dues, or loans. Paris led the field when it came to taking up loans. In other towns there was a more restrictive attitude, although Stockholm, for example, did take up substantial loans. In some cases, with Paris as the prime example, state support was provided. In Budapest the state lottery funds were used.

Another possibility, as in Paris for example, was to exploit the rise in values in order to cover the costs of implementing the plan. The very existence of a plan often meant that land values rose rapidly, and when a new street was constructed the value of the area, which thus became building land, naturally increased as well. However, the expropriation regulations were aimed largely at protecting private interests, on the one hand by not expropriating more land than was technically necessary for the implementation of a project, and on the other by guaranteeing the victims of expropriation full or sometimes even excess compensation for the market value of the ceded land. The chance of expropriating land at a low price and then selling it as plots was thus slight or non-existent. Another way in which the towns could profit from at least some of the rise in land values when new streets were being constructed, was to demand financial contributions from the plot-owners. This procedure was evidently regarded as less distasteful, and the principle of letting plot-owners contribute to the cost of streets was to become accepted towards the end of the century in several countries. In fact this system reflected earlier praxis, whereby plot-owners had been obliged to help to keep streets accessible to traffic.

In most cases public investment probably covered only a minor proportion of the total cost of the transformation of the cities. All projects were dependent for their implementation on private investment, primarily in housing property. In many places building companies played an important part, sometimes by influencing the planning as in Berlin, Rome and Stockholm, and sometimes by coming in at the implementation stage. In Brussels and Paris private companies were in charge of whole projects, thus operating on the town's behalf and in its stead.

The economic aspects of planning are closely tied up with the legal conditions. What legal force does a plan possess *vis-à-vis* the private individual, and what are the rights of land-owners who are unable to use their land in the way they had intended? Under what circumstances can a landowner be compelled to surrender his land as a result of expropriation, and how should the compensation be determined? And what is the landowner's liability as regards helping to finance measures which are undertaken by the authorities, but which also increase the value of his land, for example the construction of streets? These are the eternal problems of all public planning. What steps were taken to solve them during the period we are discussing here?

Naturally, just like private plot-owners, states or towns could make and even implement whatever plans they wanted, provided – as in Vienna – they owned the land and could therefore include guarantees in the sale that the plans would be followed after the plots were sold. On the other hand, neither state nor municipality, according to the legal principles which seem to have been firmly entrenched in most European states by the middle of the nineteenth century, could make decisions about private property except in ways expressly permitted by law. The ownership of land appears to have been regarded as a particularly inviolable right. And the capital city projects were largely aimed at areas which were not in public ownership.

The building ordinances and regulations which existed in many places in the seventeenth century or even earlier, and which became general in the nineteenth century, implied certain constraints on the basically unlimited right of a property-owner to build as he wished. They provided general stipulations applying to all property, and were probably often rather weak. Planning legislation is more problematic than general building regulations, since a plan interferes more directly in the rights of individual property-owners, and may be advantageous to one person and disadvantageous to another. Plans can also create complicated legal situations between individual

property-owners when plot boundaries are to be changed, and between property-owners and the municipality when land is to be used for streets and public space.

These problems were to some extent new. We have noted that great urban development enterprises were undertaken in many parts of Europe during the seventeenth and eighteenth centuries. New towns and new urban districts were generally established on land which was in public ownership, or which belonged to the prince who decided upon the plan. Ownership of the land thus caused no decisive problems. Street restructuring projects also enjoyed another advantage in that house-owners did not have what we today would call full rights of possession over their plots. Nor, in seventeenth-century Sweden for example, was it ever questioned that house-owners had to accept a redevelopment plan decided by the government; compensation for a plot ceded in this way was essentially limited to the offer of a roughly similar piece of land. In Sweden the new constitution established after the death of Charles XII in 1718, reduced the power of the government, leaving it in a weaker position when it came to implementing schemes for urban development; of the relatively few attempts that were made, fewer still came to anything.[5]

In several German states the planning prerogatives of the princes were evidently reinforced during the seventeenth century. Towards the end of the eighteenth century a process began whereby responsibility for planning was successively transferred to the local authorities. In Prussia the 1794 *Allgemeines Landrecht* gave the local state authority, namely the police, the right to indicate *Fluchtlinien*, i.e. the boundaries of areas which were to be reserved for streets. After the Prussian municipal reform of 1808 the *Baupolizei* became accountable to the municipal administration (with the important exception of Berlin), which thus also became responsible for the planning function.[6] This right to indicate and maintain street boundaries had long been regarded as particularly important; in the Middle Ages perhaps the most important task for the municipal building control function was to prevent building on street land.

In France too these boundary lines – the *alignements* – were assigned great importance. As far back as the reign of Henri IV a stipulation was issued according to which building permission was required for erecting buildings along traffic thoroughfares. This regulation was reinforced during the last decades of the *ancien régime* in a remarkably progressive building code for Paris, and was subsequently included in a law enacted by Napoleon in 1807, empowering all towns to draw up plans which were to indicate the desired *alignements* for all urban areas, even those not yet built. However, the municipal right to indicate the land for streets in areas intended for exploitation was never very important, partly because the courts disallowed the law.[7]

Thus the legal conditions affecting the planning of cities towards the middle of the nineteenth century were both weak and unclear, and imbued with the liberal view that the authorities should interfere as little as possible with the right of individuals to control their own property. Around this time, however, some improvements were made. In 1845 the *Baupolizei* in Prussia were given greater responsibility, including the supervision of plot layout, and the right to refuse building permission in certain cases; ten years later the towns were given the main responsibility for producing plans for urban expansion. The next important step was the 1875 law on street boundary lines (*Fluchtlinien-Gesetz*) which ratified the right and the duty of towns to produce expansion plans and gave them the authority to expropriate land for future streets. Further, a principle was adopted whereby plot-owners were to contribute to the cost of a planned street. Most of the German states soon followed suit, and adopted similar regula-

tions.[8] Italy acquired a planning tool in 1865, namely the *piano regolatore*, which referred primarily to existing structures, and the *piano di ampliamento* for expansions.[9]

In England there was no equivalent in the nineteenth century to the German or French legislation in the field of planning. When new urban areas were to be built, plans showing street and plot divisions were generally made on the initiative of the developers; the weakness, according to Sutcliffe, was that no one was responsible for constructing broad through roads. It should also be emphasized that considerable efforts were made in different local bodies to improve the sanitary standard, particularly after the 1848 Public Health Act and through slum clearances. On the whole, Sutcliffe stresses, the English urban environment was not inferior to the continental but was in fact rather better, depending among other things on the fact that wages in England were considerably higher.[10]

The Swedish 1874 building ordinances included a chapter on town plans; we have already noted that several of its stipulations about the making of town plans were ahead of their time. However, the problem of the legal force of the plans was dodged – although Albert Lindhagen, the author of the ordinances, was a prominent member of the legal profession – apart from one weak stipulation that 'a town may not be built in conflict with prevailing plans, nor expanded into areas for which there is no ratified plan'.[11] The town plans approved and ratified for Stockholm in 1879 and 1880 implied no compelling injunction on the property owners concerned, but represented rather a kind of statement of the will of the town. In principle the town apparently had the right to refuse building permission for projects in conflict with the plan, but not even this passive right went undisputed. Moreover, prevailing attitudes were marked to a great extent by the idea that the government – national or local – should interfere as little as possible in the right of private individuals to dispose of their own property. If the introduction of the building ordinances encouraged the completion of the planning operation in Stockholm, then the difficulty in implementing it was probably the most important reason why Sweden finally acquired a planning act in 1907.[12] However, this act like its later successors had negative force only: it could forbid building in any way other than that indicated in the plan, but could not impose implementation.

In the later nineteenth and early twentieth century it was customary for plans to possess only this kind of passive legal force.[13] In such a situation a town could proceed in one of two ways once a plan had been decided upon: either it could wait and hope that the plan would be realized as a result of unforced renewal, i.e. by voluntary clearances and new building undertaken by the house- and plot-owners concerned at the pace they deemed appropriate, which was an uncertain and time-consuming way of proceeding; or the town could invest actively in the implementation itself. In this last case it was difficult to avoid making extensive land acquisitions, and the possibility of expropriations – and the rules for calculating expropriation compensation – thus became a question of central importance. And, as we have seen, they generally ended up to the disadvantage of the towns.

The difficulties were thus enormous. What, then, did the results look like? 'Results' can be expressed in three ways: how far was the plan actually realized, how far did it achieve the goals intended, and what were the other effects – positive or negative – of its implementation? Here let us look at the question of the actual realization of the capital city plans described above.

First it has to be remembered that radical changes and simplifications were often introduced between the first proposals and the ratified plans. This was the case in Amsterdam, Copenhagen, Rome, Stockholm and Vienna. Hobrecht's project for Berlin and Cerdá's for Barcelona, on the other hand, were decided without any fundamental changes having been made; the same applied to Ehrenström's plan for Helsinki, Castro's plan for Madrid, Schaubert and Kleanthes's and Klenze's plans for Athens and the project for the central boulevards in Brussels.

In the course of implementation further modifications were sometimes introduced, as was the case in Athens and Vienna. Or a town might abstain from demanding realization of a plan, accepting instead changes suggested by the plot-owners or even allowing the plan to be disregarded altogether. This seems to have been the case to a greater or lesser degree in Berlin, Christiania and Madrid. The Viviani plan for Rome was only partly realized; the same applies to Cerdá's plan for Barcelona, even though his project clearly left its mark on the block and street structure in the *ensanche*, the new urban area. In Budapest the plan completed in 1872 seems to have been realized, albeit with certain revisions and adjustments as regards details; here the role of the city's General Board of Works was a powerful obstacle to changes in the plan. In Brussels the plans for the central boulevards and for the Notre-Dame-aux-Neiges district were implemented relatively quickly and systematically, with only a few minor deviations. In Stockholm the plans ratified in 1879 and 1880 were realized with only fairly small changes, which seems paradoxical in view of the severe conflicts during the decision phase. But perhaps it was felt that the lengthy discussions in the 1870s must have aired all the problems pretty thoroughly. In Copenhagen, too, the plans as finally ratified seem to have been fully implemented. Paris is a special case, since there was no ratified plan. Planning and implementation went hand in hand. However, most of the streets planned by the Emperor and Haussmann were realized during the Second Empire or in the decades immediately following. Two conclusions can be drawn from all this. One, not very surprisingly, is that plans which have been worked over and discussed before being ratified were generally realized more consistently than plans decided in a hurry. The other is that respect for ratified plans tended to increase during the later decades of the century. There is a definite down period as regards the effective force of the plans after the sovereign planning of the pre-industrial society and before the emergence of 'modern' planning during the later nineteenth century.

However, there is nothing unique or unnatural about making changes in plans. It does not in itself imply failure; rather, it is a natural consequence of the fact that planning situations change and developments do not stand still.

In planning it is always difficult to assess how far goals have been fulfilled. The execution of a major project is generally a time-consuming undertaking, and the age that experiences the finished product is often different from the one that commissioned it, with other values, problems and technical conditions. Added to which, the unintended effects are often every bit as important as the intended ones. Further, in the case of the capital city projects there were few explicit goal descriptions; the goals were obvious to all those involved and did not have to be spelled out. I shall not attempt any systematic evaluation of the separate projects here. But if one sweeping generalization can be allowed, it must surely be that, on the whole, the capital city projects did fulfil the expectations harboured by their progenitors.

To sum up: nineteenth-century planning took place during a time of expansion and extensive building. There was thus theoretically an opportunity for giving considered shape to large areas. But the legal instruments for controlling developments were weak, and planning itself was not established as a special field of knowledge. Moreover the resources at the disposal of the towns, in terms of both finances and personnel, were still meagre. Development often went its own way; and yet planning clearly helped to create more rational and more healthy environments.

NOTES

1. Planning historians have generally paid less attention to the implementation phase than to the planning phase. The execution of the plans for Vienna, which is discussed in several parts of *Die Wiener Ringstraße*, is an exception in this respect. The implementation process in Paris has also been addressed by several authors, in the first instance Pinkney (1957 and 1958), but in a relatively general way.
2. This way of tackling street-improvement projects was to have many imitators in other towns. A recent example of this has been the redevelopment of Stockholm CBD between the 1950s and 1970s, which in several ways is a striking parallel to Haussmann's regulations in Paris (see Hall, 1985).
3. Dyos (1957), pp. 261 ff; according to Tyack, though, 'the government found itself having to foot most of the bill' (1992, p. 45).
4. This section should be seen as a rather impressionistic and free-hand sketch of the problems of implementing plans, based on the overall picture that emerges from the material presented here. Almost inevitably the Swedish experience has provided the screen through which the other countries are viewed. But it is remarkable to note that, however much the administrative frames and legal solutions may vary, the fundamental problems are in many ways the same everywhere.
5. See Hall (1991), pp. 170 ff.
6. Sutcliffe (1981*b*), pp. 10 ff.
7. *Ibidem*, pp. 127 ff.
8. *Ibidem*, pp. 17 ff. Detailed reviews of the *baupolizeiliche* stipulations are provided in Baumeister (1876), pp. 246 ff and Stübben (1890), pp. 70 ff; this last includes a number of ordinances, among them the above-mentioned *Fluchtlinien-Gesetz* of 1875: 'Prussian law regarding the making and changing of streets and squares in towns and urban settlements' (pp. 520 ff).
9. Calabi (1980), p. 57.
10. Sutcliffe (1981*b*), pp. 48 ff; see also Ashworth (1954) and Cherry (1980). Fraser (1979) provides a description of the complex structure of British local government (see his treatment of the 'improvement question' in Liverpool on pp. 26 ff).

11. *Kungl. byggnadsstadga* (1874), § 9. However, the building ordinances were issued by the government and were not the subject of a joint decision by the *Riksdag* and the government together and could not therefore affect the rights which the property owners enjoyed according to civil law. This meant that, when the government approved a town plan, it regularly made the reservation that the plan should serve as a guideline, so long as it did not encroach on any person's legal rights. Furthermore, the government weakened its own statute by granting generous dispensations (Hall (1984), pp. 180 ff and (1991), pp. 179 f).

12. The difficulty in implementing the plans led Moritz Rubenson, secretary to the Stockholm City Council for many years and briefly also a member of parliament, to urge the *Riksdag* in 1884 to consider a new planning act. The *Riksdag* agreed and the government appointed an investigatory committee which recommended an act. Among other things it would not be permitted to build on land which, according to a ratified town plan, was to provide land for streets; in the case of new exploitations plot-owners were either to cede land for streets at no cost or were to contribute to the street-related expenses. This was a radical proposal for nineteenth-century Sweden, and it never became a government bill. Only after further urging and more committees and reports did Sweden acquire a town planning law in 1907 which forbade building in conflict with the town plan, and made it mandatory on the affected plot-owners to contribute to the cost of land for streets. Furthermore the opportunity was provided for creating stipulations regarding the design of buildings (Hall (1984), pp. 121 ff).

13. During the twentieth century all countries in Western Europe have probably acquired planning legislation which gives particular legal force to plans approved according to certain specified procedures. But even today, in the Nordic countries at any rate, plans have negative legal force: they imply prohibitions against building in ways other than those indicated in the plan but no obligation to implement the plan. If the municipality wants a plan to be implemented and, for reasons of his own interest a property-owner does not comply, it is up to the municipality in some way or another to make implementation of the plan attractive to the property-owner. The only way for the municipality to enforce the implementation of the plan is to take over the property concerned by purchasing or expropriating it.

25

The Role of the Capital City Projects in Planning History

In a discussion of the status and importance of the capital city projects in the context of general planning history, the following are some of the questions that should be raised:

● What was the relation between the capital city projects and earlier planning traditions?

● To what extent did the capital city projects influence one another? Is there any common denominator? Can we speak of a special type of 'capital city planning'?

● Are the capital city projects the precursors or successors of other urban projects in their respective countries? To what extent were they influenced by previous and contemporary undertakings, and to what extent have they acted as textbook examples since?

● What impact have the capital city projects had on the evolution of 'modern' town planning?

Let us start with the first point. In chapter 2 we saw that an analysis of pre-industrial town planning can usefully start from a classification of plans into three types: rectilinear grid planning, ideal city planning, and local design planning. The first category refers to a type of urban foundation and extension pattern which has existed at least since the thirteenth century, albeit to a greater or lesser extent at different times and in different regions. The aim in such cases has generally been to create straight streets intersecting at right angles, and homogeneous rectangular blocks, which in turn can be divided into uniform plots. This type of planning has not usually concerned itself with the shape or design of the buildings, which have generally been realized in accordance with simple standardized solutions. The land was generally entirely at the disposal of the particular founder which meant that planning involved no legal problems.

During the fifteenth century the question of urban development began to be discussed in a theoretical perspective. A number of projects for 'ideal cities' reveal sophisticated plan designs, in which architecturally conceived features often play an important part. There are only occasional examples of towns built entirely in accordance with ideal city conceptions, but the projects nonetheless left their mark on other town plans of a more modest kind, where the rectangular street network provides the basic structure.

From the sixteenth century onwards, and sometimes earlier, a type of local design planning began to emerge, with the creation of monumental accents such as squares, or the insertion of a building into an architectural ensemble.

As the chapters on the different cities have shown, the nineteenth-century capital city projects appear in many respects as the continuation of earlier planning traditions with similar goals, methods and solutions. Thus the fundamental principles were still the desire for rectilinearity, straight streets and uniform blocks. As before, little interest was paid to what happened inside the plot boundaries; this was regarded as essentially the plot-owner's business. Squares were conceived largely in accordance with earlier ideas about planning of monumental ensembles. In some cases, particularly in Paris, the achievements of the nineteenth century can even be seen as the direct continuation and completion of earlier projects. Nor did the two main ways of implementing the capital city projects, namely laying out streets and blocks on vacant land or redeveloping previously heavy built areas, involve anything fundamentally new. At one point in his memoirs – significantly enough, in a discussion of the sewage system – Haussmann declares with intentionally exaggerated modesty: 'We have invented nothing new . . . We are simply imitators. Our only merit is that we have dared to challenge the future, despite the scorn poured upon us and the obstructions of ignorance and habit (and worse still, of empty science!), to ensure the cleansing of the Cité-reine, the Rome Impériale of our times'[1] – a declaration that can serve to describe the relation of the capital city projects in general to earlier planning.

But the differences between the achievements of the nineteenth century and those of previous centuries in terms of planning and urban development are also striking, particularly as regards the scale of the problems and the scope of the projects. The whole urban structure is different; the blocks are larger and the streets broader. New elements include tree-planted streets and parks, not as isolated ceremonial markers, but as standard components in the urban milieu. Technological development brought new types of problems, but it also provided new opportunities for improving life in the cities. Sanitary and technical aspects came to play an increasingly important role; the laying out of blocks and streets was treated as part of a comprehensive municipal programme that embraced water and sewage facilities, embankments and bridges and, ultimately, more adequate housing. We cannot include all this under the heading of 'planning', but the need to co-ordinate the efforts of several different bodies and interests was a fundamental condition for the change in the role and content of planning, which was to take place around the end of the century.

As regards the legal force of the plans, the picture is not altogether clear-cut. New and more detailed building ordinances were in fact issued in many places, and the activities of the building authorities were made more efficient. But this sort of development constantly came up against the restrictive liberal attitude towards public interference and the great respect in which private property was held. In practice all this tended to reduce the legal force of the plans.[2] Moreover, the decision process took much longer when everything had to be done in municipal assemblies, than when princes made all the decisions. A comparison between planning in Helsinki around 1810–20 and later during the 1870s reveals this very clearly. The answer to our first main question regarding the relation between the capital city projects and earlier planning traditions, is thus that despite a certain obvious continuity a number of new problems arose and new features appeared.

Let us proceed to the second point and discuss the extent to which the capital city projects influenced one another. First it should be remembered that the nineteenth century was a time of rapid internationalization. Around the middle of the century railways and steamboats were transforming travel between countries or between capital cities into a matter of days rather than weeks or months. Developments in the graphic industry made it possible to disseminate information on a scale infinitely greater than before. The famous Great Exhibition in London in 1851 proved to be the prelude to a whole series of manifestations of a similar kind.[3] In the later decades of the century exhibitions, congresses and international organizations proliferated.

The growing opportunities for exchanging information were accompanied by a change in attitudes; science and professional activities were also becoming internationalized. It was now the natural thing to investigate the way problems were being solved in other countries. This came to apply to some extent also to urban development. In Vienna, for example, at an early stage in the planning of the Ringstraße around the beginning of 1858, instructions went out to the imperial legations in Berlin, Hamburg, London, Munich and Paris and to the general consul in Frankfurt, to submit reports on the organisation and implementation of urban development activities in connection with expansion projects in those towns.[4]

The results of this enquiry do not seem to have made much impact on the future development of the Ringstraße project. Nor, over the next few decades, was town planning a particularly important field as regards organized international cooperation. The real breakthrough did not appear until after the turn of the century, when, for instance, the first international conference to be devoted to planning questions was held in 1910. Urban development problems were of course discussed before this date at architectural congresses or social housing conferences, and even earlier at meetings addressing medical, hygienic or demographic topics, but then only in passing and as a side issue.[5] The picture is the same in the world of books and professional journals,[6] i.e. it was not until the end of the century that publications on our present theme began to appear in any great numbers. We shall return to this point below. Here it is sufficient to note that Reinhard Baumeister's book published in 1876 – *Stadt-Erweiterungen in technischer, baupolizeilicher und wirthschaftlicher Beziehung* – was an important starting-point. Before this, there had been some publications on the technicalities of urban development, such as water and sewage systems, but little on any aspects of planning proper.[7]

Although no special planning congresses were arranged or journals published, hundreds of thousands of visitors to the capital cities could see the results of the planning projects for themselves at the world exhibitions and the international congresses that sometimes accompanied them; here too the emergence of mass tourism played a part. Street improvements and the elegant new districts in many towns were often noted in the numerous newspapers and leisure journals that were now available. The chief focus of this interest was of course Paris. In time for the 1855 World Exhibition the first new streets had been opened and the Bois de Boulogne completed; the most prominent visitor, Queen Victoria, allowed Haussmann to name a street after her (Avenue Victoria). Events in Paris after this would certainly have been followed with great interest in many quarters. The new streets and parks and buildings, the dazzling festivities and public arrangements, the abundance and variety of the cultural life of the town and the innumerable offerings of entertainment and luxury, all combined to give Paris its special image as the great international metropolis.[8]

All this helped to spread knowledge of the public works in Paris and to establish Haussmann's position as an international authority on urban development. In Sweden, on the periphery of Europe, the urban development activities in Paris were referred to in a parliamentary debate as early as 1857.[9] Haussmann tells us in his memoirs that during a visit to Italy in 1870 after his retirement, he was sought out by a financial magnate (whose name he did not wish to mention), who was in the process of creating 'a great Company to transform Rome in the same way as Paris'. He suggested that Haussmann should take over 'the presidency of this Society', which the Frenchman declined to do. However,

Haussmann promised 'to show on a plan of the Eternal City, all parts of which I have carefully studied, those places where it would be practical to pierce the network of narrow tortuous streets running over rough and broken ground, which seem to me capable of best improving the traffic between the different districts.'[10] It is not known whether this promise was kept, but it seems likely that the whole thing petered out – fortunately, one is tempted to say. The episode is interesting, however, not only because it confirms Haussmann's reputation, but also because it shows that he was not averse to considering tasks of pure planning.

How important, then, was the great planning enterprise in Paris as a stimulus to others? In more general terms Haussmann's projects may have helped to turn the attention of other cities to the idea of extensive urban development activities. It is not unlikely for instance that the example of Paris may have hastened the development of the *glacis* area of Vienna, although this would have occurred anyway, if perhaps a little later. It is less certain that the street cuttings in Paris had any influence on the authorities in Prussia or Berlin. Hobrecht would probably have been given his commission in 1858, even if Haussmann had never existed. In Stockholm, too, it was population growth and new demands on the city's structure that provided the impetus behind the planning; at any rate there is no evidence that events in Paris were an instigating factor of real importance. The situation was apparently the same in Copenhagen, as well as in Madrid and Barcelona. Paris may have had a greater impact in the case of Rome and Budapest; neither of these new capital cities were particularly impressive in their physical character, and it would have seemed natural to regard the transformation of Paris as a challenge, particularly as planning in these cities did not begin until after the great Paris exhibition in 1867 when Haussmann's work was well advanced; it was then that visitors from all over Europe could admire the new boulevards and avenues

and that the status of Paris as a model was definitely established.

Napoleon III and Haussmann were obviously significant figures in urban development, but the great enterprises in the other capitals were triggered by contemporary events and would certainly have come about even without Paris showing the way. Naturally, however, other capital cities may nonetheless have learnt certain specific lessons from the experience of Paris. To what extent, then, did the concrete solutions and methods employed there provide ideas and norms for other capital cities?

We have seen how the problems and conditions varied very much from one capital city to another, and that planning around the middle of the nineteenth century in many respects followed earlier traditions. Thus the planners had no need to turn to Paris for their solutions, and anyway Haussmann's planning principles could not be applied to other places just as they were. Moreover, work on the planning of Barcelona began in the middle of the 1850s; Berlin and Vienna started in 1858, while planning began seriously in Stockholm in 1863. It is not altogether easy to find out just how much concrete information people in the different cities would have had about Haussmann's urban development project at the relevant dates. It has to be remembered, too, that no official plan existed for the work in Paris which had barely begun at the end of the 1850s, and that our present-day knowledge of Haussmann's intentions is based to a large extent on his memoirs which were not published until the 1890s.

To take Vienna first: it is obvious that the situation there was fundamentally different from that in Paris, and the solutions were naturally different too. While in Paris it was a question of constructing streets by piercing old blocks, in Vienna there was unbuilt land waiting to be exploited. The idea of having a ring road certainly derived from the *grands boulevards*, but long before the Second Empire. Perhaps the Bois de Boulogne and the other great parks in Paris may have been one source of inspiration for the emphasis on parkland in Vienna; but against this is the fact that the utilization of the *glacis* region as a green area was an old tradition.[11] And when it came to the design of the various details in the urban structure such as parks and squares, it would be difficult to prove any direct Parisian influence. Thus, if the design of the Ringstraße area was influenced at all by the more or less contemporary planning activities in the French capital, the effect was very slight.

Several writers have claimed that the Hobrecht plan for Berlin was based on Haussmann's planning work in Paris. 'The model was Haussmann's plan for Paris' says Thienel, for example.[12] This is a debatable point on several counts. First, in 1858 there was, as we have seen, no public or generally known plan for the redevelopments in Paris. Nor are there any indications that Hobrecht was interested in planning questions before he was commissioned to produce a plan for Berlin; it therefore seems unlikely that he would have known much about what was happening in the French capital. Secondly, in Berlin it was a question not of clearances in the centre, but of exploiting virgin ground. Moreover, such similarities as do exist between the Hobrecht plan and the new street system in Paris are relatively general and non-specific. If we disregard the ring boulevard at the periphery which came about as a result of a royal directive, the rather unstructured street network suggested by Hobrecht lacks a system of principal streets of the type that Haussmann created in Paris.

Hobrecht seems to have intended monumental buildings to be located as visual markers at the end of the major streets, in particular the different sections of the ring boulevard, and focal accents were of course also an essential ingredient in Haussmann's urban development programme. But this does not necessarily mean, as has sometimes been suggested, that Hobrecht was influenced by Haussmann. The

desire to create visual accents at the termination of long axial streets was not specific to Paris; it had been a recurring theme in urban development programmes ever since the Renaissance. Examples of the same kind of thinking can be found even in earlier planning in Berlin itself. When it comes to the design of squares the Hobrecht plan offers several variants, some of which might look Parisian; but Hobrecht had inspiration closer to hand in Berlin's own great monumental squares – Pariser Platz, Leipziger Platz and Belle-Alliance-Platz (now Mehringplatz) – although these in their turn go back to French models. Star-shaped places also appear in the Berlin project, but they lack the same role as those in Haussmann's Paris. In other words there is little point in seeing Hobrecht as a kind of Haussmann epigone. He continued the type of *Fluchtlinienplanung* (see pp. 339 f) which had long been applied in German towns, albeit on a larger scale and with a few little accents here and there which could have been derived from some of the seventeenth-century districts in Berlin. In so far as we want to look for more immediate models, the projects for the Köpenicker Feld lies closer to hand than Haussmann's work in Paris.[13]

Cerdá visited Paris in 1856 to study the construction of the railway there, and was greatly interested in the current improvements. Perhaps in his Barcelona plan we can discern the influence of Haussmann in the streets that cut ruthlessly through the old town, but not in the *ensanche*. Cerdá also emerges as a strikingly independent thinker. His goal was to create a model for the future, not to copy something already in existence. It also seems unlikely that the example of Paris had any influence on Castro's plan for Madrid, since he makes no mention of Haussmann's projects in his comprehensive commentary.[14]

As far as the Lindhagen plan for Stockholm is concerned, the situation is more complicated. The system of broad and absolutely straight streets which cut relentlessly through the old built area, would hardly have been envisaged without some knowledge of the street constructions in Paris; the Lindhagen Committee's project for Sveavägen can be seen as a Stockholm version of the Boulevard de Sébastopol. The two star-shaped 'squares' also recall Paris; if we want to stretch the comparison a little, we could say that their location in the urban structure more or less corresponds to that of the Place Charles de Gaulle and the Place de la Nation. Lindhagen must surely have been impressed by the work that was under way in Paris when he visited the town in 1860, just before he became involved in the planning of Stockholm. But too much should not be made of the influence of Paris. The Lindhagen plan was primarily an expansion project. Neither Haussmann nor Paris are even mentioned in the comprehensive commentary attached to the plan (on the other hand Paris was sometimes cited in the debate on the plan in the town council during the 1870s). Some such mention would have seemed natural, if the authors had considered they were following the same principles as Haussmann; Napoleon III and Haussmann still stood high in the general regard when the Lindhagen plan was published in 1866. Planning in Finland probably had as much if not more importance as a model for Lindhagen, which also indirectly meant Russian planning from the late eighteenth and early nineteenth centuries.

In the case of Brussels the influence of Paris is more obvious. In location and function the central boulevard through the *ville basse* between the railway stations Gare du Nord and Gare du Midi recalls the Boulevard de Sébastopol. Anspach certainly also saw himself as a Belgian Haussmann; he even asked the Paris Prefect for advice. The many parks and straight streets with their focal accents which were laid out during the last decade of the century outside the central city, are quite in line with Haussmann's aesthetic programme, as are the projects for the inner town supported by Leopold II.[15] However, the conditions and problems were quite different from those in

Paris; the French capital's importance as a model was hardly relevant when it came to details; it remained on a more general level. Van Niftrik's plan for Amsterdam does not have much in common with Haussmann's project, but would have involved a huge investment on the part of the town. In the debate on the plan in the municipal council, one of the reasons given for not accepting it was that the municipality did not have the same powers 'as a certain prefect on the Seine'.[16]

The direct influence of Paris might seem more likely in the case of our last two capital city projects, namely Budapest and Rome. And few if any of the capital city streets that were actually built outside France appear to correspond so closely to Haussmann's ideals in both location and design as the 'Radial road' in Budapest, the Andrássy út of today. Admittedly the great visual marker, the Millennium Monument, was not envisaged from the start, but some kind of building as a background to the street was presumably intended. Further, the ring road – the Nagykörút – corresponds fairly closely in both function and design to the inner boulevard ring in Paris, even though it has not been systematically completed on the west side of the Danube. As in Paris an outer ring, the Hungária körút, was also planned, together with several radial streets. In the old urban core a number of street-widening projects were considered, parts of which required extensive demolitions. Planning and implementation in Budapest would most likely have won Haussmann's approval. Probably Paris, at any rate on a general level, was something of an inspiration for planning in Budapest, just as the General Board of Works in the Hungarian capital was inspired by the Metropolitan Board of Works in London. Political reasons may have been one of the factors explaining why Budapest looked for ideals elsewhere than in Vienna. But the problems calling for solutions were also partly of a different kind.

In Rome the first plan proposal, the project of the Camporesi Committee, showed clear signs of Haussmann's grand scale and uncompromising approach; in the subsequent and more realistic plans the visionary element was replaced by adjustments to both topography and existing buildings, and to what was regarded as politically and economically possible. Of Haussmann's programme and aesthetic there were no longer many traces. The only street actually built that recalls Haussmann is the Via Nazionale, laid out on land that was previously largely unbuilt; but although it starts in a monumental fashion at the Piazza della Repubblica, it finishes rather ignominiously without any proper extension through the old urban structure.

Thus it seems that planning in Paris had only a minor influence on the planning solutions of other capital cities.[17] Its influence is most evident in Brussels and Budapest, although traces can also be discerned in Stockholm, for instance.[18] On the other hand it is probable that the street cuttings undertaken at a later stage in Berlin, Madrid and Vienna among others – without any direct link with the overall projects discussed here – may have been inspired in a general way by the street developments in Paris, albeit realized in a less uncompromising manner.

If at first the great urban development projects in Paris stood alone as the focus of European interest, they soon acquired a rival in the Ringstraße in Vienna, which also attracted a good deal of attention. Just as Paris had created a 'school' when it came to streets cutting through earlier structures, the development of Vienna's *glacis* area was seen as a model for similar undertakings. Nonetheless Vienna seems to have made little real impact on planning in the other capital cities. Apart from Vienna, the only towns of those studied here with similar *glacis* areas available were Amsterdam, Barcelona and Copenhagen, although Vienna's conditions were unique due to the vast suburban districts beyond the fortification area. Towards the end of the 1850s planning activities in Vienna and Barcelona

were proceeding at much the same time, albeit without any apparent contact between the two; the results were a plan for Vienna ratified in 1859 and one for Barcelona ratified in 1860 – two plans which on almost every count were each other's opposite. In Copenhagen, too, planning issues were being discussed in the late 1850s, but there was no ratified plan until 1872. Obviously the relevant actors in Copenhagen would have noted what was happening in Vienna, and this probably had certain implications for the final proposal. However, the solutions were rather different, and it is hard to identify any direct influence, except that the 'Voldgadene' might not have been built in the location ultimately chosen, without the inspiration of the Ringstraße. Van Niftrik's plan for the fortification area in Amsterdam reveals certain general features in common with the *Grundplan* for Vienna, particularly the many parks. A number of public buildings were also proposed, but compared with the *Grundplan*, van Niftrik's plan seems rather muddled and the ring road has none of the importance or dimensions of the Viennese Ringstraße.

Paris and Vienna are in a class of their own. The other projects provoked far less interest and had hardly any effect on one another. Not even the most systematic enterprise in any of our towns, namely Cerdá's planning proposal for Barcelona, appears to have been noted by the planners in any of the capital cities apart from Madrid. London is perhaps something of a special case. The town had a good deal of experience of street improvements and related technicalities, even though the various projects were not executed in the same dramatic sweep as in Paris, but were spread out over time. It would have been strange if no attempt had been made in the other capital cities to benefit from London's experience. It was certainly no coincidence that an English company was called in to lay out the central boulevard in Brussels, nor that Budapest established a board based on the Metropolitan Board of Works. But London's possible importance as a

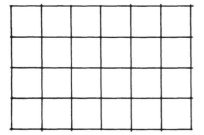 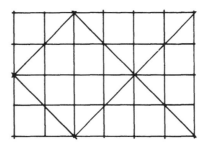 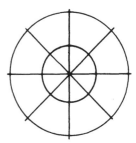

Figure 25.1 *It is perhaps possible to identify three archetypal urban street patterns: the consistently rectangular plan, the rectangular plan with diagonal main streets, and the radial plan. As has been seen, pure rectangular solutions have predominated in all periods of planned urban development, at least until the end of the nineteenth century. The radial plan launched by Renaissance theorists was only realized in a few cases, mostly in typical fortified towns. In a number of city projects during the nineteenth century, however, the same basic principle was to be applied, although on a much larger scale, by means of ring boulevards and radial exit roads. Diagonal avenues in a more or less regular rectangular street network were either planned from the beginning or were later additions – often with distinctive focal accents – when an enhanced aesthetic effect and/or a more functional standard was desired. One major influence was the regularization of streets in Rome in the sixteenth century, another was Wren's 1666 plan for London. This third type of plan can be seen as an attempt to combine the advantages of the rectangular and the radial plans.*

model seems to have been limited mainly to the execution rather than the actual design of the plans – except, perhaps, as regards the influence of its parks.

It thus seems that the different capital city projects influenced one another less than might have been expected. The features which the capital city projects had in common were in fact typical of most contemporary schemes. It is hardly possible to identify anything we could call 'capital city planning' as such, unless we mean by that the greater splendour and the imposing ensembles which were natural to the important parts of such cities, or to areas devoted to government and other significant public buildings.[19] The main reasons for this are the dissimilar local conditions, and the fact that there were as yet no specialists in 'town planning', who could systematically study and compare different solutions.

To turn now to the third of the points raised at the beginning of this chapter: what position did the capital city projects occupy in the development of urban planning in the respective countries? It is difficult to provide a well-founded and exhaustive answer to this question, mainly because little knowledge is available on the subject of urban development in various countries (although the state of scholarship varies from country to country). In most cases there was some activity in the way of planned urban expansions and the redevelopment of existing urban structures, always alongside extensive 'spontaneous' and unplanned urban growth. Very often, the railway was an important factor; the location of the station generated new districts and new streets leading into the centre of the towns, or in some cases involved a displacement of the city centre.

Let us take a brief look at these activities. In France uninhibited urban growth seems to have been the usual pattern in the larger cities.[20] Only a few new towns were founded: Pontivy and La Roche-sur-Yon during the First Empire, and the seaside resorts of Trouville and Cabourg, for example, during the Second.

PLANNING EUROPE'S CAPITAL CITIES

The plans are fairly traditional, apart from Cabourg which has a fan shape, although it is not as consistently applied as in Motala in Sweden.

There were probably no very significant redevelopments in the provincial towns prior to the big undertakings in Paris. During the Second Empire and the period immediately afterwards, however, *percées* of the same type as in Paris were carried out in several other towns such as Avignon, Lyons, Marseilles, Montpellier, Rouen and Toulouse. 'Several *rues Impériales* or *rues de l'Impératrice* were built,' writes Lavedan, 'which later became *rues de la République* or were given the name of some determined opponent of the Empire.'[21] These activities took place at the same time as the improvements in Paris; the impetus, as in the capital, was obviously Napoleon's ambition to be seen as a vigorous and enterprising ruler, while also creating jobs by launching great public projects. We should therefore be cautious of talking about 'Haussmannization' or describing Paris as the model for improvements elsewhere. Any resemblance in the results was probably due to the prevalence of common ideas and conditions, rather than to any conscious imitation of Paris. However, the improvements in the capital city must have served to encourage investment in similar projects in the provincial towns (figure 25.2).

How influential was the example of Paris in other countries, if we consider town planning as a whole, and not just planning in capital cities? Wurzer considers the French capital to be of 'exemplary importance' in Germany and even in Europe, but he makes no real attempt to support this statement.[22] However, streets which break through existing blocks according to the Haussmann model can certainly be found in many towns – a striking example is the Corso Umberto I in Naples[23] – although some caution should be exercised in invoking a direct influence. The lesson learnt from Paris may have been primarily the idea of thinking big and being bold; it was then presumably a case

of having to solve the economic, legal and design problems in appropriate ways in the different countries. What is quite certain, however, is that the French capital as it finally emerged from the projects of the Second Empire, served as a source of inspiration for the American City Beautiful Movement, and thus for planners such as Daniel Burnham, Charles McKim and Frederick Law Olmsted. The French *École des Beaux Arts* tradition enjoyed a long period of influence in American architectural circles, and the inspiration of Paris can be discerned for instance in the plans for Chicago, Philadelphia and Washington (cf. pp. 332 f).[24]

In terms of towns in general rather than capital cities, how much importance did Vienna have as a model, both inside and outside the Austrian Empire? Towards the end of the eighteenth century it began to be widely recognized that towns were not suitable as fortresses (cf. p. 267). The Emperor Joseph II decided to abandon the ramparts in Graz and in the towns of the Austrian Netherlands. In Graz it was decided in 1784 to lay out tree-planted promenades in the area of the old defence works, and similar ideas were adopted in the Netherlands. The Napoleonic wars demonstrated the ineffectiveness of the old fortifications, and in some cases Napoleon decided, for example in Brussels, to raze the ramparts to the ground. At the beginning of the nineteenth century a belt of parks was laid out in Bremen on the land formerly occupied by the fortifications, and the moats were transformed into artificial lakes (figure 25.3a). Similar projects were carried out in Frankfurt and several other towns.[25] A street encircling the old urban structure and the expansion of the built area were recurring elements in such enterprises. Gothenburg, where as far back as 1807 town and government agreed on the demolition of the ramparts, provides an early example outside Germany. When a town plan by the city architect Carl Wilhelm Carlberg was ratified the following year, it was decided that

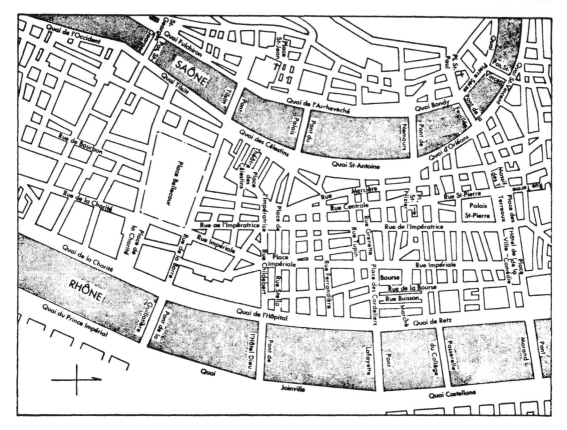

Figure 25.2 *Lyons. Contemporary with Haussmann's public works in Paris a similar programme was being implemented in Lyons under the direction of the Prefect, Claude Marius Vaïsse. As in Paris, the measures concerned water supply, sewage systems, quays and so on, but the most spectacular feature consisted of the two new streets, Rue de l'Impératrice and Rue Impériale, cutting through the slums in the centre. Similar streets were built in a number of other French towns; in Toulouse the new streets form a* grande croisée *of the Parisian type. [From Leonard (1961)]*

a tree-lined boulevard should be laid out in the *glacis* area; it is still an important element in central Gothenburg today (figure 25.3*b*).

The Ringstraße project in Vienna was thus by no means the first example but was certainly the most noted urban scheme of this kind. However, the situation in Vienna was exceptional, owing to the demand for an imperial setting with suitable sites for monumental public buildings, but also because of the wealth of funds available and the need to link the

central city with extensive suburban areas. Vienna was in a unique situation in urban development history, namely that of suddenly being able to double the size of its centre – an extraordinary opportunity which was also exploited in an extraordinary way.

After Vienna, the planning and building of areas formerly occupied by defence works became a feature of several towns, e.g. Brünn (1860), Salzburg (1861), Augsburg (1862), Stettin (1873), Mainz (1875), Nuremberg

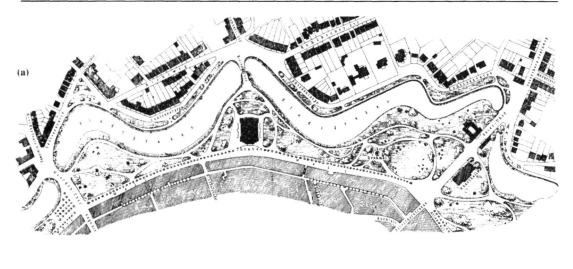

Figure 25.3 *One of the chief issues connected with urban development in Europe in the later decades of the eighteenth century and for a hundred years or so afterwards, concerned the use of land that became available for civil purposes as a result of the abandonment of a town's fortifications and artillery range. A common solution was to build some kind of ring boulevard; the model here was of course Paris. This wave of defortification came at the same time as demands were being raised for public parks and plantations, and in most places there were attempts to use part of the* glacis *as a green area. In Bremen in 1802–9, under the direction of Ch.L. Bosse, I.H.A. Altmann and others, a park was laid out within the moat area, with the moat itself preserved as open water (a). This model recurred with some variations throughout the nineteenth century. In C.W. Carlberg's town plan for Gothenburg dated 1808 (b) the moat has been retained and the*

(1879), Cologne (1881) and Danzig (1895). Vienna was certainly regarded as a given model for such projects, but there was never any question of direct imitation: the conditions, the particular requirements and the resources differed too much. Functionally speaking it was generally more a question of urban expansion and not as in Vienna of a gigantic 'infill'.[26]

In Germany, too, relatively few towns were founded during the nineteenth century; Bremerhaven is one of the rare examples (1827).[27] Destructive fires did not play the same part in urban renewal here as they did in the wooden-built Nordic towns. Hamburg was the most notable German exception; after a great fire there in 1842 the English engineer

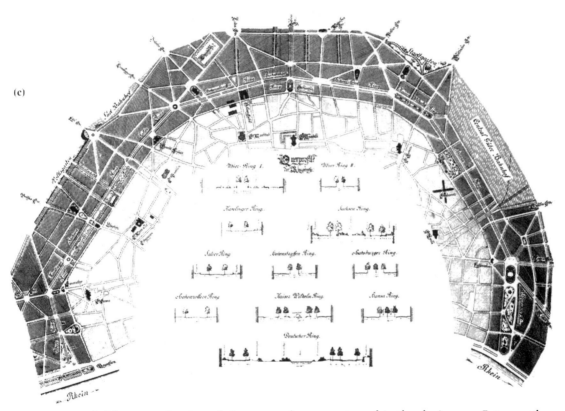

(c)

town surrounded by a ring boulevard, but no park was envisaged in the glacis area. Between the boulevard and the moat, however, several parks were laid out later, and the area inside the moat was not as heavily developed as the plan had intended. A final example of such glacis projects can be seen in Cologne, where Karl Henrici and Joseph Stübben won both the first and second prizes in the 1880 competition, which resulted in a ring road roughly 6 kilometres long. The aim at planning an entire ring as a coherent entity – as in Vienna – had been abandoned, and instead the ring road in Cologne seems to consist of a series of autonomous streets (c). There was no moat in Cologne, and green areas do not appear to have been given the same weight as before. Technical communication issues were now of central importance. The scale of the maps is not uniform. [From Stübben (1890) (a) and (c) and Schånberg (1975) (b)]

William Lindley was asked to produce a plan. The idea was clearly to use the opportunity to provide the centre with a new structure fit for a town 'which was on the way to becoming one of the foremost trading centres anywhere . . . In a word', as Schumacher put it, 'it was a question of the technological foundations appropriate to a large modern city.'[28] Lindley's proposal was the obvious product of an engineer's mind. An alternative plan paying more attention to architectural considerations was made by Gottfried Semper. Thus, just as in Barcelona a little later, an engineer's plan was confronted by another with an architectural slant. The proposal that was finally ratified was presented by a 'technical committee', whose chairman and main driver was the architect Alexis de Chateauneuf. It can be described as an independent revision of the earlier projects.

Urban development in Munich took quite a different turn. While Hamburg was a town of well-established burghers in which merchant interests were predominant, Munich was the residence of princes – perhaps around the middle of the nineteenth century the most typical of its kind among the larger German towns – and belonged in all essentials to the capital city category. During the nineteenth century two great ceremonial parades were created here, Ludwigstraße during the first half of the century – the main architects were Leo von Klenze and Friedrich von Gärtner – and Maximilianstraße in the 1850s.[29] Similar planning was undertaken in Hanover, where an architecturally designed townscape was created.

Compared with the princely plans for such towns as Hanover, Karlsruhe, Munich and Stuttgart, the Hobrecht plan for Berlin belongs to a different category; nor was it characterized by the same ambitions as the project for Hamburg. In Berlin it was a question of dividing the land between streets and blocks in an appropriate and simple manner. This type of *Fluchtlinienplanung* was also well established

in Germany when Hobrecht was given the commission. In the later decades of the nineteenth century a great many urban expansion plans were approved in Germany, particularly after the establishment of the Empire 1871.[30] The earlier of these were generally based on the same principles as the Hobrecht plan, which certainly had some influence even though most of the other plans could be described as miniature projects in comparison. Just how much importance the Berlin plan may have had as a model remains an open question.[31] Berlin was of course soon to fall into disrepute, being regarded not as an ideal but as an awful warning, a 'crime'. This note was struck as early as 1870 in an article by Ernst Bruch, 'Berlins bauliche Zukunft und der Bebauungs-plan' published in the *Deutsche Bauzeitung*. The theme was then elaborated by Rudolf Eberstadt among others, and reached a furious crescendo in 1930 in Werner Hegemann's *Das steinerne Berlin*.

In Sweden planning questions were being discussed in various towns from at least the 1860s onwards; it was often, though not always, the effects of a fire which provided the impetus for the planning activities.[32] Swedish towns which burned down more or less completely and were then planned anew included Vänersborg (1834), Karlstad (1865), Gävle (1869), Umeå (1888) and Sundsvall (1888). The 1874 building ordinances made it mandatory on all towns to produce town plans, which naturally triggered intensive planning activities. However, even prior to the 1874 building ordinances, Umeå had a plan (figure 25.4), which had been partly realized before the 1888 fire, and Gothenburg organized a town planning competition for the expansion of the city as early as 1862. In Sweden as in other countries industrialization meant that a great many new places were appearing on the map – generally, however, without any plans behind them – and some of these would in time become towns. Thus we can hardly talk of urban foundations here, except perhaps in the

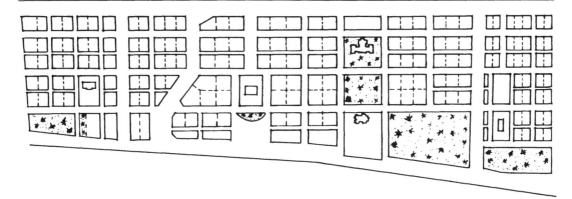

Figure 25.4 *Umeå. At the beginning of the 1860s a new town plan was made, at roughly the same time as the planning work was proceeding in Stockholm, but without any connection with the plan for the capital. Instead the models were taken from Finnish towns, primarily Vasa. After a fire in 1888 the plan shown here was ratified; it met the requirement stipulated in the 1874 building ordinances that 'esplanades' should be created by means of regularizations within the area destroyed by fire in the centre of the town. The outer parts of the town rectangle follow the design of the earlier plan. Simplified redrawing. [Stadsingenjörsarkiv, Umeå]*

case of Motala with its characteristic fan-shaped plan, which was founded during the 1820s but did not become a town until very much later.

The Lindhagen Committee's proposal for Stockholm represents a special case; the project reveals a certain general kinship with other earlier or later plans for other towns, but its wide sweep puts it in a class of its own. But, just as Cerdá based his *Teoría general de la urbanización* on the experience he gained from working on the plan for Barcelona, so must Lindhagen have exploited the lessons of the Stockholm plan when, at the beginning of the 1870s, he wrote what were to become the 1874 building ordinances – and, with these, what had been appropriate in Stockholm became the norm for all the towns in the country.

In Finland the re-planning of the capital city during the 1810s became the prelude to a long series of urban improvements and expansions.[33] However, the solution reached in Helsinki depended on the unique conditions in the town, and did not therefore readily lend itself to repetition. More important as a model was Carl Ludvig Engel's project for the re-building of Åbo after the great fire of 1827 (figure 25.5). Several Finnish towns were rebuilt after fires along much the same lines. Vasa (1855) and Tavastehus (1858) should be mentioned, although in the second of these there was no direct connection with a fire.

Early moves were also made in Norway: the Norwegian parliament approved a law in 1845 which made it mandatory upon the towns to appoint planning committees, which in turn were responsible for seeing that plans were made.[34] The law included detailed provisions about the plans; streets, for instance, were to be straight and at least 12.5 metres broad. This and similar directives had disastrous consequences when towns or districts were rebuilt after fires: the small Norwegian towns generally lay in very hilly terrain, often on steep slopes, where a rectilinear street network was totally unsuitable. Regulations along these lines were made in Risør (1861), Arendal (1863) and Drammen (1866). Among new foundations

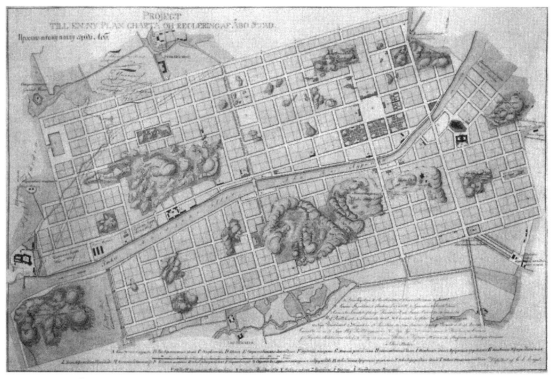

Figure 25.5 *Åbo. Carl Ludwig Engel's plan for the reconstruction of Åbo after the fire of 1827. A street grid, which was as regular as possible was created between the stretches of terrain that were too hilly to build on. A major purpose of the plan was to prevent a repetition of the disastrous fire, which is believed to have been the most severe in Nordic urban history, by replacing the densely built town with a sparser structure consisting of broader streets and smaller blocks, and by adding parks and tree-planted 'esplanades'. [Photograph from Åbo landskapsmuseum, Åbo]*

mention should be made of Gjøvik (1861). After an early start, planning in the capital city made little progress; Christiania can therefore hardly have served as a model for other Norwegian towns. The same probably applies to Copenhagen. Denmark had no towns that could compare with the capital city in size or in the type of problems that needed tackling.[35]

In the Spanish case scholars have emphasized the influence not only of the extension of Madrid but even more importantly of Barcelona, as can be seen in a whole series of subsequent *ensanches* in towns such as Bilbao

(1863), San Sebastian (1864, figure 25.6), Sabadell (1865), Elche (1866) and Bilbao (1867).[36]

In Greece several plans were produced along much the same lines as in Athens, often with a combination of right-angled and radial streets. The authors of the first ratified plan for Athens, Schaubert and Kleanthes, also produced plans for Agion and Piraeus, while Schaubert – working on his own or together with others – made plans for Eretria (figure 25.7), Levadia, Corinth, Mégara and Thebes.[37] There is little question of 'imitation' here; rather, the similarities stem from the fact that a

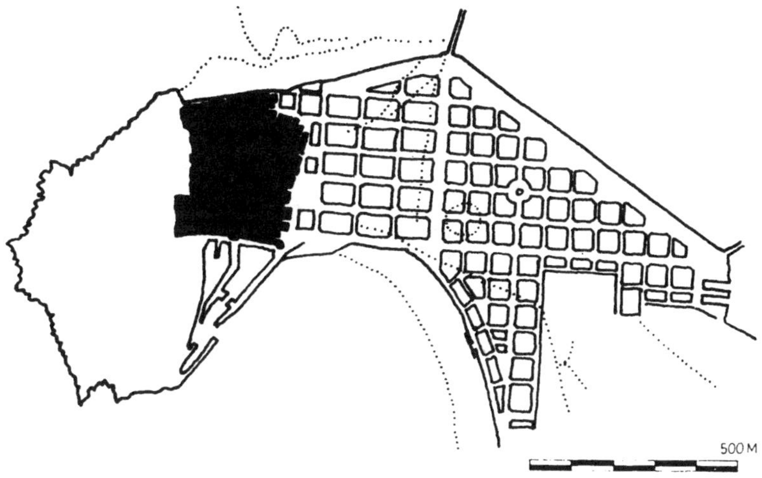

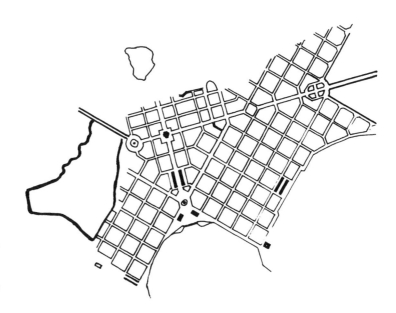

Figure 25.6 *San Sebastian. This expansion plan dated 1864 is one of many examples showing that projects for ensanches in Barcelona and Madrid acquired considerable importance as models. [From Solá-Morales et al. (1978)]*

500 M

Figure 25.7 *Eretria. Schaubert's town plan dated 1834 may serve as an example of the intensive town planning activities in many Greek towns after the liberation, primarily according to the same principles as in Athens. [Redrawing of a plan in Sinos (1974)]*

small number of planners worked in many different places, hence similarities between places were inevitable.

In Italy, where political fragmentation and late urbanization and industrialization created rather special conditions, national legislation was passed in 1865 which opened the way for the creation of *piani regolatori edilizi* and *piani di ampliamento urbano*, but as planning tools these do not seem to have acquired the importance intended. However, plans were made for Florence (figure 25.8), Milan, Naples, Padua and Venice among others.[38] No planning took place in the capital city until after plans had already been produced for several other large towns; it is therefore doubtful

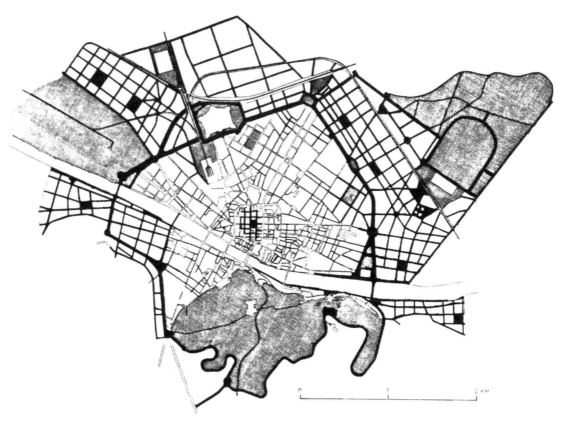

Figure 25.8 *Florence (capital of Italy 1864–71). Map of implemented regularisations. Solid black streets are newly constructed, shaded areas denote parks and gardens. [From Benevolo (1980)]*

whether Rome can have had any importance as a model. And Italian capital city planning had in fact started before Rome even became the capital, with Giuseppe Poggi's 1865 plan for Florence.

As regards other countries, the impact of planning in the respective capital cities on developments in the provincial towns, must remain an open question.

To summarize: when it comes to the influential effect of the capital city projects on other towns, we find big variations between countries, depending on such factors as the date of the projects in relation to the history of urban development in the particular country, differ-

ences in the size of the cities, and the specific requirements which had to be satisfied. That said, however, the capital city projects in some cases at least do appear to have had a certain importance as models. Generally speaking they were precursors rather than successors.

Let us finally look at the role of the capital city projects in relation to the emergence of modern urban planning. First we have to ask ourselves what we mean by the emergence of 'modern' planning. We have already noted that a number of interrelated events and processes justify dating this development to the decades around the turn of the century. The planning of towns was breaking free from its former status as a 'job on the side' for architects and engineers, and was becoming an independent field of operations, a new sphere of knowledge embracing elements of technology, design and law and developing its own set of theories about the organization of the town and of urban life and about the physical appearance of cities. At the same time a professional planning identity was evolving. In several countries urban planning was beginning to attract people who devoted their time exclusively or at any rate predominantly to it, and who regarded themselves as representing a special expertise. Increasingly, members of this new professional group were seeking contact with one another across national borders. At architectural conferences after the beginning of the twentieth century urban development issues were attracting growing attention, and in 1910 the Royal Institute of British Architects (RIBA) reported one of its meetings as the first international urban planning conference. The same year the first urban development exhibition was organized in Berlin, and several others were held over the next few years. The first professional journal, *Der Städtebau*, appeared in 1904, to be followed in 1910 by the *Town Planning Review*.[39] In several countries new laws were also passed to specify and tighten up the legal effect (Italy 1865, Prussia 1875, Saxony 1899, Sweden 1874 and 1907 and England 1909). An important innovation was the *Staffelbauordnung* or *Zonenbauordnung*,[40] which began to be applied in German towns during the 1890s. Frankfurt was first, with the building regulations introduced by the *Oberbürgermeister* Franz Adickes. The idea was to allow tall houses and a high level of building intensity in the central parts of the town, while buildings further out should be less high and less densely packed together. Zones for industrial and residential building also began to be marked out.[41] An important step had thus been taken from general prescriptions applying to all landowners in the form of building ordinances or bylaws, towards the systematic control over land use and individual building activities by means of plans.

The seminal presentation of this development appears in Sutcliffe's *Towards the Planned City* (1981b). But Sutcliffe is perhaps a little too keen to fix a specific date for the 'birth' of planning. In his view, 'planning was finally invented . . . between about 1890 and the early 1900s,'[42] even if the 'antecedents of urban planning may be traced back as far as early Antiquity.'[43] Haussmann's contribution 'came closest to planning without actually getting there'; it was, according to Sutcliffe, 'too dependent on massive investment of public funds to achieve that essential quality of planning, the power to perpetuate itself.'[44] At this point one looks for a definition of what Sutcliffe includes in his concept of planning. But there does not appear to be any comprehensive definition, beyond the author's statement in the introduction that the concepts of 'town planning', '*Städteplanung*' and '*urbanisme*' were created in the years before the First World War to express 'the deliberate ordering by public authority of the physical arrangements of towns or part of towns in order to promote their efficient and equitable functioning as economic and social units, and to create an aesthetically pleasing environment.'[45]

According to Sutcliffe's interpretation, it could be said that the first capital city project of the nineteenth century – as early as its second decade – was Ehrenström's plan for Helsinki, which corresponds fully to the quoted definition. The same applies, albeit to a varying extent, to the subsequent projects for other capital cities, and to the planning of other towns. However, it is clear that a fundamental change in attitudes towards planning occurred around the end of the nineteenth and the beginning of the twentieth centuries: it became increasingly recognized that the shaping and design of the physical environment in towns and other urban settlements should be controlled by public planning mandatory on the

individual. But this was no sudden development; rather, it was one step in a process,
partly in reaction against the increase in land
speculation that had accompanied industrialization. If we disregard the projects undertaken in the capital cities and in many other
places during the nineteenth century and even
before, and claim that planning was 'born' or
'invented' at the beginning of our own century,
we are blinding ourselves to the continuity
which did patently exist. It is more a question
of a shift in emphasis than of the start of
something entirely new. It is probably not
possible to say when such a new phase might
have begun, but the street improvements in
Paris come readily to mind as a prelude, even
though some of the most striking developments
occurred much later, at the beginning of the
present century. To identify the outbreak of
the First World War as an ending, or at any
rate a halt upon the way, is less controversial.
Finally, it should of course be remembered
that any survey of successes tends to give an
exaggerated idea of the importance and the
extent of the achievements. It has to be
remembered, that many towns still lacked any
planning worthy of the name at the beginning
of the twentieth century, and in the Nordic
countries, for instance, only Sweden was subject to planning legislation that could be called
'modern' for its times.

Certain aspects of the development outlined
above have been taken up in earlier sections,
since crucial parts of the process occurred in
the capital cities, owing to the particular
problems and projects that arose there. This
applies particularly to the dawning debate on
urban development and planning theory. On
the other hand the capital city projects probably
affected legislation and planning instruments
to a lesser extent. Of the planning legislation
mentioned above, probably only the Swedish
had any immediate connection with experience
gained in the capital.[46] In the following pages I
shall therefore look particularly at some of
the earliest publications to address urban

development, and comment on their background.

Again we can look first at developments
from the beginning of the nineteenth century,
up to about 1880. A planning tradition is
clearly evident, which although lacking a comprehensive theoretical base in the form of
written sources, was nonetheless characterized
by a systematic and rational approach: the
ideal was the rectilinear plan with large uniform
blocks; some streets designed as broader tree-
planted principal streets, sometimes with a
diagonal orientation; parks and imposing public
spaces, often with a monument or important
building as an eye-catching focus. It is important to re-assert that the basic principles are the
same, irrespective of whether it is a case of
improving earlier urban structures, laying out
new districts, or building new towns. It is not a
question of separate watertight categories;
rather, everything is based on one and the
same planning philosophy.

As part of a second tradition – if the small
number of projects realized warrants the term
– we find various proposals whose purpose was
to create alternative social forms. We have
already noted (cf. pp. 45 ff) how reflections
upon the 'ideal' social structure and physical
form for an urban community had reappeared
during the later decades of the eighteenth
century. Some noted contributions were made
to this tradition in the following century by
Utopian socialists such as Owen and Fourier,
but apart from some practical experiments like
Owen's New Lanark and Godin's *Familistère,*
these were mainly of a theoretical kind.

It is not altogether easy to assess the practical
influence of these ventures. However, the
space devoted to them in modern publications
is certainly not in proportion to their importance in concrete terms.[47] It was left to the
industrialist Titus Salt to show at Saltaire that
the model town was not merely the stuff of
dreams: it was perfectly possible to create such
a town in the real world and as part of the
existing economic and social system, possibly

encouraged by some earlier experiments in model housing. What distinguishes Saltaire from other planned towns and urban districts of the time, is that a single 'progressive' builder was able to shape the entire townscape. But the design of Saltaire testifies to the same system and the same rationalism as our capital city projects, and the community is thus equally at home in the mainstream of planning as described above as in any special 'model-city' tradition.[48] If Haussmann had been in Titus Salt's shoes, he would certainly have produced something much the same as Saltaire. In any case, Saltaire and the later industrial 'model communities', in particular Bournville and Port Sunlight, obviously made a not insignificant impact on subsequent developments.[49]

Compared with the first half of the century, the years between 1850 and 1880 saw changes of a far more dramatic kind in many European towns. The transformation of the old settings proceeded more rapidly, while the exploitation of new ground continued both more rapidly and more extensively. Like other large cities, the capitals of Europe began to assume something of the appearance that we can still recognize today. The great city of the age of industrialism was now a fact. While admiring the progress this type of city represented in hygienic terms, for instance, people also began to notice its drawbacks, in particular the frequently monotonous townscape, and the dull and often wretched living conditions in the tenement buildings which were put up by speculative developers and in which the great majority of urban dwellers had to live. It was these urban environments which people were now beginning to investigate and discuss, in face of further expected metropolitan expansion.[50] Various publications – which proved fundamental to modern town planning – appeared, either as attempts to systematize and build on the developments of the preceding decades, or as critical attacks upon them.[51]

The first important publication on town planning to appear during the nineteenth century, and perhaps the most remarkable, was Ildefonso Cerdá's voluminous *Teoría general de la urbanización y aplicación de sus principios y doctrinas á la reforma y ensanche de Barcelona* (1867), which we have discussed above (pp. 134 ff). As the title indicates this is an attempt to formulate a general theory of urban development, i.e. a system of universal rules about towns and urban life. But although the idea was to suggest universal principles, the book is largely based – as the title declares – on conditions in Barcelona and Cerdá's own project for that city. The book can be seen as a sort of manifesto for the project. Cerdá proceeds rather like a scientist, first posing a number of hypotheses about urban development, and then testing them empirically in a full-scale experiment – the plan for Barcelona – after which he finally reaches a universal theory. The scope of the book is vast, ranging from detailed prescriptions about particular points of building technology to philosophical reflections upon the nature and life of towns. The ambition is obviously to embrace everything in a single theoretical structure, in which one thing leads to another and nothing is left to chance. In its desire to achieve totality, this book has no parallel in the literature of urban development theory. It is also unique in its claim to universality combined with strong links to a particular town. The *Teoría general de la urbanización* does not appear to have aroused much attention outside Spain, either at the time or more recently. As recently as twenty-five years ago, Cerdá's name was still generally unknown even among people interested in planning history, but today he is one of the cult figures of nineteenth-century planning. Naturally this earlier neglect may have depended largely on the fact that the book was written in Spanish, and perhaps translation has been discouraged by the book's pedestrian and not infrequently long-winded style.

When it comes to works on planning theory in German, an important trigger was Rudolph

Eitelberger von Edelberg's lecture 'Über Städteanlagen und Stadtbauten', which was delivered in Vienna at the beginning of 1858 and published later the same year. It was occasioned by the discussions taking place at the time about the planning of Vienna, and its delivery coincided almost exactly with the announcement of the important competition for the planning of the *glacis* area, and it addresses a number of urban development issues.[52] But the real pioneer of urban development theory in German was Reinhard Baumeister, professor at the College of Technology in Karlsruhe and author of a long series of publications in the field, of which the most important is the lengthy (almost 500 pages) *Stadterweiterungen in technischer, baupolizeilicher und wirthschaftlicher Beziehung* published in 1876.[53] This book offers a commentary and by no means uncritical survey of the problems and lessons learned from various urban expansions schemes, including an impressing attempt to establish a new scientific field and to illuminate it from a variety of angles.[54] Apart from Cerdá's works, this is also the first in which the housing question is addressed as a central feature of urban development.

A little over ten years later, in 1890, Joseph Stübben's *Der Städtebau* appeared. This book represents a broad and systematic approach; it also established once and for all the term *Städtebau*. Stübben summarized the experiences of the preceding decades, providing a collection of examples with his own comments, so that practitioners could examine the way problems had been solved elsewhere. The aim was to span the whole professional field, from the designing of public squares and parks to laying down pipes and marking out plots. Stübben's book differs from Baumeister's not least in the wide-ranging illustrations which it provides. Baumeister concentrates more on the theoretical aspects, without any illustrations. Stübben, on the other hand, devotes a good deal more interest to the actual shaping

of the town plan, but treats the economic and legal side of things – one of Baumeister's main themes – more sketchily. German data dominate in both books, although Stübben in particular does quote many examples from other countries. Neither of these writers has created a theoretical structure in the spirit of Cerdá; they analyse the problems but do not attempt to formulate any comprehensive urban development theory. Nonetheless they both believe with Cerdá that it is possible to achieve general rules regarding optimum solutions for many of the problems of urban development.

Two other publications appeared before 1900 which proved to be of central importance, although their aims were different from those of the works we have been looking at above. These were Camillo Sitte's *Der Städte-Bau nach seinen künstlerischen Grundsätzen* (1889) and Ebenezer Howard's *Garden Cities of To-Morrow,* which appeared first in 1898 under the title *To-Morrow: A Peaceful Path to Real Reform.* Sitte, whose book has already been referred to above (pp. 330 ff), examined urban development from a perspective which Baumeister did not include – at least not in the comprehensive title of his book – namely the aesthetic. Sitte appears to have had two aims: one was to plead for a more artistic approach to urban development and the other was to derive ideas for such an approach from an analysis of earlier urban milieus. Whereas Cerdá looked forward and was eager to experiment and to try out new ideas, Sitte turned his gaze backward and sought models in the past. In this context mention should also be made of Charles Buls's *Esthétique des Villes,* published in 1893, which on the basis of the author's experience as mayor of Brussels appealed for a more preservationist approach to urban development, an idea which began to spread towards the end of the century, not least in reaction to the dramatic redevelopments in many capital city centres.

By 'garden city' Howard meant a town of a certain predetermined maximum size, in which the benefits of urban and rural living could be combined, with workplaces for the inhabitants and well-developed social functions, and surrounded by a rural zone protected from any further urbanisation. Much of his book is devoted to showing how such a town could be realized in practice. Where Sitte's book is dominated by design aspects, Howard pays little attention to such considerations. The plans which accompany his book are schematic, and it was left to Raymond Unwin to give the garden city its physical shape. Consequently, outside England, the 'garden city' came to be regarded as a building pattern rather than a social concept, and Unwin rather than Howard as its spiritual father.

It may seem surprising that Howard does not mention Saltaire, nor the industrial villages which appeared during the 1890s, namely Bournville and Port Sunlight. Admittedly the 'garden city' he describes does differ in various ways from Saltaire, for example in its bigger scale and because the surrounding green zone was to be protected from exploitation. But the actual basic idea, to lay out well-ordered communities *ex novo* as an alternative to existing settlements, is the same. Howard's prime contribution probably consisted in transforming the model city from a paternalistic phenomenon into a public facility organized according to ordered principles, and for marketing it so successfully. We might therefore ask ourselves whether Titus Salt has not been allocated too obscure a place in the history of the planned 'new towns'.

Finally, mention should be made of the concept of the *cuidad lineal* launched in Spain by Arturo Soria y Mata in 1882 as an alternative to the traditional town, in this case especially Madrid. A *cuidad lineal* should consist of a narrow ribbon-like urban structure along a transport link. A suburb – the *cuidad lineal* – was built outside Madrid inspired by this pattern.[55]

On examining the importance of the capital cities for pre-1900 works on urban development

theory, we find that Vienna features prominently in two of the publications: Eitelberger's published lecture was triggered by the pending exploitation of the *glacis* area, and Sitte's by the allegedly meagre results for the Viennese townscape. Similarly, the point of departure for Howard's *Garden Cities of To-Morrow* was the overpopulated and disorganized structure of London. Baumeister was well aware of the problems and plans of the capital cities, and quotes them often as examples. This applies even more to Stübben, although neither author discusses the towns in their role as capitals; nor do they treat them as belonging to a special 'capital city' category.

But none of the works mentioned here would have been written, or at any rate would not have been organized or focused as they were, without experience of the capital cities – of their planning or of the consequences of the absence of planning. Baumeister and Stübben – and even Cerdá in the case of Barcelona – started from their experience, from what they had seen in the various towns, and then sought with the systematic approach of the engineer to build on this. Sitte and Howard, on the other hand, are more in the agitator mould: they condemn the existing solutions and seek to transform their own visions into reality, both of them anticipating the missionary role adopted later by several twentieth-century planning ideologists.[56]

The first fifteen years of the new century were to see a great many more works on planning and urban development. The authors include Raymond Unwin, Rudolf Eberstadt, A.E. Brinckmann, Otto Wagner, Werner Hegemann, Eugen Faßbender and Patrick Geddes. The great projects of the nineteenth century now lay several decades in the past, but they were nonetheless an important part of these writers' common professional consciousness and their frames of reference. Of particular interest in this context is Werner Hegemann's *Der Städtebau nach den Ergebnissen der allgemeinen Städtebau-Ausstellung in Berlin*

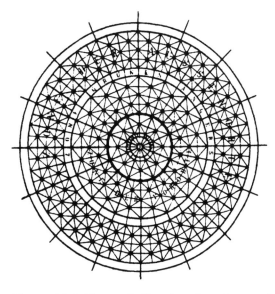

Figure 25.9 *Eugen Faßbender shared second prize in the great 1892–94 competition for a comprehensive development plan for the city of Vienna. This is a diagrammatic sketch of the proposal. The plan types described in figure 25.1 have been combined here into an urban pattern allowing for expansion by the addition of new rings round the existing city. Faßbender, like other nineteenth-century theorists, was envisaging the continuous growth of the city. Ebenezer Howard, in his book on the garden city published a few years later, was to lay the theoretical foundations for the preferred city model of the twentieth century, where expansion was to be catered for by satellite towns (cf. figure 25.10). [From Wulz (1979)]*

(1911 and 1913), which introduces and discusses problems and projects in several capital cities – chiefly Berlin – with a view to setting the present situation in a historical perspective. Some publications also refer to specific towns. *Die Großstadt, Eine Studie über diese* (1911) by Otto Wagner takes Vienna as its point of departure, but uses it as a more general example of the way a large city can be infinitely extended. Just after the turn of the century Paris was to be the subject of several noted

studies by Eugène Hénard, who can be seen as an important link between nineteenth- and twentieth-century urban development; he built on the experiences of the later nineteenth century to produce several innovations which heralded much that was later to appear in twentieth-century schemes (figure 21.2).[57] Even before this the dominating housing type in the continental capitals, namely the tenement block, had already been the subject of critical analysis, particularly in Germany. Here the focus was naturally on Berlin – 'the greatest city of tenements in the world'. Rudolf Eberstadt made the most important contribution here, in his *Handbuch des Wohnungswesens* (1909).

Around 1910, when urban development was beginning to take shape as a professional discipline, its practitioners faced two sets of problems: on the one hand, the improvement and expansion of older towns, and on the other the planning of new areas such as suburbs or completely new communities. There is no doubt at all that most planners regarded the second of these tasks as the more important and more interesting. Confronted by most of the urban environments created in the nineteenth century, they were becoming increasingly critical and pessimistic, or even plain indifferent.[58]

It is clear, however, that the capital cities did occupy a prominent position in the urban development debate, though mainly, perhaps, in their role as large towns. It was in the capitals that the negative consequences of unrestrained big-city growth were more brutally evident than elsewhere, since the capital cities were generally very much larger than the next biggest city in the respective countries. It was there that the wretched conditions were noticed and discussed not only at the local level, but also in many cases in a national context. And it was there that governments had a particular interest in intervening and trying to improve things. And it was there, as we have seen, that many great projects were undertaken, which

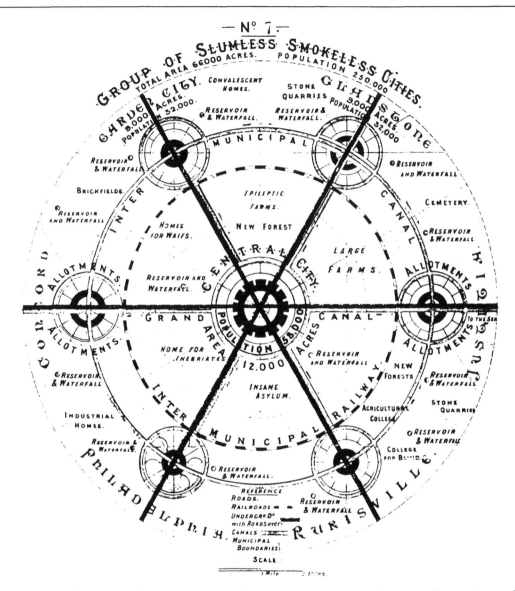

Figure 25.10 *'Diagram' illustrating the satellite expansion model, which according to Howard is 'the correct principle of a city's growth'. The figure appeared in the first edition of* To-Morrow: A Peaceful Path to Real Reform *(1898), but was omitted as being too radical from the second edition,* Garden Cities of To-Morrow *(1902). In a comparison with Faßbender's plan (figure 25.9), this can surely be said to represent a new paradigm for urban development in a new century.*

called attention to the problems of urban development and helped to build up a store of experience and knowledge. Around the end of the nineteenth and the beginning of the twenti-eth centuries the most progressive planning, as Sutcliffe has pointed out, was often to be found in towns other than the capitals.[59] But a few decades earlier, as the present study has shown, the situation was different. In several cases the most noted contributions by then were being made in the capital cities.

Thus, the great capital city projects can be said to have occupied a crucial position in planning history, as an intermediate link between pre-industrial town planning and 'modern' planning such as it evolved around the beginning of the present century, i.e. as an activity undertaken by specialists and regulated by law, based on the systematic accumulation of facts and the build-up of theory. In the evolution of modern planning the capital city projects were of central importance, certainly of far greater importance than the publications or urban experiments of the Utopians.

Today many of the townscapes which emerged as the result of nineteenth-century capital city planning appear to be an inalienable part of the European cultural heritage. They provide a solid core and a specific identity for the surrounding metropolitan regions. They exert a strong attraction not only on their own or their country's inhabitants, but on hundreds of thousands of others who are drawn there for recreation or intellectual excitement. 'Urban tourism' is now a recognized concept: in the post-industrial service society the heart of every capital city will play an ever more important part in the tourist industry, and thus also in its own and its country's economy. The nineteenth-century planners have made a contribution whose value has not fallen; on the contrary it has been rising and will continue to do so.

NOTES

1. Haussmann (1893), III, p. 351.
2. This process is discussed in several of the papers collected in Fehl and Rodriguez-Lores (1983).
3. World exhibitions were organized in London 1851 and 1862, in Paris in 1855, 1867, 1878, 1889 and 1900, in Vienna in 1873, in Philadelphia in 1876 and in Chicago in 1893. Great international exhibitions were also held in several towns, without being officially recognized as 'world fairs'. Examples among the cities discussed here are Barcelona (1888), Budapest (1896) and Stockholm (1897).
4. Special attention was to be paid to '1. Building bylaws, 2. Water supplies, 3. Sewage systems and 4. The costs and methods for technical implementation of national and municipal building' (Mollik, Reining and Wurzer (1980), pp. 406 f).
5. On this development, see Sutcliffe (1981b), pp. 163 ff.
6. Looking through copies of *The Builder* for the period 1855–82, the architect George Lázár found that the capital city projects were discussed on a few occasions only, and then generally fairly superficially. An article on the Boulevard de Sébastopol (1858, p. 257) devoted far more space to the opening ceremonies than to the street itself or its importance. Vienna is mentioned a few times (e.g. 1865, p. 411), while other capital city redevelopment projects do not seem to have been noted at all. More interest was of course paid to the problems of London, and in several articles the planning and street construction projects in Paris and London were compared, most exhaustively in 1872 in a report on a debate at the Royal Institute of British Architects (pp. 22 ff). It can be noted that in this debate the term 'general plan' was used; one of the speakers claimed that the absence of such a plan for London was the real reason why the improvements in London were so much less successful than those in Paris.

A similar survey of *Deutsche Bauzeitung* from its start in 1867 and up to 1882 revealed practically nothing on planning in foreign capitals, and very little on planning at all. Such mentions as did exist consisted mainly of short descriptions of projects for German towns. Other journals are unlikely to have offered any more material of the relevant kind.
7. On the other hand planning issues were naturally taken up in treatises and other works concerned primarily with architecture. Frechilla suggests, for example, that Léonce Reynaud's *Traité d'Architecture*, which was published in 1850–58, was of crucial importance to both Castro and Cerdá (Frechilla (1992), pp. 160 ff).
8. As early as 1858 Professor Rudolph Eitelberger, one of Vienna's leading experts on

matters of art and architecture, declared in a subsequently printed lecture entitled *Über Städteanlagen und Städtebauten*: 'Of all modern cities none can compete in importance with Paris. It is the prototype of a modern capital city in the true sense of the word' (quoted from Mollik, Reining and Wurzer (1980), p. 423). But here it is not Haussmann's Paris that is meant in the first instance.

9. Among the many international honours bestowed upon Haussmann was his appointment as Commander, First Class, of the Swedish Vasa Order. However, the foreign honours were not contingent on Haussmann's contributions as an urban planner, but were his due as Prefect of Paris.

10. Haussmann (1890), II, p. 553; *L'Œuvre du baron Haussmann*, pp. 154 f.

11. Cf. Mollik, Reining and Wurzer (1980), pp. 323 ff.

12. Thienel (1973), p. 43. Cf. also Matzerath and Thienel (1977), p. 176, and Sutcliffe (1979*b*), p. 83.

13. Hobrecht can reasonably be expected to have taken an interest in what was going on in Vienna – more than in Paris, perhaps – while he was working on the plan for Berlin. The three winning proposals in the town plan competition and the *Grundplan* as finally ratified were all published, and would almost certainly have been available in Berlin. However, the tasks in the two towns were so different that the projects produced for Vienna cannot have provided many pointers for planning in Berlin.

14. Frechilla strongly emphasizes the importance of Paris as a model for Castro, but he seems to be referring to a sort of ideal picture of Paris rather than Haussmann's actual project. In particular he suggests that the description of an ideal Paris which appears in Reynaud's *Traité d'Architecture* was a source of direct inspiration for Castro (Frechilla (1992), p. 160 f).

15. Cf. Ranieri (1973), p. 14, however. Ranieri seems to be questioning whether Leopold II's urban planning policy was inspired by Paris. This appears to depend on a misunderstanding on Ranieri's part, namely that urban planning under the Second Empire was primarily driven by the desire to promote the maintenance of law and order.

16. Wagenaar (1990), pp. 251 f.

17. An interesting debate on the street improvements in Paris and London took place at a meeting of the RIBA (the Royal Institute of British Architects) in 1872 (see note 6). Most of the speakers seem to have taken it for granted that the street-widening projects in Paris were exemplary, and the main question was why London had not been equally successful.

18. Thus Pinkney's claim that 'Rome, Stockholm, Barcelona, Madrid, all felt the influence of Napoleon's and Haussmann's work' must be taken with a pinch of salt (1958, p. 4). And the same applies to similar statements by Lavedan (*L'Œuvre du baron Haussmann*, p. 157).

19. The architectural apparatus of the capital city is discussed in Vale (1992), particularly pp. 16 ff.

20. On the development of town plans in France during the nineteenth century, see Lavedan (1960).

21. *L'Œuvre du baron Haussmann*, pp. 142 ff; see also Pinkney (1958), p. 4 and Lavedan (1960), pp. 208 ff. On activities in Lyons, see Leonard (1961).

22. Wurzer (1974), p. 22.

23. Da Seta (1981), Figs. 179–181 and 185–190; cf. also a project for Venice, reproduced in Calabi (1980), p. 60.

24. Pinkney (1958), p. 4.

25. Lichtenberger (1970), pp. 17 ff, and Mollik, Reining and Wurzer (1980), pp. 46 ff. Berlin had been deprived of its defence function as early as 1734.

26. Cf. Mollik, Reining and Wurzer (1980), pp. 428 ff. Here a number of extension projects in formerly fortified towns are reported but without any real analysis of the importance of Vienna as a model.

Perhaps Gothenburg may have been inspired to organize the planning competition of 1862 by the example of the great competition in Vienna a few years earlier.

27. For a brief survey of town-planning developments in Germany during the nineteenth century, see Wurzer (1974).

28. Schumacher (1920), p. 6 *et passim*.

29. On Munich, see Hederer (1964), pp. 128 ff *et passim*, and Hojer (1974); see also Breitling (1978).

30. A list of urban extension plans in Germany

between 1830 and 1875 can be found in Fehl and
Roderiguez-Lores (1983), pp. 360 f.
31. Sutcliffe cites an 1884 extension plan for
Düsseldorf to illustrate the repetition of 'all the
defects of the Berlin plan' (1981*b*), p. 22).
32. For a survey of planning in Sweden during
the nineteenth century, see Hall (1991).
33. On Finnish planning, see Sundman (1991)
and *Suomen Kaupunkilaitoksen historia.*
34. For a survey of planning in Norway during
the nineteenth century, see Lorange and Myhre
(1991).
35. For a study of planning in Denmark during
the nineteenth century, see Larsson and
Thomasen (1991).
36. Cf. Solá-Morales *et al.* (1978), pp. 17 ff; see
also *Plan Castro*, pp. XVII ff and Moreno Peralta
(1980).
37. Russack (1942), p. 36, Sinos (1974), pp. 45 ff
and Fountoulaki (1979), pp. 25 f, 41 and 55 ff,
and Wassenhoven (1984). According to Sinos,
both architects contributed to the Eretria plan.
38. See Calabi (1980 and 1984) and Mioni
(1980).
39. In this context mention can also be made of
La Ciudad Lineal, started in 1897 by Arturo
Soria y Mata as a journal in support of his 'linear
planning' concept, but after 1902 appearing as a
more general urban planning journal (cf. Collins
(1959*a*), p. 47 f).
40. *Staffelbauordnung* is the usual term in
southern Germany (Bavaria, Württemberg); in
Prussia and northern Germany the term *Zonenbauordnung* is used.
41. For a detailed discussion on the Frankfurt
Zonenbauordnung, see Schulz-Kleeßen (1985).
42. Sutcliffe (1981*b*), p. 205.
43. *Ibidem*, p. VIII.
44. *Ibidem*, p. 204.
45. *Ibidem*, p. VIII:
46. Perhaps an exception to this was the development of expropriation legislation, which must
have been affected by land prices and problems in
the capital cities.
47. Benevolo (1968), for example, claims that
the 'Utopian' experiments of the first half of the
nineteenth century were grounded in a holistic
political-ideological concept of society, and on a
desire to introduce more equality into the conditions of life. According to Benevolo the events of

1848 represented a break between the political
left and urban planning, which was subsequently
reduced to a purely technical activity and which
was prepared, in the service of the political
powers, to treat the environmental and hygienic
deficiencies of the industrial town symptomatic-
ally, without taking any interest in the underlying
causes of the problems. This interpretation is a
bit simplistic. To begin with, the ideas and
experiments of the Utopians must be seen as
isolated episodes, rather than as links in some
sort of systematic project for developing practicable models. Secondly, Benevolo seems to disregard the fact that a number of planners and
urban development theorists from Cerdá onwards
had a keen interest in social conditions and in the
possibilities of change. Thirdly, it must be possible
to discuss and evaluate urban planning, like any
other professional sphere, in terms of its own
conditions as an independent field of operations.
None of which means, of course, that town
planning, like every other activity in a society, is
not dependent upon the overriding political
conditions.
48. In a couple of publications Françoise Choay
has tried to systematize and schematize the
development of town planning during the nineteenth century (the following is based mainly on
Choay, 1969). All planning which, according to
Choay, starts from a critical analysis of the
'disorder' which industrialization created, is subsumed by her in the concept of 'critical planning',
which in turn is divided into two categories:
'regularization' and 'urbanism' (pp. 10 ff). By
'regularization' is meant 'that form of critical
planning whose explicit purpose is to regularize
the disordered city' (p. 15). The main example is
of course Haussmann's street improvements in
Paris. This regularizing focus in planning did not
imply, Choay continues, that there was not a
hidden order. The concept of 'urbanism', on the
other hand, is 'used to describe the process that
radically contested this hidden order and ultimately led to the *a-priori* construction of a new and
different one.' Within this tradition there are 'two
basic models of spatial organization'. 'One of
these models, looking to the future and inspired
by a vision of social progress, we shall call
progressist. The other, nostalgic in outlook, is
inspired by the vision of a cultural community

and may therefore be called *culturalist*.' Both models experienced a theoretical prelude during the early nineteenth century, which Choay calls 'pre-urbanism' (p. 31). The pre-urbanistic stage of the progressist development includes the Utopian socialists such as Owen and Fourier. The transition to the urbanist stage is represented by Soria y Mata's *ciudad lineal* and Garnier's *cité industrielle*. The real 'urbanist' stage in the 'progressist' line of development is functionalism, with Le Corbusier and Gropius as the leading names. Within the 'culturalist' category the pre-urbanistic stage starts with Pugin, Ruskin and Morris, while the pioneering figure in the urbanist stage is Sitte.

Björn Linn has simplified and clarified Choay's model, and prefers to speak of a 'regularist', a 'rationalist' and a 'humanist' line of development. The *regularist* line aims at regulating and building on the existing large city; it is above all the official public administration line. The *rationalist* line seeks a new city geared to efficiency in both whole and parts; it is closely associated with industry and the industrial way of defining and solving problems. Lastly, the *humanist* line sees the town primarily as a cultural environment and its advocates are interested in the way the town is perceived psychologically and socially; this line has its point of departure in humanistic knowledge, art and culture (see Linn (1974), p. 73.) Schemes of this kind – particularly an intricate system like Choay's – are apt to make developments seem more complicated than ever, rather than helping us to understand them. Choay's scheme also seems to suggest that there were three totally independent lines of development, which is presumably not what she means. Moreover the distinctions she makes are dubious on several counts. A good deal of the planning which Choay categorizes as 'regularist' and 'progressist' have a common goal, namely to seek rational solutions to the problems which had arisen in many towns. That the results turned out differently in the industrial model towns on the one hand and Paris, for example, on the other, is hardly surprising in view of the completely different conditions that prevailed in the two cases. The basic weakness of Choay's argument is that the features which were common to all lines of development are toned down in favour of a

partially artificial division, and that attention is drawn to single phenomena rather than to the general features in developments as a whole.

49. Among German industrial villages, mention should be made of the *Arbeiterkolonie* of the Maschinen- und Lokomotivfabrik der Hannoverschen Maschinenbau-Aktien-Gesellschaft in Linden near Hanover; here it is a question of a purely commercial investment, and a comparison serves to emphasise the social thinking which slightly earlier inspired Saltaire.

50. It could be added here that remarkably little thought was given to the location of industry.

51. A seminal work on the development of urban planning theory is Albers (1975*a*). And the first to provide a detailed account and analysis – in any language – of the late nineteenth-century theorists, was probably Paulsson (1959). Another Swedish work which should be mentioned is Linn (1974), which provides an excellent analysis on this topic.

52. Eitelberger von Edelberg's lecture is reported in Mollik, Reining and Wurzer (1980), pp. 422 ff. Even the memorandum attached to Ludwig Förster's proposal for this competition represents an admirable attempt to air a number of fundamental urban development ideas (reproduced in Mollik, Reining and Wurzer (1980), pp. 472 ff).

53. A general overview of Baumeister's written works is provided in Höffler (1976).

54. *Deutsche Bauzeitung* (1874, No. 65) presented eight 'theses on urban development' which Baumeister was to bring up at a meeting of the Union of German Architect and Engineer Associations (*Verband deutscher Architekten- und Ingenieur-Vereine*). At the meeting the architectural section was to discuss 'The main features of urban development plans in a technical, economic and legal perspective', with Baumeister himself and a Berlin master builder and contractor named Orth as reporters. There seems good reason to list these theses here (with some abbreviations and adjustments), as in many ways they anticipate the main ideas in Baumeister's major book which was published two years later, as well as representing one of the first attempts at formulating a programme for urban development:

1. Urban expansions should generally be planned for areas of considerable size, so that the conditions for the various communication systems such as streets, horse-drawn trams, steam trams, canals etc. can be taken into account, and so that categories with specific needs, such as big industry, commercial activities, quiet residential areas and so on can be kept apart.

2. To begin with only the main orientations in the street system should be marked out, at which stage existing roads and local conditions should as far as possible be taken into consideration. A more detailed division can be made when the requirements of the immediate future so demand, or they can be left to private initiatives.

3. The location of the different districts should be organized in light of the present situation or other special conditions; compulsion should be employed only in connection with hygienic regulations for industry and handicrafts.

4. The task of the building authorities is to take account of the essential interests of the residents, the neighbours and of the area as a whole *vis-à-vis* the developer. Such interests include fire safety, freedom from traffic (*sic*) and health. On the other hand all aesthetic prescriptions are to be condemned.

5. In determining the distance between buildings which provide dwelling- or work-space, a not uncommon rule as regards street façades is recommended, namely that the height should not exceed the distance between the buildings. Other regulations regarding courtyards, buildings in courtyards and so on are then superfluous.

6. It is desirable in the case of urban expansion that expropriation is simplified, and that a legal procedure is established for adjusting plots to create sites suitable for building on.

7. The municipality should have the necessary powers to acquire funds from the owners of the adjacent plots, to cover the costs of laying down the new streets. A particularly suitable way of doing this is to set a normal contribution per metre of a plot's frontage on the street.

8. No building should be undertaken on areas marked out for future streets or squares, once the plan has been legally ratified. The owner has no right to compensation on grounds of this restriction. Property-owners are personally responsible for seeing that individual new houses are accessible and that sewage disposal arrangements have been made. But the municipality should undertake to lay down and maintain a new street in its entirety, as soon as it is certain that one-third of the plots fronting the street will be occupied by houses.

55. See Collins (1959a). On the international influence of the *cuidad lineal*, see Collins (1959*b*).

56. Cf. Collins and Collins (1986), p. 44.

57. See Wolf (1968), and Evenson (1979), pp. 24 ff.

58. Cf. Albers (1975*b*).

59. Sutcliffe (1979*b*).

BIBLIOGRAPHY

This list includes only material cited in the text, and should not be regarded as a bibliographic guide.

Adam, Herman (1861) *Nemesis eller bidrag till Stockholms mysterier.* Stockholm: J.L. Brudin.

Agulhon, Maurice (1983) *The Republican Experiment, 1848–1852.* Cambridge: Cambridge University Press.

Ahlberg, Gösta (1958) *Stockholms befolknings-utveckling efter 1850.* Stockholm: Almqvist & Wiksell.

Ahnlund, Nils (1953) *Stockholms historia före Gustav Vasa.* Stockholm: Norstedts Förlag.

Albers, Gerd (1975a) *Entwicklungslinien im Städte-bau, Ideen, Thesen, Aussagen 1875–1945.* Düsseldorf: Bertelsmann.

Albers, Gerd (1975b) Der Städtebau des 19. Jahrhunderts im Urteil des 20. Jahrhunderts, in Schadendorf, Wulf (ed.) *Beiträge zur Rezeption der Kunst des 19. und 20. Jahrhunderts.* München: Prestel.

Alberti, Leon B. (1912) *Zehn Bücher über die Baukunst.* Wien: H. Heller & Cie.

Album von Berlin und Potsdam. (1925) Berlin: Globus-Verlag.

Allan, C.M. (1965) The genesis of British urban redevelopment with special reference to Glasgow. *Economic History Review.*

Allpass, John and Agergaard, Erik (1979) The city centre – for whom? in Hammarström, I. and Hall, T. (eds.) *Growth and Transformation of the Modern City.* Stockholm: Swedish Council for Building Research.

Alphand, Adolphe (1867–73) *Les Promenades de Paris* [I–IV]. Paris: Rothschild.

Améen, Lennart (1979) Det svenska esplanad-systemet. *Svensk geografisk årsbok.*

Amsterdam in kaarten, Verandering van de stad in vier eeuwen cartografie. Heinemeijer, W.F., Wagenaar, M.F. *et al.* (1987) Ede/Antwerpen: Zomer & Keuning.

Argan, Giulio C. (1969) *The Renaissance City.* New York: George Braziller.

Aristotle (1950) *Politics.* London: The Loeb Classical Library.

Ashworth, William (1954) *The Genesis of Modern British Town Planning, A Study in Economic and Social History of the Nineteenth and Twentieth Centuries.* London: Routledge and Kegan Paul.

Åström, Sven-Erik (1957a) J.A. Ehrenström, G.F. Stjernvall och Helsingfors stadsplan. *Historisk tidskrift för Finland.*

Åström, Sven-Erik (1957b) *Samhällsplanering och regionsbildning i kejsartidens Helsingfors, Studier i stadens inre differentiering, 1810–1910.* Helsinki: Helsingfors stad.

Åström, Sven-Erik (1979) Town planning in Imperial Helsingfors 1810–1910, in Hammarström, I. and Hall, T. (eds.) *Growth and Transformation of the Modern City.* Stockholm: Swedish Council for Building Research.

The Athenian Agora. (1976) Athens: American School of Classical Studies in Athens.

Athen – München. (1980) München: Bayrisches Nationalmuseum.

Atlas de Barcelona. Galera, Montserrat, Roca, Francesco and Tarragó, Salvador (eds.) (1972) Barcelona: A.T.E.

Bacon, Edmund N. (1974) *Design of Cities.* Harmondsworth: Penguin Books.

Ballon, Hilary (1991) *The Paris of Henry IV, Architecture and Urbanism.* Cambridge, Mass/London: The MIT Press.

Baltzarek, Frank, Hoffmann, Alfred and Stekl, Hannes (1975) *Wirtschaft und Gesellschaft der Wiener Stadterweiterung (= Die Wiener Ringstraße,* Vol. V). Wiesbaden: Franz Steiner Verlag.

Banik-Schweitzer, Renate (1995) »Zugleich ist auch

bei der Stadterweiterung die Regulierung der inneren Stadt im Auge zu behalten», in Fehl, Gerhard and Rodriguez-Lores, Juan (eds.) *Stadt-Umbau, Die planmäßige Erneuerung europäischer Großstädte zwischen Wiener Kongreß und Weimarer Republik*. Basel/Berlin/Boston: Birkhäuser Verlag.

Barker, Theodore C. and Robbins, Michael (1975) *A History of London Transport, Passenger Travel and the Development of the Metropolis*, 2 vols. London: Allen and Unwin.

Barnett, Jonathan (1986) *The Elusive City, Five Centuries of Design, Ambition and Miscalculation*. London: The Herbert Press.

Bastié, Jean (1964) *La croissance de la banlieu parisienne*. Paris: Presses Universitaires de France.

Bater, James H. (1976) *St. Petersburg, Industrialization and Change*. London: Edward Arnold.

Battiscombe, Georgina (1974) *Shaftesbury, A Biography of the Seventh Earl, 1801–85*. London: Constable.

Baumeister, Reinhard (1876) *Stadterweiterungen in technischer, baupolizeilicher und wirthschaftlicher Beziehung*. Berlin: Ernst und Korn.

Bédarida, François and Sutcliffe, Anthony (1981) The Street in the Structure and Life of the City, Reflections on the Nineteenth-Century London and Paris, in Stave, Bruce (ed.) *Modern Industrial Cities, History, Policy and Survival*. Beverly Hills: Sage.

Belgrand, Eugène (1873–77) *Les travaux souterrains de Paris*. Paris: Dunod.

Bell, Colin and Rose (1969) *City Fathers, The Early History of Town Planning in Britain*. Harmondsworth: Penguin Books.

Benevolo, Leonardo (1968) *The Origins of Modern Town Planning*. London: The MIT Press.

Benevolo, Leonardo (1978) *Geschichte der Architektur des 19. und 20. Jahrhunderts*, 2 vols. München: Deutscher Taschenbuch Verlag, DTV.

Benevolo, Leonardo (1980) *The History of the City*. London: Scolar Press.

Berger, Robert B. (1994) *A Royal Passion, Louis XIV as Patron of Architecture*. Cambridge: University Press.

Berlage in Amsterdam, 54 Architectural Projects. Kloos, Maarten (ed.) (1992) Amsterdam: Architectura & Natura Press.

Berlin, Stadtentwicklung im 19. Jahrhundert. (1976) Berlin: Senator für Bau- und Wohnungswesen.

Bernard, Leon (1970) *The Emerging City, Paris in the Age of Louis XIV*. Durham, North Carolina: Duke University Press.

Biris, Kostas (1966) Αι' Αθηναι απο τον 19ον εις τον 20ον αιωνα. Athens.

Blomstedt, Yrjö (1966) *Johan Albrecht Ehrenström, Gustavian och stadsbyggare*. Helsinki: Helsingfors stad.

Bobek, Hans and Lichtenberger, Elisabeth (1966) *Wien, Bauliche Gestalt und Entwicklung seit der Mitte des 19. Jahrhunderts*. Graz/Köln: Böhlau.

Brauman, Annick and Demanet, Marie (1985) *Le parc Léopold 1850–1950, Le Zoo, la cité scientifique et la ville*. Bruxelles: AAM Editions.

Braunfels, Wolfgang (1953) *Mittelalterliche Stadtbaukunst in der Toskana*. Berlin: Mann.

Braunfels, Wolfgang (1977) *Abendländische Stadtbaukunst, Herrschaftsform und Stadtbaugestalt*. Köln: DuMont Schauberg.

Braunfels, Wolfgang (1988) *Urban Design in Western Europe, Regime and Architecture, 900–1900*. Chicago: University of Chicago Press.

Breitling, Peter (1978) Die großstädtische Entwicklung Münchens im 19. Jahrhundert, in Jäger, Helmut (ed.) *Probleme des Städtewesens im industriellen Zeitalter*. Köln/Wien: Böhlau.

Breitling, Peter (1980) The role of the competition in the genesis of urban planning, Germany and Austria in the nineteenth century, in Sutcliffe, A. (ed.) *The Rise of Modern Urban Planning 1800–1914*. London: Mansell.

Broadbent, Geoffrey (1990) *Emerging Concepts in Urban Space Design*. London/New York: Van Nostrand Reinhold (International).

Broschek, Eva (1975) Die Radialstraße in Budapest. Wien: Universität Wien [doctoral dissertation, not published].

Bruschi, Arnaldo (1969) *Bramante architetto*. Bari: Laterza.

Brussel, breken, bouwen: Architectuur en stadsverfraaiing 1780–1914. (1979) Brussel: Gemeentekrediet van België.

Bruxelles, construire et reconstruire, Architecture et aménagement urbain 1780–1914. (1979) Bruxelles: Crédit Communal de Belgique.

Bruxelles, Croissance d'une capitale. Stengers, Jean (ed.) (1979) Bruxelles.

Buls, Charles (1894) *Esthétique des villes*. Bruxelles: St.-Lukasarchief [Facsimile print 1981].

Bunin, Andrej V. (1961) *Geschichte des russischen Städtebaues bis zum 19. Jahrhundert*. Berlin: Henschel.

Calabi, Donatella (1980) The genesis and special characteristics of town-planning instruments in

Italy, 1880–1914, in Sutcliffe, A. (ed.) *The Rise of Modern Urban Planning 1800–1914*. London: Mansell.

Calabi, Donatella (1984) Italy, in Wynn, Martin (ed.) *Planning and Urban Growth in Southern Europe*. London/New York: Mansell.

Caracciolo, Alberto (1969) Rome in the past hundred years. Urban expansion without industrialization. *Journal of Contemporary History*.

Caracciolo, Alberto (1974) *Roma capitale, Dal Risorgimento alla crisi dello Stato liberale*. Roma: Editori riuniti.

Cars, Jean de and Pinon, Pierre (1991) *Paris Haussmann, 'Le Paris d'Haussmann'*. Paris: Picard Éditeur.

Cartografía básica de la Ciudad de Madrid, Planos históricos, topográficos y parcelarios de los siglos XVII–XVIII, XIX y XX. (1979) Madrid: Colegio Oficial de Arquitectos de Madrid.

Cassiers, Myriam, de Beule, Michel, Forti, Alain and Miller, Jacqueline (1989) *Bruxelles, 150 ans de logements ouvriers et sociaux*. Bruxelles: Dire.

Castagnoli, Ferdinando (1971) *Orthogonal Town Planning in Antiquity*. Cambridge, Mass/London: The MIT Press.

100 ans de débat sur la ville, La formation de la ville moderne à travers les comptes rendus du conseil communal de Bruxelles 1840–1940. Brauman, Annick, Culot, Maurice, Demanet, Marie, Louis, Michel and van Loo, Anne (eds.) (1984) Bruxelles: AAM Editions.

Cerdá, Ildefonso (1968) *Teoría general de la urbanización y aplicación de sus principios y doctrinas á la reforma y ensanche de Barcelona*, 3 vols. Barcelona: Instituto de Estudios Fiscales.

Cerdá, Ildefonso (1979) *La théorie générale de l'urbanisation. Présentée et adaptée par Antonio Lopez de Aberasturi*. Paris: Éditions du Seuil.

[Cerdá, Ildefonso] (1991) *Teoría de la construcción de las ciudades, Cerdá y Barcelona*. Madrid: Instituto Nacional de Administración Pública/Ayuntamiento de Barcelona.

[Cerdá, Ildefonso] (1991) *Teoría de la viabilidad urbana, Cerdá y Madrid*. Madrid: Instituto Nacional de Administración Pública/Ayuntamiento de Madrid.

Cerdá. Urbs i territori, una visió de futur. (1994) Barcelona: Electa España/Fondació Catalana per la Recerca.

Chadwick, George F. (1966) *The Park and the Town, Public Landscape in the 19th and 20th Centuries*. London: The Architectural Press.

Chapman, Joan M. and Brian (1957) *The Life and Times of Baron Haussmann, Paris in the Second Empire*. London: Weidenfeld and Nicolson.

Cherry, Gordon E. (1980) Die Stadtplanungs-bewegung und die spätviktorianische Stadt, in Fehl, Gerhard and Rodriguez-Lores, J. (eds.) *Städtebau um die Jahrhundertwende, Materialien zur Entstehung der Disziplin Städtebau*. Köln: Deutscher Gemeindeverlag/Verlag W. Kohl-hammer.

Choay, Françoise (1965) *L'urbanisme, utopies et réalités*. Paris: Éditions du Seuil.

Choay, Françoise (1969) *The Modern City, Planning in the 19th Century*. New York: George Braziller.

Le Choléra, La première épidémie du XIXe siècle. (1958) Étude Collective présentée par Louis Chevalier. La Roche-sur-Yon: Impr. centrale de l'Ouest/Bibliotheque de la Révolution de 1848.

Collins, George R. (1959*a*) The Ciudad Lineal of Madrid. *Journal of the Society of Architectural Historians*.

Collins, George R. (1959*b*) Linear planning throughout the world. *Journal of the Society of Architectural Historians*.

Collins, George R. and Crasemann Collins, Christiane (1986) *Camillo Sitte, The Birth of Modern City Planning*. New York: Rizzoli International Publications [first edition 1965].

Couperie, Pierre (1968) *Paris au fil du temps, atlas historique d'urbanisme et d'architecture*. Paris: Éditions J. Cuénot.

Craig, Maurice (1992) *Dublin 1660–1860*. London: Penguin Books.

Croix, Horst de la (1972) *Military Considerations in City Planning, Fortifications*. New York: George Braziller.

Crouch, Dora P., Garr, Daniel J. and Mundigo, Axel I. (1982) *Spanish City Planning in North America*. Cambridge, Mass/London: The MIT Press.

Cuadernos de arquitectura y urbanismo, 100 and 101 (1974).

Czech, Hermann and Mistelbauer, Wolfgang (1977) *Das Looshaus*. Wien: Löcker & Wögenstein.

De Seta, Cesare (1981) *Napoli*. Roma/Bari: Editori Laterza.

Dybdahl, Lars (1973) *Byplan och boligmiljö efter 1800*. København: Gyldendal.

Dyos, Harold J. (1957) Urban transformation, a note on the objects of street improvements in Regency and early Victorian London. *International Review of Social History*, 2.

Edinburgh New Town Guide, The Story of the

Georgian New Town. (1984) Edinburgh: Edinburgh New Town Conservation Committee.

Eggert, Klaus (1971) *Die Ringstraße.* Wien/Hamburg: Zsolnay.

Egli, Ernst (1959, 1962, 1967) *Geschichte des Städtebaues,* 3 vols. Erlenbach/Zürich: Eugen Rentsch.

Egorov, Iurii Alekseevich (1969) *The Architectural Planning of St. Petersburg.* Athens, Ohio: Ohio University Press.

Eimer, Gerhard (1961) *Die Stadtplanung im schwedischen Ostseereich 1600–1715.* Stockholm: Svenska Bokförlaget.

Engel, Helmut (1976) Entstehung und Entwicklung des Berliner Stadtbildes seit 1700, in *Stadtidee und Stadtgestalt, Beispiel Berlin.* Berlin: Abakon Verlag.

Ericsson, Birgitta (1977) De anlagte steder på 1600–1700-tallet, in Authén Blom, Grethe (ed.) *Urbaniseringsprocessen i Norden,* Vol. 2. Oslo: Universitetsforlaget.

Eriksson, Karin (1975) *Studier i Umeå stads byggnadshistoria, Från 1621 till omkring 1895.* Umeå: Umeå universitet.

Espuche, Albert Garcia (1990) *El Quadrat d'Or: Centro de la Barcelona modernista.* Barcelona: Olimpíada Cultural/Caixa de Catalunya.

Espuche, Albert Garcia *et al.* (1991) Modernization and urban beautification: the 1888 Barcelona World's Fair. *Planning Perspectives,* 6.

Evenson, Norma (1979) *Paris, A Century of Change, 1878–1978.* New Haven/London: Yale University Press.

Faßbender, Eugen (1912) *Grundzüge der modernen Städtebaukunde.* Wien: F. Deuticke.

Fehl, Gerhard (1983) 'Stadt als Kunstwerk', 'Stadt als Geschäft', Der Übergang vom landesfürstlichen zum bürgerlichen Städtebau, beobachtet am Beispiel Karlsruhe zwischen 1800 and 1857, in Fehl, Gerhard and RodriguezLores, Juan (eds.) *Stadterweiterungen 1800–1875, Von den Anfängen des modernen Städtebaues in Deutschland.* Hamburg: Hans Christians Verlag.

Fehl, Gerhard and Rodriguez-Lores, Juan (eds.) (1983) *Stadterweiterungen 1800–1875, Von den Anfängen des modernen Städtebaues in Deutschland.* Hamburg: Hans Christians Verlag.

Fehl, Gerhard and Rodriguez-Lores, Juan (1985) *Städtebaureform 1865–1900, Von Licht, Luft und Ordnung in der Stadt der Gründerzeit; 1. Teil: Allgemeine Beiträge und Bebauungsplanung; 2. Teil: Bauordnungen, Zonenplanung und Enteignung.* Hamburg: Hans Christians Verlag.

Fehl, Gerhard and Rodriguez-Lores, Juan (1995) *Stadt-Umbau, Die planmäßige Erneuerung europäischer Großstädte zwischen Wiener Kongreß und Weimarer Republik.* Basel/Berlin/Boston: Birkhäuser Verlag.

Ferrán, A.C. and Frechilla Camoiras, Javier (1980) El ensanche de Madrid, Del Marqués de Salamanca a la operación Galaxia. *boden,* 21.

Finlayson, Geoffrey B.A.M. (1981) *The Seventh Earl of Shaftesbury 1801–85.* London: Eyre Methuen.

La formació de l'Eixample de Barcelona, Aproximacions a un fenomen urbà. (1990) Barcelona: Olimpíada Cultural.

Forssman, Erik (1981) *Karl Friedrich Schinkel, Bauwerke und Baugedanken.* München: Schnell und Steiner.

Fountoulaki, Olga (1979) *Stamatios Kleanthes 1802–1862, Ein griechischer Architekt aus der Schule Schinkels.* Karlsruhe: Dissertation, Fakultät für Architektur der Universität (TH) Karlsruhe.

Fraser, Derek (1973) *The Evolution of the British Welfare State, A History of Social Policy since the Industrial Revolution.* London: Macmillan.

Fraser, Derek (1979) *Power and Authority in the Victorian City.* Oxford: Basil Blackwell.

Frechilla Camoiras, Javier (1992) Cerdá i l'avant-projecte d'eixample de Madrid, in *Treballs sobre Cerdá i el seu Eixample a Barcelona.* Barcelona: Ministerio de Obras Públicas y Transportes/Ajuntament de Barcelona.

Fried, Robert C. (1973) *Planning the Eternal City, Roman Politics and Planning since World War II.* New Haven/London: Yale University Press.

Friedman, David (1988) *Florentine New Towns: Urban Design in the late Middle Ages.* Cambridge, Mass/London, The MIT Press.

Frommel, Christoph L. (1973) *Der römische Palastbau der Hochrenaissance,* I – III. Tübingen: Ernst Wasmuth.

Gamrath, Helge (1976) Pio IV e l'Urbanistica di Roma attorno al 1560, in *Studia romana in honorem Petri Krarup septuagenarii,* edenda curaverunt Karen Ascani. Odense: Odense University Press

Gamrath, Helge (1987) *Roma sancta renovata, Studi sull'urbanistica di Roma nella seconda metà del sec. XVI con particolare riferimento al pontificato di Sisto V (1585–1590).* Roma: 'L'Erma' di Bretschneider.

Gantner, Joseph (1928) *Grundformen der europäischen Stadt, Versuch eines historischen Aufbaues in Genealogien.* Wien: Schroll.

Garside, Patricia L. (1984) West End, East End: London, 1890–1940, in Sutcliffe A. (ed.) *Metropolis 1890–1940*. London: Mansell.

Garsou, Jules (1942) *Jules Anspach, Bourgmestre et Transformateur de Bruxelles (1829–79)*. Bruxelles: Union des imprimeries/Frameries.

Geist, Johann F. and Kürvers, K. (1980) *Das Berliner Mietshaus 1740–1862*. München: Prestel.

Gejvall, Birgit (1954) *1800-talets stockholmsbostad, En studie över den borgerliga bostadens planlösning i hyreshusen*. Stockholm: Almqvist & Wiksell.

Gelotte, Göran (1980) *Stadsplaner och bebyggelsetyper i Södertälje intill år 1910*. Stockholm: Svensk stadsmiljö, Stockholms universitet.

Gerkan, Armin von (1924) *Griechische Städteanlagen*. Berlin: W. de Gruyter & Co.

Giedion, Sigfried (1967) *Space, Time and Architecture: The Growth of a New Tradition*. Cambridge, Mass.: Harvard University Press.

Girardi, Franco, Gorio, Federico and Spagnesi, Gianfranco (1974) *L'Esquilino e la Piazza Vittorio, Una struttura urbana dell'ottocento*. Roma: Editalia.

Girouard, Mark (1987) *Cities & People, A Social and Architectural History*. New Haven/London: Yale University Press.

Goldfield, David R. and Brownell, Blaine A. (1979) *Urban America, From Downtown to No Town*. Boston: Houghton Mifflin Company.

La Grande Encyclopédie. (1885–1902) Paris: H. Lamirault et Cie.

Gruber, Karl (1952) *Die Gestalt der deutschen Stadt, Ihr Wandel aus der geistigen Ordnung der Zeiten*. Mehn: Callwey.

Guía de arquitectura y urbanismo de Madrid. Tomo I: El casco antiguo. (1982) Madrid: Servicio de Publicaciones del Colegio Oficial de Arquitectos.

Gutkind, E.A. (1964 and ff.) *International History of City Development*, Vol. 1 and following vols. London/New York: Collier-Macmillan Limited/The Free Press.

Gyllenstierna, Ebbe (1982) Napoleon III, Georges-Eugène Haussmann och parkerna i Paris. *Lustgården*.

Hall, Peter (1984) *The World Cities* (3rd ed.). London: Weidenfeld and Nicolson.

Hall, Thomas (1970) Anders Torstensson och Södermalm. *Konsthistorisk tidskrift*.

Hall, Thomas (1974) Über die Entstehung Stockholms. *Hansische Geschichtsblätter*.

Hall, Thomas (1978) *Mittelalterliche Stadtgrundrisse, Versuch einer Übersicht der Entwicklung in Deutschland und Frankreich*. Stockholm: Almqvist & Wiksell International.

Hall, Thomas (1984) Stadsplanering i vardande, Kring lagstiftning, beslutsprocess och planeringsidéer 1860–1910, in Hall, T. (ed.) *Städer i utveckling*. Stockholm: Svensk stadsmiljö, Stockholms universitet.

Hall, Thomas (1985) *'i nationell skala . . .' Studier kring cityplaneringen i Stockholm*. Stockholm: Svensk stadsmiljö, Stockholms univeritet.

Hall, Thomas (1991) Urban Planning in Sweden, in Hall, T. (ed.) *Planning and Urban Growth in the Nordic Countries*. London/New York: E. & F.N. Spon.

Hamberg, Per G. (1955) Ur renässansens illustrerade Vitruviusupplagor, ett bidrag till studiet av 1500-talets arkitekturteori. Uppsala: Typewritten manuscript.

Hamilton, George H. (1954) *The Art and Architecture of Russia*. London: Penguin Books.

Hammarström, Ingrid (1970) *Stockholm i svensk ekonomi 1850–1914*. Stockholm: Almqvist & Wiksell.

Hammarström, Ingrid (1979) Urban Growth and Building Fluctuations, Stockholm 1860–1920, in Hammarström, I. and Hall, T. (eds.) *Growth and Transformation of the Modern City*. Stockholm: Swedish Council for Building Research.

Hansen, Jens E.F. (1977) *Københavns forstadsbebyggelse i 1850'erne*. København: Akademisk Forlag.

Harouel, Jean-Louis (1993) *L'embellissement des villes, L'urbanisme français au XVIIIᵉ siècle*. Paris: Picard Editeur.

Hartmann, Sys and Villadsen, Villads (1979) *Byens huse – Byens plan*. København: Gyldendal.

[Haussmann, Georges-Eugène] (1890, 1893) *Mémoires du baron Haussmann*, 3 vols. Paris: Victor-Havard.

Hautecœur, Louis (1948) *Histoire de L'Architecture classique en France*, II. Paris: Éditions A. et J. Picard et Cᵢᵉ.

Hederer, Oswald (1964) *Leo von Klenze, Persönlichkeit und Werk*. München: Callwey.

Hegemann, Werner (1911,1913) *Der Städtebau nach den Ergebnissen der allgemeinen Städtebau-Ausstellung in Berlin*, 2 vols. Berlin: Ernst Wasmuth.

Hegemann, Werner (1930) *Das steinerne Berlin, Geschichte der größten Mietskasernenstadt der Welt*. Berlin: G. Kiepenheuer.

Heinrich, Ernst (1960) Die städtebauliche Entwicklung Berlins seit dem Ende des 18.

Jahrhunderts, in Dietrich, R. (ed.) *Berlin, Neun Kapitel seiner Geschichte*. Berlin: W. de Gruyter.

Heinrich, Ernst (1962) Der 'Hobrechtplan'. *Jahrbuch für Brandenburger Landesgeschichte*.

Helsingfors stadsplanehistoriska atlas. Stenius, Olof (ed.) (1969) Helsinki: Stiftelsen pro Helsingfors.

Henne, Alexandre and Wauters, Alphonse G. (1968–69) *Histoire de la ville de Bruxelles, nouvelle édition du texte original de 1845*. Bruxelles: Éditions 'Culture et civilisation'.

Hennebo, Dieter (1974) Der Stadtpark, in Grote, Ludwig (ed.) *Die deutsche Stadt im 19. Jahrhundert, Stadtplanung und Baugestaltung im industriellen Zeitalter*. München: Prestel.

Hennebo, Dieter and Schmidt, Erika [1977] *Entwicklung des Stadtgrüns in England von den frühen Volkswiesen bis zu den öffentlichen Parks im 19. Jahrhundert*. Hannover/Berlin: Patzer Verlag.

Hernàndez-Cros, Josep Emili, Mora, Gabriel and Pouplana, Xavier (1973) *Arquitectura de Barcelona*. Barcelona: La Gaya Ciencia.

Herrmann, Wolfgang (1985) *Laugier and Eighteenth Century French Theory*. London: A. Zwemmer.

Hibbert, Christopher (1969) *London, The Biography of a City*. London: Longmans.

Hines, Thomas S. (1974) *Burnham of Chicago, Architect and Planner*. New York: Oxford University Press.

Histoire de Bruxelles. Martens, Mina (ed.) (1979) Bruxelles: Éditions universitaires.

Histoire de Nancy. Taveneaux, René (ed.) (1978) Toulouse: R. Taveneaux.

The History of Garden Design, The Western Tradition from the Renaissance to the Present Day. Mosser, Monique and Teyssot, Georges (eds.) (1991) London: Thames and Hudson.

Hobhouse, Hermione (1975) *A History of Regent Street*. London: Macdonald and Jane's.

Höffler, Karl-Heinz (1976) *Reinhard Baumeister 1833–1917, Begründer der Wissenschaft vom Städtebau*. Karlsruhe: Universität Karlsruhe, Institut für Städtebau und Landesplanung.

Högberg, Staffan (1981) *Stockholms historia*, 2 vols. Stockholm: Bonnier Fakta.

Hojer, Gerhard (1974) München – Maximilianstraße und Maximiliansstil, in Grote, Ludwig (ed.) *Die Deutsche Stadt im 19. Jahrhundert, Stadtplanung und Baugestaltung im industriellen Zeitalter*. München: Prestel.

Höjer, Torgny (1955) *Stockholms stads drätselkommission 1814–1864*. Stockholm: Seelig.

Höjer, Torgny (1967) *Sockenstämmor och kommunalförvaltning i Stockholm fram till 1864*. Stockholm: Almqvist & Wiksell.

Howard, Ebenezer (1970) *Garden Cities of To-Morrow*. Osborn, Frederic J. (ed.). London: Faber and Faber.

Hyldtoft, Ole (1979) From Fortified Town to Modern Metropolis, Copenhagen 1840–1914, in Hammarström, I. and Hall, T. (eds.) *Growth and Transformation of the Modern City*. Stockholm: Swedish Council for Building Research.

Ildefonso Cerdá 1815–1876. Catalogo de la exposición conmemorativa del centenario de su muerte. (1976) Barcelona: Colegio de ingenieros de caminos, canales y puertos.

Insolera, Italo (1959*a*) Storia del primo Piano Regolatore di Roma, 1870–1874. *Urbanistica*, 27.

Insolera, Italo (1959*b*) I piani regolatori dal 1880 alla seconda guerra mondiale. *Urbanistica*, 28.

Insolera, Italo (1971) *Roma moderna, Un secolo di storia urbanistica 1870–1970*. Roma/Torino: G. Einaudi.

Jacquemyns, Guillaume (1936) *Histoire contemporaine du Grand Bruxelles*. Bruxelles: Vanderlinden.

Janik, Allan and Toulmin, Stephen (1973) *Wittgenstein's Vienna*. New York: Simon and Schuster.

Jensen, Rolf H. (1980) *Moderne norsk byplanlegging blir til*. Stockholm: Nordplan.

Jensen, Sigurd and Smidt, Claus M. (1982) *Rammerne sprænges. Københavns historie*, Vol. 4. København: Gyldendal.

Johansen, Kjeld (1941*a*) Befolkningsforhold, in Holm, Axel and Johansen, K. (eds.) *København 1840–1940, Det københavnske bysamfund og kommunens økonomi*. København: Nyt nordisk Forlag.

Johansen, Kjeld (1941*b*) Bolig- og byggeforhold, in Holm, Axel and Johansen, K. (eds.) *København 1840–1940, Det københavnske bysamfund og kommunens økonomi*. København: Nyt nordisk Forlag.

Jonsson, Marita (1986) *La cura dei monumenti alle origini. Restauro e scavo di monumenti antichi a Roma 1800–1830*. Stockholm: Skrifter utgivna av Svenska institutet i Rom.

Josephson, Ragnar (1918) *Stadsbyggnadskonst i Stockholm intill år 1800*. Stockholm: Nordisk bokhandel.

Josephson, Ragnar (1943) *Kungarnas Paris*. Stockholm: Natur och Kultur.

Juhasz, Lajos (1965) 'Den almindelige Plan', Reguleringsarbeidet i Christiania i den første halvpart av 1800-årene. *St. Hallvard*.

Kavli, Guthorm and Hjelde, Gunnar (1973) *Slottet i Oslo, Historien om hovedstadens kongebolig.* Oslo: Dreyer

Kieß, Walter (1991) *Urbanismus im Industriezeitalter, Von der klassizistischen Stadt zur Garden City.* Berlin: Ernst & Sohn Verlag für Architektur und technische Wissenschaften.

Klaar, Adalbert (1971) *Die Siedlungsformen Wiens.* Wien/Hamburg: Zsolnay.

Knudsen, Tim (1988*a*) International influences and professional rivalry in early Danish planning. *Planning Perspectives*, 3.

Knudsen, Tim (1988*b*) *Storbyen støbes, København mellem kaos og byplan 1840–1917.* København: Akademisk Forlag.

Knudsen, Tim (1992) The forgotten professionals. *Research in Urban Sociology*, 2.

Kostof, Spiro (1973) *The Third Rome, 1870–1950, Traffic und Glory.* Berkeley: University Art Museum.

Kostof, Spiro (1976) The drafting of a master plan for Roma capitale, An exordium. *Journal of the Society of Architectural Historians.*

Kostof, Spiro (1991) *The City Shaped, Urban Patterns and Meanings Through History.* Boston/ Toronto/London: Little, Brown and Company/ Thames and Hudson.

Kostof, Spiro (1992) *The City Assembled, The Elements of Urban Form Through History.* London: Thames and Hudson.

Krautheimer, Richard (1985) *The Rome of Alexander VII, 1655–1667.* Princeton: Princeton University Press.

Krings, Wilfried (1984) *Innenstädte in Belgien: Gestalt, Veränderung, Erhaltung (1860–1978).* Bonn: F. Dümmlers Verlag.

Kruft, Hanno-Walter (1989) *Städte in Utopia, Die Idealstadt vom 15. bis zum 18. Jahrhundert zwischen Staatsutopie und Wirklichkeit.* München: Verlag C.H. Beck.

Kubler, George A. and Soria, Martin (1959) *Art and Architecture in Spain and Portugal and their American dominions 1500 to 1800.* Harmondsworth/Baltimore: Penguin Books.

Kühn, Margarete (1979) Schinkel und der Entwurf seiner Schüler Schaubert und Kleanthes für die Neustadt Athens, in *Berlin und die Antike: Architektur, Kunstgewerbe, Malerei, Skulptur, Theater und Wissenschaft vom 16 Jh. bis heute.* Berlin: Deutsches Archäologisches Institut.

Lameyre, Gérard N. (1958) *Haussmann, 'Préfet de Paris'.* Paris: Flammarion.

Lampl, Paul (1968) *Cities and Planning in the Ancient Near East.* New York: George Braziller.

Lang, S. (1955) Sull'origine della disposizione a scacchiera nelle città medioevali in Inghilterra, Francia e Germania. *Palladio.*

Langberg, Harald (1952) *Uden for voldene, Københavns udbygning 1852–1952.* København: Den almindelige Brandforsikring for Landbygninger.

Larsson, Bo and Thomassen, Ole (1991) Urban planning in Denmark, in Hall, T. (ed.) *Planning and Urban Growth in the Nordic Countries.* London/New York: E. & F.N. Spon.

Larsson, Lars O. (1978) *Die Neugestaltung der Reichshauptstadt, Albert Speers Generalbebauungsplan für Berlin.* Stockholm: Stockholms universitet.

Lavedan, Pierre (1926) *Histoire de l'urbanisme, Antiquité et Moyen-Age.* Paris: Henri Laurens.

Lavedan, Pierre (1941) *Histoire de l'urbanisme, Renaissance et temps modernes.* Paris: Henri Laurens.

Lavedan, Pierre (1952) *Histoire de l'urbanisme, Époque contemporaine.* Paris: Henri Laurens.

Lavedan, Pierre (1960) *Les villes françaises.* Paris: Vincent Fréal.

Lavedan, Pierre (1969) *La question du déplacement de Paris et du transfert des Halles au Conseil municipal sous la monarchie de juillet.* Paris: Commission des traveaux historiques.

Lavedan, Pierre (1975) *Histoire de l'urbanisme à Paris, Nouvelle histoire de Paris*, Vol. 5. Paris: Hachette.

Lavedan, Pierre and Hugueney, Jeanne (1966) *Histoire de l'urbanisme, Antiquité.* Paris: Henri Laurens.

Lavedan, Pierre and Hugueney, Jeanne (1974) *L'Urbanisme au Moyen Age.* Genève: Droz.

Lavedan, Pierre, Hugueney, Jeanne and Henrat, Philippe (1982) *L'Urbanisme à l'époque moderne, XVIe–XVIIIe siècles.* Paris: Droz.

Leblicq, Yvon (1982) L'urbanisation de Bruxelles aux XIXe et XXe siècles (1830–1952), in *Villes en mutation XIXe–XXe siècles.* Bruxelles.

Leonard, Charlene M. (1961) *Lyon Transformed, Public Works of the Second Empire, 1853–1864.* Berkeley/Los Angeles: University of California Press.

Lewis, Richard A. (1952) *Edwin Chadwick and the Public Health Movement 1832–54.* London: Longmans.

Lhotsky, Alphons (1941) *Die Baugeschichte der Museen und der neuen Burg (= Festschrift des historischen Museums zur Feier des fünfzigjährigen*

Bestehens (1891–1941), Vol. 1). Wien/Horn: Berger.

Lichtenberger, Elisabeth (1970) *Wirtschaftsfunktion und Sozialstruktur der Wiener Ringstraße (= Die Wiener Ringstraße*, Vol. VI). Wien/Köln/Graz: Böhlau.

Lilius, Henrik (1967) *Der Pekkatori in Raahe, Studien über einen eckverschlossenen Platz und seine Gebäudetypen.* Helsinki: Weilin & Göös.

Lilius, Henrik (1968) Antikens och medeltidens regelbundna städer. *Finskt Museum.*

Lilius, Henrik (1968–69) Carl Ludvig Engels stadsplan för Åbo, Ett försök till tolkning av empirens stadsplanekonst. *Åbo stads historiska museum årsskrift.*

Lindahl, Göran (1972) Terza Roma: Teori och praktik i italiensk byggnadsvård. Typewritten manuscript.

Lindberg, Carolus and Rein, Gabriel (1950) Stadsplanering och byggnadsverksamhet, in *Helsingfors stads historia*, Vol. 3:1. Helsinki: Helsingfors stad.

Lindberg, Folke (1980) *Växande stad, Stockholms stadsfullmäktige 1862–1900.* Stockholm: Liber-Förlag.

Linn, Björn (1974) *Storgårdskvarteret, Ett bebyggelsemönsters bakgrund och karaktär.* Stockholm: Statens institut för byggnadsforskning.

Longmate, Norman (1966) *King Cholera, The Biography of a Disease.* London: H. Hamilton.

Lorange, Erik (1984) *Byen i landskapet, Rommene i byen.* Oslo: Universitetsforlaget.

Lorange, Erik (1990) *Historiske byer, Fra de eldste tider til renessansen.* Oslo: Universitetsforlaget.

Lorange, Erik (1995) *Historiske Byer, Fra renessansen til industrialismen.* Oslo: Universitetsforlaget.

Lorange, Erik and Myhre, Jan Eivind (1991) Urban planning in Norway, in Hall, T. (ed.) *Planning and Urban Growth in the Nordic Countries.* London/New York: E. & F.N. Spon.

Lorenzen, Vilhelm (1947–58) *Vore byer: Studier i bybygning fra middelalderens slutning til industrialismens gennembrud, 1536–1879*, 5 vols. København: Gad.

Lotus international, 23 (1979).

Lotz, W. (1973) Gli 883 cocchi della Roma del 1594, in Studi offerti a Giovanni Incisa della Rocchetta. *Miscellanea delle Società Romana di Storie Patria*, XXIII.

Loyer, François (1988) *Paris Nineteenth Century,*

Architecture and Urbanism. New York: Abbeville Press Publishers.

McCullough, Niall (1989) *Dublin. An Urban History.* Dublin: Anne Street Press.

Mace, Rodney (1976) *Trafalgar Square, Emblem of Empire.* London: Lawrence and Wishart.

McParland, Edward (1972) The Wide Streets Commissioners: Their importance for Dublin architecture in late 18th- early 19th century. *Quarterly Bulletin of the Irish Georgian Society*, XV.

Magnuson, Torgil (1958) *Studies in Roman Quattrocento Architecture.* Uppsala: University of Uppsala, Institute of Art History.

Magnuson, Torgil (1982) *Rome in the Age of Bernini*, Vol. 1. Stockholm: Almqvist & Wiksell International.

Magnuson, Torgil (1986) *Rome in the Age of Bernini*, Vol. II. Stockholm: Almqvist & Wiksell International.

Mansbridge, Michael (1991) *John Nash. A Complete Catalogue.* London: Phaidon Press.

Martiny, Victor-Gaston (1980) *Bruxelles, L'architecture des origines à 1900.* Bruxelles: Éd. Universitaires.

Martorell Portas, Vicente, Florensa Ferrer, Adolfo and Martorell Otzet, V. (1970) *Historia del urbanismo en Barcelona, Del Plan Cerdámioni al Area Metropolitana.* Barcelona: Comision de Urbanismo y Servicios Comunes.

Masur, Gerhard (1970) *Imperial Berlin.* New York: Basic Books.

Matzerath, Horst and Thienel, Ingrid (1977) Stadtentwicklung, Stadtplanung, Stadtentwicklungsplanung: Probleme im 19. und im 20. Jahrhundert am Beispiel der Stadt Berlin. *Die Verwaltung*, 10.

Meade, M.K. (1971) Plans of the New Town of Edinburgh. *Architectural History.*

Meeks, Carrol L.V. (1966) *Italian Architecture 1750–1914.* New Haven: Yale University Press.

Michael, Johannes M. (1969) *Entwicklungsüberlegungen und -initiativen zum Stadtplan von Athen nach dessen Erhebung zur Hauptstadt Griechenlands.* Athen: Dissertation, Technische Hochschule Aachen.

Milne, Gustav (1990) *The Great Fire of London.* London: Historical Publications Ltd.

Mioni, Alberto (1980) Industrialisation, urbanisation et changements du paysage urbain en Italie entre 1861 et 1921, in *Villes en mutation XIXe-XXe siècles.* Bruxelles.

Mitchell, Brian R. (1992) *International Historical Statistics, Europe 1750–1988*. Basingstoke: Macmillan.

Mollik, Kurt, Reining, Hermann and Wurzer, Rudolf (1980) *Planung und Verwirklichung der Wiener Ringstraßenzone (= Die Wiener Ringstraße*, Vol. III). Wiesbaden: Franz Steiner Verlag.

Monclús, Fco Javier and Oyón, José Luis (1990) Eixample i suburbanització, Trànsit tramviari i divisió social de l'espai urbà a Barcelona, 1883–1914, in *La formació de l'Eixample de Barcelona, Aproximacions a un fenomen urbá*. Barcelona: Olimpíada Cultural/Fundació Caixa de Catalunya.

Mönsterstäder, Stadsplanering i 1800-talets Sverige och i kejsarnas Ryssland och Finland. (1974) Stockholm: Arkitekturmuseet.

Moreno Peralta, Salvador (1980) El Ensanche de Malaga, *boden*, 21.

Morini, Mario (1963) *Atlante di storia dell' urbanistica*. Milano: Hoepli.

Morris, Anthony E.J. (1987) *History of Urban Form, Before the Industrial Revolutions*. Harlow/New York: Longman Group/John Wiley and Sons.

Münter, Georg (1957) *Idealstädte, Ihre Geschichte vom 15.-17. Jahrhundert*. Berlin: Henschel.

Muylle, Tine and van den Eynde, Wim (1989–90) *Schaarbeek 1830–1885, Een stedebouwkundig-historisch onderzoek naar de wording van een voorstad*. Leuven: Katholieke universiteit.

Myhre, Jan E. (1984) Fra småby til storby, Kristianias vekst i det nittende århundre, in Hall, T. (ed.) *Städer i utveckling*. Stockholm: Svensk stadsmiljö, Stockholms universitet.

Myhre, Jan E. (1990) *Hovedstaden Christiania, fra 1814–1900 (= Oslo bys historia*, Vol. 3). Oslo: Cappelen.

Mykland, Knut (1984) Hovedstadsfunksjonen, Christiania som eksempel, in Hall, T. (ed.) *Städer i utveckling*. Stockholm: Svensk stadsmiljö, Stockholms universitet.

Neale, R.S. (1990) Bath: ideology and utopia 1700–1760, in Boray, Peter (ed.) *The Eighteenth-Century Town. A Reader in English Urban History 1688–1820*. London/New York: Longman.

Nehring, Dorothee (1979) *Stadtparkanlagen in der ersten Hälfte des 19. Jahrhunderts. Ein Beitrag zur Kulturgeschichte des Landschaftsgartens*. Hannover/Berlin: Patzer Verlag.

Nilsson, Sten (1968) *European Architecture in India 1750–1850*. London: Faber and Faber.

Nisser, Marie (1970) Stadsplanering i det svenska riket 1700–1850, in Zeitler, Rudolf (ed.) *Sju uppsatser i svensk arkitekturhistoria*. Uppsala: Uppsala universitet, Konsthistoriska institutionen.

Nordenstreng, Sigurd (1908–11) *Fredrikshamns stads historia*, 3 vols. Fredrikshamn: Fredrikshamns stad.

L' Œuvre du baron Haussmann, Préfet de la Seine (1853–1870). Réau, Louis, Lavedan, Pierre and Plouin, Renée (1954) Paris: Presses Universitaires de France.

Olsen, Donald James (1964) *Town Planning in London, The Eighteenth and Nineteenth Centuries*. New Haven/London: Yale University Press.

Olsen, Donald James (1976) *The Growth of Victorian London*. London: B.T. Batsford.

Olsen, Donald James (1986) *The City as a Work of Art: London, Paris, Vienna*. New Haven/London: Yale University Press.

Owens, E.J. (1992) *The City in the Greek and Roman World*. London/New York: Routledge.

Panzini, Franco (1993) *Per i piaceri del popolo. L'evoluzione del giardino pubblico in Europa dalle origini al XX secolo*. Bologna: Zanichelli Editore.

Papageorgiou-Venetas, Alexander (1994) *Hauptstadt Athen, Ein Stadtgedanke des Klassizismus*. München/Berlin: Deutscher Kunstverlag.

Patte, Pierre (1765) *Monumens érigés en France à la gloire de Louis XV*. Paris: Patte, Saillant.

Paulsson, Gregor et al. (1950–53) *Svensk stad*, 2 vols. Stockholm: Albert Bonnier.

Paulsson, Thomas (1959) *Den glömda staden, svensk stadsplanering under 1900-talets början med särskild hänsyn till Stockholm, Idéhistoria, teori och praktik*. Stockholm: Stadsarkivet.

Pedersen, Bjørn S. (1961) Linstows planer for Karl Johans gate. *St. Hallvard*.

Pedersen, Bjørn S. (1965) Oslo i byplanhistorisk perspektiv. *St. Hallvard*.

Pérez-Pita, Estanislao (1980) Madrid, la Castellana, Consideraciones acerca del Eje Norte-Sur de Madrid. *Arquitectura*, 222.

Persigny, Jean G.V.F., duc de (1896) *Memoires du duc de Persigny*. de Laire, H., comte d'Espagny (ed.). Paris: Plon, Nourrit et Cie.

Picon, Antoine (1992) *French Architects and Engineers in the Age of Enlightenment*. Cambridge: Cambridge University Press.

Pierres et rues, Bruxelles, croissance urbaine 1780–1980. Poot, Fernand (ed.) (1982) Bruxelles: Weissenbruch.

Pinkney, David H. (1955) Napoleon III's transformation of Paris: the origins and development of the idea. *Journal of Modern History*, 27.

Pinkney, David H. (1957) Money and politics in the rebuilding of Paris, 1860–70. *Journal of Economic History*, 17.

Pinkney, David H. (1958) *Napoleon III and the Rebuilding of Paris*. Princeton: Princeton University Press.

Plan Castro. (1978) Madrid: Colegio Oficial de Arquitectos de Madrid.

Plessis, Alain (1989) *The Rise and Fall of the Second Empire 1852–1871*. Cambridge: Cambridge University Press.

Poelaert et son temps. (1980) Bruxelles: Crédit Communal de Belgique.

Poisson, Georges (1964) *Napoléon et Paris*. Paris: Berger-Levrault.

Pollak, Martha D. (1991) *Military Architecture, Cartography and the Representation of the Early Modern European City, A Checklist of Treatises on Fortification in The Newberry Library*. Chicago: The Newberry Library.

Preisich, Gábor (1960, 1964, 1969) *Budapest városépítésének története*, 3 vols. Budapest: Müszaki Könyvkiadó.

Prins, P. (1993) De ontmanteling van Amsterdam. *Vijfentachtigste Jaarboek van het Genootschap Amstelodamum*.

Puig, Jaume (1990) El projecte d'eixample Cerdá i la teoria urbanística, in *La formació de l'Eixample de Barcelona, Aproximacions a un fenomen urbà*. Barcelona: Olimpíada Cultural/Fundació Caixa de Catalunya.

Pundt, Herman G. (1972) *Schinkel's Berlin, A Study in Environmental Planning*. Cambridge, Mass.: Harvard University Press.

Råberg, Marianne (1979) The development of Stockholm since the seventeenth century, in Hammarström, I. and Hall, T. (eds.) *Growth and Transformation of the Modern City*. Stockholm: Swedish Council for Building Research.

Råberg, Marianne (1987) *Vision och verklighet. En studie kring Stockholms 1600-talsplan*. Stockholm: Kommittén för Stockholmsforskning.

Radicke, Dieter (1995) Stadterneuerung in Berlin 1871 bis 1914, Kaiser-Wilhelm-Straße und Scheunenviertel, in Fehl, Gerhard and Rodriguez-Lores, Juan (eds.) *Stadt-Umbau, Die planmäßige Erneuerung europäischer Großstädte zwischen Wiener Kongreṛ und Weimarer Republik*. Basel/Berlin/Boston: Birkhäuser Verlag.

Ranieri, Liane (1973) *Léopold II, urbaniste*. Bruxelles: Hayez.

Rasmussen, Steen E. (1949) *Byer og Bygninger skildret i Tegninger og Ord*. København: Fremad.

Rasmussen, Steen E. (1969) *København, Et bysamfunds særpræg og udvikling gennem tiderne*. København: G.E.C. Gads Forlag.

Rasmussen, Steen E. (1973) *London, den vidudbredte storby, Det nye London en storbyregion*. København: Gyldendal.

Rasmussen, Steen E. (1988) *London. The Unique City*. Cambridge, Mass./London: The MIT Press.

Rasmussen, Steen E. and Bredsdorff, Peter (1941) Bebyggelse og bebyggelseplaner, in Holm, Axel and Johansen, K. (eds.) *København 1840–1940, Det københavnske bysamfund og kommunens økonomi*. København: Nyt nordisk Forlag.

Reed, Henry H. (1950) Rome, The third sack. *Architectural Review*.

Reinisch, Ulrich (1984) *Zur räumlichen Dimension und Struktur sozialer Prozesse, Studien zu deutscher Städtebau- und Stadtplanungsgeschichte zwischen dem hohen Mittelalter und dem ausgehenden 19. Jh.* Berlin: Humboldt-Universität.

Reps, John W. (1965) *The Making of Urban America, A History of City Planning in the United States*. Princeton: Princeton University Press.

Rodriguez-Lores, Juan (1980) Ildefonso Cerdá, Die Wissenschaft des Städtebaues und der Bebauungsplan von Barcelona (1859), in Fehl, Gerhard and Rodriguez-Lores, J. (eds.) *Städtebau um die Jahrhundertwende, Materialien zur Entstehung der Disziplin Städtebau*. Köln: Deutscher Gemeindeverlag/Verlag W. Kohlhammer.

Roma, Città e piani. Torino: [without year; 3 issues of *Urbanistica*, 1957 and 1959, including Insolera's two papers from 1959].

Rosenau, Helen (1974) *The Ideal City, Its Architectural Evolution*. London: Studio Vista.

Rudberg, August E. (1862) *Förslag till ombyggnad af Stockholm stad inom broarna jemte plankarta öfver den nya regleringen*. Stockholm: A.E. Rudberg.

Russack, Hans H. (1942) *Deutsche bauen in Athen*. Berlin: Limpert-Verlag.

Saalman, Howard (1968) The Baltimore and Urbino Panels: Cosimo Roselli. *The Burlington Magazine*.

Saalman, Howard (1971) *Haussmann, Paris Transformed*. New York: G. Braziller.

Sambricio, Carlos (ed.) (1988) *La Casa de Correos,*

un edificio en la ciudad. Madrid: Comunidad de Madrid, Consejería de Política Territorial.

Saunders, Ann (1969) *Regent's Park, A Study of the Development of the Area from 1086 to the Present Day*. Newton Abbot: David and Charles.

Scandinavian Atlas of Historic Towns, Nr. 4, Uppsala. (1983) Stockholm/Odense: Odense University Press.

Schånberg, Sven (1975) *Där! sa unge kungen*. Göteborg: Byggnadsnämnden.

Schinz, Alfred (1964) *Berlin, Stadtschicksal und Städtebau*. Braunschweig/Berlin: G. Westermann.

Schmidt, Hartwig (1979) Das 'Wilhelminische Athen', Ludwig Hoffmanns Generalbebauungsplan für Athen. *architectura*.

Schorske, Carl E. (1980) *Fin-de-siècle Vienna, Politics and Culture*. New York: Alfred A. Knopf.

Schulz-Kleeßen, Wolf-E. (1985) Die Frankfurter Zonenbauordnung von 1891 als Steuerungsinstrument, Soziale und Politische Hintergründe, in Fehl, Gerhard and Rodriguez-Lores, J. (eds.) *Städtebaureform 1865–1900, Von Licht, Luft und Ordnung in der Stadt der Gründerzeit*, II. Hamburg: Christians.

Schück, Henrik, Sjöqvist, Erik and Magnuson, Torgil (1956) *Rom, en vandring genom seklerna: Senmedeltiden och renässansen*. Stockholm.

Schumacher, Fritz (1920) *Wie das Kunstwerk Hamburg nach dem großen Brande entstand, Ein Beitrag zur Geschichte des Städtebaues*. Berlin: K. Curtius.

Scott, Mel (1969) *American City Planning Since 1890, A History Commemorating the Fiftieth Anniversary of the American Institute of Planners*. Berkeley/Los Angeles: University of California Press.

Scully, Vincent J. (1969) *American Architecture and Urbanism*. London: Praeger Publishers.

Selling, Gösta (1960) Esplanadsystemet och Albert Lindhagen, Tillkomsten av 1866 års stadsplan. *St. Eriks årsbok*.

Selling, Gösta (1970) *Esplanadsystemet och Albert Lindhagen, Stadsplanering i Stockholm åren 1857–1887*. Stockholm: Stadsarkivet.

Selling, Gösta (1973) *Hur Gamla stan överlevde, Från ombyggnad till omvårdnad, 1840–1940*. Stockholm: Almqvist & Wiksell.

Selling, Gösta (1975) *Byggnadsbolag i brytningstid*, in *Studier och handlingar rörande Stockholms historia*, Vol. 4. Stockholm: Stockholms stadsarkiv.

Siklóssy, László (1931) *A Fövárosi Közmunkák Tanácsa Története, Hogyan épült Budapest 1870–1930*. Budapest.

Sinos, Stefan (1974) Die Gründung der neuen Stadt Athen. *architectura*.

Sitte, Camillo (1889) *Der Städte-Bau nach seinen künstlerischen Grundsätzen. Ein Beitrag zur Lösung modernster Fragen der Architektur und monumentalen Plastik unter besonderer Beziehung auf Wien*. Wien: Verlag von Carl Graeser.

Camillo Sitte e i suoi interpreti. Zucconi, Guido (ed.) (1992) Milano: FrancoAngeli.

Sjoberg, Gideon (1960) *The Preindustrial City, Past and Present*. New York: Free Press.

Smets, Marcel (1983) Un Prototipo, L'Apertura della Blaesstraat a Bruxelles, 1853–1860. *Storia Urbana*.

Smets, Marcel (1995) *Charles Buls, Les principes de l'art urbain*. Bruxelles: Mardaga.

Smets, Marcel and D'Herde, Dirk (1985) Die belgische Enteignungs-Gesetzgebung und ihre Anwendung als Instrument der städtebaulichen Entwicklung von Brüssel im 19. Jahrhundert, in Fehl, Gerhard and Rodriguez-Lores, J. (eds.) *Städtebaureform 1865–1900, Von Licht, Luft und Ordnung in der Stadt der Gründerzeit*, II. Hamburg: Christians.

Smith, P.J. (1980) Planning as environmental improvement: slum clearance in Victorian Edinburgh, in Sutcliffe, A. (ed.) *The Rise of Modern Urban Planning 1800–1914*. London: Mansell.

Solá-Morales, Manuel de et al. (1978) *Los ensanches (I), El Ensanche de Barcelona*. Barcelona: Escuela Tecnica Superior de Arquitectura.

Soria y Puig, Arturo (1979) *Hacia una teoría general de la urbanización, Introducción ala obra teórica de Ildefonso Cerdá (1815–76)*. Madrid: Colegio de Ingenieros de Caminos, Canales y Puertos.

Soria y Puig, Arturo (1992) El projecte i la seva circumstància, in *Treballs sobre Cerdá i el seu Eixample a Barcelona*. Barcelona: Ministerio de Obras Públicas y Transportes/Ajuntament de Barcelona.

Springer, Elisabeth (1979) *Geschichte und Kulturleben der Wiener Ringstraße (= Die Wiener Ringstraße*, Vol. II). Wiesbaden: Franz Steiner Verlag.

Die städtebauliche Entwicklung Wiens bis 1945. (1978) Wien: Verein für Geschichte der Stadt Wien.

Stanislawski, Dan (1946) The origin and spread of the grid-pattern town. *The Geographical Review.*

Stanislawski, Dan (1947) Early Spanish town planning in the New World. *The Geographical Review.*

Stenstadens arkitekter, Sju studier över arkitekternas verksamhet och betydelse vid utbyggnaden av Stockholms innerstad 1850–1930. Hall, T. (ed.) (1981) Stockholm: Akademilitteratur.

Stockholm 1897, Vol. 2, Dahlgren, E.W. (ed.) (1879) Stockholm: Beckman.

Strauss, Bertram W. and Frances (1974) *Barcelona Step by Step.* Barcelona: Teide.

Strengell, Gustaf (1922) *Staden som konstverk, En inblick i historisk stadsbyggnadskonst.* Stockholm: Bonnier.

Strindberg, August (1962) *Tjänstekvinnans son, in Skrifter av August Strindberg,* Vol. 7. Stockholm: Bonnier.

Stübben, Joseph (1890) *Der Städtebau (= Handbuch der Architecktur,* Vol. 9). Darmstadt: Arnold Bergsträsser Verlag.

Summerson, John (1978) *Georgian London.* London: Penguin Books.

Summerson, John (1980) *The Life and Work of John Nash, Architect.* London: Allen and Unwin.

Sundman, Mikael (1982) *Stages in the Growth of a Town.* Helsinki: Kyriiri Oy.

Sundman, Mikae (1991) Urban planning in Finland after 1850, in Hall, T. (ed.) *Planning and Urban Growth in the Nordic Countries.* London/New York: E. & F.N. Spon.

Suomen kaupunkilaitoksen historia, 3 vols. Vol. 1 Keskiajalta 1870-luvulle, Vol. 2, 1870-luvulta autonomian ajan loppuun and Vol. 3 Itsenäisyyden aika. (1981, 1983 and 1984) Vantaa: Suomen kaupunkiliitto.

Sutcliffe, Anthony (1970) *The Autumn of Central Paris, The Defeat of Town Planning 1850–1970.* London: Edward Arnold.

Sutcliffe, Anthony (1979a) Architecture and civic design in nineteenth century Paris, in Hammarström, I. and Hall, T. (eds.) *Growth and Transformation of the Modern City.* Stockholm: Swedish Council for Building Research.

Sutcliffe, Anthony (1979b) Environmental control and planning in European capitals 1850–1914: London, Paris and Berlin, in Hammarström, I. and Hall, T. (eds.) *Growth and Transformation of the Modern City.* Stockholm: Swedish Council for Building Research.

Sutcliffe, Anthony (1981a) *The History of Urban and Regional Planning, An Annotated Bibliography.* London: Mansell.

Sutcliffe, Anthony (1981b) *Towards the Planned City, Germany, Britain, the United States and France, 1780–1914.* Oxford: Basil Blackwell.

Sutcliffe, Anthony (1993) *Paris, An Architectural History.* New Haven/London: Yale University Press.

Tarn, John N. (1980) Housing reform and the emergence of town planning in Britain before 1914, in Sutcliffe, A. (ed.) *The Rise of Modern Urban Planning 1800–1914.* London: Mansell.

Thienel, Ingrid (1973) *Städtewachstum im Industrialisierungsprozeß des 19. Jahrhunderts: das Berliner Beispiel.* Berlin/New York: Walter de Gruyter.

Torres Capell, Manuel, Puig, Jaume and Llobet, J. (1985) *Inicis de la urbanística municipal de Barcelona. Catàleg de la mostra dels fons municipals de plans i projectes d'urbanisme, 1750–1930.* Barcelona: Ajuntament de Barcelona/CMB.

Travlos, Joannis (1960) Πολεοδομικη εξελιξις των 'Αθηνων απο των προισορικων χρονων μ χρι των ρχων τον 19ov α ωνος. Athens.

Travlos, Joannis (1971) *Pictorial Dictionary of Ancient Athens.* London/New York: Thames and Hudson/Praeger.

Treballs sobre Cerdá i el seu Eixample a Barcelona. (1992) Barcelona: Ministerio de Obras Públicas y Transportes/Ajuntament de Barcelona.

Tschira, Arnold (1959) Der sogennante Tulla-Plan zur Vergrößerung der Stadt Karlsruhe, in *Werke und Wege, Eine Festschrift für Dr. Eberhard Knittel zum 60. Geburtstag.* Karlsruhe: Braun.

Tyack, Geoffrey (1992) *Sir James Pennethorne and the Making of Victorian London.* Cambridge: Cambridge University Press.

2C – Construcción de la Ciudad. (1977), 6–7 [theme number on Cerdá].

Utlåtande med förslag till gaturegering i Stockholm af komiterade. (1867) Stockholm: Samson & W.

Valdenaire, Arthur (1926) *Friedrich Weinbrenner. Sein Leben und seine Bauten.* Karlsruhe: Verlag C.F. Müller [facsimile 1976].

Vale, Lawrence J. (1992) *Architecture, Power and National Identity.* New Haven/London: Yale University Press.

Valk, Arnold van der (1989) *Amsterdam in aanleg, Planvorming en dagelijks handelen 1850–1900.*

Amsterdam: Universiteit van Amsterdam, Planologisch en Demografisch Instituut.

Vanhamme, Marcel (1968) *Bruxelles, De bourg rural à cité mondiale.* Anvers/Bruxelles: Mercurius.

Vannelli, Valter (1979) *Economia dell'architettura in Roma liberale, Il centro urbano.* Roma: Kappa.

Verniers, Louis (1958) *Bruxelles et son agglomération de 1830 à nos jours.* Bruxelles: Éditions de la Librairie encyclopédique.

Vivienda y Urbanismo en España. (1982) Montserrat Mateu (ed.). Barcelona: Banco Hipotecario de España.

Voltaire (1879) Des Embellissements de Paris, in *Œuvres complètes*, Vol. 23. Paris: Garnier frères.

Wagenaar, Michiel (1990) *Amsterdam 1876–1914, Economisch herstel, ruimtelijke expansie en de veranderende ordening van het stedelijk grondgebruik.* Amsterdam: Universiteit van Amsterdam, Historisch Seminarium.

Wagner, Otto (1911) *Die Großstadt, Eine Studie über diese.* Wien: Kunstverlag A. Schroll & Co.

Wagner-Rieger, Renate (1970) *Wiens Architektur im 19. Jahrhundert.* Wien: Österreichischer Bundes-Verlag für Unterricht, Wissenschaft und Kunst.

Wagner-Rieger, Renate *et al.* (1969) *Das Kunstwerk im Bild* (= *Die Wiener Ringstraße*, Vol. I). Wien: Böhlau.

Ward-Perkins, John Bryan (1974) *Cities of Ancient Greece and Italy: Planning in Classical Antiquity.* New York/London: George Braziller/Sidgwick & Jackson.

Wassenhoven, Louis (1984) Greece, in Wynn, Martin (ed.) *Planning and Urban Growth in Southern Europe.* London/New York: Mansell.

Weigel, Hans (1979) *O du mein Österreich.* München: Deutscher Taschenbuch Verlag, DTV.

Wenzel, Jürgen (1989) Peter Joseph Lenné. Stadtplaner in weltbürgerlicher Absicht, in von Buttlar, Florian (ed.) *Peter Joseph Lenné. Volkspark und Arkadien.* Berlin: Nicolaische Verlagsbuchhandlung.

Die Wiener Ringstraße, Bild einer Epoche. Wagner-Rieger, Renate (ed.) (1969 ff).

William-Olsson, William (1937) *Huvuddragen av Stockholms geografiska utveckling 1850–1930.* Stockholm: Liber Förlag.

Williams, Allan M. (1984) Portugal, in Wynn, Martin (ed.) *Planning and Urban Growth in Southern Europe.* London/New York: Mansell.

Wilson, William H. (1980) The ideology, aesthetics and politics of the City Beautiful movement, in Sutcliffe, A. (ed.) *The Rise of Modern Urban Planning 1800–1914.* London: Mansell.

Wolf, Peter M. (1968) *Eugène Hénard and the Beginning of Urbanism in Paris, 1900–1914.* The Hague/Paris: International Federation for Housing and Planning/Centre de Research d'Urbanisme.

Wulz, Fritz (1976) *Stadt in Veränderung, Eine architekturpolitische Studie von Wien in den Jahren 1848 bis 1934.* Stockholm: Tekniska högskolan.

Wulz, Fritz (1979) *Wien, En arkitekturpolitisk studie av en stad i förändring, 1848–1934.* Stockholm: Byggforskningsrådet.

Wurzer, Rudolf (1974) Die Gestaltung der deutschen Stadt im 19. Jahrhundert, in Grote, Ludwig (ed.) *Die deutsche Stadt im 19. Jahrhundert, Stadtplanung und Baugestaltung im industriellen Zeitalter.* München: Prestel Verlag.

Wurzer, Rudolf (1989) Franz, Camillo und Siegfried Sitte. Ein langer Weg von der Architektur zur Stadtplanung. *Berichte zur Raumforschung und Raumplanung*, 33.

Wurzer, Rudolf (1992) Camillo Sittes Hauptwerk 'Der Städtebau nach seinen künstlerischen Grundsätzen'. Anlaß, Vorbilder und Auswirkungen. *Die alte Stadt*, 19.

Wycherley, Richard E. (1973) *How the Greeks Built Cities.* London: Macmillan.

Wynn, Martin (1984) Spain, in Wynn, M. (ed.) *Planning and Urban Growth in Southern Europe.* London/New York: Mansell.

Yarwood, Doreen (1976) *The Architecture of Britain.* London: B.T. Batsford.

Young, Ken and Garside, Patricia L. (1982) *Metropolitan London, Politics and Urban Change 1837–1981.* London: Edward Arnold.

Youngson, A.J. (1966) *The Making of Classical Edinburgh, 1750–1840.* Edinburgh: Edinburgh University Press.

Zacke, Brita (1971) *Koleraepidemin i Stockholm 1834.* Stockholm: Stadsarkivet.

van Zanten, David (1994) *Building Paris. Architectural Institutions and the Transformation of the French Capital, 1830–1870.* Cambridge: University Press.

Zola, Emile (1927) La Curée, in *Collection des Œuvres Complètes.* Paris: F. Bernouard.

Zola, Emile (1928) Au Bonheur des Dames, in *Collection des Œuvres Complètes.* Paris: F. Bernouard.

Major Events in Nineteenth-Century Planning Discussed in the Book

1859   James Hobrecht is formally appointed head of the commission for preparing plans for the surroundings of Berlin.

Cerdá gets on his own request permission by the national government to produce a plan for Barcelona (February).

The city hall of Barcelona announces a planning competition (April).

The first version of Castro's project for Madrid is completed (May).

Cerdá's plan for the *ensanche* of Barcelona is approved by the national governement (June).

The master plan (the *Grundplan*) for the Ringstraße area in Vienna is approved (September).

Antoni Rovira i Trias wins the planning competition for the *ensanche* of Barcelona (October).

1860–69

1860   Cerdá's proposal is approved once again by the national government (May).

Castro's proposal for the extension of Madrid is approved by the government (July) and printed.

A new plan for Athens is submitted by a committee and ratified with some changes 1864–65.

1862   Hobrecht's plan for Berlin is published after royal approval.

1863   An overall plan for Stockholm is commissioned from the city engineer A.W. Wallström and the master builder A.E. Rudberg. The plan is presented in sections to be started in the autumn of this year.

Victor Besme presents the first version of his metropolitan plan for Brussels.

1865   The 'demolition committee' in Copenhagen submits a new plan for the fortification area.

1866   The first overall plan for Amsterdam is produced by J.G. van Niftrik, but is rejected after lengthy discussions.

An overall plan for Stockholm is published by the Lindhagen Committee.

1867   Cerdá's *Teoría general de la urbanización y aplicación de sus principios y doctrinas á la reforma y ensanche de Barcelona* is published.

The second Great Exhibition in Paris takes place and gives visitors from all of Europe the opportunity to admire the new streets and parks.

L. Suy's proposal for the Boulevards du Centre in Brussels is submitted.

1870–79

1870   Haussmann resigns from the prefecture (January).

Victor Emmanuel's troops break the Roman wall at Porta Pia, and planning activities are immediately launched to transform Rome to a modern capital (September).

1871   A municipal committee in Copenhagen presents a proposal for the fortification area, which after ratification the following year is implemented with minor alterations.

1872   An overall plan for Rome with the engineer Alessandro Viviani as chief author is approved but not ratified by the government.

1874   Plans are produced for the redevelopment of the area Notre-Dame-aux-Neiges in Brussels.

1876   A new overall plan for Amsterdam
         is presented by J. Kalff.

         Reinhard Baumeister's *Stadter-
         weiterungen in technischer, bau-
         polizeilicher und wirthschaftlicher
         Beziehung* is published in Berlin.

1879   The master plans for the various
         areas of Stockholm are ratified this
         and the following year.

1880–89

1883   A revised plan for Rome is ratified
         by the Italian government.

1889   Camillo Sitte's *Der Städte-Bau nach
         seinen künstlerischen Grundsätzen*
         is published in Vienna.

1890–99

1890   Joseph Stübben's *Der Städtebau* is
         published in Darmstadt.

1893   The mayor of Brussels Charles Buls
         publishes his *Esthétique des villes*.

1898   Ebenezer Howard's *Garden Cities
         of To-Morrow* is published in
         London.

1899   Charles Buls resigns from his office
         as mayor of Brussels, partly in
         protest against the urban re-
         development projects supported by
         Leopold II.

Subject Index

aesthetic ideals 19, 20, 30, 47, 75, 104, 105, 230, 324–334, 349
alignements 73, 340
allées 301, 303
archeological zones 102, 106, 110, 259
architects 76, 100, 104, 131, 133, 151, 161, 175, 273, 274, 330, 356
avenues 221, 300–302

boulevards (streets labelled as such in contemporary sources) 59, 66, 68, 69, 95, 107, 111, 133, 159, 163, 164, 217, 218, 224–226, 229, 300, 301
building and development companies 144, 211, 220, 225, 226, 237, 238, 280, 338
building by-laws and ordinances (see also planning legislation) 33, 61, 119, 121, 122, 211, 219, 284, 304, 339, 340, 348, 356, 357, 361

canals 30, 31, 95, 234–237, 242
capital city planning and other urban projects 22, 351–360
capital city projects and emergence of 'modern' planning 360–368
cholera 128, 159, 265, 266, 290
City Beautiful Movement 43, 332, 333, 352
city blocks 10, 106, 136–138, 150, 151, 195, 306–308
city image 235, 310, 328
colonial towns 39–42, 140, 141

committees and commissions 33, 34, 88, 93–95, 108–110, 145, 160–162, 176, 193, 207–215, 229, 246, 256–258, 277, 278, 280, 335
communications between various areas of cities 65, 69, 79, 90, 149, 173, 177, 190, 206, 222, 224, 231, 235, 240, 259, 285, 287, 292
competitions 34, 35, 130, 140, 173–175, 180, 183, 248, 250, 274, 356, 366
compulsory purchase, see expropriation
congresses and conferences 13, 14, 346, 361
conservation, see preservation
courtyards 21, 150, 154, 239, 308
cuidad lineal 365

decision process 211–214, 258, 276–283, 345

earlier planning traditions, importance for nineteenth-century planning 309, 330, 344, 345
embankments 32, 46, 47, 94, 172, 180, 208, 253
embellishment 8, 20, 59, 171, 187, 188, 255, 284
engineers 75, 131, 133, 151, 161, 273, 274, 330, 356
esplanades 95, 299, 301, 302
explanatory commentaries to plans 100, 104, 128, 140, 145, 149, 150, 152, 210, 284
expropriations 72–74, 86, 122, 163, 225, 230, 252, 253, 257, 336–341

financing of planning projects 61, 72–74, 84, 86, 176, 177, 214, 253, 335–338
fires and fire safety 30–33, 39, 43, 46, 58, 85, 93, 94, 118, 144, 237, 285, 355–358
Fluchtlinien 191, 197, 304, 339, 340, 348, 356
focal points 19, 24–26, 34, 75, 102, 106, 121, 140, 219, 251, 252, 300, 325, 327, 329, 332, 349
fortifications and ramparts, construction of 14–17, 55, 56, 68, 118, 126, 127, 168, 169, 187, 217
fortifications and ramparts, demolition of 45, 59, 118, 128, 129, 164, 171, 172, 176, 190, 217, 237, 265–267, 282, 293, 325–355
fortification engineering, developments in 14–17, 171, 267, 352
fortress towns 14–17, 30, 46, 158, 159, 168, 169
foundations of towns 9, 12–18, 30, 31, 34, 39–42, 118

garden city idea 91, 365–367
gardens, see parks
General Board of Works (Budapest) 247, 248, 250–252, 277, 278, 335, 341, 349
glacis areas 128, 158, 165, 168, 169, 350, 352–355
grid plans and planning 8–13, 15, 30–33, 39, 41–43, 46, 47, 127, 133, 134, 152, 153, 324, 333, 344, 351

248, 250–253, 287, 300,
324, 347, 352, 354, 355
royal palaces 85, 95, 102,
105–107, 120, 121, 178,
179, 242

sanitary conditions 20, 44, 56,
63, 76, 88, 128, 203, 221,
237, 265, 288–292
sewage systems 59, 76, 223,
289, 345
slum clearance and urban
renewal 66, 72–74, 79, 88,
90, 165, 204–206, 226, 229–
231, 291–293, 353
social segregation 96, 149, 150,
196, 239, 294–296
speculation 73, 104, 154, 253,
267, 280, 281, 336, 337,
362
squares 10, 20–23, 26, 35, 39,
40, 47, 56–58, 61, 62, 71,
72, 85–88, 95, 102, 106,
107, 118–120, 124, 132–134,
138, 140, 144, 146, 148,
150, 154, 159, 160, 165,
178, 187, 188, 192, 194,
195, 221, 226, 234, 236,

251, 253, 309–315, 329–331,
348, 349
squares, star-shaped 32, 56, 59,
61, 71, 72, 102, 124, 132,
133, 163, 177, 192, 195,
206, 208, 213, 253, 287,
310, 311, 314, 348
Staffelbauordnung 197, 361
street improvements 22–25, 39,
62–78, 86–91, 148, 149,
155, 165, 180, 241, 242,
252, 260, 261, 287, 291,
292, 352
streets (see also *allées, avenues,*
boulevards and esplanades)
monumental 22–26, 59, 85,
187, 299–305, 356
radial or diagonal 24, 26,
32–34, 43, 47, 69, 102, 120,
132–134, 146, 147, 154,
248, 250–252, 259, 287,
324, 351
tree-lined 39, 47, 59, 187,
204, 210, 287, 299, 304,
315, 333
types 145, 287, 299–305
widths 107, 133, 134, 138,
172, 194, 299, 301–303, 357

suburban development 72, 91,
98, 111, 140, 155, 165, 182,
183, 226–229, 294

traffic (see also
communications) 56, 63,
285–288
traffic tunnels 206, 208, 247,
259, 260, 338

urban growth, see population
growth
urban renewal, see slum
clearance
urban tourism 259, 346, 347,
368
utopian ideas 45, 47, 79

vistas, see focal points

water supply 59, 63, 76, 289,
345
world exhibitions 55, 140, 230,
252, 318, 332, 345–347

zoning 149, 150, 154, 227, 234,
285, 294–296, 361

INDEX OF TOWNS AND CITIES

INDEX OF PERSONS